The Book of Calendars

The Book of Calendars

Frank Parise, Editor

Facts On File, Inc.
460 Park Avenue South
New York, N.Y. 10016

The Book of Calendars

Published by Facts On File, Inc.
460 Park Avenue South, New York, N.Y. 10016

Library of Congress Cataloging in Publication Data

Parise, Frank, ed.
The book of calendars

Includes index.
1. Calendars. I. Title
CE11.K4 529′.3 80-19974
ISBN 0-98196-467-8

9 8 7 6 5 4
PRINTED IN THE UNITED STATES OF AMERICA

TABLE OF CONTENTS

Introduction

Throughout history men and women have attempted to group periods of time in convenient ways to regulate or commemorate important events in their lives. Since the requirements of various civilizations differed dramatically from one another, the world's calendars historically have been extremely diverse. Primitive peoples had no written calendars but reckoned time by the passing of seasons, wet and dry periods, or the blossoming of various trees. They reckoned smaller periods of time by the various phases of the moon. But as societies became more advanced, their calendars became more complex. It became vital to measure time for agricultural, business, governmental, domestic and other reasons. The year had to be divided into smaller sections and these, in turn, into shorter periods.

How a people divided time was based on many factors: geography, astronomical knowledge, politics, religion, etc. A calendar may have dated from the birth of a religious leader as did the Zoroastrian or from the ascension of the monarch as did the ancient Babylonian. It may have been based on the movement of the moon as was the ancient Hebrew calendar or that of the sun as is our present, Gregorian calendar. Often throughout history two or more calendars were used simultaneously. Conquerors frequently imposed their calendars on subject peoples who continued to use their old means of time reckoning. Frequently religious calendars were used in conjunction with more modern civil ones.

The first practical calendar to evolve was the Egyptian, which, in turn, influenced the Roman calendar. This provided the basis for the Julian calendar, which was used in the Western World for over 1,500 years. It, in turn, was replaced by the Gregorian calendar which is currently almost universally used as a satisfactory system for dating religious holidays (frequently associated with the phases of the moon) and seasonal activities based on solar motion.

The large number of calendars has caused historians and others interested in time great problems. It is not easy to discover how ancient peoples told time, and it is extremely difficult to translate one calendar date to another calendar. The *Book of Calendars* solves this problem. It is designed as a quick reference to over 40 calendars—how they were developed, how they changed over time and where and when they were used. But this information is merely background for the central section of each chapter. Tables on over 60 calendars enable the reader to translate one calendar date to its appropriate Julian or Gregorian date. Thus the reader can discover that the Babylonian New Year fell on April 18 in 573 B.C. or that 1982 is the year 1403 in Islamic nations. One can learn the names of the months in the French Revolutionary calendar or why the Soviet calendar was discontinued in 1940. An extensive list of tables enables the researcher to trace when the Gregorian calendar was adopted by various western nations and gives complete Julian and Gregorian calendars from the birth of Christ.

The *Book of Calendars* includes information on all important calendars for which information is known. It takes the reader through history from the Babylonians and Egyptians to the modern Western world. It is not designed as a scholarly dissertation on how calendars are constructed. Instead, it is a handbook offering basic information on the structure of the calendar and extensive tables for quick conversions. It is hoped that the material presented here will excite an interest in calendars and save scholars much valuable time.

ANCIENT CALENDARS

BABYLONIAN CALENDAR

The Babylonian calendar is a good example of the general type of lunar calendar which was used in the Near and Middle East during early recorded history. Its influence extended from Greece and Egypt in the West, down the Arabian peninsula in the south, over to India in the East and northward into the Himalayas. The present Hebrew calendar is a modern example of this type of construction.

The month, and hence the year was controlled by lunar motion, occasionally adjusted to keep pace with the movement of the Sun. The calendar had 12 months of 29 or 30 days not set in a strict pattern and intercalary months of 29 or 30 days inserted to keep pace with solar motion. If the intercalation was made in the spring, it was, invariably 29 days. If in the autumn, 30. The 29 day intercalation is indicated in our tables by * and the 30 day intercalation by ** in the column giving the Babylonian date. The intercalations were arbitrary and mostly by royal decree.

As with many of the calendars of this type, the day began with sunset, which gave an uneven length of daylight and dark, the extent of the difference depending on how far north one was. The year apparently began on the new moon nearest to the vernal equinox. The first month was called Nisanu. The names of the months are indicated below with the two possible intercalary months indicated in the order they occurred when used.

Month Number	Name	Month Number	Name
1	Nisanu	7	Tashritu
2	Aiaru	8	Arahsamnu
3	Simanu	9	Kislimu
4	Duzu	10	Tebetu
5	Abu	11	Shabatu
6	Ululu	12	Addaru
	Ululu II (*)		Addaru II (**)

We have no record of how the month was divided, but it well may have been in the "decans," the equivalent of weeks, of 10 days each with the last decan either 9 or 10 days. The times and dates of holidays are largely lost or confused, but it can be assumed that there would be holidays at the new year, the anniversary of a ruler's ascension to the throne, the winter solstice, as well as new moon, planting and harvest festivals. There well may have been local festivals also, since the calendar was used over such vast territory and by so many different peoples.

This lunar calendar was used for religious purposes. For astronomical purposes the Babylonians relied on a second calendar. The solar or astronomical calendar, used by the Assyrians and Chaldeans as well, was also based on a 12 month year, with the day beginning at 6 a.m. The Babylonians invented the zodiac, and the sun determined the length of the year by its passage through the 12 signs, the moon passing through all of them in about 29½ days. Our horoscope is the direct descendant of the Babylonian system of calculation since the day (which was a 24 hour period) was broken up into 12 segments, the 12 segments into periods of 30° each, and those, in turn broken into 60 minutes and further divided into 60 seconds. The year began at the vernal equinox.

BABYLONIAN CALENDAR

Western Date Year	Babylonian 1st Nisanu		Western Date Year	Babylonian 1st Nisanu		Western Date Year	Babylonian 1st Nisanu		Western Date Year	Babylonian 1st Nisanu	
625*	23 Mar		621*	10 Mar	**	617*	25 Mar		613*	10 Apr	
624	13 Mar	**	620	29 Mar		616	14 Mar	**	612	30 Mar	
623	1 Apr		619	18 Mar	**	615	2 Apr		611	20 Mar	**
622	21 Mar		618	6 Apr		614	23 Mar	**	610	8 Apr	

Western Date Year	Babylonian 1st Nisanu		Western Date Year	Babylonian 1st Nisanu		Western Date Year	Babylonian 1st Nisanu		Western Date Year	Babylonian 1st Nisanu	
609*	27 Mar		558	3 Apr		507	8 Apr		456	14 Apr	
608	16 Mar		557*	22 Mar	*	506	29 Mar	**	455	3 Apr	
607	5 Mar	*	556	10 Apr		505*	16 Apr		454	22 Apr	
606	24 Mar	*	555	30 Mar	**	504	5 Apr		453*	11 Apr	
605*	11 Apr		554	18 Apr		503	26 Mar	*	452	1 Apr	*
604	1 Apr		553*	6 Apr	*	502	13 Apr		451	29 Apr	
603	21 Mar	**	552	25 Apr		501*	1 Apr		450	9 Apr	
602	9 Apr		551	15 Apr		500	22 Mar	**	449*	28 Mar	*
601*	29 Mar		550	4 Apr	*	499	10 Apr		448	15 Apr	
600	18 Mar	*	549*	22 Apr		498	30 Mar	*	447	5 Apr	
599	5 Apr		548	12 Apr		497*	17 Apr		446	25 Mar	*
598	26 Mar	*	547	1 Apr		496	7 Apr		445*	12 Apr	
597*	12 Apr		546	21 Mar	**	495	27 Mar	**	444	3 Apr	**
596	2 Apr	*	545*	8 Apr		494	15 Apr		443	21 Apr	
595	21 Apr		544	28 Mar	*	493*	3 Apr	**	442	10 Apr	
594	11 Apr	**	543	16 Apr		492	22 Apr		441*	30 Mar	**
593*	29 Apr		542	5 Apr		491	11 Apr		440	17 Apr	
592	18 Apr		541*	25 Mar	*	490	1 Apr	*	439	6 Apr	
591	7 Apr	**	540	13 Apr		489*	18 Apr		438	27 Mar	*
590	26 Apr		539	3 Apr		488	8 Apr		437*	13 Apr	
589*	14 Apr		538	23 Mar		487	29 Mar	*	436	3 Apr	*
588	3 Apr	*	537*	11 Mar	*	486	17 Apr		435	22 Apr	
587	22 Apr		536	30 Mar	*	485*	5 Apr		434	12 Apr	
586	12 Apr		535	17 Apr		484	25 Mar	*	433*	31 Mar	**
585*	1 Apr		534	7 Apr		483	13 Apr		432	19 Apr	
584	21 Mar	**	533*	27 Mar	**	482	2 Apr	**	431	8 Apr	
583	9 Apr		532	15 Apr		481*	20 Apr		430	28 Mar	**
582	29 Mar	**	531	4 Apr		480	10 Apr		429*	15 Apr	
581*	16 Apr		530	25 Mar	**	479	30 Mar	*	428	4 Apr	
580	6 Apr		529*	11 Apr		478	18 Apr		427	25 Mar	*
579	25 Mar	*	528	31 Mar		477*	7 Apr		426	13 Apr	
578	13 Apr		527	20 Mar	**	476	27 Mar	*	425*	2 Apr	**
577*	2 Apr	*	526	8 Apr		475	14 Apr		424	21 Apr	
576	21 Apr		525*	28 Mar	*	474	4 Apr	*	423	10 Apr	
575	11 Apr		524	16 Apr		473*	21 Apr		422	30 Mar	**
574	31 Mar	*	523	6 Apr		472	11 Apr		421*	17 Apr	
573*	18 Apr		522	26 Mar	**	471	31 Mar	**	420	6 Apr	
572	7 Apr	*	521*	13 Apr		470	20 Apr		419	26 Mar	*
571	25 Apr		520	2 Apr		469*	8 Apr		418	14 Apr	
570	15 Apr		519	22 Mar	*	468	28 Mar	*	417*	3 Apr	*
569*	3 Apr	*	518	10 Apr		467	16 Apr		416	22 Apr	
568	22 Apr		517*	29 Mar	*	466	5 Apr		415	12 Apr	
567	12 Apr		516	17 Apr		465*	24 Mar	*	414	1 Apr	*
566	1 Apr		515	7 Apr		464	12 Apr		413*	18 Apr	
565*	21 Mar		514	28 Mar	**	463	2 Apr	*	412	7 Apr	
564	10 Mar	**	513*	15 Apr		462	21 Apr		411	28 Mar	**
563	28 Mar	*	512	4 Apr		461*	10 Apr		410	16 Apr	
562	16 Apr		511	24 Mar	**	460	30 Mar	**	409*	4 Apr	
561*	5 Apr		510	12 Apr		459	18 Apr		408	25 Mar	*
560	25 Mar	*	509*	31 Mar	**	458	7 Apr		407	13 Apr	
559	13 Apr		508	19 Apr		457*	26 Mar	**	406	2 Apr	**

Western Date Year	Babylonian 1st Nisanu		Western Date Year	Babylonian 1st Nisanu		Western Date Year	Babylonian 1st Nisanu		Western Date Year	Babylonian 1st Nisanu	
405*	20 Apr		382	7 Apr		359	22 Apr		337*	18 Apr	
404	9 Apr		381*	26 Mar	*	358	11 Apr		336	8 Apr	
403	29 Mar	*	380	14 Apr		357*	30 Mar	*	335	28 Mar	**
402	17 Apr		379	4 Apr	*	356	18 Apr		334	16 Apr	
401*	6 Apr		378	17 Apr		355	8 Apr		333*	4 Apr	
400	26 Mar	*	377*	10 Apr		354	29 Mar	*	332	24 Mar	**
399	14 Apr		376	31 Mar	*	353*	15 Apr		331	12 Apr	
398	4 Apr	**	375	18 Apr		352	5 Apr		330	2 Apr	**
397*	22 Apr		374	8 Apr		351	25 Mar	*	329*	20 Apr	
396	11 Apr		373*	28 Mar	**	350	12 Apr		328	9 Apr	
395	31 Mar	**	372	16 Apr		349*	1 Apr	**	327	30 Mar	**
394	19 Apr		371	5 Apr		348	20 Apr		326	18 Apr	
393*	7 Apr		370	25 Mar	*	347	9 Apr		325*	6 Apr	
392	28 Mar	**	369*	12 Apr		346	30 Mar	*	324	26 Mar	
391	16 Apr		368	1 Apr	**	345*	17 Apr		323	14 Apr	
390	5 Apr		367	20 Apr		344	6 Apr		322	3 Apr	*
389*	25 Mar	*	366	9 Apr		343	26 Mar	*	321*	21 Apr	
388	13 Apr		365*	29 Mar	*	342	14 Apr		320	11 Apr	
387	2 Apr	*	364	17 Apr		341*	2 Apr	*	319	31 Mar	*
386	20 Apr		363	7 Apr		340	21 Apr		318	19 Apr	
385*	9 Apr	**	362	27 Mar	**	339	11 Apr		317*	7 Apr	
384	28 Apr		361*	14 Apr		338	31 Mar	*	316	27 Mar	*
383	17 Apr		360	3 Apr							

ERA OF NABONASSER

During the reign of the Chaldean king Nabonasser (747-734 B.C.), astrologers/astronomers developed a new calendar to correct the existing Babylonian soli-lunar one. It consisted of a vague solar year of 365 days with no intercalation for leap year so that every fifth year started one day earlier. The year contained 12 months of 30 days each with five days at the end. The Chaldeans used weeks of seven days; and the day began at noon.

This calendar, like the Babylonian one, was used through the Near and Mid East, even up into Greece. It was eventually adoptd by the Seleucidae. It is possible that local month names were utilized. Yet, the calendar was so closely associated with the Babylonians that those names could have been employed.

Holidays would be roughly the same as the Babylonian ones. The day of ascension of the ruling monarch would be celebrated, as would the New Year. The people undoubtedly took some notice of the solstices, particularly the winter solstice, and of the equinoxes. There would be the usual religious holidays associated with the calendar, probably some new or full moon festivals, and a planting and harvesting festival. They also noted the four seasons.

From the time of the invasion of Egypt by the Persians in the 6th century B.C. until the calendar reform in Egypt by Diocletian in 284 A.D., the Egyptian calendar was identical to that of Nabonasser.

ERA OF NABONASSER

Era of Nabonasser	Western Date (Julian) of New Year		Era of Nabonasser	Western Date (Julian) of New Year		Era of Nabonasser	Western Date (Julian) of New Year		Era of Nabonasser	Western Date (Julian) of New Year	
1	747	26 Feb	51	697*	14 Feb	101	647	1 Feb	151	597*	20 Jan
2	746	26 Feb	52	696	14 Feb	102	646	1 Feb	152	596	20 Jan
3	745*	26 Feb	53	695	13 Feb	103	645*	1 Feb	153	595	19 Jan
4	744	26 Feb	54	694	13 Feb	104	644	31 Jan	154	594	19 Jan
5	743	25 Feb	55	693*	13 Feb	105	643	31 Jan	155	593*	19 Jan
6	742	25 Feb	56	692	13 Feb	106	642	31 Jan	156	592	19 Jan
7	741*	25 Feb	57	691	12 Feb	107	641*	31 Jan	157	591	18 Jan
8	740	25 Feb	58	690	12 Feb	108	640	31 Jan	158	590	18 Jan
9	739	24 Feb	59	689*	12 Feb	109	639	30 Jan	159	589*	18 Jan
10	738	24 Feb	60	688	12 Feb	110	638	30 Jan	160	588	18 Jan
11	737*	24 Feb	61	687	11 Feb	111	637*	30 Jan	161	587	17 Jan
12	736	24 Feb	62	686	11 Feb	112	636	30 Jan	162	586	17 Jan
13	735	23 Feb	63	685*	11 Feb	113	635	29 Jan	163	585*	17 Jan
14	734	23 Feb	64	684	11 Feb	114	634	29 Jan	164	584	17 Jan
15	733*	23 Feb	65	683	10 Feb	115	633*	29 Jan	165	583	16 Jan
16	732	23 Feb	66	682	10 Feb	116	632	29 Jan	166	582	16 Jan
17	731	22 Feb	67	681*	10 Feb	117	631	28 Jan	167	581*	16 Jan
18	730	22 Feb	68	680	10 Feb	118	630	28 Jan	168	580	16 Jan
19	729*	22 Feb	69	679	9 Feb	119	629*	28 Jan	169	579	15 Jan
20	728	22 Feb	70	678	9 Feb	120	628	28 Jan	170	578	15 Jan
21	727	21 Feb	71	677*	9 Feb	121	627	27 Jan	171	577*	15 Jan
22	726	21 Feb	72	676	9 Feb	122	626	27 Jan	172	576	15 Jan
23	725*	21 Feb	73	675	8 Feb	123	625*	27 Jan	173	575	14 Jan
24	724	21 Feb	74	674	8 Feb	124	624	27 Jan	174	574	14 Jan
25	723	20 Feb	75	673*	8 Feb	125	623	26 Jan	175	573*	14 Jan
26	722	20 Feb	76	672	8 Feb	126	622	26 Jan	176	572	14 Jan
27	721*	20 Feb	77	671	7 Feb	127	621*	26 Jan	177	571	13 Jan
28	720	20 Feb	78	670	7 Feb	128	620	26 Jan	178	570	13 Jan
29	719	19 Feb	79	669*	7 Feb	129	619	25 Jan	179	569*	13 Jan
30	718	19 Feb	80	668	7 Feb	130	618	25 Jan	180	568	13 Jan
31	717*	19 Feb	81	667	6 Feb	131	617*	25 Jan	181	567	12 Jan
32	716	19 Feb	82	666	6 Feb	132	616	25 Jan	182	566	12 Jan
33	715	18 Feb	83	665*	6 Feb	133	615	24 Jan	183	565*	12 Jan
34	714	18 Feb	84	664	6 Feb	134	614	24 Jan	184	564	12 Jan
35	713*	18 Feb	85	663	5 Feb	135	613*	24 Jan	185	563	11 Jan
36	712	18 Feb	86	662	5 Feb	136	612	24 Jan	186	562	11 Jan
37	711	17 Feb	87	661*	5 Feb	137	611	23 Jan	187	561*	11 Jan
38	710	17 Feb	88	660	5 Feb	138	610	23 Jan	188	560	11 Jan
39	709*	17 Feb	89	659	4 Feb	139	609*	23 Jan	189	559	10 Jan
40	708	17 Feb	90	658	4 Feb	140	608	23 Jan	190	558	10 Jan
41	707	16 Feb	91	657*	4 Feb	141	607	22 Jan	191	557*	10 Jan
42	706	16 Feb	92	656	4 Feb	142	606	22 Jan	192	556	10 Jan
43	705*	16 Feb	93	655	3 Feb	143	605*	22 Jan	193	555	9 Jan
44	704	16 Feb	94	654	3 Feb	144	604	22 Jan	194	554	9 Jan
45	703	15 Feb	95	653*	3 Feb	145	603	21 Jan	195	553*	9 Jan
46	702	15 Feb	96	652	3 Feb	146	602	21 Jan	196	552	9 Jan
47	701*	15 Feb	97	651	2 Feb	147	601*	21 Jan	197	551	8 Jan
48	700	15 Feb	98	650	2 Feb	148	600	21 Jan	198	550	8 Jan
49	699	14 Feb	99	649*	2 Feb	149	599	20 Jan	199	549*	8 Jan
50	698	14 Feb	100	648	2 Feb	150	598	20 Jan	200	548	8 Jan

Era of Nabonasser	Western Date (Julian) of New Year		Era of Nabonasser	Western Date (Julian) of New Year		Era of Nabonasser	Western Date (Julian) of New Year		Era of Nabonasser	Western Date (Julian) of New Year	
201	547	7 Jan	252	497*	26 Dec	303	446	13 Dec	354	395	30 Nov
202	546	7 Jan	253	496	25 Dec	304	445*	13 Dec	355	394	30 Nov
203	545*	7 Jan	254	495	25 Dec	305	444	12 Dec	356	393*	30 Nov
204	544	7 Jan	255	494	25 Dec	306	443	12 Dec	357	392	29 Nov
205	543	6 Jan	256	493*	25 Dec	307	442	12 Dec	358	391	29 Nov
206	542	6 Jan	257	492	24 Dec	308	441*	12 Dec	359	390	29 Nov
207	541*	6 Jan	258	491	24 Dec	309	440	11 Dec	360	389*	29 Nov
208	540	6 Jan	259	490	24 Dec	310	439	11 Dec	361	388	28 Nov
209	539	5 Jan	260	489*	24 Dec	311	438	11 Dec	362	387	28 Nov
210	538	5 Jan	261	488	23 Dec	312	437*	11 Dec	363	386	28 Nov
211	537*	5 Jan	262	487	23 Dec	313	436	10 Dec	364	385*	28 Nov
212	536	5 Jan	263	486	23 Dec	314	435	10 Dec	365	384	27 Nov
213	535	4 Jan	264	485*	23 Dec	315	434	10 Dec	366	383	27 Nov
214	534	4 Jan	265	484	22 Dec	316	433*	10 Dec	367	382	27 Nov
215	533*	4 Jan	266	483	22 Dec	317	432	9 Dec	368	381*	27 Nov
216	532	4 Jan	267	482	22 Dec	318	431	9 Dec	369	380	26 Nov
217	531	3 Jan	268	481*	22 Dec	319	430	9 Dec	370	379	26 Nov
218	530	3 Jan	269	480	21 Dec	320	429*	9 Dec	371	378	26 Nov
219	529*	3 Jan	270	479	21 Dec	321	428	8 Dec	372	377*	26 Nov
220	528	3 Jan	271	478	21 Dec	322	427	8 Dec	373	376	25 Nov
221	527	2 Jan	272	477*	21 Dec	323	426	8 Dec	374	375	25 Nov
222	526	2 Jan	273	476	20 Dec	324	425*	8 Dec	375	374	25 Nov
223	525*	2 Jan	274	475	20 Dec	325	424	7 Dec	376	373*	25 Nov
224	524	2 Jan	275	474	20 Dec	326	423	7 Dec	377	372	24 Nov
225	523	1 Jan	276	473*	20 Dec	327	422	7 Dec	378	371	24 Nov
226	522	1 Jan	277	472	19 Dec	328	421*	7 Dec	379	370	24 Nov
227	521*	1 Jan	278	471	19 Dec	329	420	6 Dec	380	369*	24 Nov
228	520	1 Jan	279	470	19 Dec	330	419	6 Dec	381	368	23 Nov
229	520	31 Dec	280	469*	19 Dec	331	418	6 Dec	382	367	23 Nov
230	519	31 Dec	281	468	18 Dec	332	417*	6 Dec	383	366	23 Nov
231	518	31 Dec	282	467	18 Dec	333	416	5 Dec	384	365*	23 Nov
232	517*	31 Dec	283	466	18 Dec	334	415	5 Dec	385	364	22 Nov
233	516	30 Dec	284	465*	18 Dec	335	414	5 Dec	386	363	22 Nov
234	515	30 Dec	285	464	17 Dec	336	413*	5 Dec	387	362	22 Nov
235	514	30 Dec	286	463	17 Dec	337	412	4 Dec	388	361*	22 Nov
236	513*	30 Dec	287	462	17 Dec	338	411	4 Dec	389	360	21 Nov
237	512	29 Dec	288	461*	17 Dec	339	410	4 Dec	390	359	21 Nov
238	511	29 Dec	289	460	16 Dec	340	409*	4 Dec	391	358	21 Nov
239	510	29 Dec	290	459	16 Dec	341	408	3 Dec	392	357*	21 Nov
240	509*	29 Dec	291	458	16 Dec	342	407	3 Dec	393	356	20 Nov
241	508	28 Dec	292	457*	16 Dec	343	406	3 Dec	394	355	20 Nov
242	507	28 Dec	293	456	15 Dec	344	405*	3 Dec	395	354	20 Nov
243	506	28 Dec	294	455	15 Dec	345	404	2 Dec	396	353*	20 Nov
244	505*	28 Dec	295	454	15 Dec	346	403	2 Dec	397	352	19 Nov
245	504	27 Dec	296	453*	15 Dec	347	402	2 Dec	398	351	19 Nov
246	503	27 Dec	297	452	14 Dec	348	401*	2 Dec	399	350	19 Nov
247	502	27 Dec	298	451	14 Dec	349	400	1 Dec	400	349*	19 Nov
248	501*	27 Dec	299	450	14 Dec	350	399	1 Dec	401	348	18 Nov
249	500	26 Dec	300	449*	14 Dec	351	398	1 Dec	402	347	18 Nov
250	499	26 Dec	301	448	13 Dec	352	397*	1 Dec	403	346*	18 Nov
251	498	26 Dec	302	447	13 Dec	353	396	30 Nov	404	345*	18 Nov

Era of Nabonasser	Western Date (Julian) of New Year		Era of Nabonasser	Western Date (Julian) of New Year		Era of Nabonasser	Western Date (Julian) of New Year		Era of Nabonasser	Western Date (Julian) of New Year	
405	344	17 Nov	438	311	9 Nov	471	278	1 Nov	504	245*	24 Oct
406	343	17 Nov	439	310	9 Nov	472	277*	1 Nov	505	244	23 Oct
407	342	17 Nov	440	309*	9 Nov	473	276	31 Oct	506	243	23 Oct
408	341*	17 Nov	441	308	8 Nov	474	275	31 Oct	507	242	23 Oct
409	340	16 Nov	442	307	8 Nov	475	274	31 Oct	508	241*	23 Oct
410	339	16 Nov	443	306	8 Nov	476	273*	31 Oct	509	240	22 Oct
411	338	16 Nov	444	305*	8 Nov	477	272	30 Oct	510	239	22 Oct
412	337*	16 Nov	445	304	7 Nov	478	271	30 Oct	511	238	22 Oct
413	336	15 Nov	446	303	7 Nov	479	270	30 Oct	512	237*	22 Oct
414	335	15 Nov	447	302	7 Nov	480	269*	30 Oct	513	236	21 Oct
415	334	15 Nov	448	301*	7 Nov	481	268	29 Oct	514	235	21 Oct
416	333*	15 Nov	449	300	6 Nov	482	267	29 Oct	515	234	21 Oct
417	332	14 Nov	450	299	6 Nov	483	266	29 Oct	516	233*	21 Oct
418	331	14 Nov	451	298	6 Nov	484	265*	29 Oct	517	232	20 Oct
419	330	14 Nov	452	297*	6 Nov	485	264	28 Oct	518	231	20 Oct
420	329*	14 Nov	453	296	5 Nov	486	263	28 Oct	519	230	20 Oct
421	328	13 Nov	454	295	5 Nov	487	262	28 Oct	520	229*	20 Oct
422	327	13 Nov	455	294	5 Nov	488	261*	28 Oct	521	228	19 Oct
423	326	13 Nov	456	293*	5 Nov	489	260	27 Oct	522	227	19 Oct
424	325*	13 Nov	457	292	4 Nov	490	259	27 Oct	523	226	19 Oct
425	324	12 Nov	458	291	4 Nov	491	258	27 Oct	524	225*	19 Oct
426	323	12 Nov	459	290	4 Nov	492	257*	27 Oct	525	224	18 Oct
427	322	12 Nov	460	289*	4 Nov	493	256	26 Oct	526	223	18 Oct
428	321*	12 Nov	461	288	3 Nov	494	255	26 Oct	527	222	18 Oct
429	320	11 Nov	462	287	3 Nov	495	254	26 Oct	528	221*	18 Oct
430	319	11 Nov	463	286	3 Nov	496	253*	26 Oct	529	220	17 Oct
431	318	11 Nov	464	285*	3 Nov	497	252	25 Oct	530	219	17 Oct
432	317*	11 Nov	465	284	2 Nov	498	251	25 Oct	531	218	17 Oct
433	316	10 Nov	466	283	2 Nov	499	250	25 Oct	532	217*	17 Oct
434	315	10 Nov	467	282	2 Nov	500	249*	25 Oct	533	216	16 Oct
435	314	10 Nov	468	281*	2 Nov	501	248	24 Oct	534	215	16 Oct
436	313*	10 Nov	469	280	1 Nov	502	247	24 Oct	533	214	16 Oct
437	312	9 Nov	470	279	1 Nov	503	246	24 Oct	532	213*	16 Oct

MACEDONIAN CALENDAR

The Macedonian calendar is very similar to the Babylonion, which dominated the Near East during the 9th to 7th century B.C. The only difference was the date on which the New Year was celebrated: October in the Macedonian calendar, March or April in the Babylonian. Like the Babylonian calendar, the Macedonian was luni-solar, using a 354 lunar year with a periodic intercalated month of 29 or 30 days to keep it in line with solar motion. The months consisted of 29 or 30 days alternately. The intercalated month was sometimes inserted after the sixth month and sometimes at the end of the year. The Macedonians did not use either a seven or 10 day period as a "week," but they may have divided the month by full as well as new moon. Although we do not really know what festivals they celebrated, we can assume that they had planting and harvest festivals, days honoring their gods, a festival around the winter solstice, etc.

The months were named as follows:

1. Dios	30 days	7. Artemisios	30 days		
2. Apellaeus	29 days	8. Daesius	29 days		
3. Andynaeus	30 days	9. Panaemus	30 days		
4. Peritius	29 days	10. Lous	29 days		
5. Dystrus	30 days	11. Gorpiaeus	30 days		
6. Xanticus	29 days	12. Hyperberetaeus	29 days		

In the following tables, a 29 day intercalation is designated * and a 30 day intercalation ** There is no pattern to the intercalation.

MACEDONIAN CALENDAR

Western Year (Julian)	Macedonian 1st Dios (Lunar)	Int. Cal. Month	Western Year (Julian)	Macedonian 1st Dios (Lunar)	Int. Cal. Month	Western Year (Julian)	Macedonian 1st Dios (Lunar)	Int. Cal. Month	Western Year (Julian)	Macedonian 1st Dios (Lunar)	Int. Cal. Month
526	4 Oct		487	22 Sep	*	448	11 Oct		409*	29 Sep	
525*	22 Sep	*	486	11 Oct		447	30 Sep		408	17 Oct	*
524	10 Oct		485*	29 Sep		446	19 Sep	*	407	7 Oct	
523	30 Sep		484	18 Oct	*	445*	7 Oct		406	26 Sep	**
522	19 Sep	**	483	8 Oct		444	26 Sep	**	405*	14 Oct	
521*	7 Oct		482	27 Sep	**	443	14 Oct		404	4 Oct	
520	26 Sep		481*	15 Oct		442	4 Oct		403	23 Sep	*
519	15 Oct	*	480	4 Oct		441*	22 Sep	**	402	12 Oct	
518	5 Oct		479*	23 Sep	*	440	11 Oct		401*	30 Sep	
517*	23 Sep	*	478	11 Oct		439	1 Oct		400	19 Sep	*
516	12 Oct		477*	30 Sep		438	20 Sep	*	399	8 Oct	
515	1 Oct		476	20 Sep	*	437*	8 Oct		398	27 Sep	**
514	20 Sep	**	475	9 Oct		436	27 Sep	*	397*	16 Oct	
513*	8 Oct		474	28 Sep	*	435	16 Oct		396	5 Oct	
512	28 Sep		473*	16 Oct		434	8 Oct		395	25 Sep	**
511	17 Oct	**	472	6 Oct		433*	24 Sep	**	394	14 Oct	
510	6 Oct		471	25 Sep	**	432	13 Oct		393*	2 Oct	
509*	25 Sep	**	470	14 Oct		431	3 Oct		392	21 Sep	**
508	14 Oct		469*	2 Oct		430	22 Sep	**	391	10 Oct	
507	3 Oct		468	21 Sep	*	429*	10 Oct		390	29 Sep	
506	22 Sep	**	467	11 Oct		428	29 Sep		389*	17 Oct	*
505*	10 Oct		466	30 Sep		427	19 Sep	*	388	6 Oct	
504	29 Sep		465*	18 Oct	*	426	7 Oct		387	26 Sep	*
503	18 Oct	*	464	7 Oct		425*	25 Sep	**	386	15 Oct	
502	8 Oct		463	26 Sep	*	424	14 Oct		385*	3 Oct	**
501*	26 Sep		462	15 Oct		423	4 Oct		384	22 Oct	
500	16 Sep	**	461*	3 Oct		422	23 Sep	**	383	11 Oct	
499	4 Oct		460	22 Sep	**	421*	11 Oct		382	30 Sep	
498	23 Sep	*	459	11 Oct		420	1 Oct		381*	19 Sep	*
497*	11 Oct		458	1 Oct		419	20 Sep	*	380	8 Oct	
496	30 Sep		457*	20 Sep	**	418	9 Oct		379	28 Sep	*
495	20 Sep	**	456	9 Oct		417*	27 Sep	*	378	17 Oct	
494	9 Oct		455	28 Sep		416	16 Oct		377*	5 Oct	
493*	27 Sep	**	454	17 Oct		415	5 Oct		376	25 Sep	*
492	17 Oct		453*	5 Oct		414	25 Sep	*	375	14 Oct	
491	6 Oct		452	24 Sep	*	413*	13 Oct		374	3 Oct	
490	25 Sep	*	451	13 Oct		412	3 Oct		373*	21 Sep	**
489*	13 Oct		450	3 Oct		411	22 Sep	**	372	10 Oct	
488	2 Oct		449*	21 Sep	*	410	11 Oct		371	29 Sep	

Western Year (Julian)	Macedonian 1st Dios (Lunar)	Int. Cal. Month	Western Year (Julian)	Macedonian 1st Dios (Lunar)	Int. Cal. Month	Western Year (Julian)	Macedonian 1st Dios (Lunar)	Int. Cal. Month	Western Year (Julian)	Macedonian 1st Dios (Lunar)	Int. Cal. Month
370	18 Oct	*	319	24 Sep	*	268	30 Sep		217*	6 Oct	
369*	6 Oct		318	13 Oct		267	19 Sep	*	216	25 Sep	**
368	26 Sep	**	317*	2 Oct		266	8 Oct		215	14 Oct	
367	15 Oct		316	21 Sep	*	265*	27 Sep	**	214	3 Oct	
366	4 Oct		315	10 Oct		264	16 Oct		213*	21 Sep	**
365*	22 Sep	*	314	30 Sep		263	5 Oct		212	10 Oct	
364	11 Oct		313*	17 Oct	*	262	25 Sep	*	211	30 Sep	
363	30 Sep		312	6 Oct		261*	13 Oct		210	20 Sep	**
362	20 Sep	**	311	25 Sep	**	260	2 Oct		209*	8 Oct	
361*	8 Oct		310	14 Oct		259	21 Sep	**	208	27 Sep	*
360	27 Sep	**	309*	3 Oct		258	10 Oct		207	16 Oct	
359	17 Oct		308	22 Sep	**	257*	28 Sep		206	5 Oct	
358	6 Oct		307	11 Oct		256	17 Oct	*	205*	23 Sep	*
357*	24 Sep	*	306	1 Oct		255	6 Oct		204	12 Oct	
356	13 Oct		305*	19 Sep	*	254	26 Sep	*	203	2 Oct	
355	2 Oct		304	8 Oct		253*	14 Oct		202	21 Sep	**
354	21 Sep	*	303	27 Sep	*	252	3 Oct		201*	9 Oct	
353*	9 Oct		302	16 Oct		251	22 Sep	*	200	29 Sep	
352	29 Sep		301*	4 Oct		250	11 Oct		199	17 Oct	*
351	18 Oct	*	300	24 Sep	**	249*	29 Sep		198	7 Oct	
350	7 Oct		299	13 Oct		248	19 Sep	*	197*	24 Sep	**
349*	26 Sep	**	298	3 Oct		247	8 Oct		196	13 Oct	
348	14 Oct		297*	21 Sep	**	246	28 Sep	**	195	3 Oct	
347	3 Oct		296	10 Oct		245*	16 Oct		194	22 Sep	*
346	22 Sep	*	295	29 Sep		244	5 Oct		193*	10 Oct	
345*	10 Oct		294	18 Oct	**	243	25 Sep		192	30 Sep	
344	30 Sep		293*	6 Oct		242	13 Oct		191	20 Sep	*
343	20 Sep	*	292	25 Sep	**	241*	1 Oct		190	9 Oct	
342	9 Oct		291	14 Oct		240	20 Sep	**	189*	27 Sep	*
341*	27 Sep	*	290	4 Oct		239	9 Oct		188	16 Oct	
340	16 Oct		289*	22 Sep	*	238	29 Sep		187	5 Oct	
339	6 Oct		288	11 Oct		237*	17 Oct	**	186	24 Sep	**
338	25 Sep	*	287	1 Oct		236	6 Oct		185*	12 Oct	
337*	12 Oct		286	20 Sep	*	235	26 Sep	**	184	1 Oct	
336	2 Oct		285*	8 Oct		234	15 Oct		183	21 Sep	**
335	21 Sep	**	284	27 Sep	*	233*	3 Oct		182	10 Oct	
334	10 Oct		283	16 Oct		232	22 Sep	*	181*	28 Sep	
333*	29 Sep		282	5 Oct		231	11 Oct		180	17 Oct	**
332	18 Oct	**	281*	24 Sep	**	230	30 Sep		179	6 Oct	
331	7 Oct		280	13 Oct		229*	19 Sep	**	178	25 Sep	**
330	26 Sep	**	279	3 Oct		228	8 Oct		177*	13 Oct	
329*	14 Oct		278	22 Sep	**	227	28 Sep	*	176	2 Oct	
328	3 Oct		277*	9 Oct		226	17 Oct		175	22 Sep	**
327	22 Sep	**	276	28 Sep		225*	5 Oct		174	11 Oct	
326	11 Oct		275	17 Oct	**	224	24 Sep	*	173*	30 Sep	
325*	30 Sep		274	6 Oct		223	13 Oct		172	19 Sep	*
324	20 Sep		273*	25 Sep	**	222	2 Oct		171	8 Oct	
323	9 Oct		272	14 Oct		221*	20 Sep	*	170	27 Sep	*
322	28 Sep	*	271	4 Oct		220	9 Oct		169*	15 Oct	
321*	16 Oct		270	23 Sep	*	219	28 Sep		168	4 Oct	
320	5 Oct		269*	11 Oct		218	18 Oct	**	167	24 Sep	**

Western Year (Julian)	Macedonian 1st Dios (Lunar)	Int. Cal. Month
166	13 Oct	
165*	1 Oct	
164	21 Sep	**
163	9 Oct	
162	28 Sep	
161*	16 Oct	*
160	5 Oct	
159	25 Sep	*
158	14 Oct	
157*	3 Oct	
156	22 Sep	*
155	11 Oct	
154	1 Oct	
153*	19 Sep	*
152	8 Oct	
151	27 Sep	**
150	16 Oct	
149*	5 Oct	
148	24 Sep	**
147	13 Oct	
146	2 Oct	
145*	20 Sep	**
144	9 Oct	
143	28 Sep	
142	17 Oct	**
141*	5 Oct	
140	25 Sep	**
139	14 Oct	
138	5 Oct	
137*	22 Sep	*
136	11 Oct	
135	30 Sep	
134	19 Sep	*
133*	7 Oct	
132	27 Sep	*
131	16 Oct	
130	5 Oct	
129*	24 Sep	*
128	12 Oct	
127	2 Oct	
126	20 Sep	**
125*	8 Oct	
124	27 Sep	
123	16 Oct	*
122	6 Oct	
121*	25 Sep	**
120	14 Oct	
119	3 Oct	
118	22 Sep	*
117*	10 Oct	
116	29 Sep	

Western Year (Julian)	Macedonian 1st Dios (Lunar)	Int. Cal. Month
115	19 Sep	**
114	8 Oct	
113*	27 Sep	**
112	16 Oct	
111	5 Oct	
110	24 Sep	*
109*	12 Oct	
108	1 Oct	
107	20 Sep	**
106	27 Sep	
105*	27 Sep	
104	16 Oct	*
103	6 Oct	
102	26 Sep	
101*	14 Oct	
100	3 Oct	
99	22 Sep	*
98	11 Oct	
97*	29 Sep	
96	19 Sep	*
95	8 Oct	
94	28 Sep	*
93*	15 Oct	
92	5 Oct	
91	24 Sep	*
90	12 Oct	
89*	30 Sep	
88	20 Sep	**
87	9 Oct	
86	28 Sep	
85*	16 Oct	*
84	6 Oct	
83	25 Sep	**
82	14 Oct	
81*	2 Oct	
80	21 Sep	**
79	11 Oct	
78	30 Sep	
77*	19 Sep	**
76	8 Oct	
75	27 Sep	**
74	16 Oct	
73*	4 Oct	
72	23 Sep	*
71	12 Oct	
70	1 Oct	
69*	20 Sep	*
68	9 Oct	
67	28 Sep	
66	17 Oct	**
65*	5 Oct	

Western Year (Julian)	Macedonian 1st Dios (Lunar)	Int. Cal. Month
64	24 Sep	**
63	13 Oct	
62	3 Oct	
61*	21 Sep	**
60	11 Oct	
59	30 Sep	
58	20 Sep	*
57*	8 Oct	
56	27 Sep	*
55	15 Oct	
54	4 Oct	
53*	23 Sep	**
52	11 Oct	
51	1 Oct	
50	21 Sep	**
49*	9 Oct	
48	28 Sep	
47	17 Oct	**
46	6 Oct	
45*	24 Sep	**
44	13 Oct	
43	3 Oct	
42	22 Sep	**
41*	11 Oct	
40	30 Sep	
39	19 Sep	**
38	8 Oct	
37*	26 Sep	*
36	15 Oct	
35	4 Oct	
34	24 Sep	**
33*	11 Oct	
32	1 Oct	
31	20 Sep	**
30	9 Oct	
29*	27 Sep	
28	16 Oct	**
27	5 Oct	
26	25 Sep	**
25*	13 Oct	
24	3 Oct	
23	22 Sep	**
22	11 Oct	
21*	30 Sep	
20	19 Sep	*
19	7 Oct	
18	26 Sep	**
17*	14 Oct	
16	4 Oct	
15	24 Sep	**
14	12 Oct	

Western Year (Julian)	Macedonian 1st Dios (Lunar)	Int. Cal. Month
13*	1 Oct	
12	20 Sep	**
11	8 Oct	
10	28 Sep	
9*	16 Oct	*
8	5 Oct	
7	25 Sep	*
6	14 Oct	
5*	3 Oct	
4	22 Sep	**
3	11 Oct	
2	30 Sep	
1*	18 Sep	*
1	7 Oct	
2	26 Sep	**
3	15 Oct	
4*	4 Oct	
5	23 Sep	*
6	12 Oct	
7	1 Oct	
8*	19 Sep	**
9	8 Oct	
10	27 Sep	
11	16 Oct	*
12*	5 Oct	
13	25 Sep	**
14	14 Oct	
15	3 Oct	
16*	21 Sep	*
17	10 Oct	
18	29 Sep	
19	19 Sep	**
20*	7 Oct	
21	26 Sep	*
22	15 Oct	
23	5 Oct	
24*	23 Sep	*
25	11 Oct	
26	30 Sep	
27	20 Sep	*
28*	8 Oct	
29	27 Sep	
30	16 Oct	*
31	6 Oct	
32*	25 Sep	*
33	14 Oct	
34	3 Oct	
35	22 Sep	**
36*	10 Oct	
37	29 Sep	

Western Year (Julian)	Macedonian 1st Dios (Lunar)	Int. Cal. Month	Western Year (Julian)	Macedonian 1st Dios (Lunar)	Int. Cal. Month	Western Year (Julian)	Macedonian 1st Dios (Lunar)	Int. Cal. Month	Western Year (Julian)	Macedonian 1st Dios (Lunar)	Int. Cal. Month
38	19 Sep	**	48*	27 Sep		58	8 Oct		67	28 Sep	
39	8 Oct		49	17 Oct	**	59	27 Sep	**	68*	16 Oct	**
40*	26 Sep	**	50	6 Oct		60*	14 Oct		69	5 Oct	
41	15 Oct		51	25 Sep	*	61	3 Oct		70	24 Sep	*
42	4 Oct		52*	13 Oct		62	22 Sep	*	71	13 Oct	
43	23 Sep	*	53	2 Oct		63	11 Oct		72*	2 Oct	
44*	11 Oct		54	21 Sep	*	64*	30 Sep		73	21 Sep	**
45	30 Sep		55	10 Oct		65	20 Sep	**	74	10 Oct	
46	19 Sep	**	56*	29 Sep		66	9 Oct		75	30 Sep	
47	9 Oct		57	19 Sep	*						

HEBREW CALENDAR

The Jewish calendar evolved over a long period of time and is not, in its present form, an old one. The original calendar was probably primarily lunar and based on observation rather than calculation. Some time during the 7th century B.C., intercalary months began to be used to adjust the lunar year to the solar one, but they were used sporadically, and it was not until the 4th century A.D. that the calendar became fixed.

The Babylonian exile, beginning in the 6th century B.C., had a great influence on the Jewish calendar. The months, which had for the most part been designated by numbers or by agricultural information, began to be called by the Babylonian month names, and the rarely-used Hebrew names disappeared. The New Year, which had been celebrated in Nissan, was moved to Tishri, when the Babylonians celebrated theirs.

The present Jewish calendar is a luni-solar one, the years being reckoned by the sun and the months by the moon. The day is considered to begin at 6 p.m. for calendric purposes. But for religious and practical purposes it begins at sunset. The calendar day consists of 24 hours, each hour being divided into 1,080 parts, equal to about 3.3 seconds each.

The calendar is complicated by religious requirements which dictate that certain events must not occur on specific days. For example, the New Year must not fall on a Sunday, Wednesday or Friday. The Day of Atonement must not fall on a Friday or Sunday; the Day of Tabernacles must not fall on a Saturday; Passover must precede the New Year by 163 days, and Pentecost must precede the New Year by 113 days.

To circumvent these proscriptions, a system of variable year lengths is used. The month is calculated from conjunction to conjunction, which equals 29 days, 12 hours, 44 minutes, and 3⅓ seconds. To ensure that the calendar months contain an exact number of days, a system of alternating 29 and 30 days arose. The months containing 30 days are called "full" and those containing 29 are called "defective". The lengths of most of the months are fixed. However two are variable, as shown in the following table.

Tishri	30 days	Nissan	30 days
Marheshvan	variable	Iyyar	29 days
Kislev	variable	Sivan	30 days
Tebeth	29 days	Tammuz	29 days
Shebat	30 days	Ab	30 days
Adar	29 days	Ellul	29 days

We-Adar (2nd Adar, intecalary month) 30 days

The Jewish calendar employs a solar cycle of 28 years and a lunar cycle of 19 years. The intercalary month of We-Adar is used in the 3rd, 6th, 8th, 11th, 14th, 17th, and 19th years of the lunar cycle. A "complete" year is one in which both Marheshvan and Kislev are full. It will have 355 days in an ordinary year or 385 in a leap year. In a "normal" year Marheshvan is full and Kislev is defective, and there will be 354 or 384 days. Both months will be defective in a defective year, in which there will be 353 or 383 days.

The year continuing 353 days may begin on a Monday or a Saturday. The 354-day year may begin only on a Thursday. The year containing either 355 or 383 days may begin on a Monday, Thursday or Saturday; the year with 384 days begins on a Tuesday or Thursday, and the one with 355 or 385 days begins on Monday, Thursday or Saturday. Thus there are 14 possible combinations for the calendar year.

The present Jewish calendar is considered to date from the year of the Creation, or Anno Mundi 378 B.C. by the Western calendar. The year 1980 A.D. corresponds to the Jewish years 5740-41 A.M. The New Year, 1 Tishri, 5741 A.M. corresponds to September 11, 1980 A.D. It is the fourth year of the 303rd lunar cycle since the Creation and the second year of the 206th solar cycle since the Creation. The Jewish calendar is used today in Israel for all civil and religious purposes, and by Jews around the world for religious purposes.

The holy days of the Hebrew calendar are as follows:—

Tishri	1	Rosh Hashana, New Year, Feast of Trumpets
Tishri	3	Tzom Guedaliah, Fast of Guedaliah
Tishri	10	Yom Kippur, Day of Atonement
Tishri	15	(Feast of Tabernacles)
Tishri	21	Sukkoth (Last day of festival)
Tishri	22	(Feast of the 8th day)
Tishri	23	Simath Torah, Rejoicing of the Law
Kislev	25	Hanukkah, Dedication of the Temple, Feast of Lights
Tebet	10	Asarah B'Tebet, Fast, Seige of Jerusalem
Adar	13	Fast of Esther) Note: These will fall in Adar II
Adar	14	Purim) when Adar II is used.
Nisan	15	Pesach, Passover
Sivan	16	Shevouth, Pentecost
Tammuz	17	Shiveah Asar B'Tammuz, Fast, Taking of Jerusalem
Ab	9	Tishah B'Ab, Fast, Destruction of the Temple

Because a large portion of Jews resided Eastern European countries where the Julian calendar was observed prior to 1940, we have given the Julian-Gregorian overlap for 1st Tishri from 1582 through 1939.

HEBREW CALENDAR

19 Year Cycle No.	Hebrew Year	Calendar Number	Days in Year	Day of Week	Western Year	Commencement 1st of Tishri (Julian)	
199	3763	6	355	Sa	2	23	Sep
	3764	4	355	Th	3	13	Sep
	3765	10	384	Tu	4*	2	Sep
	3766	1	355	Mo	5	21	Sep
	3767	7	353	Sa	6	11	Sep
	3768	10	384	Tu	7	30	Aug
	3769	1	355	Mo	8*	17	Sep
	3770	13	385	Sa	9	7	Sep
	3771	6	355	Sa	10	27	Sep
	3772	5	354	Th	11	17	Sep
	3773	9	383	Mo	12*	5	Sep
	3774	6	355	Sa	13	23	Sep
	3775	5	354	Th	14	13	Sep
	3776	8	385	Mo	15	2	Sep
	3777	2	353	Mo	16*	21	Sep
	3778	5	354	Th	17	9	Sep
	3779	9	383	Mo	18	29	Aug
	3780	6	355	Sa	19	16	Sep
	3781	11	385	Th	20*	5	Sep
200	3782	5	354	Th	21	25	Sep
	3783	2	353	Mo	22	14	Sep
	3784	11	384	Tu	23	2	Sep
	3785	4	355	Th	24*	21	Sep
	3786	3	354	Tu	25	11	Sep
	3787	14	383	Sa	26	31	Aug
	3788	4	355	Th	27	18	Sep
	3789	10	384	Tu	28*	7	Sep
	3790	1	355	Mo	29	26	Sep
	3791	7	353	Sa	30	16	Sep
	3792	10	384	Tu	31	4	Sep
	3793	1	355	Mo	32*	22	Sep
	3794	6	355	Sa	33	12	Sep
	3795	12	383	Th	34	2	Sep
	3796	3	354	Tu	35	20	Sep

19 Year Cycle No.	Hebrew Year	Calendar Number	Days in Year	Day of Week	Western Year	Commencement 1st of Tishri (Julian)	
	3797	6	355	Sa	36*	8	Sep
	3798	12	383	Th	37	29	Aug
	3799	3	354	Tu	38	16	Sep
	3800	13	385	Sa	39	5	Sep
201	3801	1	355	Mo	40*	23	Sep
	3802	5	354	Th	41	14	Sep
	3803	9	383	Mo	42	3	Sep
	3804	6	355	Sa	43	21	Sep
	3805	5	354	Th	44*	10	Sep
	3806	8	385	Mo	45	30	Aug
	3807	2	353	Mo	46	19	Sep
	3808	11	385	Th	47	7	Sep
	3809	5	354	Th	48*	26	Sep
	3810	1	355	Mo	49	15	Sep
	3811	14	383	Sa	50	5	Sep
	3812	4	355	Th	51	23	Sep
	3813	3	354	Tu	52*	12	Sep
	3814	13	385	Sa	53	1	Sep
	3815	4	355	Th	54	19	Sep
	3816	3	354	Tu	55	9	Sep
	3817	13	385	Sa	56*	28	Aug
	3818	7	353	Sa	57	17	Sep
	3819	10	384	Tu	58	5	Sep
202	3820	1	355	Mo	59	24	Sep
	3821	7	353	Sa	60*	13	Sep
	3822	12	383	Th	61	3	Sep
	3823	3	354	Tu	62	21	Sep
	3824	6	355	Sa	63	10	Sep
	3825	11	385	Th	64*	30	Aug
	3826	3	354	Tu	65	19	Sep
	3827	9	383	Mo	66	8	Sep
	3828	6	355	Sa	67	26	Sep
	3829	4	355	Th	68*	15	Sep

	3830	10	384	Tu	69	5	Sep
	3831	2	353	Mo	70	24	Sep
	3832	4	355	Th	71	12	Sep
	3833	10	384	Tu	72*	1	Sep
	3834	1	355	Mo	73	20	Sep
	3835	7	353	Sa	74	10	Sep
	3836	10	384	Tu	75	29	Aug
	3837	1	355	Mo	76*	16	Sep
	3838	14	383	Sa	77	6	Sep
203	3839	4	355	Th	78	24	Sep
	3840	3	354	Tu	79	14	Sep
	3841	13	385	Sa	80*	2	Sep
	3842	7	353	Sa	81	22	Sep
	3843	3	354	Tu	82	10	Sep
	3844	13	385	Sa	83	30	Aug
	3945	6	355	Sa	84*	18	Sep
	3846	12	383	Th	85	8	Sep
	3847	3	354	Tu	86	26	Sep
	3848	6	355	Sa	87	15	Sep
	3849	11	385	Th	88*	4	Sep
	3850	5	354	Th	89	24	Sep
	3851	2	353	Mo	90	13	Sep
	3852	11	385	Th	91	1	Sep
	3853	4	355	Th	92*	20	Sep
	3854	3	354	Tu	93	10	Sep
	3855	14	383	Sa	94	30	Aug
	3856	5	354	Th	95	17	Sep
	3857	8	385	Mo	96*	5	Sep
204	3858	2	353	Mo	97	25	Sep
	3859	4	355	Th	98	13	Sep
	3860	10	384	Tu	99	3	Sep
	3861	1	355	Mo	100*	21	Sep
	3862	7	353	Sa	101	11	Sep
	3863	10	384	Tu	102	30	Aug
	3864	1	355	Mo	103	18	Sep
	3865	13	385	Sa	104*	7	Sep
	3866	7	353	Sa	105	27	Sep
	3867	3	354	Tu	106	15	Sep
	3868	13	385	Sa	107	4	Sep
	3869	6	355	Sa	108*	23	Sep
	3870	5	354	Th	109	13	Sep
	3871	9	383	Mo	110	2	Sep

	3872	6	355	Sa	111	20	Sep
	3873	5	354	Th	112*	9	Sep
	3874	9	383	Mo	113	29	Aug
	3875	6	355	Sa	114	16	Sep
	3876	11	385	Th	115	6	Sep
205	3877	5	354	Th	116*	25	Sep
	3878	2	353	Mo	117	14	Sep
	3879	11	385	Th	118	2	Sep
	3880	4	355	Th	119	22	Sep
	3881	1	355	Mo	120*	11	Sep
	3882	14	383	Sa	121	31	Aug
	3883	5	354	Th	122	18	Sep
	3884	8	385	Mo	123	7	Sep
	3885	1	355	Mo	124*	26	Sep
	3886	7	353	Sa	125	16	Sep
	3887	10	384	Tu	126	4	Sep
	3888	1	355	Mo	127	23	Sep
	3889	6	355	Sa	128*	12	Sep
	3890	12	383	Th	129	2	Sep
	3891	3	354	Tu	130	20	Sep
	3892	6	355	Sa	131	9	Sep
	3893	12	383	Th	132*	29	Aug
	3894	3	354	Tu	133	16	Sep
	3895	13	385	Sa	134	5	Sep
206	3896	6	355	Sa	135	25	Sep
	3897	5	354	Th	136*	14	Sep
	3898	9	383	Mo	137	3	Sep
	3899	6	355	Sa	138	21	Sep
	3900	5	354	Th	139	11	Sep
	3901	8	385	Mo	140*	30	Aug
	3902	2	353	Mo	141	19	Sep
	3903	11	385	Th	142	7	Sep
	3904	4	355	Th	143	27	Sep
	3905	3	354	Tu	144*	16	Sep
	3906	14	383	Sa	145	5	Sep
	3907	5	354	Th	146	23	Sep
	3908	1	355	Mo	147	12	Sep
	3909	12	383	Th	148*	1	Sep
	3910	1	355	Mo	149	19	Sep
	3911	3	354	Tu	150	9	Sep
	3912	13	385	Sa	151	29	Aug
	3913	7	353	Sa	152*	17	Sep
	3914	10	384	Tu	153	5	Sep

19 Year Cycle No.	Hebrew Year	Calendar Number	Days in Year	Day of Week	Western Year	Commencement 1st of Tishri (Julian)	
207	3915	1	355	Mo	154	24	Sep
	3916	6	355	Sa	155	14	Sep
	3917	12	383	Th	156*	3	Sep
	3918	3	354	Tu	157	21	Sep
	3919	7	353	Sa	158	10	Sep
	3920	10	384	Tu	159	31	Aug
	3921	1	355	Mo	160*	19	Sep
	3922	13	385	Sa	161	8	Sep
	3923	6	355	Sa	162	26	Sep
	3924	4	355	Th	163	16	Sep
	3925	10	384	Tu	164*	5	Sep
	3926	2	353	Mo	165	24	Sep
	3927	5	354	Th	166	12	Sep
	3928	8	385	Mo	167	1	Sep
	3929	1	355	Mo	168*	20	Sep
	3930	7	3353	Sa	169	10	Sep
	3931	10	384	Tu	170	29	Aug
	3932	1	355	Mo	171	17	Sep
	3933	14	383	Sa	172*	6	Sep
208	3934	4	355	Th	173	24	Sep
	3935	3	354	Tu	174	14	Sep
	3936	14	383	Sa	175	3	Sep
	3937	1	355	Mo	176*	20	Sep
	3938	3	354	Tu	177	10	Sep
	3939	13	385	Sa	178	30	Aug
	3940	6	355	Sa	179	19	Sep
	3941	12	383	Th	180*	8	Sep
	3942	3	354	Tu	181	26	Sep
	3943	6	355	Sa	182	15	Sep
	3944	11	385	Th	183	5	Sep
	3945	5	354	Th	184*	24	Sep
	3946	2	353	Mo	185	13	Sep
	3947	11	385	Th	186	1	Sep
	3948	4	355	Th	187	21	Sep
	3949	3	354	Tu	188*	10	Sep

19 Year Cycle No.	Hebrew Year	Calendar Number	Days in Year	Day of Week	Western Year	Commencement 1st of Tishri (Julian)	
	3950	14	383	Sa	189	30	Aug
	3951	5	354	Th	190	17	Sep
	3952	8	385	Mo	191	6	Sep
209	3953	2	353	Mo	192*	25	Sep
	3954	4	355	Th	193	13	Sep
	3955	10	384	Tu	194	3	Sep
	3956	1	355	Mo	195	22	Sep
	3957	7	353	Sa	196*	11	Sep
	3958	10	384	Tu	197	30	Aug
	3959	1	355	Mo	198	18	Sep
	3960	13	385	Sa	199	8	Sep
	3961	7	353	Sa	200*	27	Sep
	3962	3	354	Tu	201	15	Sep
	3963	13	385	Sa	202	4	Sep
	3964	6	355	Sa	203	24	Sep
	3965	5	354	Th	204*	13	Sep
	3966	10	384	Tu	205	3	Sep
	3967	1	355	Mo	206	22	Sep
	3968	5	354	Th	207	10	Sep
	3969	9	383	Mo	208*	29	Aug
	3970	6	355	Sa	209	16	Sep
	3971	12	383	Th	210	6	Sep
210	3972	3	354	Tu	211	24	Sep
	3973	6	355	Sa	212*	12	Sep
	3974	11	385	Th	213	2	Sep
	3975	5	354	Th	214	22	Sep
	3976	1	355	Mo	215	11	Sep
	3977	14	383	Sa	216*	31	Aug
	3978	5	354	Th	217	18	Sep
	3979	8	385	Mo	218	7	Sep
	3980	1	355	Mo	219	27	Sep
	3981	7	353	Sa	220*	16	Sep
	3982	10	384	Tu	221	4	Sep
	3983	1	355	Mo	222	23	Sep

	3984	6	355	Sa	223	13	Sep
	3985	12	383	Th	224*	2	Sep
	3986	3	354	Tu	225	20	Sep
	3987	7	353	Sa	226	9	Sep
	3988	10	384	Tu	227	28	Aug
	3989	1	355	Mo	228*	15	Sep
	3990	2	353	Mo	229	5	Sep
211	3991	7	353	Sa	230	25	Sep
	3992	3	354	Tu	221	13	Sep
	3993	13	385	Sa	232*	1	Sep
	3994	6	355	Sa	233	21	Sep
	3995	5	354	Th	234	11	Sep
	3996	8	385	Mo	235	31	Aug
	3997	2	353	Mo	236*	19	Sep
	3998	11	385	Th	237	7	Sep
	3999	5	354	Th	238	27	Sep
	4000	1	355	Mo	239	16	Sep
	4001	14	383	Sa	240*	5	Sep
	4002	4	355	Th	241	23	Sep
	4003	3	354	Tu	242	13	Sep
	4004	13	385	Sa	243	2	Sep
	4005	7	353	Sa	244*	21	Sep
	4006	3	354	Tu	245	9	Sep
	4007	14	383	Sa	246	29	Aug
	4008	5	354	Th	247	16	Sep
	4009	10	384	Tu	248*	5	Sep
212	4010	1	355	Mo	249	24	Sep
	4011	7	353	Sa	250	14	Sep
	4012	10	384	Tu	251	2	Sep
	4013	1	355	Mo	252*	20	Sep
	4014	6	355	Sa	253	10	Sep
	4015	12	383	Th	254	31	Aug
	4016	3	354	Tu	255	18	Sep
	4017	13	385	Sa	256	6	Aug
	4018	6	355	Sa	257	26	Sep
	4019	5	354	Th	258	16	Sep
	4020	8	385	Mo	259	5	Sep
	4021	2	353	Mo	260*	24	Sep
	4022	4	355	Th	261	12	Sep
	4023	10	384	Tu	262	2	Sep
	4024	1	355	Mo	263	21	Sep
	4025	7	353	Sa	264*	10	Sep

	4026	10	384	Tu	265	29	Aug
	4027	2	353	Mo	266	17	Sep
	4028	11	385	Th	267	5	Sep
213	4029	4	355	Th	268*	24	Sep
	4030	3	354	Tu	269	14	Sep
	4031	14	383	Sa	270	3	Sep
	4032	4	355	Th	271	21	Sep
	4033	3	354	Tu	272*	10	Sep
	4034	13	385	Sa	273	30	Aug
	4035	7	353	Sa	274	19	Sep
	4036	7	353	Sa	275	7	Sep
	4037	10	384	Tu	276*	25	Sep
	4038	1	355	Mo	277	15	Sep
	4039	6	355	Sa	278	5	Sep
	4040	12	383	Th	279	23	Sep
	4041	3	354	Tu	280*	11	Sep
	4042	6	355	Sa	281	1	Sep
	4043	11	385	Th	282	21	Sep
	4044	5	354	Th	283	10	Sep
	4045	2	353	Mo	284*	28	Aug
	4046	11	385	Th	285	17	Sep
	4047	5	354	Th	286	6	Sep
214	4048	9	383	Mo	287	24	Sep
	4049	6	355	Sa	288*	13	Sep
	4050	4	355	Th	289	3	Sep
	4051	10	384	Tu	290	22	Sep
	4052	2	353	Mo	291	10	Sep
	4053	4	355	Th	292*	30	Aug
	4054	10	384	Tu	293	18	Sep
	4055	1	355	Mo	294	8	Sep
	4056	14	383	Sa	295	26	Sep
	4057	4	355	Th	296*	15	Sep
	4058	3	354	Tu	297	4	Sep
	4059	11	385	Th	298	24	Sep
	4060	7	353	Sa	299	12	Sep
	4061	3	354	Tu	300*	31	Aug
	4062	13	385	Sa	301	20	Sep
	4063	6	355	Sa	302	10	Sep
	4064	5	354	Th	303	30	Aug
	4065	9	383	Mo	304*	16	Sep
	4066	6	355	Sa	305	6	Sep

19 Year Cycle No.	Hebrew Year	Calendar Number	Days in Year	Day of Week	Western Year	Commencement 1st of Tishri (Julian)
215	4067	5	354	Th	306	26 Sep
	4068	2	353	Mo	307	15 Sep
	4069	11	385	Th	308*	2 Sep
	4070	5	354	Th	309	22 Sep
	4071	1	355	Mo	310	11 Sep
	4072	14	383	Sa	311	1 Sep
	4073	5	354	Th	312*	18 Sep
	4074	8	385	Mo	313	7 Sep
	4075	2	353	Mo	314	27 Sep
	4076	4	355	Th	315	15 Sep
	4077	10	384	Tu	316*	4 Sep
	4078	1	355	Mo	317	23 Sep
	4079	7	353	Sa	318	13 Sep
	4080	10	384	Tu	319	1 Sep
	4081	1	355	Mo	320*	19 Sep
	4082	6	355	Sa	321	9 Sep
	4083	12	383	Th	322	30 Aug
	4084	3	354	Tu	323	17 Sep
	4085	13	385	Sa	324*	5 Sep
216	4086	6	355	Sa	325	25 Sep
	4087	5	354	Th	326	15 Sep
	4088	9	383	Mo	327	4 Sep
	4089	6	355	Sa	328*	21 Sep
	4090	5	354	Th	329	11 Sep
	4091	9	383	Mo	330	31 Aug
	4092	6	355	Sa	331	18 Sep
	4093	11	385	Th	332*	7 Sep
	4094	5	354	Th	333	27 Sep
	4095	2	353	Mo	334	16 Sep
	4096	11	385	Th	335	4 Sep
	4097	5	354	Th	336*	23 Sep
	4098	1	355	Mo	337	12 Sep
	4099	14	383	Sa	338	2 Sep
	4100	5	354	Th	339	20 Sep
	4101	1	355	Mo	340*	8 Sep

19 Year Cycle No.	Hebrew Year	Calendar Number	Days in Year	Day of Week	Western Year	Commencement 1st of Tishri (Julian)
	4102	13	385	Sa	341	29 Aug
	4103	7	353	Sa	342	18 Sep
	4104	10	384	Tu	343	6 Sep
217	4105	1	355	Mo	344*	24 Sep
	4106	6	355	Sa	345	14 Sep
	4107	12	383	Th	346	4 Sep
	4108	3	354	Tu	347	22 Sep
	4109	6	355	Sa	348*	10 Sep
	4110	11	385	Th	349	31 Aug
	4111	5	354	Th	350	20 Sep
	4112	9	383	Mo	351	9 Sep
	4113	6	355	Sa	352*	26 Sep
	4114	5	354	Th	353	16 Sep
	4115	9	383	Mo	354	5 Sep
	4116	6	355	Sa	355	23 Sep
	4117	5	354	Th	356*	12 Sep
	4118	8	385	Mo	357	1 Sep
	4119	2	353	Mo	358	21 Sep
	4120	5	354	Th	359	9 Sep
	4121	8	385	Mo	360*	28 Aug
	4122	1	355	Mo	361	17 Sep
	4123	14	383	Sa	362	7 Sep
218	4124	5	354	Th	363	25 Sep
	4125	1	355	Mo	364*	13 Sep
	4126	14	383	Sa	365	3 Sep
	4127	4	355	Th	366	21 Sep
	4128	3	354	Tu	367	11 Sep
	4129	13	385	Sa	368*	30 Aug
	4130	7	353	Sa	369	19 Sep
	4131	10	384	Tu	370	7 Sep
	4132	1	355	Mo	371	26 Sep
	4133	6	355	Sa	372*	15 Sep
	4134	12	383	Th	373	5 Sep
	4135	3	354	Tu	374	23 Sep

	4136	6	355	Sa	375	12	Sep
	4137	11	385	Th	376*	1	Sep
	4138	5	354	Th	377	21	Sep
	4139	2	353	Mo	378	10	Sep
	4140	11	385	Th	379	29	Aug
	4141	5	354	Th	380*	17	Sep
	4142	9	383	Mo	381	6	Sep
219	4143	6	355	Sa	382	24	Sep
	4144	5	354	Th	383	14	Sep
	4145	8	385	Mo	384*	2	Sep
	4146	2	353	Mo	385	22	Sep
	4147	4	355	Th	386	10	Sep
	4148	10	384	Tu	387	31	Aug
	4149	1	355	Mo	388*	18	Sep
	4150	14	383	Sa	389	8	Sep
	4151	5	354	Th	390	26	Sep
	4152	1	355	Mo	391	15	Sep
	4153	14	383	Sa	392*	4	Sep
	4154	4	355	Th	393	22	Sep
	4155	3	354	Tu	394	12	Sep
	4156	13	385	Sa	395	1	Sep
	4157	6	355	Sa	396*	20	Sep
	4158	5	354	Th	397	10	Sep
	4159	9	383	Mo	398	30	Aug
	4160	6	355	Sa	399	17	Sep
	4161	12	383	Th	400*	6	Sep
220	4162	3	354	Tu	401	24	Sep
	4163	6	355	Sa	402	13	Sep
	4164	11	385	Th	403	3	Sep
	4165	5	354	Th	404*	22	Sep
	4166	2	353	Mo	405	11	Sep
	4167	11	385	Th	406	30	Aug
	4168	5	354	Th	407	19	Sep
	4169	8	385	Mo	408*	7	Sep
	4170	2	353	Mo	409	27	Sep
	4171	5	354	Th	410	15	Sep
	4172	8	385	Mo	411	4	Sep
	4173	1	355	Mo	412*	23	Sep
	4174	7	353	Sa	413	13	Sep
	4175	10	384	Tu	414	1	Sep
	4176	1	355	Mo	415	20	Sep
	4177	6	355	Sa	416*	9	Sep

	4178	12	383	Th	417	30	Aug
	4179	3	354	Tu	418	17	Sep
	4180	13	385	Sa	419	6	Sep
221	4181	7	353	Sa	420*	25	Sep
	4182	3	354	Tu	421	13	Sep
	4183	13	385	Sa	422	2	Sep
	4184	6	355	Sa	423	22	Sep
	4185	5	354	Th	424*	11	Sep
	4186	9	383	Mo	425	31	Aug
	4187	6	355	Sa	426	18	Sep
	4188	11	385	Th	427	8	Sep
	4189	5	354	Th	428*	27	Sep
	4190	2	353	Mo	429	16	Sep
	4191	11	385	Th	430	4	Sep
	4192	5	354	Th	431	24	Sep
	4193	1	355	Mo	432*	12	Sep
	4194	14	383	Sa	433	2	Sep
	4195	5	354	Th	434	20	Sep
	4196	1	355	Mo	435	9	Sep
	4197	14	383	Sa	436*	29	Aug
	4198	5	354	Th	437	16	Sep
	4199	8	385	Mo	438	5	Sep
222	4200	1	355	Mo	439	25	Sep
	4201	7	353	Sa	440*	14	Sep
	4202	10	384	Tu	441	2	Sep
	4203	1	355	Mo	442	21	Sep
	4204	6	355	Sa	443	11	Sep
	4205	12	383	Th	444*	31	Aug
	4206	3	354	Tu	445	18	Sep
	4207	13	385	Sa	446	7	Sep
	4208	6	355	Sa	447	27	Sep
	4209	5	354	Th	448*	16	Sep
	4210	9	383	Mo	449	5	Sep
	4211	6	355	Sa	450	23	Sep
	4212	5	354	Th	451	13	Sep
	4213	9	383	Mo	452*	1	Sep
	4214	6	355	Sa	453	19	Sep
	4215	5	354	Th	454	9	Sep
	4216	8	385	Mo	455	29	Aug
	4217	2	353	Mo	456*	17	Sep
	4218	11	385	Th	457	5	Sep

19 Year Cycle No.	Hebrew Year	Calendar Number	Days in Year	Day of Week	Western Year	Commencement 1st of Tishri (Julian)	
223	4219	5	354	Th	458	25	Sep
	4220	1	355	Mo	459	14	Sep
	4221	14	383	Sa	460*	3	Sep
	4222	5	354	Th	461	21	Sep
	4223	1	355	Mo	462	10	Sep
	4224	14	383	Sa	463	31	Aug
	4225	4	355	Th	464*	17	Sep
	4226	10	384	Tu	465	7	Sep
	4227	1	355	Mo	466	26	Sep
	4228	7	353	Sa	467	16	Sep
	4229	10	384	Tu	468*	3	Sep
	4230	1	355	Mo	469	22	Sep
	4231	6	355	Sa	470	12	Sep
	4232	12	383	Th	471	2	Sep
	4233	3	354	Tu	472*	19	Sep
	4234	6	355	Sa	473	8	Sep
	4235	11	385	Th	474	29	Aug
	4236	5	354	Th	475	18	Sep
	4237	9	383	Mo	476*	6	Sep
224	4238	6	355	Sa	477	24	Sep
	4239	5	354	Th	478	14	Sep
	4240	9	383	Mo	479	3	Sep
	4241	6	355	Sa	480*	20	Sep
	4242	5	354	Th	481	10	Sep
	4243	8	385	Mo	482	30	Aug
	4244	2	353	Mo	483	19	Sep
	4245	11	385	Th	484*	6	Sep
	4246	5	354	Th	485	26	Sep
	4247	1	355	Mo	486	15	Sep
	4248	14	383	Sa	487	5	Sep
	4249	5	354	Th	488*	22	Sep
	4250	1	355	Mo	489	11	Sep
	4251	13	385	Sa	490	1	Sep
	4252	7	353	Sa	491	21	Sep
	4253	3	354	Tu	492*	8	Sep

19 Year Cycle No.	Hebrew Year	Calendar Number	Days in Year	Day of Week	Western Year	Commencement 1st of Tishri (Julian)	
	4254	13	385	Th	493	28	Aug
	4255	6	355	Sa	494	17	Sep
	4256	12	383	Th	495	7	Sep
225	4257	3	354	Tu	496*	24	Sep
	4258	6	355	Sa	497	13	Sep
	4259	12	383	Th	498	3	Sep
	4260	3	354	Tu	499	21	Sep
	4261	6	355	Sa	500*	9	Sep
	4262	11	385	Th	501	30	Aug
	4263	5	354	Th	502	19	Sep
	4264	9	383	Mo	503	8	Sep
	4265	6	355	Sa	504*	25	Sep
	4266	5	354	Th	505	15	Sep
	4267	8	385	Mo	506	4	Sep
	4268	2	353	Mo	507	24	Sep
	4269	5	354	Th	508*	11	Sep
	4270	8	385	Mo	509	31	Aug
	4271	1	355	Mo	510	20	Sep
	4272	7	353	Sa	511	10	Sep
	4273	10	384	Tu	512*	28	Aug
	4274	1	355	Mo	513	16	Sep
	4275	14	383	Sa	514	6	Sep
226	4276	5	354	Th	515	24	Sep
	4277	1	355	Mo	516*	12	Sep
	4278	13	385	Sa	517	2	Sep
	4279	7	353	Sa	518	22	Sep
	4280	3	354	Tu	519	10	Sep
	4281	13	385	Sa	520*	29	Aug
	4282	6	355	Sa	521	18	Sep
	4283	12	383	Th	522	8	Sep
	4284	3	354	Tu	523	26	Sep
	4285	6	355	Sa	524*	14	Sep
	4286	11	385	Th	525	4	Sep
	4287	5	353	Mo	526	24	Sep

	4288	2	353	Mo	527	13	Sep
	4289	11	385	Th	528*	31	Aug
	4290	5	353	Mo	529	20	Sep
	4291	1	355	Mo	530	9	Sep
	4292	14	383	Sa	531	30	Aug
	4293	5	353	Mo	532*	16	Sep
	4294	8	385	Mo	533	5	Sep
227	4295	11	385	Th	534	25	Sep
	4296	4	355	Th	535	13	Sep
	4297	10	384	Tu	536*	2	Sep
	4298	1	355	Mo	537	21	Sep
	4299	7	353	Sa	538	11	Sep
	4300	10	384	Tu	539	30	Aug
	4301	1	355	Mo	540*	17	Sep
	4302	14	383	Sa	541	7	Sep
	4303	4	355	Th	542	25	Sep
	4304	3	354	Tu	543	15	Sep
	4305	13	385	Sa	544*	3	Sep
	4306	6	355	Sa	545	23	Sep
	4307	5	354	Th	546	13	Sep
	4308	9	383	Mo	547	2	Sep
	4309	6	355	Sa	548*	19	Sep
	4310	5	354	Th	549	9	Sep
	4311	9	383	Mo	550	29	Aug
	4312	6	355	Sa	551	16	Sep
	4313	11	385	Th	552*	5	Sep
228	4314	5	354	Th	553	25	Sep
	4315	2	353	Mo	554	14	Sep
	4316	11	385	Th	555	2	Sep
	4317	5	354	Th	556*	21	Sep
	4318	1	355	Mo	557	10	Sep
	4319	14	383	Sa	558	31	Aug
	4320	5	354	Th	559	18	Sep
	4321	8	385	Mo	560*	6	Sep
	4322	2	353	Mo	561	26	Sep
	4323	4	355	Th	562	14	Sep
	4324	10	384	Tu	563	4	Sep
	4325	1	355	Mo	564*	22	Sep
	4326	7	353	Sa	565	12	Sep
	4327	10	384	Tu	566	31	Aug
	4328	1	355	Mo	567	19	Sep
	4329	6	355	Sa	568*	8	Sep
	4330	12	383	Th	569	29	Aug
	4331	3	354	Tu	570	16	Sep
	4332	13	385	Sa	571	5	Sep
229	4333	6	355	Sa	572*	24	Sep
	4334	5	354	Th	573	14	Sep
	4335	9	383	Mo	574	3	Sep
	4336	6	355	Sa	575	21	Sep
	4337	5	354	Th	576*	10	Sep
	4338	9	383	Mo	577	30	Aug
	4339	6	355	Sa	578	17	Sep
	4340	11	385	Th	579	7	Sep
	4341	5	354	Th	580*	26	Sep
	4342	2	353	Mo	581	15	Sep
	4343	11	385	Th	582	3	Sep
	4344	5	354	Th	583	23	Sep
	4345	1	355	Mo	584*	11	Sep
	4346	14	383	Sa	585	1	Sep
	4347	5	354	Th	586	19	Sep
	4348	1	355	Mo	587	8	Sep
	4349	13	385	Sa	588*	28	Aug
	4350	7	353	Sa	589	17	Sep
	4351	10	384	Tu	590	5	Sep
230	4352	1	355	Mo	591	24	Sep
	4353	6	355	Sa	592*	13	Sep
	4354	12	383	Th	593	3	Sep
	4355	3	354	Tu	594	21	Sep
	4356	6	355	Sa	595	10	Sep
	4357	11	385	Th	596*	30	Aug
	4358	5	354	Th	597	19	Sep
	4359	9	383	Mo	598	8	Sep
	4360	6	355	Sa	599	26	Sep
	4361	5	354	Th	600*	15	Sep
	4362	9	383	Mo	601	4	Sep
	4363	6	355	Sa	602	22	Sep
	4364	5	354	Th	603	12	Sep
	4365	8	385	Mo	604*	31	Aug
	4366	2	353	Mo	605	20	Sep
	4367	5	354	Th	606	8	Sep
	4368	8	385	Mo	607	28	Aug
	4369	1	355	Mo	608*	16	Sep
	4370	14	383	Sa	609	6	Sep

19 Year Cycle No.	Hebrew Year	Calendar Number	Days in Year	Day of Week	Western Year	Commencement 1st of Tishri (Julian)	
231	4371	5	354	Th	610	24	Sep
	4372	1	355	Mo	611	13	Sep
	4373	14	383	Sa	612*	2	Sep
	4374	4	355	Th	613	20	Sep
	4375	3	354	Tu	614	10	Sep
	4376	13	385	Sa	615	30	Aug
	4377	7	353	Sa	616*	18	Sep
	4378	10	384	Tu	617	6	Sep
	4379	1	355	Mo	618	25	Sep
	4380	6	355	Sa	619	15	Sep
	4381	12	383	Th	620*	4	Sep
	4382	3	354	Tu	621	22	Sep
	4383	6	355	Sa	622	11	Sep
	4384	11	385	Th	623	1	Sep
	4385	5	354	Th	624*	20	Sep
	4386	2	353	Mo	625	9	Sep
	4387	11	385	Th	626	28	Aug
	4388	5	354	Th	627	17	Sep
	4389	9	383	Mo	628*	5	Sep
232	4390	6	355	Sa	629	23	Sep
	4391	5	354	Th	630	13	Sep
	4392	8	385	Mo	631	2	Sep
	4393	2	353	Mo	632*	21	Sep
	4394	4	355	Th	633	9	Sep
	4395	10	384	Tu	634	30	Aug
	4396	1	355	Mo	635	18	Sep
	4397	14	383	Sa	636*	7	Sep
	4398	5	354	Th	637	25	Sep
	4399	1	355	Mo	638	14	Sep
	4400	14	383	Sa	639	4	Sep
	4401	4	355	Th	640*	21	Sep
	4402	3	354	Tu	641	11	Sep
	4403	13	385	Sa	642	31	Aug
	4404	6	355	Sa	643	20	Sep
	4405	5	354	Th	644*	9	Sep

19 Year Cycle No.	Hebrew Year	Calendar Number	Days in Year	Day of Week	Western Year	Commencement 1st of Tishri (Julian)	
	4406	9	383	Mo	645	29	Aug
	4407	6	355	Sa	646	16	Sep
	4408	12	383	Th	647	6	Sep
233	4409	3	354	Tu	648*	23	Sep
	4410	6	355	Sa	649	12	Sep
	4411	11	385	Th	650	2	Sep
	4412	5	354	Th	651	22	Sep
	4413	2	353	Mo	652*	10	Sep
	4414	11	385	Th	653	29	Aug
	4415	5	354	Th	654	18	Sep
	4416	9	383	Mo	655	7	Sep
	4417	6	355	Sa	656*	24	Sep
	4418	5	354	Th	657	14	Sep
	4419	8	385	Mo	658	3	Sep
	4420	2	353	Mo	659	23	Sep
	4421	4	355	Th	660*	10	Sep
	4422	10	384	Tu	661	31	Aug
	4423	1	355	Mo	662	19	Sep
	4424	7	353	Sa	663	9	Sep
	4425	10	384	Tu	664*	27	Aug
	4426	1	355	Mo	665	15	Sep
	4427	13	385	Sa	666	5	Sep
234	4428	7	353	Sa	667	25	Sep
	4429	3	354	Tu	668*	12	Sep
	4430	13	385	Sa	669	1	Sep
	4431	6	355	Sa	670	21	Sep
	4432	5	354	Th	671	11	Sep
	4433	9	383	Mo	672*	30	Aug
	4434	6	355	Sa	673	17	Sep
	4435	11	385	Th	674	7	Sep
	4436	5	354	Th	675	27	Sep
	4437	2	353	Mo	676*	15	Sep
	4438	11	385	Th	677	3	Sep
	4439	5	354	Th	678	23	Sep

	4440	1	355	Mo	679	12	Sep
	4441	14	383	Sa	680*	1	Sep
	4442	5	354	Th	681	19	Sep
	4443	1	355	Mo	682	8	Sep
	4444	14	383	Sa	683	29	Aug
	4445	5	354	Th	684*	15	Sep
	4446	8	385	Mo	685	4	Sep
235	4447	1	355	Mo	686	24	Sep
	4448	7	353	Sa	687	14	Sep
	4449	10	384	Tu	688*	1	Sep
	4450	1	355	Mo	689	20	Sep
	4451	6	355	Sa	690	10	Sep
	4452	12	383	Th	691	31	Aug
	4453	3	354	Tu	692*	17	Sep
	4454	13	385	Sa	693	6	Sep
	4455	6	355	Sa	694	26	Sep
	4456	5	354	Th	695	16	Sep
	4457	9	383	Mo	696*	4	Sep
	4458	6	355	Sa	697	22	Sep
	4459	5	354	Th	698	12	Sep
	4460	9	383	Mo	699	1	Sep
	4461	6	355	Sa	700*	18	Sep
	4462	5	354	Th	701	8	Sep
	4463	8	385	Mo	702	28	Aug
	4464	2	353	Mo	703	17	Sep
	4465	11	385	Th	704*	4	Sep
236	4466	5	354	Th	705	24	Sep
	4467	1	355	Mo	706	13	Sep
	4468	14	383	Sa	707	3	Sep
	4469	5	354	Th	708*	20	Sep
	4470	1	355	Mo	709	9	Sep
	4471	14	383	Sa	710	30	Aug
	4472	4	355	Th	711	17	Sep
	4473	10	384	Tu	712*	6	Sep
	4474	1	355	Mo	713	25	Sep
	4475	7	353	Sa	714	15	Sep
	4476	10	384	Tu	715	3	Sep
	4477	1	355	Mo	716*	21	Sep
	4478	6	355	Sa	717	11	Sep
	4479	12	383	Th	718	1	Sep
	4480	3	354	Tu	719	19	Sep
	4481	6	355	Sa	720*	7	Sep

	4482	11	385	Th	721	28	Aug
	4483	5	354	Th	722	17	Sep
	4484	9	383	Mo	723	6	Sep
237	4485	6	355	Sa	724*	23	Sep
	4486	5	354	Th	725	13	Sep
	4487	9	383	Mo	726	2	Sep
	4488	6	355	Sa	727	20	Sep
	4489	5	354	Th	728*	9	Sep
	4490	8	395	Mo	729	29	Aug
	4491	2	353	Mo	730	18	Sep
	4492	11	385	Th	731	6	Sep
	4493	5	354	Th	732*	25	Sep
	4494	1	355	Mo	733	14	Sep
	4495	14	383	Sa	734	4	Sep
	4496	5	354	Th	735	22	Sep
	4497	1	355	Mo	736*	10	Sep
	4498	13	385	Sa	737	31	Aug
	4499	7	353	Sa	738	20	Sep
	4500	3	354	Tu	739	8	Sep
	4501	13	385	Sa	740*	27	Aug
	4502	6	355	Sa	741	16	Sep
	4503	12	383	Th	742	6	Sep
238	4504	3	354	Tu	743	24	Sep
	4505	6	355	Sa	744*	12	Sep
	4506	12	383	Th	745	2	Sep
	4507	3	354	Tu	746	20	Sep
	4508	6	355	Sa	747	9	Sep
	4509	11	385	Th	748*	29	Aug
	4510	5	354	Th	749	18	Sep
	4511	9	383	Mo	750	7	Sep
	4512	6	355	Sa	751	25	Sep
	4513	5	354	Th	752*	14	Sep
	4514	8	385	Mo	753	3	Sep
	4515	2	353	Mo	754	23	Sep
	4516	5	354	Th	755	11	Sep
	4517	8	385	Mo	756*	30	Aug
	4518	1	355	Mo	757	19	Sep
	4519	7	353	Sa	758	9	Sep
	4520	10	384	Tu	759	28	Aug
	4521	1	355	Mo	760*	15	Sep
	4522	14	383	Sa	761	5	Sep

19 Year Cycle No.	Hebrew Year	Calendar Number	Days in Year	Day of Week	Western Year	Commencement 1st of Tishri (Julian)	
239	4523	5	354	Th	762	23	Sep
	4524	1	355	Mo	763	12	Sep
	4525	13	385	Sa	764*	1	Sep
	4526	7	353	Sa	765	21	Sep
	4527	3	354	Tu	766	9	Sep
	4528	13	385	Sa	767	29	Aug
	4529	6	355	Sa	768*	17	Sep
	4530	12	383	Th	769	7	Sep
	4531	3	354	Tu	770	25	Sep
	4532	6	355	Sa	771	14	Sep
	4533	11	385	Th	772*	3	Sep
	4534	5	354	Th	773	23	Sep
	4535	2	353	Mo	774	12	Sep
	4536	11	385	Th	775	31	Aug
	4537	5	354	Th	776*	19	Sep
	4538	1	355	Mo	777	8	Sep
	4539	14	383	Sa	778	29	Aug
	4540	5	354	Th	779	16	Sep
	4541	8	385	Mo	780*	4	Sep
240	4542	2	353	Mo	781	24	Sep
	4543	6	355	Sa	782	12	Sep
	4544	10	384	Tu	783	2	Sep
	4545	1	355	Mo	784*	20	Sep
	4546	7	353	Sa	785	10	Sep
	4547	10	384	Tu	786	29	Aug
	4548	1	355	Mo	787	17	Sep
	4549	14	383	Sa	788*	6	Sep
	4550	4	355	Th	789	24	Sep
	4551	3	354	Tu	790	14	Sep
	4552	13	385	Sa	791	3	Sep
	4553	6	355	Sa	792*	22	Sep
	4554	5	354	Th	793	12	Sep
	4555	9	383	Mo	794	1	Sep
	4556	6	355	Sa	795	19	Sep
	4557	5	354	Th	796*	8	Sep

19 Year Cycle No.	Hebrew Year	Calendar Number	Days in Year	Day of Week	Western Year	Commencement 1st of Tishri (Julian)	
	4558	9	383	Mo	797	28	Aug
	4559	6	355	Sa	798	15	Sep
	4560	11	385	Th	799	5	Sep
241	4561	5	354	Th	800*	24	Sep
	4562	2	353	Mo	801	13	Sep
	4563	11	385	Th	802	1	Sep
	4564	5	354	Th	803	21	Sep
	4565	1	355	Mo	804*	9	Sep
	4566	14	383	Sa	805	30	Aug
	4567	5	354	Th	806	17	Sep
	4568	8	385	Mo	807	6	Sep
	4569	2	353	Mo	808*	25	Sep
	4570	4	355	Th	809	13	Sep
	4571	10	384	Tu	810	3	Sep
	4572	1	355	Mo	811	22	Sep
	4573	7	353	Sa	812*	11	Sep
	4574	10	384	Tu	813	30	Aug
	4575	1	355	Mo	814	18	Sep
	4576	6	355	Sa	815	8	Sep
	4577	12	383	Th	816*	28	Aug
	4578	3	354	Tu	817	15	Sep
	4579	13	385	Sa	818	4	Sep
242	4580	6	355	Sa	819	24	Sep
	4581	5	354	Th	820*	13	Sep
	4582	9	383	Mo	821	2	Sep
	4583	6	355	Sa	822	20	Sep
	4584	5	354	Th	823	10	Sep
	4585	9	383	Mo	824*	29	Aug
	4586	6	355	Sa	825	16	Sep
	4587	11	385	Th	826	6	Sep
	4588	5	354	Th	827	26	Sep
	4589	2	353	Mo	828*	14	Sep
	4590	11	385	Th	829	2	Sep
	4591	5	354	Th	830	22	Sep

	4592	1	355	Mo	831	11	Sep
	4593	14	383	Sa	832*	31	Aug
	4594	5	354	Th	833	18	Sep
	4595	1	355	Mo	834	7	Sep
	4596	13	385	Sa	835	28	Aug
	4597	7	353	Sa	836*	16	Sep
	4598	10	384	Tu	837	4	Sep
243	4599	1	355	Mo	838	23	Sep
	4600	6	355	Sa	839	13	Sep
	4601	12	383	Th	840*	2	Sep
	4602	3	354	Tu	841	20	Sep
	4603	6	355	Sa	842	9	Sep
	4604	12	383	Th	843	30	Aug
	4605	3	354	Tu	844*	16	Sep
	4606	13	385	Sa	845	5	Sep
	4607	6	355	Sa	846	25	Sep
	4608	5	354	Th	847	15	Sep
	4609	9	383	Mo	848*	3	Sep
	4610	6	355	Sa	849	21	Sep
	4611	5	354	Th	850	11	Sep
	4612	8	385	Mo	851	31	Aug
	4613	2	353	Mo	852*	19	Sep
	4614	5	354	Th	853	7	Sep
	4615	8	385	Mo	854	27	Aug
	4616	1	355	Mo	855	16	Sep
	4617	14	383	Sa	856*	5	Sep
244	4618	5	354	Th	857	23	Sep
	4619	1	355	Mo	858	12	Sep
	4620	14	383	Sa	859	2	Sep
	4621	4	355	Th	860*	19	Sep
	4622	3	354	Tu	861	9	Sep
	4623	13	385	Sa	862	29	Aug
	4624	7	353	Sa	863	18	Sep
	4625	10	384	Tu	864*	5	Sep
	4626	1	355	Mo	865	24	Sep
	4627	6	355	Sa	866	14	Sep
	4628	12	383	Th	867	4	Sep
	4629	3	354	Tu	868*	21	Sep
	4630	6	355	Sa	869	10	Sep
	4631	11	385	Th	870	31	Aug
	4632	5	354	Th	871	20	Sep
	4633	2	353	Mo	872*	8	Sep
	4634	11	385	Th	873	27	Aug
	4635	5	354	Th	874	16	Sep
	4636	9	383	Mo	875	5	Sep
245	4637	6	355	Sa	876*	22	Sep
	4638	5	354	Th	877	12	Sep
	4639	8	385	Mo	878	1	Sep
	4640	2	353	Mo	879	21	Sep
	4641	4	355	Th	880*	8	Sep
	4642	10	384	Tu	881	29	Aug
	4643	1	355	Mo	882	17	Sep
	4644	14	383	Sa	883	7	Sep
	4645	5	354	Th	884*	24	Sep
	4646	1	355	Mo	885	13	Sep
	4647	14	383	Sa	886	3	Sep
	4648	4	355	Th	887	21	Sep
	4649	3	354	Tu	888*	10	Sep
	4650	13	385	Sa	889	30	Aug
	4651	6	355	Sa	890	19	Sep
	4652	5	354	Th	891	9	Sep
	4653	9	383	Mo	892*	28	Aug
	4654	6	355	Sa	893	15	Sep
	4655	12	383	Th	894	5	Sep
246	4656	3	354	Tu	895	23	Sep
	4657	6	355	Sa	896*	11	Sep
	4658	11	385	Th	897	1	Sep
	4659	5	354	Th	898	21	Sep
	4660	2	353	Mo	899	10	Sep
	4661	11	385	Th	900*	28	Aug
	4662	5	354	Th	901	17	Sep
	4663	9	383	Mo	902	6	Sep
	4664	6	355	Sa	903	24	Sep
	4665	5	354	Th	904*	13	Sep
	4666	8	385	Mo	905	2	Sep
	4667	2	353	Mo	906	22	Sep
	4668	4	355	Th	907	10	Sep
	4669	10	384	Tu	908*	30	Aug
	4670	1	355	Mo	909	18	Sep
	4671	7	353	Sa	910	8	Sep
	4672	10	384	Tu	911	27	Aug
	4673	1	355	Mo	912*	14	Sep
	4674	13	385	Sa	913	4	Sep

19 Year Cycle No.	Hebrew Year	Calendar Number	Days in Year	Day of Week	Western Year	Commencement 1st of Tishri (Julian)
247	4675	7	353	Sa	914	24 Sep
	4676	3	354	Tu	915	12 Sep
	4677	13	385	Sa	916*	31 Aug
	4678	6	355	Sa	917	20 Sep
	4679	5	354	Th	918	10 Sep
	4680	9	383	Mo	919	30 Aug
	4681	6	355	Sa	920*	16 Sep
	4682	11	385	Th	921	6 Sep
	4683	5	354	Th	922	26 Sep
	4684	2	353	Mo	923	15 Sep
	4685	11	385	Th	924*	2 Sep
	4686	5	354	Th	925	22 Sep
	4687	1	355	Mo	926	11 Sep
	4688	14	383	Sa	927	1 Sep
	4689	5	354	Th	928*	18 Sep
	4690	1	355	Mo	929	7 Sep
	4691	14	383	Sa	930	28 Aug
	4692	5	354	Th	931	15 Sep
	4693	8	385	Mo	932*	3 Sep
248	4694	1	355	Mo	933	23 Sep
	4695	7	353	Sa	934	13 Sep
	4696	10	384	Tu	935	1 Sep
	4697	1	355	Mo	936*	19 Sep
	4698	6	355	Sa	937	9 Sep
	4699	12	383	Th	938	30 Aug
	4700	3	354	Tu	939	17 Sep
	4701	13	385	Sa	940*	5 Sep
	4702	6	355	Sa	941	25 Sep
	4703	5	354	Th	942	15 Sep
	4704	9	383	Mo	943	4 Sep
	4705	6	355	Sa	944*	21 Sep
	4706	5	354	Th	945	11 Sep
	4707	9	383	Mo	946	31 Aug
	4708	6	355	Sa	947	18 Sep
	4709	5	354	Th	948*	7 Sep

19 Year Cycle No.	Hebrew Year	Calendar Number	Days in Year	Day of Week	Western Year	Commencement 1st of Tishri (Julian)
	4710	8	385	Mo	949	27 Aug
	4711	2	353	Mo	950	16 Sep
	4712	11	385	Th	951	4 Sep
249	4713	5	354	Th	952*	23 Sep
	4714	1	355	Mo	953	12 Sep
	4715	14	383	Sa	954	2 Sep
	4716	5	354	Th	955	20 Sep
	4717	1	355	Mo	956*	8 Sep
	4718	14	383	Sa	957	29 Aug
	4719	4	355	Th	958	16 Sep
	4720	10	384	Tu	959	6 Sep
	4721	1	355	Mo	960*	24 Sep
	4722	7	353	Sa	961	14 Sep
	4723	10	384	Tu	962	2 Sep
	4724	1	355	Mo	963	21 Sep
	4725	6	355	Sa	964*	10 Sep
	4726	12	383	Th	965	31 Aug
	4727	3	354	Tu	966	18 Sep
	4728	6	355	Sa	967	7 Sep
	4729	11	385	Th	968*	27 Aug
	4730	5	354	Th	969	16 Sep
	4731	9	383	Mo	970	5 Sep
250	4732	6	355	Sa	971	23 Sep
	4733	5	354	Th	972*	12 Sep
	4734	9	383	Mo	973	1 Sep
	4735	6	355	Sa	974	19 Sep
	4736	5	354	Th	975	9 Sep
	4737	8	385	Mo	976*	28 Aug
	4738	2	353	Mo	977	17 Sep
	4739	11	385	Th	978	5 Sep
	4740	5	354	Th	979	25 Sep
	4741	1	355	Mo	980*	13 Sep
	4742	14	383	Sa	981	3 Sep
	4743	5	354	Th	982	21 Sep

	4744	1	355	Mo	983	10	Sep
	4745	14	383	Sa	984*	30	Aug
	4746	4	355	Th	985	17	Sep
	4747	3	354	Tu	986	7	Sep
	4748	13	385	Sa	987	27	Aug
	4749	7	353	Sa	988*	15	Sep
	4750	10	384	Tu	989	3	Sep
251	4751	1	355	Mo	990	22	Sep
	4752	6	355	Sa	991	12	Sep
	4753	12	383	Th	992*	1	Sep
	4754	3	354	Tu	993	19	Sep
	4755	6	355	Sa	994	8	Sep
	4756	11	385	Th	995	29	Aug
	4757	5	354	Th	996*	17	Sep
	4758	9	383	Mo	997	6	Sep
	4759	6	355	Sa	998	24	Sep
	4760	5	354	Th	999	14	Sep
	4761	8	385	Mo	1000*	2	Sep
	4762	2	353	Mo	1001	22	Sep
	4763	5	354	Th	1002	10	Sep
	4764	8	385	Mo	1003	30	Aug
	4765	1	355	Mo	1004*	18	Sep
	4766	7	353	Sa	1005	8	Sep
	4767	10	384	Tu	1006	27	Aug
	4768	1	355	Mo	1007	15	Sep
	4769	14	383	Sa	1008*	4	Sep
252	4770	5	354	Th	1009	22	Sep
	4771	1	355	Mo	1010	11	Sep
	4772	13	385	Sa	1011	1	Sep
	4773	7	353	Sa	1012*	20	Sep
	4774	3	354	Tu	1013	8	Sep
	4775	13	385	Sa	1014	28	Aug
	4776	6	355	Sa	1015	17	Sep
	4777	12	383	Th	1016*	6	Sep
	4778	3	354	Tu	1017	24	Sep
	4779	6	355	Sa	1018	13	Sep
	4780	11	385	Th	1019	3	Sep
	4781	5	354	Th	1020*	22	Sep
	4782	2	353	Mo	1021	11	Sep
	4783	11	385	Th	1022	30	Aug
	4784	5	354	Th	1023	19	Sep
	4785	1	355	Mo	1024*	7	Sep
	4786	14	383	Sa	1025	28	Aug
	4787	5	354	Th	1026	15	Sep
	4788	8	385	Mo	1027	4	Sep
253	4789	2	353	Mo	1028*	23	Sep
	4790	5	354	Th	1029	11	Sep
	4791	8	385	Mo	1030	31	Aug
	4792	1	355	Mo	1031	20	Sep
	4793	7	353	Sa	1032*	9	Sep
	4794	10	384	Tu	1033	28	Aug
	4795	1	355	Mo	1034	16	Sep
	4796	14	383	Sa	1035	6	Sep
	4797	4	355	Th	1036*	23	Sep
	4798	3	354	Tu	1037	13	Sep
	4799	13	385	Sa	1038	2	Sep
	4800	6	355	Sa	1039	22	Sep
	4801	5	354	Th	1040*	11	Sep
	4802	9	383	Mo	1041	31	Aug
	4803	6	355	Sa	1042	18	Sep
	4804	5	354	Th	1043	8	Sep
	4805	9	383	Mo	1044*	27	Aug
	4806	6	355	Sa	1045	14	Sep
	4807	11	385	Th	1046	4	Sep
254	4808	5	354	Th	1047	24	Sep
	4809	2	353	Mo	1048*	12	Sep
	4810	11	385	Th	1049	31	Aug
	4811	5	354	Th	1050	20	Sep
	4812	1	355	Mo	1051	9	Sep
	4813	14	383	Sa	1052*	29	Aug
	4814	5	354	Th	1053	16	Sep
	4815	8	385	Mo	1054	5	Sep
	4816	2	353	Mo	1055	25	Sep
	4817	4	355	Th	1056*	12	Sep
	4818	10	384	Tu	1057	2	Sep
	4819	1	355	Mo	1058	21	Sep
	4820	7	353	Sa	1059	11	Sep
	4821	10	384	Tu	1060*	29	Aug
	4822	1	355	Mo	1061	17	Sep
	4823	6	355	Sa	1062	7	Sep
	4824	12	383	Th	1063	28	Aug
	4825	3	354	Tu	1064*	14	Sep
	4826	13	385	Sa	1065	3	Sep

19 Year Cycle No.	Hebrew Year	Calendar Number	Days in Year	Day of Week	Western Year	Commencement 1st of Tishri (Julian)	
255	4827	6	355	Sa	1066	23	Sep
	4828	5	354	Th	1067	13	Sep
	4829	9	383	Mo	1068*	1	Sep
	4830	6	355	Sa	1069	19	Sep
	4831	5	354	Th	1070	9	Sep
	4832	9	383	Mo	1071	29	Aug
	4833	6	355	Sa	1072*	15	Sep
	4834	11	385	Th	1073	5	Sep
	4835	5	354	Th	1074	25	Sep
	4836	2	353	Mo	1075	14	Sep
	4837	11	385	Th	1076*	1	Sep
	4838	5	354	Th	1077	21	Sep
	4839	1	355	Mo	1078	10	Sep
	4840	14	383	Sa	1079	31	Aug
	4841	5	354	Th	1080*	17	Sep
	4842	1	355	Mo	1081	6	Sep
	4843	13	385	Sa	1082	27	Aug
	4844	7	353	Sa	1083	16	Sep
	4845	10	384	Tu	1084*	3	Sep
256	4846	1	355	Mo	1085	22	Sep
	4847	6	355	Sa	1086	12	Sep
	4848	12	383	Th	1087	2	Sep
	4849	3	354	Tu	1088*	19	Sep
	4850	6	355	Sa	1089	8	Sep
	4851	12	383	Th	1090	29	Aug
	4852	3	354	Tu	1091	16	Sep
	4853	13	385	Sa	1092*	4	Sep
	4854	6	355	Sa	1093	24	Sep
	4855	5	354	Th	1094	14	Sep
	4856	9	383	Mo	1095	3	Sep
	4857	6	355	Sa	1096*	20	Sep
	4858	5	354	Th	1097	10	Sep
	4859	8	385	Mo	1098	30	Aug
	4860	2	353	Mo	1099	19	Sep
	4861	5	354	Th	1100*	6	Sep
	4862	8	385	Mo	1101	26	Aug
	4863	1	355	Mo	1102	15	Sep
	4864	14	383	Sa	1103	5	Sep
257	4865	5	354	Th	1104*	22	Sep
	4866	1	355	Mo	1105	11	Sep
	4867	14	383	Sa	1106	1	Sep
	4868	4	355	Th	1107	19	Sep
	4869	3	354	Tu	1108*	8	Sep
	4870	13	385	Sa	1109	28	Aug
	4871	7	353	Sa	1110	17	Sep
	4872	10	384	Tu	1111	5	Sep
	4873	1	355	Mo	1112*	23	Sep
	4874	6	355	Sa	1113	13	Sep
	4875	12	383	Th	1114	3	Sep
	4876	3	354	Tu	1115	21	Sep
	4877	6	355	Sa	1116*	9	Sep
	4878	11	385	Th	1117	30	Aug
	4879	5	354	Th	1118	19	Sep
	4880	2	353	Mo	1119	8	Sep
	4881	11	385	Th	1120*	26	Aug
	4882	5	354	Th	1121	15	Sep
	4883	9	383	Mo	1122	4	Sep
258	4884	6	355	Sa	1123	22	Sep
	4885	5	354	Th	1124*	11	Sep
	4886	8	385	Mo	1125	31	Aug
	4887	2	353	Mo	1126	20	Sep
	4888	4	355	Th	1127	8	Sep
	4889	10	384	Tu	1128*	28	Aug
	4890	1	355	Mo	1129	16	Sep
	4891	14	383	Sa	1130	6	Sep
	4892	5	354	Th	1131	24	Sep
	4893	1	355	Mo	1132*	12	Sep
	4894	14	383	Sa	1133	2	Sep
	4895	4	355	Th	1134	20	Sep

Cycle	Year		Days	Day	Year	Date	Month
	4896	3	354	Tu	1135	10	Sep
	4897	13	385	Sa	1136*	29	Aug
	4898	6	355	Sa	1137	18	Sep
	4899	5	354	Th	1138	8	Sep
	4900	9	383	Mo	1139	28	Aug
	4901	6	355	Sa	1140*	14	Sep
	4902	12	383	Th	1141	4	Sep
259	4903	3	354	Tu	1142	22	Sep
	4904	6	355	Sa	1143	11	Sep
	4905	11	385	Th	1144*	31	Aug
	4906	5	354	Th	1145	20	Sep
	4907	2	353	Mo	1146	9	Sep
	4908	11	385	Th	1147	28	Aug
	4909	5	354	Th	1148*	16	Sep
	4910	9	383	Mo	1149	5	Sep
	4911	6	355	Sa	1150	23	Sep
	4912	5	354	Th	1151	13	Sep
	4913	8	385	Mo	1152*	1	Sep
	4914	2	353	Mo	1153	21	Sep
	4915	4	355	Th	1154	9	Sep
	4916	10	384	Tu	1155	30	Aug
	4917	1	355	Mo	1156*	17	Sep
	4918	7	353	Sa	1157	7	Sep
	4919	10	384	Tu	1158	26	Aug
	4920	1	355	Mo	1159	14	Sep
	4921	13	385	Sa	1160*	3	Sep
260	4922	7	353	Sa	1161	23	Sep
	4923	3	354	Tu	1162	11	Sep
	4924	13	385	Sa	1163	31	Aug
	4925	6	355	Sa	1164*	19	Sep
	4926	5	354	Th	1165	9	Sep
	4927	9	383	Mo	1166	29	Aug
	4928	6	355	Sa	1167	16	Sep
	4929	12	383	Th	1168*	5	Sep
	4930	3	354	Tu	1169	23	Sep
	4931	6	355	Sa	1170	12	Sep
	4932	11	385	Th	1171	2	Sep
	4933	5	354	Th	1172*	21	Sep
	4934	2	353	Mo	1173	10	Sep
	4935	11	385	Th	1174	29	Aug
	4936	5	354	Th	1175	18	Sep
	4937	1	355	Mo	1176*	6	Sep
	4938	14	383	Sa	1177	27	Aug
	4939	5	354	Th	1178	14	Sep
	4940	8	385	Mo	1179	3	Sep
261	4941	1	355	Mo	1180*	22	Sep
	4942	7	353	Sa	1181	12	Sep
	4943	10	384	Tu	1182	31	Aug
	4944	1	355	Mo	1183	19	Sep
	4945	6	355	Sa	1184*	8	Sep
	4946	12	383	Th	1185	29	Aug
	4947	3	354	Tu	1186	16	Sep
	4948	13	385	Sa	1187	5	Sep
	4949	6	355	Sa	1188*	24	Sep
	4950	5	354	Th	1189	14	Sep
	4951	9	383	Mo	1190	3	Sep
	4952	6	355	Sa	1191	21	Sep
	4953	5	354	Th	1192*	10	Sep
	4954	9	383	Mo	1193	30	Aug
	4955	6	355	Sa	1194	17	Sep
	4956	5	354	Th	1195	7	Sep
	4957	8	385	Mo	1196*	26	Aug
	4958	2	353	Mo	1197	15	Sep
	4959	11	385	Th	1198	3	Sep
262	4960	5	354	Th	1199	23	Sep
	4961	1	355	Mo	1200*	11	Sep
	4962	14	383	Sa	1201	1	Sep
	4963	5	354	Th	1202	19	Sep
	4964	1	355	Mo	1203	8	Sep
	4965	14	383	Sa	1204*	28	Aug
	4966	4	355	Th	1205	15	Sep
	4967	10	384	Tu	1206	5	Sep
	4968	1	355	Mo	1207	24	Sep
	4969	7	353	Sa	1208*	13	Sep
	4970	10	384	Tu	1209	1	Sep
	4971	1	355	Mo	1210	20	Sep
	4972	6	355	Sa	1211	10	Sep
	4973	12	383	Th	1212*	30	Aug
	4974	3	354	Tu	1213	17	Sep
	4975	6	355	Sa	1214	6	Sep
	4976	11	385	Th	1215	27	Aug
	4977	5	354	Th	1216*	15	Sep
	4978	9	383	Mo	1217	4	Sep

19 Year Cycle No.	Hebrew Year	Calendar Number	Days in Year	Day of Week	Western Year	Commencement 1st of Tishri (Julian)	
263	4979	6	355	Sa	1218	22	Sep
	4980	5	354	Th	1219	12	Sep
	4981	9	383	Mo	1220*	31	Aug
	4982	6	355	Sa	1221	18	Sep
	4983	5	354	Th	1222	8	Sep
	4984	8	385	Mo	1223	28	Aug
	4985	2	353	Mo	1224*	16	Sep
	4986	11	385	Th	1225	4	Sep
	4987	5	354	Th	1226	24	Sep
	4988	1	355	Mo	1227	13	Sep
	4989	14	383	Sa	1228*	2	Sep
	4990	5	354	Th	1229	20	Sep
	4991	1	355	Mo	1230	9	Sep
	4992	14	383	Sa	1231	30	Aug
	4993	4	355	Th	1232*	16	Sep
	4994	3	354	Tu	1233	6	Sep
	4995	13	385	Sa	1234	26	Aug
	4996	7	353	Sa	1235	15	Sep
	4997	10	384	Tu	1236*	2	Sep
264	4998	1	355	Mo	1237	21	Sep
	4999	6	355	Sa	1238	11	Sep
	5000	12	383	Th	1239	1	Sep
	5001	3	354	Tu	1240*	18	Sep
	5002	6	355	Sa	1241	7	Sep
	5003	11	385	Th	1242	28	Aug
	5004	5	354	Th	1243	17	Sep
	5005	9	383	Mo	1244*	5	Sep
	5006	6	355	Sa	1245	23	Sep
	5007	5	354	Th	1246	13	Sep
	5008	9	383	Mo	1247	2	Sep
	5009	6	355	Sa	1248*	18	Sep
	5010	5	354	Th	1249	9	Sep
	5011	8	385	Mo	1250	29	Aug
	5012	2	353	Mo	1251	18	Sep
	5013	4	355	Th	1252*	5	Sep
	5014	10	384	Tu	1253	26	Aug
	5015	1	355	Mo	1254	14	Sep
	5016	14	383	Sa	1255	4	Sep
265	5017	5	354	Th	1256*	21	Sep
	5018	1	355	Mo	1257	10	Sep
	5019	13	385	Sa	1258	31	Aug
	5020	7	353	Sa	1259	20	Sep
	5021	3	354	Tu	1260*	7	Sep
	5022	13	385	Sa	1261	27	Aug
	5023	6	355	Sa	1262	16	Sep
	5024	12	383	Th	1263	6	Sep
	5025	3	354	Tu	1264*	23	Sep
	5026	6	355	Sa	1265	12	Sep
	5027	11	385	Th	1266	2	Sep
	5028	5	354	Th	1267	22	Sep
	5029	2	353	Mo	1268*	10	Sep
	5030	11	385	Th	1269	29	Aug
	5031	5	354	Th	1270	18	Sep
	5032	1	355	Mo	1271	7	Sep
	5033	14	383	Sa	1272*	27	Aug
	5034	5	354	Th	1273	14	Sep
	5035	8	385	Mo	1274	3	Sep
266	5036	2	353	Mo	1275	23	Sep
	5037	5	354	Th	1276*	10	Sep
	5038	13	385	Sa	1277	30	Aug
	5039	1	355	Mo	1278	19	Sep
	5040	7	353	Sa	1279	9	Sep
	5041	10	384	Tu	1280*	27	Aug
	5042	1	355	Mo	1281	15	Sep
	5043	14	383	Sa	1282	5	Sep
	5055	4	355	Th	1283	23	Sep
	5045	3	354	Tu	1284*	12	Sep
	5046	13	385	Sa	1285	1	Sep
	5047	6	355	Sa	1286	21	Sep

Cycle	Year		Length	Day	Year	Date	
	5048	5	354	Th	1287	11	Sep
	5049	9	383	Mo	1288*	30	Aug
	5050	6	355	Sa	1289	17	Sep
	5051	5	354	Th	1290	7	Sep
	5052	9	383	Mo	1291	27	Aug
	5053	6	355	Sa	1292*	13	Sep
	5054	11	385	Th	1293	3	Sep
267	5055	5	354	Th	1294	23	Sep
	5056	2	353	Mo	1295	12	Sep
	5057	11	385	Th	1296*	30	Aug
	5058	5	354	Th	1297	19	Sep
	5059	1	355	Mo	1298	8	Sep
	5060	14	383	Sa	1299	29	Aug
	5061	5	354	Th	1300*	15	Sep
	5062	8	385	Mo	1301	4	Sep
	5063	2	353	Mo	1302	24	Sep
	5064	4	355	Th	1303	12	Sep
	5065	10	384	Tu	1304*	1	Sep
	5066	1	355	Mo	1305	20	Sep
	5067	7	353	Sa	1306	10	Sep
	5068	10	384	Tu	1307	29	Aug
	5069	1	355	Mo	1308*	16	Sep
	5070	6	355	Sa	1309	6	Sep
	5071	12	383	Th	1310	27	Aug
	5072	3	354	Tu	1311	14	Sep
	5073	13	385	Sa	1312*	2	Sep
268	5074	6	355	Sa	1313	22	Sep
	5075	5	354	Th	1314	12	Sep
	5076	9	383	Mo	1315	1	Sep
	5077	6	355	Sa	1316*	18	Sep
	5078	5	354	Th	1317	8	Sep
	5079	9	383	Mo	1318	28	Aug
	5080	6	355	Sa	1319	15	Sep
	5081	11	385	Th	1320*	4	Sep
	5082	5	354	Th	1321	24	Sep
	5083	2	353	Mo	1322	13	Sep
	5084	11	385	Th	1323	1	Sep
	5085	5	354	Th	1324*	20	Sep
	5086	1	355	Mo	1325	9	Sep
	5087	14	383	Sa	1326	30	Aug
	5088	5	354	Th	1327	17	Sep
	5089	1	355	Mo	1328*	5	Sep
	5090	13	385	Sa	1329	26	Aug
	5091	7	353	Sa	1330	15	Sep
	5092	10	384	Tu	1331	3	Sep
269	5093	1	355	Mo	1332*	21	Sep
	5094	6	355	Sa	1333	11	Sep
	5095	12	383	Th	1334	1	Sep
	5096	3	354	Tu	1335	19	Sep
	5097	6	355	Sa	1336*	7	Sep
	5098	12	383	Th	1337	28	Aug
	5099	3	354	Tu	1338	15	Sep
	5100	13	385	Sa	1339	4	Sep
	5101	6	355	Sa	1340*	23	Sep
	5102	5	354	Th	1341	13	Sep
	5103	9	383	Mo	1342	2	Sep
	5104	6	355	Sa	1343	20	Sep
	5105	5	354	Th	1344*	9	Sep
	5106	8	385	Mo	1345	29	Aug
	5107	2	353	Mo	1346	18	Sep
	5108	5	354	Th	1347	6	Sep
	5109	8	385	Mo	1348*	25	Aug
	5110	1	355	Mo	1349	14	Sep
	5111	14	383	Sa	1350	4	Sep
270	5112	5	354	Th	1351	22	Sep
	5113	1	355	Mo	1352*	10	Sep
	5114	14	383	Sa	1353	31	Aug
	5115	5	354	Th	1354	18	Sep
	5116	1	355	Mo	1355	7	Sep
	5117	13	385	Sa	1356*	27	Aug
	5118	7	353	Sa	1357	16	Sep
	5119	10	384	Tu	1358	4	Sep
	5120	1	355	Mo	1359	23	Sep
	5121	6	355	Sa	1360*	12	Sep
	5122	12	383	Th	1361	2	Sep
	5123	3	354	Tu	1362	20	Sep
	5124	6	355	Sa	1363	9	Sep
	5125	11	385	Th	1364*	29	Aug
	5126	5	354	Th	1365	18	Sep
	5127	2	353	Mo	1366	7	Sep
	5128	11	385	Th	1367	26	Aug
	5129	5	354	Th	1368*	14	Sep
	5130	9	383	Mo	1369	3	Sep

19 Year Cycle No.	Hebrew Year	Calendar Number	Days in Year	Day of Week	Western Year	Commencement 1st of Tishri (Julian)	
271	5131	6	355	Sa	1370	21	Sep
	5132	5	354	Th	1371	11	Sep
	5133	8	385	Mo	1372*	30	Aug
	5134	2	353	Mo	1373	19	Sep
	5135	4	355	Th	1374	7	Sep
	5136	10	384	Tu	1375	28	Aug
	5137	1	355	Mo	1376*	15	Sep
	5138	14	383	Sa	1377	5	Sep
	5139	5	354	Th	1378	23	Sep
	5140	1	355	Mo	1379	12	Sep
	5141	14	383	Sa	1380*	1	Sep
	5142	4	355	Th	1381	19	Sep
	5143	3	354	Tu	1382	9	Sep
	5144	13	385	Sa	1383	29	Aug
	5145	6	355	Sa	1384*	17	Sep
	5146	5	354	Th	1385	7	Sep
	5147	9	383	Mo	1386	27	Aug
	5148	6	355	Sa	1387	14	Sep
	5149	12	383	Th	1388*	3	Sep
272	5150	3	354	Tu	1389	21	Sep
	5151	6	355	Sa	1390	10	Sep
	5152	11	383	Th	1391	31	Aug
	5153	5	354	Th	1392*	19	Sep
	5154	2	353	Mo	1393	8	Sep
	5155	11	383	Th	1394	27	Aug
	5156	5	354	Th	1395	16	Sep
	5157	9	383	Mo	1396*	4	Sep
	5158	6	355	Sa	1397	22	Sep
	5159	5	354	Th	1398	12	Sep
	5160	8	385	Mo	1399	1	Sep
	5161	2	353	Mo	1400*	20	Sep
	5162	4	355	Th	1401	8	Sep
	5163	10	384	Tu	1402	29	Aug
	5164	1	355	Mo	1403	17	Sep
	5165	7	353	Sa	1404*	6	Sep

19 Year Cycle No.	Hebrew Year	Calendar Number	Days in Year	Day of Week	Western Year	Commencement 1st of Tishri (Julian)	
	5166	10	384	Tu	1405	25	Aug
	5167	1	355	Mo	1406	13	Sep
	5168	13	385	Sa	1407	3	Sep
273	5169	7	353	Sa	1408*	22	Sep
	5170	3	354	Tu	1409	10	Sep
	5171	13	385	Sa	1410	30	Aug
	5172	6	355	Sa	1411	19	Sep
	5173	5	354	Th	1412*	8	Sep
	5174	9	383	Mo	1413	28	Aug
	5175	6	355	Sa	1414	15	Sep
	5176	12	383	Th	1415	5	Sep
	5177	3	354	Tu	1416*	22	Sep
	5178	6	355	Sa	1417	11	Sep
	5179	11	385	Th	1418	1	Sep
	5180	5	354	Th	1419	21	Sep
	5181	2	353	Mo	1420*	9	Sep
	5182	11	385	Th	1421	28	Aug
	5183	5	354	Th	1422	17	Sep
	5184	1	355	Mo	1423	6	Sep
	5185	14	383	Sa	1424*	26	Aug
	5186	5	354	Th	1425	13	Sep
	5187	8	385	Mo	1426	2	Sep
274	5188	1	355	Mo	1427	22	Sep
	5189	7	353	Sa	1428*	11	Sep
	5190	10	384	Tu	1429	30	Aug
	5191	1	355	Mo	1430	18	Sep
	5192	6	355	Sa	1431	8	Sep
	5193	12	383	Th	1432*	28	Aug
	5194	3	354	Tu	1433	15	Sep
	5195	13	385	Sa	1434	4	Sep
	5196	7	353	Sa	1435	24	Sep
	5197	3	354	Tu	1436*	11	Sep
	5198	13	385	Sa	1437	31	Aug
	5199	6	355	Sa	1438	20	Sep

	5200	5	354	Th	1439	10	Sep
	5201	9	383	Mo	1440*	29	Aug
	5202	6	355	Sa	1441	16	Sep
	5203	5	354	Th	1442	6	Sep
	5204	8	385	Mo	1443	26	Aug
	5205	2	353	Mo	1444*	14	Sep
	5206	11	385	Th	1445	2	Sep
275	5207	5	354	Th	1446	22	Sep
	5208	1	355	Mo	1447	11	Sep
	5209	14	383	Sa	1448*	31	Aug
	5210	5	354	Th	1449	18	Sep
	5211	1	355	Mo	14 50	7	Sep
	5212	14	383	Sa	1451	28	Aug
	5213	4	355	Th	1452*	14	Sep
	5214	10	384	Tu	1453	4	Sep
	5215	1	355	Mo	1454	23	Sep
	5216	7	353	Sa	1455	13	Sep
	5217	10	384	Tu	1456*	31	Aug
	5218	1	355	Mo	1457	19	Sep
	5219	6	355	Sa	1458	9	Sep
	5220	12	383	Th	1459	30	Aug
	5221	3	354	Tu	1460*	16	Sep
	5222	6	355	Sa	1461	5	Sep
	5223	11	385	Th	1462	26	Aug
	5224	5	354	Th	1463	15	Sep
	5225	9	383	Mo	1464*	3	Sep
276	5226	6	355	Sa	1465	21	Sep
	5227	5	354	Th	1466	11	Sep
	5228	9	383	Mo	1467	31	Aug
	5229	6	355	Sa	1468*	17	Sep
	5230	5	354	Th	1469	7	Sep
	5231	8	385	Mo	1470	27	Aug
	5232	2	353	Mo	1471	16	Sep
	5233	11	385	Th	1472*	3	Sep
	5234	5	354	Th	1473	23	Sep
	5235	1	355	Mo	1474	12	Sep
	5236	14	383	Sa	1475	2	Sep
	5237	5	354	Th	1476*	19	Sep
	5238	1	355	Mo	1477	8	Sep
	5239	14	383	Sa	1478	29	Aug
	5240	4	355	Th	1479	16	Sep
	5241	3	354	Tu	1480*	5	Sep
	5242	13	385	Sa	1481	25	Aug
	5243	7	353	Sa	1482	14	Sep
	5244	10	384	Tu	1483	2	Sep
277	5245	1	355	Mo	1484*	20	Sep
	5246	6	355	Sa	1485	10	Sep
	5247	12	383	Th	1486	31	Aug
	5248	3	354	Tu	1487	18	Sep
	5249	6	355	Sa	1488*	6	Sep
	5250	11	385	Th	1489	27	Aug
	5251	5	354	Th	1490	16	Sep
	5252	9	383	Mo	1491	5	Sep
	5253	6	355	Sa	1492*	22	Sep
	5254	5	354	Th	1493	12	Sep
	5255	9	383	Mo	1494	1	Sep
	5256	6	355	Sa	1495	19	Sep
	5257	5	354	Th	1496*	8	Sep
	5258	8	385	Mo	1497	28	Aug
	5259	2	353	Mo	1498	17	Sep
	5260	4	355	Th	1499	5	Sep
	5261	10	384	Tu	1500*	25	Aug
	5262	1	355	Mo	1501	13	Sep
	5263	14	383	Sa	1502	3	Sep
278	5264	5	354	Th	1503	21	Sep
	5265	1	355	Mo	1504*	9	Sep
	5266	13	385	Sa	1505	30	Aug
	5267	7	353	Sa	1506	19	Sep
	5268	3	354	Tu	1507	7	Sep
	5269	13	385	Sa	1508*	26	Aug
	5270	6	355	Sa	1509	15	Sep
	5271	12	383	Th	1510	5	Sep
	5272	3	354	Tu	1511	23	Sep
	5273	6	355	Sa	1512*	11	Sep
	5274	11	385	Th	1513	1	Sep
	5275	5	354	Th	1514	21	Sep
	5276	2	353	Mo	1515	10	Sep
	5277	11	385	Th	1516*	28	Aug
	5278	5	354	Th	1517	17	Sep
	5279	1	355	Mo	1518	6	Sep
	5280	14	383	Sa	1519	27	Aug
	5281	5	354	Th	1520*	13	Sep
	5282	8	385	Mo	1521	2	Sep

19 Year Cycle No.	Hebrew Year	Calendar Number	Days in Year	Day of Week	Western Year	Commencement 1st of Tishri (Julian)	
279	5283	2	353	Mo	1522	22	Sep
	5284	5	354	Th	1523	10	Sep
	5285	8	385	Mo	1524*	29	Aug
	5286	1	355	Mo	1525	18	Sep
	5287	7	353	Sa	1526	8	Sep
	5288	10	384	Tu	1527	27	Aug
	5289	1	355	Mo	1528*	14	Sep
	5290	14	383	Sa	1529	4	Sep
	5291	4	355	Th	1530	22	Sep
	5292	3	354	Tu	1531	12	Sep
	5293	13	385	Sa	1532*	31	Aug
	5294	6	355	Sa	1533	20	Sep
	5295	5	354	Th	1534	10	Sep
	5296	9	383	Mo	1535	30	Aug
	5297	6	355	Sa	1536*	16	Sep
	5298	5	354	Th	1537	6	Sep
	5299	9	383	Mo	1538	26	Aug
	5300	6	355	Sa	1539	13	Sep
	5301	11	385	Th	1540*	2	Sep
280	5302	5	354	Th	1541	22	Sep
	5303	2	353	Mo	1542	11	Sep
	5304	11	385	Th	1543	30	Aug
	5305	5	354	Th	1544*	18	Sep
	5306	1	355	Mo	1545	7	Sep
	5307	14	383	Sa	1546	28	Aug
	5308	5	354	Th	1547	15	Sep
	5309	8	385	Mo	1548*	3	Sep
	5310	2	353	Mo	1549	23	Sep
	5311	4	355	Th	1550	11	Sep
	5312	10	384	Tu	1551	1	Sep
	5313	1	355	Mo	1552*	19	Sep

19 Year Cycle No.	Hebrew Year	Calendar Number	Days in Year	Day of Week	Western Year	Commencement 1st of Tishri (Julian)	
	5314	7	353	Sa	1553	9	Sep
	5315	10	384	Tu	1554	28	Aug
	5316	1	355	Mo	1555	16	Sep
	5317	6	355	Sa	1556*	5	Sep
	5318	12	383	Th	1557	26	Aug
	5319	3	354	Tu	1558	13	Sep
	5320	13	385	Sa	1559	2	Sep
281	5321	6	355	Sa	1560*	21	Sep
	5322	5	354	Th	1561	11	Sep
	5323	9	383	Mo	1562	31	Aug
	5324	6	355	Sa	1563	18	Sep
	5325	5	354	Th	1564*	7	Sep
	5326	9	383	Mo	1565	27	Aug
	5327	6	355	Sa	1566	14	Sep
	5328	11	385	Th	1567	4	Sep
	5329	5	354	Th	1568*	23	Sep
	5330	2	353	Mo	1569	12	Sep
	5331	11	385	Th	1570	31	Aug
	5332	5	354	Th	1571	20	Sep
	5333	1	355	Mo	1572*	8	Sep
	5334	14	383	Sa	1573	29	Aug
	5335	5	354	Th	1574	16	Sep
	5336	1	355	Mo	1575	5	Sep
	5337	14	383	Sa	1576*	25	Aug
	5338	4	355	Th	1577	12	Sep
	5339	10	384	Tu	1578	2	Sep
282	5340	1	355	Mo	1579	21	Sep
	5341	7	353	Sa	1580*	10	Sep
	5342	10	384	Tu	1581	29	Aug
	5343	1	355	Mo	1582	17	Sep

19 Year Cycle No.	Hebrew Year	Calendar Number	Days in Year	Day of Week	Western Year	Commencement 1st of Tishri (Julian)		(Gregorian)	
	5344	6	355	Sa	1583	7	Sep	17	Sep
	5345	12	383	Th	1584*	27	Aug	6	Sep
	5346	3	354	Tu	1585	14	Sep	24	Sep
	5347	13	385	Sa	1586	3	Sep	13	Sep
	5348	6	355	Sa	1587	23	Sep	3	Oct
	5349	5	354	Th	1588*	12	Sep	22	Sep
	5350	9	383	Mo	1589	1	Sep	11	Sep
	5351	6	355	Sa	1590	19	Sep	29	Sep
	5352	5	354	Th	1591	9	Sep	19	Sep
	5353	8	385	Mo	1592*	28	Aug	7	Sep
	5354	2	353	Mo	1593	17	Sep	27	Sep
	5355	5	354	Th	1594	5	Sep	15	Sep
	5356	8	385	Mo	1595	25	Aug	4	Sep
	5357	1	355	Mo	1596*	13	Sep	23	Sep
	5358	14	383	Sa	1597	3	Sep	13	Sep
283	5359	5	354	Th	1598	21	Sep	1	Oct
	5360	1	355	Mo	1599	10	Sep	20	Sep
	5361	14	383	Sa	1600*	30	Aug	9	Sep
	5362	5	354	Th	1601	17	Sep	27	Sep
	5363	1	355	Mo	1602	6	Sep	16	Sep
	5364	13	385	Sa	1603	27	Aug	6	Sep
	5365	7	353	Sa	1604*	15	Sep	25	Sep
	5366	10	384	Tu	1605	3	Sep	13	Sep
	5367	1	355	Mo	1606	22	Sep	2	Oct
	5368	6	355	Sa	1607	12	Sep	22	Sep
	5369	12	383	Th	1608*	1	Sep	11	Sep
	5370	3	354	Tu	1609	19	Sep	29	Sep
	5371	6	355	Sa	1610	8	Sep	18	Sep
	5372	11	385	Th	1611	29	Aug	8	Sep
	5373	5	354	Th	1612*	17	Sep	27	Sep
	5374	2	353	Mo	1613	6	Sep	16	Sep
	5375	11	385	Th	1614	25	Aug	4	Sep
	5376	5	354	Th	1615	14	Sep	24	Sep
	5377	9	383	Mo	1616*	2	Sep	12	Sep
284	5378	6	355	Sa	1617	20	Sep	30	Sep
	5379	5	354	Th	1618	10	Sep	20	Sep
	5380	8	385	Mo	1619	30	Aug	9	Sep
	5381	2	353	Mo	1620*	18	Sep	28	Sep
	5382	5	354	Th	1621	6	Aug	16	Sep
	5383	8	385	Mo	1622	26	Aug	5	Sep
	5384	1	355	Mo	1623	15	Sep	25	Sep
	5385	14	383	Sa	1624*	4	Sep	14	Sep
	5386	5	354	Th	1625	22	Sep	2	Oct
	5387	1	355	Mo	1626	11	Sep	21	Sep
	5388	14	383	Sa	1627	1	Sep	11	Sep
	5389	4	355	Th	1628*	18	Sep	28	Sep
	5390	3	354	Tu	1629	8	Sep	18	Sep
	5391	13	385	Sa	1630	28	Aug	7	Sep
	5392	6	355	Sa	1631	17	Sep	27	Sep
	5393	5	354	Th	1632*	6	Sep	16	Sep
	5394	9	383	Mo	1633	26	Aug	5	Sep
	5395	6	355	Sa	1634	13	Sep	23	Sep
	5396	12	383	Th	1635	3	Sep	13	Sep
285	5397	3	354	Tu	1636*	20	Sep	30	Sep
	5398	6	355	Sa	1637	9	Sep	19	Sep
	5399	11	385	Th	1638*	30	Aug	9	Sep
	5400	5	354	Th	1639	19	Sep	29	Sep
	5401	2	353	Mo	1640*	7	Sep	17	Sep
	5402	11	385	Th	1641	26	Aug	5	Sep
	5403	5	354	Th	1642	15	Sep	25	Sep
	5404	9	383	Mo	1643	4	Sep	14	Sep
	5405	6	355	Sa	1644*	21	Sep	1	Oct
	5406	5	354	Th	1645	11	Sep	21	Sep
	5407	8	385	Mo	1646	31	Aug	10	Sep
	5408	2	353	Mo	1647	20	Sep	30	Sep
	5409	4	355	Th	1648*	7	Sep	17	Sep
	5410	10	384	Tu	1649	28	Aug	7	Sep
	5411	1	355	Mo	1650	16	Sep	26	Sep
	5412	7	353	Sa	1651	6	Sep	16	Sep
	5413	10	384	Tu	1652*	24	Aug	3	Sep
	5414	1	355	Mo	1653	12	Sep	22	Sep
	5415	13	385	Sa	1654	2	Sep	12	Sep

19 Year Cycle No.	Hebrew Year	Calendar Number	Days in Year	Day of Week	Western Year	Commencement 1st of Tishri (Julian)		(Gregorian)	
286	5416	7	353	Sa	1655	22	Sep	2	Oct
	5417	3	354	Tu	1656*	9	Sep	19	Sep
	5418	13	385	Sa	1657	29	Aug	8	Sep
	5419	6	355	Sa	1658	18	Sep	28	Sep
	5420	5	354	Th	1659	8	Sep	18	Sep
	5421	9	383	Mo	1660*	27	Aug	6	Sep
	5422	6	355	Sa	1661	14	Sep	24	Sep
	5423	12	383	Th	1662	4	Sep	14	Sep
	5424	3	354	Tu	1663	22	Sep	2	Oct
	5425	6	355	Sa	1664*	10	Sep	20	Sep
	5426	11	385	Th	1665	31	Aug	10	Sep
	5427	5	354	Th	1666	20	Sep	30	Sep
	5428	2	353	Mo	1667	9	Sep	19	Sep
	5429	11	3385	Th	1668*	27	Aug	6	Sep
	5430	5	354	Th	1669	16	Sep	26	Sep
	5431	1	355	Mo	1670	5	Sep	15	Sep
	5432	14	383	Sa	1671	26	Aug	5	Sep
	5433	5	354	Th	1672*	12	Sep	22	Sep
	5434	8	385	Mo	1673	1	Sep	11	Sep
287	5435	1	355	Mo	1674	21	Sep	1	Oct
	5436	7	353	Sa	1675	11	Sep	21	Sep
	5437	10	384	Tu	1676*	29	Aug	8	Sep
	5438	1	355	Mo	1677	17	Sep	27	Sep
	5439	6	355	Sa	1678	7	Sep	17	Sep
	5440	12	383	Th	1679	28	Aug	7	Sep
	5441	3	354	Tu	1680*	14	Sep	24	Sep
	5442	13	385	Sa	1681	3	Sep	13	Sep
	5443	7	353	Sa	1682	23	Sep	3	Oct
	5444	3	354	Tu	1683	11	Sep	21	Sep
	5445	13	385	Sa	1684*	30	Aug	9	Sep
	5446	6	355	Sa	1685	19	Sep	29	Sep
	5447	5	354	Th	1686	9	Sep	19	Sep
	5448	9	383	Mo	1687	29	Aug	8	Sep
	5449	6	355	Sa	1688*	15	Sep	25	Sep
	5450	5	354	Th	1689	5	Sep	15	Sep

19 Year Cycle No.	Hebrew Year	Calendar Number	Days in Year	Day of Week	Western Year	Commencement 1st of Tishri (Julian)		(Gregorian)	
	5451	8	385	Mo	1690	25	Aug	4	Sep
	5452	2	353	Mo	1691	14	Sep	24	Sep
	5453	11	385	Th	1692*	1	Sep	11	Sep
288	5454	5	354	Th	1693	21	Sep	1	Oct
	5455	1	355	Mo	1694	10	Sep	20	Sep
	5456	14	383	Sa	1695	31	Aug	10	Sep
	5457	5	354	Th	1696*	17	Sep	27	Sep
	5458	1	355	Mo	1697	6	Sep	16	Sep
	5459	14	383	Sa	1698	27	Aug	6	Sep
	5460	4	355	Th	1699	14	Sep	24	Sep
	5461	10	384	Tu	1700	3	Sep	14	Sep
	5462	1	355	Mo	1701	22	Sep	3	Oct
	5463	7	353	Sa	1702	12	Sep	23	Sep
	5464	10	384	Tu	1703	31	Aug	11	Sep
	5465	1	355	Mo	1704*	18	Sep	29	Sep
	5466	6	355	Sa	1705	8	Sep	19	Sep
	5467	12	383	Th	1706	29	Aug	9	Sep
	5468	3	354	Tu	1707	16	Sep	27	Sep
	5469	6	355	Sa	1708*	4	Sep	15	Sep
	5470	11	385	Sa	1709	25	Aug	5	Sep
	5471	5	354	Th	1710	14	Sep	25	Sep
	5472	9	383	Mo	1711	3	Sep	14	Sep
289	5473	6	355	Sa	1712*	20	Sep	1	Oct
	5474	5	354	Th	1713	10	Sep	21	Sep
	5475	9	383	Mo	1714	30	Aug	10	Sep
	5476	6	355	Sa	1715	17	Sep	28	Sep
	5477	5	354	Th	1716*	6	Sep	17	Sep
	5478	8	385	Mo	1717	26	Aug	6	Sep
	5479	2	353	Mo	1718	15	Sep	26	Sep
	5480	11	385	Th	1719	3	Sep	14	Sep
	5481	5	354	Th	1720*	22	Sep	3	Oct
	5482	1	355	Mo	1721	1	Sep	22	Sep
	5483	14	383	Sa	1722	1	Sep	12	Sep
	5484	5	354	Th	1723	19	Sep	30	Sep

Cycle	Year		Days	Weekday	Year				
	5485	1	355	Mo	1724*	7	Sep	18	Sep
	5486	14	383	Sa	1725	28	Aug	8	Sep
	5487	4	355	Th	1726	15	Sep	26	Sep
	5488	3	354	Tu	1727	5	Sep	16	Sep
	5489	13	385	Sa	1728*	24	Aug	4	Sep
	5490	7	353	Sa	1729	13	Sep	24	Sep
	5491	10	384	Tu	1730	1	Sep	12	Sep
290	5492	1	355	Mo	1731	20	Sep	1	Oct
	5493	6	355	Sa	1732*	9	Sep	20	Sep
	5494	12	383	Th	1733	30	Aug	10	Sep
	5495	3	354	Tu	1734	17	Sep	28	Sep
	5496	6	355	Sa	1735	6	Sep	17	Sep
	5497	11	385	Th	1736*	26	Aug	6	Sep
	5498	5	354	Th	1737	15	Sep	26	Sep
	5499	9	383	Mo	1738	4	Sep	15	Sep
	5500	6	355	Sa	1739	22	Sep	3	Oct
	5501	5	354	Th	1740*	11	Sep	22	Sep
	5502	9	383	Mo	1741	31	Aug	11	Sep
	5503	6	355	Sa	1742	18	Sep	29	Sep
	5504	5	354	Th	1743	8	Sep	19	Sep
	5505	8	385	Mo	1744*	27	Aug	7	Sep
	5506	2	353	Mo	1745	16	Sep	27	Sep
	5507	4	355	Th	1746	4	Sep	15	Sep
	5508	10	384	Tu	1747	25	Aug	5	Sep
	5509	1	355	Mo	1748*	12	Sep	23	Sep
	5510	14	383	Sa	1749	2	Sep	13	Sep
291	5511	5	354	Th	1750	20	Sep	1	Oct
	5512	1	355	Mo	1751	9	Sep	20	Sep
	5513	13	385	Sa	1752*	29	Aug	9	Sep
	5514	1	355	Mo	1753	18	Sep	29	Sep
	5515	3	354	Tu	1754	6	Sep	17	Sep
	5516	13	385	Sa	1755	26	Aug	6	Sep
	5517	6	355	Sa	1756*	14	Sep	25	Sep
	5518	12	383	Th	1757	4	Sep	15	Sep
	5519	3	354	Tu	1758	21	Sep	3	Oct
	5520	6	355	Sa	1759	11	Sep	22	Sep
	5521	12	383	Th	1760*	31	Aug	11	Sep
	5522	3	354	Tu	1761	18	Sep	29	Sep
	5523	6	355	Sa	1762	7	Sep	18	Sep
	5524	11	385	Th	1763	28	Aug	8	Sep
	5525	5	354	Th	1764*	16	Sep	27	Sep
	5526	2	353	Mo	1765	5	Sep	16	Sep
	5527	11	385	Th	1766	23	Sep	4	Oct
	5528	5	354	Th	1767	13	Sep	24	Sep
	5529	8	385	Mo	1768*	1	Sep	12	Sep
292	5530	2	353	Mo	1769	21	Sep	2	Oct
	5531	5	354	Th	1770	9	Sep	20	Sep
	5532	8	385	Mo	1771	29	Aug	9	Sep
	5533	1	355	Mo	1772*	17	Sep	28	Sep
	5534	7	353	Sa	1773	7	Sep	18	Sep
	5535	10	384	Tu	1774	26	Aug	6	Sep
	5536	1	355	Mo	1775	14	Sep	25	Sep
	5537	14	383	Sa	1776*	3	Sep	14	Sep
	5538	4	355	Th	1777	21	Sep	2	Oct
	5539	3	354	Tu	1778	11	Sep	22	Sep
	5540	13	385	Sa	1779	31	Aug	11	Sep
	5541	6	355	Sa	1780*	19	Sep	30	Sep
	5542	5	354	Th	1781	9	Sep	20	Sep
	5543	9	383	Mo	1782	29	Aug	9	Sep
	5544	6	355	Sa	1783	16	Sep	27	Sep
	5545	5	354	Th	1784*	5	Sep	16	Sep
	5546	9	383	Mo	1785	25	Aug	5	Sep
	5547	6	355	Sa	1786	12	Sep	23	Sep
	5548	11	385	Th	1787	2	Sep	13	Sep
293	5549	5	354	Th	1788*	22	Sep	3	Oct
	5550	2	353	Mo	1789	11	Sep	22	Sep
	5551	11	385	Th	1790	29	Aug	9	Sep
	5552	5	354	Th	1791	18	Sep	29	Sep
	5553	1	355	Mo	1792*	6	Sep	17	Sep
	5554	14	383	Sa	1793	27	Aug	7	Sep
	5555	5	354	Th	1794	14	Sep	25	Sep
	5556	8	385	Mo	1795	3	Sep	14	Sep
	5557	2	353	Mo	1796*	22	Sep	3	Oct
	5558	4	355	Th	1797	10	Sep	21	Sep
	5559	10	384	Tu	1798	31	Aug	11	Sep
	5560	1	355	Mo	1799	19	Sep	30	Sep
	5561	7	353	Sa	1800	8	Sep	20	Sep
	5562	10	384	Tu	1801	27	Aug	8	Sep
	5563	1	355	Mo	1802	15	Sep	27	Sep
	5564	6	355	Sa	1803	5	Sep	17	Sep
	5565	12	383	Th	1804*	25	Aug	6	Sep
	5566	3	354	Tu	1805	12	Sep	24	Sep
	5567	13	385	Sa	1806	1	Sep	13	Sep

19 Year Cycle No.	Hebrew Year	Calendar Number	Days in Year	Day of Week	Western Year	Commencement 1st of Tishri (Julian)		(Gregorian)	
294	5568	6	355	Sa	1807	21	Sep	3	Oct
	5569	5	354	Th	1808*	10	Sep	22	Sep
	5570	9	383	Mo	1809	30	Aug	11	Sep
	5571	6	355	Sa	1810	17	Sep	29	Sep
	5572	5	354	Th	1811	7	Sep	19	Sep
	5573	9	383	Mo	1812*	26	Aug	7	Sep
	5574	6	355	Sa	1813	13	Sep	25	Sep
	5575	11	385	Th	1814	3	Sep	15	Sep
	5576	5	354	Th	1815	23	Sep	5	Oct
	5577	2	353	Mo	1816*	11	Sep	23	Sep
	5578	11	385	Th	1817	30	Aug	11	Sep
	5579	5	354	Th	1818	19	Sep	1	Oct
	5580	1	355	Mo	1819	8	Sep	20	Sep
	5581	14	383	Sa	1820*	28	Aug	9	Sep
	5582	5	354	Th	1821	15	Sep	27	Sep
	5583	1	355	Mo	1822	4	Sep	16	Sep
	5584	14	383	Sa	1823	25	Aug	6	Sep
	5585	4	355	Th	1824*	11	Sep	23	Sep
	5586	10	384	Tu	1825	1	Sep	13	Sep
295	5587	1	355	Mo	1826	20	Sep	2	Oct
	5588	7	353	Sa	1827	10	Sep	22	Sep
	5589	10	384	Tu	1828*	28	Aug	9	Sep
	5590	1	354	Mo	1829	16	Sep	28	Sep
	5591	6	355	Sa	1830	6	Sep	18	Sep
	5592	12	383	Th	1831	27	Aug	8	Sep
	5593	3	354	Tu	1832*	13	Sep	25	Sep
	5594	13	385	Sa	1833	2	Sep	14	Sep
	5595	6	355	Sa	1834	22	Sep	4	Oct
	5596	5	354	Th	1835	12	Sep	24	Sep
	5597	9	383	Mo	1836*	31	Aug	12	Sep
	5598	6	355	Sa	1837	18	Sep	30	Sep
	5599	5	354	Th	1838	8	Sep	20	Sep
	5600	8	385	Mo	1839	28	Aug	9	Sep
	5601	2	353	Mo	1840*	16	Sep	28	Sep
	5602	5	354	Th	1841	4	Sep	16	Sep

19 Year Cycle No.	Hebrew Year	Calendar Number	Days in Year	Day of Week	Western Year	Commencement 1st of Tishri (Julian)		(Gregorian)	
	5603	8	385	Mo	1842	24	Aug	5	Sep
	5604	1	355	Mo	1843	13	Sep	25	Sep
	5605	14	383	Sa	1844*	2	Sep	14	Sep
296	5606	5	354	Th	1845	20	Sep	2	Oct
	5607	1	355	Mo	1846	9	Sep	21	Sep
	5608	14	383	Sa	1847	30	Aug	11	Sep
	5609	5	354	Th	1848*	16	Sep	28	Sep
	5610	1	355	Mo	1849	5	Sep	17	Sep
	5611	13	385	Sa	1850	26	Aug	7	Sep
	5612	7	353	Sa	1851	15	Sep	27	Sep
	5613	10	384	Tu	1852*	2	Sep	14	Sep
	5614	1	355	Mo	1853	21	Sep	3	Oct
	5615	6	355	Sa	1854	11	Sep	23	Sep
	5616	12	383	Th	1855	1	Sep	13	Sep
	5617	3	354	Tu	1856*	18	Sep	30	Sep
	5618	6	355	Sa	1857	7	Sep	19	Sep
	5619	11	385	Th	1858	28	Aug	9	Sep
	5620	5	354	Th	1859	17	Sep	29	Sep
	5621	2	353	Mo	1860*	5	Sep	17	Sep
	5622	11	385	Th	1861	24	Aug	5	Sep
	5623	5	354	Th	1862	13	Sep	25	Sep
	5624	9	383	Mo	1863	2	Sep	14	Sep
297	5625	6	355	Sa	1864*	19	Sep	1	Oct
	5626	5	354	Th	1865	9	Sep	21	Sep
	5627	8	385	Mo	1866	29	Aug	10	Sep
	5628	2	353	Mo	1867	18	Sep	30	Sep
	5629	5	354	Th	1868*	5	Sep	17	Sep
	5630	8	385	Mo	1869	25	Aug	6	Sep
	5631	1	355	Mo	1870	14	Sep	26	Sep
	5632	14	383	Sa	1871	4	Sep	16	Sep
	5633	5	354	Th	1872*	21	Sep	3	Oct
	5634	1	355	Mo	1873	10	Sep	22	Sep
	5635	14	383	Sa	1874	31	Aug	12	Sep
	5636	4	355	Th	1875	18	Sep	30	Sep

19 Year Cycle No.	Hebrew Year	Calendar Number	Days in Year	Day of Week	Western Year		Commencement 1st of Tishri (Gregorian)
	5637	3	354	Tu	1876*	7 Sep	19 Sep
	5638	13	385	Sa	1877	27 Aug	8 Sep
	5639	6	355	Sa	1878	16 Sep	28 Sep
	5640	5	354	Th	1879	6 Sep	18 Sep
	5641	9	383	Mo	1880*	25 Aug	6 Sep
	5642	6	355	Sa	1881	12 Sep	24 Sep
	5643	12	383	Th	1882	2 Sep	14 Sep
298	5644	3	354	Tu	1883	20 Sep	2 Oct
	5645	6	355	Sa	1884*	8 Sep	20 Sep
	5646	11	385	Th	1885	29 Aug	10 Sep
	5647	5	354	Th	1886	18 Sep	30 Sep
	5648	2	353	Mo	1887	7 Sep	19 Sep
	5649	11	385	Th	1888*	25 Aug	6 Sep
	5650	5	354	Th	1889	14 Sep	26 Sep
	5651	9	383	Mo	1890	3 Sep	15 Sep
	5652	6	355	Sa	1891	21 Sep	3 Oct
	5553	5	354	Th	1892*	10 Sep	22 Sep
	5654	8	385	Mo	1893	30 Aug	11 Sep
	5655	2	353	Mo	1894	19 Sep	1 Oct
	5656	4	355	Th	1895	7 Sep	19 Sep
	5657	10	384	Tu	1896*	27 Aug	8 Sep
	5658	1	355	Mo	1897	15 Sep	27 Sep
	5659	7	353	Sa	1898	5 Sep	17 Sep
	5660	10	384	Tu	1899	24 Aug	5 Sep
	5661	1	355	Mo	1900	11 Sep	24 Sep
	5662	14	383	Sa	1901	1 Sep	14 Sep
299	5663	4	355	Th	1902	19 Sep	2 Oct
	5664	3	354	Tu	1903	9 Sep	22 Sep
	5665	13	385	Sa	1904*	28 Aug	10 Sep
	5666	6	355	Sa	1905	17 Sep	30 Sep
	5667	5	354	Th	1906	7 Sep	20 Sep
	5668	9	383	Mo	1907	27 Aug	9 Sep
	5669	6	355	Sa	1908*	13 Sep	26 Sep
	5670	12	383	Th	1909	4 Sep	16 Sep
	5671	3	354	Tu	1910	21 Sep	4 Oct
	5672	6	355	Sa	1911	10 Sep	23 Sep
	5673	11	385	Th	1912*	30 Aug	12 Sep
	5674	5	354	Th	1913	19 Sep	2 Oct
	5675	2	353	Mo	1914	8 Sep	21 Sep
	5676	11	385	Th	1915	27 Aug	9 Sep
	5677	5	354	Th	1916*	15 Sep	28 Sep
	5678	1	355	Mo	1917	4 Sep	17 Sep
	5679	14	383	Sa	1918	25 Aug	7 Sep
	5680	5	354	Th	1919	12 Sep	25 Sep
	5681	8	385	Mo	1920*	31 Sep	13 Sep
300	5682	1	355	Mo	1921	20 Sep	3 Oct
	5683	7	353	Sa	1922	3 Sep	23 Sep
	5684	10	384	Tu	1923	29 Aug	11 Sep
	5685	1	355	Mo	1924*	16 Sep	29 Sep
	5686	6	355	Sa	1925	6 Sep	19 Sep
	5687	12	383	Th	1926	27 Aug	9 Sep
	5688	3	354	Tu	1927	14 Sep	27 Sep
	5689	13	385	Sa	1928*	2 Sep	15 Sep
	5690	7	353	Sa	1929	22 Sep	5 Oct
	5691	3	354	Tu	1930	10 Sep	23 Sep
	5692	13	385	Sa	1931	30 Aug	12 Sep
	5693	6	355	Sa	1932*	18 Sep	1 Oct
	5694	5	354	Th	1933	8 Sep	21 Sep
	5695	9	383	Mo	1934	28 Aug	10 Sep
	5696	6	355	Sa	1935	15 Sep	28 Sep
	5697	5	354	Th	1936*	4 Sep	17 Sep
	5698	8	385	Mo	1937	24 Aug	6 Sep
	5699	2	353	Mo	1938	13 Sep	26 Sep
	5700	11	385	Th	1939	1 Sep	14 Sep
301	5701	5	354	Th	1940*		3 Oct
	5702	1	355	Mo	1941		22 Sep
	5703	14	383	Sa	1942		12 Sep
	5704	5	354	Th	1943		30 Sep
	5705	1	355	Mo	1944*		18 Sep
	5706	14	383	Sa	1945		8 Sep
	5707	5	354	Th	1946		26 Sep
	5708	8	385	Mo	1947		15 Sep
	5709	1	355	Mo	1948*		4 Oct
	5710	7	353	Sa	1949		24 Sep
	5711	10	384	Tu	1950		12 Sep
	5712	1	355	Mo	1951		1 Oct

19 Year Cycle No.	Hebrew Year	Calendar Number	Days in Year	Day of Week	Western Year	Commencement 1st of Tishri (Gregorian)	
	5713	6	355	Sa	1952*	20	Sep
	5714	12	383	Th	1953	10	Sep
	5715	3	354	Tu	1954	28	Sep
	5716	6	355	Sa	1955	17	Sep
	5717	11	385	Th	1956*	6	Sep
	5718	5	354	Th	1957	26	Sep
	5719	9	383	Mo	1958	15	Sep
302	5720	6	355	Sa	1959	3	Oct
	5721	5	354	Th	1960*	22	Sep
	5722	9	383	Mo	1961	11	Sep
	5723	6	355	Sa	1962	29	Sep
	5724	5	354	Th	1963	19	Sep
	5725	8	385	Mo	1964*	7	Sep
	5726	2	353	Mo	1965	27	Sep
	5727	11	385	Th	1966	15	Sep
	5728	5	354	Th	1967	5	Oct
	5729	1	355	Mo	1968*	23	Sep
	5730	14	383	Sa	1969	13	Sep
	5731	5	354	Th	1970	1	Oct
	5732	1	355	Mo	1971	20	Sep
	5733	14	383	Sa	1972*	9	Sep
	5734	4	355	Th	1973	27	Sep
	5735	1	355	Mo	1974	17	Sep
	5736	13	385	Sa	1975	6	Sep
	5737	7	353	Sa	1976*	25	Sep
	5738	10	384	Tu	1977	13	Sep
303	5739	1	355	Mo	1978	2	Oct
	5740	6	355	Sa	1979	22	Sep
	5741	12	383	Th	1980*	11	Sep
	5742	3	354	Tu	1981	29	Sep
	5743	6	355	Sa	1982	18	Sep
	5744	11	385	Th	1983	8	Sep
	5745	5	354	Th	1984*	27	Sep
	5746	9	383	Mo	1985	16	Sep
	5747	6	355	Sa	1986	4	Oct
	5748	5	354	Th	1987	24	Sep
	5749	9	383	Mo	1988*	12	Sep
	5750	6	355	Sa	1989	30	Sep
	5751	5	354	Th	1990	20	Sep
	5752	8	385	Mo	1991	9	Sep
	5753	2	353	Mo	1992*	28	Sep
	5754	4	355	Th	1993	16	Sep
	5755	10	384	Tu	1994	6	Sep
	5756	1	355	Mo	1995	25	Sep
	5757	14	383	Sa	1996*	14	Sep
304	5758	5	354	Th	1997	2	Oct
	5759	1	355	Mo	1998	21	Sep
	5760	13	385	Sa	1999	11	Sep
	5761	7	353	Sa	2000*	30	Sep
	5762	3	354	Tu	2001	18	Sep
	5763	13	385	Sa	2002	7	Sep
	5764	6	355	Sa	2003	27	Sep
	5765	12	383	Th	2004*	16	Sep
	5766	3	354	Tu	2005	4	Oct
	5767	6	355	Sa	2006	23	Sep
	5768	12	383	Th	2007	13	Sep
	5769	3	354	Tu	2008*	30	Sep
	5770	6	355	Sa	2009	19	Sep
	5771	11	385	Th	2010	9	Sep
	5772	5	354	Th	2011	29	Sep
	5773	2	353	Mo	2012*	17	Sep
	5774	11	385	Th	2013	5	Sep
	5775	5	354	Th	2014	25	Sep
	5776	8	385	Mo	2015	14	Sep
305	5777	2	353	Mo	2016*	3	Oct
	5778	5	354	Th	2017	21	Sep
	5779	8	385	Mo	2018	10	Sep
	5780	1	355	Mo	2019	30	Sep

Cycle	Year		Days	Day	Year	Date	Month
	5781	7	353	Sa	2020*	19	Sep
	5782	10	384	Tu	2021	7	Sep
	5783	1	355	Mo	2022	26	Sep
	5784	14	383	Sa	2023	16	Sep
	5785	4	355	Th	2024*	3	Oct
	5786	3	354	Tu	2025	23	Sep
	5787	13	385	Sa	2026	12	Sep
	5788	6	355	Sa	2027	2	Oct
	5789	5	354	Th	2028*	21	Sep
	5790	9	383	Mo	2029	10	Sep
	5791	6	355	Sa	2030	28	Sep
	5792	5	354	Th	2031	18	Sep
	5793	9	383	Mo	2032*	6	Sep
	5794	6	355	Sa	2033	24	Sep
	5795	11	385	Th	2034	14	Sep
306	5796	5	354	Th	2035	4	Oct
	5797	2	353	Mo	2036*	22	Sep
	5798	11	385	Th	2037	10	Sep
	5799	5	354	Th	2038	30	Sep
	5800	1	355	Mo	2039	19	Sep
	5801	14	383	Sa	2040*	8	Sep
	5802	5	354	Th	2041	26	Sep
	5803	8	385	Mo	2042	15	Sep
	5804	2	353	Mo	2043	5	Oct
	5805	4	355	Th	2044*	22	Sep
	5806	10	384	Tu	2045	12	Sep
	5807	1	355	Mo	2046	1	Oct
	5808	7	353	Sa	2047	21	Sep
	5809	10	384	Tu	2048*	8	Sep
	5810	1	355	Mo	2049	27	Sep
	5811	6	355	Sa	2050	17	Sep
	5812	12	383	Th	2051	7	Sep
	5813	3	354	Tu	2052*	24	Sep
	5814	13	385	Sa	2053	13	Sep
307	5815	6	355	Sa	2054	3	Oct
	5816	5	354	Th	2055	23	Sep
	5817	9	383	Mo	2056*	11	Sep
	5818	6	355	Sa	2057	29	Sep
	5819	5	354	Th	2058	19	Sep
	5820	9	383	Mo	2059	8	Sep
	5821	6	355	Sa	2060*	25	Sep
	5822	11	385	Th	2061	15	Sep
	5823	5	354	Th	2062	5	Oct
	5824	2	353	Mo	2063	24	Sep
	5825	11	385	Th	2064*	11	Sep
	5826	5	354	Th	2065	1	Oct
	5827	1	355	Mo	2066	20	Sep
	5828	14	383	Sa	2067	10	Sep
	5829	5	354	Th	2068*	27	Sep
	5830	1	355	Mo	2069	16	Sep
	5831	14	383	Sa	2070	6	Sep
	5832	4	355	Th	2071	24	Sep
	5833	10	384	Tu	2072*	13	Sep
308	5834	1	355	Mo	2073	2	Oct
	5835	7	353	Sa	2074	22	Sep
	5836	10	384	Tu	2075	10	Sep
	5837	1	355	Mo	2076*	28	Sep
	5838	6	355	Sa	2077	18	Sep
	5839	12	383	Th	2078	8	Sep
	5840	3	354	Tu	2079	26	Sep
	5841	13	385	Sa	2080*	14	Sep
	5842	6	355	Sa	2081	4	Oct
	5843	5	354	Th	2082	24	Sep
	5844	9	383	Mo	2083	13	Sep
	5845	6	355	Sa	2084*	30	Sep
	5846	5	354	Th	2085	20	Sep
	5847	9	383	Mo	2086	9	Sep
	5848	6	355	Sa	2087	27	Sep
	5849	5	354	Th	2088*	16	Sep
	5850	8	385	Mo	2089	5	Sep
	5851	2	353	Mo	2090	25	Sep
	5852	11	385	Th	2091	13	Sep
309	5853	5	354	Th	2092*	2	Oct
	5854	1	355	Mo	2093	21	Sep
	5855	14	383	Sa	2094	11	Sep
	5856	5	354	Th	2095	29	Sep
	5857	1	355	Mo	2096	17	Sep
	5858	13	385	Sa	2097	7	Sep
	5859	7	353	Sa	2098	27	Sep
	5860	10	384	Tu	2099	15	Sep
	5861	1	355	Mo	2100	4	Oct
	5862	6	355	Sa	2101	24	Sep
	5863	12	383	Th	2102	14	Sep
	5864	3	354	Tu	2103	2	Oct

19 Year Cycle No.	Hebrew Year	Calendar Number	Days in Year	Day of Week	Western Year	Commencement 1st of Tishri (Gregorian)	
	5865	6	355	Sa	2104*	20	Sep
	5866	11	385	Th	2105	10	Sep
	5867	5	354	Th	2106	30	Sep
	5868	2	353	Mo	2107	19	Sep
	5869	11	385	Th	2108*	6	Sep
	5870	5	354	Th	2109	26	Sep
	5871	9	383	Mo	2110	15	Sep
310	5872	6	355	Sa	2111	3	Oct
	5873	5	354	Th	2112*	22	Sep
	5874	8	385	Mo	2113	11	Sep
	5875	2	353	Mo	2114	1	Oct
	5876	5	354	Th	2115	19	Sep
	5877	8	385	Mo	2116*	7	Sep
	5878	1	355	Mo	2117	27	Sep
	5879	14	383	Sa	2118	17	Sep
	5880	5	354	Th	2119	5	Oct
	5881	1	355	Mo	2120*	23	Sep
	5882	14	383	Sa	2121	13	Sep
	5883	4	355	Th	2122	1	Oct
	5884	3	354	Tu	2123	21	Sep
	5885	13	385	Sa	2124*	9	Sep
	5886	6	355	Sa	2125	29	Sep
	5887	5	354	Th	2126	19	Sep
	5888	9	383	Mo	2127	8	Sep
	5889	6	355	Sa	2128*	25	Sep
	5890	12	383	Th	2129	15	Sep
311	5891	3	354	Tu	2130	3	Oct
	5892	6	355	Sa	2131	22	Sep
	5893	11	385	Th	2132*	11	Sep
	5894	5	354	Th	2133	1	Oct
	5895	2	353	Mo	2134	20	Sep
	5896	11	385	Th	2135	8	Sep
	5897	5	354	Th	2136*	27	Sep
	5898	9	383	Mo	2137	16	Sep

19 Year Cycle No.	Hebrew Year	Calendar Number	Days in Year	Day of Week	Western Year	Commencement 1st of Tishri (Gregorian)	
	5899	6	355	Sa	2138	4	Oct
	5900	5	354	Th	2139	24	Sep
	5901	8	385	Mo	2140*	12	Sep
	5902	2	353	Mo	2141	2	Oct
	5903	4	355	Th	2142	20	Sep
	5904	10	384	Tu	2143	19	Sep
	5905	1	355	Mo	2144*	28	Sep
	5906	7	353	Sa	2145	18	Sep
	5907	10	384	Tu	2146	6	Sep
	5908	1	355	Mo	2147	25	Sep
	5909	14	383	Sa	2148*	14	Sep
312	5910	4	355	Th	2149	2	Oct
	5911	3	354	Tu	2150	22	Sep
	5912	13	385	Sa	2151	11	Sep
	5913	6	355	Sa	2152*	30	Sep
	5914	5	354	Th	2153	20	Sep
	5915	9	383	Mo	2154	9	Sep
	5916	6	355	Sa	2155	27	Sep
	5917	12	383	Th	2156*	16	Sep
	5918	3	354	Tu	2157	4	Oct
	5919	6	355	Sa	2158	23	Sep
	5920	11	385	Th	2159	13	Sep
	5921	5	354	Th	2160*	2	Oct
	5922	2	353	Mo	2161	21	Sep
	5923	11	385	Th	2162	9	Sep
	5924	5	354	Th	2163	29	Sep
	5925	1	355	Mo	2164*	17	Sep
	5926	14	383	Sa	2165	7	Sep
	5927	5	354	Th	2166	25	Sep
	5928	8	385	Mo	2167	14	Sep
313	5929	2	353	Mo	2168*	3	Oct
	5930	4	355	Th	2169	21	Sep
	5931	10	384	Tu	2170	11	Sep
	5932	1	355	Mo	2171	30	Sep

	5933	7	353	Sa	2172*	19	Sep
	5934	10	384	Tu	2173	7	Sep
	5935	1	355	Mo	2174	26	Sep
	5936	13	385	Sa	2175	16	Sep
	5937	7	353	Sa	2176*	5	Oct
	5938	3	354	Tu	2177	13	Sep
	5939	13	385	Sa	2178	12	Sep
	5940	6	355	Sa	2179	2	Oct
	5941	5	354	Th	2180*	21	Sep
	5942	9	383	Mo	2181	10	Sep
	5943	6	355	Sa	2182	28	Sep
	5944	5	354	Th	2183	18	Sep
	5945	8	385	Mo	2184*	6	Sep
	5946	2	353	Mo	2185	26	Sep
	5947	11	385	Th	2186	14	Sep
314	5948	5	354	Th	2187	4	Oct
	5949	1	355	Mo	2188*	22	Sep
	5950	14	383	Sa	2189	12	Sep
	5951	5	354	Th	2190	30	Sep
	5952	1	355	Mo	2191	19	Sep
	5953	14	383	Sa	2192*	8	Sep
	5954	5	354	Th	2193	26	Sep
	5955	8	385	Mo	2194	15	Sep
	5956	1	355	Mo	2195	5	Oct
	5957	7	353	Sa	2196*	24	Sep
	5958	10	384	Tu	2197	12	Sep
	5959	1	355	Mo	2198	1	Oct
	5960	6	355	Sa	2199	21	Sep
	5961	12	383	Th	2200	11	Sep
	5962	3	354	Tu	2201	29	Sep
	5963	6	355	Sa	2202	18	Sep
	5964	11	385	Th	2203	8	Sep
	5965	5	354	Th	2204*	27	Sep
	5966	9	383	Mo	2205	16	Sep

SELEUCID CALENDAR AND ERA OF ANTIOCH

In the early years of the 4th century B.C. Seleucus Necator, one of Alexander the Great's generals, founded an empire that was eventually to stretch from Asia Minor to India. Like many other middle Eastern rulers he also established a new calendar. This was essentially one that had been used in Syria for some centuries prior to his conquest and continued to be used, with some modifications, throughout the empire.

The calendar was a solar one of 365 days with an extra day every fourth year to account for solar motion. It contained 12 months of 30 days each and an extra five (or in leap year six) days at the year's end. Because the calendar was used over a large area and among different religious and ethnic groups, there were many variations. Both the Greeks in Syria and the native Syrians changed that date of the new year, while retaining all the other elements of the calendar. The Greeks began the new year on September 1 while the Syrians began it on October 9. The Macedonians in the empire continued to use their old lunar calendar.

Shortly after the Roman invasion of Syria in 64 B.C., the Syrians adopted a variation of their calendar. The major change was in the celebration of the New Year. While the Greeks in the area continued to begin the New Year in September, the Syrians moved their New Year back from October to August. This new calendar with the epoch in 48 B.C., was called the Era of Antioch.

SELEUCID CALENDAR

Seleucide Solar Year	Western Date of New Year (Julian)			Seleucide Solar Year	Western Date of New Year (Julian)			Seleucide Solar Year	Western Date of New Year (Julian)			Seleucide Solar Year	Western Date of New Year (Julian)		
1	312	2	Oct	23	290	2	Oct	45	268	2	Oct	67	246	2	Oct
2	311	2	Oct	24	289*	1	Oct	46	267	2	Oct	68	245*	1	Oct
3	310	2	Oct	25	288	2	Oct	47	266	2	Oct	69	244	2	Oct
4	309*	1	Oct	26	287	2	Oct	48	265*	1	Oct	70	243	2	Oct
5	308	2	Oct	27	286	2	Oct	49	264	2	Oct	71	242	2	Oct
6	307	2	Oct	28	285*	1	Oct	50	263	2	Oct	72	241*	1	Oct
7	306	2	Oct	29	284	2	Oct	51	262	2	Oct	73	240	2	Oct
8	305*	1	Oct	30	283	2	Oct	52	261*	1	Oct	74	239	2	Oct
9	304	2	Oct	31	282	2	Oct	53	260	2	Oct	75	238	2	Oct
10	303	2	Oct	32	281*	1	Oct	54	259	2	Oct	76	237*	1	Oct
11	302	2	Oct	33	280	2	Oct	55	258	2	Oct	77	236	2	Oct
12	301*	1	Oct	34	279	2	Oct	56	257*	1	Oct	78	235	2	Oct
13	300	2	Oct	35	278	2	Oct	57	256	2	Oct	79	234	2	Oct
14	299	2	Oct	36	277*	1	Oct	58	255	2	Oct	80	233*	1	Oct
15	298	2	Oct	37	276	2	Oct	59	254	2	Oct	81	232	2	Oct
16	297*	1	Oct	38	275	2	Oct	60	253*	1	Oct	82	231	2	Oct
17	296	2	Oct	39	274	2	Oct	61	252	2	Oct	83	230	2	Oct
18	295	2	Oct	40	273*	1	Oct	62	251	2	Oct	84	229*	1	Oct
19	294	2	Oct	41	272	2	Oct	63	250	2	Oct	85	228	2	Oct
20	293*	1	Oct	42	271	2	Oct	64	249*	1	Oct	86	227	2	Oct
21	292	2	Oct	43	270	2	Oct	65	248	2	Oct	87	226	2	Oct
22	291	2	Oct	44	269*	1	Oct	66	247	2	Oct	88	225*	1	Oct

Seleucide Solar Year	Western Date of New Year (Julian)			Seleucide Solar Year	Western Date of New Year (Julian)			Seleucide Solar Year	Western Date of New Year (Julian)			Seleucide Solar Year	Western Date of New Year (Julian)		
89	224	2	Oct	140	173*	1	Oct	191	122	2	Oct	242	71	2	Oct
90	223	2	Oct	141	172	2	Oct	192	121*	1	Oct	243	70	2	Oct
91	222	2	Oct	142	171	2	Oct	193	120	2	Oct	244	69*	1	Oct
92	221*	1	Oct	143	170	2	Oct	194	119	2	Oct	245	68	2	Oct
93	220	2	Oct	144	169*	1	Oct	195	118	2	Oct	246	67	2	Oct
94	219	2	Oct	145	168	2	Oct	196	117*	1	Oct	247	66	2	Oct
95	218	2	Oct	146	167	2	Oct	197	116	2	Oct	248	65*	1	Oct
96	217*	1	Oct	147	166	2	Oct	198	115	2	Oct	249	64	2	Oct
97	216	2	Oct	148	165*	1	Oct	199	114	2	Oct	250	63	2	Oct
98	215	2	Oct	149	164	2	Oct	200	113*	1	Oct	251	62	2	Oct
99	214	2	Oct	150	163	2	Oct	201	112	2	Oct	252	61*	1	Oct
100	213*	1	Oct	151	162	2	Oct	202	111	2	Oct	253	60	2	Oct
101	212	2	Oct	152	161*	1	Oct	203	110	2	Oct	254	59	2	Oct
102	211	2	Oct	153	160	2	Oct	204	109*	1	Oct	255	58	2	Oct
103	210	2	Oct	154	159	2	Oct	205	108	2	Oct	256	57*	1	Oct
104	209*	1	Oct	155	158	2	Oct	206	107	2	Oct	257	56	2	Oct
105	208	2	Oct	156	157*	1	Oct	207	106	2	Oct	258	55	2	Oct
106	207	2	Oct	157	156	2	Oct	208	105*	1	Oct	259	54	2	Oct
107	206	2	Oct	158	155	2	Oct	209	104	2	Oct	260	53*	1	Oct
108	205*	1	Oct	159	154	2	Oct	210	103	2	Oct	261	52	2	Oct
109	204	2	Oct	160	153*	1	Oct	211	102	2	Oct	262	51	2	Oct
110	203	2	Oct	161	152	2	Oct	212	101*	1	Oct	263	50	2	Oct
111	202	2	Oct	162	151	2	Oct	213	100	2	Oct	264	49*	1	Oct
112	201*	1	Oct	163	150	2	Oct	214	99	2	Oct	265	48	2	Oct
113	200	2	Oct	164	149*	1	Oct	215	98	2	Oct	266	47	2	Oct
114	199	2	Oct	165	148	2	Oct	216	97*	1	Oct	267	46	2	Oct
115	198	2	Oct	166	147	2	Oct	217	96	2	Oct	268	45*	1	Oct
116	197*	1	Oct	167	146	2	Oct	218	95	2	Oct	269	44	2	Oct
117	196	2	Oct	168	145*	1	Oct	219	94	2	Oct	270	43	2	Oct
118	195	2	Oct	169	144	2	Oct	220	93*	1	Oct	271	42	2	Oct
119	194	2	Oct	170	143	2	Oct	221	92	2	Oct	272	41*	1	Oct
120	193*	1	Oct	171	142	2	Oct	222	91	2	Oct	273	40	2	Oct
121	192	2	Oct	172	141*	1	Oct	223	90	2	Oct	274	39	2	Oct
122	191	2	Oct	173	140	2	Oct	224	89*	1	Oct	275	38	2	Oct
123	190	2	Oct	174	139	2	Oct	225	88	2	Oct	276	37*	1	Oct
124	189*	1	Oct	175	138	2	Oct	226	87	2	Oct	277	36	2	Oct
125	188	2	Oct	176	137*	1	Oct	227	86	2	Oct	278	35	2	Oct
126	187	2	Oct	177	136	2	Oct	228	85*	1	Oct	279	34	2	Oct
127	186	2	Oct	178	135	2	Oct	229	84	2	Oct	280	33*	1	Oct
128	185*	1	Oct	179	134	2	Oct	230	83	2	Oct	281	32	2	Oct
129	184	2	Oct	180	133*	1	Oct	231	82	2	Oct	282	31	2	Oct
130	183	2	Oct	181	132	2	Oct	232	81*	1	Oct	283	30	2	Oct
131	182	2	Oct	182	131	2	Oct	233	80	2	Oct	284	29*	1	Oct
132	181*	1	Oct	183	130	2	Oct	234	79	2	Oct	285	28	2	Oct
133	180	2	Oct	184	129*	1	Oct	235	78	2	Oct	286	27	2	Oct
134	179	2	Oct	185	128	2	Oct	236	77*	1	Oct	287	26	2	Oct
135	178	2	Oct	186	127	2	Oct	237	76	2	Oct	288	25*	1	Oct
136	177*	1	Oct	187	126	2	Oct	238	75	2	Oct	289	24	2	Oct
137	176	2	Oct	188	125*	1	Oct	239	74	2	Oct	290	23	2	Oct
138	175	2	Oct	189	124	2	Oct	240	73*	1	Oct	291	22	2	Oct
139	174	2	Oct	190	123	2	Oct	241	72	2	Oct	292	21*	1	Oct

Seleucide Solar Year	Western Date of New Year (Julian)		
293	20	2	Oct
294	19	2	Oct
295	18	2	Oct
296	17*	1	Oct
297	16	2	Oct
298	15	2	Oct
299	14	2	Oct
300	13*	1	Oct
301	12	2	Oct
302	11	2	Oct
303	10	2	Oct
304	9*	1	Oct
305	8	2	Oct
306	7	2	Oct
307	6	2	Oct
308	5*	1	Oct
309	4	2	Oct
310	3	2	Oct
311	2	2	Oct
312	1*	1	Oct
313	1	2	Oct
314	2	2	Oct
315	3	2	Oct
316	4*	1	Oct
317	5	2	Oct
318	6	2	Oct
319	7	2	Oct
320	8*	1	Oct
321	9	2	Oct
322	10	2	Oct
323	11	2	Oct
324	12*	1	Oct
325	13	2	Oct
326	14	2	Oct
327	15	2	Oct
328	16*	1	Oct
329	17	2	Oct
330	18	2	Oct
331	19	2	Oct
332	20*	1	Oct
333	21	2	Oct
334	22	2	Oct
335	23	2	Oct
336	24*	1	Oct
337	25	2	Oct
338	26	2	Oct
339	27	2	Oct
340	28*	1	Oct
341	29	2	Oct
342	30	2	Oct
343	31	2	Oct
344	32*	1	Oct
345	33	2	Oct
346	34	2	Oct
347	35	2	Oct
348	36*	1	Oct
349	37	2	Oct
350	38	2	Oct
351	39	2	Oct
352	40*	1	Oct
353	41	2	Oct
354	42	2	Oct
355	43	2	Oct
356	44*	1	Oct
357	45	2	Oct
358	46	2	Oct
359	47	2	Oct
360	48*	1	Oct
361	49	2	Oct
362	50	2	Oct
363	51	2	Oct
364	52*	1	Oct
365	53	2	Oct
366	54	2	Oct
367	55	2	Oct
368	56*	1	Oct
369	57	2	Oct
370	58	2	Oct
371	59	2	Oct
372	60*	1	Oct
373	61	2	Oct
374	62	2	Oct
375	63	2	Oct
376	64*	1	Oct
377	65	2	Oct
378	66	2	Oct
379	67	2	Oct
380	68*	1	Oct
381	69	2	Oct
382	70	2	Oct
383	71	2	Oct
384	72*	1	Oct
385	73	2	Oct
386	74	2	Oct
387	75	2	Oct
388	76*	1	Oct
389	77	2	Oct
390	78	2	Oct
391	79	2	Oct
392	80*	1	Oct
393	81	2	Oct
394	82	2	Oct
395	83	2	Oct
396	84*	1	Oct
397	85	2	Oct
398	86	2	Oct
399	87	2	Oct
400	88*	1	Oct
401	89	2	Oct
402	90	2	Oct
403	91	2	Oct
404	92*	1	Oct
405	93	2	Oct
406	94	2	Oct
407	95	2	Oct
408	96*	1	Oct
409	97	2	Oct
410	98	2	Oct
411	99	2	Oct
412	100*	1	Oct
413	101	2	Oct
414	102	2	Oct
415	103	2	Oct
416	104*	1	Oct
417	105	2	Oct
418	106	2	Oct
419	107	2	Oct
420	108*	1	Oct
421	109	2	Oct
422	110	2	Oct
423	111	2	Oct
424	112*	1	Oct
425	113	2	Oct
426	114	2	Oct
427	115	2	Oct
428	116*	1	Oct
429	117	2	Oct
430	118	2	Oct
431	119	2	Oct
432	120*	1	Oct
433	121	2	Oct
434	122	2	Oct
435	123	2	Oct
436	124*	1	Oct
437	125	2	Oct
438	126	2	Oct
439	127	2	Oct
440	128*	1	Oct
441	129	2	Oct
442	130	2	Oct
443	131	2	Oct
444	132*	1	Oct
445	133	2	Oct
446	134	2	Oct
447	135	2	Oct
448	136*	1	Oct
449	137	2	Oct
450	138	2	Oct
451	139	2	Oct
452	140*	1	Oct
453	141	2	Oct
454	142	2	Oct
455	143	2	Oct
456	144*	1	Oct
457	145	2	Oct
458	146	2	Oct
459	147	2	Oct
460	148*	1	Oct
461	149	2	Oct
462	150	2	Oct
463	151	2	Oct
464	152*	1	Oct
465	153	2	Oct
466	154	2	Oct
467	155	2	Oct
468	156*	1	Oct
469	157	2	Oct
470	158	2	Oct
471	159	2	Oct
472	160*	1	Oct
473	161	2	Oct
474	162	2	Oct
475	163	2	Oct
476	164*	1	Oct
477	165	2	Oct
478	166	2	Oct
479	167	2	Oct
480	168*	1	Oct
481	169	2	Oct
482	170	2	Oct
483	171	2	Oct
484	172*	1	Oct
485	173	2	Oct
486	174	2	Oct
487	175	2	Oct
488	176*	1	Oct
489	177	2	Oct
490	178	2	Oct
491	179	2	Oct
492	180*	1	Oct
493	181	2	Oct
494	182	2	Oct
495	183	2	Oct

Seleucide Solar Year	Western Date of New Year (Julian)	Seleucide Solar Year	Western Date of New Year (Julian)	Seleucide Solar Year	Western Date of New Year (Julian)	Seleucide Solar Year	Western Date of New Year (Julian)
496	184* 1 Oct	530	218 2 Oct	564	252* 1 Oct	598	286 2 Oct
497	185 2 Oct	531	219 2 Oct	565	253 2 Oct	599	287 2 Oct
498	186 2 Oct	532	220* 1 Oct	566	254 2 Oct	600	288* 1 Oct
499	187 2 Oct	533	221 2 Oct	567	255 2 Oct	601	289 2 Oct
500	188* 1 Oct	534	222 2 Oct	568	256* 1 Oct	602	290 2 Oct
501	189 2 Oct	535	223 2 Oct	569	257 2 Oct	603	291 2 Oct
502	190 2 Oct	536	224* 1 Oct	570	258 2 Oct	604	292* 1 Oct
503	191 2 Oct	537	225 2 Oct	571	259 2 Oct	605	293 2 Oct
504	192* 1 Oct	538	226 2 Oct	572	260* 1 Oct	606	294 2 Oct
505	193 2 Oct	539	227 2 Oct	573	261 2 Oct	607	295 2 Oct
506	194 2 Oct	540	228* 1 Oct	574	262 2 Oct	608	296* 1 Oct
507	195 2 Oct	541	229 2 Oct	575	263 2 Oct	609	297 2 Oct
508	196* 1 Oct	542	230 2 Oct	576	264* 1 Oct	610	298 2 Oct
509	197 2 Oct	543	231 2 Oct	577	265 2 Oct	611	299 2 Oct
510	198 2 Oct	544	232* 1 Oct	578	266 2 Oct	612	300* 1 Oct
511	199 2 Oct	545	233 2 Oct	579	267 2 Oct	613	301 2 Oct
512	200* 1 Oct	546	234 2 Oct	580	268* 1 Oct	614	302 2 Oct
513	201 2 Oct	547	235 2 Oct	581	269 2 Oct	615	303 2 Oct
514	202 2 Oct	548	236* 1 Oct	582	270 2 Oct	616	304* 1 Oct
515	203 2 Oct	549	237 2 Oct	583	271 2 Oct	617	305 2 Oct
516	204* 1 Oct	550	238 2 Oct	584	272* 1 Oct	618	306 2 Oct
517	205 2 Oct	551	239 2 Oct	585	273 2 Oct	619	307 2 Oct
518	206 2 Oct	552	240* 1 Oct	586	274 2 Oct	620	308* 1 Oct
519	207 2 Oct	553	241 2 Oct	587	275 2 Oct	621	309 2 Oct
520	208* 1 Oct	554	242 2 Oct	588	276* 1 Oct	622	310 2 Oct
521	209 2 Oct	555	243 2 Oct	589	277 2 Oct	623	311 2 Oct
522	210 2 Oct	556	244* 1 Oct	590	278 2 Oct	624	312* 1 Oct
523	211 2 Oct	557	245 2 Oct	591	279 2 Oct	625	313 2 Oct
524	212* 1 Oct	558	246 2 Oct	592	280* 1 Oct	626	314 2 Oct
525	213 2 Oct	559	247 2 Oct	593	281 2 Oct	627	315 2 Oct
526	214 2 Oct	560	248* 1 Oct	594	282 2 Oct	628	316* 1 Oct
527	215 2 Oct	561	249 2 Oct	595	283 2 Oct	629	317 2 Oct
528	216* 1 Oct	562	250 2 Oct	596	284* 1 Oct	630	318 2 Oct
529	217 2 Oct	563	251 2 Oct	597	285 2 Oct		

SYRO-MACEDONIAN (GREEK)

Syro-Macedonian (Greek)	Western Date of New Year (Julian)	Syro-Macedonian (Greek)	Western Date of New Year (Julian)	Syro-Macedonian (Greek)	Western Date of New Year (Julian)	Syro-Macedonian (Greek)	Western Date of New Year (Julian)
1	312 B.C. 1 Sep	10	303 11 Sep	19	294 31 Aug	28	285* 1 Sep
2	311 1 Sep	11	302 31 Aug	20	293* 1 Sep	29	284 1 Sep
3	310 31 Aug	12	301* 1 Sep	21	292 1 Sep	30	283 1 Sep
4	309* 1 Sep	13	300 1 Sep	22	291 1 Sep	31	282 31 Aug
5	308 1 Sep	14	299 1 Sep	23	290 31 Aug	32	281* 1 Sep
6	307 1 Sep	15	298 31 Aug	24	289* 1 Sep	33	280 1 Sep
7	306 31 Aug	16	297* 1 Sep	25	288 1 Sep	34	279 1 Sep
8	305* 1 Sep	17	296 1 Sep	26	287 1 Sep	35	278 31 Aug
9	304 1 Sep	18	295 1 Sep	27	286 31 Aug	36	277* 1 Sep

Syro-Macedonian (Greek)	Western Date of New Year (Julian)	
37	276	1 Sep
38	275	1 Sep
39	274	31 Aug
40	273*	1 Sep
41	272	1 Sep
42	271	1 Sep
43	270	31 Aug
44	269*	1 Sep
45	268	1 Sep
46	267	1 Sep
47	266	31 Aug
48	265*	1 Sep
49	264	1 Sep
50	263	1 Sep
51	262	31 Aug
52	261*	1 Sep
53	260	1 Sep
54	259	1 Sep
55	258	31 Aug
56	257*	1 Sep
57	256	1 Sep
58	255	1 Sep
59	254	31 Aug
60	253*	1 Sep
61	252	1 Sep
62	251	1 Sep
63	250	31 Aug
64	249*	1 Sep
65	248	1 Sep
66	247	1 Sep
67	246	31 Aug
68	245*	1 Sep
69	244	1 Sep
70	243	1 Sep
71	242	31 Aug
72	241*	1 Sep
73	240	1 Sep
74	239	1 Sep
75	238	31 Aug
76	237*	1 Sep
77	236	1 Sep
78	235	1 Sep
79	234	31 Aug
80	233*	1 Sep
81	232	1 Sep
82	231	1 Sep
83	230	31 Aug
84	229*	1 Sep
85	228	1 Sep
86	227	1 Sep
87	226	31 Aug
88	225*	1 Sep
89	224	1 Sep
90	223	1 Sep
91	222	31 Aug
92	221*	1 Sep
93	220	1 Sep
94	219	1 Sep
95	218	31 Aug
96	217*	1 Sep
97	216	1 Sep
98	215	1 Sep
99	214	31 Aug
100	213*	1 Sep
101	212	1 Sep
102	211	1 Sep
103	210	31 Aug
104	209*	1 Sep
105	208	1 Sep
106	207	1 Sep
107	206	31 Aug
108	205*	1 Sep
109	204	1 Sep
110	203	1 Sep
111	202	31 Aug
112	201*	1 Sep
113	200	1 Sep
114	199	1 Sep
115	198	31 Aug
116	197*	1 Sep
117	196	1 Sep
118	195	1 Sep
119	194	31 Aug
120	193*	1 Sep
121	192	1 Sep
122	191	1 Sep
123	190	31 Aug
124	189*	1 Sep
125	188	1 Sep
126	187	1 Sep
127	186	31 Aug
128	185*	1 Sep
129	184	1 Sep
130	183	1 Sep
131	182	31 Aug
132	181*	1 Sep
133	180	1 Sep
134	179	1 Sep
135	178	31 Aug
136	177*	1 Sep
137	176	1 Sep
138	175	1 Sep
139	174	31 Aug
140	173*	1 Sep
141	172	1 Sep
142	171	1 Sep
143	170	31 Aug
144	169*	1 Sep
145	168	1 Sep
146	167	1 Sep
147	166	31 Aug
148	165*	1 Sep
149	164	1 Sep
150	163	1 Sep
151	162	31 Aug
152	161*	1 Sep
153	160	1 Sep
154	159	1 Sep
155	158	31 Aug
156	157*	1 Sep
157	156	1 Sep
158	155	1 Sep
159	154	31 Aug
160	153*	1 Sep
161	152	1 Sep
162	151	1 Sep
163	150	31 Aug
164	149*	1 Sep
165	148	1 Sep
166	147	1 Sep
167	146	31 Aug
168	145*	1 Sep
169	144	1 Sep
170	143	1 Sep
171	142	31 Aug
172	141*	1 Sep
173	140	1 Sep
174	139	1 Sep
175	138	31 Aug
176	137*	1 Sep
177	136	1 Sep
178	135	1 Sep
179	134	31 Aug
180	133*	1 Sep
181	132	1 Sep
182	131	1 Sep
183	130	31 Aug
184	129*	1 Sep
185	128	1 Sep
186	127	1 Sep
187	126	31 Aug
188	125*	1 Sep
189	124	1 Sep
190	123	1 Sep
191	122	31 Aug
192	121*	1 Sep
193	120	1 Sep
194	119	1 Sep
195	118	31 Aug
196	117*	1 Sep
197	116	1 Sep
198	115	1 Sep
199	114	31 Aug
200	113*	1 Sep
201	112	1 Sep
202	111	1 Sep
203	110	31 Aug
204	109*	1 Sep
205	108	1 Sep
206	107	1 Sep
207	106	31 Aug
208	105*	1 Sep
209	104	1 Sep
210	103	1 Sep
211	102	31 Aug
212	101*	1 Sep
213	100	1 Sep
214	99	1 Sep
215	98	31 Aug
216	97*	1 Sep
217	96	1 Sep
218	95	1 Sep
219	94	31 Aug
220	93*	1 Sep
221	92	1 Sep
222	91	1 Sep
223	90	31 Aug
224	89*	1 Sep
225	88	1 Sep
226	87	1 Sep
227	86	31 Aug
228	85*	1 Sep
229	84	1 Sep
230	83	1 Sep
231	82	31 Aug
232	81*	1 Sep
233	80	1 Sep
234	79	1 Sep
235	78	31 Aug
236	77*	1 Sep
237	76	1 Sep
238	75	1 Sep
239	74	31 Aug
240	73*	1 Sep

Syro-Macedonian (Greek)	Western Date of New Year (Julian)		Syro-Macedonian (Greek)	Western Date of New Year (Julian)		Syro-Macedonian (Greek)	Western Date of New Year (Julian)		Syro-Macedonian (Greek)	Western Date of New Year (Julian)	
241	72	1 Sep	247	66	31 Aug	253	60	1 Sep	259	54	31 Aug
242	71	1 Sep	248	65*	1 Sep	254	59	1 Sep	260	53*	1 Sep
243	70	31 Aug	249	64	1 Sep	255	58	31 Aug	261	52	1 Sep
244	69*	1 Sep	250	63	1 Sep	256	57*	1 Sep	262	51	1 Sep
245	68	1 Sep	251	62	31 Aug	257	56	1 Sep	263	50	31 Aug
246	67	1 Sep	252	61*	1 Sep	258	55	1 Sep	264	49*	1 Sep

SYRO-MACEDONIAN (SYRIAN)

Syro-Macedonian (Syrian)	Western Date of New Year (Julian)		Syro-Macedonian (Syrian)	Western Date of New Year (Julian)		Syro-Macedonian (Syrian)	Western Date of New Year (Julian)		Syro-Macedonian (Syrian)	Western Date of New Year (Julian)	
1	313*	9 Oct	36	278	8 Oct	71	243	9 Oct	106	208	9 Oct
2	312	9 Oct	37	277*	9 Oct	72	242	8 Oct	107	207	9 Oct
3	311	9 Oct	38	276	9 Oct	73	241*	9 Oct	108	206	8 Oct
4	310	8 Oct	39	275	9 Oct	74	240	9 Oct	109	205*	9 Oct
5	309*	9 Oct	40	274	8 Oct	75	239	9 Oct	110	204	9 Oct
6	308	9 Oct	41	273*	9 Oct	76	238	8 Oct	111	203	9 Oct
7	307	9 Oct	42	272	9 Oct	77	237*	9 Oct	112	202	8 Oct
8	306	8 Oct	43	271	9 Oct	78	236	9 Oct	113	201*	9 Oct
9	305*	9 Oct	44	270	8 Oct	79	235	9 Oct	114	200	9 Oct
10	304	9 Oct	45	269*	9 Oct	80	234	8 Oct	115	199	9 Oct
11	303	9 Oct	46	268	9 Oct	81	233*	9 Oct	116	198	8 Oct
12	302	8 Oct	47	267	9 Oct	82	232	9 Oct	117	197*	9 Oct
13	301*	9 Oct	48	266	8 Oct	83	231	9 Oct	118	196	9 Oct
14	300	9 Oct	49	265*	9 Oct	84	230	8 Oct	119	195	9 Oct
15	299	9 Oct	50	264	9 Oct	85	229*	9 Oct	120	194	8 Oct
16	298	8 Oct	51	263	9 Oct	86	228	9 Oct	121	193*	9 Oct
17	297*	9 Oct	52	262	8 Oct	87	227	9 Oct	122	192	9 Oct
18	296	9 Oct	53	261*	9 Oct	88	226	8 Oct	123	191	9 Oct
19	295	9 Oct	54	260	9 Oct	89	225*	9 Oct	124	190	8 Oct
20	294	8 Oct	55	259	9 Oct	90	224	9 Oct	125	189*	9 Oct
21	293*	9 Oct	56	258	8 Oct	91	223	9 Oct	126	188	9 Oct
22	292	9 Oct	57	257*	9 Oct	92	222	8 Oct	127	187	9 Oct
23	291	9 Oct	58	256	9 Oct	93	221*	9 Oct	128	186	8 Oct
24	290	8 Oct	59	255	9 Oct	94	220	9 Oct	129	185*	9 Oct
25	289*	9 Oct	60	254	8 Oct	95	219	9 Oct	130	184	9 Oct
26	288	9 Oct	61	253*	9 Oct	96	218	8 Oct	131	183	9 Oct
27	287	9 Oct	62	252	9 Oct	97	217*	9 Oct	132	182	8 Oct
28	286	8 Oct	63	251	9 Oct	98	216	9 Oct	133	181*	9 Oct
29	285*	9 Oct	64	250	8 Oct	99	215	9 Oct	134	180	9 Oct
30	284	9 Oct	65	249*	9 Oct	100	214	8 Oct	135	179	9 Oct
31	283	9 Oct	66	248	9 Oct	101	213*	9 Oct	136	178	8 Oct
32	282	8 Oct	67	247	9 Oct	102	212	9 Oct	137	177*	9 Oct
33	281*	9 Oct	68	246	8 Oct	103	211	9 Oct	138	176	9 Oct
34	280	9 Oct	69	245*	9 Oct	104	210	8 Oct	139	175	9 Oct
35	279	9 Oct	70	244	9 Oct	105	209*	9 Oct	140	174	8 Oct

Syro-Macedonian (Syrian)	Western Date of New Year (Julian)			Syro-Macedonian (Syrian)	Western Date of New Year (Julian)			Syro-Macedonian (Syrian)	Western Date of New Year (Julian)			Syro-Macedonian (Syrian)	Western Date of New Year (Julian)		
141	173*	9	Oct	173	141*	9	Oct	205	109*	9	Oct	236	78	8	Oct
142	172	9	Oct	174	140	9	Oct	206	108	9	Oct	237	77*	9	Oct
143	171	9	Oct	175	139	9	Oct	207	107	9	Oct	238	76	9	Oct
144	170	8	Oct	176	138	8	Oct	208	106	8	Oct	239	75	9	Oct
145	169*	9	Oct	177	137*	9	Oct	209	105*	9	Oct	240	74	8	Oct
146	168	9	Oct	178	136	9	Oct	210	104	9	Oct	241	73*	9	Oct
147	167	9	Oct	179	135	9	Oct	211	103	9	Oct	242	72	9	Oct
148	166	8	Oct	180	134	8	Oct	212	102	8	Oct	243	71	9	Oct
149	165*	9	Oct	181	133*	9	Oct	213	101*	9	Oct	244	70	8	Oct
150	164	9	Oct	182	132	9	Oct	214	100	9	Oct	245	69*	9	Oct
151	163	9	Oct	183	131	9	Oct	215	99	9	Oct	246	68	9	Oct
152	162	8	Oct	184	130	8	Oct	216	98	8	Oct	247	67	9	Oct
153	161*	9	Oct	185	129*	9	Oct	217	97*	9	Oct	248	66	8	Oct
154	160	9	Oct	186	128	9	Oct	218	96	9	Oct	249	65*	9	Oct
155	159	9	Oct	187	127	9	Oct	219	95	9	Oct	250	64	9	Oct
156	158	8	Oct	188	126	8	Oct	220	94	8	Oct	251	63	9	Oct
157	157*	9	Oct	189	125*	9	Oct	221	93*	9	Oct	252	62	8	Oct
158	156	9	Oct	190	124	9	Oct	222	92	9	Oct	253	61*	9	Oct
159	155	9	Oct	191	123	9	Oct	223	91	9	Oct	254	60	9	Oct
160	154	8	Oct	192	122	8	Oct	224	90	8	Oct	255	59	9	Oct
161	153*	9	Oct	193	121*	9	Oct	225	89*	9	Oct	256	58	8	Oct
162	152	9	Oct	194	120	9	Oct	226	88	9	Oct	257	57*	9	Oct
163	151	9	Oct	195	119	9	Oct	227	87	9	Oct	258	56	9	Oct
164	150	8	Oct	196	118	8	Oct	228	86	8	Oct	259	55	9	Oct
165	149*	9	Oct	197	117*	9	Oct	229	85*	9	Oct	260	54	8	Oct
166	148	9	Oct	198	116	9	Oct	230	84	9	Oct	261	53*	9	Oct
167	147	9	Oct	199	115	9	Oct	231	83	9	Oct	262	52	9	Oct
168	146	8	Oct	200	114	8	Oct	232	82	8	Oct	263	51	9	Oct
169	145*	9	Oct	201	113*	9	Oct	233	81*	9	Oct	264	50	8	Oct
170	144	9	Oct	202	112	9	Oct	234	80	9	Oct	265	49*	9	Oct
171	143	9	Oct	203	111	9	Oct	235	79	8	Oct	266	48	9	Oct
172	142	8	Oct	204	110	8	Oct								

ERA OF ANTIOCH (GREEK)

Era of Antioch Greek	Western Date (Julian) of New Year			Era of Antioch Greek	Western Date (Julian) of New Year			Era of Antioch Greek	Western Date (Julian) of New Year			Era of Antioch Greek	Western Date (Julian) of New Year		
1	48	4	Sep	9	40	4	Sep	17	32	4	Sep	25	24	4	Sep
2	47	5	Sep	10	39	5	Sep	18	31	5	Sep	26	23	5	Sep
3	46	5	Sep	11	38	5	Sep	19	30	5	Sep	27	22	5	Sep
4	45*	5	Sep	12	37*	5	Sep	20	29*	5	Sep	28	21*	5	Sep
5	44	4	Sep	13	36	4	Sep	21	28	4	Sep	29	20	4	Sep
6	43	5	Sep	14	35	5	Sep	22	27	5	Sep	30	19	5	Sep
7	42	5	Sep	15	34	5	Sep	23	26	5	Sep	31	18	5	Sep
8	41*	5	Sep	16	33*	5	Sep	24	25*	5	Sep	32	17*	5	Sep

Era of Antioch Greek	Western Date (Julian) of New Year			Era of Antioch Greek	Western Date (Julian) of New Year			Era of Antioch Greek	Western Date (Julian) of New Year			Era of Antioch Greek	Western Date (Julian) of New Year		
33	16	4	Sep	82	34	5	Sep	132	84*	5	Sep	182	134	5	Sep
34	15	5	Sep	83	35	5	Sep	133	85	4	Sep	183	135	5	Sep
35	14	5	Sep	84	36*	5	Sep	134	86	5	Sep	184	136*	5	Sep
36	13*	5	Sep	85	37	4	Sep	135	87	5	Sep	185	137	4	Sep
37	12	4	Sep	86	38	5	Sep	136	88*	5	Sep	186	138	5	Sep
38	11	5	Sep	87	39	5	Sep	137	89	4	Sep	187	139	5	Sep
39	10	5	Sep	88	40*	5	Sep	138	90	5	Sep	188	140*	5	Sep
40	9*	5	Sep	89	41	4	Sep	139	91	5	Sep	189	141	4	Sep
41	8	4	Sep	90	42	5	Sep	140	92*	5	Sep	190	142	5	Sep
42	7	5	Sep	91	43	5	Sep	141	93	4	Sep	191	143	5	Sep
43	6	5	Sep	92	44*	5	Sep	142	94	5	Sep	192	144*	5	Sep
44	5*	5	Sep	93	45	4	Sep	143	95	5	Sep	193	145	4	Sep
45	4	4	Sep	94	46	5	Sep	144	96*	5	Sep	194	146	5	Sep
46	3	5	Sep	95	47	5	Sep	145	97	4	Sep	195	147	5	Sep
47	2	5	Sep	96	48*	5	Sep	146	98	5	Sep	196	148*	5	Sep
48	1*	5	Sep	97	49	4	Sep	147	99	5	Sep	197	149	4	Sep
				98	50	5	Sep	148	100*	5	Sep	198	150	5	Sep
49	1	4	Sep	99	51	5	Sep	149	101	4	Sep	199	151	5	Sep
50	2	5	Sep	100	52*	5	Sep	150	102	5	Sep	200	152*	5	Sep
51	3	5	Sep	101	53	4	Sep	151	103	5	Sep	201	153	4	Sep
52	4*	5	Sep	102	54	5	Sep	152	104*	5	Sep	202	154	5	Sep
53	5	4	Sep	103	55	5	Sep	153	105	4	Sep	203	155	5	Sep
54	6	5	Sep	104	56*	5	Sep	154	106	5	Sep	204	156*	5	Sep
55	7	5	Sep	105	57	4	Sep	155	107	5	Sep	205	157	4	Sep
56	8*	5	Sep	106	58	5	Sep	156	108*	5	Sep	206	158	5	Sep
57	9	4	Sep	107	59	5	Sep	157	109	4	Sep	207	159	5	Sep
58	10	5	Sep	108	60*	5	Sep	158	110	5	Sep	208	160*	5	Sep
59	11	5	Sep	109	61	4	Sep	159	111	5	Sep	209	161	4	Sep
60	12*	5	Sep	110	62	5	Sep	160	112*	5	Sep	210	162	5	Sep
61	13	4	Sep	111	63	5	Sep	161	113	4	Sep	211	163	5	Sep
62	14	5	Sep	112	64*	5	Sep	162	114	5	Sep	212	164*	5	Sep
63	15	5	Sep	113	65	4	Sep	163	115	5	Sep	213	165	4	Sep
64	16*	5	Sep	114	66	5	Sep	164	116*	5	Sep	214	166	5	Sep
65	17	4	Sep	115	67	5	Sep	165	117	4	Sep	215	167	5	Sep
66	18	5	Sep	116	68*	5	Sep	166	118	5	Sep	216	168*	5	Sep
67	19	5	Sep	117	69	4	Sep	167	119	5	Sep	217	169	4	Sep
68	20*	5	Sep	118	70	5	Sep	168	120*	5	Sep	218	170	5	Sep
69	21	4	Sep	119	71	5	Sep	169	121	4	Sep	219	171	5	Sep
70	22	5	Sep	120	72*	5	Sep	170	122	5	Sep	220	172*	5	Sep
71	23	5	Sep	121	73	4	Sep	171	123	5	Sep	221	173	4	Sep
72	24*	5	Sep	122	74	5	Sep	172	124*	5	Sep	222	174	5	Sep
73	25	4	Sep	123	75	5	Sep	173	125	4	Sep	223	175	5	Sep
74	26	5	Sep	124	76*	5	Sep	174	126	5	Sep	224	176*	5	Sep
75	27	5	Sep	125	77	4	Sep	175	127	5	Sep	225	177	4	Sep
76	28*	5	Sep	126	78	5	Sep	176	128*	5	Sep	226	178	5	Sep
77	29	4	Sep	127	79	5	Sep	177	129	4	Sep	227	179	5	Sep
78	30	5	Sep	128	80*	5	Sep	178	130	5	Sep	228	180*	5	Sep
79	31	5	Sep	129	81	4	Sep	179	131	5	Sep	229	181	4	Sep
80	32*	5	Sep	130	82	5	Sep	180	132*	5	Sep	230	182	5	Sep
81	33	4	Sep	131	83	5	Sep	181	133	4	Sep	231	183	5	Sep

Era of Antioch Greek	Western Date (Julian) of New Year		
232	184*	5	Sep
233	185	4	Sep
234	186	5	Sep
235	187	5	Sep
236	188*	5	Sep
237	189	4	Sep
238	190	5	Sep
239	191	5	Sep
240	192*	5	Sep
241	193	4	Sep
242	194	5	Sep
243	195	5	Sep
244	196*	5	Sep
245	197	4	Sep
246	198	5	Sep
247	199	5	Sep
248	200*	5	Sep
249	201	4	Sep
250	202	5	Sep
251	203	5	Sep
252	204*	5	Sep
253	205	4	Sep
254	206	5	Sep
255	207	5	Sep
256	208*	5	Sep
257	209	4	Sep

Era of Antioch Greek	Western Date (Julian) of New Year		
258	210	5	Sep
259	211	5	Sep
260	212*	5	Sep
261	213	4	Sep
262	214	5	Sep
263	215	5	Sep
264	216*	5	Sep
265	217	4	Sep
266	218	5	Sep
267	219	5	Sep
268	220*	5	Sep
269	221	4	Sep
270	222	5	Sep
271	223	5	Sep
272	224*	5	Sep
273	225	4	Sep
274	226	5	Sep
275	227	5	Sep
276	228*	5	Sep
277	229	4	Sep
278	230	5	Sep
279	231	5	Sep
280	232*	5	Sep
281	233	4	Sep
282	234	5	Sep

Era of Antioch Greek	Western Date (Julian) of New Year		
283	235	5	Sep
284	236*	5	Sep
285	237	4	Sep
286	238	5	Sep
287	239	5	Sep
288	240*	5	Sep
289	241	4	Sep
290	242	5	Sep
291	243	5	Sep
292	244*	5	Sep
293	245	4	Sep
294	246	5	Sep
295	247	5	Sep
296	248*	5	Sep
297	249	4	Sep
298	250	5	Sep
299	251	5	Sep
300	252*	5	Sep
301	253	4	Sep
302	254	5	Sep
303	255	5	Sep
304	256*	5	Sep
305	257	4	Sep
306	258	5	Sep
307	259	5	Sep

Era of Antioch Greek	Western Date (Julian) of New Year		
308	260*	5	Sep
309	261	4	Sep
310	262	5	Sep
311	263	5	Sep
312	264*	5	Sep
313	265	4	Sep
314	266	5	Sep
315	267	5	Sep
316	268*	5	Sep
317	269	4	Sep
318	270	5	Sep
319	271	5	Sep
320	272*	5	Sep
321	273	4	Sep
322	274	5	Sep
323	275	5	Sep
324	276*	5	Sep
325	277	4	Sep
326	278	5	Sep
327	279	5	Sep
328	280*	5	Sep
329	281	4	Sep
330	282	5	Sep
331	283	5	Sep
332	284*	5	Sep

ERA OF ANTIOCH (SYRIAN)

Era of Antioch Syrian	Western Date (Julian) of New Year		
1	48	9	Aug
2	47	9	Aug
3	46	9	Aug
4	45*	8	Aug
5	44	9	Aug
6	43	9	Aug
7	42	9	Aug
8	41*	8	Aug
9	40	9	Aug
10	39	9	Aug
11	38	9	Aug
12	37*	8	Aug
13	36	9	Aug
14	35	9	Aug
15	34	9	Aug

Era of Antioch Syrian	Western Date (Julian) of New Year		
16	33*	8	Aug
17	32	9	Aug
18	31	9	Aug
19	30	9	Aug
20	29*	8	Aug
21	28	9	Aug
22	27	9	Aug
23	26	9	Aug
24	25*	8	Aug
25	24	9	Aug
26	23	9	Aug
27	22	9	Aug
28	21*	8	Aug
29	20	9	Aug
30	19	9	Aug

Era of Antioch Syrian	Western Date (Julian) of New Year		
31	18	9	Aug
32	17*	8	Aug
33	16	9	Aug
34	15	9	Aug
35	14	9	Aug
36	13*	8	Aug
37	12	9	Aug
38	11	9	Aug
39	10	9	Aug
40	9*	8	Aug
41	8	9	Aug
42	7	9	Aug
43	6	9	Aug
44	5*	8	Aug
45	4	9	Aug

Era of Antioch Syrian	Western Date (Julian) of New Year		
46	3	9	Aug
47	2	9	Aug
48	1*	8	Aug
49	1	9	Aug
50	2	9	Aug
51	3	9	Aug
52	4*	8	Aug
53	5	9	Aug
54	6	9	Aug
55	7	9	Aug
56	8*	8	Aug
57	9	9	Aug
58	10	9	Aug
59	11	9	Aug
60	12*	8	Aug

Era of Antioch Syrian	Western Date (Julian) of New Year			Era of Antioch Syrian	Western Date (Julian) of New Year			Era of Antioch Syrian	Western Date (Julian) of New Year			Era of Antioch Syrian	Western Date (Julian) of New Year		
61	13	9	Aug	111	63	9	Aug	161	113	9	Aug	211	163	9	Aug
62	14	9	Aug	112	64*	8	Aug	162	114	9	Aug	212	164*	8	Aug
63	15	9	Aug	113	65	9	Aug	163	115	9	Aug	213	165	9	Aug
64	16*	8	Aug	114	66	9	Aug	164	116*	8	Aug	214	166	9	Aug
65	17	9	Aug	115	67	9	Aug	165	117	9	Aug	215	167	9	Aug
66	18	9	Aug	116	68*	8	Aug	166	118	9	Aug	216	168*	8	Aug
67	19	9	Aug	117	69	9	Aug	167	119	9	Aug	217	169	9	Aug
68	20*	8	Aug	118	70	9	Aug	168	120*	8	Aug	218	170	9	Aug
69	21	9	Aug	119	71	9	Aug	169	121	9	Aug	219	171	9	Aug
70	22	9	Aug	120	72*	8	Aug	170	122	9	Aug	220	172*	8	Aug
71	23	9	Aug	121	73	9	Aug	171	123	9	Aug	221	173	9	Aug
72	24*	8	Aug	122	74	9	Aug	172	124*	8	Aug	222	174	9	Aug
73	25	9	Aug	123	75	9	Aug	173	125	9	Aug	223	175	9	Aug
74	26	9	Aug	124	76*	8	Aug	174	126	9	Aug	224	176*	8	Aug
75	27	9	Aug	125	77	9	Aug	175	127	9	Aug	225	177	9	Aug
76	28*	8	Aug	126	78	9	Aug	176	128*	8	Aug	226	178	9	Aug
77	29	9	Aug	127	79	9	Aug	177	129	9	Aug	227	179	9	Aug
78	30	9	Aug	128	80*	8	Aug	178	130	9	Aug	228	180*	8	Aug
79	31	9	Aug	129	81	9	Aug	179	131	9	Aug	229	181	9	Aug
80	32*	8	Aug	130	82	9	Aug	180	132*	8	Aug	230	182	9	Aug
81	33	9	Aug	131	83	9	Aug	181	133	9	Aug	231	183	9	Aug
82	34	9	Aug	132	84*	8	Aug	182	134	9	Aug	232	184*	8	Aug
83	35	9	Aug	133	85	9	Aug	183	135	9	Aug	233	185	9	Aug
84	36*	8	Aug	134	86	9	Aug	184	136*	8	Aug	234	186	9	Aug
85	37	9	Aug	135	87	9	Aug	185	137	9	Aug	235	187	9	Aug
86	38	9	Aug	136	88*	8	Aug	186	138	9	Aug	236	188*	8	Aug
87	39	9	Aug	137	89	9	Aug	187	139	9	Aug	237	189	9	Aug
88	40*	8	Aug	138	90	9	Aug	188	140*	8	Aug	238	190	9	Aug
89	41	9	Aug	139	91	9	Aug	189	141	9	Aug	239	191	9	Aug
90	42	9	Aug	140	92*	8	Aug	190	142	9	Aug	240	192*	8	Aug
91	43	9	Aug	141	93	9	Aug	191	143	9	Aug	241	193	9	Aug
92	44*	8	Aug	142	94	9	Aug	192	144*	8	Aug	242	194	9	Aug
93	45	9	Aug	143	95	9	Aug	193	145	9	Aug	243	195	9	Aug
94	46	9	Aug	144	96*	8	Aug	194	146	9	Aug	244	196*	8	Aug
95	47	9	Aug	145	97	9	Aug	195	147	9	Aug	245	197	9	Aug
96	48*	8	Aug	146	98	9	Aug	196	148*	8	Aug	246	198	9	Aug
97	49	9	Aug	147	99	9	Aug	197	149	9	Aug	247	199	9	Aug
98	50	9	Aug	148	100*	8	Aug	198	150	9	Aug	248	200*	8	Aug
99	51	9	Aug	149	101	9	Aug	199	151	9	Aug	249	201	9	Aug
100	52*	8	Aug	150	102	9	Aug	200	152*	8	Aug	250	202	9	Aug
101	53	9	Aug	151	103	9	Aug	201	153	9	Aug	251	203	9	Aug
102	54	9	Aug	152	104*	8	Aug	202	154	9	Aug	252	204*	8	Aug
103	55	9	Aug	153	105	9	Aug	203	155	9	Aug	253	205	9	Aug
104	56*	8	Aug	154	106	9	Aug	204	156*	8	Aug	254	206	9	Aug
105	57	9	Aug	155	107	9	Aug	205	157	9	Aug	255	207	9	Aug
106	58	9	Aug	156	108*	8	Aug	206	158	9	Aug	256	208*	8	Aug
107	59	9	Aug	157	109	9	Aug	207	159	9	Aug	257	209	9	Aug
108	60*	8	Aug	158	110	9	Aug	208	160*	8	Aug	258	210	9	Aug
109	61	9	Aug	159	111	9	Aug	209	161	9	Aug	259	211	9	Aug
110	62	9	Aug	160	112*	8	Aug	210	162	9	Aug	260	212*	8	Aug

Era of Antioch Syrian	Western Date (Julian) of New Year	Era of Antioch Syrian	Western Date (Julian) of New Year	Era of Antioch Syrian	Western Date (Julian) of New Year	Era of Antioch Syrian	Western Date (Julian) of New Year
261	213 9 Aug	279	231 9 Aug	297	249 9 Aug	315	267 9 Aug
262	214 9 Aug	280	232* 8 Aug	298	250 9 Aug	316	268* 8 Aug
263	215 9 Aug	281	233 9 Aug	299	251 9 Aug	317	269 9 Aug
264	216* 8 Aug	282	234 9 Aug	300	252* 8 Aug	318	270 9 Aug
265	217 9 Aug	283	235 9 Aug	301	253 9 Aug	319	271 9 Aug
266	218 9 Aug	284	236* 8 Aug	302	254 9 Aug	320	272* 8 Aug
267	219 9 Aug	285	237 9 Aug	303	255 9 Aug	321	273 9 Aug
268	220* 8 Aug	286	238 9 Aug	304	256* 8 Aug	322	274 9 Aug
269	221 9 Aug	287	239 9 Aug	305	257 9 Aug	323	275 9 Aug
270	222 9 Aug	288	240* 8 Aug	306	258 9 Aug	324	276* 8 Aug
271	223 9 Aug	289	241 9 Aug	307	259 9 Aug	325	277 9 Aug
272	224* 8 Aug	290	242 9 Aug	308	260* 8 Aug	326	278 9 Aug
273	225 9 Aug	291	243 9 Aug	309	261 9 Aug	327	279 9 Aug
274	226 9 Aug	292	244* 8 Aug	310	262 9 Aug	328	280* 8 Aug
275	227 9 Aug	293	245 9 Aug	311	263 9 Aug	329	281 9 Aug
276	228* 8 Aug	294	246 9 Aug	312	264* 8 Aug	330	282 9 Aug
277	229 9 Aug	295	247 9 Aug	313	265 9 Aug	331	283 9 Aug
278	230 9 Aug	296	248* 8 Aug	314	266 9 Aug	332	284* 8 Aug

THE OLYMPIAD ERA

The Olympiad was the most celebrated and ancient era of the Greeks. Its name was taken from the games held every four years at Olympia in honor of Zeus. These games became the greatest festival in ancient Greece, one of both religious and political importance. Success in the games gave honor not only to the individual but also to his family and his state. In 264 B.C., Timaeus of Sicily began using the games as a system of dating, beginning the era in 776 B.C., the year traditionally given as the commencement of the games.

The Attic calendar was a luni-solar one of 12 months of alternately 29 or 30 days with a period intercalculation of 29 or 30 days. When the intercalcary month was used, it always fell after the sixth month. Initially the intercalation was made every second year, but this made the year too long, and it became necessary to omit the intercalation periodically. This was done on an irregular basis.

The month began on the day when the moon would first show after conjunction. It was divided into decades, or periods of 10 days. The last decade contained nine days in the "hollow" or 29 day months. For the first two decades of each month, days were counted forward in sequence, e.g. 1st day 1st decade, 2nd day 1st decade, etc. The third decade, however, could also be counted backward from the end of the month to the first day of the third decade. This backward count was generally used when the month contained only 29 days. The last day of any month was always called "Old and New"

because astronomically the moon would be temporarily invisible while in conjunction with the sun.

The Attic months are as follows:

1.	Hecatombaeon	30 days
2.	Metageitnion	29 days
3.	Boedromion	30 days
4.	Pyanepsion	29 days
5.	Maemacterion	30 days
6.	Poseideon	29 days
7.	Gamelion	30 days
8.	Anthesterion	29 days
9.	Elaphebolion	30 days
10.	Munychion	29 days
11.	Thargelion	30 days
12.	Scirophorion	29 days

Poseideon II 29 or 30 days when used.

The year began at the summer solstice, which fell around July 2 at the inception of the calendar in 776 B.C. The Olympic games were always held on the eleventh through the fifteenth day after the New Moon following the summer stolstice.

OLYMPIC ERA

Olympiad Year	Western Date of New Year	
1	776	9 Jul
II	775	
III	774	
IV	773*	
2	772	24 Jun
II	771	
III	770	
IV	769*	
3	768	10 Jul
II	767	
III	766	
IV	765*	
4	764	25 Jun
II	763	
III	762	
IV	761*	
5	760	12 Jul
II	759	
III	758	
IV	757*	
6	756	27 Jun
II	755	
III	754	
IV	753*	
7	752	13 Jul
II	751	
III	750	
IV	749*	
8	748	29 Jun
II	747	
III	746	
IV	745*	
9	744	14 Jul
II	743	
III	742	
IV	741*	
10	740	1 Jul
II	739	

Olympiad Year	Western Date of New Year	
III	738	
IV	737*	
11	736	16 Jul
II	735	
III	734	
IV	733*	
12	732	2 Jul
II	731	
III	730	
IV	729*	
13	728	17 Jul
II	727	
III	726	
IV	725*	
14	724	4 Jul
II	723	
III	722	
IV	721*	
15	720	19 Jul
II	719	
III	718	
IV	717*	
16	716	5 Jul
II	715	
III	714	
IV	713*	
17	712	21 Jun
II	711	
III	710	
IV	709*	
18	708	7 Jul
II	707	
III	706	
IV	705*	
19	704	23 Jun
II	703	
III	702	
IV	701*	

Olympiad Year	Western Date of New Year	
20	700	8 Jul
II	699	
III	698	
IV	697*	
21	696	24 Jun
II	695	
III	694	
IV	693*	
22	692	9 Jul
II	691	
III	690	
IV	689*	
23	688	26 Jun
II	687	
III	686	
IV	685*	
24	684	11 Jul
II	683	
III	682	
IV	681*	
25	680	28 Jun
II	679	
III	678	
IV	677*	
26	676	12 Jul
II	675	
III	674	
IV	673*	
27	672	29 Jun
II	671	
III	670	
IV	669*	
28	668	14 Jul
II	667	
III	666	
IV	665*	
29	664	30 Jun
II	663	

Olympiad Year	Western Date of New Year	
III	662	
IV	661*	
30	660	16 Jul
II	659	
III	658	
IV	657*	
31	656	2 Jul
II	655	
III	654	
IV	653*	
32	652	18 Jul
II	651	
III	650	
IV	649*	
33	648	3 Jul
II	647	
III	646	
IV	645*	
34	644	19 Jul
II	643	
III	642	
IV	641*	
35	640	4 Jul
II	639	
III	638	
IV	637*	
36	636	21 Jun
II	635	
III	634	
IV	633*	
37	632	6 Jul
II	631	
III	630	
IV	629*	
38	628	23 Jun
II	627	
III	626	
IV	625*	

Olympiad Year	Western Date of New Year		Olympiad Year	Western Date of New Year		Olympiad Year	Western Date of New Year		Olympiad Year	Western Date of New Year	
39	624	8 Jul	IV	573*		III	522		II	471	
II	623		52	572	3 Jul	IV	521*		III	470	
III	622		II	571		65	520	29 Jun	IV	469*	
IV	621*		III	570		II	519		78	468	24 Jun
40	620	24 Jun	IV	569*		III	518		II	467	
II	619		53	568	18 Jul	IV	517*		III	466	
III	618		II	567		66	516	13 Jul	IV	465*	
IV	617*		III	566		II	515		79	464	9 Jul
41	616	10 Jun	IV	565*		III	514		II	463	
II	615		54	564	5 Jul	IV	513*		III	462	
III	614		II	563		67	512	30 Jun	IV	461*	
IV	613*		III	562		II	511		80	460	25 Jun
42	612	25 Jun	IV	561*		III	510		II	459	
II	611		55	560	20 Jul	IV	509*		III	458	
III	610		II	559		68	508	15 Jul	IV	457*	
IV	609*		III	558		II	507		81	456	10 Jul
43	608	11 Jul	IV	557*		III	506		II	455	
II	607		56	556	6 Jul	IV	505*		III	454	
III	606		II	555		69	504	1 Jul	IV	453*	
IV	605*		III	554		II	503		82	452	26 Jun
44	604	27 Jul	IV	553*		III	502		II	451	
II	603		57	552	22 Jun	IV	501*		III	450	
III	602		II	551		70	500	17 Jul	IV	449*	
IV	601*		III	550		II	499		83	448	12 Jul
45	600	13 Jul	IV	549*		III	498		II	447	
II	599		58	548	8 Jul	IV	497*		III	446	
III	598		II	547		71	496	3 Jul	IV	445*	
IV	597*		III	546		II	495		84	444	28 Jun
46	596	28 Jun	IV	545*		III	494		II	443	
II	595		59	544	23 Jun	IV	493*		III	442	
III	594		II	543		72	492	18 Jul	IV	441*	
IV	593*		III	542		II	491		85	440	14 Jul
47	592	14 Jul	IV	541*		III	490		II	439	
II	591		60	540	9 Jul	IV	489*		III	438	
III	590		II	539		73	488	4 Jul	IV	437*	
IV	589*		III	538		II	487		86	436	29 Jun
48	588	30 Jun	IV	537*		III	486		II	435	
II	587		61	536	25 Jun	IV	485*		III	434	
III	586		II	535		74	484	21 Jun	IV	433*	
IV	585*		III	534		II	483		87	432	15 Jul
49	584	16 Jul	IV	533*		III	482		II	431	
II	583		62	532	10 Jul	IV	481*		III	430	
III	582		II	531		75	480	5 Jul	IV	429*	
IV	581*		III	530		II	479		88	428	1 Jul
50	580	1 Jul	IV	529*		III	478		II	427	
II	579		63	528	27 Jun	IV	477*		III	426	
III	578		II	527		76	476	22 Jun	IV	425*	
IV	577*		III	526		II	475		89	424	17 Jul
51	576	17 Jul	IV	525*		III	474		II	423	
II	575		64	524	12 Jul	IV	473*		III	422	
III	574		II	523		77	472	7 Jul	IV	421*	

Olympiad Year	Western Date of New Year	
90	420	2 Jul
II	419	
III	418	
IV	417*	
91	416	18 Jul
II	415	
III	414	
IV	413*	
92	412	4 Jul
II	411	
III	410	
IV	409*	
93	408	19 Jul
II	407	
III	406	
IV	405*	
94	404	6 Jul
II	403	
III	402	
IV	401*	
95	400	21 Jun
II	399	
III	398	
IV	397*	
96	396	7 Jul
II	395	
III	394	
IV	393*	
97	392	23 Jun
II	391	
III	390	
IV	389*	
98	388	9 Jul
II	387	
III	386	
IV	385*	
99	384	24 Jun
II	383	
III	382	
IV	381*	
100	380	10 Jul
II	379	
III	378	
IV	377*	
101	376	26 Jun
II	375	
III	374	
IV	373*	
102	372	12 Jul
II	371	
III	370	

Olympiad Year	Western Date of New Year	
IV	369*	
103	368	28 Jun
II	367	
III	366	
IV	365*	
104	364	13 Jul
II	363	
III	362	
IV	361*	
105	360	30 Jun
II	359	
III	358	
IV	357*	
106	356	14 Jul
II	355	
III	354	
IV	353*	
107	352	1 Jul
II	351	
III	350	
IV	349*	
108	348	16 Jul
II	347	
III	346	
IV	345*	
109	344	3 Jul
II	343	
III	342	
IV	341*	
110	340	18 Jul
II	339	
III	338	
IV	337*	
111	336	4 Jul
II	335	
III	334	
IV	333*	
112	332	19 Jul
II	331	
III	330	
IV	329*	
113	328	5 Jul
II	327	
III	326	
IV	325*	
114	324	21 Jun
II	323	
III	322	
IV	321*	
115	320	7 Jul
II	319	

Olympiad Year	Western Date of New Year	
III	318	
IV	317*	
116	316	23 Jun
II	315	
III	314	
IV	313*	
117	312	8 Jul
II	311	
III	310	
IV	309*	
118	308	25 Jun
II	307	
III	306	
IV	305*	
119	304	10 Jul
II	303	
III	302	
IV	301*	
120	300	26 Jun
II	299	
III	298	
IV	297*	
121	296	11 Jul
II	295	
III	294	
IV	293*	
122	292	28 Jun
II	291	
III	290	
IV	289*	
123	288	13 Jul
II	287	
III	286	
IV	285*	
124	284	29 Jun
II	283	
III	282	
IV	281*	
125	280	15 Jul
II	279	
III	278	
IV	277*	
126	276	30 Jun
II	275	
III	274	
IV	273*	
127	272	16 Jul
II	271	
III	270	
IV	269*	
128	268	2 Jul

Olympiad Year	Western Date of New Year	
II	267	
III	266	
IV	265*	
129	264	18 Jul
II	263	
III	262	
IV	261*	
130	260	3 Jul
II	259	
III	258	
IV	257*	
131	256	19 Jul
II	255	
III	254	
IV	253*	
132	252	5 Jul
II	251	
III	250	
IV	249*	
133	248	21 Jun
II	247	
III	246	
IV	245*	
134	244	7 Jul
II	243	
III	242	
IV	241*	
135	240	23 Jun
II	239	
III	238	
IV	237*	
136	236	8 Jul
II	235	
III	234	
IV	233*	
137	232	24 Jun
II	231	
III	230	
IV	229*	
138	228	10 Jul
II	227	
III	226	
IV	225*	
139	224	25 Jun
II	223	
III	222	
IV	221*	
140	220	12 Jul
II	219	
III	218	
IV	217*	

Olympiad Year	Western Date of New Year	
141	216	27 Jun
II	215	
III	214	
IV	213*	
142	212	13 Jul
II	211	
III	210	
IV	209*	
143	208	29 Jun
II	207	
III	206	
IV	205*	
144	204	14 Jul
II	203	
III	202	
IV	201*	
145	200	30 Jun
II	199	
III	198	
IV	197*	
146	196	16 Jul
II	195	
III	194	
IV	193*	
147	192	2 Jul
II	191	
III	190	
IV	189*	
148	188	17 Jul
II	187	
III	186	
IV	185*	
149	184	4 Jul
II	183	
III	182	
IV	181*	
150	180	18 Jul
II	179	
III	178	
IV	177*	
151	176	5 Jul
II	175	
III	174	
IV	173*	
152	172	21 Jun
II	171	
III	170	
IV	169*	
153	168	7 Jul
II	167	
III	166	
IV	165*	
154	164	22 Jun
II	163	
III	162	
IV	161*	
155	160	8 Jul
II	159	
III	158	
IV	157*	
156	156	24 Jun
II	155	
III	154	
IV	153*	
157	152	9 Jul
II	151	
III	150	
IV	149*	
158	148	26 Jun
II	147	
III	146	
IV	145*	
159	144	11 Jul
II	143	
III	142	
IV	141*	
160	140	27 Jun
II	139	
III	138	
IV	137*	
161	136	12 Jul
II	135	
III	134	
IV	133*	
162	132	29 Jun
II	131	
III	130	
IV	129*	
163	128	14 Jul
II	127	
III	126	
IV	125*	
164	124	30 Jun
II	123	
III	122	
IV	121*	
165	120	16 Jul
II	119	
III	118	
IV	117*	
166	116	1 Jul
II	115	
III	114	
IV	113*	
167	112	17 Jul
II	111	
III	110	
IV	109*	
168	108	3 Jul
II	107	
III	106	
IV	105*	
169	104	19 Jul
II	103	
III	102	
IV	101*	
170	100	4 Jul
II	99	
III	98	
IV	97*	
171	96	21 Jun
II	95	
III	94	
IV	93*	
172	92	6 Jul
II	91	
III	90	
IV	89*	
173	88	22 Jun
II	87	
III	86	
IV	85*	
174	84	8 Jul
II	83	
III	82	
IV	81*	
175	80	24 Jun
II	79	
III	78	
IV	77*	
176	76	9 Jul
II	75	
III	74	
IV	73*	
177	72	25 Jun
II	71	
III	70	
IV	69*	
178	68	11 Jul
II	67	
III	66	
IV	65*	
179	64	26 Jun
II	63	
III	62	
IV	61*	
180	60	13 Jul
II	59	
III	58	
IV	57*	
181	56	28 Jun
II	55	
III	54	
IV	53*	
182	52	14 Jul
II	51	
III	50	
IV	49*	
183	48	29 Jun
II	47	
III	46	
IV	45*	
184	44	15 Jul
II	43	
III	42	
IV	41*	
185	40	1 Jul
II	39	
III	38	
IV	37*	
186	36	17 Jul
II	35	
III	34	
IV	33*	
187	32	3 Jul
II	31	
III	30	
IV	29*	
188	28	18 Jul
II	27	
III	26	
IV	25*	
189	24	5 Jul
II	23	
III	22	
IV	21*	
190	20	20 Jun
II	19	
III	18	
IV	17*	
191	16	6 Jul
II	15	
III	14	
IV	13*	

Olympiad Year	Western Date of New Year		Olympiad Year	Western Date of New Year		Olympiad Year	Western Date of New Year		Olympiad Year	Western Date of New Year	
192	12	22 Jun	III	39		II	90		230	141	21 Jun
II	11		IV	40*		III	91		II	142	
III	10		205	41	16 Jul	IV	92*		III	143	
IV	9*		II	42		218	93	12 Jul	IV	144*	
193	8	8 Jul	III	43		II	94		231	145	7 Jul
II	7		IV	44*		III	95		II	146	
III	6		206	45	3 Jul	IV	96*		III	147	
IV	5*		II	46		219	97	28 Jun	IV	148*	
194	4	23 Jun	III	47		II	98		232	149	23 Jun
II	3		IV	48*		III	99		II	150	
III	2		207	49	18 Jul	IV	100*		III	151	
IV	1*		II	50		220	101	14 Jul	IV	152*	
			III	51		II	102		233	153	9 Jul
195	1		IV	52*		III	103		II	154	
II	2		208	53	4 Jul	IV	104*		III	155	
III	3		II	54		221	105	29 Jun	IV	156*	
IV	4*		III	55		II	106		234	157	24 Jun
196	5	25 Jun	IV	56*		III	107		II	158	
II	6		209	57	20 Jul	IV	108*		III	159	
III	7		II	58		222	109	15 Jul	IV	160*	
IV	8*		III	59		II	110		235	161	10 Jul
197	9	10 Jul	IV	60*		III	111		II	162	
II	10		210	61	5 Jul	IV	112*		III	163	
III	11		II	62		223	113	30 Jun	IV	164*	
IV	12*		III	63		II	114		236	165	26 Jun
198	13	27 Jun	IV	64*		III	115		II	166	
II	14		211	65	22 Jun	IV	116*		III	167	
III	15		II	66		224	117	17 Jul	IV	168*	
IV	16*		III	67		II	118		237	169	12 Jul
199	17	12 Jul	IV	68*		III	119		II	170	
II	18		212	69	7 Jul	IV	120*		III	171	
III	19		II	70		225	121	2 Jul	IV	172*	
IV	20*		III	71		II	122		238	173	28 Jun
200	21	28 Jun	IV	72*		III	123		II	174	
II	22		213	73	24 Jun	IV	124*		III	175	
III	23		II	74		226	125	18 Jul	IV	176*	
IV	24*		III	75		II	126		239	177	13 Jul
201	25	13 Jul	IV	76*		III	127		II	178	
II	26		214	77	8 Jul	IV	128*		III	179	
III	27		II	78		227	129	4 Jul	IV	180*	
IV	28*		III	79		II	130		240	181	29 Jun
202	29	30 Jun	IV	80*		III	131		II	182	
II	30		215	81	25 Jun	IV	132*		III	183	
III	31		II	82		228	133	19 Jul	IV	184*	
IV	32*		III	83		II	134		241	185	14 Jul
203	33	15 Jul	IV	84*		III	135		II	186	
II	34		216	85	10 Jul	IV	136*		III	187	
III	35		II	86		229	137	6 Jul	IV	188*	
IV	36*		III	87		II	138		242	189	1 Jul
204	37	1 Jul	IV	88*		III	139		II	190	
II	38		217	89	26 Jun	IV	140*		III	191	

Olympiad Year	Western Date of New Year		Olympiad Year	Western Date of New Year		Olympiad Year	Western Date of New Year		Olympiad Year	Western Date of New Year	
IV	192*		III	243		II	294		**281**	345	15 Jul
243	193	16 Jul	IV	244*		III	295		II	346	
II	194		**256**	245	11 Jul	IV	296*		III	347	
III	195		II	246		**269**	297	6 Jul	IV	348*	
IV	196*		III	247		II	298		**282**	349	2 Jul
244	197	3 Jul	IV	248*		III	299		II	350	
II	198		**257**	249	28 Jun	IV	300*		III	351	
III	199		II	250		**270**	301	23 Jun	IV	352*	
IV	200*		III	251		II	302		**283**	353	17 Jul
245	201	17 Jul	IV	252*		III	303		II	354	
II	202		**258**	253	13 Jul	IV	304*		III	355	
III	203		II	254		**271**	305	8 Jul	IV	356*	
IV	204*		III	255		II	306		**284**	357	4 Jul
246	205	4 Jul	IV	256*		III	307		II	358	
II	206		**259**	257	29 Jun	IV	308*		III	359	
III	207		II	258		**272**	309	24 Jun	IV	360*	
IV	208*		III	259		II	310		**285**	361	18 Jul
247	209	19 Jul	IV	260*		III	311		II	362	
II	210		**260**	261	15 Jul	IV	312*		III	363	
III	211		II	262		**273**	313	10 Jul	IV	364*	
IV	212*		III	263		II	314		**286**	365	5 Jul
248	213	5 Jul	IV	264*		III	315		II	366	
II	214		**261**	265	30 Jun	IV	316*		III	367	
III	215		II	266		**274**	317	25 Jun	IV	368*	
IV	216*		III	267		II	318		**287**	369	20 Jul
249	217	21 Jun	IV	268*		III	319		II	370	
II	218		**262**	269	16 Jul	IV	320*		III	371	
III	219		II	270		**275**	321	11 Jul	IV	372*	
IV	220*		III	271		II	322		**288**	373	6 Jul
250	221	7 Jul	IV	272*		III	323		II	374	
II	222		**263**	273	2 Jul	IV	324*		III	375	
III	223		II	275		**276**	325	27 Jun	IV	376*	
IV	224*		III	275		II	326		**289**	377	22 Jun
251	225	23 Jun	IV	276*		III	327		II	378	
II	226		**264**	277	18 Jul	IV	328*		III	379	
III	227		II	278		**277**	329	13 Jul	IV	380*	
IV	228*		III	279		II	330		**290**	381	8 Jul
252	229	8 Jul	IV	280*		III	331		II	382	
II	230		**265**	281	3 Jul	IV	332*		III	383	
III	231		II	282		**278**	333	28 Jun	IV	384*	
IV	232*		III	283		II	334		**291**	385	24 Jun
253	233	25 Jun	IV	284*		III	335		II	386	
II	234		**266**	285	19 Jul	IV	336*		III	387	
III	235		II	286		**279**	337	14 Jul	IV	388*	
IV	236*		III	287		II	338		**292**	389	9 Jul
254	237	9 Jul	IV	288*		III	339		II	390	
II	238		**267**	289	5 Jul	IV	340*		III	391	
III	239		II	290		**280**	341	30 Jun	IV	392*	
IV	240*		III	291		II	342		**293**	393	26 Jun
255	241	26 Jun	IV	292*		III	343		II	394	
II	242		**268**	293	21 Jun	IV	344*		III	395	

Olympiad Year	Western Date of New Year		Olympiad Year	Western Date of New Year		Olympiad Year	Western Date of New Year		Olympiad Year	Western Date of New Year	
IV	396*		IV	408*		III	419		II	430	
294	397	10 Jul	**297**	409	29 Jun	IV	420*		III	431	
II	398		II	410		**300**	421	15 Jul	IV	432*	
III	399		III	411		II	422		**303**	433	3 Jul
IV	400*		IV	412*		III	423		II	434	
295	401	27 Jun	**298**	413	14 Jul	IV	424*		III	435	
II	402		II	414		**301**	425	1 Jul	IV	436*	
III	403		III	415		II	426		**304**	437	19 Jul
IV	404*		IV	416*		III	427		II	438	
296	405	12 Jul	**299**	417	30 Jun	IV	428*		III	439	
II	406		II	418		**302**	429	17 Jul	IV	440*	
III	407										

THE ERA OF TYRE

The Phoenicians were a seafaring people who, by 600 B.C. had stretched their influence from the eastern coast of the Mediterranean to Carthage in Africa, Marseille in France and Cadiz in Spain. Each of these farflung cities was an outpost in their trading empire. During their early history, the Phoenicians used the Babylonian, Assyrian and Chaldean calendars in turn. Between the fifth and third centuries B.C., wars with Greece increased Greek influence in Phoenicia. And in 333-332 B.C. Tyre, one of Phoenicia's major city states, was conquered by Alexander the Great. Sometime after the conquest, around 125 B.C. according to later historians, the area adopted a calendar similar in structure to that of the Macedonian Greeks, one that also used Greek names for months. However, the new year was celebrated 17 days later. Several years after the Roman conquest, the calendar was abandoned.

ERA OF TYRE

Tyre (Phoenician) Year	Western Date (Julian) of New Year		Tyre (Phoenician) Year	Western Date (Julian) of New Year		Tyre (Phoenician) Year	Western Date (Julian) of New Year		Tyre (Phoenician) Year	Western Date (Julian) of New Year	
1	125*	19 Oct	14	112	19 Oct	27	99	19 Oct	40	86	18 Oct
2	124	19 Oct	15	111	19 Oct	28	98	18 Oct	41	85*	19 Oct
3	123	19 Oct	16	110	18 Oct	29	97*	19 Oct	42	84	19 Oct
4	122	18 Oct	17	109*	19 Oct	30	96	19 Oct	43	83	19 Oct
5	121*	18 Oct	18	108	19 Oct	31	95	19 Oct	44	82	18 Oct
6	120	19 Oct	19	107	19 Oct	32	94	18 Oct	45	81*	19 Oct
7	119	19 Oct	20	106	18 Oct	33	93*	19 Oct	46	80	19 Oct
8	118	18 Oct	21	105*	19 Oct	34	92	19 Oct	47	79	19 Oct
9	117*	19 Oct	22	104	19 Oct	35	91	19 Oct	48	78	18 Oct
10	116	19 Oct	23	103	19 Oct	36	90	18 Oct	49	77*	19 Oct
11	115	19 Oct	24	102	18 Oct	37	89*	19 Oct	50	76	19 Oct
12	114	18 Oct	25	101*	19 Oct	38	88	19 Oct	51	75	19 Oct
13	113*	19 Oct	26	100	19 Oct	39	87	19 Oct	52	74	18 Oct

Tyre (Phoenician) Year	Western Date (Julian) of New Year		Tyre (Phoenician) Year	Western Date (Julian) of New Year		Tyre (Phoenician) Year	Western Date (Julian) of New Year		Tyre (Phoenician) Year	Western Date (Julian) of New Year	
53	73*	19 Oct	60	66	18 Oct	67	59	19 Oct	73	53*	19 Oct
54	72	19 Oct	61	65*	19 Oct	68	58	18 Oct	74	52	19 Oct
55	71	19 Oct	62	64	19 Oct	69	57*	19 Oct	75	51	19 Oct
56	70	18 Oct	63	63	19 Oct	70	56	19 Oct	76	50	18 Oct
57	69*	19 Oct	64	62	18 Oct	71	55	19 Oct	77	49*	19 Oct
58	68	19 Oct	65	61*	19 Oct	72	54	18 Oct	78	48	19 Oct
59	67	19 Oct	66	60	19 Oct						

ROMAN CALENDARS

The earliest Roman calendar, traditionally ascribed to Romulus, the legendary founder of Rome, consisted of 10 months; March (31 days), April (29 days), May (31 days), June (29 days), Quintilis (31 days), Sextilis (29 days), September (29 days), October (31 days), November (29 days) and December (29 days). Extra days or months were added to fill out the remaining 365 days of the solar year.

When Numa Pompilius became king of Rome around 715 B.C., he reformed the calendar, adding January (29 days) and February (28 days) to the end of the year. He also adopted a lunar calendar of 354 days, but because even numbers were considered unlucky, an extra day was added, making the year 355 days.

While this improved the calendar, it did not solve all the problems involved. Every four years there were four days too many. More importantly, the Pontifex Maximus, which had charge of the calendar, began using intercalations for political purposes—for extending the terms of prominent politicians or giving extra holidays. These practices made the calendar almost meaningless by the time Julius Caesar undertook reform. (See Julian Calendar)

The Romans divided each month into three sections: Kalends (the first day of the month), Nones (the 7th day in March, May, July and October; the 5th day in other months) and Ides (the 15th day in March, May, July and October and the 13th in the remaining months) Days were counted before a section, not after it. Thus February 3 was the third of the Nones of February. The reason for this arrangement has never been discovered.

CALENDAR OF NUMA POMPILIUS

	January		February		March		April		May		June
1.	Calend.	1.	Calend.	1.	Calend.	1.	Calend.	1.	Calend.	1.	Calend.
2.	IV	2.	IV	2.	VI	2.	IV	2.	VI	2.	IV
3.	III	3.	III	3.	V	3.	III	3.	V	3.	III
4.	Prid.	4.	Prid.	4.	IV	4.	Prid.	4.	IV	4.	Prid.
5.	Non.	5.	Non.	5.	III	5.	Non.	5.	III	5.	Non.
6.	VIII	6.	VIII	6.	Prid.	6.	VIII	6.	Prid.	6.	VIII
7.	VII	7.	VII	7.	Non.	7.	VII	7.	Non.	7.	VII
8.	VI	8.	VI	8.	VIII	8.	VI	8.	VIII	8.	VI
9.	V	9.	V	9.	VII	9.	V	9.	VII	9.	V
10.	IV	10.	IV	10.	VI	10.	IV	10.	VI	10.	IV
11.	III	11.	III	11.	V	11.	III	11.	V	11.	III
12.	Prid.	12.	Prid.	12.	IV	12.	Prid.	12.	IV	12.	Prid.
13.	Id.	13.	Id.	13.	III	13.	Id.	13.	III	13.	Id.
14.	XVII	14.	XVI	14.	Prid.	14.	XVIII	14.	Prid.	14.	XVII
15.	XVI	15.	XV	15.	Id.	15.	XVII	15.	Id.	15.	XVI
16.	XV	16.	XIV	16.	XVII	16.	XVI	16.	XVII	16.	XV
17.	XIV	17.	XIII	17.	XVI	17.	XV	17.	XVI	17.	XIV
18.	XIII	18.	XII	18.	XV	18.	XIV	18.	XV	18.	XIII
19.	XII	19.	XI	19.	XIV	19.	XIII	19.	XIV	19.	XII
20.	XI	20.	X	20.	XIII	20.	XII	20.	XIII	20.	XI
21.	X	21.	IX	21.	XII	21.	XI	21.	XII	21.	X
22.	IX	22.	VIII	22.	XI	22.	X	22.	XI	22.	IX
23.	VIII	23.	VII	23.	X	23.	IX	23.	X	23.	VIII
24.	VII	24.	VI	24.	IX	24.	VIII	24.	IX	24.	VII
25.	VI	25.	V	25.	VIII	25.	VII	25.	VIII	25.	VI
26.	V	26.	IV	26.	VII	26.	VI	26.	VII	26.	V
27.	IV	27.	III.	27.	VI	27.	V	27.	VI	27.	IV
28.	III	28.	Prid.	28.	V	28.	IV	28.	V	28.	III
29.	Prid.			29.	IV	29.	III	29.	IV	29.	Prid.
				30.	III	30.	Prid.	30.	III		
				31.	Prid.			31.	Prid.		

	Quintilis.		Sextilis.		September.		October.		November.		December.
1.	Calend.	1.	Calend.	1.	Calend.	1.	Calend.	1.	Calend.	1.	Calend.
2.	VI	2.	IV	2.	IV	2.	VI	2.	IV	2.	IV
3.	V	3.	III	3.	III	3.	V	3.	III	3.	III
4.	IV	4.	Prid.	4.	Prid.	4.	IV	4.	Prid.	4.	Prid.
5.	III	5.	Non.	5.	Non.	5.	III	5.	Non.	5.	Non.
6.	Prid.	6.	VIII	6.	VIII	6.	Prid.	6.	VIII	6.	VIII
7.	Non.	7.	VII	7.	VII	7.	Non.	7.	VII	7.	VII
8.	VIII	8.	VI	8.	VI	8.	VIII	8.	VI	8.	VI
9.	VII	9.	V	9.	V	9.	VII	9.	V	9.	V
10.	VI	10.	IV	10.	IV	10.	VI	10.	IV	10.	IV
11.	V	11.	III	11.	III	11.	V	11.	III	11.	III
12.	IV	12.	Prid.	12.	Prid.	12.	IV	12.	Prid.	12.	Prid.
13.	III	13.	Id.	13.	Id.	13.	III	13.	Id.	13.	Id.
14.	Prid.	14.	XVII	14.	XVII	14.	Prid.	14.	XVII	14.	XVII
15.	Id.	15.	XVI	15.	XVI	15.	Id.	15.	XVI	15.	XVI
16.	XVII	16.	XV	16.	XV	16.	XVII	16.	XV	16.	XV
17.	XVI	17.	XIV	17.	XIV	17.	XVI	17.	XIV	17.	XIV
18.	XV	18.	XIII	18.	XIII	18.	XV	18.	XIII	18.	XIII
19.	XIV	19.	XII	19.	XII	19.	XIV	19.	XII	19.	XII
20.	XIII	20.	XI	20.	XI	20.	XIII	20.	XI	20.	XI
21.	XII	21.	X	21.	X	21.	XII	21.	X	21.	X
22.	XI	22.	IX	22.	IX	22.	XI	22.	IX	22.	IX
23.	X	23.	VIII	23.	VIII	23.	X	23.	VIII	23.	VIII
24.	IX	24.	VII	24.	VII	24.	IX	24.	VII	24.	VII
25.	VIII	25.	VI	25.	VI	25.	VIII	25.	VI	25.	VI
26.	VII	26.	V	26.	V	26.	VII	26.	V	26.	V
27.	VI	27.	IV	27.	IV	27.	VI	27.	IV	27.	IV
28.	V	28.	III	28.	III	28.	V	28.	III	28.	III
29.	IV	29.	Prid.	29.	Prid.	29.	IV	29.	Prid.	29.	Prid.
30.	III					30.	III				
31.	Prid.					31.	Prid.				

CALENDAR OF ROMULUS

March.		April.		May.		June.		Quintilis.	
1.	Calend.	1.	Calend.	1.	Calend.	1.	Calend.	1.	Calend.
2.	VI	2.	IV	2.	VI	2.	IV	2.	VI
3.	V	3.	III	3.	V	3.	III	3.	V
4.	IV	4.	Prid.	4.	IV	4.	Prid.	4.	IV
5.	III	5.	Non.	5.	III	5.	Non.	5.	III
6.	Prid.	6.	VIII	6.	Prid.	6.	VIII	6.	Prid.
7.	Non.	7.	VII	7.	Non.	7.	VII	7.	Non.
8.	VIII	8.	VI	8.	VIII	8.	VI	8.	VIII
9.	VII	9.	V	9.	VII	9.	V	9.	VII
10.	VI	10.	IV	10.	VI	10.	IV	10.	VI
11.	V	11.	III	11.	V	11.	III	11.	V
12.	IV	12.	Prid.	12.	IV	12.	Prid.	12.	IV
13.	III	13.	Id.	13.	III	13.	Id.	13.	III
14.	Prid.	14.	XVIII	14.	Prid.	14.	XVIII	14.	Prid.
15.	Id.	15.	XVII	15.	Id.	15.	XVII	15.	Id.
16.	XVII	16.	XVI	16.	XVII	16.	XVI	16.	XVII
17.	XVI	17.	XV	17.	XVI	17.	XV	17.	XVI
18.	XV	18.	XIV	18.	XV	18.	XIV	18.	XV
19.	XIV	19.	XIII	19.	XIV	19.	XIII	19.	XIV
20.	XIII	20.	XII	20.	XIII	20.	XII	20.	XIII
21.	XII	21.	XI	21.	XII	21.	XI	21.	XII
22.	XI	22.	X	22.	XI	22.	X	22.	XI
23.	X	23.	IX	23.	X	23.	IX	23.	X
24.	IX	24.	VIII	24.	IX	24.	VIII	24.	IX
25.	VIII	25.	VII	25.	VIII	25.	VII	25.	VIII
26.	VII	26.	VI	26.	VII	26.	VI	26.	VII
27.	VI	27.	V	27.	VI	27.	V	27.	VI
28.	V	28.	IV	28.	V	28.	IV	28.	V
29.	IV	29.	III	29.	IV	29.	III	29.	IV
30.	III	30.	Prid.	30.	III	30.	Prid.	30.	III
31.	Prid.			31.	Prid.			31.	Prid.

CALENDAR OF ROMULUS

Sextilis.		September.		October.		November.		December.	
1.	Calend.	1.	Calend.	1.	Calend.	1.	Calend.	1.	Calend.
2.	IV	2.	IV	2.	VI	2.	IV	2.	IV
3.	III	3.	III	3.	V	3.	III	3.	III
4.	Prid.	4.	Prid.	4.	IV	4.	Prid.	4.	Prid.
5.	Non.	5.	Non.	5.	III	5.	Non.	5.	Non.
6.	VIII	6.	VIII	6.	Prid.	6.	VIII	6.	VIII
7.	VII	7.	VII	7.	Non.	7.	VII	7.	VII
8.	VI	8.	VI	8.	VIII	8.	VI	8.	VI
9.	V	9.	V	9.	VII	9.	V	9.	V
10.	IV	10.	IV	10.	VI	10.	IV	10.	IV
11.	III	11.	III	11.	V	11.	III	11.	III
12.	Prid.	12.	Prid.	12.	IV	12.	Prid.	12.	Prid.
13.	Id.	13.	Id.	13.	III	13.	Id.	13.	Id.
14.	XVIII	14.	XVIII	14.	Prid.	14.	XVIII	14.	XVIII
15.	XVII	15.	XVII	15.	Id.	15.	XVII	15.	XVII
16.	XVI	16.	XVI	16.	XVII	16.	XVI	16.	XVI
17.	XV	17.	XV	17.	XVI	17.	XV	17.	XV
18.	XIV	18.	XIV	18.	XV	18.	XIV	18.	XIV
19.	XIII	19.	XIII	19.	XIV	19.	XIII	19.	XIII
20.	XII	20.	XII	20.	XIII	20.	XII	20.	XII
21.	XI	21.	XI	21.	XII	21.	XI	21.	XI
22.	X	22.	X	22.	XI	22.	X	22.	X
23.	IX	23.	IX	23.	X	23.	IX	23.	IX
24.	VIII	24.	VIII	24.	IX	24.	VIII	24.	VIII
25.	VII	25.	VII	25.	VIII	25.	VII	25.	VII
26.	VI	26.	VI	26.	VII	26.	VI	26.	VI
27.	V	27.	V	27.	VI	27.	V	27.	V
28.	IV	28.	IV	28.	V	28.	IV	28.	IV
29.	III	29.	III	29.	IV	29.	III	29.	III
30.	Prid.	30.	Prid.	30.	III	30.	Prid.	30.	Prid.
				31.	Prid.				

THE ERA OF THE ARMENIANS

The Era of the Armenians was established in the middle of the sixth century A.D. as Christianity began to move into the area. Previously residents had used both the Greek and the Babylonian Chaldean calendars. They had no standard calendar of their own.

Like many others employed in the region, the Armenian calendar is based on the vague solar year of 365 days only, with no allowance for leap year. It had a seven day week. Holidays were a combination of the traditional pre-Christian feasts and the Christian ones celebrated by the church during that particular period. Residents used local names for months and days. Some sections utilized the local Armenian dialect; others Arabic and still others Greek, a reflection of the ethnic composition of the area.

When Christianity became fully established in the 13th century, the Armenian calendar was replaced by the Julian.

ERA OF THE ARMENIANS

Era of Armenians	Western Date (Julian) of New Year		Era of Armenians	Western Date (Julian) of New Year		Era of Armenians	Western Date (Julian) of New Year		Era of Armenians	Western Date (Julian) of New Year	
1	552*	9 Jul	33	584*	1 Jul	65	616*	23 Jun	97	648*	15 Jun
2	553	9 Jul	34	585	1 Jul	66	617	23 Jun	98	649	15 Jun
3	554	9 Jul	35	586	1 Jul	67	618	23 Jun	99	650	15 Jun
4	555	9 Jul	36	587	1 Jul	68	619	23 Jun	100	651	15 Jun
5	556*	8 Jul	37	588*	30 Jun	69	620*	22 Jun	101	652*	14 Jun
6	557	8 Jul	38	589	30 Jun	70	621	22 Jun	102	653	14 Jun
7	558	8 Jul	39	590	30 Jun	71	622	22 Jun	103	654	14 Jun
8	559	8 Jul	40	591	30 Jun	72	623	22 Jun	104	655	14 Jun
9	560*	7 Jul	41	592*	29 Jun	73	624*	21 Jun	105	656*	13 Jun
10	561	7 Jul	42	593	29 Jun	74	625	21 Jun	106	657	13 Jun
11	562	7 Jul	43	594	29 Jun	75	626	21 Jun	107	658	13 Jun
12	563	7 Jul	44	595	29 Jun	76	627	21 Jun	108	659	13 Jun
13	564*	6 Jul	45	596*	28 Jun	77	628*	20 Jun	109	660*	12 Jun
14	565	6 Jul	46	597	28 Jun	78	629	20 Jun	110	661	12 Jun
15	566	6 Jul	47	598	28 Jun	79	630	20 Jun	111	662	12 Jun
16	567	6 Jul	48	599	28 Jun	80	631	20 Jun	112	663	12 Jun
17	568*	5 Jul	49	600*	27 Jun	81	632*	19 Jun	113	664*	11 Jun
18	569	5 Jul	50	601	27 Jun	82	633	19 Jun	114	665	11 Jun
19	570	5 Jul	51	602	27 Jun	83	634	19 Jun	115	666	11 Jun
20	571	5 Jul	52	603	27 Jun	84	635	19 Jun	116	667	11 Jun
21	572*	4 Jul	53	604*	26 Jun	85	636*	18 Jun	117	668*	10 Jun
22	573	4 Jul	54	605	26 Jun	86	637	18 Jun	118	669	10 Jun
23	574	4 Jul	55	606	26 Jun	87	638	18 Jun	119	670	10 Jun
24	575	4 Jul	56	607	26 Jun	88	639	18 Jun	120	671	10 Jun
25	576*	3 Jul	57	608*	25 Jun	89	640*	17 Jun	121	672*	9 Jun
26	577	3 Jul	58	609	25 Jun	90	641	17 Jun	122	673	9 Jun
27	578	3 Jul	59	610	25 Jun	91	642	17 Jun	123	674	9 Jun
28	579	3 Jul	60	611	25 Jun	92	643	17 Jun	124	675	9 Jun
29	580*	2 Jul	61	612*	24 Jun	93	644*	16 Jun	125	676*	8 Jun
30	581	2 Jul	62	613	24 Jun	94	645	16 Jun	126	677	8 Jun
31	582	2 Jul	63	614	24 Jun	95	646	16 Jun	127	678	8 Jun
32	583	2 Jul	64	615	24 Jun	96	647	16 Jun	128	679	8 Jun

Era of Armenians	Western Date (Julian) of New Year	Era of Armenians	Western Date (Julian) of New Year	Era of Armenians	Western Date (Julian) of New Year	Era of Armenians	Western Date (Julian) of New Year
129	680* 7 Jun	179	730 26 May	229	780* 13 May	279	830 1 May
130	681 7 Jun	180	731 26 May	230	781 13 May	280	831 1 May
131	682 7 Jun	181	732* 25 May	231	782 13 May	281	832* 30 Apr
132	683 7 Jun	182	733 25 May	232	783 13 May	282	833 30 Apr
133	684* 6 Jun	183	734 25 May	233	784* 12 May	283	834 30 Apr
134	685 6 Jun	184	735 25 May	234	785 12 May	284	835 30 Apr
135	686 6 Jun	185	736* 24 May	235	786 12 May	285	836* 29 Apr
136	687 6 Jun	186	737 24 May	236	787 12 May	286	837 29 Apr
137	688* 5 Jun	187	738 24 May	237	788* 11 May	287	838 29 Apr
138	689 5 Jun	188	739 24 May	238	789 11 May	288	839 29 Apr
139	690 5 Jun	189	740* 23 May	239	790 11 May	289	840* 28 Apr
140	691 5 Jun	190	741 23 May	240	791 11 May	290	841 28 Apr
141	692* 4 Jun	191	742 23 May	241	792* 10 May	291	842 28 Apr
142	693 4 Jun	192	743 23 May	242	793 10 May	292	843 28 Apr
143	694 4 Jun	193	744* 22 May	243	794 10 May	293	844* 27 Apr
144	695 4 Jun	194	745 22 May	244	795 10 May	294	845 27 Apr
145	696* 3 Jun	195	746 22 May	245	796* 9 May	295	846 27 Apr
146	697 3 Jun	196	747 22 May	246	797 9 May	296	847 27 Apr
147	698 3 Jun	197	748* 21 May	247	798 9 May	297	848* 26 Apr
148	699 3 Jun	198	749 21 May	248	799 9 May	298	849 26 Apr
149	700* 2 Jun	199	750 21 May	249	800* 8 May	299	850 26 Apr
150	701 2 Jun	200	751 21 May	250	801 8 May	300	851 26 Apr
151	702 2 Jun	201	752* 20 May	251	802 8 May	301	852* 25 Apr
152	703 2 Jun	202	753 20 May	252	803 8 May	302	853 25 Apr
153	704* 1 Jun	203	754 20 May	253	804* 7 May	303	854 25 Apr
154	705 1 Jun	204	755 20 May	254	805 7 May	304	855 25 Apr
155	706 1 Jun	205	756* 19 May	255	806 7 May	305	856* 24 Apr
156	707 1 Jun	206	757 19 May	256	807 7 May	306	857 24 Apr
157	708* 31 May	207	758 19 May	257	808* 6 May	307	858 24 Apr
158	709 31 May	208	759 19 May	258	809 6 May	308	859 24 Apr
159	710 31 May	209	760* 18 May	259	810 6 May	309	860* 23 Apr
160	711 31 May	210	761 18 May	260	811 6 May	310	861 23 Apr
161	712* 30 May	211	762 18 May	261	812* 5 May	311	862 23 Apr
162	713 30 May	212	763 18 May	262	813 5 May	312	863 23 Apr
163	714 30 May	213	764* 17 May	263	814 5 May	313	864* 22 Apr
164	715 30 May	214	765 17 May	264	815 5 May	314	865 22 Apr
165	716* 29 May	215	766 17 May	265	816* 4 May	315	866 22 Apr
166	717 29 May	216	767 17 May	266	817 4 May	316	867 22 Apr
167	718 29 May	217	768* 16 May	267	818 4 May	317	868* 21 Apr
168	719 29 May	218	769 16 May	268	819 4 May	318	869 21 Apr
169	720* 28 May	219	770 16 May	269	820* 3 May	319	870 21 Apr
170	721 28 May	220	771 16 May	270	821 3 May	320	871 21 Apr
171	722 28 May	221	772* 15 May	271	822 3 May	321	872* 20 Apr
172	723 28 May	222	773 15 May	272	823 3 May	322	873 20 Apr
173	724* 27 May	223	774 15 May	273	824* 2 May	323	874 20 Apr
174	725 27 May	224	775 15 May	274	825 2 May	324	875 20 Apr
175	726 27 May	225	776* 14 May	275	826 2 May	325	876* 19 Apr
176	727 27 May	226	777 14 May	276	827 2 May	326	877 19 Apr
177	728* 26 May	227	778 14 May	277	828* 1 May	327	878 19 Apr
178	729 26 May	228	779 14 May	278	829 1 May	328	879 19 Apr

Era of Armenians	Western Date (Julian) of New Year	Era of Armenians	Western Date (Julian) of New Year	Era of Armenians	Western Date (Julian) of New Year	Era of Armenians	Western Date (Julian) of New Year
329	880* 18 Apr	379	930 6 Apr	429	980* 24 Mar	479	1030 12 Mar
330	881 18 Apr	380	931 6 Apr	430	981 24 Mar	480	1031 12 Mar
331	882 18 Apr	381	932* 5 Apr	431	982 24 Mar	481	1032* 11 Mar
332	883 18 Apr	382	933 5 Apr	432	983 24 Mar	482	1033 11 Mar
333	884* 17 Apr	383	934 5 Apr	433	984* 23 Mar	483	1034 11 Mar
334	885 17 Apr	384	935 5 Apr	434	985 23 Mar	484	1035 11 Mar
335	886 17 Apr	385	936* 4 Apr	435	986 23 Mar	485	1036* 10 Mar
336	887 17 Apr	386	937 4 Apr	436	987 23 Mar	486	1037 10 Mar
337	888* 16 Apr	387	938 4 Apr	437	988* 22 Mar	487	1038 10 Mar
338	889 16 Apr	388	939 4 Apr	438	989 22 Mar	488	1039 10 Mar
339	890 16 Apr	389	940* 3 Apr	439	990 22 Mar	489	1040* 9 Mar
340	891 16 Apr	390	941 3 Apr	440	991 22 Mar	490	1041 9 Mar
341	892* 15 Apr	391	942 3 Apr	441	992* 21 Mar	491	1042 9 Mar
342	893 15 Apr	392	943 3 Apr	442	993 21 Mar	492	1043 9 Mar
343	894 15 Apr	393	944* 2 Apr	443	994 21 Mar	493	1044* 8 Mar
344	895 15 Apr	394	945 2 Apr	444	995 21 Mar	494	1045 8 Mar
345	896* 14 Apr	395	946 2 Apr	445	996* 20 Mar	495	1046 8 Mar
346	897 14 Apr	396	947 2 Apr	446	997 20 Mar	496	1047 8 Mar
347	898 14 Apr	397	948* 1 Apr	447	998 20 Mar	497	1048* 7 Mar
348	899 14 Apr	398	949 1 Apr	448	999 20 Mar	498	1049 7 Mar
349	900* 13 Apr	399	950 1 Apr	449	1000* 19 Mar	499	1050 7 Mar
350	901 13 Apr	400	951 1 Apr	450	1001 19 Mar	500	1051 7 Mar
351	902 13 Apr	401	952* 31 Mar	451	1002 19 Mar	501	1052* 6 Mar
352	903 13 Apr	402	953 31 Mar	452	1003 19 Mar	502	1053 6 Mar
353	904* 12 Apr	403	954 31 Mar	453	1004* 18 Mar	503	1054 6 Mar
354	905 12 Apr	404	955 31 Mar	454	1005 18 Mar	504	1055 6 Mar
355	906 12 Apr	405	956* 30 Mar	455	1006 18 Mar	505	1056* 5 Mar
356	907 12 Apr	406	957 30 Mar	456	1007 18 Mar	506	1057 5 Mar
357	908* 11 Apr	407	958 30 Mar	457	1008* 17 Mar	507	1058 5 Mar
358	909 11 Apr	408	959 30 Mar	458	1009 17 Mar	508	1059 5 Mar
359	910 11 Apr	409	960* 29 Mar	459	1010 17 Mar	509	1060* 4 Mar
360	911 11 Apr	410	961 29 Mar	460	1011 17 Mar	510	1061 4 Mar
361	912* 10 Apr	411	962 29 Mar	461	1012* 16 Mar	511	1062 4 Mar
362	913 10 Apr	412	963 29 Mar	462	1013 16 Mar	512	1063 4 Mar
363	914 10 Apr	413	964* 28 Mar	463	1014 16 Mar	513	1064* 3 Mar
364	915 10 Apr	414	965 28 Mar	464	1015 16 Mar	514	1065 3 Mar
365	916* 9 Apr	415	966 28 Mar	465	1016* 15 Mar	515	1066 3 Mar
366	917 9 Apr	416	967 28 Mar	466	1017 15 Mar	516	1067 3 Mar
367	918 9 Apr	417	968* 27 Mar	467	1018 15 Mar	517	1068* 2 Mar
368	919 9 Apr	418	969 27 Mar	468	1019 15 Mar	518	1069 2 Mar
369	920* 8 Apr	419	970 27 Mar	469	1020* 14 Mar	519	1070 2 Mar
370	921 8 Apr	420	971 27 Mar	470	1021 14 Mar	520	1071 2 Mar
371	922 8 Apr	421	972 26 Mar	471	1022 14 Mar	521	1072* 1 Mar
372	923 8 Apr	422	973 26 Mar	472	1023 14 Mar	522	1073 1 Mar
373	924* 7 Apr	423	974 26 Mar	473	1024* 13 Mar	523	1074 1 Mar
374	925 7 Apr	424	975 26 Mar	474	1025 13 Mar	524	1075 1 Mar
375	926 7 Apr	425	976* 25 Mar	475	1026 13 Mar	525	1076* 29 Feb
376	927 7 Apr	426	977 25 Mar	476	1027 13 Mar	526	1077 28 Feb
377	928* 6 Apr	427	978 25 Mar	477	1028* 12 Mar	527	1078 28 Feb
378	929 6 Apr	428	979 25 Mar	478	1029 12 Mar	528	1079 28 Feb

Era of Armenians	Western Date (Julian) of New Year	Era of Armenians	Western Date (Julian) of New Year	Era of Armenians	Western Date (Julian) of New Year	Era of Armenians	Western Date (Julian) of New Year
529	1080* 28 Feb	579	1130 15 Feb	629	1180* 3 Feb	679	1230 21 Jan
530	1081 27 Feb	580	1131 15 Feb	630	1181 2 Feb	680	1231 21 Jan
531	1082 27 Feb	581	1132* 15 Feb	631	1182 2 Feb	681	1232* 21 Jan
532	1083 27 Feb	582	1133 14 Feb	632	1183 2 Feb	682	1233 20 Jan
533	1084* 27 Feb	583	1134 14 Feb	633	1184* 2 Feb	683	1234 20 Jan
534	1085 26 Feb	584	1135 14 Feb	634	1185 1 Feb	684	1235 20 Jan
535	1086 26 Feb	585	1136* 14 Feb	635	1186 1 Feb	685	1236* 20 Jan
536	1087 26 Feb	586	1137 13 Feb	636	1187 1 Feb	686	1237 19 Jan
537	1088* 26 Feb	587	1138 13 Feb	637	1188* 1 Feb	687	1238 19 Jan
538	1089 25 Feb	588	1139 13 Feb	638	1189 31 Jan	688	1239 19 Jan
539	1090 25 Feb	589	1140* 13 Feb	639	1190 31 Jan	689	1240* 19 Jan
540	1091 25 Feb	590	1141 12 Feb	640	1191 31 Jan	690	1241 18 Jan
541	1092* 25 Feb	591	1142* 12 Feb	641	1192* 31 Jan	691	1242 18 Jan
542	1093 24 Feb	592	1143 12 Feb	642	1193 30 Jan	692	1243 18 Jan
543	1094 24 Feb	593	1144* 12 Feb	643	1194 30 Jan	693	1244* 18 Jan
544	1095 24 Feb	594	1145 11 Feb	644	1195 30 Jan	694	1245 17 Jan
545	1096* 24 Feb	595	1146 11 Feb	645	1196* 30 Jan	695	1246 17 Jan
546	1097 23 Feb	596	1147 11 Feb	646	1197 29 Jan	696	1247 17 Jan
547	1098 23 Feb	597	1148* 11 Feb	647	1198 29 Jan	697	1248* 17 Jan
548	1099 23 Feb	598	1149 10 Feb	648	1199 29 Jan	698	1249 16 Jan
549	1100* 23 Feb	599	1150 10 Feb	649	1200* 29 Jan	699	1250 16 Jan
550	1101 22 Feb	600	1151 10 Feb	650	1201 28 Jan	700	1251 16 Jan
551	1102 22 Feb	601	1152* 10 Feb	651	1202 28 Jan	701	1252* 16 Jan
552	1103 22 Feb	602	1153 9 Feb	652	1203 28 Jan	702	1253 15 Jan
553	1104* 22 Feb	603	1154 9 Feb	653	1204* 28 Jan	703	1254 15 Jan
554	1105 21 Feb	604	1155 9 Feb	654	1205 27 Jan	704	1255 15 Jan
555	1106 21 Feb	605	1156* 9 Feb	655	1206 27 Jan	705	1256* 15 Jan
556	1107 21 Feb	606	1157 8 Feb	656	1207 27 Jan	706	1257 14 Jan
557	1108* 21 Feb	607	1158 8 Feb	657	1208* 27 Jan	707	1258 14 Jan
558	1109 20 Feb	608	1159 8 Feb	658	1209 26 Jan	708	1259 14 Jan
559	1110 20 Feb	609	1160* 8 Feb	659	1210 26 Jan	709	1260* 14 Jan
560	1111 20 Feb	610	1161 7 Feb	660	1211 26 Jan	710	1261 13 Jan
561	1112* 20 Feb	611	1162 7 Feb	661	1212* 26 Jan	711	1262 13 Jan
562	1113 19 Feb	612	1163 7 Feb	662	1213 25 Jan	712	1263 13 Jan
563	1114 19 Feb	613	1164* 7 Feb	663	1214 25 Jan	713	1264* 13 Jan
564	1115 19 Feb	614	1165 6 Feb	664	1215 25 Jan	714	1265 12 Jan
565	1116* 19 Feb	615	1166 6 Feb	665	1216* 25 Jan	715	1266 12 Jan
566	1117 18 Feb	616	1167 6 Feb	666	1217 24 Jan	716	1267 12 Jan
567	1118 18 Feb	617	1168* 6 Feb	667	1218 24 Jan	717	1268* 12 Jan
568	1119 18 Feb	618	1169 5 Feb	668	1219 24 Jan	718	1269 11 Jan
569	1120* 18 Feb	619	1170 5 Feb	669	1220* 24 Jan	719	1270 11 Jan
570	1121 17 Feb	620	1171 5 Feb	670	1221 23 Jan	720	1271 11 Jan
571	1122 17 Feb	621	1172* 5 Feb	671	1222 23 Jan	721	1272* 11 Jan
572	1123 17 Feb	622	1173 4 Feb	672	1223 23 Jan	722	1273 10 Jan
573	1124* 17 Feb	623	1174 4 Feb	673	1224* 23 Jan	723	1274 10 Jan
574	1125 16 Feb	624	1175 4 Feb	674	1225 22 Jan	724	1275 10 Jan
575	1126 16 Feb	625	1176* 4 Feb	675	1226 22 Jan	725	1276* 10 Jan
576	1127 16 Feb	626	1177 3 Feb	676	1227 22 Jan	726	1277 9 Jan
577	1128* 16 Feb	627	1178 3 Feb	677	1228* 22 Jan	727	1278 9 Jan
578	1129 15 Feb	628	1179 3 Feb	678	1229 21 Jan	728	1279 9 Jan

Era of Armenians	Western Date (Julian) of New Year		Era of Armenians	Western Date (Julian) of New Year		Era of Armenians	Western Date (Julian) of New Year		Era of Armenians	Western Date (Julian) of New Year	
729	1280*	9 Jan	735	1286	7 Jan	740	1291	6 Jan	745	1296*	5 Jan
730	1281	8 Jan	736	1287	7 Jan	741	1292*	6 Jan	746	1297	4 Jan
731	1282	8 Jan	737	1288*	7 Jan	742	1293	5 Jan	747	1298	4 Jan
732	1283	8 Jan	738	1289	6 Jan	743	1294	5 Jan	748	1299	4 Jan
733	1284*	8 Jan	739	1290	6 Jan	744	1295	5 Jan	749	1300*	4 Jan
734	1285	7 Jan									

THE ISLAMIC CALENDAR

The Islamic calendar is computed from the Hejira, the flight of Mohammed from Mecca to Medina. The epoch is Mohammed's arrival in Medina, considered to be sunset July 16, 622 A.D. by the majority of Muslims. (A minority which reckons the day from midnight to midnight uses July 15 as the epoch.)

The calendar is a purely lunar one, that is, the year contains only 354 days. It does not take into consideration the solar revolution, so the calendar consistently moves back 11 days for each solar year. Periodically one day is added for a leap year. In the case of those using July 16 as the epoch, the leap day is added to the second, fifth, seventh, 10th, 13th, 16th, 18th, 21st, 24th, 26th and 29th years of a 30 year cycle. When July 15 is used as the epoch, the 15th, rather than the 16th year has a leap day added. Otherwise the intercalations are the same.

The months of the Islamic calendar contain, alternately, 29 or 30 days. The last month which may have either number. The extra day is intercalated at regular intervals because the moon's orbit is just over 29½ days long. The months, standard to the Islamic world are:

1. Muharram	30 days
2. Safar	29 days
3. Rabi I	30 days
4. Rabi II	29 days
5. Jumada I	30 days
6. Jumada II	29 days
7. Rajab	30 days
8. Sha'ban	29 days
9. Ramadan	30 days
10. Shawwal	29 days
11. Dhu al-Qada	30 days
12. Dhu al-Hijjah	29 or 30 days

The Islamic month begins when two responsible witnesses claim they can see the first crescent of the new moon. They then go before the qadi (judge), who, if he decides they are correct, informs a mufti (interpreter of the law). He, in turn, announces that the new month has begun. Prior to the coming of the telephone and telegraph, complications could arise if the weather was cloudy. Each local group decided independently just when the month actually started, and the day could, on occasion, be later than the calendar indication. It has become customary among Middle Eastern Muslims to accept the verdict of Cairo on when the month begins.

The Islamic calendar uses a week of seven days, the names of which vary from place to place. They are invariably connected to solar, lunar and planetary motion. The only day with a standard name is el Jumah, or the "day of gathering," the equivalent of the Hebrew Sabbath and the Christian Sunday. This day is Friday and is considered the first of the week. Because Mohammed entered Medina at sunset, the Muslim day runs from sundown to sundown. Therefore the week begins at sundown on Friday and runs through to the sundown of the following Friday.

The Islamic calendar contains one major fast period and two major feasts. During the month of Ramadan no food or drink may be taken from sunrise until it is dark enough to see the stars. Immediately following Ramadan is a feast period known as Eed es Sagheer. It lasts for three days, or from the first through the third of Shawwal. The other major feast, Eed el Keeber or Kurban, is celebrated from the 10th through the 13th or 14th of the last month of the Islamic year, Dhu al Hijjah. Whether it continues for three or four days is determined by whether or not there is an intercalary day added to that year. The feast celebrates Abraham's attempt to sacrifice his son, Isaac.

There are several other feast and fast days that are celebrated through the Islamic world. The fast of Yom Ashoora may be celebrated for the first ten days of Moharram, the key day being either the 9th or 10th day, depending on the moon's position. Feast days occur on the 12th day of the third month (Rabi I), Mohammed's birthday, in the fourth month (Rabi II) celebrating el Hoseyn's birthday (el Hoseyn was Mohammed's son), and in the seventh month (Rejab), celebrating Mohammed's ascension to Heaven.

The era of the Hejira is used by many different peoples, often in conjunction with another calendar. The era is the official one in Saudi Arabia, Yeman and the smaller nations in the Persian Gulf. It is used with the Christian calendar in Egypt, Syria, Jordan and Morocco. Muslims throughout the world use it for religious purposes. There have been some attempts to modify the calendar and make it conform with the more prevalent Christian one. During the 17th century Turkey adopted the Julian year while retaining the Muslim era. In the late 19th century, Turkey dropped the Islamic calendar and for official purposes adopted the Gregorian. Iran, during the mid 20th century adopted a solar calendar with Persian names for months and the Muslim era.

ISLAMIC CALENDAR

Year of Hegira	Western Date (Julian) of Islamic New Year	Year of Hegira	Western Date (Julian) of Islamic New Year	Year of Hegira	Western Date (Julian) of Islamic New Year	Year of Hegira	Western Date (Julian) of Islamic New Year
1	16 Jul 622	17	23 Jan 638	33	2 Aug 653	49	9 Feb 669
2*	5 Jul 623	18*	12 Jan 639	34	22 Jul 654	50	29 Jan 670
3	24 Jun 624*	19	2 Jan 640*	35*	11 Jul 655	51*	18 Jan 671
4	13 Jun 625	20	21 Dec 640*	36	30 Jun 656*	52	8 Jan 672*
5*	2 Jun 626	21*	10 Dec 641	37*	19 Jun 657	53	27 Dec 672*
6	23 May 627	22	30 Nov 642	38	9 Jun 658	54*	16 Dec 673
7*	11 May 628*	23	19 Nov 643	39	29 May 659	55	6 Dec 674
8	1 May 629	24*	7 Nov 644*	40*	17 May 660*	56*	25 Nov 675
9	20 Apr 630	25	28 Oct 645	41	7 May 661	57	14 Nov 676*
10*	9 Apr 631	26*	17 Oct 646	42	26 Apr 662	58	3 Nov 677
11	29 Mar 632*	27	7 Oct 647	43*	15 Apr 663	59*	23 Oct 678
12	18 Mar 633	28	25 Sep 648*	44	4 Apr 664*	60	13 Oct 679
13*	7 Mar 634	29*	14 Sep 649	45	24 Mar 665	61	1 Oct 680*
14	25 Feb 635	30	4 Sep 650	46*	13 Mar 666	62*	20 Sep 681
15	14 Feb 636*	31	24 Aug 651	47	3 Mar 667	63	10 Sep 682
16*	2 Feb 637	32*	12 Aug 652*	48*	20 Feb 668*	64	30 Aug 683

Year of Hegira	Western Date (Julian) of Islamic New Year	Year of Hegira	Western Date (Julian) of Islamic New Year	Year of Hegira	Western Date (Julian) of Islamic New Year	Year of Hegira	Western Date (Julian) of Islamic New Year
65*	18 Aug 684*	115	21 Feb 733	165	26 Aug 781	215*	25 Feb 830
66	8 Aug 685	116*	10 Feb 734	166*	15 Aug 782	216	18 Feb 831
67*	28 Jul 686	117	31 Jan 735	167	5 Aug 783	217*	7 Feb 832*
68	18 Jul 687	118	20 Jan 736*	168*	24 Jul 784*	218	27 Jan 833
69	6 Jul 688*	119*	8 Jan 737	169	14 Jul 785	219	16 Jan 834
70*	25 Jun 689	120	29 Dec 737	170	3 Jul 786	220*	5 Jan 835
71	15 Jun 690	121	18 Dec 738	171*	22 Jun 787	221	26 Dec 835*
72	4 Jun 691	122*	7 Dec 739	172	11 Jun 788*	222	14 Dec 836*
73*	23 May 692*	123	26 Nov 740*	173	31 May 789	223*	3 Dec 837
74	13 May 693	124	15 Nov 741	174*	20 May 790	224	23 Nov 838
75	2 May 694	125*	4 Nov 742	175	10 May 791	225	12 Nov 839
76*	21 Apr 695	126	25 Oct 743	176*	28 Apr 792*	226*	31 Oct 840*
77	10 Apr 696*	127*	13 Oct 744*	177	18 Apr 793	227	21 Oct 841
78	30 Mar 697	128	3 Oct 745	178	7 Apr 794	228*	10 Oct 842
79	20 Mar 698	129	22 Sep 746	179*	27 Mar 795	229	30 Sep 843
80	9 Mar 699	130*	11 Sep 747	180	16 Mar 796*	230	18 Sep 844*
81*	26 Feb 700*	131	31 Aug 748*	181	5 Mar 797	231*	7 Sep 845
82	15 Feb 701	132	20 Aug 749	182*	22 Feb 798	232	28 Aug 846
83	4 Feb 702	133*	9 Aug 750	183	12 Feb 799	233	17 Aug 847
84*	24 Jan 703	134	30 Jul 751	184	1 Feb 800*	234*	5 Aug 848*
85	14 Jan 704*	135	18 Jul 752*	185*	20 Jan 801	235	26 Jul 849
86*	2 Jan 705	136*	7 Jul 753	186	10 Jan 802	236*	15 Jul 850
87	23 Dec 705	137	27 Jun 754	187*	30 Dec 802	237	5 Jul 851
88	12 Dec 706	138*	16 Jun 755	188	20 Dec 803	238	23 Jun 852*
89*	1 Dec 707	139	5 Jun 756*	189	8 Dec 804*	239*	12 Jun 853
90	20 Nov 708*	140	25 May 757	190*	27 Nov 805	240	2 Jun 854
91	9 Nov 709	141*	14 May 758	191	17 Nov 806	241	22 May 855
92*	29 Oct 710	142	4 May 759	192	6 Nov 807	242*	10 May 856*
93	19 Oct 711	143	22 Apr 760*	193*	25 Oct 808*	243	30 Apr 857
94	7 Oct 712*	144*	11 Apr 761	194	15 Oct 809	244	19 Apr 858
95*	26 Sep 713	145	1 Apr 762	195	4 Oct 810	245*	8 Apr 859
96	16 Sep 714	146*	21 Mar 763	196*	23 Sep 811	246	28 Mar 860*
97*	5 Sep 715	147	10 Mar 764*	197	12 Sep 812*	247*	17 Mar 861
98	25 Aug 716*	148	27 Feb 765	198	1 Sep 813	248	7 Mar 862
99	14 Aug 717	149*	16 Feb 766	199	22 Aug 814	249	24 Feb 863
100*	3 Aug 718	150	6 Feb 767	200	11 Aug 815	250*	13 Feb 864*
101	24 Jul 719	151	26 Jan 768*	201*	30 Jul 816*	251	2 Feb 865
102	12 Jul 720*	152*	14 Jan 769	202	20 Jul 817	252	22 Jan 866
103*	1 Jul 721	153	4 Jan 770	203	9 Jul 818	253*	11 Jan 867
104	21 Jun 722	154	24 Dec 770	204*	28 Jun 819	254	1 Jan 868*
105	10 Jun 723	155*	13 Dec 771	205	17 Jun 820*	255	20 Dec 868*
106*	29 May 724*	156	2 Dec 772*	206*	6 Jun 821	256*	9 Dec 869
107	19 May 725	157*	21 Nov 773	207	27 May 822	257	29 Nov 870
108*	8 May 726	158	11 Nov 774	208	16 May 823	258*	18 Nov 871
109	28 Apr 727	159	31 Oct 775	209*	4 May 824*	259	7 Nov 872*
110	16 Apr 728*	160*	19 Oct 776*	210	24 Apr 825	260	27 Oct 873
111*	5 Apr 729	161	9 Oct 777	211	13 Apr 826	261*	16 Oct 874
112	26 Mar 730	162	28 Sep 778	212*	2 Apr 827	262	6 Oct 875
113	15 Mar 731	163*	17 Sep 779	213	22 Mar 828*	263	24 Sep 876*
114*	3 Mar 732*	164	6 Sep 780*	214	11 Mar 829	264*	13 Sep 877

Year of Hegira	Western Date (Julian) of Islamic New Year	Year of Hegira	Western Date (Julian) of Islamic New Year	Year of Hegira	Western Date (Julian) of Islamic New Year	Year of Hegira	Western Date (Julian) of Islamic New Year
265	3 Sep 878	316*	25 Feb 928*	367*	19 Aug 977	418	11 Feb 1027
266*	23 Aug 879	317	14 Feb 929	368	9 Aug 978	419*	31 Jan 1028*
267	12 Aug 880*	318*	3 Feb 930	369	29 Jul 979	420	20 Jan 1029
268	1 Aug 881	319	24 Jan 931	370*	17 Jul 980*	421	9 Jan 1030
269*	21 Jul 882	320	13 Jan 932*	371	7 Jul 981	422*	29 Dec 1030
270	11 Jul 883	321*	1 Jan 933	372	26 Jun 982	423	19 Dec 1031
271	29 Jun 884	322	22 Dec 933	373*	15 Jun 983	424	7 Dec 1032*
272*	8 Jun 886	323	11 Dec 934	374	4 Jun 984*	425	26 Nov 1033
273	8 Jun 886	324*	30 Nov 935	375	24 May 985	426	16 Nov 1034
274	28 May 887	325	19 Nov 936*	376*	13 May 986	427*	5 Nov 1035
275*	16 May 888*	326*	8 Nov 937	377	3 May 987	428	25 Oct 1036*
276	6 May 889	327	29 Oct 938	378*	21 Apr 988*	429	14 Oct 1037
277*	25 Apr 890	328	18 Oct 939	379	11 Apr 989	430*	3 Oct 1038
278	15 Apr 891	329*	6 Oct 940*	380	31 Mar 990	431	23 Sep 1039
279	3 Apr 892*	330	26 Sep 941	381*	20 Mar 991	432	11 Sep 1040*
280*	23 Mar 893	331	15 Sep 942	382	9 Mar 992*	433*	31 Aug 1041
281	13 Mar 894	332*	4 Sep 943	383	26 Feb 993	434	21 Aug 1042
282	2 Mar 895	333	24 Aug 944*	384*	15 Feb 994	435	10 Aug 1043
283*	19 Feb 896*	334	13 Aug 945	385	5 Feb 995	436*	29 Jul 1044*
284	8 Feb 897	335*	2 Aug 946	386*	25 Feb 996*	437	19 Jul 1045
285	28 Jan 898	336	23 Jul 947	387	14 Jan 997	438	8 Jul 1046
286*	17 Jan 899	337*	11 Jul 948*	388	3 Jan 998	439	28 Jun 1047
287	7 Jan 900*	338	1 Jul 949	389*	23 Dec 998	440	16 Jun 1048*
288*	26 Dec 900*	339	20 Jun 950	390	13 Dec 999	441*	5 Jun 1049
289	16 Dec 901	340*	9 Jun 951	391	1 Dec 1000*	442	26 May 1050
290	5 Dec 902	341	29 May 952*	392*	20 Nov 1001	443	15 May 1051
291*	24 Nov 903	342	18 May 953	393	10 Nov 1002	444*	3 May 1052
292	13 Nov 904*	343*	7 May 954	394	30 Oct 1003	445	23 Apr 1053
293	2 Nov 905	344	27 Apr 955	395*	18 Oct 1004*	446*	12 Apr 1054
294*	22 Oct 906	345	15 Apr 956*	396	8 Oct 1005	447	2 Apr 1055
295	12 Oct 907	346*	4 Apr 957	397*	27 Sep 1006	448	21 Mar 1056*
296*	30 Sep 908*	347	25 Mar 958	398	17 Sep 1007	449*	10 Mar 1057
297	20 Sep 909	348*	14 Mar 959	399	5 Sep 1008*	450	28 Feb 1058
298	9 Sep 910	349	3 Mar 960*	400*	25 Aug 1009	451	17 Feb 1059
299*	29 Aug 911	350	20 Feb 961	401	15 Aug 1010	452*	6 Feb 1060*
300	18 Aug 912*	351*	9 Feb 962	402	4 Aug 1011	453	26 Jan 1061
301	7 Aug 913	352	30 Jan 963	403*	23 Jul 1012*	454	15 Jan 1062
302*	27 Jul 914	353	19 Jan 964*	404	13 Jul 1013	455*	4 Jan 1063
303	17 Jul 915	354*	7 Jan 965	405	3 Jul 1014	456	25 Dec 1063
304	5 Jul 916*	355	28 Dec 965	406*	21 Jun 1015	457*	13 Dec 1064*
305*	24 Jun 917	356*	17 Dec 966	407	10 Jun 1016*	458	3 Dec 1065
306	14 Jun 918	357	7 Dec 967	408*	30 May 1017	459	22 Nov 1066
307*	3 Jun 919	358	25 Nov 968*	409	20 May 1018	460*	11 Nov 1067
308	23 May 920*	359*	14 Nov 969	410	9 May 1019	461	31 Oct 1068*
309	12 May 921	360	4 Nov 970	411*	27 Apr 1020*	462	20 Oct 1069
310*	1 May 922	361	24 Oct 971	412	17 Apr 1021	463*	9 Oct 1070
311	21 Apr 923	362*	12 Oct 972*	413	6 Apr 1022	464	29 Sep 1071
312	9 Apr 924*	363	2 Oct 973	414*	26 Mar 1023	465	17 Sep 1072*
313*	29 Mar 925	364	21 Sep 974	415	15 Mar 1024*	466*	6 Sep 1073
314	19 Mar 926	365*	10 Sep 975	416*	4 Mar 1025	467	27 Aug 1074
315	8 Mar 927	366	30 Aug 976*	417	22 Feb 1026	468*	16 Aug 1075

Year of Hegira	Western Date (Julian) of Islamic New Year	Year of Hegira	Western Date (Julian) of Islamic New Year	Year of Hegira	Western Date (Julian) of Islamic New Year	Year of Hegira	Western Date (Julian) of Islamic New Year
469	5 Aug 1076*	520*	27 Jan 1126*	571	22 Jul 1175	622	13 Jan 1225
470	25 Jul 1077	521	17 Jan 1127	572*	10 Jul 1176*	623	2 Jan 1226
471*	14 Jul 1078	522	6 Jan 1128*	573	30 Jun 1177	624*	22 Dec 1226
472	4 Jul 1079	523*	25 Dec 1128*	574	19 Jun 1178	625	12 Dec 1227
473	22 Jun 1080*	524	15 Dec 1129	575*	8 Jun 1179	626*	30 Nov 1228*
474*	11 Jun 1081	525	4 Dec 1130	576	28 May 1180*	627	20 Nov 1229
475	1 Jun 1082	526*	23 Nov 1131	577*	17 May 1181	628	9 Nov 1230
476*	21 May 1083	527	12 Nov 1132*	578	7 May 1182	629*	29 Oct 1231
477	10 May 1084*	528*	1 Nov 1133	579	26 Apr 1183	630	18 Oct 1232*
478	29 Apr 1085	529	22 Oct 1134	580*	14 Apr 1184*	631	7 Oct 1233
479*	18 Apr 1086	530	11 Oct 1135	581	4 Apr 1185	632*	26 Sep 1234
480	8 Apr 1087	531*	29 Sep 1136*	582	24 Mar 1186	633	16 Sep 1235
481	27 Mar 1088*	532	19 Sep 1137	583*	13 Mar 1187	634	4 Sep 1236*
482*	16 Mar 1089	533	8 Sep 1138	584	2 Mar 1188*	635*	24 Aug 1237
483	6 Mar 1090	534*	28 Aug 1139	585	19 Feb 1189	636	14 Aug 1238
484	23 Feb 1091	535	17 Aug 1140*	586*	8 Feb 1190	637*	3 Aug 1239
485*	12 Feb 1092*	536*	6 Aug 1141	587	29 Jan 1191	638	23 Jul 1240*
486	1 Feb 1093	537	27 Jul 1142	588*	18 Jan 1192*	639	12 Jul 1241
487*	21 Jan 1094	538	16 Jul 1143	589	7 Jan 1193	640*	1 Jul 1242
488	11 Jan 1095	539*	4 Jul 1144*	590	27 Dec 1193	641	21 Jun 1243
489	31 Dec 1095	540	24 Jun 1145	591*	16 Dec 1194	642	9 Jun 1244*
490*	19 Dec 1096*	541	13 Jun 1146	592	6 Dec 1195	643*	29 May 1245
491	9 Dec 1097	542*	2 Jun 1147	593	24 Nov 1196*	644	19 May 1246
492	28 Nov 1098	543	22 May 1148*	594*	13 Nov 1197	645	8 May 1247
493*	17 Nov 1099	544	11 May 1149	595	3 Nov 1198	646*	26 Apr 1248*
494	6 Nov 1100*	545*	30 Apr 1150	596*	23 Oct 1199	647	16 Apr 1249
495	26 Oct 1101	546	20 Apr 1151	597	12 Oct 1200*	648*	5 Apr 1250
496*	15 Oct 1102	547*	8 Apr 1152*	598	1 Oct 1201	649	26 Mar 1251
497	5 Oct 1103	548	27 Mar 1153	599*	20 Sep 1202	650	14 Mar 1252*
498*	23 Sep 1104*	549	18 Mar 1154	600	10 Sep 1203	651*	3 Mar 1253
499	13 Sep 1105	550*	7 Mar 1155	601	29 Aug 1204*	652	21 Feb 1254
500	2 Sep 1106	551	25 Feb 1156*	602*	18 Aug 1205	653	10 Feb 1255
501*	22 Aug 1107	552	13 Feb 1157	603	8 Aug 1206	654*	30 Jan 1256*
502	11 Aug 1108*	553*	2 Feb 1158	604	28 Jul 1207	655	19 Jan 1257
503	31 Jul 1109	554	23 Jan 1159	605*	16 Jul 1208*	656*	8 Jan 1258
504*	20 Jul 1110	555	12 Jan 1160*	606	6 Jul 1209	657	29 Dec 1258
505	10 Jul 1111	556	31 Dec 1160*	607*	25 Jun 1210	658	18 Dec 1259
506*	28 Jun 1112*	557	21 Dec 1161	608	15 Jun 1211	659*	6 Dec 1260*
507	18 Jun 1113	558*	10 Dec 1162	609	3 Jun 1212*	660	26 Nov 1261
508	7 Jun 1114	559	30 Nov 1163	610*	23 May 1213	661	15 Nov 1262
509*	27 May 1115	560	18 Nov 1164*	611	13 May 1214	662*	4 Nov 1263
510	16 May 1116*	561*	7 Nov 1165	612	2 May 1215	663	24 Oct 1264*
511	5 May 1117	562	28 Oct 1166	613*	20 Apr 1216*	664	13 Oct 1265
512*	24 Apr 1118	563	17 Oct 1167	614	10 Apr 1217	665*	2 Oct 1266
513	14 Apr 1119	564*	5 Oct 1168*	615	30 Mar 1218	666	22 Sep 1267
514	2 Apr 1120*	565	25 Sep 1169	616*	19 Mar 1219	667*	10 Sep 1268*
515*	22 Mar 1121	566*	14 Sep 1170	617	8 Mar 1220*	668	31 Aug 1269
516	12 Mar 1122	567	4 Sep 1171	618*	25 Feb 1221	669	20 Aug 1270
517*	1 Mar 1123	568	23 Aug 1172*	619	15 Feb 1222	670*	9 Aug 1271
518	19 Feb 1124*	569*	12 Aug 1173	620	4 Feb 1223	671	29 Jul 1272*
519	7 Feb 1125	570	2 Aug 1174	621*	24 Jan 1224*	672	18 Jul 1273

Year of Hegira	Western Date (Julian) of Islamic New Year	Year of Hegira	Western Date (Julian) of Islamic New Year	Year of Hegira	Western Date (Julian) of Islamic New Year	Year of Hegira	Western Date (Julian) of Islamic New Year
673*	7 Jul 1274	724	30 Dec 1323	775	23 Jun 1373	826*	15 Dec 1422
674	27 Jun 1275	725*	18 Dec 1324*	776*	12 Jun 1374	827	5 Dec 1423
675	15 Jun 1276*	726	8 Dec 1325	777	2 Jun 1375	828*	23 Nov 1424*
676*	4 Jun 1277	727*	27 Nov 1326	778	21 May 1376*	829	13 Nov 1425
677	25 May 1278	728	17 Nov 1327	779*	10 May 1377	830	2 Nov 1426
678*	14 May 1279	729	5 Nov 1328*	780	30 Apr 1378	831*	22 Oct 1427
679	3 May 1280*	730*	25 Oct 1329	781	19 Apr 1379	832	11 Oct 1428*
680	22 Apr 1281	731	15 Oct 1330	782*	7 Apr 1380	833	30 Sep 1429
681*	11 Apr 1282	732	4 Oct 1331	783	28 Mar 1381	834*	19 Sep 1430
682	1 Apr 1283	733*	22 Sep 1332*	784	17 Mar 1382	835	9 Sep 1431
683	20 Mar 1284*	734	12 Sep 1333	785*	6 Mar 1383	836*	28 Aug 1432*
684*	9 Mar 1285	735	1 Sep 1334	786	24 Feb 1384*	837	18 Aug 1433
685	27 Feb 1286	736*	21 Aug 1335	787*	12 Feb 1385	838	7 Aug 1434
686*	16 Feb 1287	737	10 Aug 1336*	788	2 Feb 1386	839*	27 Jul 1435
687	6 Feb 1288*	738*	30 Jul 1337	789	22 Jan 1387	840	16 Jul 1436*
688	25 Jan 1289	739	20 Jul 1338	790*	11 Jan 1388*	841	5 Jul 1437
689*	14 Jan 1290	740	9 Jul 1339	791	31 Dec 1388*	842*	24 Jun 1438
690	4 Jan 1291	741*	27 Jun 1340*	792	20 Dec 1389	843	14 Jun 1439
691	24 Dec 1291	742	17 Jun 1341	793*	9 Dec 1390	844	2 Jun 1440*
692*	12 Dec 1292*	743	6 Jun 1342	794	29 Nov 1391	845*	22 May 1441
693	2 Dec 1293	744*	26 May 1343	795	17 Nov 1392*	846	12 May 1442
694	21 Nov 1294	745	15 May 1344*	796*	6 Nov 1393	847*	1 May 1443
695*	10 Nov 1295	746*	4 May 1345	797	27 Oct 1394	848	20 Apr 1444*
696	30 Oct 1296*	747	24 Apr 1346	798*	16 Oct 1395	849	9 Apr 1445
697*	19 Oct 1297	748	13 Apr 1347	799	5 Oct 1396*	850*	29 Mar 1446
698	9 Oct 1298	749*	1 Apr 1348*	800	24 Sep 1397	851	19 Mar 1447
699	28 Sep 1299	750	22 Mar 1349	801*	13 Sep 1398	852	7 Mar 1448*
700*	16 Sep 1300*	751	11 Mar 1350	802	3 Sep 1399	853*	24 Feb 1449
701	5 Sep 1301	752*	28 Feb 1351	803	22 Aug 1400*	854	14 Feb 1450
702	26 Aug 1302	753	18 Feb 1352*	804*	11 Aug 1401	855	3 Feb 1451
703*	15 Aug 1303	754	6 Feb 1353	805	1 Aug 1402	856*	23 Jan 1452*
704	4 Aug 1304*	755*	26 Jan 1354	806*	21 Jul 1403	857	12 Jan 1453
705	24 Jul 1305	756	16 Jan 1355	807	10 Jul 1404*	858*	1 Jan 1454
706*	13 Jul 1306	757*	5 Jan 1356*	808	29 Jun 1405	859	22 Dec 1454
707	3 Jul 1307	758	25 Dec 1356*	809*	18 Jun 1406	860	11 Dec 1455
708*	21 Jun 1308*	759	15 Dec 1357	810	8 Jun 1407	861*	29 Nov 1456*
709	11 Jun 1309	760*	3 Dec 1358	811	27 May 1408*	862	19 Nov 1457
710	31 May 1310	761	23 Nov 1359	812*	16 May 1409	863	8 Nov 1458
711*	20 May 1311	762	11 Nov 1360*	813	6 May 1410	864*	28 Oct 1459
712	9 May 1312*	763*	31 Oct 1361	814	25 Apr 1411	865	17 Oct 1460*
713	28 Apr 1313	764	21 Oct 1362	815*	13 Apr 1412*	866*	6 Oct 1461
714*	17 Apr 1314	765	10 Oct 1363	816	3 Apr 1413	867	26 Sep 1462
715	7 Apr 1315	766*	28 Sep 1364*	817*	23 Mar 1414	868	15 Sep 1463
716*	26 Mar 1316*	767	18 Sep 1365	818	13 Mar 1415	869*	3 Sep 1464*
717	16 Mar 1317	768*	7 Sep 1366	819	1 Mar 1416*	870	23 Aug 1465
718	5 Mar 1318	769	28 Aug 1367	820*	18 Feb 1417	871	13 Aug 1466
719*	22 Feb 1319	770	16 Aug 1368*	821	8 Feb 1418	872*	2 Aug 1467
720	12 Feb 1320*	771*	5 Aug 1369	822	28 Jan 1419	873	22 Jul 1468*
721	31 Jan 1321	772	26 Jul 1370	823*	17 Jan 1420*	874	11 Jul 1469
722*	20 Jan 1322	773	15 Jul 1371	824	6 Jan 1421	875*	30 Jun 1470
723	10 Jan 1323	774*	3 Jul 1372*	825	26 Dec 1421	876	20 Jun 1471

Year of Hegira	Western Date (Julian) of Islamic New Year	Year of Hegira	Western Date (Julian) of Islamic New Year	Year of Hegira	Western Date (Julian) of Islamic New Year	Year of Hegira	Western Date (Julian) of Islamic New Year
877*	8 Jun 1472*	906	28 Jul 1500*	935*	15 Sep 1528*	964	4 Nov 1556*
878	29 May 1473	907*	17 Jul 1501	936	5 Sep 1529	965*	24 Oct 1557
879	18 May 1474	908	7 Jul 1502	937*	25 Aug 1530	966	14 Oct 1558
880*	7 May 1475	909	26 Jun 1503	938	15 Aug 1531	967*	3 Oct 1559
881	26 Apr 1476*	910*	14 Jun 1504*	939	3 Aug 1532*	968	22 Sep 1560*
882	15 Apr 1477	911	4 Jun 1505	940*	23 Jul 1533	969	11 Sep 1561
883*	4 Apr 1478	912	24 May 1506	941	13 Jul 1534	970*	31 Aug 1562
884	25 Mar 1479	913*	13 May 1507	942	2 Jul 1535	971	21 Aug 1563
885	13 Mar 1480*	914	2 May 1508*	943*	20 Jun 1536*	972	9 Aug 1564*
886*	2 Mar 1481	915	21 Apr 1509	944	10 Jun 1537	973*	29 Jul 1565
887	20 Feb 1482	916*	10 Apr 1510	945	30 May 1538	974	19 Jul 1566
888*	9 Feb 1483	917	31 Mar 1511	946*	19 May 1539	975	8 Jul 1567
889	3 Jan 1484*	918*	19 Mar 1512*	947	8 May 1540*	976*	26 Jun 1568*
890	18 Jan 1485	919	9 Mar 1513	948*	27 Apr 1541	977	16 Jun 1569
891*	7 Jan 1486	920	26 Feb 1514	949	17 Apr 1542	978*	5 Jun 1570
892	28 Dec 1486	921*	15 Feb 1515	950	6 Apr 1543	979	26 May 1571
893	17 Dec 1487	922	5 Feb 1516	951*	25 Mar 1544*	980	14 May 1572*
894*	5 Dec 1488*	923	24 Jan 1517	952	15 Mar 1545	981*	3 May 1573
895	25 Nov 1489	924*	13 Jan 1518	953	4 Mar 1546	982	23 Apr 1574
896*	14 Nov 1490	925	3 Jan 1519	954*	21 Feb 1547	983	12 Apr 1575
897	4 Nov 1491	926*	23 Dec 1519	955	11 Feb 1548*	984*	31 Mar 1576
898	23 Oct 1492*	927	12 Dec 1520*	956*	30 Jan 1549	985	21 Mar 1577
899*	12 Oct 1493	928	1 Dec 1521	957	20 Jan 1550	986*	10 Mar 1578
900	2 Oct 1494	929*	20 Nov 1522	958	9 Jan 1551	987	28 Feb 1579
901	21 Sep 1495	930	10 Nov 1523	959*	29 Dec 1551	988	17 Feb 1580*
902*	9 Sep 1496*	931	29 Oct 1524*	960	18 Dec 1552*	989*	5 Feb 1581
903	30 Aug 1497	932*	18 Oct 1525	961	7 Dec 1553	990	26 Jan 1582
904	19 Aug 1498	933	8 Oct 1526	962*	26 Nov 1554		
905*	8 Aug 1499	934	27 Sep 1527	963	16 Nov 1555		

Year of Hegira	Western Date (Julian) of Islamic New Year		Western Date (Gregorian) of Islamic New Year	
991	25 Jan	1583	15 Jan	1583
992*	4 Jan	1584*	14 Jan	1584*
993	24 Dec	1584*	3 Jan	1585
994	13 Dec	1585	23 Dec	1585
995*	2 Dec	1586	12 Dec	1586
996	22 Nov	1587	2 Dec	1587
997*	10 Nov	1588*	20 Nov	1588*
998	31 Oct	1589	10 Nov	1589
999	20 Oct	1590	30 Oct	1590
1000*	9 Oct	1591	19 Oct	1591
1001	28 Sep	1592*	8 Sep	1592*
1002	17 Sep	1593	27 Sep	1593
1003*	6 Sep	1594	16 Sep	1594
1004	27 Aug	1595	6 Sep	1595
1005	15 Aug	1596*	28 Aug	1596*
1006*	4 Aug	1597	14 Aug	1597
1007	25 Jul	1598	4 Aug	1598

Year of Hegira	Western Date (Julian) of Islamic New Year		Western Date (Gregorian) of Islamic New Year	
1008*	14 Jul	1599	24 Jul	1599
1009	3 Jul	1600*	13 Jul	1600*
1010	22 Jun	1601	2 Jul	1601
1011*	11 Jun	1602	21 Jun	1602
1012	1 Jun	1603	11 Jun	1603
1013	20 May	1604*	30 May	1604*
1014*	9 May	1605	19 May	1605
1015	29 Apr	1606	9 May	1606
1016*	18 Apr	1607	28 Apr	1607
1017	7 Apr	1608*	17 Apr	1608*
1018	27 Mar	1609	6 Apr	1609
1019*	16 Mar	1610	26 Mar	1610
1020	6 Mar	1611	16 Mar	1611
1021	23 Feb	1612*	4 Mar	1612*
1022*	11 Feb	1613	21 Feb	1613
1023	1 Feb	1614	11 Feb	1614
1024	21 Jan	1615	31 Jan	1615

Year of Hegira	Western Date (Julian) of Islamic New Year		(Gregorian)	
1025*	10 Jan	1616*	20 Jan	1616*
1026	30 Dec	1616*	9 Jan	1617
1027*	19 Dec	1617	29 Dec	1617
1028	9 Dec	1618	19 Dec	1618
1029	28 Nov	1619	8 Dec	1619
1030*	16 Nov	1620*	26 Nov	1620*
1031	6 Nov	1621	16 Nov	1621
1032	26 Oct	1622	5 Nov	1622
1033*	16 Oct	1623	25 Oct	1623
1034	4 Oct	1624*	14 Oct	1624*
1035	23 Sep	1625	3 Oct	1625
1036*	12 Sep	1626	22 Sep	1626
1037	2 Sep	1627	12 Sep	1627
1038*	21 Aug	1628*	31 Aug	1628*
1039	11 Aug	1629	21 Aug	1629
1040	31 Jul	1630	10 Aug	1630
1041*	20 Jul	1631	30 Jul	1631
1042	9 Jul	1632*	19 Jul	1632*
1043	28 Jun	1633	8 Jul	1633
1044*	17 Jun	1634	27 Jun	1634
1045	7 Jun	1635	17 Jun	1635
1046*	26 May	1636*	5 Jun	1636*
1047	16 May	1637	26 May	1637
1048	5 May	1638	15 May	1638
1049*	24 Apr	1639	4 May	1639
1050	13 Apr	1640*	23 Apr	1640*
1051	2 Apr	1641	12 Apr	1641
1052*	22 Mar	1642	1 Apr	1642
1053	12 Mar	1643	22 Mar	1643
1054	29 Feb	1644*	10 Mar	1644*
1055*	17 Feb	1645	27 Feb	1645
1056	7 Feb	1646	17 Feb	1646
1057*	27 Jan	1647	6 Feb	1647
1058	17 Jan	1648*	27 Jan	1648*
1059	5 Jan	1649	15 Jan	1649
1060*	25 Dec	1649	4 Jan	1650
1061	15 Dec	1650	25 Dec	1650
1062	4 Dec	1651	14 Dec	1651
1063*	22 Nov	1652*	2 Dec	1652*
1064	12 Nov	1653	22 Nov	1653
1065	1 Nov	1654	11 Nov	1654
1066*	21 Oct	1655	21 Oct	1655
1067	10 Oct	1656*	20 Oct	1656*
1068*	29 Sep	1657	9 Oct	1657
1069	19 Sep	1658	29 Sep	1658
1070	8 Sep	1659	18 Sep	1659
1071*	27 Aug	1660*	6 Sep	1660*
1072	17 Aug	1661	27 Aug	1661
1073	6 Aug	1662	16 Aug	1662
1074*	26 Jul	1663	5 Aug	1663
1075	15 Jul	1664*	25 Jul	1664*

Year of Hegira	Western Date (Julian) of Islamic New Year		(Gregorian)	
1076*	4 Jul	1665	14 Jul	1665
1077	24 Jun	1666	4 Jul	1666
1078	13 Jun	1667	23 Jun	1667
1079*	1 Jun	1668*	11 Jun	1668*
1080	22 May	1669	1 Jun	1669
1081	11 May	1670	21 May	1670
1082*	30 Apr	1671	10 May	1671
1083	19 Apr	1672*	29 Apr	1672*
1084	8 Apr	1673	18 Apr	1673
1085*	28 Mar	1674	7 Apr	1674
1086	18 Mar	1675	28 Mar	1675
1087*	6 Mar	1676*	16 Mar	1676*
1088	24 Feb	1677	6 Mar	1677
1089	13 Feb	1678	23 Feb	1678
1090*	2 Feb	1679	12 Feb	1679
1091	23 Jan	1680*	2 Feb	1680*
1092	11 Jan	1681	21 Jan	1681
1093*	31 Dec	1681	10 Jan	1682
1094	21 Dec	1682	31 Dec	1682
1095	10 Dec	1683	20 Dec	1683
1096*	28 Nov	1684*	8 Dec	1684*
1097	18 Nov	1685	28 Nov	1685
1098*	7 Nov	1686	17 Nov	1686
1099	28 Oct	1687	7 Nov	1687
1100	16 Oct	1688*	26 Oct	1688*
1101*	5 Oct	1689	15 Oct	1689
1102	25 Sep	1690	5 Oct	1690
1103	14 Sep	1691	24 Sep	1691
1104*	2 Sep	1692*	12 Sep	1692*
1105	23 Aug	1693	2 Sep	1693
1106*	12 Aug	1694	22 Aug	1694
1107	2 Aug	1695	12 Aug	1695
1108	21 Jul	1696*	31 Jul	1696*
1109*	10 Jul	1697	20 Jul	1697
1110	30 Jun	1698	10 Jul	1698
1111	19 Jun	1699	29 Jun	1699
1112*	7 Jun	1700*	18 Jun	1700
1113	28 May	1701	8 Jun	1701
1114	17 May	1702	28 May	1702
1115*	6 May	1703	17 May	1703
1116	25 Apr	1704*	6 May	1704*
1117*	14 Apr	1705	25 Apr	1705
1118	4 Apr	1706	15 Apr	1706
1119	24 Mar	1707	4 Apr	1707
1120*	12 Mar	1708*	23 Mar	1708*
1121	2 Mar	1709	13 Mar	1709
1122	19 Feb	1710	2 Mar	1710
1123*	8 Feb	1711	19 Feb	1711
1124	29 Jan	1712*	9 Feb	1712*
1125	17 Jan	1713	28 Jan	1713
1126*	6 Jan	1714	17 Jan	1714

Year of Hegira	Western Date (Julian) of Islamic New Year	Western Date (Gregorian) of Islamic New Year
1127	27 Dec 1714	7 Jan 1715
1128*	16 Dec 1715	27 Dec 1715
1129	5 Dec 1716*	16 Dec 1716*
1130	24 Nov 1717	5 Dec 1717
1131*	13 Nov 1718	24 Nov 1718
1132	3 Nov 1719	14 Nov 1719
1133	22 Oct 1720*	2 Nov 1720*
1134*	11 Oct 1721	22 Oct 1721
1135	1 Oct 1722	12 Oct 1722
1136*	20 Sep 1723	1 Oct 1723
1137	9 Sep 1724*	20 Sep 1724*
1138	29 Aug 1725	9 Sep 1725
1139*	18 Aug 1726	29 Aug 1726
1140	8 Aug 1727	19 Aug 1727
1141	27 Jul 1728*	7 Aug 1728*
1142*	16 Jul 1729	27 Jul 1729
1143	6 Jul 1730	17 Jul 1730
1144	25 Jun 1731	6 Jul 1731
1145*	13 Jun 1732*	24 Jun 1732*
1146	3 Jun 1733	14 Jun 1733

Year of Hegira	Western Date (Julian) of Islamic New Year	Western Date (Gregorian) of Islamic New Year
1147*	23 May 1734	3 Jun 1734
1148	13 May 1735	24 May 1735
1149	1 May 1736*	12 May 1736*
1150*	20 Apr 1737	1 May 1737
1151	10 Apr 1738	21 Apr 1738
1152	30 Mar 1739	10 Apr 1739
1153*	18 Mar 1740*	29 Mar 1740*
1154	8 Mar 1741	19 Mar 1741
1155	25 Feb 1742	8 Mar 1742
1156*	14 Feb 1743	25 Feb 1743
1157	4 Feb 1744*	15 Feb 1744*
1158*	23 Jan 1745	3 Feb 1745
1159	13 Jan 1746	24 Jan 1746
1160	2 Jan 1747	13 Jan 1747
1161*	22 Dec 1747	2 Jan 1748*
1162	11 Dec 1748*	22 Dec 1748*
1163	30 Nov 1749	11 Dec 1749
1164*	19 Nov 1750	30 Nov 1750
1165	9 Nov 1751	20 Nov 1751

Year of Hegira	Western Date (Julian) of Islamic New Year
1166*	8 Nov 1762*
1167	29 Oct 1763
1168	18 Oct 1754
1169*	7 Oct 1755
1170	26 Sep 1756*
1171	15 Sep 1757
1172*	4 Sep 1758
1173	25 Aug 1759
1174	13 Aug 1760*
1175*	2 Aug 1761
1176	23 Jul 1762
1177*	12 Jul 1763
1178	1 Jul 1764*
1179	20 Jun 1765
1180*	9 Jun 1766
1181	30 May 1767
1182	18 May 1768*
1183*	7 May 1769
1184	27 Apr 1770
1185	16 Apr 1771
1186*	4 Apr 1772*
1187	25 Mar 1773
1188*	14 Mar 1774
1189	4 Mar 1775
1190	21 Feb 1776*

Year of Hegira	Western Date (Julian) of Islamic New Year
1191*	19 Feb 1777
1192	30 Jan 1778
1193	19 Jan 1779
1194*	8 Jan 1780*
1195	28 Dec 1780*
1196*	17 Dec 1781
1197	7 Dec 1782
1198	26 Nov 1783
1199*	14 Nov 1784*
1200	4 Nov 1785
1201	24 Oct 1786
1202*	13 Oct 1787
1203	2 Oct 1788*
1204	21 Sep 1789
1205*	10 Sep 1790
1206	31 Aug 1791
1207*	19 Aug 1792*
1208	9 Aug 1793
1209	29 Jul 1794
1210*	18 Jul 1795
1211	7 Jul 1796*
1212	26 Jun 1797
1213*	15 Jun 1798
1214	5 Jun 1799
1215	25 May 1800

Year of Hegira	Western Date (Julian) of Islamic New Year
1216*	14 May 1801
1217	4 May 1802
1218*	23 Apr 1803
1219	12 Apr 1804*
1220	1 Apr 1805
1221*	21 Mar 1806
1222	11 Mar 1807
1223	28 Feb 1808*
1224*	16 Feb 1809
1225	6 Feb 1810
1226*	26 Jan 1811
1227	16 Jan 1812*
1228	4 Jan 1813
1229*	24 Dec 1813
1230	14 Dec 1814
1231	3 Dec 1815
1232*	12 Nov 1816*
1233	11 Nov 1817
1234	31 Oct 1818
1235*	20 Oct 1819
1236	9 Oct 1820*
1237*	28 Sep 1821
1238	18 Sep 1822
1239	7 Sep 1823
1240*	26 Aug 1824*

Year of Hegira	Western Date (Julian) of Islamic New Year
1241	16 Aug 1825
1242	5 Aug 1826
1243*	25 Jul 1827
1244	14 Jul 1828*
1245	3 Jul 1829
1246*	22 Jun 1830
1247	12 Jun 1831
1248*	31 May 1832*
1249	21 May 1833
1250	10 May 1834
1251*	20 Apr 1835
1252	18 Apr 1836*
1253	7 Apr 1837
1254*	27 Mar 1838
1255	17 Mar 1839
1256*	5 Mar 1840*
1257	23 Feb 1841
1258	12 Feb 1842
1259*	1 Feb 1843
1260	22 Jan 1844*
1261	10 Jan 1845
1262*	30 Dec 1845
1263	20 Dec 1846*
1264	9 Dec 1847
1265*	27 Nov 1848*

Year of Hegira	Western Date (Julian) of Islamic New Year	Year of Hegira	Western Date (Julian) of Islamic New Year	Year of Hegira	Western Date (Julian) of Islamic New Year	Year of Hegira	Western Date (Julian) of Islamic New Year
1266	17 Nov 1849	1318	1 May 1900	1370	13 Oct 1950	1422	26 Mar 2001
1267*	6 Nov 1850	1319*	20 Apr 1901	1371*	2 Oct 1951	1423*	15 Mar 2002
1268	27 Oct 1851	1320	10 Apr 1902	1372	21 Sep 1952*	1424	5 Mar 2003
1269	15 Oct 1852*	1321	30 Mar 1903	1373	10 Sep 1953	1425	22 Feb 2004*
1270*	4 Oct 1853	1322*	18 Mar 1904*	1374*	30 Aug 1954	1426*	10 Feb 2005
1271	24 Sep 1854	1323	8 Mar 1905	1375	20 Aug 1955	1427	31 Jan 2006
1272	13 Sep 1855	1324	25 Feb 1906	1376*	8 Aug 1956*	1428*	20 Jan 2007
1273*	1 Sep 1856*	1325	14 Feb 1907	1377	29 Jul 1957	1429	10 Jan 2008*
1274	22 Aug 1857	1326	4 Feb 1908*	1378	18 Jul 1958	1430	29 Dec 2008*
1275	11 Aug 1858	1327*	23 Jan 1909	1379*	7 Jul 1959	1431*	18 Dec 2009
1276*	31 Jul 1859	1328	13 Jan 1910	1380	26 Jun 1960*	1432	8 Dec 2010
1277*	20 Jul 1860*	1329	2 Jan 1911	1381	15 Jun 1961	1433	27 Nov 2011
1278*	9 Jul 1861	1330*	22 Dec 1911	1382*	4 Jun 1962	1434*	15 Nov 2012*
1279	29 Jun 1862	1331	11 Dec 1912*	1383	25 May 1963	1435	5 Nov 2013
1280	18 Jun 1863	1332	30 Nov 1913	1384	13 May 1964*	1436*	25 Oct 2014
1281*	6 Jun 1864*	1333*	19 Nov 1914	1385*	2 May 1965	1437	15 Oct 2015
1282	27 May 1865	1334	9 Nov 1915	1386	22 Apr 1966	1438	3 Oct 2016*
1283	16 May 1866	1335	28 Oct 1916*	1387*	11 Apr 1967	1439*	22 Sep 2017
1284*	5 May 1867	1336*	17 Oct 1917	1388	31 Mar 1968*	1440	12 Sep 2018
1285	24 Apr 1868*	1337	7 Oct 1918	1389	20 Mar 1969	1441	1 Sep 2019
1286*	13 Apr 1869	1338*	26 Sep 1919	1390*	9 Mar 1970	1442*	20 Aug 2020*
1287	3 Apr 1870	1339	15 Sep 1920*	1391	27 Feb 1971	1443	10 Aug 2021
1288	23 Mar 1871	1340	4 Sep 1921	1392	16 Feb 1972*	1444	30 Jul 2022
1289*	11 Mar 1872*	1341*	24 Aug 1922	1393*	4 Feb 1973	1445*	19 Jul 2023
1290	1 Mar 1873	1342	14 Aug 1923	1394	25 Jan 1974	1446	8 Jul 2024*
1291	18 Feb 1874	1343	2 Aug 1924*	1395	14 Jan 1975	1447*	27 Jun 2025
1292*	7 Feb 1875	1344*	22 Jul 1925	1396*	3 Jan 1976*	1448	17 Jun 2026
1293	28 Jan 1876*	1345	12 Jul 1926	1397	23 Dec 1976*	1449	6 Jun 2027
1294	16 Jan 1877	1346*	1 Jul 1927	1398*	12 Dec 1977	1450*	25 May 2028
1295*	5 Jan 1878	1347	20 Jun 1928*	1399	2 Dec 1978	1451	15 May 2029
1296	26 Dec 1878	1348	9 Jun 1929	1400	21 Nov 1979	1452	4 May 2030
1297*	15 Dec 1879	1349*	29 May 1930	1401*	9 Nov 1980*	1453*	23 Apr 2031
1298	4 Dec 1880*	1350	19 May 1931	1402	30 Oct 1981	1454	12 Apr 2032*
1299	23 Nov 1881	1351	7 May 1932*	1403	19 Oct 1982	1455	1 Apr 2033
1300*	12 Nov 1882	1352*	26 Apr 1933	1404*	8 Oct 1983	1456*	21 Mar 2034
1301	2 Nov 1883	1353	16 Apr 1934	1405	27 Sep 1984*	1457	11 Mar 2035
1302	21 Oct 1884*	1354	5 Apr 1935	1406*	16 Sep 1985	1458*	28 Feb 2036*
1303*	10 Oct 1885	1355*	24 Mar 1936*	1407	6 Sep 1986	1459	17 Feb 2037
1304	30 Sep 1886	1356	14 Mar 1937	1408	26 Aug 1987	1460	6 Feb 2038
1305	19 Sep 1887	1357*	3 Mar 1938	1409*	14 Aug 1988*	1461*	26 Jan 2039
1306*	7 Sep 1888*	1358	21 Feb 1939	1410	4 Aug 1989	1462	16 Jan 2040*
1307	28 Aug 1889	1359	10 Feb 1940*	1411	24 Jul 1990	1463	4 Jan 2041
1308*	17 Aug 1890	1360*	29 Jan 1941	1412*	13 Jul 1991	1464*	24 Dec 2041
1309	7 Aug 1891	1361	19 Jan 1942	1413	2 Jul 1992*	1465	14 Dec 2042
1310	26 Jul 1892*	1362	8 Jan 1943	1414	21 Jun 1993	1466*	3 Dec 2043
1311*	15 Jul 1893	1363*	28 Dec 1943	1415*	10 Jun 1994	1467	22 Nov 2044*
1312	5 Jul 1894	1364	17 Dec 1944*	1416	31 May 1995	1468	11 Nov 2045
1313	24 Jun 1895	1365	6 Dec 1945	1417*	19 May 1996*	1469*	31 Oct 2046
1314*	12 Jun 1896*	1366*	25 Nov 1946	1418	9 May 1997	1470	21 Oct 2047
1315	2 Jun 1897	1367	15 Nov 1947	1419	28 Apr 1998		
1316*	22 May 1898	1368*	3 Nov 1948*	1420*	17 Apr 1999		
1317	12 May 1899	1369	24 Oct 1949	1421	6 Apr 2000*		

FASLI (SOOR SAN)

The Soor San calendar is one of several bearing the surname Fasli or Fuzli which came into being prior to the advent of Islam. It was constructed as a correction for the vague year of 365 days which was in general use throughout Asia Minor and, to some degree, in India. The Soor San (and other Fasli calendars) uses a year of 365 days and adds an extra day every fourth year for the leap year. It contains 12 months of 30 days each with the extra five or six days added to the end of the year.

The Soor San calendar follows another rather interesting complicated structure in the form of cycles of 10, 100 and 1,000 years—somewhat similar to our structure of decades, centuries and millenia. The decades are calculated by repeating the first nine years and adding a suffix indicating the number of the decade to the 10th year. The name changes at the century, and the same process is followed, except that every 10th year the indication for the century is given. The name changes again at the millenium and the name of the millenium, century and decade are used every 10th year. We do the same thing in calling a year 110 or 125 or 1240 or 1981.

The calendar begins in late May in the Julian calendar and since the changeover to Gregorian, in early June. The month names, in their Arabic order, are as follows:

1. Baune	5. Babe	9. Mashir Amshir
2. Abib	6. Hatur	10. Buramat
3. Meshri	7. Kyak	11. Barsude
4. Tot	8. Tabe	12. Bashans

This calendar was in general use in Asia Minor. It has been frequently dropped in one area only to be resurrected in others. In some cases the beginning of the year was changed to conform to local needs. It is still employed in the Near and Mid East.

SOOR SAN CALENDAR

Soor San Year	Arabic Year as it is Spoken	Western Date (Julian) of New Year	Soor San Year	Arabic Year as it is Spoken	Western Date (Julian) of New Year
1	San Ahadi	600* 24 May	24	San Arba	623 25 May
2	San Isni	601 25 May	25	San Khams	624* 24 May
3	San Salas	602 25 May	26	San Sita	625 25 May
4	San Arba	603 25 May	27	San Saba	626 25 May
5	San Khams	604* 24 May	28	San Samani	627 25 May
6	San Sita	605 25 May	29	San Tisa	628* 24 May
7	San Saba	606 25 May	30	San Salatin	629 25 May
8	San Samani	607 25 May	31	San Ahadi	630 25 May
9	San Tisa	608* 24 May	32	San Isni	631 25 May
10	San Ashar	609 25 May	33	San Salas	632* 24 May
11	San Ahadi	610 25 May	34	San Arba	633 25 May
12	San Isni	611 25 May	35	San Khams	634 25 May
13	San Salas	612* 24 May	36	San Sita	635 25 May
14	San Arba	613 25 May	37	San Saba	636* 24 May
15	San Khams	614 25 May	38	San Samani	637 25 May
16	San Sita	615 25 May	39	San Tisa	638 25 May
17	San Saba	616* 24 May	40	San Arbain	639 25 May
18	San Samani	617 25 May	41	San Ahadi	640* 24 May
19	San Tisa	618 25 May	42	San Isni	641 25 May
20	San Ishrin	619 25 May	43	San Salas	642 25 May
21	San Ahadi	620* 24 May	44	San Arbas	643 25 May
22	San Isni	621 25 May	45	San Khams	644* 24 May
23	San Salas	622 25 May	46	San Sita	645 25 May

Soor San Year	Arabic Year as it is Spoken	Western Date (Julian) of New Year	Soor San Year	Arabic Year as it is Spoken	Western Date (Julian) of New Year
47	San Saba	646 25 May	98	San Samani	697 25 May
48	San Samani	647 25 May	99	San Tisa	698 25 May
49	San Tisa	648* 24 May	100	San Mayat	699 25 May
50	San Khamsin	649 25 May	101	San Ahadi	700* 24 May
51	San Ahadi	650 25 May	102	San Isni	701 25 May
52	San Isni	651 25 May	103	San Salas	702 25 May
53	San Sadas	652* 24 May	104	San Arba	703 25 May
54	San Arba	653 25 May	105	San Khams	704* 24 May
55	San Khams	654 25 May	106	San Sita	705 25 May
56	San Sita	655 25 May	107	San Saba	706 25 May
57	San Saba	656* 24 May	108	San Samani	707 25 May
58	San Samani	657 25 May	109	San Tisa	708* 24 May
59	San Tisa	658 25 May	110	San Ashar mayat	709 25 May
60	San Sitain	659 25 May	111	San Ahadi	710 25 May
61	San Ahadi	660* 24 May	112	San Isni	711 25 May
62	San Isni	661 25 May	113	San Salas	712* 24 May
63	San Salas	662 25 May	114	San Arba	713 25 May
64	San Arba	663 25 May	115	San Khams	714 25 May
65	San Khams	664* 24 May	116	San Sita	715 25 May
66	San Sita	665 25 May	117	San Saba	716* 24 May
67	San Saba	666 25 May	118	San Samani	717 25 May
68	San Samani	667 25 May	119	San Tisa	718 25 May
69	San Tisa	668* 24 May	120	San Ishrin mayat	719 25 May
70	San Sabain	669 25 May	121	San Ahadi	720* 24 May
71	San Ahadi	670 25 May	122	San Isni	721 25 May
72	San Isni	671 25 May	123	San Salas	722 25 May
73	San Salas	672* 24 May	124	San Arba	723 25 May
74	San Arba	673 25 May	125	San Khams	724* 24 May
75	San Khams	674 25 May	126	San Sita	725 25 May
76	San Sita	675 25 May	127	San Saba	726 25 May
77	San Saba	676* 24 May	128	San Samani	727 25 May
78	San Samani	677 25 May	129	San Tisa	728* 24 May
79	San Tisa	678 25 May	130	San Salatin mayat	729 25 May
80	San Samanin	679 25 May	131	San Ahadi	730 25 May
81	San Ahadi	680* 24 May	132	San Isni	731 25 May
82	San Isni	681 25 May	133	San Salas	732* 24 May
83	San Salas	682 25 May	134	San Arba	733 25 May
84	San Arba	683 25 May	135	San Khams	734 25 May
85	San Khams	684* 24 May	136	San Sita	735 25 May
86	San Sita	685 25 May	137	San Saba	736* 24 May
87	San Saba	686 25 May	138	San Samani	737 25 May
88	San Samani	687 25 May	139	San Tisa	738 25 May
89	San Tisa	688* 24 May	140	San Arbain mayat	739 25 May
90	San Tisa-in	689 25 May	141	San Ahadi	740* 24 May
91	San Ahadi	690 25 May	142	San Isni	741 25 May
92	San Isni	691 25 May	143	San Salas	742 25 May
93	San Salas	692* 24 May	144	San Arba	743 25 May
94	San Arba	693 25 May	145	San Khams	744* 24 May
95	San Khams	694 25 May	146	San Sita	745 25 May
96	San Sita	695 25 May	147	San Saba	746 25 May
97	San Saba	696* 24 May	148	San Samani	747 25 May

Soor San Year	Arabic Year as it is Spoken	Western Date (Julian) of New Year	Soor San Year	Arabic Year as it is Spoken	Western Date (Julian) of New Year
149	San Tisa	748* 24 May	200	San Miatin	799 25 May
150	San Khamsin mayat	749 25 May	201	San Ahadi	800* 24 May
151	San Ahadi	750 25 May	202	San Isni	801 25 May
152	San Isni	751 25 May	203	San Salas	802 25 May
153	San Salas	752* 24 May	204	San Arba	803 25 May
154	San Arba	753 25 May	205	San Khams	804* 24 May
155	San Khams	754 25 May	206	San Sita	805 25 May
156	San Sita	755 25 May	207	San Saba	806 25 May
157	San Saba	756* 24 May	208	San Samani	807 25 May
158	San Samani	757 25 May	209	San Tisa	808* 24 May
159	San Tisa	758 25 May	210	San Ashar miatin	809 25 May
160	San Sitain mayat	759 25 May	211	San Ahadi	810 25 May
161	San Ahadi	760* 24 May	212	San Isni	811 25 May
162	San Isni	761 25 May	213	San Salas	812* 24 May
163	San Salas	762 25 May	214	San Arba	813 25 May
164	San Arba	763 25 May	215	San Khams	814 25 May
165	San Khams	764* 24 May	216	San Sita	815 25 May
166	San Sita	765 25 May	217	San Saba	816* 24 May
167	San Saba	766 25 May	218	San Samani	817 25 May
168	San Samani	767 25 May	219	San Tisa	818 25 May
169	San Tisa	768* 24 May	220	San Ishrin miatin	819 25 May
170	San Sabain mayat	769 25 May	221	San Ahadi	820* 24 May
171	San Ahadi	770 25 May	222	San Isni	821 25 May
172	San Isni	771 25 May	223	San Salas	822 25 May
173	San Salas	772* 24 May	224	San Arba	823 25 May
174	San Arba	773 25 May	225	San Khams	824* 24 May
175	San Khams	774 25 May	226	San Sita	825 25 May
176	San Sita	775 25 May	227	San Saba	826 25 May
177	San Saba	776* 24 May	228	San Samani	827 25 May
178	San Samani	777 25 May	229	San Tisa	828* 24 May
179	San Tisa	778 25 May	230	San Salatin miatin	829 25 May
180	San Samanin mayat	779 25 May	231	San Ahadi	830 25 May
181	San Ahadi	780* 24 May	232	San Isni	831 25 May
182	San Isni	781 25 May	233	San Salas	832* 24 May
183	San Salas	782 25 May	234	San Arba	833 25 May
184	San Arba	783 25 May	235	San Khams	834 25 May
185	San Khams	784* 24 May	236	San Sita	835 25 May
186	San Sita	785 25 May	237	San Saba	836* 24 May
187	San Saba	786 25 May	238	San Samani	837 25 May
188	San Samani	787 25 May	239	San Tisa	838 25 May
189	San Tisa	788* 24 May	240	San Arbain miatin	839 25 May
190	San Tisain mayat	789 25 May	241	San Ahadi	840* 24 May
191	San Ahadi	790 25 May	242	San Isni	841 25 May
192	San Isni	791 25 May	243	San Salas	842 25 May
193	San Salas	792* 24 May	244	San Arba	843 25 May
194	San Arba	793 25 May	245	San Khams	844* 24 May
195	San Khams	794 25 May	246	San Sita	845 25 May
196	San Sita	795 25 May	247	San Saba	846 25 May
197	San Saba	796* 24 May	248	San Samani	847 25 May
198	San Samani	797 25 May	249	San Tisa	848* 24 May
199	San Tisa	798 25 May	250	San khamsin miatin	849 25 May

Soor San Year	Arabic Year as it is Spoken	Western Date (Julian) of New Year
251	San Ahadi	850 25 May
252	San Isni	851 25 May
253	San Salas	852* 24 May
254	San Arba	853 25 May
255	San Khams	854 25 May
256	San Sita	855 25 May
257	San Saba	856* 24 May
258	San Samani	857 25 May
259	San Tisa	858 25 May
260	San Sitain miatin	859 25 May
261	San Ahadi	860* 24 May
262	San Isni	861 25 May
263	San Salas	862 25 May
264	San Arba	863 25 May
265	San Khams	864* 24 May
266	San Sita	865 25 May
267	San Saba	866 25 May
268	San Samani	867 25 May
269	San Tisa	868* 24 May
270	San Sabain miatin	869 25 May
271	San Ahadi	870 25 May
272	San Isni	871 25 May
273	San Salas	872* 24 May
274	San Arba	873 25 May
275	San Khams	874 25 May
276	San Sita	875 25 May
277	San Saba	876* 24 May
278	San Samani	877 25 May
279	San Tisa	878 25 May
280	San Samanin miatin	879 25 May
281	San Ahadi	880* 24 May
282	San Isni	881 25 May
283	San Salas	882 25 May
284	San Arba	883 25 May
285	San Khams	884* 24 May
286	San Sita	885 25 May
287	San Saba	886 25 May
288	San Samani	887 25 May
289	San Tisa	888* 24 May
290	San Tisa miatin	889 25 May
291	San Ahadi	890 25 May
292	San Isni	891 25 May
293	San Salas	892* 24 May
294	San Arba	893 25 May
295	San Khams	894 25 May
296	San Sita	895 25 May
297	San Saba	896* 24 May
298	San Samani	897 25 May
299	San Tisa	898 25 May
300	San Salas mayat	899 25 May
301	San Ahadi	900* 24 May
302	San Isni	901 25 May
303	San Salas	902 25 May
304	San Arba	903 25 May
305	San Khams	904* 24 May
306	San Sita	905 25 May
307	San Saba	906 25 May
308	San Samani	907 25 May
309	San Tisa	908* 24 May
310	San Ashar Salas mayat	909 25 May
311	San Ahadi	910 25 May
312	San Isni	911 25 May
313	San Salas	912* 24 May
314	San Arba	913 25 May
315	San Khams	914 25 May
316	San Sita	915 25 May
317	San Saba	916* 24 May
318	San Samani	917 25 May
319	San Tisa	918 25 May
320	San Ishrin Salas mayat	919 25 May
321	San Ahadi	920* 24 May
322	San Isni	921 25 May
323	San Salas	922 25 May
324	San Arba	923 25 May
325	San Khams	924* 24 May
326	San Sita	925 25 May
327	San Saba	926 25 May
328	San Samani	927 25 May
329	San Tisa	928* 24 May
330	San Salatin Salas mayat	929 25 May
331	San Ahadi	930 25 May
332	San Isni	931 25 May
333	San Salas	932* 24 May
334	San Arba	933 25 May
335	San Khams	934 25 May
336	San Sita	935 25 May
337	San Saba	936* 24 May
338	San Samani	937 25 May
339	San Tisa	938 25 May
340	San Arbain Salas mayat	939 25 May
341	San Ahadi	940* 24 May
342	San Isni	941 25 May
343	San Salas	942 25 May
344	San Arba	943 25 May
345	San Khams	944* 24 May
346	San Sita	945 25 May
347	San Saba	946 25 May
348	San Samani	947 25 May
349	San Tisa	948* 24 May
350	San Khamsin salas mayat	949 25 May

Soor San Year	Arabic Year as it is Spoken	Western Date (Julian) of New Year
351	San Ahadi	950 25 May
352	San Isni	951 25 May
353	San Salas	952* 24 May
354	San Arba	953 25 May
355	San Khams	954 25 May
356	San Sita	955 25 May
357	San Saba	956* 24 May
358	San Samani	957 25 May
359	San Tisa	958 25 May
360	San Sitain Salas mayat	959 25 May
361	San Ahadi	960* 24 May
362	San Isni	961 25 May
363	San Salas	962 25 May
364	San Arba	963 25 May
365	San Khams	964* 24 May
366	San Sita	965 25 May
367	San Saba	966 25 May
368	San Samani	967 25 May
369	San Tisa	968* 24 May
370	San Sabain Salas mayat	969 25 May
371	San Ahadi	970 25 May
372	San Isni	971 25 May
373	San Salas	972* 24 May
374	San Arba	973 25 May
375	San Khams	974 25 May
376	San Sita	975 25 May
377	San Saba	976* 24 May
378	San Samani	977 25 May
379	San Tisa	978 25 May
380	San Samanin Salas mayat	979 25 May
381	San Ahadi	980* 24 May
382	San Isni	981 25 May
383	San Salas	982 25 May
384	San Arba	983 25 May
385	San Khams	984* 24 May
386	San Sita	985 25 May
387	San Saba	986 25 May
388	San Samani	987 25 May
389	San Tisa	988* 24 May
390	San Tisain Salas mayat	989 25 May
391	San Ahadi	990 25 May
392	San Isni	991 25 May
393	San Salas	992* 24 May
394	San Arba	993 25 May
395	San Khams	994 25 May
396	San Sita	995 25 May
397	San Saba	996* 24 May
398	San Samani	997 25 May
399	San Tisa	998 25 May
400	San Arbain mayat	999 25 May
401	San Ahadi	1000* 24 May
402	San Isni	1001 25 May
403	San Salas	1002 25 May
404	San Arba	1003 25 May
405	San Khams	1004* 24 May
406	San Sita	1005 25 May
407	San Saba	1006 25 May
408	San Samani	1007 25 May
409	San Tisa	1008* 24 May
410	San Ashar arba mayat	1009 25 May
411	San Ahadi	1010 25 May
412	San Isni	1011 25 May
413	San Salas	1012* 24 May
414	San Arba	1013 25 May
415	San Khams	1014 25 May
416	San Sita	1015 25 May
417	San Saba	1016* 24 May
418	San Samani	1017 25 May
419	San Tisa	1018 25 May
420	San Ishrin arba mayat	1019 25 May
421	San Ahadi	1020* 24 May
422	San Isni	1021 25 May
423	San Salas	1022 25 May
424	San Arba	1023 25 May
425	San Khams	1024* 24 May
426	San Sita	1025 25 May
427	San Saba	1026 25 May
428	San Samani	1027 25 May
429	San Tisa	1028* 24 May
430	San Salatin arba mayat	1029 25 May
431	San Ahadi	1030 25 May
432	San Isni	1031 25 May
433	San Salas	1032* 24 May
434	San Arba	1033 25 May
435	San Khams	1034 25 May
436	San Sita	1035 25 May
437	San Saba	1036* 24 May
438	San Samani	1037 25 May
439	San Tisa	1038 25 May
440	San Arbain arba mayat	1039 25 May
441	San Ahadi	1040* 24 May
442	San Isni	1041 25 May
443	San Salas	1042 25 May
444	San Arba	1043 25 May

Soor San Year	Arabic Year as it is Spoken	Western Date (Julian) of New Year	Soor San Year	Arabic Year as it is Spoken	Western Date (Julian) of New Year
445	San Khams	1044* 24 May	491	San Ahadi	1090 25 May
446	San Sita	1045 25 May	492	San Salas	1091 25 May
447	San Saba	1046 25 May	493	San Salas	1092* 24 May
448	San Samani	1047 25 May	494	San Arba	1093 25 May
449	San Tisa	1048* 24 May	495	San Khams	1094 25 May
450	San Khamsin arba mayat	1049 25 May	496	San Sita	1095 25 May
			497	San Saba	1096* 24 May
451	San Ahadi	1050 25 May	498	San Samani	1097 25 May
452	San Isni	1051 25 May	499	San Tisa	1098 25 May
453	San Salas	1052* 24 May	500	San Khams mayat	1099 25 May
454	San Arba	1053 25 May	501	San Ahadi	1100* 24 May
455	San Khams	1054 25 May	502	San Isni	1101 25 May
456	San Sita	1055 25 May	503	San Salas	1102 25 May
457	San Saba	1056* 24 May	504	Sam Arba	1103 25 May
458	San Samani	1057 25 May	505	San Khams	1104* 24 May
459	San Tisa	1058 25 May	506	San Sita	1105 25 May
460	San Sitain arba mayat	1059 25 May	507	San Saba	1106 25 May
			508	San Samani	1107 25 May
461	San Ahadi	1060* 24 May	509	San Tisa	1108* 24 May
462	San Isni	1061 25 May	510	San Ashar Khams mayat	1109 25 May
463	San Salas	1062 25 May	511	San Ahadi	1110 25 May
464	San Arba	1063 25 May	512	San Isni	1111 25 May
465	San Khams	1064* 24 May	513	San Salas	1112* 24 May
466	San Sita	1065 25 May	514	San Arba	1113 25 May
467	San Saba	1066 25 May	515	San Khams	1114 25 May
468	San Samani	1067 25 May	516	San Sita	1115 25 May
469	San Tisa	1068* 24 May	517	San Saba	1116* 24 May
470	San Sabain arba mayat	1069 25 May	518	San Samani	1117 25 May
			519	San Tisa	1118 25 May
471	San Ahadi	1070 25 May	520	San Ishrin Khams	1119 25 May
472	San Isni	1071 25 May	521	San Ahadi	1120* 24 May
473	San Salas	1072* 24 May	522	San Isni	1121 25 May
474	San Arba	1073 25 May	523	San Salas	1122 25 May
475	San Khams	1074 25 May	524	San Arba	1123 25 May
476	San Sita	1075 25 May	525	San Khams	1124* 24 May
477	San Saba	1076* 24 May	526	San Sita	1125 25 May
478	San Samani	1077 25 May	527	San Saba	1126 25 May
479	San Tisa	1078 25 May	528	San Samani	1127 25 May
480	San Samanin arba mayat	1079 25 May	529	San Tisa	1128* 24 May
			530	San Salatin Khams	1129 25 May
481	San Ahadi	1080* 24 May	531	San Ahadi	1130 25 May
482	San Isni	1081 25 May	532	San Isni	1131 25 May
483	San Salas	1082 25 May	533	San Salas	1132* 24 May
484	San Arba	1083 25 May	534	San Arba	1133 25 May
485	San Khams	1084* 24 May	535	San Khams	1134 25 May
486	San Sita	1085 25 May	536	San Sita	1135 25 May
487	San Saba	1086 25 May	537	San Saba	1136* 24 May
488	San Samani	1087 25 May	538	San Samani	1137 25 May
489	San Tisa	1088* 24 May	539	San Tisa	1138 25 May
490	San Tisain arba mayat	1089 25 May	540	San Arbain Khams	1139 25 May
			541	San Ahadi	1140* 24 May

Soor San Year	Arabic Year as it is Spoken	Western Date (Julian) of New Year
542	San Isni	1141 25 May
543	San Salas	1142 25 May
544	San Arba	1143 25 May
545	San Khams	1144* 24 May
546	San Sita	1145 25 May
547	San Saba	1146 25 May
548	San Samani	1147 25 May
549	San Tisa	1148* 24 May
550	San Khamsin Khams mayat	1149 25 May
551	San Ahadi	1150 25 May
552	San Isni	1151 25 May
553	San Salas	1152* 24 May
554	San Arba	1153 25 May
555	San Khams	1154 25 May
556	San Sita	1155 25 May
557	San Saba	1156* 24 May
558	San Samani	1157 25 May
559	San Tisa	1158 25 May
560	San Sitain Khams mayat	1159 25 May
561	San Ahadi	1160* 24 May
562	San Isni	1161 25 May
563	San Salas	1162 25 May
564	San Arba	1163 25 May
565	San Khams	1164* 24 May
566	San Sita	1165 25 May
567	San Saba	1166 25 May
568	San Samani	1167 25 May
569	San Tisa	1168* 24 May
570	San Sabain Khams mayat	1169 25 May
571	San Ahadi	1170 25 May
572	San Isni	1171 25 May
573	San Salas	1172* 24 May
574	San Arba	1173 25 May
575	San Khams	1174 25 May
576	San Sita	1175 25 May
577	San Saba	1176* 24 May
578	San Samani	1177 25 May
579	San Tisa	1178 25 May
580	San Samanin Khams mayat	1179 25 May
581	San Ahadi	1180* 24 May
582	San Isni	1181 25 May
583	San Salas	1182 25 May
584	San Arba	1183 25 May
585	San Khams	1184* 24 May
586	San Sita	1185 25 May
587	San Saba	1186 25 May
588	San Samani	1187 25 May
589	San Tisa	1188* 24 May
590	San Tisain Khams mayat	1189 25 May
591	San Ahadi	1190 25 May
592	San Isni	1191 25 May
593	San Salas	1192* 24 May
594	San Arba	1193 25 May
595	San Khams	1194 25 May
596	San Sita	1195 25 May
597	San Saba	1196* 24 May
598	San Samani	1197 25 May
599	San Tisa	1198 25 May
600	San Sita mayat	1199 25 May
601	San Ahadi	1200* 24 May
602	San Isni	1201 25 May
603	San Salas	1202 25 May
604	San Arba	1203 25 May
605	San Khams	1204* 24 May
606	San Sita	1205 25 May
607	San Saba	1206 25 May
608	San Samani	1207 25 May
609	San Tisa	1208* 24 May
610	San Ashar sita mayat	1209 25 May
611	San Ahadi	1210 25 May
612	San Isni	1211 25 May
613	San Salas	1212* 24 May
614	San Arba	1213 25 May
615	San Khams	1214 25 May
616	San Sita	1215 25 May
617	San Saba	1216* 24 May
618	San Samani	1217 25 May
619	San Tisa	1218 25 May
620	San Ishrin sita mayat	1219 25 May
621	San Ahadi	1220* 24 May
622	San Isni	1221 25 May
623	San Salas	1222 25 May
624	San Arba	1223 25 May
625	San Khams	1224* 24 May
626	San Sita	1225 25 May
627	San Saba	1226 25 May
628	San Samani	1227 25 May
629	San Tisa	1228* 24 May
630	San Salatin sita mayat	1229 25 May
631	San Ahadi	1230 25 May
632	San Isni	1231 25 May
633	San Salas	1232* 24 May
634	San Arba	1233 25 May
635	San Khams	1234 25 May
636	San Sita	1235 25 May
637	San Saba	1236* 24 May
638	San Samani	1237 25 May
639	San Tisa	1238 25 May
640	San Arbain sita mayat	1239 25 May
641	San Ahadi	1240* 24 May

Soor San Year	Arabic Year as it is Spoken	Western Date (Julian) of New Year	Soor San Year	Arabic Year as it is Spoken	Western Date (Julian) of New Year
642	San Isni	1241 25 May	693	San Salas	1292* 24 May
643	San Salas	1242 25 May	694	San Arba	1293 25 May
644	San Arba	1243 25 May	695	San Khams	1294 25 May
645	San Khams	1244* 24 May	696	San Sita	1295 25 May
646	San Sita	1245 25 May	697	San Saba	1296* 24 May
647	San Saba	1246 25 May	698	San Samani	1297 25 May
648	San Samani	1247 25 May	699	San Tisa	1298 25 May
649	San Tisa	1248* 24 May	700	San Saba mayat	1299 25 May
650	San Khamsin sita mayat	1249 25 May	701	San Ahadi	1300* 24 May
651	San Ahadi	1250 25 May	702	San Isni	1301 25 May
652	San Isni	1251 25 May	703	San Salas	1302 25 May
653	San Salas	1252* 24 May	704	San Arba	1303 25 May
654	San Arba	1253 25 May	705	San Khams	1304* 24 May
655	San Khams	1254 25 May	706	San Sita	1305 25 May
656	San Sita	1255 25 May	707	San Saba	1306 25 May
657	San Saba	1256* 24 May	708	San Samani	1307 25 May
658	San Samani	1257 25 May	709	San Tisa	1308* 24 May
659	San Tisa	1258 25 May	710	San Ashar Saba mayat	1309 25 May
660	San Sitain Sita mayat	1259 25 May	711	San Ahadi	1310 25 May
661	San Ahadi	1260* 24 May	712	San Isni	1311 25 May
662	San Isni	1261 25 May	713	San Salas	1312* 24 May
663	San Salas	1262 25 May	714	San Arba	1313 25 May
664	San Arba	1263 25 May	715	San Khams	1314 25 May
665	San Khams	1264* 24 May	716	San Sita	1315 25 May
666	San Sita	1265 25 May	717	San Saba	1316* 24 May
667	San Saba	1266 25 May	718	San Samani	1317 25 May
668	San Samani	1267 25 May	719	San Tisa	1318 25 May
669	San Tisa	1268* 24 May	720	San Ishrin Saba mayat	1319 25 May
670	San Sabain Sita mayat	1269 25 May	721	San Ahadi	1320* 24 May
671	San Ahadi	1270 25 May	722	San Isni	1321 25 May
672	San Isni	1271 25 May	723	San Salas	1322 25 May
673	San Salas	1272* 24 May	724	San Arba	1323 25 May
674	San Arba	1273 25 May	725	San Khams	1324* 24 May
675	San Khams	1274 25 May	726	San Sita	1325 25 May
676	San Sita	1275 25 May	727	San Saba	1326 25 May
677	San Saba	1276* 24 May	728	San Samani	1327 25 May
678	San Samani	1277 25 May	729	San Tisa	1328* 24 May
679	San Tisa	1278 25 May	730	San Salatin Saba mayat	1329 25 May
680	San Samanin Sita mayat	1279 25 May	731	San Ahadi	1330 25 May
681	San Ahadi	1280* 24 May	732	San Isni	1331 25 May
682	San Isni	1281 25 May	733	San Salas	1332* 24 May
683	San Salas	1282 25 May	734	San Arba	1333 25 May
684	San Arba	1283 25 May	735	San Khams	1334 25 May
685	San Khams	1284* 24 May	736	San Sita	1335 25 May
686	San Sita	1285 25 May	737	San Saba	1336* 24 May
687	San Saba	1286 25 May	738	San Samani	1337 25 May
688	San Samani	1287 25 May	739	San Tisa	1338 25 May
689	San Tisa	1288* 24 May	740	San Arbain Saba mayat	1339 25 May
690	San Tisain Sita mayat	1289 25 May	741	San Ahadi	1340* 24 May
691	San Ahadi	1290 25 May	742	San Isni	1341 25 May
692	San Isni	1291 25 May	743	San Salas	1342 25 May

Soor San Year	Arabic Year as it is Spoken	Western Date (Julian) of New Year
744	San Arba	1343 25 May
745	San Khams	1344* 24 May
746	San Sita	1345 25 May
747	San Saba	1346 25 May
748	San Samani	1347 25 May
749	San Tisa	1348* 24 May
750	San Khamsin Saba mayat	1349 25 May
751	San Ahadi	1350 25 May
752	San Isni	1351 25 May
753	San Salas	1352* 24 May
754	San Arba	1353 25 May
755	San Khams	1354 25 May
756	San Sita	1355 25 May
757	San Saba	1356* 24 May
758	San Samani	1357 25 May
759	San Tisa	1358 25 May
760	San Sitain Saba mayat	1359 25 May
761	San Ahadi	1360* 24 May
762	San Isni	1361 25 May
763	San Salas	1362 25 May
764	San Arba	1363 25 May
765	San Khams	1364* 24 May
766	San Sita	1365 25 May
767	San Saba	1366 25 May
768	San Samani	1367 25 May
769	San Tisa	1368* 24 May
770	San Sabain Saba mayat	1369 25 May
771	San Ahadi	1370 25 May
772	San Isni	1371 25 May
773	San Salas	1372* 24 May
774	San Arba	1373 25 May
775	San Khams	1374 25 May
776	San Sita	1375 25 May
777	San Saba	1376* 24 May
778	San Samani	1377 25 May
779	San Tisa	1378 25 May
780	San Samanin Saba mayat	1379 25 May
781	San Ahadi	1380* 24 May
782	San Isni	1381 25 May
783	San Salas	1382 25 May
784	San Arba	1383 25 May
785	San Khams	1384* 24 May
786	San Sita	1385 25 May
787	San Saba	1386 25 May
788	San Samani	1387 25 May
789	San Tisa	1388* 24 May
790	San Tisain Saba mayat	1389 25 May
791	San Ahadi	1390 25 May
792	San Isni	1391 25 May
793	San Salas	1392* 24 May
794	San Arba	1393 25 May
795	San Khams	1394 25 May
796	San Sita	1395 25 May
797	San Saba	1396* 24 May
798	San Samani	1397 25 May
799	San Tisa	1398 25 May
800	San Samani mayat	1399 25 May
801	San Ahadi	1400* 24 May
802	San Isni	1401 25 May
803	San Salas	1402 25 May
804	San Arba	1403 25 May
805	San Khams	1404* 24 May
806	San Sita	1405 25 May
807	San Saba	1406 25 May
808	San Samani	1407 25 May
809	San Tisa	1408* 24 May
810	San Ashar Samani mayat	1409 25 May
811	San Ahadi	1410 25 May
812	San Isni	1411 25 May
813	San Salas	1412* 24 May
814	San Arba	1413 25 May
815	San Khams	1414 25 May
816	San Sita	1415 25 May
817	San Saba	1416* 24 May
818	San Samani	1417 25 May
819	San Tisa	1418 25 May
820	San Ishrin Samani mayat	1419 25 May
821	San Ahadi	1420* 24 May
822	San Isni	1421 25 May
823	San Salas	1422 25 May
824	San Arba	1423 25 May
825	San Khams	1424* 24 May
826	San Sita	1425 25 May
827	San Saba	1426 25 May
828	San Samani	1427 25 May
829	San Tisa	1428* 24 May
830	San Salatin Samani mayat	1429 25 May
831	San Ahadi	1430 25 May
832	San Isni	1431 25 May
833	San Salas	1432* 24 May
834	San Arba	1433 25 May
835	San Khams	1434 25 May
836	San Sita	1435 25 May
837	San Saba	1436* 24 May
838	San Samani	1437 25 May
839	San Tisa	1438 25 May
840	San Arbain Samani mayat	1439 25 May
841	San Ahadi	1440* 24 May
842	San Isni	1441 25 May
843	San Salas	1442 25 May

Soor San Year	Arabic Year as it is Spoken	Western Date (Julian) of New Year
844	San Arba	1443 25 May
845	San Khams	1444* 24 May
846	San Sita	1445 25 May
847	San Saba	1446 25 May
848	San Samani	1447 25 May
849	San Tisa	1448* 24 May
850	San Khamsain Samani mayat	1449 25 May
851	San Ahadi	1450 25 May
852	San Isni	1451 25 May
853	San Salas	1452* 24 May
854	San Arba	1453 25 May
855	San Khams	1454 25 May
856	San Sita	1455 25 May
857	San Saba	1456* 24 May
858	San Samani	1457 25 May
859	San Tisa	1458 25 May
860	San Sitain Samani mayat	1459 25 May
861	San Ahadi	1460* 24 May
862	San Isni	1461 25 May
863	San Salas	1462 25 May
864	San Arba	1463 25 May
865	San Khams	1464* 24 May
866	San Sita	1465 25 May
867	San Saba	1466 25 May
868	San Samani	1467 25 May
869	San Tisa	1468* 24 May
870	San Sabain Samani mayat	1469 25 May
871	San Ahadi	1470 25 May
872	San Isni	1471 25 May
873	San Salas	1472* 24 May
874	San Arba	1473 25 May
875	San Khams	1474 25 May
876	San Sita	1475 25 May
877	San Saba	1476* 24 May
878	San Samani	1477 25 May
879	San Tisa	1478 25 May
880	San Samanin Samani mayat	1479 25 May
881	San Ahadi	1480* 24 May
882	San Isni	1481 25 May
883	San Salas	1482 25 May
884	San Arba	1483 25 May
885	San Khams	1484* 24 May
886	San Sita	1485 25 May
887	San Saba	1486 25 May
888	San Samani	1487 25 May
889	San Tisa	1488* 24 May
890	San Tisain Samani mayat	1489 25 May
891	San Ahadi	1490 25 May
892	San Isni	1491 25 May
893	San Salas	1492* 24 May
894	San Arba	1493 25 May
895	San Khams	1494 25 May
896	San Sita	1495 25 May
897	San Saba	1496* 24 May
898	San Samani	1497 25 May
899	San Tisa	1498 25 May
900	San Tisa mayat	1499 25 May
901	San Ahadi	1500* 24 May
902	San Isni	1501 25 May
903	San Salas	1502 25 May
904	San Arba	1503 25 May
905	San Khams	1504* 24 May
906	San Sita	1505 25 May
907	San Saba	1506 25 May
908	San Samani	1507 25 May
909	San Tisa	1508* 24 May
910	San Ashar Tisa mayat	1509 25 May
911	San Ahadi	1510 25 May
912	San Isni	1511 25 May
913	San Salas	1512* 24 May
914	San Arba	1513 25 May
915	San Khams	1514 25 May
916	San Sita	1515 25 May
917	San Saba	1516* 24 May
918	San Samani	1517 25 May
919	San Tisa	1518 25 May
920	San Ishrin Tisa mayat	1519 25 May
921	San Ahadi	1520* 24 May
922	San Isni	1521 25 May
923	San Salas	1522 25 May
924	San Arba	1523 25 May
925	San Khams	1524* 24 May
926	San Sita	1525 25 May
927	San Saba	1526 25 May
928	San Samani	1527 25 May
929	San Tisa	1528* 24 May
930	San Salatin Tisa mayat	1529 25 May
931	San Ahadi	1530 25 May
932	San Isni	1531 25 May
933	San Salas	1532* 24 May
934	San Arba	1533 25 May
935	San Khams	1534 25 May
936	San Sita	1535 25 May
937	San Saba	1536* 24 May
938	San Samani	1537 25 May
939	San Tisa	1538 25 May
940	San Arbain Tisa mayat	1539 25 May
941	San Ahadi	1540* 24 May
942	San Isni	1541 25 May

Soor San Year	Arabic Year as it is Spoken	Western Date (Julian) of New Year	
943	San Salas	1542	25 May
944	San Arba	1543	25 May
945	San Khams	1544*	24 May
946	San Sita	1545	25 May
947	San Saba	1546	25 May
948	San Samani	1547	25 May
949	San Tisa	1548*	24 May
950	San Khamsin Tisa mayat	1549	25 May
951	San Ahadi	1550	25 May
952	San Isni	1551	25 May
953	San Salas	1552*	24 May
954	San Arba	1553	25 May
955	San Khams	1554	25 May
956	San Sita	1555	25 May
957	San Saba	1556*	24 May
958	San Samani	1557	25 May
959	San Tisa	1558	25 May
960	San Sitain Tisa mayat	1559	25 May
961	San Ahadi	1560*	24 May
962	San Isni	1561	25 May
963	San Salas	1562	25 May
964	San Arba	1563	25 May
965	San Khams	1564*	24 May
966	San Sita	1565	25 May
967	San Saba	1566	25 May
968	San Samani	1567	25 May
969	San Tisa	1568*	24 May
970	San Sabain Tisa mayat	1569	25 May
971	San Ahadi	1570	25 May
972	San Isni	1571	25 May
973	San Salas	1572*	24 May
974	San Arba	1573	25 May
975	San Khams	1574	25 May
976	San Sita	1575	25 May
977	San Saba	1576*	24 May
978	San Samani	1577	25 May
979	San Tisa	1578	25 May
980	San Samanin Tisa mayat	1579	25 May
981	San Ahadi	1580*	24 May
982	San Isni	1581	25 May
983	San Salas	1582	25 May

Soor San Year	Arabic Year as it is Spoken	Western Date (Julian)		(Gregorian) of New Year
984	San Arba	1583	25 May	4 Jun
985	San Khams	1584*	24 May	3 Jun
986	San Sita	1585	25 May	4 Jun
987	San Saba	1586	25 May	4 Jun
988	San Samani	1587	25 May	4 Jun
989	San Tisa	1588*	24 May	3 Jun
990	San Tisain Tisa mayat	1589	25 May	4 Jun
991	San Ahadi	1590	25 May	4 Jun
992	San Isni	1591	25 May	4 Jun
993	San Salas	1592*	24 May	3 Jun
994	San Arba	1593	25 May	4 Jun
995	San Khams	1594	25 May	4 Jun
996	San Sita	1595	25 May	4 Jun
997	San Saba	1596*	24 May	3 Jun
998	San Samani	1597	25 May	4 Jun
999	San Tisa	1598	25 May	4 Jun
1000	San Alf	1599	25 May	4 Jun
1001	San Ahadi	1600*	24 May	3 Jun
1002	San Isni	1601	25 May	4 Jun
1003	San Salas	1602	25 May	4 Jun
1004	San Arba	1603	25 May	4 Jun
1005	San Khams	1604*	24 May	3 Jun
1006	San Sita	1605	25 May	4 Jun
1007	San Saba	1606	25 May	4 Jun
1008	San Samani	1607	25 May	4 Jun
1009	San Tisa	1608*	24 May	3 Jun
1010	San Ashar-o-alf	1609	25 May	4 Jun
1011	San Ahadi	1610	25 May	4 Jun
1012	San Isni	1611	25 May	4 Jun
1013	San Salas	1612*	24 May	3 Jun
1014	San Arba	1613	25 May	4 Jun
1015	San Khams	1614	25 May	4 Jun
1016	San Sita	1615	25 May	4 Jun
1017	San Saba	1616*	24 May	3 Jun
1018	San Samani	1617	25 May	4 Jun
1019	San Tisa	1618	25 May	4 Jun
1020	San Ishrin-o-alf	1619	25 May	4 Jun
1021	San Ahadi	1620*	24 May	3 Jun
1022	San Isni	1621	25 May	4 Jun
1023	San Salas	1622	25 May	4 Jun
1024	San Arba	1623	25 May	4 Jun
1025	San Khams	1624*	24 May	3 Jun
1026	San Sita	1625	25 May	4 Jun
1027	San Saba	1626	25 May	4 Jun
1028	San Samani	1627	25 May	4 Jun
1029	San Tisa	1628*	24 May	3 Jun
1030	San Salatin-o-alf	1629	25 May	4 Jun
1031	San Ahadi	1630	25 May	4 Jun
1032	San Isni	1631	25 May	4 Jun
1033	San Salas	1632*	24 May	3 Jun
1034	San Arba	1633	25 May	4 Jun
1035	San Khams	1634	25 May	4 Jun

Soor San Year	Arabic Year as it is Spoken	Western Date (Julian) of New Year		(Gregorian)
1036	San Sita	1635	25 May	4 Jun
1037	San Saba	1636*	24 May	3 Jun
1038	San Samani	1637	25 May	4 Jun
1039	San Tisa	1638	25 May	4 Jun
1040	San Arbain-o-alf	1639	25 May	4 Jun
1041	San Ahadi	1640*	24 May	3 Jun
1042	San Isni	1641	25 May	4 Jun
1043	San Salas	1642	25 May	4 Jun
1044	San Arba	1643	25 May	4 Jun
1045	San Khams	1644*	24 May	3 Jun
1046	San Sita	1645	25 May	4 Jun
1047	San Saba	1646	25 May	4 Jun
1048	San Samani	1647	25 May	4 Jun
1049	San Tisa	1648*	24 May	3 Jun
1050	San Khamsin-o-alf	1649	25 May	4 Jun
1051	San Ahadi	1650	25 May	4 Jun
1052	San Isni	1651	25 May	4 Jun
1053	San Salas	1652*	24 May	3 Jun
1054	San Arba	1653	25 May	4 Jun
1055	San Khams	1654	25 May	4 Jun
1056	San Sita	1655	25 May	4 Jun
1057	San Saba	1656*	24 May	3 Jun
1058	San Samani	1657	25 May	4 Jun
1059	San Tisa	1658	25 May	4 Jun
1060	San Sitain-o-alf	1659	25 May	4 Jun
1061	San Ahadi	1660*	24 May	3 Jun
1062	San Isni	1661	25 May	4 Jun
1063	San Salas	1662	25 May	4 Jun
1064	San Arba	1663	25 May	4 Jun
1065	San Khams	1664*	24 May	3 Jun
1066	San Sita	1665	25 May	4 Jun
1067	San Saba	1666	25 May	4 Jun
1068	San Samani	1667	25 May	4 Jun
1069	San Tisa	1668*	24 May	3 Jun
1070	San Sabain-o-alf	1669	25 May	4 Jun
1071	San Ahadi	1670	25 May	4 Jun
1072	San Isni	1671	25 May	4 Jun
1073	San Salas	1672*	24 May	3 Jun
1074	San Arba	1673	25 May	4 Jun
1075	San Khams	1674	25 May	4 Jun
1076	San Sita	1675	25 May	4 Jun
1077	San Saba	1676*	24 May	3 Jun
1078	San Samani	1677	25 May	4 Jun
1079	San Tisa	1678	25 May	4 Jun
1080	San Samanin-o-alf	1679	25 May	4 Jun
1081	San Ahadi	1680*	24 May	3 Jun
1082	San Isni	1681	25 May	4 Jun
1083	San Salas	1682	25 May	4 Jun
1084	San Arba	1683	25 May	4 Jun
1085	San Khams	1684*	24 May	3 Jun
1086	San Sita	1685	25 May	4 Jun
1087	San Saba	1686	25 May	4 Jun
1088	San Samani	1687	25 May	4 Jun
1089	San Tisa	1688*	24 May	3 Jun
1090	San Tisain-o-alf	1689	25 May	4 Jun
1091	San Ahadi	1690	25 May	4 Jun
1092	San Isni	1691	25 May	4 Jun
1093	San Salas	1692*	24 May	3 Jun
1094	San Arba	1693	25 May	4 Jun
1095	San Khams	1694	25 May	4 Jun
1096	San Sita	1695	25 May	4 Jun
1097	San Saba	1696*	24 May	3 Jun
1098	San Samani	1697	25 May	4 Jun
1099	San Tisa	1698	25 May	4 Jun
1100	San Mayat-o-alf	1699	25 May	4 Jun
1101	San Ahadi	1700	24 May	4 Jun
1102	San Isni	1701	25 May	5 Jun
1103	San Salas	1702	25 May	5 Jun
1104	San Arba	1703	25 May	5 Jun
1105	San Khams	1704*	24 May	4 Jun
1106	San Sita	1705	25 May	5 Jun
1107	San Saba	1706	25 May	5 Jun
1108	San Samani	1707	25 May	5 Jun
1109	San Tisa	1708*	24 May	4 Jun
1110	San Ashar mayat-o-alf	1709	25 May	5 Jun
1111	San Ahadi	1710	25 May	5 Jun
1112	San Isni	1711	25 May	5 Jun
1113	San Salas	1712*	24 May	4 Jun
1114	San Arba	1713	25 May	5 Jun
1115	San Khams	1714	25 May	5 Jun
1116	San Sita	1715	25 May	5 Jun
1117	San Saba	1716*	24 May	4 Jun
1118	San Samani	1717	25 May	5 Jun
1119	San Tisa	1718	25 May	5 Jun
1120	San Ishrin mayat-o-alf	1719	25 May	5 Jun
1121	San Ahadi	1720*	24 May	4 Jun
1122	San Isni	1721	25 May	5 Jun
1123	San Salas	1722	25 May	5 Jun
1124	San Arba	1723	25 May	5 Jun
1125	San Khams	1724*	24 May	4 Jun
1126	San Sita	1725	25 May	5 Jun
1127	San Saba	1726	25 May	5 Jun
1128	San Samani	1727	25 May	5 Jun
1129	San Tisa	1728*	24 May	4 Jun
1130	San Salatin mayat-o-alf	1729	25 May	5 Jun
1131	San Ahadi	1730	25 May	5 Jun
1132	San Isni	1731	25 May	5 Jun
1133	San Salas	1732*	24 May	4 Jun
1134	San Arba	1733	25 May	5 Jun

Soor San Year	Arabic Year as it is Spoken	Western Date (Julian)	(Gregorian) of New Year	
1135	San Khams	25 May	5 Jun	1734
1136	San Sita	25 May	5 Jun	1735
1137	San Saba	24 May	4 Jun	1736*
1138	San Samani	25 May	5 Jun	1737
1139	San Tisa	25 May	5 Jun	1738
1140	San Arbain mayat-o-alf	25 May	5 Jun	1739
1141	San Ahadi	24 May	4 Jun	1740*
1142	San Isni	25 May	5 Jun	1741
1143	San Salas	25 May	5 Jun	1742
1144	San Arba	25 May	5 Jun	1743
1145	San Khams	24 May	4 Jun	1744*
1146	San Sita	25 May	5 Jun	1745
1147	San Saba	25 May	5 Jun	1746
1148	San Samani	25 May	5 Jun	1747
1149	San Tisa	24 May	4 Jun	1748*
1150	San Khamsin mayat-o-alf	25 May	5 Jun	1749
1151	San Ahadi	25 May	5 Jun	1750
1152	San Isni	25 May	5 Jun	1751
1153	San Salas	24 May	4 Jun	1752*

Soor San Year	Arabic Year as it is Spoken	Western Date (Gregorian) of New Year	
1154	San Arba	Jun 5	1753
1155	San Khams	Jun 5	1754
1156	San Sita	Jun 5	1755
1157	San Saba	Jun 4	1756*
1158	San Samani	Jun 5	1757
1159	San Tisa	Jun 5	1758
1160	San Sitain mayat-o-alf	Jun 5	1759
1161	San Ahadi	Jun 4	1760*
1162	San Isni	Jun 5	1761
1163	San Salas	Jun 5	1762
1164	San Arba	Jun 5	1763
1165	San Khams	Jun 4	1764*
1166	San Sita	Jun 5	1765
1167	San Saba	Jun 5	1766
1168	San Samani	Jun 5	1767
1169	San Tisa	Jun 4	1768*
1170	San Sabain mayat-o-alf	Jun 5	1769
1171	San Ahadi	Jun 5	1770
1172	San Isni	Jun 5	1771
1173	San Salas	Jun 4	1772*
1174	San Arba	Jun 5	1773
1175	San Khams	Jun 5	1774
1176	San Sita	Jun 5	1775

Soor San Year	Arabic Year as it is Spoken	Western Date (Gregorian) of New Year	
1177	San Saba	1776*	4 Jun
1178	San Samani	1777	5 Jun
1179	San Tisa	1778	5 Jun
1180	San Samanin mayat-o-alf	1779	5 Jun
1181	San Ahadi	1780*	4 Jun
1182	San Isni	1781	5 Jun
1183	San Salas	1782	5 Jun
1184	San Arba	1783	5 Jun
1185	San Khams	1784*	4 Jun
1186	San Sita	1785	5 Jun
1187	San Saba	1786	5 Jun
1188	San Samani	1787	5 Jun
1189	San Tisa	1788*	4 Jun
1190	San Tisain mayat-o-alf	1789	5 Jun
1191	San Ahadi	1790	5 Jun
1192	San Isni	1791	5 Jun
1193	San Salas	1792*	4 Jun
1194	San Arba	1793	5 Jun
1195	San Khams	1794	5 Jun
1196	San Sita	1795	5 Jun
1197	San Saba	1796*	4 Jun
1198	San Samani	1797	5 Jun
1199	San Tisa	1798	5 Jun
1200	San Miatin-o-alf	1799	5 Jun
1201	San Ahadi	1800	5 Jun
1202	San Isni	1801	6 Jun
1203	San Salas	1802	6 Jun
1204	San Arba	1803	6 Jun
1205	San Khams	1804*	5 Jun
1206	San Sita	1805	6 Jun
1207	San Saba	1806	6 Jun
1208	San Samani	1807	6 Jun
1209	San Tisa	1808*	5 Jun
1210	San Ashar Miatin-o-alf	1809	6 Jun
1211	San Ahadi	1810	6 Jun
1212	San Isni	1811	6 Jun
1213	San Salas	1812*	5 Jun
1214	San Arba	1813	6 Jun
1215	San Khams	1814	6 Jun
1216	San Sita	1815	6 Jun
1217	San Saba	1816*	5 Jun
1218	San Samani	1817	6 Jun
1219	San Tisa	1818	6 Jun
1220	San Ishrin Miatin-o-alf	1819	6 Jun
1221	San Ahadi	1820*	5 Jun
1222	San Isni	1821	6 Jun
1223	San Salas	1822	6 Jun

Soor San Year	Arabic Year as it is Spoken	Western Date (Gregorian) of New Year	
1224	San Arba	1823	6 Jun
1225	San Khams	1824*	5 Jun
1226	San Sita	1825	6 Jun
1227	San Saba	1826	6 Jun
1228	San Samani	1827	6 Jun
1229	San Tisa	1828*	5 Jun
1230	San Salatin Miatin-o-alf	1829	6 Jun
1231	San Ahadi	1830	6 Jun
1232	San Isni	1831	6 Jun
1233	San Salas	1832*	5 Jun
1234	San Arba	1833	6 Jun
1235	San Khams	1834	6 Jun
1236	San Sita	1835	6 Jun
1237	San Saba	1836*	5 Jun
1238	San Samani	1837	6 Jun
1239	San Tisa	1838	6 Jun
1240	San Arbain miatin-o-alf	1839	6 Jun
1241	San Ahadi	1840*	5 Jun
1242	San Isni	1841	6 Jun
1243	San Salas	1842	6 Jun
1244	San Arba	1843	6 Jun
1245	San Khams	1844*	5 Jun
1246	San Sita	1845	6 Jun
1247	San Saba	1846	6 Jun
1248	San Samani	1847	6 Jun
1249	San Tisa	1848*	5 Jun
1250	San Khamsin miatin-o-alf	1849	6 Jun
1251	San Ahadi	1850	6 Jun
1252	San Isni	1851	6 Jun
1253	San Salas	1852*	5 Jun
1254	San Arba	1853	6 Jun
1255	San Khams	1854	6 Jun
1256	San Sita	1855	6 Jun
1257	San Saba	1856*	5 Jun
1258	San Samani	1857	6 Jun
1259	San Tisa	1858	6 Jun
1260	San Sitain miatin-o-alf	1859	6 Jun
1261	San Ahadi	1860*	5 Jun
1262	San Isni	1861	6 Jun
1263	San Salas	1862	6 Jun
1264	San Arba	1863	6 Jun
1265	San Khams	1864*	5 Jun
1266	San Sita	1865	6 Jun
1267	San Saba	1866	6 Jun
1268	San Samani	1867	6 Jun
1269	San Tisa	1868*	5 Jun
1270	San Sabain miatin-o-alf	1869	6 Jun
1271	San Ahadi	1870	6 Jun
1272	San Isni	1871	6 Jun
1273	San Salas	1872*	5 Jun
1274	San Arba	1873	6 Jun
1275	San Khams	1874	6 Jun
1276	San Sita	1875	6 Jun
1277	San Saba	1876*	5 Jun
1278	San Samani	1877	6 Jun
1279	San Tisa	1878	6 Jun
1280	San Samanin miatin-o-alf	1879	6 Jun
1281	San Ahadi	1880*	5 Jun
1282	San Isni	1881	6 Jun
1283	San Salas	1882	6 Jun
1284	San Arba	1883	6 Jun
1285	San Khams	1884*	5 Jun
1286	San Sita	1885	6 Jun
1287	San Saba	1886	6 Jun
1288	San Samani	1887	6 Jun
1289	San Tisa	1888*	5 Jun
1290	San Tisain miatin-o-alf	1889	6 Jun
1291	San Ahadi	1890	6 Jun
1292	San Isni	1891	6 Jun
1293	San Salas	1892*	5 Jun
1294	San Arba	1893	6 Jun
1295	San Khams	1894	6 Jun
1296	San Sita	1895	6 Jun
1297	San Saba	1896*	5 Jun
1298	San Samani	1897	6 Jun
1299	San Tisa	1898	6 Jun
1300	San Salas miatin-o-alf	1899	6 Jun
1301	San Ahadi	1900	6 Jun
1302	San Isni	1901	7 Jun
1303	San Salas	1902	7 Jun
1304	San Arba	1903	7 Jun
1305	San Khams	1904*	6 Jun
1306	San Sita	1905	7 Jun
1307	San Saba	1906	7 Jun
1308	San Samani	1907	7 Jun
1309	San Tisa	1908*	6 Jun
1310	San Ashar Salas miatin-o-alf	1909	7 Jun
1311	San Ahadi	1910	7 Jun
1312	San Isni	1911	7 Jun
1313	San Salas	1912*	6 Jun
1314	San Arba	1913	7 Jun

Soor San Year	Arabic Year as it is Spoken	Western Date (Gregorian) of New Year	
1315	San Khams	1914	7 Jun
1316	San Sita	1915	7 Jun
1317	San Saba	1916*	6 Jun
1318	San Samani	1917	7 Jun
1319	San Tisa	1918	7 Jun
1320	San Ishrin Salas miatin-o-alf	1919	7 Jun
1321	San Ahadi	1920*	6 Jun
1322	San Isni	1921	7 Jun
1323	San Salas	1922	7 Jun
1324	San Arba	1923	7 Jun
1325	San Khams	1924*	6 Jun
1326	San Sita	1925	7 Jun
1327	San Saba	1926	7 Jun
1328	San Samani	1927	7 Jun
1329	San Tisa	1928*	6 Jun
1330	San Salatin Salas miatin-o-alf	1929	7 Jun
1331	San Ahadi	1930	7 Jun
1332	San Isni	1931	7 Jun
1333	San Salas	1932*	6 Jun
1334	San Arba	1933	7 Jun
1335	San Khams	1934	7 Jun
1336	San Sita	1935	7 Jun
1337	San Saba	1936*	6 Jun
1338	San Samani	1937	7 Jun
1339	San Tisa	1938	7 Jun
1340	San Arbain Salas mayat-o-alf	1939	7 Jun
1341	San Ahadi	1940*	6 Jun
1342	San Isni	1941	7 Jun
1343	San Salas	1942	7 Jun
1344	San Arba	1943	7 Jun
1345	San Khams	1944*	6 Jun
1346	San Sita	1945	7 Jun
1347	San Saba	1946	7 Jun
1348	San Samani	1947	7 Jun
1349	San Tisa	1948*	6 Jun
1350	San Khamsin Salas mayat-o-alf	1949	7 Jun
1351	San Ahadi	1950	7 Jun
1352	San Isni	1951	7 Jun
1353	San Salas	1952*	6 Jun
1354	San Arba	1953	7 Jun
1355	San Khams	1954	7 Jun
1356	San Sita	1955	7 Jun
1357	San Saba	1956*	6 Jun
1358	San Samani	1957	7 Jun

Soor San Year	Arabic Year as it is Spoken	Western Date (Gregorian) of New Year	
1359	San Tisa	1958	7 Jun
1360	San Sitain Salas mayat-o-alf	1959	7 Jun
1361	San Ahadi	1960*	6 Jun
1362	San Isni	1961	7 Jun
1363	San Salas	1962	7 Jun
1364	San Arba	1963	7 Jun
1365	San Khams	1964*	6 Jun
1366	San Sita	1965	7 Jun
1367	San Saba	1966	7 Jun
1368	San Samani	1967	7 Jun
1369	San Tisa	1968*	6 Jun
1370	San Sabain Salas mayat-o-alf	1969	7 Jun
1371	San Ahadi	1970	7 Jun
1372	San Isni	1971	7 Jun
1373	San Salas	1972*	6 Jun
1374	San Arba	1973	7 Jun
1375	San Khams	1974	7 Jun
1376	San Sita	1975	7 Jun
1377	San Saba	1976*	6 Jun
1378	San Samani	1977	7 Jun
1379	San Tisa	1978	7 Jun
1380	San Samanin Salas mayat-o-alf	1979	7 Jun
1381	San Ahadi	1980*	6 Jun
1382	San Isni	1981	7 Jun
1383	San Salas	1982	7 Jun
1384	San Arba	1983	7 Jun
1385	San Khams	1984*	6 Jun
1386	San Sita	1985	7 Jun
1387	San Saba	1986	7 Jun
1388	San Samani	1987	7 Jun
1389	San Tisa	1988*	6 Jun
1390	San Tisain Salas mayat-o-alf	1989	7 Jun
1391	San Ahadi	1990	7 Jun
1392	San Isni	1991	7 Jun
1393	San Salas	1992*	6 Jun
1394	San Arba	1993	7 Jun
1395	San Khams	1994	7 Jun
1396	San Sita	1995	7 Jun
1397	San Saba	1996*	6 Jun
1398	San Samani	1997	7 Jun
1399	San Tisa	1998	7 Jun
1400	San Arba mayat-o-alf	1999	7 Jun
1401	San Ahadi	1200*	6 Jun

ZOROASTRIAN CALENDAR

The Zoroastrians began their calendar with the birth of their founder, the prophet Zoroaster, on March 3, 389 B.C. The calendar was a vague solar year of 365 days. It contained 12 months of 30 days each, with five additional days at the end of the year. It did not use a leap year, nor did it divide the months into weeks or decades (10-day "week"). Each of the 30 days had its own name and was spoken of in the same way we use a number for the month day name.

The months were called:

1. Furvurdeen	5. Amerdad	9. Adur
2. Ardibehest	6. Sherever	10. Deh
3. Khordad	7. Moher	11. Bahman
4. Tir	8. Aban	12. Aspendadmad

The days of the month are called:

1. Hormazd	6. Khordad	11. Khurshed	16. Meher	21. Ram	26. Ashtad
2. Bahman	7. Amerdad	12. Mhor	17. Serosh	22. Guvad	27. Asman
3. Ardibehest	8. Depadur	13. Tir	18. Rashne	23. Depdin	28. Zamiad
4. Shrerever	9. Adur	14. Gosh	19. Furvurdeen	24. Din	29. Maharesphand
5. Aspundad	10. Aban	15. Depmhel	20. Behram	25. Ashasang	30. Aniram

The five extra days at the end of the year are called:

1. Ahnuvud 2. Ushtuvad 3. Spentamud
4. Vohi-Kshusthra and 5. Vahishtusht

The Zoroastrian calendar was well established over all of Asia Minor by 300 B.C. and, during the subsequent 23 centuries, has continued to be used wherever Zoroaster's teachings prevailed. The only exception is among the Persian Zoroastrians who, about the 7th century A.D. began to use the calendar of Yezdezred. The Zoroastrian calendar today is used primarily in the Bombay district of India, although it is also employed in some other isolated pockets in Asia Minor.

ZOROASTERIAN CALENDAR

Zoroasterian Year	Western Date (Julian) of New Year	Zoroasterian Year	Western Date (Julian) of New Year	Zoroasterian Year	Western Date (Julian) of New Year	Zoroasterian Year	Western Date (Julian) of New Year
1	388 3 Mar	21	368 26 Feb	41	348 21 Feb	61	328 16 Feb
2	387 3 Mar	22	367 26 Feb	42	347 21 Feb	62	327 16 Feb
3	386 3 Mar	23	366 26 Feb	43	346 21 Feb	63	326 16 Feb
4	385* 3 Mar	24	365* 26 Feb	44	345* 21 Feb	64	325* 16 Feb
5	384 2 Mar	25	364 25 Feb	45	344 20 Feb	65	324 15 Feb
6	383 2 Mar	26	363 25 Feb	46	343 20 Feb	66	323 15 Feb
7	382 2 Mar	27	362 25 Feb	47	342 20 Feb	67	322 15 Feb
8	381* 2 Mar	28	361* 25 Feb	48	341* 20 Feb	68	321* 15 Feb
9	380 1 Mar	29	360 24 Feb	49	340 19 Feb	69	320 14 Feb
10	379 1 Mar	30	359 24 Feb	50	339 19 Feb	70	319 14 Feb
11	378 1 Mar	31	358 24 Feb	51	338 19 Feb	71	318 14 Feb
12	377* 1 Feb	32	357* 24 Feb	52	337* 19 Feb	72	317* 14 Feb
13	376 28 Feb	33	356 23 Feb	53	336 18 Feb	73	316 13 Feb
14	375 28 Feb	34	355 23 Feb	54	335 18 Feb	74	315 13 Feb
15	374 28 Feb	35	354 23 Feb	55	334 18 Feb	75	314 13 Feb
16	373* 28 Feb	36	353* 23 Feb	56	333* 18 Feb	76	313* 13 Feb
17	372 27 Feb	37	352 22 Feb	57	332 17 Feb	77	312 12 Feb
18	371 27 Feb	38	351 22 Feb	58	331 17 Feb	78	311 12 Feb
19	370 27 Feb	39	350 22 Feb	59	330 17 Feb	79	310 12 Feb
20	369* 27 Feb	40	349* 22 Feb	60	329* 17 Feb	80	309* 12 Feb

Zoroasterian Year	Western Date (Julian) of New Year	
81	308	11 Feb
82	307	11 Feb
83	306	11 Feb
84	305*	11 Feb
85	304	10 Feb
86	303	10 Feb
87	304	10 Feb
88	301*	10 Feb
89	300	9 Feb
90	299	9 Feb
91	298	9 Feb
92	297*	9 Feb
93	296	8 Feb
94	295	8 Feb
95	294	8 Feb
96	293*	8 Feb
97	292	7 Feb
98	291	7 Feb
99	290	7 Feb
100	289*	7 Feb
101	288	6 Feb
102	287	6 Feb
103	286	6 Feb
104	285*	6 Feb
105	284	5 Feb
106	283	5 Feb
107	282	5 Feb
108	281*	5 Feb
109	280	4 Feb
110	279	4 Feb
111	278	4 Feb
112	277*	4 Feb
113	276	3 Feb
114	275	3 Feb
115	274	3 Feb
116	273*	3 Feb
117	272	2 Feb
118	271	2 Feb
119	270	2 Feb
120	269*	2 Feb
121	268	1 Feb
122	267	1 Feb
123	266	1 Feb
124	265*	1 Feb
125	264	31 Jan
126	263	31 Jan
127	262	31 Jan
128	261*	31 Jan
129	260	30 Jan
130	259	30 Jan
131	258	30 Jan
132	257*	30 Jan
133	256	29 Jan
134	255	29 Jan
135	254	29 Jan
136	253*	29 Jan
137	252	28 Jan
138	251	28 Jan
139	250	28 Jan
140	249*	28 Jan
141	248	27 Jan
142	247	27 Jan
143	246	27 Jan
144	245*	27 Jan
145	244	26 Jan
146	243	26 Jan
147	242	26 Jan
148	241*	26 Jan
149	240	25 Jan
150	239	25 Jan
151	238	25 Jan
152	237*	25 Jan
153	236	24 Jan
154	235	24 Jan
155	234	24 Jan
156	233*	24 Jan
157	232	23 Jan
158	231	23 Jan
159	230	23 Jan
160	229*	23 Jan
161	228	22 Jan
162	227	22 Jan
163	226	22 Jan
164	225*	22 Jan
165	224	21 Jan
166	223	21 Jan
167	222	21 Jan
168	221*	21 Jan
169	220	20 Jan
170	219	20 Jan
171	218	20 Jan
172	217*	20 Jan
173	216	19 Jan
174	215	19 Jan
175	214	19 Jan
176	213*	19 Jan
177	212	18 Jan
178	211	18 Jan
179	210	18 Jan
180	209*	18 Jan
181	208	17 Jan
182	207	17 Jan
183	206	17 Jan
184	205*	17 Jan
185	204	16 Jan
186	203	16 Jan
187	202	16 Jan
188	201*	16 Jan
189	200	15 Jan
190	199	15 Jan
191	198	15 Jan
192	197*	15 Jan
193	196	14 Jan
194	195	14 Jan
195	194	14 Jan
196	193*	14 Jan
197	192	13 Jan
198	191	13 Jan
199	190	13 Jan
200	189*	13 Jan
201	188	12 Jan
202	187	12 Jan
203	186	12 Jan
204	185*	12 Jan
205	184	11 Jan
206	183	11 Jan
207	182	11 Jan
208	181*	11 Jan
209	180	10 Jan
210	179	10 Jan
211	178	10 Jan
212	177*	10 Jan
213	176	9 Jan
214	175	9 Jan
215	174	9 Jan
216	173*	9 Jan
217	172	8 Jan
218	171	8 Jan
219	170	8 Jan
220	169*	8 Jan
221	168	7 Jan
222	167	7 Jan
223	166	7 Jan
224	165*	7 Jan
225	164	6 Jan
226	163	6 Jan
227	162	6 Jan
228	161*	6 Jan
229	160	5 Jan
230	159	5 Jan
231	158	5 Jan
232	157*	5 Jan
233	156	4 Jan
234	155	4 Jan
235	154	4 Jan
236	153*	4 Jan
237	152	3 Jan
238	151	3 Jan
239	150	3 Jan
240	149*	3 Jan
241	148	2 Jan
242	147	2 Jan
243	146	2 Jan
244	145*	2 Jan
245	144	1 Jan
246	143	1 Jan
247	142	1 Jan
248	141*	1 Dec
249	141*	31 Dec
250	140	31 Dec
251	139	31 Dec
252	138	31 Dec
253	137*	30 Dec
254	136	30 Dec
255	135	30 Dec
256	134	30 Dec
257	133*	29 Dec
258	132	29 Dec
259	131	29 Dec
260	130	29 Dec
261	129*	28 Dec
262	128	28 Dec
263	127	28 Dec
264	126	28 Dec
265	125*	27 Dec
266	124	27 Dec
267	123	27 Dec
268	122	27 Dec
269	121*	26 Dec
270	120	26 Dec
271	119	26 Dec
272	118	26 Dec
273	117*	25 Dec
274	116	25 Dec
275	115	25 Dec
276	114	25 Dec
277	113*	24 Dec
278	112	24 Dec
279	111	24 Dec
280	110	24 Dec
281	109*	23 Dec
282	108	23 Dec
283	107	23 Dec
284	106	23 Dec
285	105*	22 Dec
286	104	22 Dec
287	103	22 Dec
288	102	22 Dec

Zoroasterian Year	Western Date (Julian) of New Year		Zoroasterian Year	Western Date (Julian) of New Year		Zoroasterian Year	Western Date (Julian) of New Year		Zoroasterian Year	Western Date (Julian) of New Year	
289	101*	21 Dec	341	49*	8 Dec	393	4*	25 Nov	445	56*	12 Nov
290	100	21 Dec	342	48	8 Dec	394	5	25 Nov	446	57	12 Nov
291	99	21 Dec	343	47	8 Dec	395	6	25 Nov	447	58	12 Nov
292	98	21 Dec	344	46	8 Dec	396	7	25 Nov	448	59	12 Nov
293	97*	20 Dec	345	45*	7 Dec	397	8*	24 Nov	449	60*	11 Nov
294	96	20 Dec	346	44	7 Dec	398	9	24 Nov	450	61	11 Nov
295	95	20 Dec	347	43	7 Dec	399	10	24 Nov	451	62	11 Nov
296	94	20 Dec	348	42	7 Dec	400	11	24 Nov	452	63	11 Nov
297	93*	19 Dec	349	41*	6 Dec	401	12*	23 Nov	453	64*	10 Nov
298	92	19 Dec	350	40	6 Dec	402	13	23 Nov	454	65	10 Nov
299	91	19 Dec	351	39	6 Dec	403	14	23 Nov	455	66	10 Nov
300	90	19 Dec	352	38	6 Dec	404	15	23 Nov	456	67	10 Nov
301	89*	18 Dec	353	37*	5 Dec	405	16*	22 Nov	457	68*	9 Nov
302	88	18 Dec	354	36	5 Dec	406	17	22 Nov	458	69	9 Nov
303	87	18 Dec	355	35	5 Dec	407	18	22 Nov	459	70	9 Nov
304	86	18 Dec	356	34	5 Dec	408	19	22 Nov	460	71	9 Nov
305	85*	17 Dec	357	33*	4 Dec	409	20*	21 Nov	461	72*	8 Nov
306	84	17 Dec	358	32	4 Dec	410	21	21 Nov	462	73	8 Nov
307	83	17 Dec	359	31	4 Dec	411	22	21 Nov	463	74	8 Nov
308	82	17 Dec	360	30	4 Dec	412	23	21 Nov	464	75	8 Nov
309	81*	16 Dec	361	29*	3 Dec	413	24*	20 Nov	465	76*	7 Nov
310	80	16 Dec	362	28	3 Dec	414	25	20 Nov	466	77	7 Nov
311	79	16 Dec	363	27	3 Dec	415	26	20 Nov	467	78	7 Nov
312	78	16 Dec	364	26	3 Dec	416	27	20 Nov	468	79	7 Nov
313	77*	15 Dec	365	25*	2 Dec	417	28*	19 Nov	469	80*	6 Nov
314	76	15 Dec	366	24	2 Dec	418	29	19 Nov	470	81	6 Nov
315	75	15 Dec	367	23	2 Dec	419	30	19 Nov	471	82	6 Nov
316	74	15 Dec	368	22	2 Dec	420	31	19 Nov	472	83	6 Nov
317	73*	14 Dec	369	21*	1 Dec	421	32*	18 Nov	473	84*	5 Nov
318	72	14 Dec	370	20	1 Dec	422	33	18 Nov	474	85	5 Nov
319	71	14 Dec	371	19	1 Dec	423	34	18 Nov	475	86	5 Nov
320	70	14 Dec	372	18	1 Dec	424	35	18 Nov	476	87	5 Nov
321	69*	13 Dec	373	17*	30 Nov	425	36*	17 Nov	477	88*	4 Nov
322	68	13 Dec	374	16	30 Nov	426	37	17 Nov	478	89	4 Nov
323	67	13 Dec	375	15	30 Nov	427	38	17 Nov	479	90	4 Nov
324	66	13 Dec	376	14	30 Nov	428	39	17 Nov	480	91	4 Nov
325	65*	12 Dec	377	13*	29 Nov	429	40*	16 Nov	481	92*	3 Nov
326	64	12 Dec	378	12	29 Nov	430	41	16 Nov	482	93	3 Nov
327	63	12 Dec	379	11	29 Nov	431	42	16 Nov	483	94	3 Nov
328	62	12 Dec	380	10	29 Nov	432	43	16 Nov	484	95	3 Nov
329	61*	11 Dec	381	9*	28 Nov	433	44*	15 Nov	485	96*	2 Nov
330	60	11 Dec	382	8	28 Nov	434	45	15 Nov	486	97	2 Nov
331	59	11 Dec	383	7	28 Nov	435	46	15 Nov	487	98	2 Nov
332	58	11 Dec	384	6	28 Nov	436	47	15 Nov	488	99	2 Nov
333	57*	10 Dec	385	5*	27 Nov	437	48*	14 Nov	489	100*	1 Nov
334	56	10 Dec	386	4	27 Nov	438	49	14 Nov	490	101	1 Nov
335	55	10 Dec	387	3	27 Nov	439	50	14 Nov	491	102	1 Nov
336	54	10 Dec	388	2	27 Nov	440	51	14 Nov	492	103	1 Nov
337	53*	9 Dec	389	1*	26 Nov	441	52*	13 Nov	493	104*	31 Oct
338	52	9 Dec	390	1	26 Nov	442	53	13 Nov	494	105	31 Oct
339	51	9 Dec	391	2	26 Nov	443	54	13 Nov	495	106	31 Oct
340	50	9 Dec	392	3	26 Nov	444	55	13 Nov	496	107	31 Oct

Zoroasterian Year	Western Date (Julian) of New Year	Zoroasterian Year	Western Date (Julian) of New Year	Zoroasterian Year	Western Date (Julian) of New Year	Zoroasterian Year	Western Date (Julian) of New Year
497	108* 30 Oct	549	160* 17 Oct	601	212* 4 Oct	653	264* 21 Sep
498	109 30 Oct	550	161 17 Oct	602	213 4 Oct	654	265 21 Sep
499	110 30 Oct	551	162 17 Oct	603	214 4 Oct	655	266 21 Sep
500	111 30 Oct	552	163 17 Oct	604	215 4 Oct	656	267 21 Sep
501	112* 29 Oct	553	164* 16 Oct	605	216* 3 Oct	657	268* 20 Sep
502	113 29 Oct	554	165 16 Oct	606	217 3 Oct	658	269 20 Sep
503	114 29 Oct	555	166 16 Oct	607	218 3 Oct	659	270 20 Sep
504	115 29 Oct	556	167 16 Oct	608	219 3 Oct	660	271 20 Sep
505	116* 28 Oct	557	168* 15 Oct	609	220* 2 Oct	661	272* 19 Sep
506	117 28 Oct	558	169 15 Oct	610	221 2 Oct	662	273 19 Sep
507	118 28 Oct	559	170 15 Oct	611	222 2 Oct	663	274 19 Sep
508	119 28 Oct	560	171 15 Oct	612	223 2 Oct	664	275 19 Sep
509	120* 27 Oct	561	172* 14 Oct	613	224* 1 Oct	665	276* 18 Sep
510	121 27 Oct	562	173 14 Oct	614	225 1 Oct	666	277 18 Sep
511	122 27 Oct	563	174 14 Oct	615	226 1 Oct	667	278 18 Sep
512	123 27 Oct	564	175 14 Oct	616	227 1 Oct	668	279 18 Sep
513	124* 26 Oct	565	176* 13 Oct	617	228* 30 Sep	669	280* 17 Sep
514	125 26 Oct	566	177 13 Oct	618	229 30 Sep	670	281 17 Sep
515	126 26 Oct	567	178 13 Oct	619	230 30 Sep	671	282 17 Sep
516	127 26 Oct	568	179 13 Oct	620	231 30 Sep	672	283 17 Sep
517	128* 25 Oct	569	180* 12 Oct	621	232* 29 Sep	673	284* 16 Sep
518	129 25 Oct	570	181 12 Oct	622	233 29 Sep	674	285 16 Sep
519	130 25 Oct	571	182 12 Oct	623	234 29 Sep	675	286 16 Sep
520	131 25 Oct	572	183 12 Oct	624	235 29 Sep	676	287 16 Sep
521	132* 24 Oct	573	184* 11 Oct	625	236* 28 Sep	677	288* 15 Sep
522	133 24 Oct	574	185 11 Oct	626	237 28 Sep	678	289 15 Sep
523	134 24 Oct	575	186 11 Oct	627	238 28 Sep	679	290 15 Sep
524	135 24 Oct	576	187 11 Oct	628	239 28 Sep	680	291 15 Sep
525	136* 23 Oct	577	188* 10 Oct	629	240* 27 Sep	681	292* 14 Sep
526	137 23 Oct	578	189 10 Oct	630	241 27 Sep	682	293 14 Sep
527	138 23 Oct	579	190 10 Oct	631	242 27 Sep	683	294 14 Sep
528	139 23 Oct	580	191 10 Oct	632	243 27 Sep	684	295 14 Sep
529	140* 22 Oct	581	192* 9 Oct	633	244* 26 Sep	685	296* 13 Sep
530	141 22 Oct	582	193 9 Oct	634	245 26 Sep	686	297 13 Sep
531	142 22 Oct	583	194 9 Oct	635	246 26 Sep	687	298 13 Sep
532	143 22 Oct	584	195 9 Oct	636	247 26 Sep	688	299 13 Sep
533	144* 21 Oct	585	196* 8 Oct	637	248* 25 Sep	689	300* 12 Sep
534	145 21 Oct	586	197 8 Oct	638	249 25 Sep	690	301 12 Sep
535	146 21 Oct	587	198 8 Oct	639	250 25 Sep	691	302 12 Sep
536	147 21 Oct	588	199 8 Oct	640	251 25 Sep	692	303 12 Sep
537	148* 20 Oct	589	200* 7 Oct	641	252* 24 Sep	693	304* 11 Sep
538	149 20 Oct	590	201 7 Oct	642	253 24 Sep	694	305 11 Sep
539	150 20 Oct	591	202 7 Oct	643	254 24 Sep	695	306 11 Sep
540	151 20 Oct	592	203 7 Oct	644	255 24 Sep	696	307 11 Sep
541	152* 19 Oct	593	204* 6 Oct	645	256* 23 Sep	697	308* 10 Sep
542	153 19 Oct	594	205 6 Oct	646	257 23 Sep	698	309 10 Sep
543	154 19 Oct	595	206 6 Oct	647	258 23 Sep	699	310 10 Sep
544	155 19 Oct	596	207 6 Oct	648	259 23 Sep	700	311 10 Sep
545	156* 18 Oct	597	208* 5 Oct	649	260* 22 Sep	701	312* 9 Sep
546	157 18 Oct	598	209 5 Oct	650	261 22 Sep	702	313 9 Sep
547	158 18 Oct	599	210 5 Oct	651	262 22 Sep	703	314 9 Sep
548	159 18 Oct	600	211 5 Oct	652	263 22 Sep	704	315 9 Sep

Zoroastrian Year	Western Date (Julian) of New Year	Zoroastrian Year	Western Date (Julian) of New Year	Zoroastrian Year	Western Date (Julian) of New Year	Zoroastrian Year	Western Date (Julian) of New Year
705	316* 8 Sep	757	368* 26 Aug	809	420* 13 Aug	861	472* 31 Jul
706	317 8 Sep	758	369 26 Aug	810	421 13 Aug	862	473 31 Jul
707	318 8 Sep	759	370 26 Aug	811	422 13 Aug	863	474 31 Jul
708	319 8 Sep	760	371 26 Aug	812	423 13 Aug	864	475 31 Jul
709	320* 7 Sep	761	372* 25 Aug	813	424* 12 Aug	865	476* 30 Jul
710	321 7 Sep	762	373 25 Aug	814	425 12 Aug	866	477 30 Jul
711	322 7 Sep	763	374 25 Aug	815	426 12 Aug	867	478 30 Jul
712	323 7 Sep	764	375 25 Aug	816	427 12 Aug	868	479 30 Jul
713	324* 6 Sep	765	376* 24 Aug	817	428* 11 Aug	869	480* 29 Jul
714	325 6 Sep	766	377 24 Aug	818	429 11 Aug	870	481 29 Jul
715	326 6 Sep	767	378 24 Aug	819	430 11 Aug	871	482 29 Jul
716	327 6 Sep	768	379 24 Aug	820	431 11 Aug	872	483 29 Jul
717	328* 5 Sep	769	380* 23 Aug	821	432* 10 Aug	873	484* 28 Jul
718	329 5 Sep	770	381 23 Aug	822	433 10 Aug	874	485 28 Jul
719	330 5 Sep	771	382 23 Aug	823	434 10 Aug	875	486 28 Jul
720	331 5 Sep	772	383 23 Aug	824	435 10 Aug	876	487 28 Jul
721	332* 4 Sep	773	384* 22 Aug	825	436* 9 Aug	877	488* 27 Jul
722	333 4 Sep	774	385 22 Aug	826	437 9 Aug	878	489 27 Jul
723	334 4 Sep	775	386 22 Aug	827	438 9 Aug	879	490 27 Jul
724	335 4 Sep	776	387 22 Aug	828	439 9 Aug	880	491 27 Jul
725	336* 3 Sep	777	388* 21 Aug	829	440* 8 Aug	881	492* 26 Jul
726	337 3 Sep	778	389 21 Aug	830	441 8 Aug	882	493 26 Jul
727	338 3 Sep	779	390 21 Aug	831	442 8 Aug	883	494 26 Jul
728	339 3 Sep	780	391 21 Aug	832	443 8 Aug	884	495 26 Jul
729	340* 2 Sep	781	392* 20 Aug	833	444* 7 Aug	885	496* 25 Jul
730	341 2 Sep	782	393 20 Aug	834	445 7 Aug	886	497 25 Jul
731	342 2 Sep	783	394 20 Aug	835	446 7 Aug	887	498 25 Jul
732	343 2 Sep	784	395 20 Aug	836	447 7 Aug	888	499 25 Jul
733	344* 1 Sep	785	396* 19 Aug	837	448* 6 Aug	889	500* 24 Jul
734	345 1 Sep	786	397 19 Aug	838	449 6 Aug	890	501 24 Jul
735	346 1 Sep	787	398 19 Aug	839	450 6 Aug	891	502 24 Jul
736	347 1 Sep	788	399 19 Aug	840	451 6 Aug	892	503 24 Jul
737	348* 31 Aug	789	400* 18 Aug	841	452* 5 Aug	893	504* 23 Jul
738	349 31 Aug	790	401 18 Aug	842	453 5 Aug	894	505 23 Jul
739	350 31 Aug	791	402 18 Aug	843	454 5 Aug	895	506 23 Jul
740	351 31 Aug	792	403 18 Aug	844	455 5 Aug	896	507 23 Jul
741	352* 30 Aug	793	404* 17 Aug	845	456* 4 Aug	897	508* 22 Jul
742	353 30 Aug	794	405 17 Aug	846	457 4 Aug	898	509 22 Jul
743	354 30 Aug	795	406 17 Aug	847	458 4 Aug	899	510 22 Jul
744	355 30 Aug	796	407 17 Aug	848	459 4 Aug	900	511 22 Jul
745	356* 29 Aug	797	408* 16 Aug	849	460* 3 Aug	901	512* 21 Jul
746	357 29 Aug	798	409 16 Aug	850	461 3 Aug	902	513 21 Jul
747	358 29 Aug	799	410 16 Aug	851	462 3 Aug	903	514 21 Jul
748	359 29 Aug	800	411 16 Aug	852	463 3 Aug	904	515 21 Jul
749	360* 28 Aug	801	412* 15 Aug	853	464* 2 Aug	905	516* 20 Jul
750	361 28 Aug	802	413 15 Aug	854	465 2 Aug	906	517 20 Jul
751	362 28 Aug	803	414 15 Aug	855	466 2 Aug	907	518 20 Jul
752	363 28 Aug	804	415 15 Aug	856	467 2 Aug	908	519 20 Jul
753	364* 27 Aug	805	416* 14 Aug	857	468* 1 Aug	909	520* 19 Jul
754	365 27 Aug	806	417 14 Aug	858	469 1 Aug	910	521 19 Jul
755	366 27 Aug	807	418 14 Aug	859	470 1 Aug	911	522 19 Jul
756	367 27 Aug	808	419 14 Aug	860	471 1 Aug	912	523 19 Jul

Zoroasterian Year	Western Date (Julian) of New Year	
913	524*	18 Jul
914	525	18 Jul
915	526	18 Jul
916	527	18 Jul
917	528*	17 Jul
918	529	17 Jul
919	530	17 Jul
920	531	17 Jul
921	532*	16 Jul
922	533	16 Jul
923	534	16 Jul
924	535	16 Jul
925	536*	15 Jul
926	537	15 Jul
927	538	15 Jul
928	539	15 Jul
929	540*	14 Jul
930	541	14 Jul
931	542	14 Jul
932	543	14 Jul
933	544*	13 Jul
934	545	13 Jul
935	546	13 Jul
936	547	13 Jul
937	548*	12 Jul
938	549	12 Jul
939	550	12 Jul
940	551	12 Jul
941	552*	11 Jul
942	553	11 Jul
943	554	11 Jul
944	555	11 Jul
945	556*	10 Jul
946	557	10 Jul
947	558	10 Jul
948	559	10 Jul
949	560*	9 Jul
950	561	9 Jul
951	562	9 Jul
952	563	9 Jul
953	564*	8 Jul
954	565	8 Jul
955	566	8 Jul
956	567	8 Jul
957	568*	7 Jul
958	569	7 Jul
959	570	7 Jul
960	571	7 Jul
961	572*	6 Jul
962	573	6 Jul
963	574	6 Jul
964	575	6 Jul

Zoroasterian Year	Western Date (Julian) of New Year	
965	576*	5 Jul
966	577	5 Jul
967	578	5 Jul
968	579	5 Jul
969	580*	4 Jul
970	581	4 Jul
971	582	4 Jul
972	583	4 Jul
973	584*	3 Jul
974	585	3 Jul
975	586	3 Jul
976	587	3 Jul
977	588*	2 Jul
978	589	2 Jul
979	590	2 Jul
980	591	2 Jul
981	592*	1 Jul
982	593	1 Jul
983	594	1 Jul
984	595	1 Jul
985	596*	30 Jun
986	597	30 Jun
987	598	30 Jun
988	599	30 Jun
989	600*	29 Jun
990	601	29 Jun
991	602	29 Jun
992	603	29 Jun
993	604*	28 Jun
994	605	28 Jun
995	606	28 Jun
996	607	28 Jun
997	608*	27 Jun
998	609	27 Jun
999	610	27 Jun
1000	611	27 Jun
1001	612*	26 Jun
1002	613	26 Jun
1003	614	26 Jun
1004	615	26 Jun
1005	616*	25 Jun
1006	617	25 Jun
1007	618	25 Jun
1008	619	25 Jun
1009	620*	24 Jun
1010	621	24 Jun
1011	622	24 Jun
1012	623	24 Jun
1013	624*	23 Jun
1014	625	23 Jun
1015	626	23 Jun
1016	627	23 Jun

Zoroasterian Year	Western Date (Julian) of New Year	
1017	628*	22 Jun
1018	629	22 Jun
1019	630	22 Jun
1020	631	22 Jun
1021	632*	21 Jun
1022	633	21 Jun
1023	634	21 Jun
1024	635	21 Jun
1025	636*	20 Jun
1026	637	20 Jun
1027	638	20 Jun
1028	639	20 Jun
1029	640*	19 Jun
1030	641	19 Jun
1031	642	19 Jun
1032	643	19 Jun
1033	644*	18 Jun
1034	645	18 Jun
1035	646	18 Jun
1036	647	18 Jun
1037	648*	17 Jun
1038	649	17 Jun
1039	650	17 Jun
1040	651	17 Jun
1041	652*	16 Jun
1042	653	16 Jun
1043	654	16 Jun
1044	655	16 Jun
1045	656*	15 Jun
1046	657	15 Jun
1047	658	15 Jun
1048	659	15 Jun
1049	660*	14 Jun
1050	661	14 Jun
1051	662	14 Jun
1052	663	14 Jun
1053	664*	13 Jun
1054	665	13 Jun
1055	666	13 Jun
1056	667	13 Jun
1057	668*	12 Jun
1058	669	12 Jun
1059	670	12 Jun
1060	671	12 Jun
1061	672*	11 Jun
1062	673	11 Jun
1063	674	11 Jun
1064	675	11 Jun
1065	676*	10 Jun
1066	677	10 Jun
1067	678	10 Jun
1068	679	10 Jun

Zoroasterian Year	Western Date (Julian) of New Year	
1069	680*	9 Jun
1070	681	9 Jun
1071	682	9 Jun
1072	683	9 Jun
1073	684*	8 Jun
1074	685	8 Jun
1075	686	8 Jun
1076	687	8 Jun
1077	688*	7 Jun
1078	689	7 Jun
1079	690	7 Jun
1080	691	7 Jun
1081	692*	6 Jun
1082	693	6 Jun
1083	694	6 Jun
1084	695	6 Jun
1085	696*	5 Jun
1086	697	5 Jun
1087	698	5 Jun
1088	699	5 Jun
1089	700*	4 Jun
1090	701	4 Jun
1091	702	4 Jun
1092	703	4 Jun
1093	704*	3 Jun
1094	705	3 Jun
1095	706	3 Jun
1096	707	3 Jun
1097	708*	2 Jun
1098	709	2 Jun
1099	710	2 Jun
1100	711	2 Jun
1101	712*	1 Jun
1102	713	1 Jun
1103	714	1 Jun
1104	715	1 Jun
1105	716*	31 May
1106	717	31 May
1107	718	31 May
1108	719	31 May
1109	720*	30 May
1110	721	30 May
1111	722	30 May
1112	723	30 May
1113	724*	29 May
1114	725	29 May
1115	726	29 May
1116	727	29 May
1117	728*	28 May
1118	729	28 May
1119	730	28 May
1120	731	28 May

Zoroasterian Year	Western Date (Julian) of New Year	Zoroasterian Year	Western Date (Julian) of New Year	Zoroasterian Year	Western Date (Julian) of New Year	Zoroasterian Year	Western Date (Julian) of New Year
1121	732* 27 May	1173	784* 14 May	1225	836* 1 May	1277	888* 18 Apr
1122	733 27 May	1174	785 14 May	1226	837 1 May	1278	889 18 Apr
1123	734 27 May	1175	786 14 May	1227	838 1 May	1279	890 18 Apr
1124	735 27 May	1176	787 14 May	1228	839 1 May	1280	891 18 Apr
1125	736* 26 May	1177	788* 13 May	1229	840* 30 Apr	1281	892* 17 Apr
1126	737 26 May	1178	789 13 May	1230	841 30 Apr	1282	893 17 Apr
1127	738 26 May	1179	790 13 May	1231	842 30 Apr	1283	894 17 Apr
1128	739 26 May	1180	791 13 May	1232	843 30 Apr	1284	895 17 Apr
1129	740* 25 May	1181	792* 12 May	1233	844* 29 Apr	1285	896* 16 Apr
1130	741 25 May	1182	793 12 May	1234	845 29 Apr	1286	897 16 Apr
1131	742 25 May	1183	794 12 May	1235	846 29 Apr	1287	898 16 Apr
1132	743 25 May	1184	795 12 May	1236	847 29 Apr	1288	899 16 Apr
1133	744* 24 May	1185	796* 11 May	1237	848* 28 Apr	1289	900* 15 Apr
1134	745 24 May	1186	797 11 May	1238	849 28 Apr	1290	901 15 Apr
1135	746 24 May	1187	798 11 May	1239	850 28 Apr	1291	902 15 Apr
1136	747 24 May	1188	799 11 May	1240	851 28 Apr	1292	903 15 Apr
1137	748* 23 May	1189	800* 10 May	1241	852* 27 Apr	1293	904* 14 Apr
1138	749 23 May	1190	801 10 May	1242	853 27 Apr	1294	905 14 Apr
1139	750 23 May	1191	802 10 May	1243	854 27 Apr	1295	906 14 Apr
1140	751 23 May	1192	803 10 May	1244	855 27 Apr	1296	907 14 Apr
1141	752* 22 May	1193	804* 9 May	1245	856* 26 Apr	1297	908* 13 Apr
1142	753 22 May	1194	805 9 May	1246	857 26 Apr	1298	909 13 Apr
1143	754 22 May	1195	806 9 May	1247	858 26 Apr	1299	910 13 Apr
1144	755 22 May	1196	807 9 May	1248	859 26 Apr	1300	911 13 Apr
1145	756* 21 May	1197	808* 8 May	1249	860* 25 Apr	1301	912* 12 Apr
1146	757 21 May	1198	809 8 May	1250	861 25 Apr	1302	913 12 Apr
1147	758 21 May	1199	810 8 May	1251	862 25 Apr	1303	914 12 Apr
1148	759 21 May	1200	811 8 May	1252	863 25 Apr	1304	915 12 Apr
1149	760* 20 May	1201	812* 7 May	1253	864* 24 Apr	1305	916* 11 Apr
1150	761 20 May	1202	813 7 May	1254	865 24 Apr	1306	917 11 Apr
1151	762 20 May	1203	814 7 May	1255	866 24 Apr	1307	918 11 Apr
1152	763 20 May	1204	815 7 May	1256	867 24 Apr	1308	919 11 Apr
1153	764* 19 May	1205	816* 6 May	1257	868* 23 Apr	1309	920* 10 Apr
1154	765 19 May	1206	817 6 May	1258	869 23 Apr	1310	921 10 Apr
1155	766 19 May	1207	818 6 May	1259	870 23 Apr	1311	922 10 Apr
1156	767 19 May	1208	819 6 May	1260	871 23 Apr	1312	923 10 Apr
1157	768* 18 May	1209	820* 5 May	1261	872* 22 Apr	1313	924* 9 Apr
1158	769 18 May	1210	821 5 May	1262	873 22 Apr	1314	925 9 Apr
1159	770 18 May	1211	822 5 May	1263	874 22 Apr	1315	926 9 Apr
1160	771 18 May	1212	823 5 May	1264	875 22 Apr	1316	927 9 Apr
1161	772* 17 May	1213	824* 4 May	1265	876* 21 Apr	1317	928* 8 Apr
1162	773 17 May	1214	825 4 May	1266	877 21 Apr	1318	929 8 Apr
1163	774 17 May	1215	826 4 May	1267	878 21 Apr	1319	930 8 Apr
1164	775 17 May	1216	827 4 May	1268	879 21 Apr	1320	931 8 Apr
1165	776* 16 May	1217	828* 3 May	1269	880* 20 Apr	1321	932* 7 Apr
1166	777 16 May	1218	829 3 May	1270	881 20 Apr	1322	933 7 Apr
1167	778 16 May	1219	830 3 May	1271	882 20 Apr	1323	934 7 Apr
1168	779 16 May	1220	831 3 May	1272	883 20 Apr	1324	935 7 Apr
1169	780* 15 May	1221	832* 2 May	1273	884* 19 Apr	1325	936* 6 Apr
1170	781 15 May	1222	833 2 May	1274	885 19 Apr	1326	937 6 Apr
1171	782 15 May	1223	834 2 May	1275	886 19 Apr	1327	938 6 Apr
1172	783 15 May	1224	835 2 May	1276	887 19 Apr	1328	939 6 Apr

Zoroasterian Year	Western Date (Julian) of New Year	Zoroasterian Year	Western Date (Julian) of New Year	Zoroasterian Year	Western Date (Julian) of New Year	Zoroasterian Year	Western Date (Julian) of New Year
1329	940* 5 Apr	1381	992* 23 Mar	1433	1044* 10 Mar	1485	1096* 26 Feb
1330	941 5 Apr	1382	993 23 Mar	1434	1045 10 Mar	1486	1097 25 Feb
1331	942 5 Apr	1383	994 23 Mar	1435	1046 10 Mar	1487	1098 25 Feb
1332	943 5 Apr	1384	995 23 Mar	1436	1047 10 Mar	1488	1099 25 Feb
1333	944* 4 Apr	1385	996* 22 Mar	1437	1048* 9 Mar	1489	1100* 25 Feb
1334	945 4 Apr	1386	997 22 Mar	1438	1049 9 Mar	1490	1101 24 Feb
1335	946 4 Apr	1387	998 22 Mar	1439	1050 9 Mar	1491	1102 24 Feb
1336	947 4 Apr	1388	999 22 Mar	1440	1051 9 Mar	1492	1103 24 Feb
1337	948* 3 Apr	1389	1000* 21 Mar	1441	1052* 8 Mar	1493	1104* 24 Feb
1338	949 3 Apr	1390	1001 21 Mar	1442	1053 8 Mar	1494	1105 23 Feb
1339	950 3 Apr	1391	1002 21 Mar	1443	1054 8 Mar	1495	1106 23 Feb
1340	951 3 Apr	1392	1003 21 Mar	1444	1055 8 Mar	1496	1107 23 Feb
1341	952* 2 Apr	1393	1004* 20 Mar	1445	1056* 7 Mar	1497	1108* 23 Feb
1342	953 2 Apr	1394	1005 20 Mar	1446	1057 7 Mar	1498	1109 22 Feb
1343	954 2 Apr	1395	1006 20 Mar	1447	1058 7 Mar	1499	1110 22 Feb
1344	955 2 Apr	1396	1007 20 Mar	1448	1059 7 Mar	1500	1111 22 Feb
1345	956* 1 Apr	1397	1008* 19 Mar	1449	1060* 6 Mar	1501	1112* 22 Feb
1346	957 1 Apr	1398	1009 19 Mar	1450	1061 6 Mar	1502	1113 21 Feb
1347	958 1 Apr	1399	1010 19 Mar	1451	1062 6 Mar	1503	1114 21 Feb
1348	959 1 Apr	1400	1011 19 Mar	1452	1063 6 Mar	1504	1115 21 Feb
1349	960* 31 Mar	1401	1012* 18 Mar	1453	1064* 5 Mar	1505	1116* 21 Feb
1350	961 31 Mar	1402	1013 18 Mar	1454	1065 5 Mar	1506	1117 20 Feb
1351	962 31 Mar	1403	1014 18 Mar	1455	1066 5 Mar	1507	1118 20 Feb
1352	963 31 Mar	1404	1015 18 Mar	1456	1067 5 Mar	1508	1119 20 Feb
1353	964* 30 Mar	1405	1016* 17 Mar	1457	1068* 4 Mar	1509	1120* 20 Feb
1354	965 30 Mar	1406	1017 17 Mar	1458	1069 4 Mar	1510	1121 19 Feb
1355	966 30 Mar	1407	1018 17 Mar	1459	1070 4 Mar	1511	1122 19 Feb
1356	967 30 Mar	1408	1019 17 Mar	1460	1071 4 Mar	1512	1123 19 Feb
1357	968* 29 Mar	1409	1020* 16 Mar	1461	1072* 3 Mar	1513	1124* 19 Feb
1358	969 29 Mar	1410	1021 16 Mar	1462	1073 3 Mar	1514	1125 18 Feb
1359	970 29 Mar	1411	1022 16 Mar	1463	1074 3 Mar	1515	1126 18 Feb
1360	971 29 Mar	1412	1023 16 Mar	1464	1075 3 Mar	1516	1127 18 Feb
1361	972* 28 Mar	1413	1024* 15 Mar	1465	1076* 2 Mar	1517	1128* 18 Feb
1362	973 28 Mar	1414	1025 15 Mar	1466	1077 2 Mar	1518	1129 17 Feb
1363	974 28 Mar	1415	1026 15 Mar	1467	1078 2 Mar	1519	1130 17 Feb
1364	975 28 Mar	1416	1027 15 Mar	1468	1079 2 Mar	1520	1131 17 Feb
1365	976* 27 Mar	1417	1028* 14 Mar	1469	1080* 1 Mar	1521	1132* 17 Feb
1366	977 27 Mar	1418	1029 14 Mar	1470	1081 1 Mar	1522	1133 16 Feb
1367	978 27 Mar	1419	1030 14 Mar	1471	1082 1 Mar	1523	1134 16 Feb
1368	979 27 Mar	1420	1031 14 Mar	1472	1083 1 Mar	1524	1135 16 Feb
1369	980* 26 Mar	1421	1032* 13 Mar	1473	1084* 29 Feb	1525	1136* 16 Feb
1370	981 26 Mar	1422	1033 13 Mar	1474	1085 28 Feb	1526	1137 15 Feb
1371	982 26 Mar	1423	1034 13 Mar	1475	1086 28 Feb	1527	1138 15 Feb
1372	983 26 Mar	1424	1035 13 Mar	1476	1087 28 Feb	1528	1139 15 Feb
1373	984* 25 Mar	1425	1036* 12 Mar	1477	1088* 28 Feb	1529	1140* 15 Feb
1374	985 25 Mar	1426	1037 12 Mar	1478	1089 27 Feb	1530	1141 14 Feb
1375	986 25 Mar	1427	1038 12 Mar	1479	1090 27 Feb	1531	1142 14 Feb
1376	987 25 Mar	1428	1039 12 Mar	1480	1091 27 Feb	1532	1143 14 Feb
1377	988* 24 Mar	1429	1040* 11 Mar	1481	1092* 27 Feb	1533	1144* 14 Feb
1378	989 24 Mar	1430	1041 11 Mar	1482	1093 26 Feb	1534	1145 13 Feb
1379	990 24 Mar	1431	1042 11 Mar	1483	1094 26 Feb	1535	1146 13 Feb
1380	991 24 Mar	1432	1043 11 Mar	1484	1095 26 Feb	1536	1147 13 Feb

Zoroasterian Year	Western Date (Julian) of New Year	Zoroasterian Year	Western Date (Julian) of New Year	Zoroasterian Year	Western Date (Julian) of New Year	Zoroasterian Year	Western Date (Julian) of New Year
1537	1148* 13 Feb	1589	1200* 31 Jan	1641	1252* 18 Jan	1693	1304* 5 Jan
1538	1149 12 Feb	1590	1201 30 Jan	1642	1253 17 Jan	1694	1305 4 Jan
1539	1150 12 Feb	1591	1202 30 Jan	1643	1254 17 Jan	1695	1306 4 Jan
1540	1151 12 Feb	1592	1203 30 Jan	1644	1255 17 Jan	1696	1307 4 Jan
1541	1152* 12 Feb	1593	1204* 30 Jan	1645	1256* 17 Jan	1697	1308* 4 Jan
1542	1153 11 Feb	1594	1205 29 Jan	1646	1257 16 Jan	1698	1309 3 Jan
1543	1154 11 Feb	1595	1206 29 Jan	1647	1258 16 Jan	1699	1310 3 Jan
1544	1155 11 Feb	1596	1207 29 Jan	1648	1259 16 Jan	1700	1311 3 Jan
1545	1156* 11 Feb	1597	1208* 29 Jan	1649	1260* 16 Jan	1701	1312* 3 Jan
1546	1157 10 Feb	1598	1209 28 Jan	1650	1261 15 Jan	1702	1313 2 Jan
1547	1158 10 Feb	1599	1210 28 Jan	1651	1262 15 Jan	1703	1314 2 Jan
1548	1159 10 Feb	1600	1211 28 Jan	1652	1263 15 Jan	1704	1315 2 Jan
1549	1160* 10 Feb	1601	1212* 28 Jan	1653	1264* 15 Jan	1705	1316* 2 Jan
1550	1161 9 Feb	1602	1213 27 Jan	1654	1265 14 Jan	1706	1317 1 Jan
1551	1162 9 Feb	1603	1214 27 Jan	1655	1266 14 Jan	1707	1318 1 Jan
1552	1163 9 Feb	1604	1215 27 Jan	1656	1267 14 Jan	1708	1319 1 Jan
1553	1164* 9 Feb	1605	1216* 27 Jan	1657	1268* 14 Jan	1709	1320* 1 Jan
1554	1165 8 Feb	1606	1217 26 Jan	1658	1269 13 Jan	1710	1321 31 Dec
1555	1166 8 Feb	1607	1218 26 Jan	1659	1270 13 Jan	1711	1321 31 Dec
1556	1167 8 Feb	1608	1219 26 Jan	1660	1271 13 Jan	1712	1322 31 Dec
1557	1168* 8 Feb	1609	1220* 26 Jan	1661	1272* 13 Jan	1713	1323 31 Dec
1558	1169 7 Feb	1610	1221 25 Jan	1662	1273 12 Jan	1714	1324* 30 Dec
1559	1170 7 Feb	1611	1222 25 Jan	1663	1274 12 Jan	1715	1325 30 Dec
1560	1171 7 Feb	1612	1223 25 Jan	1664	1275 12 Jan	1716	1326 30 Dec
1561	1172* 7 Feb	1613	1224* 25 Jan	1665	1276* 12 Jan	1717	1327 30 Dec
1562	1173 6 Feb	1614	1225 24 Jan	1666	1277 11 Jan	1718	1328* 29 Dec
1563	1174 6 Feb	1615	1226 24 Jan	1667	1278 11 Jan	1719	1329 29 Dec
1564	1175 6 Feb	1616	1227 24 Jan	1668	1279 11 Jan	1720	1330 29 Dec
1565	1176* 6 Feb	1617	1228* 24 Jan	1669	1280* 11 Jan	1721	1331 29 Dec
1566	1177 5 Feb	1618	1229 23 Jan	1670	1281 10 Jan	1722	1332* 28 Dec
1567	1178 5 Feb	1619	1230 23 Jan	1671	1282 10 Jan	1723	1333 28 Dec
1568	1179 5 Feb	1620	1231 23 Jan	1672	1283 10 Jan	1724	1334 28 Dec
1569	1180* 5 Feb	1621	1232* 23 Jan	1673	1284* 10 Jan	1725	1335 28 Dec
1570	1181 4 Feb	1622	1233 22 Jan	1674	1285 9 Jan	1726	1336* 27 Dec
1571	1182 4 Feb	1623	1234 22 Jan	1675	1286 9 Jan	1727	1337 27 Dec
1572	1183 4 Feb	1624	1235 22 Jan	1676	1287 9 Jan	1728	1338 27 Dec
1573	1184* 4 Feb	1625	1236* 22 Jan	1677	1288* 9 Jan	1729	1339 27 Dec
1574	1185 3 Feb	1626	1237 21 Jan	1678	1289 8 Jan	1730	1340* 26 Dec
1575	1186 3 Feb	1627	1238 21 Jan	1679	1290 8 Jan	1731	1341 26 Dec
1576	1187 3 Feb	1628	1239 21 Jan	1680	1291 8 Jan	1732	1342 26 Dec
1577	1188* 3 Feb	1629	1240* 21 Jan	1681	1292* 8 Jan	1733	1343 26 Dec
1578	1189 2 Feb	1630	1241 20 Jan	1682	1293 7 Jan	1734	1344* 25 Dec
1579	1190 2 Feb	1631	1242 20 Jan	1683	1294 7 Jan	1735	1345 25 Dec
1580	1191 2 Feb	1632	1243 20 Jan	1684	1295 7 Jan	1736	1346 25 Dec
1581	1192* 2 Feb	1633	1244* 20 Jan	1685	1296* 7 Jan	1737	1347 25 Dec
1582	1193 1 Feb	1634	1245 19 Jan	1686	1297 6 Jan	1738	1348* 24 Dec
1583	1194 1 Feb	1635	1246 19 Jan	1687	1298 6 Jan	1739	1349 24 Dec
1584	1195 1 Feb	1636	1247 19 Jan	1688	1299 6 Jan	1740	1350 24 Dec
1585	1196* 1 Feb	1637	1248* 19 Jan	1689	1300* 6 Jan	1741	1351 24 Dec
1586	1197 31 Jan	1638	1249 18 Jan	1690	1301 5 Jan	1742	1352* 23 Dec
1587	1198 31 Jan	1639	1250 18 Jan	1691	1302 5 Jan	1743	1353 23 Dec
1588	1199 31 Jan	1640	1251 18 Jan	1692	1303 5 Jan	1744	1354 23 Dec

Zoroasterian Year	Western Date (Julian) of New Year	Zoroasterian Year	Western Date (Julian) of New Year	Zoroasterian Year	Western Date (Julian) of New Year	Zoroasterian Year	Western Date (Julian) of New Year
1745	1355 23 Dec	1797	1407 10 Dec	1849	1459 27 Nov	1901	1511 14 Nov
1746	1356* 22 Dec	1798	1408* 9 Dec	1850	1460* 26 Nov	1902	1512* 13 Nov
1747	1357 22 Dec	1799	1409 9 Dec	1851	1461 26 Nov	1903	1513 13 Nov
1748	1358 22 Dec	1800	1410 9 Dec	1852	1462 26 Nov	1904	1514 13 Nov
1749	1359 22 Dec	1801	1411 9 Dec	1853	1463 26 Nov	1905	1515 13 Nov
1750	1360* 21 Dec	1802	1412* 8 Dec	1854	1464* 25 Nov	1906	1516* 12 Nov
1751	1361 21 Dec	1803	1413 8 Dec	1855	1465 25 Nov	1907	1517 12 Nov
1752	1362 21 Dec	1804	1414 8 Dec	1856	1466 25 Nov	1908	1518 12 Nov
1753	1363 21 Dec	1805	1415 8 Dec	1857	1467 25 Nov	1909	1519 12 Nov
1754	1364* 20 Dec	1806	1416* 7 Dec	1858	1468* 24 Nov	1910	1520* 11 Nov
1755	1365 20 Dec	1807	1417 7 Dec	1859	1469 24 Nov	1911	1521 11 Nov
1756	1366 20 Dec	1808	1418 7 Dec	1860	1470 24 Nov	1912	1522 11 Nov
1757	1367 20 Dec	1809	1419 7 Dec	1861	1471 24 Nov	1913	1523 11 Nov
1758	1368* 19 Dec	1810	1420* 6 Dec	1862	1472* 23 Nov	1914	1524* 10 Nov
1759	1369 19 Dec	1811	1421 6 Dec	1863	1473 23 Nov	1915	1525 10 Nov
1760	1370 19 Dec	1812	1422 6 Dec	1864	1474 23 Nov	1916	1526 10 Nov
1761	1371 19 Dec	1813	1423 6 Dec	1865	1475 23 Nov	1917	1527 10 Nov
1762	1372* 18 Dec	1814	1424* 5 Dec	1866	1476* 22 Nov	1918	1528* 9 Nov
1763	1373 18 Dec	1815	1425 5 Dec	1867	1477 22 Nov	1919	1529 9 Nov
1764	1374 18 Dec	1816	1426 5 Dec	1868	1478 22 Nov	1920	1530 9 Nov
1765	1375 18 Dec	1817	1427 5 Dec	1869	1479 22 Nov	1921	1531 9 Nov
1766	1376* 17 Dec	1818	1428* 4 Dec	1870	1480* 21 Nov	1922	1532* 8 Nov
1767	1377 17 Dec	1819	1429 4 Dec	1871	1481 21 Nov	1923	1533 8 Nov
1768	1378 17 Dec	1820	1430 4 Dec	1872	1482 21 Nov	1924	1534 8 Nov
1769	1379 17 Dec	1821	1431 4 Dec	1873	1483 21 Nov	1925	1535 8 Nov
1770	1380* 16 Dec	1822	1432* 3 Dec	1874	1484* 20 Nov	1926	1536* 7 Nov
1771	1381 16 Dec	1823	1433 3 Dec	1875	1485 20 Nov	1927	1537 7 Nov
1772	1382 16 Dec	1824	1434 3 Dec	1876	1486 20 Nov	1928	1538 7 Nov
1773	1383 16 Dec	1825	1435 3 Dec	1877	1487 20 Nov	1929	1539 7 Nov
1774	1384* 15 Dec	1826	1436* 2 Dec	1878	1488* 19 Nov	1930	1540* 6 Nov
1775	1385 15 Dec	1827	1437 2 Dec	1879	1489 19 Nov	1931	1541 6 Nov
1776	1386 15 Dec	1828	1438 2 Dec	1880	1490 19 Nov	1932	1542 6 Nov
1777	1387 15 Dec	1829	1439 2 Dec	1881	1491 19 Nov	1933	1543 6 Nov
1778	1388* 14 Dec	1830	1440* 1 Dec	1882	1492* 18 Nov	1934	1544* 5 Nov
1779	1389 14 Dec	1831	1441 1 Dec	1883	1493 18 Nov	1935	1545 5 Nov
1780	1390 14 Dec	1832	1442 1 Dec	1884	1494 18 Nov	1936	1546 5 Nov
1781	1391 14 Dec	1833	1443 1 Dec	1885	1495 18 Nov	1937	1547 5 Nov
1782	1392* 13 Dec	1834	1444* 30 Nov	1886	1496* 17 Nov	1938	1548* 4 Nov
1783	1393 13 Dec	1835	1445 30 Nov	1887	1497 17 Nov	1939	1549 4 Nov
1784	1394 13 Dec	1836	1446 30 Nov	1888	1498 17 Nov	1940	1550 4 Nov
1785	1395 13 Dec	1837	1447 30 Nov	1889	1499 17 Nov	1941	1551 4 Nov
1786	1396* 12 Dec	1838	1448* 29 Nov	1890	1500* 16 Nov	1942	1552* 3 Nov
1787	1397 12 Dec	1839	1449 29 Nov	1891	1501 16 Nov	1943	1553 3 Nov
1788	1398 12 Dec	1840	1450 29 Nov	1892	1502 16 Nov	1944	1554 3 Nov
1789	1399 12 Dec	1841	1451 29 Nov	1893	1503 16 Nov	1945	1555 3 Nov
1790	1400* 11 Dec	1842	1452* 28 Nov	1894	1504* 15 Nov	1946	1556* 2 Nov
1791	1401 11 Dec	1843	1453 28 Nov	1895	1505 15 Nov	1947	1557 2 Nov
1792	1402 11 Dec	1844	1454 28 Nov	1896	1506 15 Nov	1948	1558 2 Nov
1793	1403 11 Dec	1845	1455 28 Nov	1897	1507 15 Nov	1949	1559 2 Nov
1794	1404* 10 Dec	1846	1456* 27 Nov	1898	1508* 14 Nov	1950	1560* 1 Nov
1795	1405 10 Dec	1847	1457 27 Nov	1899	1509 14 Nov	1951	1561 1 Nov
1796	1406 10 Dec	1848	1458 27 Nov	1900	1510 14 Nov	1952	1562 1 Nov

Zoroasterian Year	Western Date (Julian) of New Year		Zoroasterian Year	Western Date (Julian) of New Year		Zoroasterian Year	Western Date (Julian) of New Year		Zoroasterian Year	Western Date (Julian) of New Year	
1953	1563	1 Nov	1958	1568*	30 Oct	1963	1573	29 Oct	1968	1578	28 Oct
1954	1564*	31 Oct	1959	1569	30 Oct	1964	1574	29 Oct	1969	1579	28 Oct
1955	1565	31 Oct	1960	1570	30 Oct	1965	1575	29 Oct	1970	1580*	27 Oct
1956	1566	31 Oct	1961	1571	30 Oct	1966	1576*	28 Oct	1971	1581	27 Oct
1957	1567	31 Oct	1962	1572*	29 Oct	1967	1577	28 Oct			

Zoroasterian Year	Western Date (Julian) of New Year		Western Date (Gregorian) of New Year	Zoroasterian Year	Western Date (Julian) of New Year		Western Date (Gregorian) of New Year	Zoroasterian Year	Western Date (Julian) of New Year		Western Date (Gregorian) of New Year
1972	1582	27 Oct	6 Nov	2013	1623	17 Oct	27 Oct	2054	1664*	6 Oct	16 Oct
1973	1583	27 Oct	6 Nov	2014	1624*	16 Oct	26 Oct	2055	1665	6 Oct	16 Oct
1974	1584*	26 Oct	5 Nov	2015	1625	16 Oct	26 Oct	2056	1666	6 Oct	16 Oct
1975	1585	26 Oct	5 Nov	2016	1626	16 Oct	26 Oct	2057	1667	6 Oct	16 Oct
1976	1586	26 Oct	5 Nov	2017	1627	16 Oct	26 Oct	2058	1668*	5 Oct	15 Oct
1977	1587	26 Oct	5 Nov	2018	1628*	15 Oct	25 Oct	2059	1669	5 Oct	15 Oct
1978	1588*	25 Oct	4 Nov	2019	1629	15 Oct	25 Oct	2060	1670	5 Oct	15 Oct
1979	1589	25 Oct	4 Nov	2020	1630	15 Oct	25 Oct	2061	1671	5 Oct	15 Oct
1980	1590	25 Oct	4 Nov	2021	1631	15 Oct	25 Oct	2062	1672*	4 Oct	14 Oct
1981	1591	25 Oct	4 Nov	2022	1632*	14 Oct	24 Oct	2063	1673	4 Oct	14 Oct
1982	1592*	24 Oct	3 Nov	2023	1633	14 Oct	24 Oct	2064	1674	4 Oct	14 Oct
1983	1593	24 Oct	3 Nov	2024	1634	14 Oct	24 Oct	2065	1675	4 Oct	14 Oct
1984	1594	24 Oct	3 Nov	2025	1635	14 Oct	24 Oct	2066	1676*	3 Oct	13 Oct
1985	1595	24 Oct	3 Nov	2026	1636*	13 Oct	23 Oct	2067	1677	3 Oct	13 Oct
1986	1596*	23 Oct	2 Nov	2027	1637	13 Oct	23 Oct	2068	1678	3 Oct	13 Oct
1987	1597	23 Oct	2 Nov	2028	1638	13 Oct	23 Oct	2069	1679	3 Oct	13 Oct
1988	1598	23 Oct	2 Nov	2029	1639	13 Oct	23 Oct	2070	1680*	2 Oct	12 Oct
1989	1599	23 Oct	2 Nov	2030	1640*	12 Oct	22 Oct	2071	1681	2 Oct	12 Oct
1990	1600*	22 Oct	1 Nov	2031	1641	12 Oct	22 Oct	2072	1682	2 Oct	12 Oct
1991	1601	22 Oct	1 Nov	2032	1642	12 Oct	22 Oct	2073	1683	2 Oct	12 Oct
1992	1602	22 Oct	1 Nov	2033	1643	12 Oct	22 Oct	2074	1684*	1 Oct	11 Oct
1993	1603	22 Oct	1 Nov	2034	1644*	11 Oct	21 Oct	2075	1685	1 Oct	11 Oct
1994	1604*	21 Oct	31 Oct	2035	1645	11 Oct	21 Oct	2076	1686	1 Oct	11 Oct
1995	1605	21 Oct	31 Oct	2036	1646	11 Oct	21 Oct	2077	1687	1 Oct	11 Oct
1996	1606	21 Oct	31 Oct	2037	1647	11 Oct	21 Oct	2078	1688*	30 Sep	10 Oct
1997	1607	21 Oct	31 Oct	2038	1648*	10 Oct	20 Oct	2079	1689	30 Sep	10 Oct
1998	1608*	20 Oct	30 Oct	2039	1649	10 Oct	20 Oct	2080	1690	30 Sep	10 Oct
1999	1609	20 Oct	30 Oct	2040	1650	10 Oct	20 Oct	2081	1691	30 Sep	10 Oct
2000	1610	20 Oct	30 Oct	2041	1651	10 Oct	20 Oct	2082	1692*	29 Sep	9 Oct
2001	1611	20 Oct	30 Oct	2042	1652*	9 Oct	19 Oct	2083	1693	29 Sep	9 Oct
2002	1612*	19 Oct	29 Oct	2043	1653	9 Oct	19 Oct	2084	1694	29 Sep	9 Oct
2003	1613	19 Oct	29 Oct	2044	1654	9 Oct	19 Oct	2085	1695	29 Sep	9 Oct
2004	1614	19 Oct	29 Oct	2045	1655	9 Oct	19 Oct	2086	1696*	28 Sep	8 Oct
2005	1615	19 Oct	29 Oct	2046	1656*	8 Oct	18 Oct	2087	1697	28 Sep	8 Oct
2006	1616*	18 Oct	28 Oct	2047	1657	8 Oct	18 Oct	2088	1698	28 Sep	8 Oct
2007	1617	18 Oct	28 Oct	2048	1658	8 Oct	18 Oct	2089	1699	28 Sep	8 Oct
2008	1618	18 Oct	28 Oct	2049	1659	8 Oct	18 Oct	2090	1700	27 Sep	8 Oct
2009	1619	18 Oct	28 Oct	2050	1660*	7 Oct	17 Oct	2091	1701	27 Sep	8 Oct
2010	1620*	17 Oct	27 Oct	2051	1661	7 Oct	17 Oct	2092	1702	27 Sep	8 Oct
2011	1621	17 Oct	27 Oct	2052	1662	7 Oct	17 Oct	2093	1703	27 Sep	8 Oct
2012	1622	17 Oct	27 Oct	2053	1663	7 Oct	17 Oct	2094	1704*	26 Sep	7 Oct

Zoroasterian Year	Western Date of New Year (Julian)		Western Date of New Year (Gregorian)
2095	1705	26 Sep	7 Oct
2096	1706	26 Sep	7 Oct
2097	1707	26 Sep	7 Oct
2098	1708*	25 Sep	6 Oct
2099	1709	25 Sep	6 Oct
2100	1710	25 Sep	6 Oct
2101	1711	25 Sep	6 Oct
2102	1712*	24 Sep	5 Oct
2103	1713	24 Sep	5 Oct
2104	1714	24 Sep	5 Oct
2105	1715	24 Sep	5 Oct
2106	1716*	23 Sep	4 Oct
2107	1717	23 Sep	4 Oct
2108	1718	23 Sep	4 Oct
2109	1719	23 Sep	4 Oct
2110	1720*	22 Sep	3 Oct

Zoroasterian Year	Western Date of New Year (Julian)		Western Date of New Year (Gregorian)
2111	1721	22 Sep	3 Oct
2112	1722	22 Sep	3 Oct
2113	1723	22 Sep	3 Oct
2114	1724*	21 Sep	2 Oct
2115	1725	21 Sep	2 Oct
2116	1726	21 Sep	2 Oct
2117	1727	21 Sep	2 Oct
2118	1728*	20 Sep	1 Oct
2119	1729	20 Sep	1 Oct
2120	1730	20 Sep	1 Oct
2121	1731	20 Sep	1 Oct
2122	1732*	19 Sep	30 Sep
2123	1733	19 Sep	30 Sep
2124	1734	19 Sep	30 Sep
2125	1735	19 Sep	30 Sep
2126	1736*	18 Sep	29 Sep

Zoroasterian Year	Western Date of New Year (Julian)		Western Date of New Year (Gregorian)
2127	1737	18 Sep	29 Sep
2128	1738	18 Sep	29 Sep
2129	1739	18 Sep	29 Sep
2130	1740*	17 Sep	28 Sep
2131	1741	17 Sep	28 Sep
2132	1742	17 Sep	28 Sep
2133	1743	17 Sep	28 Sep
2134	1744*	16 Sep	27 Sep
2135	1745	16 Sep	27 Sep
2136	1746	16 Sep	27 Sep
2137	1747	16 Sep	27 Sep
2138	1748*	15 Sep	26 Sep
2139	1749	15 Sep	26 Sep
2140	1750	15 Sep	26 Sep
2141	1751	15 Sep	26 Sep

Zoroasterian Year	Western Date (Julian) of New Year	
2142	1752*	25 Sep
1243	1753	25 Sep
2144	1754	25 Sep
2145	1755	25 Sep
2146	1756*	24 Sep
2147	1757	24 Sep
2148	1758	24 Sep
2149	1759	24 Sep
2150	1760*	23 Sep
2151	1761	23 Sep
2152	1762	23 Sep
2153	1763	23 Sep
2154	1764*	22 Sep
2155	1765	22 Sep
2156	1766	22 Sep
2157	1767	22 Sep
2158	1768*	21 Sep
2159	1769	21 Sep
2160	1770	21 Sep
2161	1771	21 Sep
2162	1772*	20 Sep
2163	1773	20 Sep
2164	1774	20 Sep
2165	1775	20 Sep
2166	1776*	19 Sep
2167	1777	19 Sep

Zoroasterian Year	Western Date (Julian) of New Year	
2168	1778	19 Sep
2169	1779	19 Sep
2170	1780*	18 Sep
2171	1781	18 Sep
2172	1782	18 Sep
2173	1783	18 Sep
2174	1784*	17 Sep
2175	1785	17 Sep
2176	1786	17 Sep
2177	1787	17 Sep
2178	1788*	16 Sep
2179	1789	16 Sep
2180	1790	16 Sep
2181	1791	16 Sep
2182	1792*	15 Sep
2183	1793	15 Sep
2184	1794	15 Sep
2185	1795	15 Sep
2186	1796*	14 Sep
2187	1797	14 Sep
2188	1798	14 Sep
2189	1799	14 Sep
2190	1800	14 Sep
2191	1801	14 Sep
2192	1802	14 Sep
2193	1803	14 Sep

Zoroasterian Year	Western Date (Julian) of New Year	
2194	1804*	13 Sep
2195	1805	13 Sep
2196	1806	13 Sep
2197	1807	13 Sep
2198	1808*	12 Sep
2199	1809	12 Sep
2200	1810	12 Sep
2201	1811	12 Sep
2202	1812*	11 Sep
2203	1813	11 Sep
2204	1814	11 Sep
2205	1815	11 Sep
2206	1816*	10 Sep
2207	1817	10 Sep
2208	1818	10 Sep
2209	1819	10 Sep
2210	1820*	9 Sep
2211	1821	9 Sep
2212	1822	9 Sep
2213	1823	9 Sep
2214	1824*	8 Sep
2215	1825	8 Sep
2216	1826	8 Sep
2217	1827	8 Sep
2218	1828*	7 Sep
2219	1829	7 Sep

Zoroasterian Year	Western Date (Julian) of New Year	
2220	1830	7 Sep
2221	1831	7 Sep
2222	1832*	6 Sep
2223	1833	6 Sep
2224	1834	6 Sep
2225	1835	6 Sep
2226	1836*	5 Sep
2227	1837	5 Sep
2228	1838	5 Sep
2229	1839	5 Sep
2230	1840*	4 Sep
2231	1841	4 Sep
2232	1842	4 Sep
2233	1843	4 Sep
2234	1844*	3 Sep
2235	1845	3 Sep
2236	1846	3 Sep
2237	1847	3 Sep
2238	1848*	2 Sep
2239	1849	2 Sep
2240	1850	2 Sep
2241	1851	2 Sep
2242	1852*	1 Sep
2243	1853	1 Sep
2244	1854	1 Sep
2245	1855	1 Sep

Zoroasterian Year	Western Date (Julian) of New Year	
2246	1856*	31 Aug
2247	1857	31 Aug
2248	1858	31 Aug
2249	1859	31 Aug
2250	1860*	30 Aug
2251	1861	30 Aug
2252	1862	30 Aug
2253	1863	30 Aug
2254	1864*	29 Aug
2255	1865	29 Aug
2256	1866	29 Aug
2257	1867	29 Aug
2258	1868*	28 Aug
2259	1869	28 Aug
2260	1870	28 Aug
2261	1871	28 Aug
2262	1872*	27 Aug
2263	1873	27 Aug
2264	1874	27 Aug
2265	1875	27 Aug
2266	1876*	26 Aug
2267	1877	26 Aug
2268	1878	26 Aug
2269	1879	26 Aug
2270	1880*	25 Aug
2271	1881	25 Aug
2272	1882	25 Aug
2273	1883	25 Aug
2274	1884*	24 Aug
2275	1885	24 Aug
2276	1886	24 Aug
2277	1887	24 Aug
2278	1888*	23 Aug
2279	1889	23 Aug
2280	1890	23 Aug
2281	1891	23 Aug
2282	1892*	22 Aug
2283	1893	22 Aug
2284	1894	22 Aug
2285	1895	22 Aug
2286	1896*	21 Aug
2287	1897	21 Aug
2288	1898	21 Aug
2289	1899	21 Aug
2290	1900	21 Aug
2291	1901	21 Aug
2292	1902	21 Aug
2293	1903	21 Aug
2294	1904*	20 Aug
2295	1905	20 Aug
2296	1906	20 Aug
2297	1907	20 Aug
2298	1908*	19 Aug
2299	1909	19 Aug
2300	1910	19 Aug
2301	1911	19 Aug
2302	1912*	18 Aug
2303	1913	18 Aug
2304	1914	18 Aug
2305	1915	18 Aug
2306	1916*	17 Aug
2307	1917	17 Aug
2308	1918	17 Aug
2309	1919	17 Aug
2310	1920*	16 Aug
2311	1921	16 Aug
2312	1922	16 Aug
2313	1923	16 Aug
2314	1924*	15 Aug
2315	1925	15 Aug
2316	1926	15 Aug
2317	1927	15 Aug
2318	1928*	14 Aug
2319	1929	14 Aug
2320	1930	14 Aug
2321	1931	14 Aug
2322	1932*	13 Aug
2323	1933	13 Aug
2324	1934	13 Aug
2325	1935	13 Aug
2326	1936*	12 Aug
2327	1937	12 Aug
2328	1938	12 Aug
2329	1939	12 Aug
2330	1940*	11 Aug
2331	1941	11 Aug
2332	1942	11 Aug
2333	1943	11 Aug
2334	1944*	10 Aug
2335	1945	10 Aug
2336	1946	10 Aug
2337	1947	10 Aug
2338	1948*	9 Aug
2339	1949	9 Aug
2340	1950	9 Aug
2341	1951	9 Aug
2342	1952*	8 Aug
2343	1953	8 Aug
2344	1954	8 Aug
2345	1955	8 Aug
2346	1956*	7 Aug
2347	1957	7 Aug
2348	1958	7 Aug
2349	1959	7 Aug
2350	1960*	6 Aug
2351	1961	6 Aug
2352	1962	6 Aug
2353	1963	6 Aug
2354	1964*	5 Aug
2355	1965	5 Aug
2356	1966	5 Aug
2357	1967	5 Aug
2358	1968*	4 Aug
2359	1969	4 Aug
2360	1970	4 Aug
2361	1971	4 Aug
2362	1972*	3 Aug
2363	1973	3 Aug
2364	1974	3 Aug
2365	1975	3 Aug
2366	1976*	2 Aug
2367	1977	2 Aug
2368	1978	2 Aug
2369	1979	2 Aug
2370	1980*	1 Aug
2371	1981	1 Aug
2372	1982	1 Aug
2373	1983	1 Aug
2374	1984*	31 Jul
2375	1985	31 Jul
2376	1986	31 Jul
2377	1987	31 Jul
2378	1988*	30 Jul
2379	1989	30 Jul
2380	1990	30 Jul
2381	1991	30 Jul
2382	1992*	29 Jul
2383	1993	29 Jul
2384	1994	29 Jul
2385	1995	29 Jul
2386	1996*	28 Jul
2387	1997	28 Jul
2388	1998	28 Jul
2389	1999	28 Jul
2390	2000*	27 Jul

YEZDEZRED AND JELALI CALENDARS

In the times of the ancient Persian Kings, as with so many eastern kingdoms, a new epoch was begun with the ascension of the king to the throne. The day of that ascension was considered day one of year one; and the New Year day falling on the anniversary. When Yezdezred mounted the throne on June 16, 632 A.D., a new epoch began. He was to be the last hereditary Persian King for many centuries. At the time, most of the Persians were Zoroastrians and used the Zoroastrian calendar. It was noted that the Zoroastrian calendar was only five days (although over 900 years) in disagreement with the Zezdezred calendar. Because the date of the New Year was so close in both calendars and each used a year of 365 days (and, consequently lost a day every 4 years) most of the Persian Zoroastrians and later some of the Zoroastrians of India, accepted the Yezdezred calendar. The remainder of the sect did not.

Nearly 1,100 years later, in 1720 A.D., a learned Zoroastrian priest from Persia went to Surat in Western India to instruct the Zoroastrians there. He noted that due to precision and varying calendar calculations, there was a month difference between the Yezdezred calendar in use in Persia, and that used in Surat. He made a notation of the fact but paid no further attention. In 1744 A.D. another Indian priest in Surat established a sect which he called "Kudmi" Zoroastrians, after the Kudmi or Yezdezred calendar which they accepted. The other Zoroastrians in the area became known as "Shensoy" and continued to use the calendar which was a month behind the "Kudmi" calendar. Other than this, there is no difference in the two sects.

The arrangement of the year remained as 12 months of 30 days each with 5 *gatha* days at the end of the year, and the local month names continued to be used.

In Persia, for tax revenue purposes only, an intercalory month was added to the tax calendar every 120 years. That, for tax purposes, brought the calendar in line with solar motion, but it did not affect the everyday or religious calendar in any way.

Around 1077 A.D. Sultan Jelaledin Malik Shah bin Alkh Ashlan Suljookee of Persia reformed the Yezdezred calendar in order to make it conform with solar motion. A committee of astroler/astronomers, led by Omar Khayyam, created a calendar setting the new year at the vernal equinox. Like the Yezdezred calendar it contained 12 months, consisting of 30 days each, with five days added to the end of the year. But, every fourth year another day was added to bring the calendar in line with solar motion. This new calendar was called the Jelali, after the Sultan. The committee of astrologers suggested that it run concurrently with the Yezdezred, called the "Kudmi." The simultaneous use of the calendars occurred on February 25 in the Yezdezred calendar and March 17 in the Jelali, a difference of 20 days. That difference increased by one day every four years. The Jelali calendar finally fell into disuse, except among a few isolated peoples.

YEZDEZRED CALENDAR

Yezdezred Year	Western Date of New Year (Julian)	Yezdezred Year	Western Date of New Year (Julian)	Yezdezred Year	Western Date of New Year (Julian)	Yezdezred Year	Western Date of New Year (Julian)
1	16 Jun 632*	22	11 Jun 653	43	6 Jun 674	64	1 Jun 695
2	16 Jun 633	23	11 Jun 654	44	6 Jun 675	65	31 May 696*
3	16 Jun 634	24	11 Jun 655	45	5 Jun 676*	66	31 May 697
4	16 Jun 635	25	10 Jun 656*	46	5 Jun 677	67	31 May 698
5	15 Jun 636*	26	10 Jun 657	47	5 Jun 678	68	31 May 699
6	15 Jun 637	27	10 Jun 658	48	5 Jun 679	69	30 May 700*
7	15 Jun 638	28	10 Jun 659	49	4 Jun 680*	70	30 May 701
8	15 Jun 639	29	9 Jun 660*	50	4 Jun 681	71	30 May 702
9	14 Jun 640*	30	9 Jun 661	51	4 Jun 682	72	30 May 703
10	14 Jun 641	31	9 Jun 662	52	4 Jun 683	73	29 May 704*
11	14 Jun 642	32	9 Jun 663	53	3 Jun 684*	74	29 May 705
12	14 Jun 643	33	8 Jun 664*	54	3 Jun 685	75	29 May 706
13	13 Jun 644*	34	8 Jun 665	55	3 Jun 686	76	29 May 707
14	13 Jun 645	35	8 Jun 666	56	3 Jun 687	77	28 May 708*
15	13 Jun 646	36	8 Jun 667	57	2 Jun 688*	78	28 May 709
16	13 Jun 647	37	7 Jun 668*	58	2 Jun 689	79	28 May 710
17	12 Jun 648*	38	7 Jun 669	59	2 Jun 690	80	28 May 711
18	12 Jun 649	39	7 Jun 670	60	2 Jun 691	81	27 May 712*
19	12 Jun 650	40	7 Jun 671	61	1 Jun 692*	82	27 May 713
20	12 Jun 651	41	6 Jun 672*	62	1 Jun 693	83	27 May 714
21	11 Jun 652*	42	6 Jun 673	63	1 Jun 694	84	27 May 715

Yezdezred Year	Western Date of New Year (Julian)		Yezdezred Year	Western Date of New Year (Julian)		Yezdezred Year	Western Date of New Year (Julian)		Yezdezred Year	Western Date of New Year (Julian)	
85	26 May	716*	136	14 May	767	187	1 May	818	238	18 Apr	869
86	26 May	717	137	13 May	768*	188	1 May	819	239	18 Apr	870
87	26 May	718	138	13 May	769	189	30 Apr	820*	240	18 Apr	871
88	26 May	719	139	13 May	770	190	30 Apr	821	241	17 Apr	872*
89	25 May	720*	140	13 May	771	191	30 Apr	822	242	17 Apr	873
90	25 May	721	141	12 May	772*	192	30 Apr	823	243	17 Apr	874
91	25 May	722	142	12 May	773	193	29 Apr	824*	244	17 Apr	875
92	25 May	723	143	12 May	774	194	29 Apr	825	245	16 Apr	876*
93	24 May	724*	144	12 May	775	195	29 Apr	826	246	16 Apr	877
94	24 May	725	145	11 May	776*	196	29 Apr	827	247	16 Apr	878
95	24 May	726	146	11 May	777	197	28 Apr	828*	248	16 Apr	879
96	24 May	727	147	11 May	778	198	28 Apr	829	249	15 Apr	880*
97	23 May	728*	148	11 May	779	199	28 Apr	830	250	15 Apr	881
98	23 May	729	149	10 May	780*	200	28 Apr	831	251	15 Apr	882
99	23 May	730	150	10 May	781	201	27 Apr	832*	252	15 Apr	883
100	23 May	731	151	10 May	782	202	27 Apr	833	253	14 Apr	884*
101	22 May	732*	152	10 May	783	203	27 Apr	834	254	14 Apr	885
102	22 May	733	153	9 May	784*	204	27 Apr	835	255	14 Apr	886
103	22 May	734	154	9 May	785	205	26 Apr	836*	256	14 Apr	887
104	22 May	735	155	9 May	786	206	26 Apr	837	257	13 Apr	888*
105	21 May	736*	156	9 May	787	207	26 Apr	838	258	13 Apr	889
106	21 May	737	157	8 May	788*	208	26 Apr	839	259	13 Apr	890
107	21 May	738	158	8 May	789	209	25 Apr	840*	260	13 Apr	891
108	21 May	739	159	8 May	790	210	25 Apr	841	261	12 Apr	892*
109	20 May	740*	160	8 May	791	211	25 Apr	842	262	12 Apr	893
110	20 May	741	161	7 May	792*	212	25 Apr	843	263	12 Apr	894
111	20 May	742	162	7 May	793	213	24 Apr	844*	264	12 Apr	895
112	20 May	743	163	7 May	794	214	24 Apr	845	265	11 Apr	896*
113	19 May	744*	164	7 May	795	215	24 Apr	846	266	11 Apr	897
114	19 May	745	165	6 May	796*	216	24 Apr	847	267	11 Apr	898
115	19 May	746	166	6 May	797	217	23 Apr	848*	268	11 Apr	899
116	19 May	747	167	6 May	798	218	23 Apr	849	269	10 Apr	900*
117	18 May	748*	168	6 May	799	219	23 Apr	850	270	10 Apr	901
118	18 May	749	169	5 May	800*	220	23 Apr	851	271	10 Apr	902
119	18 May	750	170	5 May	801	221	22 Apr	852*	272	10 Apr	903
120	18 May	751	171	5 May	802	222	22 Apr	853	273	9 Apr	904*
121	17 May	752*	172	5 May	803	223	22 Apr	854	274	9 Apr	905
122	17 May	753	173	4 May	804*	224	22 Apr	855	275	9 Apr	906
123	17 May	754	174	4 May	805	225	21 Apr	856*	276	9 Apr	907
124	17 May	755	175	4 May	806	226	21 Apr	857	277	8 Apr	908*
125	16 May	756*	176	4 May	807	227	21 Apr	858	278	8 Apr	909
126	16 May	757	177	3 May	808*	228	21 Apr	859	279	8 Apr	910
127	16 May	758	178	3 May	809	229	20 Apr	860*	280	8 Apr	911
128	16 May	759	179	3 May	810	230	20 Apr	861	281	7 Apr	912*
129	15 May	760*	180	3 May	811	231	20 Apr	862	282	7 Apr	913
130	15 May	761	181	2 May	812*	232	20 Apr	863	283	7 Apr	914
131	15 May	762	182	2 May	813	233	19 Apr	864*	284	7 Apr	915
132	15 May	763	183	2 May	814	234	19 Apr	865	285	6 Apr	916*
133	14 May	764*	184	2 May	815	235	19 Apr	866	286	6 Apr	917
134	14 May	765	185	1 May	816*	236	19 Apr	867	287	6 Apr	918
135	14 May	766	186	1 May	817	237	18 Apr	868*	288	6 Apr	919

Yezdezred Year	Western Date of New Year (Julian)	
289	5 Apr	920*
290	5 Apr	921
291	5 Apr	922
292	5 Apr	923
293	4 Apr	924*
294	4 Apr	925
295	4 Apr	926
296	4 Apr	927
297	3 Apr	928*
298	3 Apr	929
299	3 Apr	930
300	3 Apr	931
301	2 Apr	932*
302	2 Apr	933
303	2 Apr	934
304	2 Apr	935
305	1 Apr	936*
306	1 Apr	937
307	1 Apr	938
308	1 Apr	939
309	31 Mar	940*
310	31 Mar	941
311	31 Mar	942
312	31 Mar	943
313	30 Mar	944*
314	30 Mar	945
315	30 Mar	946
316	30 Mar	947
317	29 Mar	948*
318	29 Mar	949
319	29 Mar	950
320	29 Mar	951
321	28 Mar	952*
322	28 Mar	953
323	28 Mar	954
324	28 Mar	955
325	27 Mar	956*
326	27 Mar	957
327	27 Mar	958
328	27 Mar	959
329	26 Mar	960*
330	26 Mar	961
331	26 Mar	962
332	26 Mar	963
333	25 Mar	964*
334	25 Mar	965
335	25 Mar	966
336	25 Mar	967
337	24 Mar	968*
338	24 Mar	969
339	24 Mar	970
340	24 Mar	971
341	23 Mar	972*
342	23 Mar	973
343	23 Mar	974
344	23 Mar	975
345	22 Mar	976*
346	22 Mar	977
347	22 Mar	978
348	22 Mar	979
349	21 Mar	980*
350	21 Mar	981
351	21 Mar	982
352	21 Mar	983
353	20 Mar	984*
354	20 Mar	985
355	20 Mar	986
356	20 Mar	987
357	19 Mar	988*
358	19 Mar	989
359	19 Mar	990
360	19 Mar	991
361	18 Mar	992*
362	18 Mar	993
363	18 Mar	994
364	18 Mar	995
365	17 Mar	996*
366	17 Mar	997
367	17 Mar	998
368	17 Mar	999
369	16 Mar	1000*
370	16 Mar	1001
371	16 Mar	1002
372	16 Mar	1003
373	15 Mar	1004*
374	15 Mar	1005
375	15 Mar	1006
376	15 Mar	1007
377	14 Mar	1008*
378	14 Mar	1009
379	14 Mar	1010
380	14 Mar	1011
381	13 Mar	1012*
382	13 Mar	1013
383	13 Mar	1014
384	13 Mar	1015
385	12 Mar	1016*
386	12 Mar	1017
387	12 Mar	1018
388	12 Mar	1019
389	11 Mar	1020*
390	11 Mar	1021
391	11 Mar	1022
392	11 Mar	1023
393	10 Mar	1024*
394	10 Mar	1025
395	10 Mar	1026
396	10 Mar	1027
397	9 Mar	1028*
398	9 Mar	1029
399	9 Mar	1030
400	9 Mar	1031
401	8 Mar	1032*
402	8 Mar	1033
403	8 Mar	1034
404	8 Mar	1035
405	7 Mar	1036*
406	7 Mar	1037
407	7 Mar	1038
408	7 Mar	1039
409	6 Mar	1040*
410	6 Mar	1041
411	6 Mar	1042
412	6 Mar	1043
413	5 Mar	1044*
414	5 Mar	1045
415	5 Mar	1046
416	5 Mar	1047
417	4 Mar	1048*
418	4 Mar	1049
419	4 Mar	1050
420	4 Mar	1051
421	3 Mar	1052*
422	3 Mar	1053
423	3 Mar	1054
424	3 Mar	1055
425	2 Mar	1056*
426	2 Mar	1057
427	2 Mar	1058
428	2 Mar	1059
429	1 Mar	1060*
430	1 Mar	1061
431	1 Mar	1062
432	1 Mar	1063
433	29 Feb	1064*
434	28 Feb	1065
435	28 Feb	1066
436	28 Feb	1067
437	28 Feb	1068*
438	27 Feb	1069
439	27 Feb	1070
440	27 Feb	1071
441	27 Feb	1072*
442	26 Feb	1073
443	26 Feb	1074
444	26 Feb	1075
445	26 Feb	1076*
446	25 Feb	1077
447	25 Feb	1078
448	25 Feb	1079
449	25 Feb	1080*
450	24 Feb	1081
451	24 Feb	1082
452	24 Feb	1083
453	24 Feb	1084*
454	23 Feb	1085
455	23 Feb	1086
456	23 Feb	1087
457	23 Feb	1088*
458	22 Feb	1089
459	22 Feb	1090
460	22 Feb	1091
461	22 Feb	1092*
462	21 Feb	1093
463	21 Feb	1094
464	21 Feb	1095
465	21 Feb	1096*
466	20 Feb	1097
467	20 Feb	1098
468	20 Feb	1099
469	20 Feb	1100*
470	19 Feb	1101
471	19 Feb	1102
472	19 Feb	1103
473	19 Feb	1104*
474	18 Feb	1105
475	18 Feb	1106
476	18 Feb	1107
477	18 Feb	1108*
478	17 Feb	1109
479	17 Feb	1110
480	17 Feb	1111
481	17 Feb	1112*
482	16 Feb	1113
483	16 Feb	1114
484	16 Feb	1115
485	16 Feb	1116*
486	15 Feb	1117
487	15 Feb	1118
488	15 Feb	1119
489	15 Feb	1120*
490	14 Feb	1121
491	14 Feb	1122
492	14 Feb	1123

Yezdezred Year	Western Date of New Year (Julian)	Yezdezred Year	Western Date of New Year (Julian)	Yezdezred Year	Western Date of New Year (Julian)	Yezdezred Year	Western Date of New Year (Julian)
493	14 Feb 1124*	544	1 Feb 1175	595	19 Jan 1226	646	6 Jan 1277
494	13 Feb 1125	545	1 Feb 1176*	596	19 Jan 1227	647	6 Jan 1278
495	13 Feb 1126	546	31 Jan 1177	597	19 Jan 1228*	648	6 Jan 1279
496	13 Feb 1127	547	31 Feb 1178	598	18 Jan 1229	649	6 Jan 1280*
497	13 Feb 1128*	548	31 Feb 1179	599	18 Jan 1230	650	5 Jan 1281
498	12 Feb 1129	549	31 Jan 1180*	600	18 Jan 1231	651	5 Jan 1282
499	12 Feb 1130	550	30 Jan 1181	601	18 Jan 1232*	652	5 Jan 1283
500	12 Feb 1131	551	30 Jan 1182	602	17 Jan 1233	653	5 Jan 1284*
501	12 Feb 1132*	552	30 Jan 1183	603	17 Jan 1234	654	4 Jan 1285
502	11 Feb 1133	553	30 Jan 1184*	604	17 Jan 1235	655	4 Jan 1286
503	11 Feb 1134	554	29 Jan 1185	605	17 Jan 1236*	656	4 Jan 1287
504	11 Feb 1135	555	29 Jan 1186	606	16 Jan 1237	657	4 Jan 1288*
505	11 Feb 1136*	556	29 Jan 1187	607	16 Jan 1238	658	3 Jan 1289
506	10 Feb 1137	557	29 Jan 1188*	608	16 Jan 1239	659	3 Jan 1290
507	10 Feb 1138	558	28 Jan 1189	609	16 Jan 1240*	660	3 Jan 1291
508	10 Feb 1139	559	28 Jan 1190	610	15 Jan 1241	661	3 Jan 1292*
509	10 Feb 1140*	560	28 Jan 1191	611	15 Jan 1242	662	2 Jan 1293
510	9 Feb 1141	561	28 Jan 1192*	612	15 Jan 1243	663	2 Jan 1294
511	9 Feb 1142	562	27 Jan 1193	613	15 Jan 1244*	664	2 Jan 1295
512	9 Feb 1143	563	27 Jan 1194	614	14 Jan 1245	665	2 Jan 1296*
513	9 Feb 1144*	564	27 Jan 1195	615	14 Jan 1246	666	1 Jan 1297
514	8 Feb 1145	565	27 Jan 1196*	616	14 Jan 1247	667	1 Jan 1298
515	8 Feb 1146	566	26 Jan 1197	617	14 Jan 1248*	668	1 Jan 1299
516	8 Feb 1147	567	26 Jan 1198	618	13 Jan 1249	669	1 Jan 1300*
517	8 Feb 1148*	568	26 Jan 1199	619	13 Jan 1250	670	31 Dec 1300*
518	7 Feb 1149	569	26 Jan 1200*	620	13 Jan 1251	671	31 Dec 1301
519	7 Feb 1150	570	25 Jan 1201	621	13 Jan 1252*	672	31 Dec 1302
520	7 Feb 1151	571	25 Jan 1202	622	12 Jan 1253	673	31 Dec 1303
521	7 Feb 1152*	572	25 Jan 1203	623	12 Jan 1254	674	30 Dec 1304*
522	6 Feb 1153	573	25 Jan 1204*	624	12 Jan 1255	675	30 Dec 1305
523	6 Feb 1154	574	24 Jan 1205	625	12 Jan 1256*	676	30 Dec 1306
524	6 Feb 1155	575	24 Jan 1206	626	11 Jan 1257	677	30 Dec 1307
525	6 Feb 1156*	576	24 Jan 1207	627	11 Jan 1258	678	29 Dec 1308*
526	5 Feb 1157	577	24 Jan 1208*	628	11 Jan 1259	679	29 Dec 1309
527	5 Feb 1158	578	23 Jan 1209	629	11 Jan 1260*	680	29 Dec 1310
528	5 Feb 1159	579	23 Jan 1210	630	10 Jan 1261	681	29 Dec 1311
529	5 Feb 1160*	580	23 Jan 1211	631	10 Jan 1262	682	28 Dec 1312*
530	4 Feb 1161	581	23 Jan 1212*	632	10 Jan 1263	683	28 Dec 1313
531	4 Feb 1162	582	22 Jan 1213	633	10 Jan 1264*	684	28 Dec 1314
532	4 Feb 1163	583	22 Jan 1214	634	9 Jan 1265	685	28 Dec 1315
533	4 Feb 1164*	584	22 Jan 1215	635	9 Jan 1266	686	27 Dec 1316*
534	3 Feb 1165	585	22 Jan 1216*	636	9 Jan 1267	687	27 Dec 1317
535	3 Feb 1166	586	21 Jan 1217	637	9 Jan 1268*	688	27 Dec 1318
536	3 Feb 1167	587	21 Jan 1218	638	8 Jan 1269	689	27 Dec 1319
537	3 Feb 1168*	588	21 Jan 1219	639	8 Jan 1270	690	26 Dec 1320*
538	2 Feb 1169	589	21 Jan 1220*	640	8 Jan 1271	691	26 Dec 1321
539	2 Feb 1170	590	20 Jan 1221	641	8 Jan 1272*	692	26 Dec 1322
540	2 Feb 1171	591	20 Jan 1222	642	7 Jan 1273	693	26 Dec 1323
541	2 Feb 1172*	592	20 Jan 1223	643	7 Jan 1274	694	25 Dec 1324*
542	1 Feb 1173	593	20 Jan 1224*	644	7 Jan 1275	695	25 Dec 1325
543	1 Feb 1174	594	19 Jan 1225	645	7 Jan 1276*	696	25 Dec 1326

Yezdezred Year	Western Date of New Year (Julian)	Yezdezred Year	Western Date of New Year (Julian)	Yezdezred Year	Western Date of New Year (Julian)	Yezdezred Year	Western Date of New Year (Julian)
697	25 Dec 1327	748	12 Dec 1378	799	29 Nov 1429	850	16 Nov 1480*
698	24 Dec 1328*	749	12 Dec 1379	800	29 Nov 1430	851	16 Nov 1481
699	24 Dec 1329	750	11 Dec 1380*	801	29 Nov 1431	852	16 Nov 1482
700	24 Dec 1330	751	11 Dec 1381	802	28 Nov 1432*	853	16 Nov 1483
701	24 Dec 1331	752	11 Dec 1382	803	28 Nov 1433	854	15 Nov 1484*
702	23 Dec 1332*	753	11 Dec 1383	804	28 Nov 1434	855	15 Nov 1485
703	23 Dec 1333	754	10 Dec 1384*	805	28 Nov 1435	856	15 Nov 1486
704	23 Dec 1334	755	10 Dec 1385	806	27 Nov 1436*	857	15 Nov 1487
705	23 Dec 1335	756	10 Dec 1386	807	27 Nov 1437	858	14 Nov 1488*
706	22 Dec 1336*	757	10 Dec 1387	808	27 Nov 1438	859	14 Nov 1489
707	22 Dec 1337	758	9 Dec 1388*	809	27 Nov 1439	860	14 Nov 1490
708	22 Dec 1338	759	9 Dec 1389	810	26 Nov 1440*	861	14 Nov 1491
709	22 Dec 1339	760	9 Dec 1390	811	26 Nov 1441	862	13 Nov 1492*
710	21 Dec 1340*	761	9 Dec 1391	812	26 Nov 1442	863	13 Nov 1493
711	21 Dec 1341	762	8 Dec 1392*	813	26 Nov 1443	864	13 Nov 1494
712	21 Dec 1342	763	8 Dec 1393	814	25 Nov 1444*	865	13 Nov 1495
713	21 Dec 1343	764	8 Dec 1394	815	25 Nov 1445	866	12 Nov 1496*
714	20 Dec 1344*	765	8 Dec 1395	816	25 Nov 1446	867	12 Nov 1497
715	20 Dec 1345	766	7 Dec 1396*	817	25 Nov 1447	868	12 Nov 1498
716	20 Dec 1346	767	7 Dec 1397	818	24 Nov 1448*	869	12 Nov 1499
717	20 Dec 1347	768	7 Dec 1398	819	24 Nov 1449	870	11 Nov 1500*
718	19 Dec 1348*	769	7 Dec 1399	820	24 Nov 1450	871	11 Nov 1501
719	19 Dec 1349	770	6 Dec 1400*	821	24 Nov 1451	872	11 Nov 1502
720	19 Dec 1350	771	6 Dec 1401	822	23 Nov 1452*	873	11 Nov 1503
721	19 Dec 1351	772	6 Dec 1402	823	23 Nov 1453	874	10 Nov 1504*
722	18 Dec 1352*	773	6 Dec 1403	824	23 Nov 1454	875	10 Nov 1505
723	18 Dec 1353	774	5 Dec 1404*	825	23 Nov 1455	876	10 Nov 1506
724	18 Dec 1354	775	5 Dec 1405	826	22 Nov 1456*	877	10 Nov 1507
725	18 Dec 1355	776	5 Dec 1406	827	22 Nov 1457	878	9 Nov 1508*
726	17 Dec 1356*	777	5 Dec 1407	828	22 Nov 1458	879	9 Nov 1509
727	17 Dec 1357	778	4 Dec 1408*	829	22 Nov 1459	880	9 Nov 1510
728	17 Dec 1358	779	4 Dec 1409	830	21 Nov 1460*	881	9 Nov 1511
729	17 Dec 1359	780	4 Dec 1410	831	21 Nov 1461	882	8 Nov 1512*
730	16 Dec 1360*	781	4 Dec 1411	832	21 Nov 1462	883	8 Nov 1513
731	16 Dec 1361	782	3 Dec 1412*	833	21 Nov 1463	884	8 Nov 1514
732	16 Dec 1362	783	3 Dec 1413	834	20 Nov 1464*	885	8 Nov 1515
733	16 Dec 1363	784	3 Dec 1414	835	20 Nov 1465	886	7 Nov 1516*
734	15 Dec 1364*	785	3 Dec 1415	836	20 Nov 1466	887	7 Nov 1517
735	15 Dec 1365	786	2 Dec 1416*	837	20 Nov 1467	888	7 Nov 1518
736	15 Dec 1366	787	2 Dec 1417	838	19 Nov 1468*	889	7 Nov 1519
737	15 Dec 1367	788	2 Dec 1418	839	19 Nov 1469	890	6 Nov 1520*
738	14 Dec 1368*	789	2 Dec 1419	840	19 Nov 1470	891	6 Nov 1521
739	14 Dec 1369	790	1 Dec 1420*	841	19 Nov 1471	892	6 Nov 1522
740	14 Dec 1370	791	1 Dec 1421	842	18 Nov 1472*	893	6 Nov 1523
741	14 Dec 1371	792	1 Dec 1422	843	18 Nov 1473	894	5 Nov 1524*
742	13 Dec 1372*	793	1 Dec 1423	844	18 Nov 1474	895	5 Nov 1525
743	13 Dec 1373	794	30 Nov 1424*	845	18 Nov 1475	896	5 Nov 1526
744	13 Dec 1374	795	30 Nov 1425	846	17 Nov 1476*	897	5 Nov 1527
745	13 Dec 1375	796	30 Nov 1426	847	17 Nov 1477	898	4 Nov 1528*
746	12 Dec 1376*	797	30 Nov 1427	848	17 Nov 1478	899	4 Nov 1529
747	12 Dec 1377	798	29 Nov 1428*	849	17 Nov 1479	900	4 Nov 1530

Yezdezred Year	Western Date of New Year (Julian)	Yezdezred Year	Western Date of New Year (Julian)	Yezdezred Year	Western Date of New Year (Julian)	Yezdezred Year	Western Date of New Year (Julian)
901	4 Nov 1531	914	31 Oct 1544*	927	28 Oct 1557	940	25 Oct 1570
902	3 Nov 1532*	915	31 Oct 1545	928	28 Oct 1558	941	25 Oct 1571
903	3 Nov 1533	916	31 Oct 1546	929	28 Oct 1559	942	24 Oct 1572*
904	3 Nov 1534	917	31 Oct 1547	930	27 Oct 1560*	943	24 Oct 1573
905	3 Nov 1535	918	30 Oct 1548*	931	27 Oct 1561	944	24 Oct 1574
906	2 Nov 1536*	919	30 Oct 1549	932	27 Oct 1562	945	24 Oct 1575
907	2 Nov 1537	920	30 Oct 1550	933	27 Oct 1563	946	23 Oct 1576*
908	2 Nov 1538	921	30 Oct 1551	934	26 Oct 1564*	947	23 Oct 1577
909	2 Nov 1539	922	29 Oct 1552*	935	26 Oct 1565	948	23 Oct 1578
910	1 Nov 1540*	923	29 Oct 1553	936	26 Oct 1566	949	23 Oct 1579
911	1 Nov 1541	924	29 Oct 1554	937	26 Oct 1567	950	22 Oct 1580*
912	1 Nøv 1542	925	29 Oct 1555	938	25 Oct 1568*		
913	1 Nov 1543	926	28 Oct 1556*	939	25 Oct 1569		

Yezdezred Year	Western Date of New Year (Gregorian)		(Julian)	Yezdezred Year	Western Date of New Year (Gregorian)		(Julian)	Yezdezred Year	Western Date of New Year (Gregorian)		(Julian)
952	1 Nov	22 Oct	1582	900	25 Oct	15 Oct	1610	928	18 Oct	8 Oct	1638
953	1 Nov	22 Oct	1583	901	25 Oct	15 Oct	1611	929	18 Oct	8 Oct	1639
954	31 Oct	21 Oct	1584*	902	24 Oct	14 Oct	1612*	930	17 Oct	7 Oct	1640*
955	31 Oct	21 Oct	1585	903	24 Oct	14 Oct	1613	931	17 Oct	7 Oct	1641
956	31 Oct	21 Oct	1586	904	24 Oct	14 Oct	1614	932	17 Oct	7 Oct	1642
957	31 Oct	21 Oct	1587	905	24 Oct	14 Oct	1615	933	17 Oct	7 Oct	1643
958	30 Oct	20 Oct	1588*	906	23 Oct	13 Oct	1616*	934	16 Oct	6 Oct	1644*
959	30 Oct	20 Oct	1589	907	23 Oct	13 Oct	1617	935	16 Oct	6 Oct	1645
960	30 Oct	20 Oct	1590	908	23 Oct	13 Oct	1618	936	16 Oct	6 Oct	1646
961	30 Oct	20 Oct	1591	909	23 Oct	13 Oct	1619	937	16 Oct	6 Oct	1647
962	29 Oct	19 Oct	1592*	910	22 Oct	12 Oct	1620*	938	15 Oct	5 Oct	1648*
963	29 Oct	19 Oct	1593	911	22 Oct	12 Oct	1621	939	15 Oct	5 Oct	1649
964	29 Oct	19 Oct	1594	912	22 Oct	12 Oct	1622	940	15 Oct	5 Oct	1650
965	29 Oct	19 Oct	1595	913	22 Oct	12 Oct	1623	941	15 Oct	5 Oct	1651
966	28 Oct	18 Oct	1596*	914	21 Oct	11 Oct	1624*	942	14 Oct	4 Oct	1652*
967	28 Oct	18 Oct	1597	915	21 Oct	11 Oct	1625	943	14 Oct	4 Oct	1653
968	28 Oct	18 Oct	1598	916	21 Oct	11 Oct	1626	944	14 Oct	4 Oct	1654
969	28 Oct	18 Oct	1599	917	21 Oct	11 Oct	1627	945	14 Oct	4 Oct	1655
970	27 Oct	17 Oct	1600*	918	20 Oct	10 Oct	1628*	946	13 Oct	3 Oct	1656*
971	27 Oct	17 Oct	1601	919	20 Oct	10 Oct	1629	947	13 Oct	3 Oct	1657
972	27 Oct	17 Oct	1602	920	20 Oct	10 Oct	1630	948	13 Oct	3 Oct	1658
973	27 Oct	17 Oct	1603	921	20 Oct	10 Oct	1631	949	13 Oct	3 Oct	1659
974	26 Oct	16 Oct	1604*	922	19 Oct	9 Oct	1632*	950	12 Oct	2 Oct	1660*
975	26 Oct	16 Oct	1605	923	19 Oct	9 Oct	1633	951	12 Oct	2 Oct	1661
976	26 Oct	16 Oct	1606	924	19 Oct	9 Oct	1634	952	12 Oct	2 Oct	1662
897	26 Oct	16 Oct	1607	925	19 Oct	9 Oct	1635	953	12 Oct	2 Oct	1663
898	25 Oct	15 Oct	1608*	926	18 Oct	8 Oct	1636*	954	11 Oct	1 Oct	1664*
899	25 Oct	15 Oct	1609	927	18 Oct	8 Oct	1637	955	11 Oct	1 Oct	1665

Yezdezred Year	Western Date of New Year (Gregorian)		
	(Gregorian)	(Julian)	
956	11 Oct	1 Oct	1666
957	11 Oct	1 Oct	1667
958	10 Oct	30 Sep	1668*
959	10 Oct	30 Sep	1669
960	10 Oct	30 Sep	1670
961	10 Oct	30 Sep	1671
962	9 Oct	29 Sep	1672*
963	9 Oct	29 Sep	1673
964	9 Oct	29 Sep	1674
965	9 Oct	29 Sep	1675
966	8 Oct	28 Sep	1676*
967	8 Oct	28 Sep	1677
968	8 Oct	28 Sep	1678
969	8 Oct	28 Sep	1679
970	7 Oct	27 Sep	1680*
971	7 Oct	27 Sep	1681
972	7 Oct	27 Sep	1682
973	7 Oct	27 Sep	1683
974	6 Oct	26 Sep	1684*
975	6 Oct	26 Sep	1685
976	6 Oct	26 Sep	1686
977	6 Oct	26 Sep	1687
978	5 Oct	25 Sep	1688*
979	5 Oct	25 Sep	1689
980	5 Oct	25 Sep	1690
981	5 Oct	25 Sep	1691
982	4 Oct	24 Sep	1692*
983	4 Oct	24 Sep	1693
984	4 Oct	24 Sep	1694

Yezdezred Year	Western Date of New Year		
	(Gregorian)	(Julian)	
985	4 Oct	24 Sep	1695
986	3 Oct	23 Sep	1696*
987	3 Oct	23 Sep	1697
988	3 Oct	23 Sep	1698
989	3 Oct	23 Sep	1699
990	3 Oct	22 Sep	1700*
991	3 Oct	22 Sep	1701
992	3 Oct	22 Sep	1702
993	3 Oct	22 Sep	1703
994	2 Oct	21 Sep	1704*
995	2 Oct	21 Sep	1705
996	2 Oct	21 Sep	1706
997	2 Oct	21 Sep	1707
998	1 Oct	20 Sep	1708*
999	1 Oct	20 Sep	1709
1000	1 Oct	20 Sep	1710
1001	1 Oct	20 Sep	1711
1002	30 Sep	19 Sep	1712*
1003	30 Sep	19 Sep	1713
1004	30 Sep	19 Sep	1714
1005	30 Sep	19 Sep	1715
1006	29 Sep	18 Sep	1716*
1007	29 Sep	18 Sep	1717
1008	29 Sep	18 Sep	1718
1009	29 Sep	18 Sep	1719
1010	28 Sep	17 Sep	1720*
1011	28 Sep	17 Sep	1721
1012	28 Sep	17 Sep	1722
1013	28 Sep	17 Sep	1723

Yezdezred Year	Western Date of New Year		
	(Gregorian)	(Julian)	
1014	27 Sep	16 Sep	1724*
1015	27 Sep	16 Sep	1725
1016	27 Sep	16 Sep	1726
1017	27 Sep	16 Sep	1727
1018	26 Sep	15 Sep	1728*
1019	26 Sep	15 Sep	1729
1020	26 Sep	15 Sep	1730
1021	26 Sep	15 Sep	1731
1022	25 Sep	14 Sep	1732*
1023	25 Sep	14 Sep	1733
1024	25 Sep	14 Sep	1734
1025	25 Sep	14 Sep	1735
1026	24 Sep	13 Sep	1736*
1027	24 Sep	13 Sep	1737
1028	24 Sep	13 Sep	1738
1029	24 Sep	13 Sep	1739
1030	23 Sep	12 Sep	1740*
1031	23 Sep	12 Sep	1741
1032	23 Sep	12 Sep	1742
1033	23 Sep	12 Sep	1743
1034	22 Sep	11 Sep	1744*
1035	22 Sep	11 Sep	1745
1036	22 Sep	11 Sep	1746
1037	22 Sep	11 Sep	1747
1038	21 Sep	10 Sep	1748*
1039	21 Sep	10 Sep	1749
1040	21 Sep	10 Sep	1750
1041	21 Sep	10 Sep	1751

Yezdezred Year	Western Date of New Year (Julian)	
1042	20 Sep	1752*
1043	20 Sep	1753
1044	20 Sep	1754
1045	20 Sep	1755
1046	19 Sep	1756*
1047	19 Sep	1757
1048	19 Sep	1758
1049	19 Sep	1759
1050	18 Sep	1760*
1051	18 Sep	1761
1052	18 Sep	1762
1053	18 Sep	1763
1054	17 Sep	1764*
1055	17 Sep	1765

Yezdezred Year	Western Date of New Year (Julian)	
1056	17 Sep	1766
1057	17 Sep	1767
1058	16 Sep	1768*
1059	16 Sep	1769
1060	16 Sep	1770
1061	16 Sep	1771
1062	15 Sep	1772*
1063	15 Sep	1773
1064	15 Sep	1774
1075	15 Sep	1775
1066	14 Sep	1776*
1067	14 Sep	1777
1068	14 Sep	1778
1069	14 Sep	1779

Yezdezred Year	Western Date of New Year (Julian)	
1070	13 Sep	1780*
1071	13 Sep	1781
1072	13 Sep	1782
1073	13 Sep	1783
1074	12 Sep	1784*
1075	12 Sep	1785
1076	12 Sep	1786
1077	12 Sep	1787
1078	11 Sep	1788*
1079	11 Sep	1789
1080	11 Sep	1790
1081	11 Sep	1791
1082	10 Sep	1792*
1083	10 Sep	1793

Yezdezred Year	Western Date of New Year (Julian)	
1084	10 Sep	1794
1085	10 Sep	1795
1086	9 Sep	1796*
1087	9 Sep	1797
1088	9 Sep	1798
1089	9 Sep	1799
1090	9 Sep	1800
1091	9 Sep	1801
1092	9 Sep	1802
1093	9 Sep	1803
1094	8 Sep	1804*
1095	8 Sep	1805
1096	8 Sep	1806
1097	8 Sep	1807

Yezdezred Year	Western Date of New Year (Julian)		Yezdezred Year	Western Date of New Year (Julian)		Yezdezred Year	Western Date of New Year (Julian)		Yezdezred Year	Western Date of New Year (Julian)	
1098	7 Sep	1808*	1147	26 Aug	1857	1196	15 Aug	1906	1245	3 Aug	1955
1099	7 Sep	1809	1148	26 Aug	1858	1197	15 Aug	1907	1246	2 Aug	1956*
1100	7 Sep	1810	1149	26 Aug	1859	1198	14 Aug	1908*	1247	2 Aug	1957
1101	7 Sep	1811	1150	25 Aug	1860*	1199	14 Aug	1909	1248	2 Aug	1958
1102	6 Sep	1812*	1151	25 Aug	1861	1200	14 Aug	1910	1249	2 Aug	1959
1103	6 Sep	1813	1152	25 Aug	1862	1201	14 Aug	1911	1250	1 Aug	1960*
1104	6 Sep	1814	1153	25 Aug	1863	1202	13 Aug	1912*	1251	1 Aug	1961
1105	6 Sep	1815	1154	24 Aug	1864*	1203	13 Aug	1913	1252	1 Aug	1962
1106	5 Sep	1816*	1155	24 Aug	1865	1204	13 Aug	1914	1253	1 Aug	1963
1107	5 Sep	1817	1156	24 Aug	1866	1205	13 Aug	1915	1254	31 Jul	1964*
1108	5 Sep	1818	1157	24 Aug	1867	1206	12 Aug	1916*	1255	31 Jul	1965
1109	5 Sep	1819	1158	23 Aug	1868*	1207	12 Aug	1917	1256	31 Jul	1966
1110	4 Sep	1820*	1159	23 Aug	1869	1208	12 Aug	1918	1257	31 Jul	1967
1111	4 Sep	1821	1160	23 Aug	1870	1209	12 Aug	1919	1258	30 Jul	1968*
1112	4 Sep	1822	1161	23 Aug	1871	1210	11 Aug	1920*	1259	30 Jul	1969
1113	4 Sep	1823	1162	22 Aug	1872*	1211	11 Aug	1921	1260	30 Jul	1970
1114	3 Sep	1824*	1163	22 Aug	1873	1212	11 Aug	1922	1261	30 Jul	1971
1115	3 Sep	1825	1164	22 Aug	1874	1213	11 Aug	1923	1262	29 Jul	1972*
1116	3 Sep	1826	1165	22 Aug	1875	1214	10 Aug	1924*	1263	29 Jul	1973
1117	3 Sep	1827	1166	21 Aug	1876*	1215	10 Aug	1925	1264	29 Jul	1974
1118	2 Sep	1828*	1167	21 Aug	1877	1216	10 Aug	1926	1265	29 Jul	1975
1119	2 Sep	1829	1168	21 Aug	1878	1217	10 Aug	1927	1266	28 Jul	1976*
1120	2 Sep	1830	1169	21 Aug	1879	1218	9 Aug	1928*	1267	28 Jul	1977
1121	2 Sep	1831	1170	20 Aug	1880*	1219	9 Aug	1929	1268	28 Jul	1978
1122	1 Sep	1832*	1171	20 Aug	1881	1220	9 Aug	1930	1269	28 Jul	1979
1123	1 Sep	1833	1172	20 Aug	1882	1221	9 Aug	1931	1270	27 Jul	1980*
1124	1 Sep	1834	1173	20 Aug	1883	1222	8 Aug	1932*	1271	27 Jul	1981
1125	1 Sep	1835	1174	19 Aug	1884*	1223	8 Aug	1933	1272	27 Jul	1982
1126	31 Aug	1836*	1175	19 Aug	1885	1224	8 Aug	1934	1273	27 Jul	1983
1127	31 Aug	1837	1176	19 Aug	1886	1225	8 Aug	1935	1274	26 Jul	1984*
1128	31 Aug	1838	1177	19 Aug	1887	1226	7 Aug	1936*	1275	26 Jul	1985
1129	31 Aug	1839	1178	18 Aug	1888*	1227	7 Aug	1937	1276	26 Jul	1986
1130	30 Aug	1840*	1179	18 Aug	1889	1228	7 Aug	1938	1277	26 Jul	1987
1131	30 Aug	1841	1180	18 Aug	1890	1229	7 Aug	1939	1278	25 Jul	1988*
1132	30 Aug	1842	1181	18 Aug	1891	1230	6 Aug	1940*	1279	25 Jul	1989
1133	30 Aug	1843	1182	17 Aug	1892*	1231	6 Aug	1941	1280	25 Jul	1990
1134	29 Aug	1844*	1183	17 Aug	1893	1232	6 Aug	1942	1281	25 Jul	1991
1135	29 Aug	1845	1184	17 Aug	1894	1233	6 Aug	1943	1282	24 Jul	1992*
1136	29 Aug	1846	1185	17 Aug	1895	1234	5 Aug	1944*	1283	24 Jul	1993
1137	29 Aug	1847	1186	16 Aug	1896*	1235	5 Aug	1945	1284	24 Jul	1994
1138	28 Aug	1848*	1187	16 Aug	1897	1236	5 Aug	1946	1285	24 Jul	1995
1139	28 Aug	1849	1188	16 Aug	1898	1237	5 Aug	1947	1286	23 Jul	1996*
1140	28 Aug	1850	1189	16 Aug	1899	1238	4 Aug	1948*	1287	23 Jul	1997
1141	28 Aug	1851	1190	16 Aug	1900	1239	4 Aug	1949	1288	23 Jul	1998
1142	27 Aug	1852*	1191	16 Aug	1901	1240	4 Aug	1950	1289	23 Jul	1999
1143	27 Aug	1853	1192	16 Aug	1902	1241	4 Aug	1951	1290	22 Jul	1200*
1144	27 Aug	1854	1193	16 Aug	1903	1242	3 Aug	1952*	1291	22 Jul	1201
1145	27 Aug	1855	1194	15 Aug	1904*	1243	3 Aug	1953	1292	22 Jul	1202
1146	26 Aug	1856*	1195	15 Aug	1905	1244	3 Aug	1954	1293	22 Jul	1203

JELALI CALENDAR

Jelali Year	Western Date (Julian)	Jelali Year	Western Date (Julian)	Jelali Year	Western Date (Julian)	Jelali Year	Western Date (Julian)
1	1078 17 Mar	49	1126 17 Mar	97	1174 16 Mar	145	1222 16 Mar
2	1079 17 Mar	50	1127 17 Mar	98	1175 16 Mar	146	1223 16 Mar
3	1080* 17 Mar	51	1128* 17 Mar	99	1176* 16 Mar	147	1224* 16 Mar
4*	1081 16 Mar	52*	1129 16 Mar	100*	1177 15 Mar	148*	1225 15 Mar
5	1082 17 Mar	53	1130 17 Mar	101	1178 16 Mar	149	1226 16 Mar
6	1083 17 Mar	54	1131 17 Mar	102	1179 16 Mar	150	1227 16 Mar
7	1084* 17 Mar	55	1132* 17 Mar	103	1180* 16 Mar	151	1228* 16 Mar
8*	1085 16 Mar	56*	1133 16 Mar	104*	1181 15 Mar	152*	1229 15 Mar
9	1086 17 Mar	57	1134 17 Mar	105	1182 16 Mar	153	1230 16 Mar
10	1087 17 Mar	58	1135 17 Mar	106	1183 16 Mar	154	1231 16 Mar
11	1088* 17 Mar	59	1136* 17 Mar	107	1184* 16 Mar	155	1232* 16 Mar
12*	1089 16 Mar	60*	1137 16 Mar	108*	1185 15 Mar	156*	1233 15 Mar
13	1090 17 Mar	61	1138 17 Mar	109	1186 16 Mar	157	1234 15 Mar
14	1091 17 Mar	62	1139 17 Mar	110	1187 16 Mar	158	1235 15 Mar
15	1092* 17 Mar	63	1140* 17 Mar	111	1188* 16 Mar	159	1236* 15 Mar
16*	1093 16 Mar	64*	1141 16 Mar	112*	1189 15 Mar	160*	1237 14 Mar
17	1094 17 Mar	65	1142 16 Mar	113	1190 16 Mar	161	1238 15 Mar
18	1095 17 Mar	66	1143 16 Mar	114	1191 16 Mar	162	1239 15 Mar
19	1096* 17 Mar	67	1144* 16 Mar	115	1192* 16 Mar	163	1240* 15 Mar
20*	1097 16 Mar	68*	1145 15 Mar	116*	1193 15 Mar	164*	1241 14 Mar
21	1098 17 Mar	69	1146 16 Mar	117	1194 16 Mar	165	1242 15 Mar
22	1099 17 Mar	70	1147 16 Mar	118	1195 16 Mar	166	1243 15 Mar
23	1100* 17 Mar	71	1148* 16 Mar	119	1196* 16 Mar	167	1244* 15 Mar
24*	1101 16 Mar	72*	1149 15 Mar	120*	1197 15 Mar	168*	1245 14 Mar
25	1102 17 Mar	73	1150 16 Mar	121	1198 16 Mar	169	1246 15 Mar
26	1103 17 Mar	74	1151 16 Mar	122	1199 16 Mar	170	1247 15 Mar
27	1104* 17 Mar	75	1152* 16 Mar	123	1200* 16 Mar	171	1248* 15 Mar
28*	1105 16 Mar	76*	1153 15 Mar	124*	1201 15 Mar	172*	1249 14 Mar
29	1106 17 Mar	77	1154 16 Mar	125	1202 16 Mar	173	1250 15 Mar
30	1107 17 Mar	78	1155 16 Mar	126	1203 16 Mar	174	1251 15 Mar
31	1108* 17 Mar	79	1156* 16 Mar	127	1204* 16 Mar	175	1252* 15 Mar
32*	1109 16 Mar	80*	1157 15 Mar	128*	1205 15 Mar	176*	1253 14 Mar
33	1110 17 Mar	81	1158 16 Mar	129	1206 16 Mar	177	1254 15 Mar
34	1111 17 Mar	82	1159 16 Mar	130	1207 16 Mar	178	1255 15 Mar
35	1112* 17 Mar	83	1160* 16 Mar	131	1208* 16 Mar	179	1256* 15 Mar
36*	1113 16 Mar	84*	1161 15 Mar	132*	1209 15 Mar	180*	1257 14 Mar
37	1114 17 Mar	85	1162 16 Mar	133	1210 16 Mar	181	1258 15 Mar
38	1115 17 Mar	86	1163 16 Mar	134	1211 16 Mar	182	1259 15 Mar
39	1116* 17 Mar	87	1164* 16 Mar	135	1212* 16 Mar	183	1260* 15 Mar
40*	1117 16 Mar	88*	1165 15 Mar	136*	1213 15 Mar	184*	1261 14 Mar
41	1118 17 Mar	89	1166 16 Mar	137	1214 16 Mar	185	1262 15 Mar
42	1119 17 Mar	90	1167 16 Mar	138	1215 16 Mar	186	1263 15 Mar
43	1120* 17 Mar	91	1168* 16 Mar	139	1216* 16 Mar	187	1264* 15 Mar
44*	1121 16 Mar	92*	1169 15 Mar	140*	1217 15 Mar	188*	1265 14 Mar
45	1122 17 Mar	93	1170 16 Mar	141	1218 16 Mar	189	1266 15 Mar
46	1123 17 Mar	94	1171 16 Mar	142	1219 16 Mar	190	1267 15 Mar
47	1124* 17 Mar	95	1172* 16 Mar	143	1220* 16 Mar	191	1268* 15 Mar
48*	1125 16 Mar	96*	1173 15 Mar	144*	1221 15 Mar	192*	1269 14 Mar

Jelali Year	Western Date (Julian)	Jelali Year	Western Date (Julian)	Jelali Year	Western Date (Julian)	Jelali Year	Western Date (Julian)
193	1270 15 Mar	245	1322 15 Mar	297	1374 14 Mar	349	1426 13 Mar
194	1271 15 Mar	246	1323 15 Mar	298	1375 14 Mar	350	1427 13 Mar
195	1272* 15 Mar	247	1324* 15 Mar	299	1376* 14 Mar	351	1428* 13 Mar
196*	1273 14 Mar	248*	1325 14 Mar	300*	1377 13 Mar	352*	1429 12 Mar
197	1274 15 Mar	249	1326 14 Mar	301	1378 14 Mar	353	1430 13 Mar
198	1275 15 Mar	250	1327 14 Mar	302	1379 14 Mar	354	1431 13 Mar
199	1276* 15 Mar	251	1328* 14 Mar	303	1380* 14 Mar	355	1432* 13 Mar
200*	1277 14 Mar	252*	1329 13 Mar	304*	1381 13 Mar	356*	1433 12 Mar
201	1278 15 Mar	253	1330 14 Mar	305	1382 14 Mar	357	1434 13 Mar
202	1279 15 Mar	254	1331 14 Mar	306	1383 14 Mar	358	1435 13 Mar
203	1280* 15 Mar	255	1332* 14 Mar	307	1384* 14 Mar	359	1436* 13 Mar
204*	1281 14 Mar	256*	1333 13 Mar	308*	1385 13 Mar	360*	1437 12 Mar
205	1282 15 Mar	257	1334 14 Mar	309	1386 14 Mar	361	1438 13 Mar
206	1283 15 Mar	258	1335 14 Mar	310	1387 14 Mar	362	1439 13 Mar
207	1284* 15 Mar	259	1336* 14 Mar	311	1388* 14 Mar	363	1440* 13 Mar
208*	1285 14 Mar	260*	1337 13 Mar	312*	1389 13 Mar	364*	1441 12 Mar
209	1286 15 Mar	261	1338 14 Mar	313	1390 14 Mar	365	1442 13 Mar
210	1287 15 Mar	262	1339 14 Mar	314	1391 14 Mar	366	1443 13 Mar
211	1288* 15 Mar	263	1340* 14 Mar	315	1392* 14 Mar	367	1444* 13 Mar
212*	1289 14 Mar	264*	1341 13 Mar	316*	1393 13 Mar	368*	1445 12 Mar
213	1290 15 Mar	265	1342 14 Mar	317	1394 14 Mar	369	1446 13 Mar
214	1291 15 Mar	266	1343 14 Mar	318	1395 14 Mar	370	1447 13 Mar
215	1292* 15 Mar	267	1344* 14 Mar	319	1396* 14 Mar	371	1448* 13 Mar
216*	1293 14 Mar	268*	1345 13 Mar	320*	1397 13 Mar	372*	1449 12 Mar
217	1294 15 Mar	269	1346 14 Mar	321	1398 14 Mar	373	1450 13 Mar
218	1295 15 Mar	270	1347 14 Mar	322	1399 14 Mar	374	1451 13 Mar
219	1296* 15 Mar	271	1348* 14 Mar	323	1400* 14 Mar	375	1452* 13 Mar
220*	1297 14 Mar	272*	1349 13 Mar	324*	1401 13 Mar	376*	1453 12 Mar
221	1298 15 Mar	273	1350 14 Mar	325	1402 14 Mar	377	1454 13 Mar
222	1299 15 Mar	274	1351 14 Mar	326	1403 14 Mar	378	1455 13 Mar
223	1300* 15 Mar	275	1352* 14 Mar	327	1404* 14 Mar	379	1456* 13 Mar
224*	1301 14 Mar	276*	1353 13 Mar	328*	1405 13 Mar	380*	1457 12 Mar
225	1302 15 Mar	277	1354 14 Mar	329	1406 14 Mar	381	1458 13 Mar
226	1303 15 Mar	278	1355 14 Mar	330	1407 14 Mar	382	1459 13 Mar
227	1304* 15 Mar	279	1356* 14 Mar	331	1408* 14 Mar	383	1460* 13 Mar
228*	1305 14 Mar	280*	1357 13 Mar	332*	1409 13 Mar	384*	1461 12 Mar
229	1306 15 Mar	281	1358 14 Mar	333	1410 14 Mar	385	1462 13 Mar
230	1307 15 Mar	282	1359 14 Mar	334	1411 14 Mar	386	1463 13 Mar
231	1308* 15 Mar	283	1360* 14 Mar	335	1412* 14 Mar	387	1464* 13 Mar
232*	1309 14 Mar	284*	1361 13 Mar	336*	1413 13 Mar	388*	1465 12 Mar
233	1310 15 Mar	285	1362 14 Mar	337	1414 14 Mar	389	1466 13 Mar
234	1311 15 Mar	286	1363 14 Mar	338	1415 14 Mar	390	1467 13 Mar
235	1312* 15 Mar	287	1364* 14 Mar	339	1416* 14 Mar	391	1468* 13 Mar
236*	1313 14 Mar	288*	1365 13 Mar	340*	1417 13 Mar	392*	1469 12 Mar
237	1314 15 Mar	289	1366 14 Mar	341	1418 14 Mar	393	1470 13 Mar
238	1315 15 Mar	290	1367 14 Mar	342	1419 14 Mar	394	1471 13 Mar
239	1316* 15 Mar	291	1368* 14 Mar	343	1420* 14 Mar	395	1472* 13 Mar
240*	1317 14 Mar	292*	1369 13 Mar	344*	1421 13 Mar	396*	1473 12 Mar
241	1318 15 Mar	293	1370 14 Mar	345	1422 14 Mar	397	1474 13 Mar
242	1319 15 Mar	294	1371 14 Mar	346	1423 14 Mar	398	1475 13 Mar
243	1320* 15 Mar	295	1372* 14 Mar	347	1424* 14 Mar	399	1476* 13 Mar
244*	1321 14 Mar	296*	1373 13 Mar	348*	1425 13 Mar	400*	1477 12 Mar

Jelali Year	Western Date (Julian)		Jelali Year	Western Date (Julian)		Jelali Year	Western Date (Julian)		Jelali Year	Western Date (Julian)	
401	1478	13 Mar	428*	1505	12 Mar	455	1532*	12 Mar	482	1559	12 Mar
402	1479	13 Mar	429	1506	13 Mar	456*	1533	11 Mar	483	1560*	12 Mar
403	1480*	13 Mar	430	1507	13 Mar	457	1534	12 Mar	484*	1561	11 Mar
404*	1481	12 Mar	431	1508*	13 Mar	458	1535	12 Mar	485	1562	12 Mar
405	1482	13 Mar	432*	1509	12 Mar	459	1536*	12 Mar	486	1563	12 Mar
406	1483	13 Mar	433	1510	13 Mar	460*	1537	11 Mar	487	1564*	12 Mar
407	1484*	13 Mar	434	1511	13 Mar	461	1538	12 Mar	488*	1565	11 Mar
408*	1485	12 Mar	435	1512*	13 Mar	462	1539	12 Mar	489	1566	12 Mar
409	1486	13 Mar	436*	1513	12 Mar	463	1540*	12 Mar	490	1567	12 Mar
410	1487	13 Mar	437	1514	13 Mar	464*	1541	11 Mar	491	1568*	12 Mar
411	1488*	13 Mar	438	1515	13 Mar	465	1542	12 Mar	492*	1569	11 Mar
412*	1489	12 Mar	439	1516*	13 Mar	466	1543	12 Mar	493	1570	12 Mar
413	1490	13 Mar	440*	1517	12 Mar	467	1544*	12 Mar	494	1571	12 Mar
414	1491	13 Mar	441	1518	13 Mar	468*	1545	11 Mar	495	1572*	12 Mar
415	1492*	13 Mar	442	1519	13 Mar	469	1546	12 Mar	496*	1573	11 Mar
416*	1493	12 Mar	443	1520*	13 Mar	470	1547	12 Mar	497	1574	12 Mar
417	1494	13 Mar	444*	1521	12 Mar	471	1548*	12 Mar	498	1575	12 Mar
418	1495	13 Mar	445	1522	13 Mar	472*	1549	11 Mar	499	1576*	12 Mar
419	1496*	13 Mar	446	1523	13 Mar	473	1550	12 Mar	500*	1577	11 Mar
420*	1497	12 Mar	447	1524*	13 Mar	474	1551	12 Mar	501	1578	12 Mar
421	1498	13 Mar	448*	1525	12 Mar	475	1552*	12 Mar	502	1579	12 Mar
422	1499	13 Mar	449	1526	13 Mar	476*	1553	11 Mar	503	1580*	12 Mar
423	1500*	13 Mar	450	1527	13 Mar	477	1554	12 Mar	504*	1581	11 Mar
424*	1501	12 Mar	451	1528*	13 Mar	478	1555	12 Mar	505	1582	12 Mar
425	1502	13 Mar	452*	1529	12 Mar	479	1556*	12 Mar			
426	1503	13 Mar	453	1530	12 Mar	480*	1557	11 Mar			
427	1504*	13 Mar	454	1531	12 Mar	481	1558	12 Mar			

Jelali Year	Western Date of New Year	(Julian)	(Gregorian)	Jelali Year	Western Date of New Year	(Julian)	(Gregorian)	Jelali Year	Western Date of New Year	(Julian)	(Gregorian)
506	1583	12 Mar	22 Mar	525	1602	12 Mar	22 Mar	544*	1621	11 Mar	21 Mar
507	1584*	12 Mar	22 Mar	526	1603	12 Mar	22 Mar	545	1622	12 Mar	22 Mar
508*	1585	11 Mar	21 Mar	527	1604*	12 Mar	22 Mar	546	1623	12 Mar	22 Mar
509	1586	12 Mar	22 Mar	528*	1605	11 Mar	21 Mar	547	1624*	12 Mar	22 Mar
510	1587	12 Mar	22 Mar	529	1606	12 Mar	22 Mar	548*	1625	11 Mar	21 Mar
511	1588*	12 Mar	22 Mar	530	1607	12 Mar	22 Mar	549	1626	12 Mar	22 Mar
512*	1589	11 Mar	21 Mar	531	1608*	12 Mar	22 Mar	550	1627	12 Mar	22 Mar
513	1590	12 Mar	22 Mar	532*	1609	11 Mar	21 Mar	551	1628*	12 Mar	22 Mar
514	1591	12 Mar	22 Mar	533	1610	12 Mar	22 Mar	552*	1629	11 Mar	21 Mar
515	1592*	12 Mar	22 Mar	534	1611	12 Mar	22 Mar	553	1630	12 Mar	22 Mar
516*	1593	11 Mar	21 Mar	535	1612*	12 Mar	22 Mar	554	1631	12 Mar	22 Mar
517	1594	12 Mar	22 Mar	536*	1613	11 Mar	21 Mar	555	1632*	12 Mar	22 Mar
518	1595	12 Mar	22 Mar	537	1614	12 Mar	22 Mar	556*	1633	11 Mar	21 Mar
519	1596*	12 Mar	22 Mar	538	1615	12 Mar	22 Mar	557	1634	12 Mar	22 Mar
520*	1597	11 Mar	21 Mar	539	1616*	12 Mar	22 Mar	558	1635	12 Mar	22 Mar
521	1598	12 Mar	22 Mar	540*	1617	11 Mar	21 Mar	559	1636*	12 Mar	22 Mar
522	1599	12 Mar	22 Mar	541	1618	12 Mar	22 Mar	560*	1637	11 Mar	21 Mar
523	1600*	12 Mar	22 Mar	542	1619	12 Mar	22 Mar	561	1638	12 Mar	22 Mar
524*	1601	11 Mar	21 Mar	543	1620*	12 Mar	22 Mar	562	1639	12 Mar	22 Mar

Jelali Year	Western Date of New Year (Julian)		(Gregorian)
563	1640*	12 Mar	22 Mar
564*	1641	11 Mar	21 Mar
565	1642	12 Mar	22 Mar
566	1643	12 Mar	22 Mar
567	1644*	12 Mar	22 Mar
568*	1645	11 Mar	21 Mar
569	1646	11 Mar	21 Mar
570	1647	11 Mar	21 Mar
571	1648*	11 Mar	21 Mar
572*	1649	10 Mar	20 Mar
573	1650	11 Mar	21 Mar
574	1651	11 Mar	21 Mar
575	1652*	11 Mar	21 Mar
576*	1653	10 Mar	20 Mar
577	1654	11 Mar	21 Mar
578	1655	11 Mar	21 Mar
579	1656*	11 Mar	21 Mar
580*	1657	10 Mar	20 Mar
581	1658	11 Mar	21 Mar
582	1659	11 Mar	21 Mar
583	1660*	11 Mar	21 Mar
584*	1661	10 Mar	20 Mar
585	1662	11 Mar	21 Mar
586	1663	11 Mar	21 Mar
587	1664*	11 Mar	21 Mar
588*	1665	10 Mar	20 Mar
589	1666	11 Mar	21 Mar
590	1667	11 Mar	21 Mar
591	1668*	11 Mar	21 Mar
592*	1669	10 Mar	20 Mar
593	1670	11 Mar	21 Mar
594	1671	11 Mar	21 Mar
595	1672*	11 Mar	21 Mar
596*	1673	10 Mar	20 Mar
597	1674	11 Mar	21 Mar
598	1675	11 Mar	21 Mar
599	1676*	11 Mar	21 Mar
600*	1677	10 Mar	20 Mar

Jelali Year	Western Date of New Year (Julian)		(Gregorian)
601	1678	11 Mar	21 Mar
602	1679	11 Mar	21 Mar
603	1680*	11 Mar	21 Mar
604*	1681	10 Mar	20 Mar
605	1682	11 Mar	21 Mar
606	1683	11 Mar	21 Mar
607	1684*	11 Mar	21 Mar
608*	1685	10 Mar	20 Mar
609	1686	11 Mar	21 Mar
610	1687	11 Mar	21 Mar
611	1688*	11 Mar	21 Mar
612*	1689	10 Mar	20 Mar
613	1690	11 Mar	21 Mar
614	1691	11 Mar	21 Mar
615	1692*	11 Mar	21 Mar
616*	1693	10 Mar	20 Mar
617	1694	11 Mar	21 Mar
618	1695	11 Mar	21 Mar
619	1696*	11 Mar	21 Mar
620*	1697	10 Mar	20 Mar
621	1698	11 Mar	21 Mar
622	1699	11 Mar	21 Mar
623	1700	11 Mar	22 Mar
624*	1701	10 Mar	21 Mar
625	1702	11 Mar	22 Mar
626	1703	11 Mar	22 Mar
627	1704*	11 Mar	22 Mar
628*	1705	10 Mar	21 Mar
629	1706	11 Mar	22 Mar
630	1707	11 Mar	22 Mar
631	1708*	11 Mar	22 Mar
632*	1709	10 Mar	21 Mar
633	1710	11 Mar	22 Mar
634	1711	11 Mar	22 Mar
635	1712*	11 Mar	22 Mar
636*	1713	10 Mar	21 Mar
637	1714	11 Mar	22 Mar

Jelali Year	Western Date of New Year (Julian)		(Gregorian)
638	1715	11 Mar	22 Mar
639	1716*	11 Mar	22 Mar
640*	1717	10 Mar	21 Mar
641	1718	11 Mar	22 Mar
642	1719	11 Mar	22 Mar
643	1720*	11 Mar	22 Mar
644*	1721	10 Mar	21 Mar
645	1722	11 Mar	22 Mar
646	1723	11 Mar	22 Mar
647	1724*	11 Mar	22 Mar
648*	1725	10 Mar	21 Mar
649	1726	11 Mar	22 Mar
650	1727	11 Mar	22 Mar
651	1728*	11 Mar	22 Mar
652*	1729	10 Mar	21 Mar
653	1730	11 Mar	22 Mar
654	1731	11 Mar	22 Mar
655	1732*	11 Mar	22 Mar
656*	1733	10 Mar	21 Mar
657	1734	11 Mar	22 Mar
658	1735	11 Mar	22 Mar
659	1736*	11 Mar	22 Mar
660*	1737	10 Mar	21 Mar
661	1738	11 Mar	22 Mar
662	1739	11 Mar	22 Mar
663	1740*	11 Mar	22 Mar
664*	1741	10 Mar	21 Mar
665	1742	11 Mar	22 Mar
666	1743	11 Mar	22 Mar
667	1744*	11 Mar	22 Mar
668*	1745	10 Mar	21 Mar
669	1746	11 Mar	22 Mar
670	1747	11 Mar	22 Mar
671	1748*	11 Mar	22 Mar
672*	1749	10 Mar	21 Mar
673	1750	11 Mar	22 Mar
674	1751	11 Mar	22 Mar

Jelali Year	Western Date (Julian)	
675	1752*	22 Mar
676*	1753	21 Mar
677	1754	22 Mar
678	1755	22 Mar
679	1756*	22 Mar
680*	1757	21 Mar
681	1758	22 Mar

Jelali Year	Western Date (Julian)	
682	1759	22 Mar
683	1760*	22 Mar
684*	1761	21 Mar
685	1762	22 Mar
686	1763	22 Mar
687	1764*	22 Mar
688*	1765	21 Mar

Jelali Year	Western Date (Julian)	
689	1766	22 Mar
690	1767	22 Mar
691	1768*	22 Mar
692*	1769	21 Mar
693	1770	22 Mar
694	1771	22 Mar
695	1772*	22 Mar

Jelali Year	Western Date (Julian)	
696*	1773	21 Mar
697	1774	22 Mar
698	1775	22 Mar
699	1776*	22 Mar
700*	1777	21 Mar
701	1778	22 Mar
702	1779	22 Mar

Jelali Year	Western Date (Julian)	Jelali Year	Western Date (Julian)	Jelali Year	Western Date (Julian)	Jelali Year	Western Date (Julian)
703	1780* 22 Mar	754	1831 23 Mar	805	1882 23 Mar	856*	1933 23 Mar
704*	1781 21 Mar	755	1832* 23 Mar	806	1883 23 Mar	857	1934 24 Mar
705	1782 22 Mar	756*	1833 22 Mar	807	1884* 23 Mar	858	1935 24 Mar
706	1783 22 Mar	757	1834 23 Mar	808*	1885 22 Mar	859	1936* 24 Mar
707	1784* 22 Mar	758	1835 23 Mar	809	1886 23 Mar	860*	1937 23 Mar
708*	1785 21 Mar	759	1836* 23 Mar	810	1887 23 Mar	861	1938 24 Mar
709	1786 22 Mar	760*	1837 22 Mar	811	1888* 23 Mar	862	1939 24 Mar
710	1787 22 Mar	761	1838 23 Mar	812*	1889 22 Mar	863	1940* 24 Mar
711	1788* 22 Mar	762	1839 23 Mar	813	1890 23 Mar	864*	1941 23 Mar
712*	1789 21 Mar	763	1840* 23 Mar	814	1891 23 Mar	865	1942 24 Mar
713	1790 22 Mar	764*	1841 22 Mar	815	1892* 23 Mar	866	1943 24 Mar
714	1791 22 Mar	765	1842 23 Mar	816*	1893 22 Mar	867	1944* 24 Mar
715	1792* 22 Mar	766	1843 23 Mar	817	1894 23 Mar	868*	1945 23 Mar
716*	1793 21 Mar	767	1844* 23 Mar	818	1895 23 Mar	869	1946 24 Mar
717	1794 22 Mar	768*	1845 22 Mar	819	1896* 23 Mar	870	1947 24 Mar
718	1795 22 Mar	769	1846 23 Mar	820*	1897 22 Mar	871	1948* 24 Mar
719	1796* 22 Mar	770	1847 23 Mar	821	1898 23 Mar	872*	1949 23 Mar
720*	1797 21 Mar	771	1848* 23 Mar	822	1899 23 Mar	873	1950 24 Mar
721	1798 22 Mar	772*	1849 22 Mar	823	1900 24 Mar	874	1951 24 Mar
722	1799 22 Mar	773	1850 23 Mar	824*	1901 23 Mar	875	1952* 24 Mar
723	1800 23 Mar	774	1851 23 Mar	825	1902 24 Mar	876*	1953 23 Mar
724*	1801 22 Mar	775	1852* 23 Mar	826	1903 24 Mar	877	1954 24 Mar
725	1802 23 Mar	776*	1853 22 Mar	827	1904* 24 Mar	878	1955 24 Mar
726	1803 23 Mar	777	1854 23 Mar	828*	1905 23 Mar	879	1956* 24 Mar
727	1804* 23 Mar	778	1855 23 Mar	829	1906 24 Mar	880*	1957 23 Mar
728*	1805 22 Mar	779	1856* 23 Mar	830	1907 24 Mar	881	1958 24 Mar
729	1806 23 Mar	780*	1857 22 Mar	831	1908* 24 Mar	882	1959 24 Mar
730	1807 23 Mar	781	1858 23 Mar	832*	1909 23 Mar	883	1960* 24 Mar
731	1808* 23 Mar	782	1859 23 Mar	833	1910 24 Mar	884*	1961 23 Mar
732*	1809 22 Mar	783	1860* 23 Mar	834	1911 24 Mar	885	1962 24 Mar
733	1810 23 Mar	784*	1861 22 Mar	835	1912* 24 Mar	886	1963 24 Mar
734	1811 23 Mar	785	1862 23 Mar	836*	1913 23 Mar	887	1964* 24 Mar
735	1812* 23 Mar	786	1863 23 Mar	837	1914 24 Mar	888*	1965 23 Mar
736*	1813 22 Mar	787	1864* 23 Mar	838	1915 24 Mar	889	1966 24 Mar
737	1814 23 Mar	788*	1865 22 Mar	839	1916* 24 Mar	890	1967 24 Mar
738	1815 23 Mar	789	1866 23 Mar	840*	1917 23 Mar	891	1968* 24 Mar
739	1816* 23 Mar	790	1867 23 Mar	841	1918 24 Mar	892*	1969 23 Mar
740*	1817 22 Mar	791	1868* 23 Mar	842	1919 24 Mar	893	1970 24 Mar
741	1818 23 Mar	792*	1869 22 Mar	843	1920* 24 Mar	894	1971 24 Mar
742	1819 23 Mar	793	1870 23 Mar	844*	1921 23 Mar	895	1972* 24 Mar
743	1820* 23 Mar	794	1871 23 Mar	845	1922 24 Mar	896*	1973 23 Mar
744*	1821 22 Mar	795	1872* 23 Mar	846	1923 24 Mar	897	1974 24 Mar
745	1822 23 Mar	796*	1873 22 Mar	847	1924* 24 Mar	898	1975 24 Mar
746	1823 23 Mar	797	1874 23 Mar	848*	1925 23 Mar	899	1976* 24 Mar
747	1824* 23 Mar	798	1875 23 Mar	849	1926 24 Mar	900*	1977 23 Mar
748*	1825 22 Mar	799	1876* 23 Mar	850	1927 24 Mar	901	1978 24 Mar
749	1826 23 Mar	800*	1877 22 Mar	851	1928* 24 Mar	902	1979 24 Mar
750	1827 23 Mar	801	1878 23 Mar	852*	1929 23 Mar	903	1980* 24 Mar
751	1828* 23 Mar	802	1879 23 Mar	853	1930 24 Mar	904*	1981 23 Mar
752*	1829 22 Mar	803	1880* 23 Mar	854	1931 24 Mar	905	1982 24 Mar
753	1830 23 Mar	804*	1881 22 Mar	855	1932* 24 Mar	906	1983 24 Mar

Jelali Year	Western Date (Julian)		Jelali Year	Western Date (Julian)		Jelali Year	Western Date (Julian)		Jelali Year	Western Date (Julian)	
907	1984*	24 Mar	912*	1989	23 Mar	916*	1993	23 Mar	920*	1997	23 Mar
908*	1985	23 Mar	913	1990	24 Mar	917	1994	24 Mar	921	1998	24 Mar
909	1986	24 Mar	914	1991	24 Mar	918	1995	24 Mar	922	1999	24 Mar
910	1987	24 Mar	915	1992*	24 Mar	919	1996*	24 Mar	923	2000*	24 Mar
911	1988*	24 Mar									

AFRICA

AFRICA

Until recently, historians assumed that there were no major civilizations in Africa except Egypt. But archeological finds over the past 20 years have rapidly disclosed that this was not the case. On the west coast and in central Africa five large empires once existed—Nok, Benin, Mali, Songhay, Kanem Bornu and Ancient Ghana. There are also traces of extensive cities thought to date back to the 6th century B.C. and some of these were still in existence in the 19th century. Zimbabwe, Napungubwe, Zany, Engaruka, Khami, Penhalonga, Niekerk and Bigo have all been rediscovered in the southeast or south central part of the continent. Some, such as Zimbabwe, appear in the Arabic records because they were centers of trade with the countries across the Arab Gulf and Indian Oceans. Indications of how these inhabitants measured time are lost, or may never have existed, but it is unlikely that such extensive empires and trading cities had no written calendar of some sort.

Throughout its history, Africa was the object of numerous invasions. Persians overran Egypt in the 6th century B.C. The Greeks came as conquerers in the 3rd century B.C. to be followed later by the Romans. After the collapse of the Roman Empire, Africa was not disturbed by foreign invaders until a vast flux of Islamic peoples spread across the north during the late 7th and early 8th centuries A.D. Europeans arrived still later. While there was some exploration of Africa before the 14th century, it was not until Henry the Navigator's day that European colonies began to be established along the west coast. And it was still more than three centuries later before northern Europeans began their invasion of the central and southern parts of Africa. Each succeeding invasion brought with it a new group of people who introduced its own calendar which was used in conjunction with earlier ones.

Among Africa's disparate peoples—of Negroid, Semetic, Berber and Hametic—time was regulated by their way of life. Some were hunters, some were farmers, some were nomads. Generally speaking the black African peoples, like all peoples with unwritten calendars, kept time chiefly by correlating the motion of the moon with the annual seasons: in this case a wet, a growing and a hot season. These people recognized the times of the solstices and equinoxes as well as the rising and setting of the particularly bright stars. Sirius, the brightest of these, played a prominent part in the calendar. Planetary motion was noted and these ancient peoples had a fairly good reckoning of eclipse periodicity. The astronomical phenomenon enabled them to fix fairly accurately the dates of particular rulers and events which had profoundly affected them. While they had no astronomy as we know it, they were also able to figure the times of their religious observances. Most of them considered the period around the winter solstice to be the beginning of the year. Unfortunately, the coming of the white man and the imposition of his religion and customs resulted in much of the richness of the native customs being lost.

In and around the great desert, time was reckoned differently. The people here measured time by the passage of the moon and the seasons, which changed only from blazingly hot to quite cold, particularly at night. They were largely nomadic people, wandering over the desert areas or living in oases in the desert, sparse now, but perhaps more plentiful 2000 years ago, as indicated by extensive ruins in the area. When the Romans and later the Moslims conquered this area they brought their calendar with them.

The Mediterranean coast of Africa was the site of countless invasions. With the resulting mixture of peoples, many different calendars were used concurrently. Aside from the ancient Egyptian calendar, the Era of Nabonassar, a calendar used by the Chaldeans, Babylonians and others from the eastern shores of the Mediterranean was also employed. So too, during long and often overlapping periods were the calendars of the Greeks, Macedonians, Seleucids, Romans, Hebrews, etc. The calendar from the Abyssinian and Egyptian Eras was also utilized. Particularly in Alexandria, the calendar of the Julius Africanus Era of Antioch was employed by Greeks there. The following eras were used in this area:

The ABYSSINIAN ERA is said to have begun in 5493 B.C., about the same time as the founding of Egypt.

The JULIUS AFRICANUS ERA OF ANTIOCH is said to have begun in 5413 B.C.; its New Year is thought to have begun in the autumn.

The ALEXANDRIAN ERA is reputed to have begun on August 29, 5502 B.C.

The ERA OF DIOCLETIAN or ERA OF THE MARTYRS, variously given as August 29 and/or September 17, 284 A.D. It superceded the Alexandrian Era.

The ROMAN ERA is generally accepted as having begun April 24, 753 B.C., but several other dates have been given.

The ERA OF NABONASSAR began on February 26, 747 B.C., a Wednesday, at noon.

The EGYPTIAN ERA, like the Era of Nabonassar, also began on February 26, 747 B.C. Both of these eras had 365 days only. Leap year was unaccounted for. By 38 B.C., the New Year in the Egyptian Era had retreated to August 29, at which time it was declared that the New Year be fixed for that date.

EGYPT

Like all other peoples, the early Egyptians first devised a lunar calendar. As the centuries went by, this calendar was altered in an attempt to bring it into line with solar motion. Eventually a solar calendar was devised based on a year of 360 days. However it still used lunar motion to a great degree in determining religious feasts and festivals. This 360 day calendar, like so many others, was changed during the 8th century B.C. to one of 365 days. The extra five days was simply added to the end of the year.

The Egyptian calendar is the only one that is based on a geophysical rather than merely an astronomical fact. Egypt depended on the adequate rising and flooding of the Nile; each year as the Nile flooded, it brought down soil from the mountains to the Egyptian plain, enabling the people to establish an agricultural system which supported the civilization. During the early empire, the Nile began flooding in the last half of July. Modern calculations claim that the Dog Star, Sirius, the brightest star in the heavens, had its helical rising a few days before the expected rise in the river. Hence, the Egyptians considered the star a herald of the coming flood, and Sirius became an object of worship. If the flood was inadequate, this meant a period of famine; if it was excessive, planting would be delayed and again famine would result. So it was around the flood, as well as around solar and lunar motion that the early Egyptian calendar and its attendant religious observances was built, rather than the astronomical observations and calculations farther to the east across the Red Sea and the Persian Gulf.

In the 6th century B.C. the Persians overran Egypt, bringing their calendar with them. The Era of Nabonassar (see page xxx) was used by the Egyptians and the peoples of Kush and Nubia, or what is now Ethiopia and Abyssinia. In the 3rd century B.C. the Greeks invaded the area, introducing the Alexandrian Era. In the 1st century B.C. the Romans swarmed over northern Africa, particularly Egypt, and the new calendar of Julius Caesar was established (see page 294).

During the first century A.D. Christianity began to find its way down into upper Egypt and into Abyssinia, and a large number of people in these areas turned to this new religious belief. The peoples around the eastern coast of the Mediterranean and North Africa also began to accept these tenets as the Roman Empire began to collapse and Christian authorities grew stronger. Alexandria became one of the Christian strongholds. Then, in the late 7th and early 8th centuries A.D. a wave of Islam swept across Africa, and while Alexandria held firm, the other areas, with two exceptions, bowed to Islam, were converted and adopted the Islamic calendar.

The two peoples who did not opt for Islam were the early Christians in upper Egypt whom we now call the Copts, and their neighbors to the south, the Ethiopians. The sweep of Islam, however, cut them off from their Christian fellows for more than a thousand years. It was probably because of this isolation that the Coptic and Ethiopian churches never adopted the Western calendar. Instead these two isolated pockets of Christianity continued to employ the Alexandrian Era of 5502 B.C.; the Ethiopians dated their epoch from August 29, 7 A.D.; the Copts from August 29, 284 A.D.

Except for the number of the years, the two calendars were identical. The year had 365 days with an extra day every fourth year. It was divided into 12 months of 30 days each, with the extra five or six days added to the end of the year. The Ethiopians call these five or six extra days Pagnem or Quaggimi, and the leap year Kadis Yojannis. The Copts call the five days Nisi and the six days Kebus. Both the Copts and the Ethiopians celebrate Christmas on the 28th day of the fourth month in common years and the 29th in leap years. Good Friday begins on the morning of the day on which the Jews begin their Passover at 6 p.m., so that Easter always falls on the second full day of Passover. They observe a seven day week, the Holy Day of which is Sunday. The day begins at 6 a.m.

The Ethiopians made few concessions, if any, to Islam. They continued to use the old Ethiopian names for the months, while the Copts, who lived in much closer contact with the Arabs, gradually forgot Coptic as a language and adopted Arabic instead. The Coptic month names are known (they are the same as the Egyptian ones) and are still used for ecclesiastical purposes. The Arabic names are in daily use.

Month Number	Ethiopian Name	Coptic Name	Arabic Name
1	Maskarram	Thoth	Tot
2	Tekemt	Paophi	Babe
3	Hadar	Athyr	Hatur
4	Tahsas	Cohiac	Kyak
5	Tarr	Tybi	Tobe
6	Yekatit	Mesir	Mashir Amshir
7	Magawit	Phamenoth	Buramat
8	Miaziah	Pharmouti	Baramude
9	Genbot	Pachons	Bashans
10	Sanni	Payni	Baune
11	Hamle	Epiphi	Abib
12	Nas'hi	Mesori	Meshri

COPTIC CALENDAR

Coptic Year	Western Date (Julian) of New Year	Coptic Year	Western Date (Julian) of New Year	Coptic Year	Western Date (Julian) of New Year	Coptic Year	Western Date (Julian) of New Year
1	283 29 Aug	9	291 29 Aug	17	299 29 Aug	25	307 29 Aug
2	284* 29 Aug	10	292* 30 Aug	18	300* 30 Aug	26	308* 30 Aug
3	285 29 Aug	11	293 29 Aug	19	301 29 Aug	27	309 29 Aug
4*	286 29 Aug	12*	294 29 Aug	20*	302 29 Aug	28*	310 29 Aug
5	287 29 Aug	13	295 29 Aug	21	303 29 Aug	29	311 29 Aug
6	288* 30 Aug	14	296* 30 Aug	22	304* 30 Aug	30	312* 30 Aug
7	289 29 Aug	15	297 29 Aug	23	305 29 Aug	31	313 29 Aug
8*	290 29 Aug	16*	298 29 Aug	24*	306 29 Aug	32*	314 29 Aug

Coptic Year	Western Date (Julian) of New Year	Coptic Year	Western Date (Julian) of New Year	Coptic Year	Western Date (Julian) of New Year	Coptic Year	Western Date (Julian) of New Year
33	315 29 Aug	84*	366 29 Aug	135	417 29 Aug	186	468* 29 Aug
34	316* 30 Aug	85	367 30 Aug	136	418 29 Aug	187	469 29 Aug
35	317 29 Aug	86	368* 29 Aug	137	419 30 Aug	188	470 29 Aug
36*	318 29 Aug	87	369 29 Aug	138	420* 29 Aug	189	471 30 Aug
37	319 29 Aug	88*	370 29 Aug	139	421 29 Aug	190	472* 29 Aug
38	320* 30 Aug	89	371 30 Aug	140	422 29 Aug	191	473 29 Aug
39	321 29 Aug	90	372* 29 Aug	141	423 30 Aug	192	474 29 Aug
40*	322 29 Aug	91	373 29 Aug	142	424* 29 Aug	193	475 30 Aug
41	323 29 Aug	92*	374 29 Aug	143	425 29 Aug	194	476* 29 Aug
42	324* 30 Aug	93	375 30 Aug	144	426 29 Aug	195	477 29 Aug
43	325 29 Aug	94	376* 29 Aug	145	427 30 Aug	196	478 29 Aug
44*	326 29 Aug	95	377 29 Aug	146	428* 29 Aug	197	479 30 Aug
45	327 29 Aug	96*	378 29 Aug	147	429 29 Aug	198	480* 29 Aug
46	328* 30 Aug	97	379 30 Aug	148	430 29 Aug	199	481 29 Aug
47	329 29 Aug	98	380* 29 Aug	149	431 30 Aug	200	482 29 Aug
48*	330 29 Aug	99	381 29 Aug	150	432* 29 Aug	201	483 30 Aug
49	331 29 Aug	100*	382 29 Aug	151	433 29 Aug	202	484* 29 Aug
50	332* 30 Aug	101	383 30 Aug	152	434 29 Aug	203	485 29 Aug
51	333 29 Aug	102	384* 29 Aug	153	435 30 Aug	204	486 29 Aug
52*	334 29 Aug	103	385 29 Aug	154	436* 29 Aug	205	487 30 Aug
53	335 30 Aug	104*	386 29 Aug	155	437 29 Aug	206	488* 29 Aug
54	336* 29 Aug	105	387 30 Aug	156	438 29 Aug	207	489 29 Aug
55	337 29 Aug	106	388* 29 Aug	157	439 30 Aug	208	490 29 Aug
56*	338 29 Aug	107	389 29 Aug	158	440* 29 Aug	209	491 30 Aug
57	339 30 Aug	108	390 29 Aug	159	441 29 Aug	210	492* 29 Aug
58	340* 29 Aug	109	391 30 Aug	160	442 29 Aug	211	493 29 Aug
59	341 29 Aug	110	392* 29 Aug	161	443 30 Aug	212	494 29 Aug
60*	342 29 Aug	111	393 29 Aug	162	444* 29 Aug	213	495 30 Aug
61	343 30 Aug	112	394 29 Aug	163	445 29 Aug	214	496* 29 Aug
62	344* 29 Aug	113	395 30 Aug	164	446 29 Aug	215	497 29 Aug
63	345 29 Aug	114	396* 29 Aug	165	447 30 Aug	216	498 29 Aug
64*	346 29 Aug	115	397 29 Aug	166	448* 29 Aug	217	499 30 Aug
65	347 30 Aug	116	398 29 Aug	167	449 29 Aug	218	500* 29 Aug
66	348* 29 Aug	117	399 30 Aug	168	450 29 Aug	219	501 29 Aug
67	349 29 Aug	118	400* 29 Aug	169	451 30 Aug	220	502 29 Aug
68*	350 29 Aug	119	401 29 Aug	170	452* 29 Aug	221	503 30 Aug
69	351 30 Aug	120	402 29 Aug	171	453 29 Aug	222	504* 29 Aug
70	352* 29 Aug	121	403 30 Aug	172	454 29 Aug	223	505 29 Aug
71	353 29 Aug	122	404* 29 Aug	173	455 30 Aug	224	506 29 Aug
72*	354 29 Aug	123	405 29 Aug	174	456* 20 Aug	225	507 30 Aug
73	355 30 Aug	124	406 29 Aug	175	457 29 Aug	226	508* 29 Aug
74	356* 29 Aug	125	407 30 Aug	176	458 29 Aug	227	509 29 Aug
75	357 29 Aug	126	408* 29 Aug	177	459 30 Aug	228	510 29 Aug
76*	358 29 Aug	127	409 29 Aug	178	460* 29 Aug	229	511 30 Aug
77	359 30 Aug	128	410 29 Aug	179	461 29 Aug	230	512* 29 Aug
78	360* 29 Aug	129	411 30 Aug	180	462 29 Aug	231	513 29 Aug
79	361 29 Aug	130	412* 29 Aug	181	463 30 Aug	232	514 29 Aug
80*	362 29 Aug	131	413 29 Aug	182	464* 29 Aug	233	515 30 Aug
81	363 30 Aug	132	414 29 Aug	183	465 29 Aug	234	516* 29 Aug
82	364* 29 Aug	133	415 30 Aug	184	466 29 Aug	235	517 29 Aug
83	365 29 Aug	134	416* 29 Aug	185	467 30 Aug	236	518 29 Aug

Coptic Year	Western Date (Julian) of New Year	Coptic Year	Western Date (Julian) of New Year	Coptic Year	Western Date (Julian) of New Year	Coptic Year	Western Date (Julian) of New Year
237	519 30 Aug	288	570 29 Aug	339	621 29 Aug	390	672* 29 Aug
238	520* 29 Aug	289	571 30 Aug	340	622 29 Aug	391	673 29 Aug
239	521 29 Aug	290	572* 29 Aug	341	623 30 Aug	392	674 29 Aug
240	522 29 Aug	291	573 29 Aug	342	624* 29 Aug	393	675 30 Aug
241	523 30 Aug	292	574 29 Aug	343	625 29 Aug	394	676* 29 Aug
242	524* 29 Aug	293	575 30 Aug	344	626 29 Aug	395	677 29 Aug
243	525 29 Aug	294	576* 29 Aug	345	627 30 Aug	396	678 29 Aug
244	526 29 Aug	295	577 29 Aug	346	628* 29 Aug	397	679 30 Aug
245	527 30 Aug	296	578 29 Aug	347	629 29 Aug	398	680* 29 Aug
246	528* 29 Aug	297	579 30 Aug	348	630 29 Aug	399	681 29 Aug
247	529 29 Aug	298	580* 29 Aug	349	631 30 Aug	400	682 29 Aug
248	530 29 Aug	299	581 29 Aug	350	632* 29 Aug	401	683 30 Aug
249	531 30 Aug	300	582 29 Aug	351	633 29 Aug	402	684* 29 Aug
250	532* 29 Aug	301	583 30 Aug	352	634 29 Aug	403	685 29 Aug
251	533 29 Aug	302	584* 29 Aug	353	635 30 Aug	404	686 29 Aug
252	534 29 Aug	303	585 29 Aug	354	636* 29 Aug	405	687 30 Aug
253	535 30 Aug	304	586 29 Aug	355	637 29 Aug	406	688* 29 Aug
254	536* 29 Aug	305	587 30 Aug	356	638 29 Aug	407	689 29 Aug
255	537 29 Aug	306	588* 29 Aug	357	639 30 Aug	408	690 29 Aug
256	538 29 Aug	307	589 29 Aug	358	640* 29 Aug	409	691 30 Aug
257	539 30 Aug	308	590 29 Aug	359	641 29 Aug	410	692* 29 Aug
258	540* 29 Aug	309	591 30 Aug	360	642 29 Aug	411	693 29 Aug
259	541 29 Aug	310	592* 29 Aug	361	643 30 Aug	412	694 29 Aug
260	542 29 Aug	311	593 29 Aug	362	644* 29 Aug	413	695 30 Aug
261	543 30 Aug	312	594 29 Aug	363	645 29 Aug	414	696* 29 Aug
262	544* 29 Aug	313	595 30 Aug	364	646 29 Aug	415	697 29 Aug
263	545 29 Aug	314	596* 29 Aug	365	647 30 Aug	416	698 29 Aug
264	546 29 Aug	315	597 29 Aug	366	648* 29 Aug	417	699 30 Aug
265	547 30 Aug	316	598 29 Aug	367	649 29 Aug	418	700* 29 Aug
266	548* 29 Aug	317	599 30 Aug	368	650 29 Aug	419	701 29 Aug
267	549 29 Aug	318	600* 29 Aug	369	651 30 Aug	420	702 29 Aug
268	550 29 Aug	319	601 29 Aug	370	652* 29 Aug	421	703 30 Aug
269	551 30 Aug	320	602 29 Aug	371	653 29 Aug	422	704* 29 Aug
270	552* 29 Aug	321	603 30 Aug	372	654 29 Aug	423	705 29 Aug
271	553 29 Aug	322	604* 29 Aug	373	655 30 Aug	424	706 29 Aug
272	554 29 Aug	323	605 29 Aug	374	656* 29 Aug	425	707 30 Aug
273	555 30 Aug	324	606 29 Aug	375	657 29 Aug	426	708* 29 Aug
274	556* 29 Aug	325	607 30 Aug	376	658 29 Aug	427	709 29 Aug
275	557 29 Aug	326	608* 29 Aug	377	659 30 Aug	428	710 29 Aug
276	558 29 Aug	327	609 29 Aug	378	660* 29 Aug	429	711 30 Aug
277	559 30 Aug	328	610 29 Aug	379	661 29 Aug	430	712* 29 Aug
278	560* 29 Aug	329	611 30 Aug	380	662 29 Aug	431	713 29 Aug
279	561 29 Aug	330	612* 29 Aug	381	663 30 Aug	432	714 29 Aug
280	562 29 Aug	331	613 29 Aug	382	664* 29 Aug	433	715 30 Aug
281	563 30 Aug	332	614 29 Aug	383	665 29 Aug	434	716* 29 Aug
282	564* 29 Aug	333	615 30 Aug	384	666 29 Aug	435	717 29 Aug
283	565 29 Aug	334	616* 29 Aug	385	667 30 Aug	436	718 29 Aug
284	566 29 Aug	335	617 29 Aug	386	668* 29 Aug	437	719 30 Aug
285	567 30 Aug	336	618 29 Aug	387	669 29 Aug	438	720* 29 Aug
286	568* 29 Aug	337	619 30 Aug	388	670 29 Aug	439	721 29 Aug
287	569 29 Aug	338	620* 29 Aug	389	671 30 Aug	440	722 29 Aug

Coptic Year	Western Date (Julian) of New Year	Coptic Year	Western Date (Julian) of New Year	Coptic Year	Western Date (Julian) of New Year	Coptic Year	Western Date (Julian) of New Year
441	723 30 Aug	492	774 29 Aug	543	825 29 Aug	594	876* 29 Aug
442	724* 29 Aug	493	775 30 Aug	544	826 29 Aug	595	877 29 Aug
443	725 29 Aug	494	776* 29 Aug	545	827 30 Aug	596	878 29 Aug
444	726 29 Aug	495	777 29 Aug	546	828* 29 Aug	597	879 30 Aug
445	727 30 Aug	496	778 29 Aug	547	829 29 Aug	598	880* 29 Aug
446	728* 29 Aug	497	779 30 Aug	548	830 29 Aug	599	881 29 Aug
447	729 29 Aug	498	780* 29 Aug	549	831 30 Aug	600	882 29 Aug
448	730 29 Aug	499	781 29 Aug	550	832* 29 Aug	601	883 30 Aug
449	731 30 Aug	500	782 29 Aug	551	833 29 Aug	602	884* 29 Aug
450	732* 29 Aug	501	783 30 Aug	552	834 29 Aug	603	885 29 Aug
451	733 29 Aug	502	784* 29 Aug	553	835 30 Aug	604	886 29 Aug
452	734 29 Aug	503	785 29 Aug	554	836* 29 Aug	605	887 30 Aug
453	735 30 Aug	504	786 29 Aug	555	837 29 Aug	606	888* 29 Aug
454	736* 29 Aug	505	787 30 Aug	556	838 29 Aug	607	889 29 Aug
455	737 29 Aug	506	788* 29 Aug	557	839 30 Aug	608	890 29 Aug
456	738 29 Aug	507	789 29 Aug	558	840* 29 Aug	609	891 30 Aug
457	739 30 Aug	508	790 29 Aug	559	841 29 Aug	610	892* 29 Aug
458	740* 29 Aug	509	791 30 Aug	560	842 29 Aug	611	893 29 Aug
459	741 29 Aug	510	792* 29 Aug	561	843 30 Aug	612	894 29 Aug
460	742 29 Aug	511	793 29 Aug	562	844* 29 Aug	613	895 30 Aug
461	743 30 Aug	512	794 29 Aug	563	845 29 Aug	614	896* 29 Aug
462	744* 29 Aug	513	795 30 Aug	564	846 29 Aug	615	897 29 Aug
463	745 29 Aug	514	796* 29 Aug	565	847 30 Aug	616	898 29 Aug
464	746 29 Aug	515	797 29 Aug	566	848* 29 Aug	617	899 30 Aug
465	747 30 Aug	516	798 29 Aug	567	849 29 Aug	618	900* 29 Aug
466	748* 29 Aug	517	799 30 Aug	568	850 29 Aug	619	901 29 Aug
467	749 29 Aug	518	800* 29 Aug	569	851 30 Aug	620	902 29 Aug
468	750 29 Aug	519	801 29 Aug	570	852* 29 Aug	621	903 30 Aug
469	751 30 Aug	520	802 29 Aug	571	853 29 Aug	622	904 29 Aug
470	752* 29 Aug	521	803 30 Aug	572	854 29 Aug	623	905 29 Aug
471	753 29 Aug	522	804* 29 Aug	573	855 30 Aug	624	906 29 Aug
472	754 29 Aug	523	805 29 Aug	574	856* 29 Aug	625	907 30 Aug
473	755 30 Aug	524	806 29 Aug	575	857 29 Aug	626	908* 29 Aug
474	756* 29 Aug	525	807 30 Aug	576	858 29 Aug	627	909 29 Aug
475	757 29 Aug	526	808* 29 Aug	577	859 30 Aug	628	910 29 Aug
476	758 29 Aug	527	809 29 Aug	578	860* 29 Aug	629	911 30 Aug
477	759 30 Aug	528	810 29 Aug	579	861 29 Aug	630	912* 29 Aug
478	760* 29 Aug	529	811 30 Aug	580	862 29 Aug	631	913 29 Aug
479	761 29 Aug	530	812* 29 Aug	581	863 30 Aug	632	914 29 Aug
480	762 29 Aug	531	813 29 Aug	582	864* 29 Aug	633	915 30 Aug
481	763 30 Aug	532	814 29 Aug	583	865 29 Aug	634	916* 29 Aug
482	764* 29 Aug	533	815 30 Aug	584	866 29 Aug	635	917 29 Aug
483	765 29 Aug	534	816* 29 Aug	585	867 30 Aug	636	918 29 Aug
484	766 29 Aug	535	817 29 Aug	586	868* 29 Aug	637	919 30 Aug
485	767 30 Aug	536	818 29 Aug	587	869 29 Aug	638	920* 29 Aug
486	768* 29 Aug	537	819 30 Aug	588	870 29 Aug	639	921 29 Aug
487	769 29 Aug	538	820* 29 Aug	589	871 30 Aug	640	922 29 Aug
488	770 29 Aug	539	821 29 Aug	590	872* 29 Aug	641	923 30 Aug
489	771 30 Aug	540	822 29 Aug	591	873 29 Aug	642	924* 29 Aug
490	772* 29 Aug	541	823 30 Aug	592	874 29 Aug	643	925 29 Aug
491	773 29 Aug	542	824* 29 Aug	593	875 30 Aug	644	926 29 Aug

Coptic Year	Western Date (Julian) of New Year	Coptic Year	Western Date (Julian) of New Year	Coptic Year	Western Date (Julian) of New Year	Coptic Year	Western Date (Julian) of New Year
645	927 30 Aug	696	978 29 Aug	747	1029 29 Aug	798	1080* 29 Aug
646	928* 29 Aug	697	979 30 Aug	748	1030 29 Aug	799	1081 29 Aug
647	929 29 Aug	698	980* 29 Aug	749	1031 30 Aug	800	1082 29 Aug
648	930 29 Aug	699	981 29 Aug	750	1032* 29 Aug	801	1083 30 Aug
649	931 30 Aug	700	982 29 Aug	751	1033 29 Aug	802	1084* 29 Aug
650	932* 29 Aug	701	983 30 Aug	752	1034 29 Aug	803	1085 29 Aug
651	933 29 Aug	702	984* 29 Aug	753	1035 30 Aug	804	1086 29 Aug
652	934 29 Aug	703	985 29 Aug	754	1036* 29 Aug	805	1087 30 Aug
653	935 30 Aug	704	986 29 Aug	755	1037 29 Aug	806	1088* 29 Aug
654	936* 29 Aug	705	987 30 Aug	756	1038 29 Aug	807	1089 29 Aug
655	937 29 Aug	706	988* 29 Aug	757	1039 30 Aug	808	1090 29 Aug
656	938 29 Aug	707	989 29 Aug	758	1040* 29 Aug	809	1091 30 Aug
657	939 30 Aug	708	990 29 Aug	759	1041 29 Aug	810	1092* 29 Aug
658	940* 29 Aug	709	991 30 Aug	760	1042 29 Aug	811	1093 29 Aug
659	941 29 Aug	710	992* 29 Aug	761	1043 30 Aug	812	1094 29 Aug
660	942 29 Aug	711	993 29 Aug	762	1044* 29 Aug	813	1095 30 Aug
661	943 30 Aug	712	994 29 Aug	763	1045 29 Aug	814	1096* 29 Aug
662	944* 29 Aug	713	995 30 Aug	764	1046 29 Aug	815	1097 29 Aug
663	945 29 Aug	714	996* 29 Aug	765	1047 30 Aug	816	1098 29 Aug
664	946 29 Aug	715	997 29 Aug	766	1048* 29 Aug	817	1099 30 Aug
665	947 30 Aug	716	998 29 Aug	767	1049 29 Aug	818	1100* 29 Aug
666	948* 29 Aug	717	999 30 Aug	768	1050 29 Aug	819	1101 29 Aug
667	949 29 Aug	718	1000* 29 Aug	769	1051 30 Aug	820	1102 29 Aug
668	950 29 Aug	719	1001 29 Aug	770	1052* 29 Aug	821	1103 30 Aug
669	951 30 Aug	720	1002 29 Aug	771	1053 29 Aug	822	1104* 29 Aug
670	952* 29 Aug	721	1003 30 Aug	772	1054 29 Aug	823	1105 29 Aug
671	953 29 Aug	722	1004* 29 Aug	773	1055 30 Aug	824	1106 29 Aug
672	954 29 Aug	723	1005 29 Aug	774	1056* 29 Aug	825	1107 30 Aug
673	955 30 Aug	724	1006 29 Aug	775	1057 29 Aug	826	1108* 29 Aug
674	956* 29 Aug	725	1007 30 Aug	776	1058 29 Aug	827	1109 29 Aug
675	957 29 Aug	726	1008* 29 Aug	777	1059 30 Aug	828	1110 29 Aug
676	958 29 Aug	727	1009 29 Aug	778	1060* 29 Aug	829	1111 30 Aug
677	959 30 Aug	728	1010 29 Aug	779	1061 29 Aug	830	1112* 29 Aug
678	960* 29 Aug	729	1011 30 Aug	780	1062 29 Aug	831	1113 29 Aug
679	961 29 Aug	730	1012* 29 Aug	781	1063 30 Aug	832	1114 29 Aug
680	962 29 Aug	731	1013 29 Aug	782	1064* 29 Aug	833	1115 30 Aug
681	963 30 Aug	732	1014 29 Aug	783	1065 29 Aug	834	1116* 29 Aug
682	964* 29 Aug	733	1015 30 Aug	784	1066 29 Aug	835	1117 29 Aug
683	965 29 Aug	734	1016* 29 Aug	785	1067 30 Aug	836	1118 29 Aug
684	966 29 Aug	735	1017 29 Aug	786	1068* 29 Aug	837	1119 30 Aug
685	967 30 Aug	736	1018 29 Aug	787	1069 29 Aug	838	1120* 29 Aug
686	968* 29 Aug	737	1019 30 Aug	788	1070 29 Aug	839	1121 29 Aug
687	969 29 Aug	738	1020* 29 Aug	789	1071 30 Aug	840	1122 29 Aug
688	970 29 Aug	739	1021 29 Aug	790	1072* 29 Aug	841	1123 30 Aug
689	971 30 Aug	740	1022 29 Aug	791	1073 29 Aug	842	1124* 29 Aug
690	972* 29 Aug	741	1023 30 Aug	792	1074 29 Aug	843	1125 29 Aug
691	973 29 Aug	742	1024* 29 Aug	793	1075 30 Aug	844	1126 29 Aug
692	974 29 Aug	743	1025 29 Aug	794	1076* 29 Aug	845	1127 30 Aug
693	975 30 Aug	744	1026 29 Aug	795	1077 29 Aug	846	1128* 29 Aug
694	976* 29 Aug	745	1027 30 Aug	796	1078 29 Aug	847	1129 29 Aug
695	977 29 Aug	746	1028* 29 Aug	797	1079 30 Aug	848	1130 29 Aug

Coptic Year	Western Date (Julian) of New Year	Coptic Year	Western Date (Julian) of New Year	Coptic Year	Western Date (Julian) of New Year	Coptic Year	Western Date (Julian) of New Year
849	1131 30 Aug	900	1182 29 Aug	951	1233 29 Aug	1002	1284* 29 Aug
850	1132* 29 Aug	901	1183 30 Aug	952	1234 29 Aug	1003	1285 29 Aug
851	1133 29 Aug	902	1184* 29 Aug	953	1235 30 Aug	1004	1286 29 Aug
852	1134 29 Aug	903	1185 29 Aug	954	1236* 29 Aug	1005	1287 30 Aug
853	1135 30 Aug	904	1186 29 Aug	955	1237 29 Aug	1006	1288* 29 Aug
854	1136* 29 Aug	905	1187 30 Aug	956	1238 29 Aug	1007	1289 29 Aug
855	1137 29 Aug	906	1188* 29 Aug	957	1239 30 Aug	1008	1290 29 Aug
856	1138 29 Aug	907	1189 29 Aug	958	1240* 29 Aug	1009	1291 30 Aug
857	1139 30 Aug	908	1190 29 Aug	959	1241 29 Aug	1010	1292* 29 Aug
858	1140* 29 Aug	909	1191 30 Aug	960	1242 29 Aug	1011	1293 29 Aug
859	1141 29 Aug	910	1192* 29 Aug	961	1243 30 Aug	1012	1294 29 Aug
860	1142 29 Aug	911	1193 29 Aug	962	1244* 29 Aug	1013	1295 30 Aug
861	1143 30 Aug	912	1194 29 Aug	963	1245 29 Aug	1014	1296* 29 Aug
862	1144* 29 Aug	913	1195 30 Aug	964	1246 29 Aug	1015	1297 29 Aug
863	1145 29 Aug	914	1196* 29 Aug	965	1247 30 Aug	1016	1298 29 Aug
864	1146 29 Aug	915	1197 29 Aug	966	1248* 29 Aug	1017	1299 30 Aug
865	1147 30 Aug	916	1198 29 Aug	967	1249 29 Aug	1018	1300* 29 Aug
866	1148* 29 Aug	917	1199 30 Aug	968	1250 29 Aug	1019	1301 29 Aug
867	1149 29 Aug	918	1200* 29 Aug	969	1251 30 Aug	1020	1302 29 Aug
868	1150 29 Aug	919	1201 29 Aug	970	1252* 29 Aug	1021	1303 30 Aug
869	1151 30 Aug	920	1202 29 Aug	971	1253 29 Aug	1022	1304* 29 Aug
870	1152* 29 Aug	921	1203 30 Aug	972	1254 29 Aug	1023	1305 29 Aug
871	1153 29 Aug	922	1204* 29 Aug	973	1255 30 Aug	1024	1306 29 Aug
872	1154 29 Aug	923	1205 29 Aug	974	1256* 29 Aug	1025	1307 30 Aug
873	1155 30 Aug	924	1206 29 Aug	975	1257 29 Aug	1026	1308* 29 Aug
874	1156* 29 Aug	925	1207 30 Aug	976	1258 29 Aug	1027	1309 29 Aug
875	1157 29 Aug	926	1208* 29 Aug	977	1259 30 Aug	1028	1310 29 Aug
876	1158 29 Aug	927	1209 29 Aug	978	1260* 29 Aug	1029	1311 30 Aug
877	1159 30 Aug	928	1210 29 Aug	979	1261 29 Aug	1030	1312* 29 Aug
878	1160* 29 Aug	929	1211 30 Aug	980	1262 29 Aug	1031	1313 29 Aug
879	1161 29 Aug	930	1212* 29 Aug	981	1263 30 Aug	1032	1314 29 Aug
880	1162 29 Aug	931	1213 29 Aug	982	1264* 29 Aug	1033	1315 30 Aug
881	1163 30 Aug	932	1214 29 Aug	983	1265 29 Aug	1034	1316* 29 Aug
882	1164* 29 Aug	933	1215 30 Aug	984	1266 29 Aug	1035	1317 29 Aug
883	1165 29 Aug	934	1216* 29 Aug	985	1267 30 Aug	1036	1318 29 Aug
884	1166 29 Aug	935	1217 29 Aug	986	1268* 29 Aug	1037	1319 30 Aug
885	1167 30 Aug	936	1218 29 Aug	987	1269 29 Aug	1038	1320* 29 Aug
886	1168* 29 Aug	937	1219 30 Aug	988	1270 29 Aug	1039	1321 29 Aug
887	1169 29 Aug	938	1220* 29 Aug	989	1271 30 Aug	1040	1322 29 Aug
888	1170 29 Aug	939	1221 29 Aug	990	1272* 29 Aug	1041	1323 30 Aug
889	1171 30 Aug	940	1222 29 Aug	991	1273 29 Aug	1042	1324* 29 Aug
890	1172* 29 Aug	941	1223 30 Aug	992	1274 29 Aug	1043	1325 29 Aug
891	1173 29 Aug	942	1224* 29 Aug	993	1275 30 Aug	1044	1326 29 Aug
892	1174 29 Aug	943	1225 29 Aug	994	1276* 29 Aug	1045	1327 30 Aug
893	1175 30 Aug	944	1226 29 Aug	995	1277 29 Aug	1046	1328* 29 Aug
894	1176* 29 Aug	945	1227 30 Aug	996	1278 29 Aug	1047	1329 29 Aug
895	1177 29 Aug	946	1228* 29 Aug	997	1279 30 Aug	1048	1330 29 Aug
896	1178 29 Aug	947	1229 29 Aug	998	1280* 29 Aug	1049	1331 30 Aug
897	1179 30 Aug	948	1230 29 Aug	999	1281 29 Aug	1050	1332* 29 Aug
898	1180* 29 Aug	949	1231 30 Aug	1000	1282 29 Aug	1051	1333 29 Aug
899	1181 29 Aug	950	1232* 29 Aug	1001	1283 30 Aug	1052	1334 29 Aug

Coptic Year	Western Date (Julian) of New Year	Coptic Year	Western Date (Julian) of New Year	Coptic Year	Western Date (Julian) of New Year	Coptic Year	Western Date (Julian) of New Year
1053	1335 30 Aug	1104	1386 29 Aug	1155	1437 29 Aug	1206	1488* 29 Aug
1054	1336* 29 Aug	1105	1387 30 Aug	1156	1438 29 Aug	1207	1489 29 Aug
1055	1337 29 Aug	1106	1388* 29 Aug	1157	1439 30 Aug	1208	1490 29 Aug
1056	1338 29 Aug	1107	1389 29 Aug	1158	1440* 29 Aug	1209	1491 30 Aug
1057	1339 30 Aug	1108	1390 29 Aug	1159	1441 29 Aug	1210	1492* 29 Aug
1058	1340* 29 Aug	1109	1391 30 Aug	1160	1442 29 Aug	1211	1493 29 Aug
1059	1341 29 Aug	1110	1392 29 Aug	1161	1443 30 Aug	1212	1494 29 Aug
1060	1342 29 Aug	1111	1393 29 Aug	1162	1444* 29 Aug	1213	1495 30 Aug
1061	1343 30 Aug	1112	1394 29 Aug	1163	1445 29 Aug	1214	1496* 29 Aug
1062	1344* 29 Aug	1113	1395 30 Aug	1164	1446 29 Aug	1215	1497 29 Aug
1063	1345 29 Aug	1114	1396* 29 Aug	1165	1447 30 Aug	1216	1498 29 Aug
1064	1346 29 Aug	1115	1397 29 Aug	1166	1448* 29 Aug	1217	1499 30 Aug
1065	1347 30 Aug	1116	1398 29 Aug	1167	1449 29 Aug	1218	1500* 29 Aug
1066	1348* 29 Aug	1117	1399 30 Aug	1168	1450 29 Aug	1219	1501 29 Aug
1067	1349 29 Aug	1118	1400* 29 Aug	1169	1451 30 Aug	1220	1502 29 Aug
1068	1350 29 Aug	1119	1401 29 Aug	1170	1452* 29 Aug	1221	1503 30 Aug
1069	1351 30 Aug	1120	1402 29 Aug	1171	1453 29 Aug	1222	1504* 29 Aug
1070	1352* 29 Aug	1121	1403 30 Aug	1172	1454 29 Aug	1223	1505 29 Aug
1071	1353 29 Aug	1122	1404* 29 Aug	1173	1455 30 Aug	1224	1506 29 Aug
1072	1354 29 Aug	1123	1405 29 Aug	1174	1456* 29 Aug	1225	1507 30 Aug
1073	1355 30 Aug	1124	1406 29 Aug	1175	1457 29 Aug	1226	1508* 29 Aug
1074	1356* 29 Aug	1125	1407 30 Aug	1176	1458 29 Aug	1227	1509 29 Aug
1075	1357 29 Aug	1126	1408* 29 Aug	1177	1459 30 Aug	1228	1510 29 Aug
1076	1358 29 Aug	1127	1409 29 Aug	1178	1460* 29 Aug	1229	1511 30 Aug
1077	1359 30 Aug	1128	1410 29 Aug	1179	1461 29 Aug	1230	1512* 29 Aug
1078	1360* 29 Aug	1129	1411 30 Aug	1180	1462 29 Aug	1231	1513 29 Aug
1079	1361 29 Aug	1130	1412 29 Aug	1181	1463 30 Aug	1232	1514 29 Aug
1080	1362 29 Aug	1131	1413 29 Aug	1182	1464* 29 Aug	1233	1515 30 Aug
1081	1363 30 Aug	1132	1414 29 Aug	1183	1465 29 Aug	1234	1516* 29 Aug
1082	1364* 29 Aug	1133	1415 30 Aug	1184	1466 29 Aug	1235	1517 29 Aug
1083	1365 29 Aug	1134	1416* 29 Aug	1185	1467 30 Aug	1236	1518 29 Aug
1084	1366 29 Aug	1135	1417 29 Aug	1186	1468* 29 Aug	1237	1519 30 Aug
1085	1367 30 Aug	1136	1418 29 Aug	1187	1469 29 Aug	1238	1520* 29 Aug
1086	1368* 29 Aug	1137	1419 30 Aug	1188	1470 29 Aug	1239	1521 29 Aug
1087	1369 29 Aug	1138	1420* 29 Aug	1189	1471 30 Aug	1240	1522 29 Aug
1088	1370 29 Aug	1139	1421 29 Aug	1190	1472* 29 Aug	1241	1523 30 Aug
1089	1371 30 Aug	1140	1422 29 Aug	1191	1473 29 Aug	1242	1524* 29 Aug
1090	1372* 29 Aug	1141	1423 30 Aug	1192	1474 29 Aug	1243	1525 29 Aug
1091	1373 29 Aug	1142	1424* 29 Aug	1193	1475 30 Aug	1244	1526 29 Aug
1092	1374 29 Aug	1143	1425 29 Aug	1194	1476* 29 Aug	1245	1527 30 Aug
1093	1375 30 Aug	1144	1426 29 Aug	1195	1477 29 Aug	1246	1528* 29 Aug
1094	1376* 29 Aug	1145	1427 30 Aug	1196	1479 29 Aug	1247	1529 29 Aug
1095	1377 29 Aug	1146	1428* 29 Aug	1197	1479 30 Aug	1248	1530 29 Aug
1096	1378 29 Aug	1147	1429 29 Aug	1198	1480* 29 Aug	1249	1531 30 Aug
1097	1379 30 Aug	1148	1430 29 Aug	1199	1481 29 Aug	1250	1532* 29 Aug
1098	1380* 29 Aug	1149	1431 30 Aug	1200	1482 29 Aug	1251	1533 29 Aug
1099	1381 29 Aug	1150	1432* 29 Aug	1201	1483 30 Aug	1252*	1534 29 Aug
1100	1382 29 Aug	1151	1433 29 Aug	1202	1484* 29 Aug	1253	1535 30 Aug
1101	1383 30 Aug	1152	1434 29 Aug	1203	1485 29 Aug	1254	1536* 29 Aug
1102	1384* 29 Aug	1153	1435 30 Aug	1204	1486 29 Aug	1255	1537 29 Aug
1103	1385 29 Aug	1154	1436* 29 Aug	1205	1487 30 Aug	1256*	1538 29 Aug

Coptic Year	Western Date (Julian) of New Year	
1257	1539	30 Aug
1258	1540*	29 Aug
1259	1541	29 Aug
1260*	1542	29 Aug
1261	1543	30 Aug
1262	1544*	29 Aug
1263	1545	29 Aug
1264*	1546	29 Aug
1265	1547	30 Aug
1266	1548*	29 Aug
1267	1549	29 Aug

Coptic Year	Western Date (Julian) of New Year	
1268*	1550	29 Aug
1269	1551	30 Aug
1270	1552*	29 Aug
1271	1553	29 Aug
1272*	1554	29 Aug
1273	1555	30 Aug
1274	1556*	29 Aug
1275	1557	29 Aug
1276*	1558	29 Aug
1277	1559	30 Aug
1278	1560*	29 Aug

Coptic Year	Western Date (Julian) of New Year	
1279	1561	29 Aug
1280*	1562	29 Aug
1281	1563	30 Aug
1282	1564*	29 Aug
1283	565	29 Aug
1284*	1566	29 Aug
1285	1567	30 Aug
1286	1568*	29 Aug
1287	1569	29 Aug
1288*	1570	29 Aug
1289	1571	30 Aug

Coptic Year	Western Date (Julian) of New Year	
1290	1572*	29 Aug
1291	1573	29 Aug
1292*	1574	29 Aug
1293	1575	30 Aug
1294	1576*	29 Aug
1295	1577	29 Aug
1296*	1578	29 Aug
1297	1579	30 Aug
1298	1580*	29 Aug
1299	1581	29 Aug
1300*	1582	29 Aug

Coptic Year	Western Date (Julian) of New Year		(Gregorian)
1301	1583	30 Aug	9 Sep
1302	1584*	29 Aug	8 Sep
1303	1585	29 Aug	8 Sep
1304*	1586	29 Aug	8 Sep
1305	1587	30 Aug	9 Sep
1306	1588*	29 Aug	8 Sep
1307	1589	29 Aug	8 Sep
1308*	1590	29 Aug	8 Sep
1309	1591	30 Aug	9 Sep
1310	1592*	29 Aug	8 Sep
1311	1593	29 Aug	8 Sep
1312	1594	29 Aug	8 Sep
1313	1595	30 Aug	9 Sep
1314	1596*	29 Aug	8 Sep
1315	1597	29 Aug	8 Sep
1316*	1598	29 Aug	8 Sep
1317	1599	30 Aug	9 Sep
1318	1600*	29 Aug	8 Sep
1319	1601	29 Aug	8 Sep
1320*	1602	29 Aug	8 Sep
1321	1603	30 Aug	9 Sep
1322	1604*	29 Aug	8 Sep
1323	1605	29 Aug	8 Sep
1324*	1606	29 Aug	8 Sep
1325	1607	30 Aug	9 Sep
1326	1608*	29 Aug	8 Sep
1327	1609	29 Aug	8 Sep
1328*	1610	29 Aug	8 Sep
1329	1611	30 Aug	9 Sep
1330	1612*	29 Aug	8 Sep
1331	1613	29 Aug	8 Sep
1332*	1614	29 Aug	8 Sep
1333	1615	30 Aug	9 Sep
1334	1616*	29 Aug	8 Sep

Coptic Year	Western Date (Julian) of New Year		(Gregorian)
1335	1617	29 Aug	8 Sep
1336*	1618	29 Aug	8 Sep
1337	1619	30 Aug	9 Sep
1338	1620*	29 Aug	8 Sep
1339	1621	29 Aug	8 Sep
1340*	1622	29 Aug	8 Sep
1341	1623	30 Aug	9 Sep
1342	1624*	29 Aug	8 Sep
1343	1625	29 Aug	8 Sep
1344*	1626	29 Aug	8 Sep
1345	1627	30 Aug	9 Sep
1346	1628*	29 Aug	8 Sep
1347	1629	29 Aug	8 Sep
1348*	1630	29 Aug	8 Sep
1349	1631	30 Aug	9 Sep
1350	1632*	29 Aug	8 Sep
1351	1633	29 Aug	8 Sep
1352*	1634	29 Aug	8 Sep
1353	1635	30 Aug	9 Sep
1354	1636*	29 Aug	8 Sep
1355	1637	29 Aug	8 Sep
1356*	1638	29 Aug	8 Sep
1357	1639	30 Aug	9 Sep
1358	1640*	29 Aug	8 Sep
1359	1641	29 Aug	8 Sep
1360*	1642	29 Aug	8 Sep
1361	1643	30 Aug	9 Sep
1362	1644*	29 Aug	8 Sep
1363	1645	29 Aug	8 Sep
1364*	1646	29 Aug	8 Sep
1365	1647	30 Aug	9 Sep
1366	1648*	29 Aug	8 Sep
1367	1649	29 Aug	8 Sep
1368*	1650	29 Aug	8 Sep

Coptic Year	Western Date (Julian) of New Year		(Gregorian)
1369	1651	30 Aug	9 Sep
1370	1652*	29 Aug	8 Sep
1371	1653	29 Aug	8 Sep
1372*	1654	29 Aug	8 Sep
1373	1655	30 Aug	9 Sep
1374	1656*	29 Aug	8 Sep
1375	1657	29 Aug	8 Sep
1376*	1658	29 Aug	8 Sep
1377	1659	30 Aug	9 Sep
1378	1660*	29 Aug	8 Sep
1379	1661	29 Aug	8 Sep
1380*	1662	29 Aug	8 Sep
1381	1663	30 Aug	9 Sep
1382	1664*	29 Aug	8 Sep
1383	1665	29 Aug	8 Sep
1384*	1666	29 Aug	8 Sep
1385	1667	30 Aug	9 Sep
1386	1668*	29 Aug	8 Sep
1387	1669	29 Aug	8 Sep
1388*	1670	29 Aug	8 Sep
1389	1671	30 Aug	9 Sep
1390	1672*	29 Aug	8 Sep
1391	1673	29 Aug	8 Sep
1392*	1674	29 Aug	8 Sep
1393	1675	30 Aug	9 Sep
1394	1676*	29 Aug	8 Sep
1395	1677	29 Aug	8 Sep
1396*	1678	29 Aug	8 Sep
1397	1679	30 Aug	9 Sep
1398	1680*	29 Aug	8 Sep
1399	1681	29 Aug	8 Sep
1400*	1682	29 Aug	8 Sep
1401	1683	30 Aug	9 Sep
1402	1684*	29 Aug	8 Sep

Coptic Year	Western Date (Julian) of New Year		Western Date (Gregorian) of New Year
1403	1685	29 Aug	8 Sep
1404*	1686	29 Aug	8 Sep
1405	1687	30 Aug	9 Sep
1406	1688*	29 Aug	8 Sep
1407	1689	29 Aug	8 Sep
1408*	1690	29 Aug	8 Sep
1409	1691	30 Aug	9 Sep
1410	1962*	29 Aug	8 Sep
1411	1693	29 Aug	8 Sep
1412*	1694	29 Aug	8 Sep
1413	1695	30 Aug	9 Sep
1414	1696*	29 Aug	8 Sep
1415	1697	29 Aug	8 Sep
1416*	1698	29 Aug	8 Sep
1417	1699	30 Aug	9 Sep
1418	1700	29 Aug	8 Sep
1419	1701	29 Aug	9 Sep
1420*	1702	29 Aug	9 Sep
1421	1703	30 Aug	10 Sep
1422	1704*	29 Aug	9 Sep
1423	1705	29 Aug	9 Sep
1424*	1706	29 Aug	9 Sep
1425	1707	30 Aug	10 Sep

Coptic Year	Western Date (Julian) of New Year		Western Date (Gregorian) of New Year
1426	1708*	29 Aug	9 Sep
1427	1709	29 Aug	9 Sep
1428*	1710	29 Aug	9 Sep
1429	1711	30 Aug	10 Sep
1430	1712*	29 Aug	9 Sep
1431	1713	29 Aug	9 Sep
1432*	1714	29 Aug	9 Sep
1433	1715	30 Aug	10 Sep
1434	1716*	29 Aug	9 Sep
1435	1717	29 Aug	9 Sep
1436*	1718	29 Aug	9 Sep
1437	1719	30 Aug	10 Sep
1438	1720*	29 Aug	9 Sep
1439	1721	29 Aug	9 Sep
1440*	1722	29 Aug	9 Sep
1441	1723	30 Aug	10 Sep
1442	1724*	29 Aug	9 Sep
1443	1725	29 Aug	9 Sep
1444*	1726	29 Aug	9 Sep
1445	1727	30 Aug	10 Sep
1446	1728*	29 Aug	9 Sep
1447	1729	29 Aug	9 Sep
1448*	1730	29 Aug	9 Sep

Coptic Year	Western Date (Julian) of New Year		Western Date (Gregorian) of New Year
1449	1731	30 Aug	10 Sep
1450	1732*	29 Aug	9 Sep
1451	1733	29 Aug	9 Sep
1452*	1734	29 Aug	9 Sep
1453	1735	30 Aug	10 Sep
1454	1736*	29 Aug	9 Sep
1455	1737	29 Aug	9 Sep
1456*	1738	29 Aug	9 Sep
1457	1739	30 Aug	10 Sep
1458	1740*	29 Aug	9 Sep
1459	1741	29 Aug	9 Sep
1460*	1742	29 Aug	9 Sep
1461	1743	30 Aug	10 Sep
1462	1744*	29 Aug	9 Sep
1463	1745	29 Aug	9 Sep
1464*	1746	29 Aug	9 Sep
1465	1747	30 Aug	10 Sep
1466	1748*	29 Aug	9 Sep
1467	1749	29 Aug	9 Sep
1468*	1750	29 Aug	9 Sep
1469	1751	30 Aug	10 Sep

Coptic Year	Western Date (Julian) of New Year	
1470	1752*	9 Sep
1471	1753	9 Sep
1472*	1754	9 Sep
1473	1755	10 Sep
1474	1756*	9 Sep
1475	1757	9 Sep
1476*	1758	9 Sep
1477	1759	10 Sep
1478	1760*	9 Sep
1479	1761	9 Sep
1480*	1762	9 Sep
1481	1763	10 Sep
1482	1764*	9 Sep
1483	1765	9 Sep
1484*	1766	9 Sep
1485	1767	10 Sep
1486	1768*	9 Sep
1487	1769	9 Sep
1488*	1770	9 Sep
1489	1771	10 Sep

Coptic Year	Western Date (Julian) of New Year	
1490	1772*	9 Sep
1491	1773	9 Sep
1492*	1774	9 Sep
1493	1775	10 Sep
1494	1776*	9 Sep
1495	1777	9 Sep
1496*	1778	9 Sep
1497	1779	10 Sep
1498	1780*	9 Sep
1499	1781	9 Sep
1500*	1782	9 Sep
1501	1783	10 Sep
1502	1784*	9 Sep
1503	1785	9 Sep
1504*	1786	9 Sep
1505	1787	10 Sep
1506	1788*	9 Sep
1507	1789	9 Sep
1508*	1790	9 Sep
1509	1791	10 Sep

Coptic Year	Western Date (Julian) of New Year	
1510	1792*	9 Sep
1511	1793	9 Sep
1512*	1794	9 Sep
1513	1795	10 Sep
1514	1796*	9 Sep
1515	1797	9 Sep
1516*	1798	9 Sep
1517	1799	10 Sep
1518	1800	9 Sep
1519	1801	10 Sep
1520*	1802	10 Sep
1521	1803	11 Sep
1522	1804*	10 Sep
1523	1805	10 Sep
1524*	1806	10 Sep
1525	1807	11 Sep
1526	1808*	10 Sep
1527	1809	10 Sep
1528*	1810	10 Sep
1529	1811	11 Sep

Coptic Year	Western Date (Julian) of New Year	
1530	1812*	10 Sep
1531	1813	10 Sep
1532*	1814	10 Sep
1533	1815	11 Sep
1534	1816*	10 Sep
1535	1817	10 Sep
1536*	1818	10 Sep
1537	1819	11 Sep
1538	1820*	10 Sep
1539	1821	10 Sep
1540*	1822	10 Sep
1541	1823	11 Sep
1542	1824*	10 Sep
1543	1825	10 Sep
1544*	1826	10 Sep
1545	1827	11 Sep
1546	1828*	10 Sep
1547	1829	10 Sep
1548*	1830	10 Sep
1549	1831	11 Sep

Coptic Year	Western Date (Julian) of New Year	Coptic Year	Western Date (Julian) of New Year	Coptic Year	Western Date (Julian) of New Year	Coptic Year	Western Date (Julian) of New Year
1550	1832* 10 Sep	1600*	1882 10 Sep	1650	1932* 11 Sep	1700*	1982 11 Sep
1551	1833 10 Sep	1601	1883 11 Sep	1651	1933 11 Sep	1701	1983 12 Sep
1552*	1834 10 Sep	1602	1884* 10 Sep	1652*	1934 11 Sep	1702	1984* 11 Sep
1553	1835 11 Sep	1603	1885 10 Sep	1653	1935 12 Sep	1703	1985 11 Sep
1554	1836* 10 Sep	1604*	1886 10 Sep	1654	1936* 11 Sep	1704*	1986 11 Sep
1555	1837 10 Sep	1605	1887 11 Sep	1655	1937 11 Sep	1705	1987 12 Sep
1556*	1838 10 Sep	1606	1888* 10 Sep	1656*	1938 11 Sep	1706	1988* 11 Sep
1557	1839 11 Sep	1607	1889 10 Sep	1657	1939 12 Sep	1707	1989 11 Sep
1558	1840* 10 Sep	1608*	1890 10 Sep	1658	1940* 11 Sep	1708*	1990 11 Sep
1559	1841 10 Sep	1609	1891 11 Sep	1659	1941 11 Sep	1709	1991 12 Sep
1560*	1842 10 Sep	1610	1892* 10 Sep	1660*	1942 11 Sep	1710	1992* 11 Sep
1561	1843 11 Sep	1611	1893 10 Sep	1661	1943 12 Sep	1711	1993 11 Sep
1562	1844* 10 Sep	1612*	1894 10 Sep	1662	1944* 11 Sep	1712*	1994 11 Sep
1563	1845 10 Sep	1613	1895 11 Sep	1663	1945 11 Sep	1713	1995 12 Sep
1564*	1846 10 Sep	1614	1896* 10 Sep	1664*	1946 11 Sep	1714	1996* 11 Sep
1565	1847 11 Sep	1615	1897 10 Sep	1665	1947 12 Sep	1715	1997 11 Sep
1566	1848* 10 Sep	1616*	1898 10 Sep	1666	1948* 11 Sep	1716*	1998 11 Sep
1567	1849 10 Sep	1617	1899 11 Sep	1667	1949 11 Sep	1717	1999 12 Sep
1568*	1850 10 Sep	1618	1900 10 Sep	1668*	1950 11 Sep	1718	2000* 11 Sep
1569	1851 11 Sep	1619	1901 11 Sep	1669	1951 12 Sep	1719	2001 11 Sep
1570	1852* 10 Sep	1620*	1902 11 Sep	1670	1952* 11 Sep	1720*	2002 11 Sep
1571	1853 10 Sep	1621	1903 12 Sep	1671	1953 11 Sep	1721	2003 12 Sep
1572*	1854 10 Sep	1622	1904* 11 Sep	1672*	1954 11 Sep	1722	2004* 11 Sep
1573	1855 11 Sep	1623	1905 11 Sep	1673	1955 12 Sep	1723	2005 11 Sep
1574	1856* 10 Sep	1624*	1906 11 Sep	1674	1956* 11 Sep	1724*	2006 11 Sep
1575	1857 10 Sep	1625	1907 12 Sep	1675	1957 11 Sep	1725	2007 12 Sep
1576*	1858 10 Sep	1626	1908* 11 Sep	1676*	1958 11 Sep	1726	2008* 11 Sep
1577	1859 11 Sep	1627	1909 11 Sep	1677	1959 12 Sep	1727	2009 11 Sep
1578	1860* 10 Sep	1628*	1910 11 Sep	1678	1960* 11 Sep	1728*	2010 11 Sep
1579	1861 10 Sep	1629	1911 12 Sep	1679	1961 11 Sep	1729	2011 12 Sep
1580*	1862 10 Sep	1630	1912* 11 Sep	1680*	1962 11 Sep	1730	2012* 11 Sep
1581	1863 11 Sep	1631	1913 11 Sep	1681	1963 12 Sep	1731	2013 11 Sep
1582	1864* 10 Sep	1632*	1914 11 Sep	1682	1964* 11 Sep	1732*	2014 11 Sep
1583	1865 10 Sep	1633	1915 12 Sep	1683	1965 11 Sep	1733	2015 12 Sep
1584*	1866 10 Sep	1634	1916* 11 Sep	1684*	1966 11 Sep	1734	2016* 11 Sep
1585	1867 11 Sep	1635	1917 11 Sep	1685	1967 12 Sep	1735	2017 11 Sep
1586	1868* 10 Sep	1636*	1918 11 Sep	1686	1968* 11 Sep	1736*	2018 11 Sep
1587	1869 10 Sep	1637	1919 12 Sep	1687	1969 11 Sep	1737	2019 12 Sep
1588*	1870 10 Sep	1638	1920* 11 Sep	1688*	1970 11 Sep	1738	2020* 11 Sep
1589	1871 11 Sep	1639	1921 11 Sep	1689	1971 12 Sep	1739	2021 11 Sep
1590	1872* 10 Sep	1640*	1922 11 Sep	1690	1972* 11 Sep	1740*	2022 11 Sep
1591	1873 10 Sep	1641	1923 12 Sep	1691	1973 11 Sep	1741	2023 12 Sep
1592*	1874 10 Sep	1642	1924* 11 Sep	1692*	1974 11 Sep	1742	2024* 11 Sep
1593	1875 11 Sep	1643	1925 11 Sep	1693	1975 12 Sep	1743	2025 11 Sep
1594	1876* 10 Sep	1644*	1926 11 Sep	1694	1976* 11 Sep	1744*	2026 11 Sep
1595	1877 10 Sep	1645	1927 12 Sep	1695	1977 11 Sep	1745	2027 12 Sep
1596*	1878 10 Sep	1646	1928* 11 Sep	1696*	1978 11 Sep	1746	2028* 11 Sep
1597	1879 11 Sep	1647	1929 11 Sep	1697	1979 12 Sep	1747	2029 11 Sep
1598	1880* 10 Sep	1648*	1930 11 Sep	1698	1980* 11 Sep	1748*	2030 11 Sep
1599	1881 10 Sep	1649	1931 12 Sep	1699	1981 11 Sep	1749	2031 12 Sep

Coptic Year	Western Date (Julian) of New Year	Coptic Year	Western Date (Julian) of New Year	Coptic Year	Western Date (Julian) of New Year	Coptic Year	Western Date (Julian) of New Year
1750	2032* 11 Sep	1755	2037 11 Sep	1760*	2042 11 Sep	1765	2047 12 Sep
1751	2033 11 Sep	1756*	2038 11 Sep	1761	2043 12 Sep	1766	2048* 11 Sep
1752*	2034 11 Sep	1757	2039 12 Sep	1762	2044* 11 Sep	1767	2049 11 Sep
1753	2035 12 Sep	1758	2040* 11 Sep	1763	2045 11 Sep	1768*	2050 11 Sep
1754	2036* 11 Sep	1759	2041 11 Sep	1764*	2046 11 Sep		

ETHIOPIAN CALENDAR

Ethiopian Year	Western Date (Julian) Ethiopian New Year	Ethiopian Year	Western Date (Julian) Ethiopian New Year	Ethiopian Year	Western Date (Julian) Ethiopian New Year	Ethiopian Year	Western Date (Julian) Ethiopian New Year
1	7 29 Aug	33	39 30 Aug	65	71 30 Aug	97	103 30 Aug
2	8* 30 Aug	34	40* 29 Aug	66	72* 29 Aug	98	104* 29 Aug
3	9 29 Aug	35	41 29 Aug	67	73 29 Aug	99	105 29 Aug
4*	10 29 Aug	36*	42 29 Aug	68*	74 29 Aug	100*	106 29 Aug
5	11 30 Aug	37	43 30 Aug	69	75 30 Aug	101	107 30 Aug
6	12* 29 Aug	38	44* 29 Aug	70	76* 29 Aug	102	108* 29 Aug
7	13 29 Aug	39	45 29 Aug	71	77 29 Aug	103	109 29 Aug
8*	14 29 Aug	40*	46 29 Aug	72*	78 29 Aug	104*	110 29 Aug
9	15 30 Aug	41	47 30 Aug	73	79 30 Aug	105	111 30 Aug
10	16* 29 Aug	42	48* 29 Aug	74	80* 29 Aug	106	112* 29 Aug
11	17 29 Aug	43	49 29 Aug	75	81 29 Aug	107	113 29 Aug
12*	18 29 Aug	44*	50 29 Aug	76*	82 29 Aug	108	114 29 Aug
13	19 30 Aug	45	51 30 Aug	77	83 30 Aug	109	115 30 Aug
14	20* 29 Aug	46	52* 29 Aug	78	84* 29 Aug	110	116* 29 Aug
15	21 29 Aug	47	53 29 Aug	79	85 29 Aug	111	117 29 Aug
16*	22 29 Aug	48*	54 29 Aug	80*	86 29 Aug	112	118 29 Aug
17	23 30 Aug	49	55 30 Aug	81	87 30 Aug	113	119 30 Aug
18	24* 29 Aug	50	56* 29 Aug	82	88* 29 Aug	114	120* 29 Aug
19	25 29 Aug	51	57 29 Aug	83	89 29 Aug	115	121 29 Aug
20*	26 29 Aug	52*	58 29 Aug	84*	90 29 Aug	116	122 29 Aug
21	27 30 Aug	53	59 30 Aug	85	91 30 Aug	117	123 30 Aug
22	28* 29 Aug	54	60* 29 Aug	86	92* 29 Aug	118	124* 29 Aug
23	29 29 Aug	55	61 29 Aug	87	93 29 Aug	119	125 29 Aug
24*	30 29 Aug	56*	62 29 Aug	88*	94 29 Aug	120	126 29 Aug
25	31 30 Aug	57	63 30 Aug	89	95 30 Aug	121	127 30 Aug
26	32* 29 Aug	58	64* 29 Aug	90	96* 29 Aug	122	128* 29 Aug
27	33 29 Aug	59	65 29 Aug	91	97 29 Aug	123	129 29 Aug
28*	34 29 Aug	60*	66 29 Aug	92*	98 29 Aug	124	130 29 Aug
29	35 30 Aug	61	67 30 Aug	93	99 30 Aug	125	131 30 Aug
30	36* 29 Aug	62	68* 29 Aug	94	100* 29 Aug	126	132* 29 Aug
31	37 29 Aug	63	69 29 Aug	95	101 29 Aug	127	133 29 Aug
32*	38 29 Aug	64*	70 29 Aug	96*	102 29 Aug	128	134 29 Aug

Ethiopian Year	Western Date (Julian) Ethiopian New Year	Ethiopian Year	Western Date (Julian) Ethiopian New Year	Ethiopian Year	Western Date (Julian) Ethiopian New Year	Ethiopian Year	Western Date (Julian) Ethiopian New Year
129	135 30 Aug	179	185 29 Aug	229	235 30 Aug	279	285 29 Aug
130	136* 29 Aug	180	186 29 Aug	230	236* 29 Aug	280	286 29 Aug
131	137 29 Aug	181	187 30 Aug	231	237 29 Aug	281	287 30 Aug
132	138 29 Aug	182	188* 29 Aug	232	238 29 Aug	282	288* 29 Aug
133	139 30 Aug	183	189 29 Aug	233	239 30 Aug	283	289 29 Aug
134	140* 29 Aug	184	190 29 Aug	234	240* 29 Aug	284	290 29 Aug
135	141 29 Aug	185	191 30 Aug	235	241 29 Aug	285	291 30 Aug
136	142 29 Aug	186	192* 29 Aug	236	242 29 Aug	286	292* 29 Aug
137	143 30 Aug	187	193 29 Aug	237	243 30 Aug	287	293 29 Aug
138	144* 29 Aug	188	194 29 Aug	238	244* 29 Aug	288	294 29 Aug
139	145 29 Aug	189	195 30 Aug	239	245 29 Aug	289	295 30 Aug
140	146 29 Aug	190	196* 29 Aug	240	246 29 Aug	290	296* 29 Aug
141	147 30 Aug	191	197 29 Aug	241	247 30 Aug	291	297 29 Aug
142	148* 29 Aug	192	198 29 Aug	242	248* 29 Aug	292	298 29 Aug
143	149 29 Aug	193	199 30 Aug	243	249 29 Aug	293	299 30 Aug
144	150 29 Aug	194	200* 29 Aug	244	250 29 Aug	294	300* 29 Aug
145	151 30 Aug	195	201 29 Aug	245	251 30 Aug	295	301 29 Aug
146	152* 29 Aug	196	202 29 Aug	246	252* 29 Aug	296	302 29 Aug
147	153 29 Aug	197	203 30 Aug	247	253 29 Aug	297	303 30 Aug
148	154 29 Aug	198	204* 29 Aug	248	254 29 Aug	298	304* 29 Aug
149	155 30 Aug	199	205 29 Aug	249	255 30 Aug	299	305 29 Aug
150	156* 29 Aug	200	206 29 Aug	250	256* 29 Aug	300	306 29 Aug
151	157 29 Aug	201	207 30 Aug	251	257 29 Aug	301	307 30 Aug
152	158 29 Aug	202	208* 29 Aug	252	258 29 Aug	302	308* 29 Aug
153	159 30 Aug	203	209 29 Aug	253	259 30 Aug	303	309 29 Aug
154	160* 29 Aug	204	210 29 Aug	254	260* 29 Aug	304	310 29 Aug
155	161 29 Aug	205	211 30 Aug	255	261 29 Aug	305	311 30 Aug
156	162 29 Aug	206	212* 29 Aug	256	262 29 Aug	306	312* 29 Aug
157	163 30 Aug	207	213 29 Aug	257	263 30 Aug	307	313 29 Aug
158	164* 29 Aug	208	214 29 Aug	258	264* 29 Aug	308	314 29 Aug
159	165 29 Aug	209	215 30 Aug	259	265 29 Aug	309	315 30 Aug
160	166 29 Aug	210	216* 29 Aug	260	266 29 Aug	310	316* 29 Aug
161	167 30 Aug	211	217 29 Aug	261	267 30 Aug	311	317 29 Aug
162	168* 29 Aug	212	218 29 Aug	262	268* 29 Aug	312	318 29 Aug
163	169 29 Aug	213	219 30 Aug	263	269 29 Aug	313	319 30 Aug
164	170 29 Aug	214	220* 29 Aug	264	270 29 Aug	314	320* 29 Aug
165	171 30 Aug	215	221 29 Aug	265	271 30 Aug	315	321 29 Aug
166	172* 29 Aug	216	222 29 Aug	266	272* 29 Aug	316	322 29 Aug
167	173 29 Aug	217	223 30 Aug	267	273 29 Aug	317	323 30 Aug
168	174 29 Aug	218	224* 29 Aug	268	274 29 Aug	318	324* 29 Aug
169	175 30 Aug	219	225 29 Aug	269	275 30 Aug	319	325 29 Aug
170	176* 29 Aug	220	226 29 Aug	270	276* 29 Aug	320	326 29 Aug
171	177 29 Aug	221	227 30 Aug	271	277 29 Aug	321	327 30 Aug
172	178 29 Aug	222	228* 29 Aug	272	278 29 Aug	322	328* 29 Aug
173	179 30 Aug	223	229 29 Aug	273	279 30 Aug	323	329 29 Aug
174	180* 29 Aug	224	230 29 Aug	274	280* 29 Aug	324	330 29 Aug
175	181 29 Aug	225	231 30 Aug	275	281 29 Aug	325	331 30 Aug
176	182 29 Aug	226	232* 29 Aug	276	282 29 Aug	326	332* 29 Aug
177	183 30 Aug	227	233 29 Aug	277	283 30 Aug	327	333 29 Aug
178	184* 29 Aug	228	234 29 Aug	278	284* 29 Aug	328	334 29 Aug

Ethiopian Year	Western Date (Julian) Ethiopian New Year
329	335 30 Aug
330	336* 29 Aug
331	337 29 Aug
332	338 29 Aug
333	339 30 Aug
334	340* 29 Aug
335	341 29 Aug
336	342 29 Aug
337	343 30 Aug
338	344* 29 Aug
339	345 29 Aug
340	346 29 Aug
341	347 30 Aug
342	348* 29 Aug
343	349 29 Aug
344	350 29 Aug
345	351 30 Aug
346	352* 29 Aug
347	353 29 Aug
348	354 29 Aug
349	355 30 Aug
350	356* 29 Aug
351	357 29 Aug
352	358 29 Aug
353	359 30 Aug
354	360* 29 Aug
355	361 29 Aug
356	362 29 Aug
357	363 30 Aug
358	364* 29 Aug
359	365 29 Aug
360	366 29 Aug
361	367 30 Aug
362	368* 29 Aug
363	369 29 Aug
364	370 29 Aug
365	371 30 Aug
366	372* 29 Aug
367	373 29 Aug
368	374 29 Aug
369	375 30 Aug
370	376* 29 Aug
371	377 29 Aug
372	378 29 Aug
373	379 30 Aug
374	380* 29 Aug
375	381 29 Aug
376	382 29 Aug
377	383 30 Aug
378	384* 29 Aug
379	385 29 Aug
380	386 29 Aug
381	387 30 Aug
382	388* 29 Aug
383	389 29 Aug
384	390 29 Aug
385	391 30 Aug
386	392* 29 Aug
387	393 29 Aug
388	394 29 Aug
389	395 30 Aug
390	396* 29 Aug
391	397 29 Aug
392	398 29 Aug
393	399 30 Aug
394	400* 29 Aug
395	401 29 Aug
396	402 29 Aug
397	403 30 Aug
398	404* 29 Aug
399	405 29 Aug
400	406 29 Aug
401	407 30 Aug
402	408* 29 Aug
403	409 29 Aug
404	410 29 Aug
405	411 30 Aug
406	412* 29 Aug
407	413 29 Aug
408	414 29 Aug
409	415 30 Aug
410	416* 29 Aug
411	417 29 Aug
412	418 29 Aug
413	419 30 Aug
414	420* 29 Aug
415	421 29 Aug
416	422 29 Aug
417	423 30 Aug
418	424* 29 Aug
419	425 29 Aug
420	426 29 Aug
421	427 30 Aug
422	428* 29 Aug
423	429 29 Aug
424	430 29 Aug
425	431 30 Aug
426	432* 29 Aug
427	433 29 Aug
428	434 29 Aug
429	435 30 Aug
430	436* 29 Aug
431	437 29 Aug
432	438 29 Aug
433	439 30 Aug
434	440* 29 Aug
435	441 29 Aug
436	442 29 Aug
437	443 30 Aug
438	444* 29 Aug
439	445 29 Aug
440	446 29 Aug
441	447 30 Aug
442	448* 29 Aug
443	449 29 Aug
444	450 29 Aug
445	451 30 Aug
446	452* 29 Aug
447	453 29 Aug
448	454 29 Aug
449	455 30 Aug
450	456* 29 Aug
451	457 29 Aug
452	458 29 Aug
453	459 30 Aug
454	460* 29 Aug
455	461 29 Aug
456	462 29 Aug
457	463 30 Aug
458	464* 29 Aug
459	465 29 Aug
460	466 29 Aug
461	467 30 Aug
462	468* 29 Aug
463	469 29 Aug
464	470 29 Aug
465	471 30 Aug
466	472* 29 Aug
467	473 29 Aug
468	474 29 Aug
469	475 30 Aug
470	476* 29 Aug
471	477 29 Aug
472	478 29 Aug
473	479 30 Aug
474	480* 29 Aug
475	481 29 Aug
476	482 29 Aug
477	483 30 Aug
478	484* 29 Aug
479	485 29 Aug
480	486 29 Aug
481	487 30 Aug
482	488* 29 Aug
483	489 29 Aug
484	490 29 Aug
485	491 30 Aug
486	492* 29 Aug
487	493 29 Aug
488	494 29 Aug
489	495 30 Aug
490	496* 29 Aug
491	497 29 Aug
492	498 29 Aug
493	499 30 Aug
494	500* 29 Aug
495	501 29 Aug
496	502 29 Aug
497	503 30 Aug
498	504* 29 Aug
499	505 29 Aug
500	506 29 Aug
501	507 30 Aug
502	508* 29 Aug
503	509 29 Aug
504	510 29 Aug
505	511 30 Aug
506	512* 29 Aug
507	513 29 Aug
508	514 29 Aug
509	515 30 Aug
510	516* 29 Aug
511	517 29 Aug
512	518 29 Aug
513	519 30 Aug
514	520* 29 Aug
515	521 29 Aug
516	522 29 Aug
517	523 30 Aug
518	524* 29 Aug
519	525 29 Aug
520	526 29 Aug
521	527 30 Aug
522	528* 29 Aug
523	529 29 Aug
524	530 29 Aug
525	531 30 Aug
526	532* 29 Aug
527	533 29 Aug
528	534 29 Aug

Ethiopian Year	Western Date (Julian) Ethiopian New Year	Ethiopian Year	Western Date (Julian) Ethiopian New Year	Ethiopian Year	Western Date (Julian) Ethiopian New Year	Ethiopian Year	Western Date (Julian) Ethiopian New Year
529	535 30 Aug	579	585 29 Aug	629	635 30 Aug	679	685 29 Aug
530	536* 29 Aug	580	586 29 Aug	630	636* 29 Aug	680	686 29 Aug
531	537 29 Aug	581	587 30 Aug	631	637 29 Aug	681	687 30 Aug
532	538 29 Aug	582	588* 29 Aug	632	638 29 Aug	682	688* 29 Aug
533	539 30 Aug	583	589 29 Aug	633	639 30 Aug	683	689 29 Aug
534	540* 29 Aug	584	590 29 Aug	634	640* 29 Aug	684	690 29 Aug
535	541 29 Aug	585	591 30 Aug	635	641 29 Aug	685	691 30 Aug
536	542 29 Aug	586	592* 29 Aug	636	642 29 Aug	686	692* 29 Aug
537	543 30 Aug	587	593 29 Aug	637	743 30 Aug	687	693 29 Aug
538	544* 29 Aug	588	594 29 Aug	638	644* 29 Aug	688	694 29 Aug
539	545 29 Aug	589	595 30 Aug	639	645 29 Aug	689	695 30 Aug
540	546 29 Aug	590	596* 29 Aug	640	646 29 Aug	690	696* 29 Aug
541	547 30 Aug	591	597 29 Aug	641	647 30 Aug	691	697 29 Aug
542	548* 29 Aug	592	598 29 Aug	642	648* 29 Aug	692	698 29 Aug
543	549 29 Aug	593	599 30 Aug	643	649 29 Aug	693	699 30 Aug
544	550 29 Aug	594	600* 29 Aug	644	650 29 Aug	694	700* 29 Aug
545	551 30 Aug	595	601 29 Aug	645	651 30 Aug	695	701 29 Aug
546	552* 29 Aug	596	602 29 Aug	646	652* 29 Aug	696	702 29 Aug
547	553 29 Aug	597	603 30 Aug	647	653 29 Aug	697	703 30 Aug
548	554 29 Aug	598	604* 29 Aug	648	654 29 Aug	698	704* 29 Aug
549	555 30 Aug	599	605 29 Aug	649	655 30 Aug	699	705 29 Aug
550	556* 29 Aug	600	606 29 Aug	650	656* 29 Aug	700	706 29 Aug
551	557 29 Aug	601	607 30 Aug	651	657 29 Aug	701	707 30 Aug
552	558 29 Aug	602	608* 29 Aug	652	658 29 Aug	702	708* 29 Aug
553	559 30 Aug	603	609 29 Aug	653	659 30 Aug	703	709 29 Aug
554	560* 29 Aug	604	610 29 Aug	654	660* 29 Aug	704	710 29 Aug
555	561 29 Aug	605	611 30 Aug	655	661 29 Aug	705	711 30 Aug
556	562 29 Aug	606	612* 29 Aug	656	662 29 Aug	706	712* 29 Aug
557	563 30 Aug	607	613 29 Aug	657	663 30 Aug	707	713 29 Aug
558	564* 29 Aug	608	614 29 Aug	658	664* 29 Aug	708	714 29 Aug
559	565 29 Aug	609	615 30 Aug	659	665 29 Aug	709	715 30 Aug
560	566 29 Aug	610	616* 29 Aug	660	666 29 Aug	710	716* 29 Aug
561	567 30 Aug	611	617 29 Aug	661	667 30 Aug	711	717 29 Aug
562	568* 29 Aug	612	618 29 Aug	662	668* 29 Aug	712	718 29 Aug
563	569 29 Aug	613	619 30 Aug	663	669 29 Aug	713	719 30 Aug
564	570 29 Aug	614	620* 29 Aug	664	670 29 Aug	714	720* 29 Aug
565	571 30 Aug	615	621 29 Aug	665	671 30 Aug	715	721 29 Aug
566	572* 29 Aug	616	622 29 Aug	666	672* 29 Aug	716	722 29 Aug
567	573 29 Aug	617	623 30 Aug	667	673 29 Aug	717	723 30 Aug
568	574 29 Aug	618	624* 29 Aug	668	674 29 Aug	718	724* 29 Aug
569	575 30 Aug	619	625 29 Aug	669	675 30 Aug	719	725 29 Aug
570	576* 29 Aug	620	626 29 Aug	670	676* 29 Aug	720	726 29 Aug
571	577 29 Aug	621	627 30 Aug	671	677 29 Aug	721	727 30 Aug
572	578 29 Aug	622	628* 29 Aug	672	678 29 Aug	722	728* 29 Aug
573	579 30 Aug	623	629 29 Aug	673	679 30 Aug	723	729 29 Aug
574	580* 29 Aug	624	630 29 Aug	674	680* 29 Aug	724	730 29 Aug
575	581 29 Aug	625	631 30 Aug	675	681 29 Aug	725	731 30 Aug
576	582 29 Aug	626	632* 29 Aug	676	682 29 Aug	726	732* 29 Aug
577	583 30 Aug	627	633 29 Aug	677	683 30 Aug	727	733 29 Aug
578	584* 29 Aug	628	634 29 Aug	678	684* 29 Aug	728	734 29 Aug

Ethiopian Year	Western Date (Julian) Ethiopian New Year	Ethiopian Year	Western Date (Julian) Ethiopian New Year	Ethiopian Year	Western Date (Julian) Ethiopian New Year	Ethiopian Year	Western Date (Julian) Ethiopian New Year
729	735 30 Aug	779	785 29 Aug	829	835 30 Aug	879	885 29 Aug
730	736* 29 Aug	780	786 29 Aug	830	836* 29 Aug	880	886 29 Aug
731	737 29 Aug	781	787 30 Aug	831	837 29 Aug	881	887 30 Aug
732	738 29 Aug	782	788* 29 Aug	832	838 29 Aug	882	888* 29 Aug
733	739 30 Aug	783	789 29 Aug	833	839 30 Aug	883	889 29 Aug
734	740* 29 Aug	784	790 29 Aug	834	840* 29 Aug	884	890 29 Aug
735	741 29 Aug	785	791 30 Aug	835	841 29 Aug	885	891 30 Aug
736	742 29 Aug	786	792* 29 Aug	836	842 29 Aug	886	892* 29 Aug
737	743 30 Aug	787	793 29 Aug	837	843 30 Aug	887	893 29 Aug
738	744* 29 Aug	788	794 29 Aug	838	844* 29 Aug	888	894 29 Aug
739	745 29 Aug	789	795 30 Aug	839	845 29 Aug	889	895 30 Aug
740	746 29 Aug	790	796* 29 Aug	840	846 29 Aug	890	896* 29 Aug
741	747 30 Aug	791	797 29 Aug	841	847 30 Aug	891	897 29 Aug
742	748* 29 Aug	792	798 29 Aug	842	848* 29 Aug	892	898 29 Aug
743	749 29 Aug	793	799 30 Aug	843	849 29 Aug	893	899 30 Aug
744	750 29 Aug	794	800* 29 Aug	844	850 29 Aug	894	900* 29 Aug
745	751 30 Aug	795	801 29 Aug	845	851 30 Aug	895	901 29 Aug
746	752* 29 Aug	796	802 29 Aug	846	852* 29 Aug	896	902 29 Aug
747	753 29 Aug	797	803 30 Aug	847	853 29 Aug	897	903 30 Aug
748	754 29 Aug	798	804* 29 Aug	848	854 29 Aug	898	904* 29 Aug
749	755 30 Aug	799	805 29 Aug	849	855 30 Aug	899	905 29 Aug
750	756* 29 Aug	800	806 29 Aug	850	856* 29 Aug	900	906 29 Aug
751	757 29 Aug	801	807 30 Aug	851	857 29 Aug	901	907 30 Aug
752	758 29 Aug	802	808* 29 Aug	852	858 29 Aug	902	908* 29 Aug
753	759 30 Aug	803	809 29 Aug	853	859 30 Aug	903	909 29 Aug
754	760* 29 Aug	804	810 29 Aug	854	860* 29 Aug	904	910 29 Aug
755	761 29 Aug	805	811 30 Aug	855	861 29 Aug	905	911 30 Aug
756	762 29 Aug	806	812* 29 Aug	856	862 29 Aug	906	912* 29 Aug
757	763 30 Aug	807	813 29 Aug	857	863 30 Aug	907	913 29 Aug
758	764* 29 Aug	808	814 29 Aug	858	864* 29 Aug	908	914 29 Aug
759	765 29 Aug	809	815 30 Aug	859	865 29 Aug	909	915 30 Aug
760	766 29 Aug	810	816* 29 Aug	860	866 29 Aug	910	916* 29 Aug
761	767 30 Aug	811	817 29 Aug	861	867 30 Aug	911	917 29 Aug
762	768* 29 Aug	812	818 29 Aug	862	868* 29 Aug	912	918 29 Aug
763	769 29 Aug	813	819 30 Aug	863	869 29 Aug	913	919 30 Aug
764	770 29 Aug	814	820* 29 Aug	864	870 29 Aug	914	920* 29 Aug
765	771 30 Aug	815	821 29 Aug	865	871 30 Aug	915	921 29 Aug
766	772* 29 Aug	816	822 29 Aug	866	872* 29 Aug	916	922 29 Aug
767	773 29 Aug	817	823 30 Aug	867	873 29 Aug	917	923 30 Aug
768	774 29 Aug	818	824* 29 Aug	868	874 29 Aug	918	924* 29 Aug
769	775 30 Aug	819	825 29 Aug	869	875 30 Aug	919	925 29 Aug
770	776* 29 Aug	820	826 29 Aug	870	876* 29 Aug	920	926 29 Aug
771	777 29 Aug	821	827 30 Aug	871	877 29 Aug	921	927 30 Aug
772	778 29 Aug	822	828* 29 Aug	872	878 29 Aug	922	928* 29 Aug
773	779 30 Aug	823	829 29 Aug	873	879 30 Aug	923	929 29 Aug
774	780* 29 Aug	824	830 29 Aug	874	880* 29 Aug	924	930 29 Aug
775	781 29 Aug	825	831 30 Aug	875	881 29 Aug	925	931 30 Aug
776	782 29 Aug	826	832* 29 Aug	876	882 29 Aug	926	932* 29 Aug
777	783 30 Aug	827	833 29 Aug	877	883 30 Aug	927	933 29 Aug
778	784* 29 Aug	828	834 29 Aug	878	884* 29 Aug	928	934 29 Aug

Ethiopian Year	Western Date (Julian) Ethiopian New Year	Ethiopian Year	Western Date (Julian) Ethiopian New Year	Ethiopian Year	Western Date (Julian) Ethiopian New Year	Ethiopian Year	Western Date (Julian) Ethiopian New Year
929	935 30 Aug	979	985 29 Aug	1029	1035 30 Aug	1079	1085 29 Aug
930	936* 29 Aug	980	986 29 Aug	1030	1036* 29 Aug	1080	1086 29 Aug
931	937 29 Aug	981	987 30 Aug	1031	1037 29 Aug	1081	1087 30 Aug
932	938 29 Aug	982	988* 29 Aug	1032	1038 29 Aug	1082	1088* 29 Aug
933	939 30 Aug	983	989 29 Aug	1033	1039 30 Aug	1083	1089 29 Aug
934	940* 29 Aug	984	990 29 Aug	1034	1040* 29 Aug	1084	1090 29 Aug
935	941 29 Aug	985	991 30 Aug	1035	1041 29 Aug	1085	1091 30 Aug
936	942 29 Aug	986	992* 29 Aug	1036	1042 29 Aug	1086	1092* 29 Aug
937	943 30 Aug	987	993 29 Aug	1037	1043 30 Aug	1087	1093 29 Aug
938	944* 29 Aug	988	994 29 Aug	1038	1044* 29 Aug	1088	1094 29 Aug
939	945 29 Aug	989	995 30 Aug	1039	1045 29 Aug	1089	1095 30 Aug
940	946 29 Aug	990	996* 29 Aug	1040	1046 29 Aug	1090	1096* 29 Aug
941	947 30 Aug	991	997 29 Aug	1041	1047 30 Aug	1091	1097 29 Aug
942	948* 29 Aug	992	998 29 Aug	1042	1048* 29 Aug	1092	1098 29 Aug
943	949 29 Aug	993	999 30 Aug	1043	1049 29 Aug	1093	1099 30 Aug
944	950 29 Aug	994	1000* 29 Aug	1044	1050 29 Aug	1094	1100* 29 Aug
945	951 30 Aug	995	1001 29 Aug	1045	1051 30 Aug	1095	1101 29 Aug
946	952* 29 Aug	996	1002 29 Aug	1046	1052* 29 Aug	1096	1102 29 Aug
947	953 29 Aug	997	1003 30 Aug	1047	1053 29 Aug	1097	1103 30 Aug
948	954 29 Aug	998	1004* 29 Aug	1048	1054 29 Aug	1098	1104* 29 Aug
949	955 30 Aug	999	1005 29 Aug	1049	1055 30 Aug	1099	1105 29 Aug
950	956* 29 Aug	1000	1006 29 Aug	1050	1056* 29 Aug	1100	1106 29 Aug
951	957 29 Aug	1001	1007 30 Aug	1051	1057 29 Aug	1101	1107 30 Aug
952	958 29 Aug	1002	1008* 29 Aug	1052	1058 29 Aug	1102	1108* 29 Aug
953	959 30 Aug	1003	1009 29 Aug	1053	1059 30 Aug	1103	1109 29 Aug
954	960* 29 Aug	1004	1010 29 Aug	1054	1060* 29 Aug	1104	1110 29 Aug
955	961 29 Aug	1005	1011 30 Aug	1055	1061 29 Aug	1105	1111 30 Aug
956	962 29 Aug	1006	1012* 29 Aug	1056	1062 29 Aug	1106	1112* 29 Aug
957	963 30 Aug	1007	1013 29 Aug	1057	1063 30 Aug	1107	1113 29 Aug
958	964* 29 Aug	1008	1014 29 Aug	1058	1064* 29 Aug	1108	1114 29 Aug
959	965 29 Aug	1009	1015 30 Aug	1059	1065 29 Aug	1109	1115 30 Aug
960	966 29 Aug	1010	1016* 29 Aug	1060	1066 29 Aug	1110	1116* 29 Aug
961	967 30 Aug	1011	1017 29 Aug	1061	1067 30 Aug	1111	1117 29 Aug
962	968* 29 Aug	1012	1018 29 Aug	1062	1068* 29 Aug	1112	1118 29 Aug
963	969 29 Aug	1013	1019 30 Aug	1063	1069 29 Aug	1113	1119 30 Aug
964	970 29 Aug	1014	1020* 29 Aug	1064	1070 29 Aug	1114	1120* 29 Aug
965	971 30 Aug	1015	1021 29 Aug	1065	1071 30 Aug	1115	1121 29 Aug
966	972* 29 Aug	1016	1022 29 Aug	1066	1072* 29 Aug	1116	1122 29 Aug
967	973 29 Aug	1017	1023 30 Aug	1067	1073 29 Aug	1117	1123 30 Aug
968	974 29 Aug	1018	1024* 29 Aug	1068	1074 29 Aug	1118	1124* 29 Aug
969	975 30 Aug	1019	1025 29 Aug	1069	1075 30 Aug	1119	1125 29 Aug
970	976* 29 Aug	1020	1026 29 Aug	1070	1076* 29 Aug	1120	1126 29 Aug
971	977 29 Aug	1021	1027 30 Aug	1071	1077 29 Aug	1121	1127 30 Aug
972	978 29 Aug	1022	1028* 29 Aug	1072	1078 29 Aug	1122	1128* 29 Aug
973	979 30 Aug	1023	1029 29 Aug	1073	1079 30 Aug	1123	1129 29 Aug
974	880* 29 Aug	1024	1030 29 Aug	1074	1080* 29 Aug	1124	1130 29 Aug
975	881 29 Aug	1025	1031 30 Aug	1075	1081 29 Aug	1125	1131 30 Aug
976	882 29 Aug	1026	1032* 29 Aug	1076	1082 29 Aug	1126	1132* 29 Aug
977	883 30 Aug	1027	1033 29 Aug	1077	1083 30 Aug	1127	1133 29 Aug
978	984* 29 Aug	1028	1034 29 Aug	1078	1084* 29 Aug	1128	1134 29 Aug

Ethiopian Year	Western Date (Julian) Ethiopian New Year	Ethiopian Year	Western Date (Julian) Ethiopian New Year	Ethiopian Year	Western Date (Julian) Ethiopian New Year	Ethiopian Year	Western Date (Julian) Ethiopian New Year
1129	1135 30 Aug	1179	1185 29 Aug	1229	1235 30 Aug	1279	1285 29 Aug
1130	1136* 29 Aug	1180	1186 29 Aug	1230	1236* 29 Aug	1280	1286 29 Aug
1131	1137 29 Aug	1181	1187 30 Aug	1231	1237 29 Aug	1281	1287 30 Aug
1132	1138 29 Aug	1182	1188* 29 Aug	1232	1238 29 Aug	1282	1288* 29 Aug
1133	1139 30 Aug	1183	1189 29 Aug	1233	1239 30 Aug	1283	1289 29 Aug
1134	1140* 29 Aug	1184	1190 29 Aug	1234	1240* 29 Aug	1284	1290 29 Aug
1135	1141 29 Aug	1185	1191 30 Aug	1235	1241 29 Aug	1285	1291 30 Aug
1136	1142 29 Aug	1186	1192* 29 Aug	1236	1242 29 Aug	1286	1292* 29 Aug
1137	1143 30 Aug	1187	1193 29 Aug	1237	1243 30 Aug	1287	1293 29 Aug
1138	1144* 29 Aug	1188	1194 29 Aug	1238	1244* 29 Aug	1288	1294 29 Aug
1139	1145 29 Aug	1189	1195 30 Aug	1239	1245 29 Aug	1289	1295 30 Aug
1140	1146 29 Aug	1190	1196* 29 Aug	1240	1246 29 Aug	1290	1296* 29 Aug
1141	1147 30 Aug	1191	1197 29 Aug	1241	1247 30 Aug	1291	1297 29 Aug
1142	1148* 29 Aug	1192	1198 29 Aug	1242	1248* 29 Aug	1292	1298 29 Aug
1143	1149 29 Aug	1193	1199 30 Aug	1243	1249 29 Aug	1293	1299 30 Aug
1144	1150 29 Aug	1194	1200* 29 Aug	1244	1250 29 Aug	1294	1300* 29 Aug
1145	1151 30 Aug	1195	1201 29 Aug	1245	1251 30 Aug	1295	1301 29 Aug
1146	1152* 29 Aug	1196	1202 29 Aug	1246	1252* 29 Aug	1296	1302 29 Aug
1147	1153 29 Aug	1197	1203 30 Aug	1247	1253 29 Aug	1297	1303 30 Aug
1148	1154 29 Aug	1198	1204* 29 Aug	1248	1254 29 Aug	1298	1304* 29 Aug
1149	1155 30 Aug	1199	1205 29 Aug	1249	1255 30 Aug	1299	1305 29 Aug
1150	1156* 29 Aug	1200	1206 29 Aug	1250	1256* 29 Aug	1300	1306 29 Aug
1151	1157 29 Aug	1201	1207 30 Aug	1251	1257 29 Aug	1301	1307 30 Aug
1152	1158 29 Aug	1202	1208* 29 Aug	1252	1258 29 Aug	1302	1308* 29 Aug
1153	1159 30 Aug	1203	1209 29 Aug	1253	1259 30 Aug	1303	1309 29 Aug
1154	1160* 29 Aug	1204	1210 29 Aug	1254	1260* 29 Aug	1304	1310 29 Aug
1155	1161 29 Aug	1205	1211 30 Aug	1255	1261 29 Aug	1305	1311 30 Aug
1156	1162 29 Aug	1206	1212* 29 Aug	1256	1262 29 Aug	1306	1312* 29 Aug
1157	1163 30 Aug	1207	1213 29 Aug	1257	1263 30 Aug	1307	1313 29 Aug
1158	1164* 29 Aug	1208	1214 29 Aug	1258	1264* 29 Aug	1308	1314 29 Aug
1159	1165 29 Aug	1209	1215 30 Aug	1259	1265 29 Aug	1309	1315 30 Aug
1160	1166 29 Aug	1210	1216* 29 Aug	1260	1266 29 Aug	1310	1316* 29 Aug
1161	1167 30 Aug	1211	1217 29 Aug	1261	1267 30 Aug	1311	1317 29 Aug
1162	1168* 29 Aug	1212	1218 29 Aug	1262	1268* 29 Aug	1312	1318 29 Aug
1163	1169 29 Aug	1213	1219 30 Aug	1263	1269 29 Aug	1313	1319 30 Aug
1164	1170 29 Aug	1214	1220* 29 Aug	1264	1270 29 Aug	1314	1320* 29 Aug
1165	1171 30 Aug	1215	1221 29 Aug	1265	1271 30 Aug	1315	1321 29 Aug
1166	1172* 29 Aug	1216	1222 29 Aug	1266	1272* 29 Aug	1316	1322 29 Aug
1167	1173 29 Aug	1217	1223 30 Aug	1267	1273 29 Aug	1317	1323 30 Aug
1168	1174 29 Aug	1218	1224* 29 Aug	1268	1274 29 Aug	1318	1324* 29 Aug
1169	1175 30 Aug	1219	1225 29 Aug	1269	1275 30 Aug	1319	1325 29 Aug
1170	1176* 29 Aug	1220	1226 29 Aug	1270	1276* 29 Aug	1320	1326 29 Aug
1171	1177 29 Aug	1221	1227 30 Aug	1271	1277 29 Aug	1321	1327 30 Aug
1172	1178 29 Aug	1222	1228* 29 Aug	1272	1278 29 Aug	1322	1328* 29 Aug
1173	1179 30 Aug	1223	1229 29 Aug	1273	1279 30 Aug	1323	1329 29 Aug
1174	1180* 29 Aug	1224	1230 29 Aug	1274	1280* 29 Aug	1324	1330 29 Aug
1175	1181 29 Aug	1225	1231 30 Aug	1275	1281 29 Aug	1325	1331 30 Aug
1176	1182 29 Aug	1226	1232* 29 Aug	1276	1282 29 Aug	1326	1332* 29 Aug
1177	1183 30 Aug	1227	1233 29 Aug	1277	1283 30 Aug	1327	1333 29 Aug
1178	1184* 29 Aug	1228	1234 29 Aug	1278	1284* 29 Aug	1328	1334 29 Aug

Ethiopian Year	Western Date (Julian) Ethiopian New Year	Ethiopian Year	Western Date (Julian) Ethiopian New Year	Ethiopian Year	Western Date (Julian) Ethiopian New Year	Ethiopian Year	Western Date (Julian) Ethiopian New Year
1329	1335 30 Aug	1379	1385 29 Aug	1429	1435 30 Aug	1479	1485 29 Aug
1330	1336* 29 Aug	1380	1386 29 Aug	1430	1436* 29 Aug	1480	1486 29 Aug
1331	1337 29 Aug	1381	1387 30 Aug	1431	1437 29 Aug	1481	1487 30 Aug
1332	1338 29 Aug	1382	1388* 29 Aug	1432	1438 29 Aug	1482	1488* 29 Aug
1333	1339 30 Aug	1383	1389 29 Aug	1433	1439 30 Aug	1483	1489 29 Aug
1334	1340* 29 Aug	1384	1390 29 Aug	1434	1440* 29 Aug	1484	1490 29 Aug
1335	1341 29 Aug	1385	1391 30 Aug	1435	1441 29 Aug	1485	1491 30 Aug
1336	1342 29 Aug	1386	1392* 29 Aug	1436	1442 29 Aug	1486	1492* 29 Aug
1337	1343 30 Aug	1387	1393 29 Aug	1437	1443 30 Aug	1487	1493 29 Aug
1338	1344* 29 Aug	1388	1394 29 Aug	1438	1444* 29 Aug	1488	1494 29 Aug
1339	1345 29 Aug	1389	1395 30 Aug	1439	1445 29 Aug	1489	1495 30 Aug
1340	1346 29 Aug	1390	1396* 29 Aug	1440	1446 29 Aug	1490	1496* 29 Aug
1341	1347 30 Aug	1391	1397 29 Aug	1441	1447 30 Aug	1491	1497 29 Aug
1342	1348* 29 Aug	1392	1398 29 Aug	1442	1448* 29 Aug	1492	1498 29 Aug
1343	1349 29 Aug	1393	1399 30 Aug	1443	1449 29 Aug	1493	1499 30 Aug
1344	1350 29 Aug	1394	1400* 29 Aug	1444	1450 29 Aug	1494	1500* 29 Aug
1345	1351 30 Aug	1395	1401 29 Aug	1445	1451 30 Aug	1495	1501 29 Aug
1346	1352* 29 Aug	1396	1402 29 Aug	1446	1452* 29 Aug	1496	1502 29 Aug
1347	1353 29 Aug	1397	1403 30 Aug	1447	1453 29 Aug	1497	1503 30 Aug
1348	1354 29 Aug	1398	1404* 29 Aug	1448	1454 29 Aug	1498	1504* 29 Aug
1349	1355 30 Aug	1399	1405 29 Aug	1449	1455 30 Aug	1499	1505 29 Aug
1350	1356* 29 Aug	1400	1406 29 Aug	1450	1456* 29 Aug	1500	1506 29 Aug
1351	1357 29 Aug	1401	1407 30 Aug	1451	1457 29 Aug	1501	1507 30 Aug
1352	1358 29 Aug	1402	1408* 29 Aug	1452	1458 29 Aug	1502	1508* 29 Aug
1353	1359 30 Aug	1403	1409 29 Aug	1453	1459 30 Aug	1503	1509 29 Aug
1354	1360* 29 Aug	1404	1410 29 Aug	1454	1460* 29 Aug	1504	1510 29 Aug
1355	1361 29 Aug	1405	1411 30 Aug	1455	1461 29 Aug	1505	1511 30 Aug
1356	1362 29 Aug	1406	1412* 29 Aug	1456	1462 29 Aug	1506	1512* 29 Aug
1357	1363 30 Aug	1407	1413 29 Aug	1457	1463 30 Aug	1507	1513 29 Aug
1358	1364* 29 Aug	1408	1414 29 Aug	1458	1464* 29 Aug	1508	1514 29 Aug
1359	1365 29 Aug	1409	1415 30 Aug	1459	1465 29 Aug	1509	1515 30 Aug
1360	1366 29 Aug	1410	1416* 29 Aug	1460	1466 29 Aug	1510	1516* 29 Aug
1361	1367 30 Aug	1411	1417 29 Aug	1461	1467 30 Aug	1511	1517 29 Aug
1362	1368* 29 Aug	1412	1418 29 Aug	1462	1468* 29 Aug	1512	1518 29 Aug
1363	1369 29 Aug	1413	1419 30 Aug	1463	1469 29 Aug	1513	1519 30 Aug
1364	1370 29 Aug	1414	1420* 29 Aug	1464	1470 29 Aug	1514	1520* 29 Aug
1365	1371 30 Aug	1415	1421 29 Aug	1465	1471 30 Aug	1515	1521 29 Aug
1366	1372* 29 Aug	1416	1422 29 Aug	1466	1472* 29 Aug	1516	1522 29 Aug
1367	1373 29 Aug	1417	1423 30 Aug	1467	1473 29 Aug	1517	1523 30 Aug
1368	1374 29 Aug	1418	1424* 29 Aug	1468	1474 29 Aug	1518	1524* 29 Aug
1369	1375 30 Aug	1419	1425 29 Aug	1469	1475 30 Aug	1519	1525 29 Aug
1370	1376* 29 Aug	1420	1426 29 Aug	1470	1476* 29 Aug	1520	1526 29 Aug
1371	1377 29 Aug	1421	1427 30 Aug	1471	1477 29 Aug	1521	1527 30 Aug
1372	1378 29 Aug	1422	1428* 29 Aug	1472	1478 29 Aug	1522	1528* 29 Aug
1373	1379 30 Aug	1423	1429 29 Aug	1473	1479 30 Aug	1523	1529 29 Aug
1374	1380* 29 Aug	1424	1430 29 Aug	1474	1480* 29 Aug	1524	1530 29 Aug
1375	1381 29 Aug	1425	1431 30 Aug	1475	1481 29 Aug	1525	1531 30 Aug
1376	1382 29 Aug	1426	1432* 29 Aug	1476	1482 29 Aug	1526	1532* 29 Aug
1377	1383 30 Aug	1427	1433 29 Aug	1477	1483 30 Aug	1527	1533 29 Aug
1378	1384* 29 Aug	1428	1434 29 Aug	1478	1484* 29 Aug	1528	1534 29 Aug

Ethiopian Year	Western Date (Julian) Ethiopian New Year		Ethiopian Year	Western Date (Julian) Ethiopian New Year		Ethiopian Year	Western Date (Julian) Ethiopian New Year		Ethiopian Year	Western Date (Julian) Ethiopian New Year	
1529	1535	30 Aug	1541	1547	30 Aug	1553	1559	30 Aug	1565	1571	30 Aug
1530	1536*	29 Aug	1542	1548*	29 Aug	1554	1560*	29 Aug	1566	1572*	29 Aug
1531	1537	29 Aug	1543	1549	29 Aug	1555	1561	29 Aug	1567	1573	29 Aug
1532	1538	29 Aug	1544	1550	29 Aug	1556	1562	29 Aug	1568*	1574	29 Aug
1533	1539	30 Aug	1545	1551	30 Aug	1557	1563	30 Aug	1569	1575	30 Aug
1534	1540*	29 Aug	1546	1552*	29 Aug	1558	1564*	29 Aug	1570	1576*	29 Aug
1535	1541	29 Aug	1547	1553	29 Aug	1559	1565	29 Aug	1571	1577	29 Aug
1536	1542	29 Aug	1548	1554	29 Aug	1560	1566	29 Aug	1572*	1578	29 Aug
1537	1543	30 Aug	1549	1555	30 Aug	1561	1567	30 Aug	1573	1579	30 Aug
1538	1544*	29 Aug	1550	1556*	29 Aug	1562	1568*	29 Aug	1574	1580*	29 Aug
1539	1545	29 Aug	1551	1557	29 Aug	1563	1569	29 Aug	1575	1581	29 Aug
1540	1546	29 Aug	1552	1558	29 Aug	1564*	1570	29 Aug	1576*	1582	29 Aug

Ethiopian Year	Western Date of New Year (Julian)		(Gregorian)	Ethiopian Year	Western Date of New Year (Julian)		(Gregorian)	Ethiopian Year	Western Date of New Year (Julian)		(Gregorian)
1577	1583	30 Aug	9 Sep	1607	1613	29 Aug	8 Sep	1637	1643	30 Aug	9 Sep
1578	1584*	29 Aug	8 Sep	1608*	1614	29 Aug	8 Sep	1638	1644*	29 Aug	8 Sep
1579	1585	29 Aug	8 Sep	1609	1615	30 Aug	9 Sep	1639	1645	29 Aug	8 Sep
1580*	1586	29 Aug	8 Sep	1610	1616*	29 Aug	8 Sep	1640*	1646	29 Aug	8 Sep
1581	1587	30 Aug	9 Sep	1611	1617	29 Aug	8 Sep	1641	1647	30 Aug	9 Sep
1582	1588*	29 Aug	8 Sep	1612*	1618	29 Aug	8 Sep	1642	1648*	29 Aug	8 Sep
1583	1589	29 Aug	8 Sep	1613	1619	30 Aug	9 Sep	1643	1649	29 Aug	8 Sep
1584*	1590	29 Aug	8 Sep	1614	1620*	29 Aug	8 Sep	1644*	1650	29 Aug	8 Sep
1585	1591	30 Aug	9 Sep	1615	1621	29 Aug	8 Sep	1645	1651	30 Aug	9 Sep
1586	1592*	29 Aug	8 Sep	1616*	1622	29 Aug	8 Sep	1646	1652*	29 Aug	8 Sep
1587	1593	29 Aug	8 Sep	1617	1623	30 Aug	9 Sep	1647	1653	29 Aug	8 Sep
1588*	1594	29 Aug	8 Sep	1618	1624*	29 Aug	8 Sep	1648*	1654	29 Aug	8 Sep
1589	1595	30 Aug	9 Sep	1619	1625	29 Aug	8 Sep	1649	1655	30 Aug	9 Sep
1590	1596*	29 Aug	8 Sep	1620*	1626	29 Aug	8 Sep	1650	1656*	29 Aug	8 Sep
1591	1597	29 Aug	8 Sep	1621	1627	30 Aug	9 Sep	1651	1657	29 Aug	8 Sep
1592*	1598	29 Aug	8 Sep	1622	1628*	29 Aug	8 Sep	1652*	1658	29 Aug	8 Sep
1593	1599	30 Aug	9 Sep	1623	1629	29 Aug	8 Sep	1653	1659	30 Aug	9 Sep
1594	1600*	29 Aug	8 Sep	1624*	1630	29 Aug	8 Sep	1654	1660*	29 Aug	8 Sep
1595	1601	29 Aug	8 Sep	1625	1631	30 Aug	9 Sep	1655	1661	29 Aug	8 Sep
1596*	1602	29 Aug	8 Sep	1626	1632*	29 Aug	8 Sep	1656*	1662	29 Aug	8 Sep
1597	1603	30 Aug	9 Sep	1627	1633	29 Aug	8 Sep	1657	1663	30 Aug	9 Sep
1598	1604*	29 Aug	8 Sep	1628*	1634	29 Aug	8 Sep	1658	1664*	29 Aug	8 Sep
1599	1605	29 Aug	8 Sep	1629	1635	30 Aug	9 Sep	1659	1665	29 Aug	8 Sep
1600*	1606	29 Aug	8 Sep	1630	1636*	29 Aug	8 Sep	1660*	1666	29 Aug	8 Sep
1601	1607	30 Aug	9 Sep	1631	1637	29 Aug	8 Sep	1661	1667	30 Aug	9 Sep
1602	1608*	29 Aug	8 Sep	1632*	1638	29 Aug	8 Sep	1662	1668*	29 Aug	8 Sep
1603	1609	29 Aug	8 Sep	1633	1639	30 Aug	9 Sep	1663	1669	29 Aug	8 Sep
1604*	1610	29 Aug	8 Sep	1634	1640*	29 Aug	8 Sep	1664*	1670	29 Aug	8 Sep
1605	1611	30 Aug	9 Sep	1635	1641	29 Aug	8 Sep	1665	1671	30 Aug	9 Sep
1606	1612*	29 Aug	8 Sep	1636*	1642	29 Aug	8 Sep	1666	1672*	29 Aug	8 Sep

Ethiopian Year	Western Date (Julian) of New Year	Western Date (Gregorian) of New Year
1667	1673 29 Aug	8 Sep
1668*	1674 29 Aug	8 Sep
1669	1675 30 Aug	9 Sep
1670	1676* 29 Aug	8 Sep
1671	1677 29 Aug	8 Sep
1672*	1678 29 Aug	8 Sep
1673	1679 30 Aug	9 Sep
1674	1680* 29 Aug	8 Sep
1675	1681 29 Aug	8 Sep
1676*	1682 29 Aug	8 Sep
1677	1683 30 Aug	9 Sep
1678	1684* 29 Aug	8 Sep
1679	1685 29 Aug	8 Sep
1680*	1686 29 Aug	8 Sep
1681	1687 30 Aug	9 Sep
1682	1688* 29 Aug	8 Sep
1683	1689 29 Aug	8 Sep
1684*	1690 29 Aug	8 Sep
1685	1691 30 Aug	9 Sep
1686	1692* 29 Aug	8 Sep
1687	1693 29 Aug	8 Sep
1688*	1694 29 Aug	8 Sep
1689	1695 30 Aug	9 Sep
1690	1696* 29 Aug	8 Sep
1691	1697 29 Aug	8 Sep
1692*	1698 29 Aug	8 Sep
1693	1699 30 Aug	9 Sep

Ethiopian Year	Western Date (Julian) of New Year	Western Date (Gregorian) of New Year
1694	1700* 29 Aug	8 Sep
1695	1701 29 Aug	9 Sep
1696*	1702 29 Aug	9 Sep
1697	1703 30 Aug	10 Sep
1698	1704* 29 Aug	9 Sep
1699	1705 29 Aug	9 Sep
1700*	1706 29 Aug	9 Sep
1701	1707 30 Aug	10 Sep
1702	1608* 29 Aug	9 Sep
1703	1709 29 Aug	9 Sep
1704*	1710 29 Aug	9 Sep
1705	1711 30 Aug	10 Sep
1706	1712* 29 Aug	9 Sep
1707	1713 29 Aug	9 Sep
1708*	1714 29 Aug	9 Sep
1709	1715 30 Aug	10 Sep
1710	1716* 29 Aug	9 Sep
1711	1717 29 Aug	9 Sep
1712*	1718 29 Aug	9 Sep
1713	1719 30 Aug	10 Sep
1714	1720* 29 Aug	9 Sep
1715	1721 29 Aug	9 Sep
1716*	1722 29 Aug	9 Sep
1717	1723 30 Aug	10 Sep
1718	1724* 29 Aug	9 Sep
1719	1725 29 Aug	9 Sep
1720*	1726 29 Aug	9 Sep

Ethiopian Year	Western Date (Julian) of New Year	Western Date (Gregorian) of New Year
1721	1727 30 Aug	10 Sep
1722	1728* 29 Aug	9 Sep
1723	1729 29 Aug	9 Sep
1724*	1730 29 Aug	9 Sep
1725	1731 30 Aug	10 Sep
1726	1732* 29 Aug	9 Sep
1727	1733 29 Aug	9 Sep
1728*	1734 29 Aug	9 Sep
1729	1735 30 Aug	10 Sep
1730	1736* 29 Aug	9 Sep
1731	1737 29 Aug	9 Sep
1732*	1738 29 Aug	9 Sep
1733	1739 30 Aug	10 Sep
1734	1740* 29 Aug	9 Sep
1735	1741 29 Aug	9 Sep
1736*	1742 29 Aug	9 Sep
1737	1743 30 Aug	10 Sep
1738	1744* 29 Aug	9 Sep
1739	1745 29 Aug	9 Sep
1740*	1746 29 Aug	9 Sep
1741	1747 30 Aug	10 Sep
1742	1748* 29 Aug	9 Sep
1743	1749 29 Aug	9 Sep
1744*	1750 29 Aug	9 Sep
1745	1751 30 Aug	10 Sep

Ethiopian Year	Western Date (Gregorian) of New Year
1746	1752* 9 Sep
1747	1753 9 Sep
1748*	1754 9 Sep
1749	1755 10 Sep
1750	1756* 9 Sep
1751	1757 9 Sep
1752*	1758 9 Sep
1753	1759 10 Sep
1754	1760* 9 Sep
1755	1761 9 Sep
1756*	1762 9 Sep
1757	1763 10 Sep
1758	1764* 9 Sep
1759	1765 9 Sep
1760*	1766 9 Sep

Ethiopian Year	Western Date (Gregorian) of New Year
1761	1767 10 Sep
1762	1768* 9 Sep
1763	1769 9 Sep
1764*	1770 9 Sep
1765	1771 10 Sep
1766	1772* 9 Sep
1767	1773 9 Sep
1768*	1774 9 Sep
1769	1775 10 Sep
1770	1776* 9 Sep
1771	1777 9 Sep
1772*	1778 9 Sep
1773	1779 10 Sep
1774	1780* 9 Sep
1775	1781 9 Sep

Ethiopian Year	Western Date (Gregorian) of New Year
1776*	1782 9 Sep
1777	1783 10 Sep
1778	1784* 9 Sep
1779	1785 9 Sep
1780*	1786 9 Sep
1781	1787 10 Sep
1782	1788* 9 Sep
1783	1789 9 Sep
1784*	1790 9 Sep
1785	1791 10 Sep
1786	1792* 9 Sep
1787	1793 9 Sep
1788*	1794 9 Sep
1789	1795 10 Sep
1790	1796* 9 Sep

Ethiopian Year	Western Date (Gregorian) of New Year
1791	1797 9 Sep
1792*	1798 9 Sep
1793	1799 10 Sep
1794	1800 9 Sep
1795	1801 10 Sep
1796*	1802 10 Sep
1797	1803 11 Sep
1798	1804* 10 Sep
1799	1805 10 Sep
1800*	1806 10 Sep
1801	1807 11 Sep
1802	1808* 10 Sep
1803	1809 10 Sep
1804*	1810 10 Sep
1805	1811 11 Sep

Ethiopian Year	Western Date (Gregorian) of New Year	Ethiopian Year	Western Date (Gregorian) of New Year	Ethiopian Year	Western Date (Gregorian) of New Year	Ethiopian Year	Western Date (Gregorian) of New Year
1806	1812* 10 Sep	1857	1863 11 Sep	1908*	1914 11 Sep	1959	1965 11 Sep
1807	1813 10 Sep	1858	1864* 10 Sep	1909	1915 12 Sep	1960*	1966 11 Sep
1808*	1814 10 Sep	1859	1865 10 Sep	1910	1916* 11 Sep	1961	1967 12 Sep
1809	1815 11 Sep	1860*	1866 10 Sep	1911	1917 11 Sep	1962	1968* 11 Sep
1810	1816* 10 Sep	1861	1867 11 Sep	1912*	1918 11 Sep	1963	1969 11 Sep
1811	1817 10 Sep	1862	1868* 10 Sep	1913	1919 12 Sep	1964*	1970 11 Sep
1812*	1818 10 Sep	1863	1869 10 Sep	1914	1920* 11 Sep	1965	1971 12 Sep
1813	1819 11 Sep	1864*	1870 10 Sep	1915	1921 11 Sep	1966	1972* 11 Sep
1814	1820* 10 Sep	1865	1871 11 Sep	1916*	1922 11 Sep	1967	1973 11 Sep
1815	1821 10 Sep	1866	1872* 10 Sep	1917	1923 12 Sep	1968*	1974 11 Sep
1816*	1822 10 Sep	1867	1873 10 Sep	1918	1924* 11 Sep	1969	1975 12 Sep
1817	1823 11 Sep	1868*	1874 10 Sep	1919	1925 11 Sep	1970	1976* 11 Sep
1818	1824* 10 Sep	1869	1875 11 Sep	1920*	1926 11 Sep	1971	1977 11 Sep
1819	1825 10 Sep	1870	1876* 10 Sep	1921	1927 12 Sep	1972*	1978 11 Sep
1820*	1826 10 Sep	1871	1877 10 Sep	1922	1928* 11 Sep	1973	1979 12 Sep
1821	1827 11 Sep	1872*	1878 10 Sep	1923	1929 11 Sep	1974	1980* 11 Sep
1822	1828* 10 Sep	1873	1879 11 Sep	1924*	1930 11 Sep	1975	1981 11 Sep
1823	1829 10 Sep	1874	1880* 10 Sep	1925	1931 12 Sep	1976*	1982 11 Sep
1824*	1830 10 Sep	1875	1881 10 Sep	1926	1932* 11 Sep	1977	1983 12 Sep
1825	1831 11 Sep	1876*	1882 10 Sep	1927	1933 11 Sep	1978	1984* 11 Sep
1826	1832* 10 Sep	1877	1883 11 Sep	1928*	1934 11 Sep	1979	1985 11 Sep
1827	1833 10 Sep	1878	1884* 10 Sep	1929	1935 12 Sep	1980*	1986 11 Sep
1828*	1834 10 Sep	1879	1885 10 Sep	1930	1936* 11 Sep	1981	1987 12 Sep
1829	1835 11 Sep	1880*	1886 10 Sep	1931	1937 11 Sep	1982	1988* 11 Sep
1830	1836* 10 Sep	1881	1887 11 Sep	1932*	1938 11 Sep	1983	1989 11 Sep
1831	1837 10 Sep	1882	1888* 10 Sep	1933	1939 12 Sep	1984*	1990 11 Sep
1832*	1838 10 Sep	1883	1889 10 Sep	1934	1940* 11 Sep	1985	1991 12 Sep
1833	1839 11 Sep	1884*	1890 10 Sep	1935	1941 11 Sep	1986	1992* 11 Sep
1834	1840* 10 Sep	1885	1891 11 Sep	1936*	1942 11 Sep	1987	1993 11 Sep
1835	1841 10 Sep	1886	1892* 10 Sep	1937	1943 12 Sep	1988*	1994 11 Sep
1836*	1842 10 Sep	1887	1893 10 Sep	1938	1944* 11 Sep	1989	1995 12 Sep
1837	1843 11 Sep	1888*	1894 10 Sep	1939	1945 11 Sep	1990	1996* 11 Sep
1838	1844* 10 Sep	1889	1895 11 Sep	1940*	1946 11 Sep	1991	1997 11 Sep
1839	1845 10 Sep	1890	1896* 10 Sep	1941	1947 12 Sep	1992*	1998 11 Sep
1840*	1846 10 Sep	1891	1897 10 Sep	1942	1948* 11 Sep	1993	1999 12 Sep
1841	1847 11 Sep	1892*	1898 10 Sep	1943	1949 11 Sep	1994	2000* 11 Sep
1842	1848* 10 Sep	1893	1899 11 Sep	1944*	1950 11 Sep	1995	2001 11 Sep
1843	1849 10 Sep	1894	1900 10 Sep	1945	1951 12 Sep	1996*	2002 11 Sep
1844*	1850 10 Sep	1895	1901 11 Sep	1946	1952* 11 Sep	1997	2003 12 Sep
1845	1851 11 Sep	1896*	1902 11 Sep	1947	1953 11 Sep	1998	2004* 11 Sep
1846	1852* 10 Sep	1897	1903 12 Sep	1948*	1954 11 Sep	1999	2005 11 Sep
1847	1853 10 Sep	1898	1904* 11 Sep	1949	1955 12 Sep	2000*	2006 11 Sep
1848*	1854 10 Sep	1899	1905 11 Sep	1950	1956* 11 Sep	2001	2007 12 Sep
1849	1855 11 Sep	1900*	1906 11 Sep	1951	1957 11 Sep	2002	2008* 11 Sep
1850	1856* 10 Sep	1901	1907 12 Sep	1952*	1958 11 Sep	2003	2009 11 Sep
1851	1857 10 Sep	1902	1908* 11 Sep	1953	1959 12 Sep	2004*	2010 11 Sep
1852*	1858 10 Sep	1903	1909 11 Sep	1954	1960* 11 Sep	2005	2011 12 Sep
1853	1859 11 Sep	1904*	1910 11 Sep	1955	1961 11 Sep	2006	2012* 11 Sep
1854	1860* 10 Sep	1905	1911 12 Sep	1956*	1962 11 Sep	2007	2013 11 Sep
1855	1861 10 Sep	1906	1912* 11 Sep	1957	1963 12 Sep	2008*	2014 11 Sep
1856*	1862 10 Sep	1907	1913 11 Sep	1958	1964* 11 Sep	2009	2015 12 Sep

Ethiopian Year	Western Date (Gregorian) of New Year		Ethiopian Year	Western Date (Gregorian) of New Year		Ethiopian Year	Western Date (Gregorian) of New Year		Ethiopian Year	Western Date (Gregorian) of New Year	
2010	2016*	11 Sep	2028*	2034	11 Sep	2046	2052*	11 Sep	2064*	2070	11 Sep
2011	2017	11 Sep	2029	2035	12 Sep	2047	2053	11 Sep	2065	2071	12 Sep
2012*	2018	11 Sep	2030	2036*	11 Sep	2048*	2054	11 Sep	2066	2072*	11 Sep
2013	2019	12 Sep	2031	2037	11 Sep	2049	2055	12 Sep	2067	2073	11 Sep
2014	2020*	11 Sep	2032*	2038	11 Sep	2050	2056*	11 Sep	2068*	2074	11 Sep
2015	2021	11 Sep	2033	2039	12 Sep	2051	2057	11 Sep	2069	2075	12 Sep
2016*	2022	11 Sep	2034	2040*	11 Sep	2052*	2058	11 Sep	2070	2076*	11 Sep
2017	2023	12 Sep	2035	2041	11 Sep	2053	2059	12 Sep	2071	2077	11 Sep
2018	2024*	11 Sep	2036*	2042	11 Sep	2054	2060*	11 Sep	2072*	2078	11 Sep
2019	2025	11 Sep	2037	2043	12 Sep	2055	2061	11 Sep	2073	2079	12 Sep
2020*	2026	11 Sep	2038	2044*	11 Sep	2056*	2062	11 Sep	2074	2080*	11 Sep
2021	2027	12 Sep	2039	2045	11 Sep	2057	2063	12 Sep	2075	2081	11 Sep
2022	2028*	11 Sep	2040*	2046	11 Sep	2058	2064*	11 Sep	2076*	2082	11 Sep
2023	2029	11 Sep	2041	2047	12 Sep	2059	2065	11 Sep	2077	2083	12 Sep
2024*	2030	11 Sep	2042	2048*	11 Sep	2060*	2066	11 Sep	2078	2084*	11 Sep
2025	2031	12 Sep	2043	2049	11 Sep	2061	2067	12 Sep	2079	2085	11 Sep
2026	2032*	11 Sep	2044*	2050	11 Sep	2062	2068*	11 Sep	2080*	2086	11 Sep
2027	2033	11 Sep	2045	2051	12 Sep	2063	2069	11 Sep			

MODERN NEAR EAST

IRAN

The area that we now know as Iran has used many calendars throughout its history. During the early period, it employed the Babylonian and Zoroastrian calendars; later it utilized the Islamic. In the past two centuries four were used extensively: the Gregorian (primarily in larger cities and in foreign commercial correspondence), the Iranian Lunar Hegira, the Borji and the Iranian Solar Hegira. A fifth, the Turco-Mongolian, was used in several areas as well.

The Iranian version of the Lunar Hegira calendar differs considerably from both the Arabic and Afghanistani versions of it. Like these, it follows a strictly lunar year and begins the epoch with July 16, 622 A.D. It contains months of 29 and 30 days and uses a one-day intercalation for leap year. However, the distribution of the 29 and 30 day months is not consistent; neither is the intercalation.

The Borji, or zodiac, calendar was used extensively during the last half of the 19th and the beginning of the 20th centuries. Occasionally it was the official calendar of the area. In this calendar the beginning of the month corresponded with the date of entry of the sun into the various signs of the zodiac. Although officially the month names were given in Arabic, the Iranians also used Farsee names.

Zodiac	Arabic	Farsee
Aries	Ḥamal	Barre
Taurus	T̲hur	Gaw
Gemini	Jawzā'	Dopeykar
Cancer	Saratān	Kharchang
Leo	Asȧd	Shir
Virgo	Sunbula	Khushe
Libra	Mīzān	Terazu
Scorpio	'Aqrab	Kazhdom
Sagittarius	Qaws	Kaman
Capricorn	Jadī	Bozghale
Aquarius	Dalw	Dul
Pisces	Hūt	Mahi

In 1925 Reza Shah Pahlevi replaced the Borji calendar with the Iranian Solar. It was based on the solar year, used Persian names for months and retained the Muslim Era. During 1976 and 1977 the government experimented with placing the epoch at 599 B.C. when Cyrus, founder of the Persian Empire, was enthroned. The calendar was called the Shahinshah Era. However, this was found impractical, and in 1978, the era reverted to 622 A.D. to conform with the year of the Hegira.

The names of the months and their beginning dates are as follows:

Farvadin—March 21	Mehr—September 23
Ordibehesht—April 21	Aban—October 23
Khordad—May 22	Azar—November 22
Tir—June 22	Dey—December 22
Amordad—July 23	Bahman—January 21
Shahrivar—August 23	Esfand—February 20

Because the first day of the first month of the calendar always occurs at the equinox, the intercalated day for leap year is always added to the last day of the last month.

LUNAR HEGIRA

Lunar Hegira Year	Gregorian Year	Muharram	Safar	Rabi I	Rabi II	Jumada I	Jumada II	Rajab	Shaban	Ramadan	Shawwal	Dhul-Qa'da	Dhul-Hijja
		Number of Days in Month											
1268*	1851	30	29	30	30	30	29	30	29	30	29	30	29
1269*	1852*	29	30	29	30	30	29	30	30	29	30	29	30
1270	1853	29	30	29	29	30	29	30	30	29	30	30	29
1271*	1854	30	29	30	29	29	30	29	30	29	30	30	30
1272	1855	29	30	29	30	29	29	30	29	30	29	30	30
1273*	1856*	29	30	30	29	30	29	30	29	29	30	30	30
1274	1857	29	30	30	29	30	30	29	30	29	29	29	30
1275*	1858	30	29	30	29	30	30	30	29	30	29	29	30
1276	1859	29	30	29	30	29	30	30	29	30	29	30	29
1277*	1860*	30	29	30	29	29	30	30	29	30	30	29	30
1278	1861	29	30	29	30	29	29	30	29	30	30	29	30
1279	1862	30	30	29	29	30	29	29	30	29	30	29	30
1280	1863	30	30	30	29	29	30	29	29	30	29	30	29
1281*	1864*	30	30	30	29	30	29	30	29	29	30	29	30
1282	1865	29	30	30	29	30	29	30	30	29	30	29	30
1283*	1866	30	29	30	29	30	29	30	30	30	29	30	29
1284*	1286	29	30	29	30	29	29	30	30	30	29	30	30
1285	1868*	29	29	30	29	29	30	29	30	30	29	30	30
1286	1869	29	30	29	30	29	29	30	29	30	29	30	30
1287	1870	30	29	30	29	29	30	29	30	29	30	29	30
1288	1871	30	29	30	29	30	29	30	29	30	29	30	29
1289*	1872*	30	29	30	30	29	30	29	30	30	29	29	30
1290	1873	29	30	29	30	29	30	30	30	29	30	29	29
1291*	1874	30	29	29	30	29	30	30	30	30	29	30	29
1292	1875	29	30	29	29	30	29	30	30	30	29	30	29
1293	1876*	30	29	30	29	29	30	29	30	30	29	30	29
1294	1877	30	30	29	30	29	39	30	30	29	30	29	29
1295*	1878)	30	30	30	29	30	29	30	30	29	29	29	30
1296	1878)	29	30	30	29	30	30	29	30	30	29	29	29
1297*	1879	30	29	30	29	30	30	30	29	30	30	29	29
1298	1880*	29	30	29	30	29	30	29	30	30	30	29	29
1299*	1881	30	29	30	29	29	30	30	29	30	30	30	29
1300	1882	29	30	29	30	29	29	30	30	29	30	30	29
1301	1883	30	29	30	29	30	29	30	29	29	30	30	29
1302	1884*	30	29	30	30	29	30	29	30	29	29	30	29

1303*	1885	30	29	30	30	30	29	30	29	30	29	29	30
1304	1886	29	29	30	30	30	29	30	30	29	30	29	29
1305*	1887	30	29	29	30	30	30	29	30	30	29	30	29
1306	1888*	29	30	29	30	29	30	29	30	30	29	30	29
1307	1889	30	29	30	29	30	29	30	29	30	29	30	29
1308	1890	30	30	29	30	29	30	29	29	30	29	30	29
1309*	1891	30	30	30	29	30	29	30	29	29	30	29	30
1310	1892*	29	30	30	30	29	30	29	30	29	29	30	29
1311*	1893	30	29	30	30	29	30	30	29	30	29	29	30
1312	1895	29	30	29	30	30	29	30	30	29	30	29	29
1313*	1896*	30	29	30	29	30	29	30	29	30	30	29	30
1315	1897	30	30	29	30	29	29	30	29	29	30	30	30
1316	1898	30	30	30	29	30	29	29	30	29	30	30	29
1317*	1899	30	30	30	30	29	30	29	29	30	29	29	30
1318	1900	29	30	30	30	29	30	29	30	29	30	29	29
1319*	1901	30	29	30	30	29	30	29	30	30	29	30	29
1320*	1902	30	29	29	30	30	29	29	30	30	29	30	30
1321	1903	29	30	29	29	30	29	29	30	30	29	30	30
1322	1904*	30	29	29	30	29	30	29	29	30	29	30	30
1323	1905	30	29	30	30	29	29	30	29	29	30	29	30
1324	1906	30	30	29	30	29	30	29	30	29	29	30	29
1325*	1907	30	30	29	30	29	30	30	29	30	29	30	29
1326*	1908*	29	30	29	30	29	30	30	29	30	30	29	30
1327	1909	29	29	30	29	30	29	30	30	29	30	30	29
1328*	1910	30	29	30	29	29	29	30	30	29	30	30	30
1329	1911)	29	30	29	29	30	29	29	30	30	29	30	30
1330	1911)	29	30	30	29	30	29	29	29	30	30	29	30
1331	1912*	29	30	30	30	29	29	30	29	30	29	30	29
1332*	1913	30	29	30	30	29	30	29	30	29	30	29	30
1333	1914	29	29	30	30	29	30	29	30	30	30	29	29
1334*	1915	30	29	29	30	29	30	30	29	30	30	30	29
1335*	1916*	29	30	29	29	30	29	30	29	30	30	30	30
1336	1917	29	29	30	29	29	30	29	30	29	30	30	30
1337	1918	29	29	30	30	29	29	30	29	30	29	30	30
1338	1919	29	30	29	30	30	29	29	30	29	30	29	30
1339	1920*	29	29	30	30	30	29	30	29	30	29	30	29
1340*	1921	29	30	29	30	30	30	29	30	30	29	29	30
1341	1922	29	29	30	29	30	30	29	30	30	29	30	29
1342*	1923	30	29	29	30	29	30	29	30	30	30	29	30
1343	1924*	29	29	30	29	30	29	30	29	30	29	30	30
1344	1925	29	30	29	30	29	30	29	30	29	30	29	30
1345	1926	29	30	30	29	30	30	29	29	30	29	29	30
1346	1927	29	30	30	29	30	30	30	29	29	30	29	29
1347*	1928*	30	29	30	30	29	30	30	29	30	29	30	29
1348*	1929	29	30	29	30	30	29	30	30	29	30	29	30

Lunar Hegira Year	Gregorian Year	Muharram	Safar	Rabi I	Rabi II	Jumada I	Jumada II	Rajab	Shaban	Ramadan	Shawwal	Dhul-Qa'da	Dhul-Hijja
		Number of Days in Month											
1349	1930	29	29	30	29	30	30	29	30	29	30	30	29
1350	1931	30	29	29	30	29	30	29	30	29	30	30	29
1351	1932*	30	30	29	30	29	30	29	29	30	29	30	29
1352*	1933	30	30	29	30	30	29	30	29	29	30	29	30
1353	1934	29	30	30	30	29	30	29	30	29	29	30	29
1354*	1935	29	30	29	30	30	30	30	29	29	30	29	30
1355	1936*	29	29	30	30	29	30	30	29	30	29	30	29
1356*	1937	30	29	29	30	30	29	30	29	30	30	29	30
1357	1938	29	30	29	30	29	30	29	29	30	30	29	30
1358	1939	30	29	30	29	30	29	29	30	29	30	29	30
1359	1940*	30	30	29	30	29	30	29	29	30	29	29	30
1360*	1941	30	30	29	30	30	29	30	29	29	30	29	30
1361	1942	29	30	30	29	30	30	29	30	29	29	30	29
1362*	1943	30	29	30	29	30	30	29	30	29	30	29	30
1363	1944*	29	30	29	30	29	29	30	30	29	30	30	29
1364*	1945)	30	30	29	29	30	29	29	30	30	29	30	30
1365	1945)	29	30	30	29	29	29	30	29	30	29	30	30
1366	1946	30	29	30	29	30	29	29	30	29	29	30	30
1367	1947	30	30	29	30	29	30	29	29	30	29	30	29
1368*	1948*	30	29	30	30	29	30	30	29	29	30	29	30
1369	1949	29	30	29	30	29	30	30	29	30	29	30	29
1370*	1950	30	29	30	29	30	29	30	29	30	30	30	29
1371	1951	29	30	29	30	29	29	30	29	30	30	30	29
1372*	1952*	30	30	29	29	30	29	29	30	29	30	30	30
1373	1953	29	30	29	30	29	30	29	29	30	29	30	30
1374	1954	29	30	30	29	30	29	30	29	29	30	29	30
1375	1955	29	30	30	29	30	30	29	30	29	29	30	29
1376*	1956*	30	29	30	29	30	30	29	30	30	29	30	29
1377*	1957	29	30	29	29	30	29	29	30	30	30	30	30
1378	1958*	29	29	30	29	29	30	29	30	30	30	29	30
1379	1959	30	29	29	30	29	29	30	29	30	30	29	30
1380	1960*	30	29	30	29	30	29	29	30	30	29	29	30
1381	1961	30	29	30	30	29	30	29	30	29	29	30	29
1382*	1962	30	29	30	30	29	30	30	29	30	29	29	30
1383*	1963	29	30	30	29	30	30	30	29	30	30	29	29

1384*	1964*	30	29	29	30	29	30	30	30	29	30	30	29
1385*	1965	29	30	29	29	30	29	30	30	29	30	30	30
1386	1966	29	29	30	29	29	30	29	30	29	30	30	30
1387	1967	29	30	29	30	29	30	29	29	30	29	30	30
1388	1968*	29	30	30	29	39	29	30	29	30	29	30	29
1389	1969	29	30	30	29	30	30	29	30	29	29	30	29
1390*	1970	30	29	30	29	30	30	30	29	30	29	30	29
1391*	1971	29	30	29	29	30	30	30	29	30	30	29	30
1392	1972*	29	29	30	29	29	30	30	29	30	30	29	30
1393	1973	30	29	29	30	29	30	30	30	29	30	29	30
1394	1974	30	30	29	30	29	29	30	29	29	30	29	30
1395#	1975	30	30	29	30	29	30	29	30	29	29	29	29
1396*	1976*	30	29	30	30	30	29	30	29	30	29	29	30
1397	1977	30	29	29	30	30	30	29	30	29	30	29	29
1398	1978	30	29	30	29	29	29	30	30	29	30	29	30

#—the Iranian Lunar Hegira Year 1395 was deficient and contained only 353 days.

BORJI IRANIAN SOLAR

Iranian Borji Solar				Gregorian		
Year	0° of Sign	Date	Days in Month	Year	Date	Days in Month
1230*	♈	1 Ḥamal	31	1851	21 Mar	31
	♉	1 Thur	31		21 Apr	30
	♊	1 Jawzā'	32		22 May	31
	♋	1 Saratān	31		23 Jun	30
	♌	1 Asâd	31		24 Jul	31
	♍	1 Sunbula	31		24 Aug	31
	♎	1 Mīzān	30		24 Sep	30
	♏	1 'Aqrab	30		24 Oct	31
	♐	1 Qaws	29		23 Nov	30
	♑	1 Jadī	29		23 Dec	31
	♒	1 Dalw	30	1852*	21 Jan	31
	♓	1 Hūt	30		20 Feb	29
1231	♈	1 Ḥamal	31	1852*	21 Mar	31
	♉	1 Thur	31		21 Apr	30
	♊	1 Jawzā'	31		22 May	31
	♋	1 Saratān	31		23 Jun	30
	♌	1 Asâd	32		24 Jul	31
	♍	1 Sunbula	31		24 Aug	31
	♎	1 Mīzān	30		24 Sep	30
	♏	1 'Aqrab	30		24 Oct	31
	♐	1 Qaws	29		23 Nov	30
	♑	1 Jadī	30		23 Dec	31
	♒	1 Dalw	29	1853	21 Jan	31
	♓	1 Hūt	30		20 Feb	28
1232	♈	1 Ḥamal	31	1853	21 Mar	31
	♉	1 Thur	31		20 Apr	30
	♊	1 Jawzā'	32		21 May	31
	♋	1 Saratān	31		22 Jun	30
	♌	1 Asâ	31		23 Jul	31
	♍	1 Sunbula	31		23 Aug	31
	♎	1 Mīzān	30		23 Sep	30
	♏	1 'Aqrab	30		24 Oct	31
	♐	1 Qaws	30		22 Nov	30
	♑	1 Jadī	29		22 Dec	31
	♒	1 Dalw	30	1854	20 Jan	31
	♓	1 Hūt	30		19 Feb	28
1233	♈	1 Ḥamal	31	1854	21 Mar	31
	♉	1 Thur	31		21 Apr	30
	♊	1 Jawzā'	31		22 May	31
	♋	1 Saratān	31		22 Jun	30
	♌	1 Asâd	32		23 Jul	31

Iranian Boriji Solar				Gregorian		
Year	0° of Sign	Date	Days in Month	Year	Date	Days in Month
	♍	1 Sunbula	31		24 Aug	31
	♎	1 Mīzān	30		24 Sep	30
	♏	1 'Aqrab	30		24 Oct	31
	♐	1 Qaws	29		23 Nov	30
	♑	1 Jadī	30		22 Dec	31
	♒	1 Dalw	29	1855	21 Jan	31
	♓	1 Hūt	30		19 Feb	28
1234*	♈	1 Ḥamal	31	1855	21 Mar	31
	♉	1 Thur	31		21 Apr	30
	♊	1 Jawzā'	32		22 May	31
	♋	1 Saratān	31		22 Jun	30
	♌	1 Asâd	31		24 Jul	31
	♍	1 Sunbula	31		24 Aug	31
	♎	1 Mīzān	30		24 Sep	30
	♏	1 'Aqrab	30		24 Oct	31
	♐	1 Qaws	29		23 Nov	30
	♑	1 Jadī	29		23 Dec	31
	♒	1 Dalw	30	1856*	21 Jan	31
	♓	1 Hūt	30		20 Feb	29
1235	♈	1 Ḥamal	31	1856*	21 Mar	31
	♉	1 Thur	31		20 Apr	30
	♊	1 Jawzā'	32		21 May	31
	♋	1 Saratān	31		21 Jun	30
	♌	1 Asâd	31		23 Jul	31
	♍	1 Sunbula	31		23 Aug	31
	♎	1 Mīzān	30		23 Sep	30
	♏	1 'Aqrab	30		23 Oct	31
	♐	1 Qaws	30		22 Nov	30
	♑	1 Jadī	29		22 Dec	31
	♒	1 Dalw	30	1857	20 Jan	31
	♓	1 Hūt	30		19 Feb	28
1236	♈	1 Ḥamal	31	1857	21 Mar	31
	♉	1 Thur	31		20 Apr	30
	♊	1 Jawzā'	32		21 May	31
	♋	1 Saratān	31		22 Jun	30
	♌	1 Asâd	31		23 Jul	31
	♍	1 Sunbula	31		23 Aug	31
	♎	1 Mīzān	30		23 Sep	30
	♏	1 'Aqrab	30		24 Oct	31
	♐	1 Qaws	30		22 Nov	30
	♑	1 Jadī	29		22 Dec	31

Iranian Boriji Solar				Gregorian		
Year	0° of Sign	Date	Days in Month	Year	Date	Days in Month
	♒	1 Dalw	30	1858	20 Jan	31
	♓	1 Hūt	30		19 Feb	28
1237	♈	1 Ḥamal	31	1858	21 Mar	31
	♉	1 Thur	31		21 Apr	30
	♊	1 Jawzā'	32		22 May	31
	♋	1 Saratān	31		22 Jun	30
	♌	1 Asȧd	31		23 Jul	31
	♍	1 Sunbula	31		24 Aug	31
	♎	1 Mīzān	30		23 Sep	30
	♏	1 'Aqrab	30		24 Oct	31
	♐	1 Qaws	29		23 Nov	30
	♑	1 Jadī	29		22 Dec	31
	♒	1 Dalw	30	1859	21 Jan	31
	♓	1 Hūt	30		19 Feb	28
1238*	♈	1 Ḥamal	31	1859	21 Mar	31
	♉	1 Thur	31		21 Apr	30
	♊	1 Jawzā'	31		22 May	31
	♋	1 Saratān	32		22 Jun	30
	♌	1 Asȧd	31		24 Jul	31
	♍	1 Sunbula	31		24 Aug	31
	♎	1 Mīzān	30		24 Sep	30
	♏	1 'Aqrab	30		24 Oct	31
	♐	1 Qaws	29		23 Nov	30
	♑	1 Jadī	30		22 Dec	31
	♒	1 Dalw	30	1860*	21 Jan	31
	♓	1 Hūt	30		20 Feb	29
1239	♈	1 Ḥamal	30	1860*	21 Mar	31
	♉	1 Thur	31		20 Apr	30
	♊	1 Jawzā'	31		21 May	31
	♋	1 Saratān	32		21 Jun	30
	♌	1 Asȧd	31		23 Jul	31
	♍	1 Sunbula	31		23 Aug	31
	♎	1 Mīzān	30		23 Sep	30
	♏	1 'Aqrab	30		23 Oct	31
	♐	1 Qaws	30		22 Nov	30
	♑	1 Jadī	29		22 Dec	31
	♒	1 Dalw	30	1861	20 Jan	31
	♓	1 Hūt	30		19 Feb	28
1240	♈	1 Ḥamal	30	1861	21 Mar	31
	♉	1 Thur	31		20 Apr	30
	♊	1 Jawzā'	32		21 May	31
	♋	1 Saratān	31		22 Jun	30

Iranian Boriji Solar				Gregorian		
Year	0° of Sign	Date	Days in Month	Year	Date	Days in Month
	♌	1 Asȧd	31		23 Jul	31
	♍	1 Sunbula	31		23 Aug	31
	♎	1 Mīzān	31		23 Sep	30
	♏	1 'Aqrab	29		24 Oct	31
	♐	1 Qaws	30		22 Nov	30
	♑	1 Jadī	29		22 Dec	31
	♒	1 Dalw	30	1862	20 Jan	31
	♓	1 Hūt	30		19 Feb	28
1241	♈	1 Ḥamal	30	1862	21 Mar	31
	♉	1 Thur	32		20 Apr	30
	♊	1 Jawzā'	31		22 May	31
	♋	1 Saratān	31		22 Jun	30
	♌	1 Asȧd	32		23 Jul	31
	♍	1 Sunbula	30		24 Aug	31
	♎	1 Mīzān	31		23 Sep	30
	♏	1 'Aqrab	30		24 Oct	31
	♐	1 Qaws	29		23 Nov	30
	♑	1 Jadī	30		22 Dec	31
	♒	1 Dalw	29	1863	21 Jan	31
	♓	1 Hūt	30		19 Feb	28
1242	♈	1 Ḥamal	31	1863	21 Mar	31
	♉	1 Thur	31		21 Apr	30
	♊	1 Jawzā'	31		22 May	31
	♋	1 Saratān	32		22 Jun	30
	♌	1 Asȧd	31		24 Jul	31
	♍	1 Sunbula	31		24 Aug	31
	♎	1 Mīzān	30		24 Sep	30
	♏	1 'Aqrab	30		24 Oct	31
	♐	1 Qaws	29		23 Nov	30
	♑	1 Jadī	30		22 Dec	31
	♒	1 Dalw	29	1864*	21 Jan	31
	♓	1 Hūt	30		19 Feb	29
1243	♈	1 Ḥamal	31	1864*	20 Mar	31
	♉	1 Thur	31		20 Apr	30
	♊	1 Jawzā'	31		21 May	31
	♋	1 Saratān	32		21 Jun	30
	♌	1 Asȧd	31		23 Jul	31
	♍	1 Sunbula	31		23 Aug	31
	♎	1 Mīzān	30		23 Sep	30
	♏	1 'Aqrab	30		23 Oct	31
	♐	1 Qaws	30		22 Nov	30
	♑	1 Jadī	29		22 Dec	31
	♒	1 Dalw	30	1865	20 Jan	31
	♓	1 Hūt	30		19 Feb	28

Iranian Boriji Solar				Gregorian		
Year	0° of Sign	Date	Days in Month	Year	Date	Days in Month
1244	♈	1 Ḥamal	30	1865	21 Mar	31
	♉	1 Thur	31		20 Apr	30
	♊	1 Jawzā'	32		21 May	31
	♋	1 Saratān	31		22 Jun	30
	♌	1 Asȧd	31		23 Jul	31
	♍	1 Sunbula	31		23 Aug	31
	♎	1 Mīzān	30		23 Sep	30
	♏	1 'Aqrab	29		24 Oct	31
	♐	1 Qaws	30		22 Nov	30
	♑	1 Jadī	29		22 Dec	31
	♒	1 Dalw	30	1866	20 Jan	31
	♓	1 Hūt	30		19 Feb	28
1245	♈	1 Ḥamal	30	1866	21 Mar	31
	♉	1 Thur	31		20 Apr	30
	♊	1 Jawzā'	32		21 May	31
	♋	1 Saratān	31		22 Jun	30
	♌	1 Asȧd	32		23 Jul	31
	♍	1 Sunbula	30		24 Aug	31
	♎	1 Mīzān	31		23 Sep	30
	♏	1 'Aqrab	30		24 Oct	31
	♐	1 Qaws	29		23 Nov	30
	♑	1 Jadī	30		22 Dec	31
	♒	1 Dalw	29	1867	21 Jan	31
	♓	1 Hūt	30		19 Feb	28
1246	♈	1 Ḥamal	31	1867	21 Mar	31
	♉	1 Thur	31		21 Apr	30
	♊	1 Jawzā'	31		22 May	31
	♋	1 Saratān	32		22 Jun	30
	♌	1 Asȧd	31		24 Jul	31
	♍	1 Sunbula	31		24 Aug	31
	♎	1 Mīzān	30		24 Sep	30
	♏	1 'Aqrab	30		24 Oct	31
	♐	1 Qaws	29		23 Nov	30
	♑	1 Jadī	30		22 Dec	31
	♒	1 Dalw	29	1868*	21 Jan	31
	♓	1 Hūt	30		19 Feb	29
1247*	♈	1 Ḥamal	31	1868*	20 Mar	31
	♉	1 Thur	31		20 Apr	30
	♊	1 Jawzā'	31		21 May	31
	♋	1 Saratān	32		21 Jun	30
	♌	1 Asȧd	31		23 Jul	31
	♍	1 Sunbula	31		23 Aug	31
	♎	1 Mīzān	31		23 Sep	30
	♏	1 'Aqrab	30		23 Oct	31
	♐	1 Qaws	30		22 Nov	30
	♑	1 Jadī	29		22 Dec	31
	♒	1 Dalw	30	1869	20 Jan	31
	♓	1 Hūt	30		19 Feb	28
1248	♈	1 Ḥamal	30	1869	29 Mar	31
	♉	1 Thur	31		20 Apr	30
	♊	1 Jawzā'	32		21 May	31
	♋	1 Saratān	31		22 Jun	30
	♌	1 Asȧd	31		23 Jul	31
	♍	1 Sunbula	31		23 Aug	31
	♎	1 Mīzān	31		23 Sep	30
	♏	1 'Aqrab	29		24 Oct	31
	♐	1 Qaws	30		22 Nov	30
	♑	1 Jadī	29		22 Dec	31
	♒	1 Dalw	30	1870	20 Jan	31
	♓	1 Hūt	30		19 Feb	28
1249	♈	1 Ḥamal	30	1870	21 Mar	31
	♉	1 Thur	31		20 Apr	30
	♊	1 Jawzā'	32		21 May	31
	♋	1 Saratān	31		22 Jun	30
	♌	1 Asȧd	32		23 Jul	31
	♍	1 Sunbula	30		24 Aug	31
	♎	1 Mīzān	31		23 Sep	30
	♏	1 'Aqrab	30		24 Oct	31
	♐	1 Qaws	29		23 Nov	30
	♑	1 Jadī	30		22 Dec	31
	♒	1 Dalw	29	1871	21 Jan	31
	♓	1 Hūt	30		19 Feb	28
1250	♈	1 Ḥamal	31	1871	21 Mar	31
	♉	1 Thur	31		21 Apr	30
	♊	1 Jawzā'	31		22 May	31
	♋	1 Saratān	31		22 Jun	30
	♌	1 Asȧd	32		23 Jul	31
	♍	1 Sunbula	31		24 Aug	31
	♎	1 Mīzān	30		24 Sep	30
	♏	1 'Aqrab	30		24 Oct	31
	♐	1 Qaws	29		23 Nov	30
	♑	1 Jadī	30		22 Dec	31
	♒	1 Dalw	29	1872*	21 Jan	31
	♓	1 Hūt	30		19 Feb	29
1251*	♈	1 Ḥamal	31	1872*	20 Mar	31
	♉	1 Thur	31		20 Apr	30

Iranian Boriji Solar				Gregorian		
Year	0° of Sign	Date	Days in Month	Year	Date	Days in Month
	♊	1 Jawzā'	31		21 May	31
	♋	1 Saratān	32		21 Jun	30
	♌	1 Asȧd	31		23 Jul	31
	♍	1 Sunbula	31		23 Aug	31
	♎	1 Mīzān	30		23 Sep	30
	♏	1 'Aqrab	30		23 Oct	31
	♐	1 Qaws	30		22 Nov	30
	♑	1 Jadī	29		22 Dec	31
	♒	1 Dalw	30	1873	20 Jan	31
	♓	1 Hūt	30		19 Feb	28
1252	♈	1 Ḥamal	30	1873	21 Mar	31
	♉	1 Thur	31		20 Apr	30
	♊	1 Jawzā'	32		21 May	31
	♋	1 Saratān	31		22 Jun	30
	♌	1 Asȧd	31		23 Jul	31
	♍	1 Sunbula	31		23 Aug	31
	♎	1 Mīzān	30		23 Sep	30
	♏	1 'Aqrab	30		23 Oct	31
	♐	1 Qaws	30		22 Nov	30
	♑	1 Jadī	29		22 Dec	31
	♒	1 Dalw	30	1874	20 Jan	31
	♓	1 Hūt	30		19 Feb	28
1253	♈	1 Ḥamal	30	1874	21 Mar	31
	♉	1 Thur	31		20 Apr	30
	♊	1 Jawzā'	32		21 May	31
	♋	1 Saratān	31		22 Jun	30
	♌	1 Asȧd	31		23 Jul	31
	♍	1 Sunbula	31		23 Aug	31
	♎	1 Mīzān	31		23 Sep	30
	♏	1 'Aqrab	30		24 Oct	31
	♐	1 Qaws	29		23 Nov	30
	♑	1 Jadī	30		22 Dec	31
	♒	1 Dalw	29	1875	21 Jan	31
	♓	1 Hūt	30		19 Feb	28
1254	♈	1 Ḥamal	31	1875	21 Mar	31
	♉	1 Thur	31		21 Apr	30
	♊	1 Jawzā'	31		22 May	31
	♋	1 Saratān	31		22 Jun	30
	♌	1 Asȧd	32		23 Jul	31
	♍	1 Sunbula	31		24 Aug	31
	♎	1 Mīzān	30		24 Sep	30
	♏	1 'Aqrab	30		24 Oct	31
	♐	1 Qaws	29		23 Nov	30

Iranian Boriji Solar				Gregorian		
Year	0° of Sign	Date	Days in Month	Year	Date	Days in Month
	♑	1 Jadī	30		22 Dec	31
	♒	1 Dalw	29	1876*	21 Jan	31
	♓	1 Hūt	30		19 Feb	29
1255*	♈	1 Ḥamal	31	1876*	21 Mar	31
	♉	1 Thur	31		21 Apr	30
	♊	1 Jawzā'	31		22 May	31
	♋	1 Saratān	32		22 Jun	30
	♌	1 Asȧd	31		23 Jul	31
	♍	1 Sunbula	31		24 Aug	31
	♎	1 Mīzān	30		24 Sep	30
	♏	1 'Aqrab	30		24 Oct	31
	♐	1 Qaws	30		23 Nov	30
	♑	1 Jadī	29		22 Dec	31
	♒	1 Dalw	30	1877	21 Jan	31
	♓	1 Hūt	30		19 Feb	28
1256	♈	1 Ḥamal	30	1877	21 Mar	31
	♉	1 Thur	31		20 Apr	30
	♊	1 Jawzā'	31		21 May	31
	♋	1 Saratān	32		21 Jun	30
	♌	1 Asȧd	31		23 Jul	31
	♍	1 Sunbula	31		23 Aug	31
	♎	1 Mīzān	30		23 Sep	30
	♏	1 'Aqrab	30		23 Oct	31
	♐	1 Qaws	30		22 Nov	30
	♑	1 Jadī	29		22 Dec	31
	♒	1 Dalw	30	1878	20 Jan	31
	♓	1 Hūt	30		19 Feb	28
1257	♈	1 Ḥamal	30	1878	21 Mar	31
	♉	1 Thur	31		20 Apr	30
	♊	1 Jawzā'	31		21 May	31
	♋	1 Saratān	32		22 Jun	30
	♌	1 Asȧd	31		23 Jul	31
	♍	1 Sunbula	31		23 Aug	31
	♎	1 Mīzān	31		23 Sep	30
	♏	1 'Aqrab	30		24 Oct	31
	♐	1 Qaws	29		23 Nov	30
	♑	1 Jadī	30		22 Dec	31
	♒	1 Dalw	29	1879	21 Jan	31
	♓	1 Hūt	29		19 Feb	28
1258	♈	1 Ḥamal	31	1879	21 Mar	31
	♉	1 Thur	31		21 Apr	30
	♊	1 Jawzā'	31		22 May	31

Iranian Borji Solar				Gregorian		
Year	0° of Sign	Date	Days in Month	Year	Date	Days in Month
	♋	1 Saratān	31		22 Jun	30
	♌	1 Asâd	32		23 Jul	31
	♍	1 Sunbula	31		24 Aug	31
	♎	1 Mīzān	30		24 Sep	30
	♏	1 'Aqrab	30		24 Oct	31
	♐	1 Qaws	29		23 Nov	30
	♑	1 Jadī	30		22 Dec	31
	♒	1 Dalw	29	1880*	21 Jan	31
	♓	1 Hūt	30		19 Feb	29
1259*	♈	1 Ḥamal	31	1880	21 Mar	31
	♉	1 Thur	31		20 Apr	30
	♊	1 Jawzā'	31		21 May	31
	♋	1 Saratān	32		21 Jun	30
	♌	1 Asâd	31		23 Jul	31
	♍	1 Sunbula	31		23 Aug	31
	♎	1 Mīzān	30		23 Sep	30
	♏	1 'Aqrab	30		23 Oct	31
	♐	1 Qaws	30		22 Nov	30
	♑	1 Jadī	29		22 Dec	31
	♒	1 Dalw	30	1881	20 Jan	31
	♓	1 Hūt	30		19 Feb	28
1260	♈	1 Ḥamal	30	1881	21 Mar	31
	♉	1 Thur	31		20 Apr	30
	♊	1 Jawzā'	31		21 May	31
	♋	1 Saratān	32		21 Jun	30
	♌	1 Asâd	31		23 Jul	31
	♍	1 Sunbula	31		23 Aug	31
	♎	1 Mīzān	30		23 Sep	30
	♏	1 'Aqrab	30		23 Oct	31
	♐	1 Qaws	30		22 Nov	30
	♑	1 Jadī	29		22 Dec	31
	♒	1 Dalw	30	1882	20 Jan	31
	♓	1 Hūt	30		19 Feb	28
1261	♈	1 Ḥamal	30	1882	21 Mar	31
	♉	1 Thur	31		20 Apr	30
	♊	1 Jawzā'	31		21 May	31
	♋	1 Saratān	32		22 Jun	30
	♌	1 Asâd	31		23 Jul	31
	♍	1 Sunbula	31		23 Aug	31
	♎	1 Mīzān	31		23 Sep	30
	♏	1 'Aqrab	30		24 Oct	31
	♐	1 Qaws	29		23 Nov	30
	♑	1 Jadī	29		22 Dec	31

Iranian Boriji Solar				Gregorian		
Year	0° of Sign	Date	Days in Month	Year	Date	Days in Month
	♒	1 Dalw	30	1883	20 Jan	31
	♓	1 Hūt	30		19 Feb	28
1262	♈	1 Ḥamal	31	1883	21 Mar	31
	♉	1 Thur	31		21 Apr	30
	♊	1 Jawzā'	31		22 May	31
	♋	1 Saratān	31		22 Jun	30
	♌	1 Asâd	32		23 Jul	31
	♍	1 Sunbula	31		24 Aug	31
	♎	1 Mīzān	30		24 Sep	30
	♏	1 'Aqrab	30		24 Oct	31
	♐	1 Qaws	29		23 Nov	30
	♑	1 Jadī	30		22 Dec	31
	♒	1 Dalw	29	1884*	21 Jan	31
	♓	1 Hūt	30		19 Feb	29
1263*	♈	1 Ḥamal	31	1884*	20 Mar	31
	♉	1 Thur	31		20 Apr	30
	♊	1 Jawzā'	31		21 May	31
	♋	1 Saratān	32		21 Jun	30
	♌	1 Asâd	31		23 Jul	31
	♍	1 Sunbula	31		23 Aug	31
	♎	1 Mīzān	30		23 Sep	30
	♏	1 'Aqrab	30		23 Oct	31
	♐	1 Qaws	30		22 Nov	30
	♑	1 Jadī	29		22 Dec	31
	♒	1 Dalw	30	1885	20 Jan	31
	♓	1 Hūt	30		19 Feb	28
1264	♈	1 Ḥamal	30	1885	21 Mar	31
	♉	1 Thur	31		20 Apr	30
	♊	1 Jawzā'	31		21 May	31
	♋	1 Saratān	32		21 Jun	30
	♌	1 Asâd	31		23 Jul	31
	♍	1 Sunbula	31		23 Aug	31
	♎	1 Mīzān	30		23 Sep	30
	♏	1 'Aqrab	30		23 Oct	31
	♐	1 Qaws	30		22 Nov	30
	♑	1 Jadī	29		22 Dec	31
	♒	1 Dalw	30	1886	20 Jan	31
	♓	1 Hūt	30		19 Feb	28
1265	♈	1 Ḥamal	30	1886	21 Mar	31
	♉	1 Thur	31		20 Apr	30
	♊	1 Jawzā'	32		21 May	31
	♋	1 Saratān	31		22 Jun	30

Iranian Borji Solar				Gregorian		
Year	0° of Sign	Date	Days in Month	Year	Date	Days in Month
	♌	1 Asȧd	31		23 Jul	31
	♍	1 Sunbula	31		23 Aug	31
	♎	1 Mīzān	31		23 Sep	30
	♏	1 'Aqrab	30		24 Oct	31
	♐	1 Qaws	29		23 Nov	30
	♑	1 Jadī	29		22 Dec	31
	♒	1 Dalw	30	1887	20 Jan	31
	♓	1 Hūt	30		19 Feb	28
1266	♈	1 Ḥamal	31	1887	21 Mar	31
	♉	1 Thur	31		21 Apr	30
	♊	1 Jawzā'	31		22 May	31
	♋	1 Saratān	31		22 Jun	30
	♌	1 Asȧd	32		23 Jul	31
	♍	1 Sunbula	31		24 Aug	31
	♎	1 Mīzān	30		24 Sep	30
	♏	1 'Aqrab	30		24 Oct	31
	♐	1 Qaws	29		23 Nov	30
	♑	1 Jadī	30		22 Dec	31
	♒	1 Dalw	29	1888*	21 Jan	31
	♓	1 Hūt	29		19 Feb	29
1267*	♈	1 Ḥamal	31	1888*	20 Mar	31
	♉	1 Thur	31		20 Apr	30
	♊	1 Jawzā'	31		21 May	31
	♋	1 Saratān	32		21 Jun	30
	♌	1 Asȧd	31		23 Jul	31
	♍	1 Sunbula	31		23 Aug	31
	♎	1 Mīzān	30		23 Sep	30
	♏	1 'Aqrab	30		23 Oct	31
	♐	1 Qaws	30		22 Nov	30
	♑	1 Jadī	29		22 Dec	31
	♒	1 Dalw	30	1889	20 Jan	31
	♓	1 Hūt	30		19 Feb	28
1268	♈	1 Ḥamal	30	1889	21 Mar	31
	♉	1 Thur	31		20 Apr	30
	♊	1 Jawzā'	31		21 May	31
	♋	1 Saratān	32		21 Jun	30
	♌	1 Asȧd	31		23 Jul	31
	♍	1 Sunbula	31		23 Aug	31
	♎	1 Mīzān	30		23 Sep	30
	♏	1 'Aqrab	30		23 Oct	31
	♐	1 Qaws	30		22 Nov	30
	♑	1 Jadī	29		22 Dec	31
	♒	1 Dalw	30	1890	20 Jan	31
	♓	1 Hūt	30		19 Feb	28

Iranian Borji Solar				Gregorian		
Year	0° of Sign	Date	Days in Month	Year	Date	Days in Month
1269	♈	1 Ḥamal	30	1890	21 Mar	31
	♉	1 Thur	31		20 Apr	30
	♊	1 Jawzā'	32		21 May	31
	♋	1 Saratān	31		22 Jun	30
	♌	1 Asȧd	31		23 Jul	31
	♍	1 Sunbula	31		23 Aug	31
	♎	1 Mīzān	31		23 Sep	30
	♏	1 'Aqrab	29		24 Oct	31
	♐	1 Qaws	30		22 Nov	30
	♑	1 Jadī	29		22 Dec	31
	♒	1 Dalw	30	1891	20 Jan	31
	♓	1 Hūt	30		19 Feb	28
1270	♈	1 Ḥamal	31	1891	21 Mar	31
	♉	1 Thur	31		21 Apr	30
	♊	1 Jawzā'	31		22 May	31
	♋	1 Saratān	31		22 Jun	30
	♌	1 Asȧd	32		23 Jul	31
	♍	1 Sunbula	30		24 Aug	31
	♎	1 Mīzān	31		23 Sep	30
	♏	1 'Aqrab	20		24 Oct	31
	♐	1 Qaws	29		23 Nov	30
	♑	1 Jadī	30		22 Dec	31
	♒	1 Dalw	29	1892*	21 Jan	31
	♓	1 Hūt	30		19 Feb	29
1271*	♈	1 Ḥamal	31	1892*	20 Mar	31
	♉	1 Thur	31		20 Apr	30
	♊	1 Jawzā'	31		21 May	31
	♋	1 Saratān	32		21 Jun	30
	♌	1 Asȧd	31		23 Jul	31
	♍	1 Sunbula	31		23 Aug	31
	♎	1 Mīzān	30		23 Sep	30
	♏	1 'Aqrab	30		23 Oct	31
	♐	1 Qaws	29		22 Nov	30
	♑	1 Jadī	30		21 Dec	31
	♒	1 Dalw	30	1893	20 Jan	31
	♓	1 Hūt	30		19 Feb	28
1272	♈	1 Ḥamal	30	1893	21 Mar	31
	♉	1 Thur	30		20 Apr	30
	♊	1 Jawzā'	31		21 May	31
	♋	1 Saratān	32		21 Jun	30
	♌	1 Asȧd	31		23 Jul	31
	♍	1 Sunbula	31		23 Aug	31
	♎	1 Mīzān	30		23 Sep	30

Iranian Boriji Solar				Gregorian		
Year	0° of Sign	Date	Days in Month	Year	Date	Days in Month
	♏	1 ʻAqrab	30		23 Oct	31
	♐	1 Qaws	30		22 Nov	30
	♑	1 Jadī	29		22 Dec	31
	♒	1 Dalw	30	1894	20 Jan	31
	♓	1 Hūt	30		19 Feb	28
1273	♈	1 Ḥamal	30	1894	21 Mar	31
	♉	1 Thur	31		20 Apr	30
	♊	1 Jawzāʼ	32		21 May	31
	♋	1 Saratān	31		22 Jun	30
	♌	1 Asåd	31		23 Jul	31
	♍	1 Sunbula	31		23 Aug	31
	♎	1 Mīzān	31		23 Sep	30
	♏	1 ʻAqrab	29		24 Oct	31
	♐	1 Qaws	30		22 Nov	30
	♑	1 Jadī	29		22 Dec	31
	♒	1 Dalw	30	1895	20 Jan	31
	♓	1 Hūt	30		19 Feb	28
1274	♈	1 Ḥamal	30	1895	21 Mar	31
	♉	1 Thur	31		20 Apr	30
	♊	1 Jawzāʼ	32		21 May	31
	♋	1 Saratān	31		22 Jun	30
	♌	1 Asåd	32		23 Jul	31
	♍	1 Sunbula	30		24 Aug	31
	♎	1 Mīzān	31		23 Sep	30
	♏	1 ʻAqrab	30		24 Oct	31
	♐	1 Qaws	29		23 Nov	30
	♑	1 Jadī	30		22 Dec	31
	♒	1 Dalw	29	1896*	21 Jan	31
	♓	1 Hūt	30		19 Feb	29
1275	♈	1 Ḥamal	31	1896	20 Mar	31
	♉	1 Thur	31		20 Apr	30
	♊	1 Jawzāʼ	31		21 May	31
	♋	1 Saratān	32		21 Jun	30
	♌	1 Asåd	31		23 Jul	31
	♍	1 Sunbula	31		23 Aug	31
	♎	1 Mīzān	30		23 Sep	30
	♏	1 ʻAqrab	30		23 Oct	31
	♐	1 Qaws	29		22 Nov	30
	♑	1 Jadī	30		21 Dec	31
	♒	1 Dalw	30	1897	22 Jan	31
	♓	1 Hūt	29		18 Feb	28
1276*	♈	1 Ḥamal	31	1897	20 Mar	31
	♉	1 Thur	31		20 Apr	30

Iranian Boriji Solar				Gregorian		
Year	0° of Sign	Date	Days in Month	Year	Date	Days in Month
	♊	1 Jawzāʼ	31		21 May	31
	♋	1 Saratān	32		21 Jun	30
	♌	1 Asåd	31		23 Jul	31
	♍	1 Sunbula	31		23 Aug	31
	♎	1 Mīzān	30		23 Sep	30
	♏	1 ʻAqrab	30		23 Oct	31
	♐	1 Qaws	30		22 Nov	30
	♑	1 Jadī	29		22 Dec	31
	♒	1 Dalw	30	1898	20 Jan	31
	♓	1 Hūt	30		19 Feb	28
1277	♈	1 Ḥamal	30	1898	21 Mar	31
	♉	1 Thur	31		20 Apr	30
	♊	1 Jawzāʼ	32		21 May	31
	♋	1 Saratān	31		22 Jun	30
	♌	1 Asåd	31		23 Jul	31
	♍	1 Sunbula	31		23 Aug	31
	♎	1 Mīzān	31		23 Sep	30
	♏	1 ʻAqrab	29		24 Oct	31
	♐	1 Qaws	30		22 Nov	30
	♑	1 Jadī	29		22 Dec	31
	♒	1 Dalw	30	1899	20 Jan	31
	♓	1 Hūt	30		19 Feb	28
1278	♈	1 Ḥamal	30	1899	21 Mar	31
	♉	1 Thur	31		20 Apr	30
	♊	1 Jawzāʼ	32		21 May	31
	♋	1 Saratān	31		22 Jun	30
	♌	1 Asåd	32		23 Jul	31
	♍	1 Sunbula	30		24 Aug	31
	♎	1 Mīzān	31		23 Sep	30
	♏	1 ʻAqrab	30		24 Oct	31
	♐	1 Qaws	29		23 Nov	30
	♑	1 Jadī	30		22 Dec	31
	♒	1 Dalw	29	1900	21 Jan	31
	♓	1 Hūt	30		19 Feb	28
1279	♈	1 Ḥamal	31	1900	21 Mar	31
	♉	1 Thur	31		21 Apr	30
	♊	1 Jawzāʼ	31		22 May	31
	♋	1 Saratān	31		22 Jun	30
	♌	1 Asåd	32		23 Jul	31
	♍	1 Sunbula	31		24 Aug	31
	♎	1 Mīzān	30		24 Sep	30
	♏	1 ʻAqrab	30		24 Oct	31
	♐	1 Qaws	29		23 Nov	30

Iranian Boriji Solar				Gregorian		
Year	0° of Sign	Date	Days in Month	Year	Date	Days in Month
	♑	1 Jadī	30		22 Dec	31
	♒	1 Dalw	29	1901	21 Jan	31
	♓	1 Hūt	30		19 Feb	28
1280*	♈	1 Ḥamal	31	1901	21 Mar	31
	♉	1 Thur	31		21 Apr	30
	♊	1 Jawzā'	31		22 May	31
	♋	1 Saratān	32		22 Jun	30
	♌	1 Asȧd	31		24 Jul	31
	♍	1 Sunbula	31		24 Aug	31
	♎	1 Mīzān	30		24 Sep	30
	♏	1 'Aqrab	30		24 Oct	31
	♐	1 Qaws	30		23 Nov	30
	♑	1 Jadī	29		23 Dec	31
	♒	1 Dalw	30	1902	21 Jan	31
	♓	1 Hūt	30		20 Feb	28
1281	♈	1 Ḥamal	30	1902	22 Mar	31
	♉	1 Thur	31		21 Apr	30
	♊	1 Jawzā'	32		22 May	31
	♋	1 Saratān	31		23 Jun	30
	♌	1 Asȧd	31		24 Jul	31
	♍	1 Sunbula	31		24 Aug	31
	♎	1 Mīzān	31		24 Sep	30
	♏	1 'Aqrab	29		25 Oct	31
	♐	1 Qaws	30		23 Nov	30
	♑	1 Jadī	29		23 Dec	31
	♒	1 Dalw	30	1903	21 Jan	31
	♓	1 Hūt	30		20 Feb	28
1282	♈	1 Ḥamal	30	1903	22 Mar	31
	♉	1 Thur	30		21 Apr	30
	♊	1 Jawzā'	32		22 May	31
	♋	1 Saratān	31		23 Jun	30
	♌	1 Asȧd	31		24 Jul	31
	♍	1 Sunbula	31		24 Aug	31
	♎	1 Mīzān	31		24 Sep	30
	♏	1 'Aqrab	30		25 Oct	31
	♐	1 Qaws	29		24 Nov	30
	♑	1 Jadī	30		23 Dec	31
	♒	1 Dalw	29	1904*	22 Jan	31
	♓	1 Hūt	30		20 Feb	29
1283	♈	1 Ḥamal	31	1904*	21 Mar	31
	♉	1 Thur	31		21 Apr	30
	♊	1 Jawzā'	31		22 May	31

Iranian Boriji Solar				Gregorian		
Year	0° of Sign	Date	Days in Month	Year	Date	Days in Month
	♋	1 Saratān	31		22 Jun	30
	♌	1 Asȧd	32		23 Jul	31
	♍	1 Sunbula	31		24 Aug	31
	♎	1 Mīzān	30		24 Sep	30
	♏	1 'Aqrab	30		24 Oct	31
	♐	1 Qaws	29		23 Nov	30
	♑	1 Jadī	30		22 Dec	31
	♒	1 Dalw	29	1905	21 Jan	31
	♓	1 Hūt	30		19 Feb	28
1284*	♈	1 Ḥamal	31	1905	21 Mar	31
	♉	1 Thur	31		21 Apr	30
	♊	1 Jawzā'	31		22 May	31
	♋	1 Saratān	32		22 Jun	30
	♌	1 Asȧd	31		24 Jul	31
	♍	1 Sunbula	31		24 Aug	31
	♎	1 Mīzān	30		24 Sep	30
	♏	1 'Aqrab	30		24 Oct	31
	♐	1 Qaws	30		23 Nov	30
	♑	1 Jadī	29		23 Dec	31
	♒	1 Dalw	30	1906	21 Jan	31
	♓	1 Hūt	30		20 Feb	28
1285	♈	1 Ḥamal	30	1906	22 Mar	31
	♉	1 Thur	31		21 Apr	30
	♊	1 Jawzā'	31		22 May	31
	♋	1 Saratān	32		22 Jun	30
	♌	1 Asȧd	31		24 Jul	31
	♍	1 Sunbula	31		24 Aug	31
	♎	1 Mīzān	30		24 Sep	30
	♏	1 'Aqrab	30		24 Oct	31
	♐	1 Qaws	29		23 Nov	30
	♑	1 Jadī	30		23 Dec	31
	♒	1 Dalw	30	1907	21 Jan	31
	♓	1 Hūt	30		20 Feb	28
1286	♈	1 Ḥamal	30	1907	22 Mar	31
	♉	1 Thur	31		21 Apr	30
	♊	1 Jawzā'	32		22 May	31
	♋	1 Saratān	31		23 Jun	30
	♌	1 Asȧd	31		24 Jul	31
	♍	1 Sunbula	31		24 Aug	31
	♎	1 Mīzān	31		24 Sep	30
	♏	1 'Aqrab	30		25 Oct	31
	♐	1 Qaws	29		24 Nov	30
	♑	1 Jadī	30		23 Dec	31

Iranian Boriji Solar				Gregorian		
Year	0° of Sign	Date	Days in Month	Year	Date	Days in Month
	♒	1 Dalw	29	1908*	22 Jan	31
	♓	1 Hūt	30		29 Feb	29
1287	♈	1 Ḥamal	31	1908*	21 Mar	31
	♉	1 T̲h̲ur	31		21 Apr	30
	♊	1 Jawzā'	31		22 May	31
	♋	1 Saratān	31		22 Jun	30
	♌	1 Asȧd	32		23 Jul	31
	♍	1 Sunbula	31		24 Aug	31
	♎	1 Mīzān	30		24 Sep	30
	♏	1 'Aqrab	30		24 Oct	31
	♐	1 Qaws	29		23 Nov	30
	♑	1 Jadī	30		22 Dec	31
	♒	1 Dalw	29	1909	21 Jan	31
	♓	1 Hūt	30		19 Feb	28
1288*	♈	1 Ḥamal	31	1909	21 Mar	31
	♉	1 T̲h̲ur	31		21 Apr	30
	♊	1 Jawzā'	31		22 May	31
	♋	1 Saratān	32		22 Jun	30
	♌	1 Asȧd	31		24 Jul	31
	♍	1 Sunbula	31		24 Aug	31
	♎	1 Mīzān	30		24 Sep	30
	♏	1 'Aqrab	30		24 Oct	31
	♐	1 Qaws	30		23 Nov	30
	♑	1 Jadī	29		23 Dec	31
	♒	1 Dalw	30	1910	21 Jan	31
	♓	1 Hūt	30		20 Feb	28
1289	♈	1 Ḥamal	30	1910	22 Mar	31
	♉	1 T̲h̲ur	31		21 Apr	30
	♊	1 Jawzā'	31		22 May	31
	♋	1 Saratān	32		22 Jun	30
	♌	1 Asȧd	31		24 Jul	31
	♍	1 Sunbula	31		24 Aug	31
	♎	1 Mīzān	30		24 Sep	30
	♏	1 'Aqrab	30		24 Oct	31
	♐	1 Qaws	30		23 Nov	30
	♑	1 Jadī	29		23 Dec	31
	♒	1 Dalw	30	1911	21 Jan	31
	♓	1 Hūt	30		20 Feb	28
1290	♈	1 Ḥamal	30	1911	22 Mar	31
	♉	1 T̲h̲ur	31		21 Apr	30
	♊	1 Jawzā'	32		22 May	31
	♋	1 Saratān	31		23 Jun	30

Iranian Boriji Solar				Gregorian		
Year	0° of Sign	Date	Days in Month	Year	Date	Days in Month
	♌	1 Asȧd	31		24 Jul	31
	♍	1 Sunbula	31		24 Aug	31
	♎	1 Mīzān	31		24 Sep	30
	♏	1 'Aqrab	30		25 Oct	31
	♐	1 Qaws	29		24 Nov	30
	♑	1 Jadī	30		23 Dec	31
	♒	1 Dalw	29	1912*	22 Jan	31
	♓	1 Hūt	30		20 Feb	29
1291	♈	1 Ḥamal	31	1912*	21 Mar	31
	♉	1 T̲h̲ur	31		21 Apr	30
	♊	1 Jawzā'	31		22 May	31
	♋	1 Saratān	31		22 Jun	30
	♌	1 Asȧd	32		23 Jul	31
	♍	1 Sunbula	31		24 Aug	31
	♎	1 Mīzān	30		24 Sep	30
	♏	1 'Aqrab	30		24 Oct	31
	♐	1 Qaws	29		23 Nov	30
	♑	1 Jadī	30		22 Dec	31
	♒	1 Dalw	29	1913	21 Jan	31
	♓	1 Hūt	30		19 Feb	28
1292*	♈	1 Ḥamal	31	1913	21 Mar	31
	♉	1 T̲h̲ur	31		21 Apr	30
	♊	1 Jawzā'	31		22 May	31
	♋	1 Saratān	32		22 Jun	30
	♌	1 Asȧd	31		24 Jul	31
	♍	1 Sunbula	31		24 Aug	31
	♎	1 Mīzān	30		24 Sep	30
	♏	1 'Aqrab	30		24 Oct	31
	♐	1 Qaws	30		23 Nov	30
	♑	1 Jadī	29		23 Dec	31
	♒	1 Dalw	30	1914	21 Jan	31
	♓	1 Hūt	30		20 Feb	28
1293	♈	1 Ḥamal	30	1914	22 Mar	31
	♉	1 T̲h̲ur	31		21 Apr	30
	♊	1 Jawzā'	31		22 May	31
	♋	1 Saratān	32		22 Jun	30
	♌	1 Asȧd	31		24 Jul	31
	♍	1 Sunbula	31		24 Aug	31
	♎	1 Mīzān	30		24 Sep	30
	♏	1 'Aqrab	30		24 Oct	31
	♐	1 Qaws	30		23 Nov	30
	♑	1 Jadī	29		23 Dec	31
	♒	1 Dalw	30	1915	21 Jan	31
	♓	1 Hūt	30		20 Feb	28

Iranian Boriji Solar				Gregorian		
Year	0° of Sign	Date	Days in Month	Year	Date	Days in Month
1294	♈	1 Ḥamal	30	1915	22 Mar	31
	♉	1 Thur	31		21 Apr	30
	♊	1 Jawzā'	32		22 May	31
	♋	1 Saratān	31		23 Jun	30
	♌	1 Asåd	31		24 Jul	31
	♍	1 Sunbula	31		24 Aug	31
	♎	1 Mīzān	31		24 Sep	30
	♏	1 'Aqrab	30		25 Oct	31
	♐	1 Qaws	29		24 Nov	30
	♑	1 Jadī	30		23 Dec	31
	♒	1 Dalw	29	1916*	22 Jan	31
	♓	1 Hūt	30		19 Feb	29
1295	♈	1 Ḥamal	31	1916*	21 Mar	31
	♉	1 Thur	31		21 Apr	30
	♊	1 Jawzā'	31		22 May	31
	♋	1 Saratān	31		22 Jun	30
	♌	1 Asåd	32		23 Jul	31
	♍	1 Sunbula	31		24 Aug	31
	♎	1 Mīzān	30		24 Sep	30
	♏	1 'Aqrab	30		24 Oct	31
	♐	1 Qaws	29		23 Nov	30
	♑	1 Jadī	30		22 Dec	31
	♒	1 Dalw	29	1917	21 Jan	31
	♓	1 Hūt	30		19 Feb	28
1296*	♈	1 Ḥamal	31	1917	21 Mar	31
	♉	1 Thur	31		21 Apr	30
	♊	1 Jawzā'	31		22 May	31
	♋	1 Saratān	32		22 Jun	30
	♌	1 Asåd	31		24 Jul	31
	♍	1 Sunbula	31		24 Aug	31
	♎	1 Mīzān	30		24 Sep	30
	♏	1 'Aqrab	30		24 Oct	31
	♐	1 Qaws	30		23 Nov	30
	♑	1 Jadī	29		23 Dec	31
	♒	1 Dalw	30	1918	21 Jan	31
	♓	1 Hūt	30		20 Feb	28
1297	♈	1 Ḥamal	30	1918	22 Mar	31
	♉	1 Thur	31		21 Apr	30
	♊	1 Jawzā'	31		22 May	31
	♋	1 Saratān	32		22 Jun	30
	♌	1 Asåd	31		24 Jul	31
	♍	1 Sunbula	31		24 Aug	31
	♎	1 Mīzān	30		24 Sep	30

Iranian Boriji Solar				Gregorian		
Year	0° of Sign	Date	Days in Month	Year	Date	Days in Month
	♏	1 'Aqrab	30		24 Oct	31
	♐	1 Qaws	30		23 Nov	30
	♑	1 Jadī	29		23 Dec	31
	♒	1 Dalw	30	1919	21 Jan	31
	♓	1 Hūt	30		20 Feb	28
1298	♈	1 Ḥamal	30	1919	22 Mar	31
	♉	1 Thur	31		21 Apr	30
	♊	1 Jawzā'	32		22 May	31
	♋	1 Saratān	31		23 Jun	30
	♌	1 Asåd	31		24 Jul	31
	♍	1 Sunbula	31		24 Aug	31
	♎	1 Mīzān	31		24 Sep	30
	♏	1 'Aqrab	30		25 Oct	31
	♐	1 Qaws	29		24 Nov	30
	♑	1 Jadī	29		23 Dec	31
	♒	1 Dalw	30	1920*	21 Jan	31
	♓	1 Hūt	30		20 Feb	29
1299	♈	1 Ḥamal	31	1920*	21 Mar	31
	♉	1 Thur	31		21 Apr	30
	♊	1 Jawzā'	31		22 May	31
	♋	1 Saratān	31		22 Jun	30
	♌	1 Asåd	32		23 Jul	31
	♍	1 Sunbula	30		24 Aug	31
	♎	1 Mīzān	31		23 Sep	30
	♏	1 'Aqrab	30		24 Oct	31
	♐	1 Qaws	29		23 Nov	30
	♑	1 Jadī	30		22 Dec	31
	♒	1 Dalw	30	1921	21 Jan	31
	♓	1 Hūt	30		19 Feb	28
1300*	♈	1 Ḥamal	31	1921	21 Mar	31
	♉	1 Thur	31		21 Apr	30
	♊	1 Jawzā'	31		22 May	31
	♋	1 Saratān	32		22 Jun	30
	♌	1 Asåd	31		24 Jul	31
	♍	1 Sunbula	31		24 Aug	31
	♎	1 Mīzān	30		24 Sep	30
	♏	1 'Aqrab	30		24 Oct	31
	♐	1 Qaws	30		23 Nov	30
	♑	1 Jadī	29		23 Dec	31
	♒	1 Dalw	30	1922	21 Jan	31
	♓	1 Hūt	30		20 Feb	28
1301	♈	1 Ḥamal	30	1922	22 Mar	31
	♉	1 Thur	31		21 Apr	30

Iranian Boriji Solar				Gregorian		
Year	0° of Sign	Date	Days in Month	Year	Date	Days in Month
	♊	1 Jawzā'	31		22 May	31
	♋	1 Saratān	32		22 Jun	30
	♌	1 Asȧd	31		24 Jul	31
	♍	1 Sunbula	31		24 Aug	31
	♎	1 Mīzān	30		24 Sep	30
	♏	1 'Aqrab	30		24 Oct	31
	♐	1 Qaws	30		23 Nov	30
	♑	1 Jadī	29		23 Dec	31
	♒	1 Dalw	30	1923	21 Jan	31
	♓	1 Hūt	30		20 Feb	28
1302	♈	1 Ḥamal	30	1923	22 Mar	31
	♉	1 Thur	31		21 Apr	30
	♊	1 Jawzā'	32		22 May	31
	♋	1 Saratān	31		23 Jun	30
	♌	1 Asȧd	31		24 Jul	31
	♍	1 Sunbula	31		24 Aug	31
	♎	1 Mīzān	31		24 Sep	30
	♏	1 'Aqrab	29		25 Oct	31
	♐	1 Qaws	30		23 Nov	30
	♑	1 Jadī	29		23 Dec	31
	♒	1 Dalw	30	1924*	21 Jan	31
	♓	1 Hūt	30		20 Feb	29
1303	♈	1 Ḥamal	30	1924	21 Mar	31
	♉	1 Thur	31		20 Apr	30
	♊	1 Jawzā'	32		21 May	31
	♋	1 Saratān	31		22 Jun	30
	♌	1 Asȧd	32		23 Jul	31
	♍	1 Sunbula	30		24 Aug	31
	♎	1 Mīzān	31		23 Sep	30
	♏	1 'Aqrab	30		24 Oct	31
	♐	1 Qaws	29		23 Nov	30
	♑	1 Jadī	30		22 Dec	31
	♒	1 Dalw	29	1925	21 Jan	31
	♓	1 Hūt	30		19 Feb	28

IRANIAN SOLAR HEGIRA

Solar Hegira Year	Western (Gregorian) Year	Solar Hegira Year	Western (Gregorian) Year	Solar Hegira Year	Western (Gregorian) Year
1304*	1925	1329*	1950	1354*	1975
1305	1926	1330	1951	1355 (2535 Sh.)	1976
1306	1927	1331	1952*	1356 (2536 Sh.)	1977
1307	1928*	1332	1953	1357	1978
1308	1929	1333*	1954	1358*	1979
1309*	1930	1334	1955	1359	1980*
1310	1931	1333	1956*	1360	1981
1311	1932*	1336	1957	1361	1982
1312	1933	1337*	1958	1362*	1983
1313*	1934	1338	1959	1363	1984*
1314	1935	1339	1960*	1364	1985
1315	1936*	1340	1961	1365	1986
1316	1937	1341	1962	1366*	1987
1317*	1938	1342*	1963	1367	1988*
1318	1939	1343	1964*	1368	1989
1319	1940*	1344	1964	1369	1990

Solar Hegira Year	Western (Gregorian) Year	Solar Hegira Year	Western (Gregorian) Year	Solar Hegira Year	Western (Gregorian) Year
1320	1941	1345	1966	1370*	1991
1321*	1942	1346*	1967	1371	1992*
1322	1943	1347	1968*	1372	1993
1323	1944*	1348	1969	1373	1994
1324	1945	1349	1970	1374	1995
1325*	1946	1350*	1971	1375*	1996*
1326	1947	1351	1972*	1376	1997
1327	1948*	1352	1973	1377	1998
1328	1949	1353	1974	1378	1999

AFGHANISTAN

Modern Afghanis utilize three calendars: the Gregorian (for commercial purposes), a variant of the lunar Hegira and a variant of the Iranian Solar.

Like the Arabic lunar Hegira calendar the Afghani variation uses July 15, 622 A.D. as its epoch. It also contains 12 months with the odd months (1-11) having 30 days and the even months (2-12) having 29 days. The last month has 29 days in a common year and 30 days in a leap year. The names of the months are as follows:

Arabic	Eastern Afghani Pushtoo	Western Afghani Pushtoo
1. Muharram	Hasan wa huseyn	Hasan huseyn
2. Safar	Gul shakara	Sapara, thapara
3. Rabi al-awwal	Rumbey chor, Wrumbey chor	Lumrey khor
4. Rabi ath-thani	Dwayema chor	Dwaheyma khor
5. Jumada al-ulya	Dreyema chor	Dreyma khor
6. Jumada al-akhira	Thalorema chor	Thalarema khor
7. Rajab	Do Hadai miasht, Bzerga miasht	Do hadai taali miasht
8. Shaban	Shawkadar, Do shawkadare miasht	Barat, Barate miasht
9. Ramadan	Rozha, Do rozha miasht	Rozha, Do rozha miasht
10. Shawwal	Warukay achtar	Kuchnay akhtar, Do kuchni akhtar
11. Dhul-Qa'da	Miyana miasht	Miyana
12. Dhul-Hijja	Loy achtar	Loy akhtar

Between 1956 and 1963 the Afghanis made some changes in intercalating for the leap years. These changes are tabulated below.

Beginning Western Date	Days in Afghani month (Arabic Names)				Afghani Year
	Shaban	Ramadan	Shawwal	Dhul-Qa'da	
21 Mar 1956*	30	30	29	30	1375 A.H.
21 Mar 1957	29	30	29	30	1376* A.H.
20 Feb 1958	30	29	30	29	1377* A.H.

Beginning Western Date	Days in Afghani month (Arabic Names) Shaban	Ramadan	Shawwal	Dhul-Qa'da	Afghani Year
20 Feb 1959	29	29	30	30	1378 A.H.
21 Feb 1960*	29	30	29	30	1379 A.H.
21 Jan 1961	29	30	29	30	1380 A.H.
21 Jan 1962	29	30	29	30	1381 A.H.
21 Jan 1963	30	29	30	29	1382* A.H.
22 Dec 1963	30	30	29	30	1383 A.H.

The 19th and 20th century Iranian Zodiacal calendar, (the "Borji" solar Hegira calendar) also was adopted in Afghanistan and is called "Shamsi" in Pushtoo. There are eight leap years in a 33 year cycle for this calendar, the first seven of which occur every fourth year. The eighth leap year occurs in the last or 33rd year of the cycle. Usually both the Arabic and the Pushtoo names for the months are given. The months are those of the signs of the Zodiac, beginning with Aries.

Zodiac	Arabic	Pushtoo
Aries	Hamal	Wray
Taurus	Thur	Ghwayay
Gemini	Jawza	Ghbargulay
Cancer	Saratan	Chungash
Leo	Asad	Zmaray
Virgo	Sunbula	Wazhay
Libra	Mizan	Tala
Scorpio	Aqrab	Laram
Sagittarius	Qaws	Linda
Capricorn	Jadi	Marghumay
Aquarius	Dalw	Salwagha
Pisces	Hut	Kab

This calendar continued in use until 1958 (1377 Shamsi) when it was decided to bring it into line with the Iranian solar calendar which Iran had adopted in 1925. Due to some differences in the application of leap year, and a difference in the placing of the short month, between 1955 and 1963 A.D. (1334-1342 Shamsi), it varied somewhat from the Iranian calendar. The table below shows the number of days per month for the relevant years.

Shamshi Month	Shamshi year numbers								
Wray	31	31	31	31	31	31	31	31	31
Ghwayay	31	31	31	31	31	31	31	31	31
Ghbargulay	32	32	32	31	31	31	31	31	31
Chungash	31	31	31	31	31	31	31	31	31
Zmaray	31	31	31	31	31	31	31	31	31
Wazhay	31	31	31	31	31	31	31	31	31
Tala	30	30	30	30	30	30	30	30	30
Laram	30	30	30	30	30	30	30	30	30
Linda	29	29	29	30	30	30	30	30	30
Marghumay	29	29	29	30	29	29	29	30	30
Salwagha	30	30	30	30	30	30	30	30	30
Kab	30	30	30	30	30	30	30	30	29

Since 1968 (1347 Shamsi) the Afghani solar calendar has been identical with Iranian Solar calendar.

1334	1339
1335	1340
1336	1341*
1337*	1342
1338	

INDIA

INDIAN CALENDARS

When India gained its independence in the mid-20th century, it found itself faced with not less than 30 calendars, differing in when the era and year began, and to some extent in the method of reckoning time. This diversity had its roots in the nation's history. About 3,000 B.C., a calendar called the Kali Yuga came into use. But, because India had no astronomical observatories and astronomers could not directly observe the heavenly bodies, data differed from region to region. Thus the calendar became diversified throughout the subcontinent. With the advent of Muslim rule in 1200 A.D., the lunar Hejira calendar was adopted for administrative purposes and for Muslim religious purposes. It was employed until 1757 except for a brief period (1556-1605) when Emperor Akbar banned it and introduced his own calendar. In 1757, the British brought the Gregorian calendar, which was still utilized for official purposes at the time of India's independence. Regional calendars based on the Kali Yuga, however, survived the political changes and were also used. Each state of India had its own civil calendar of local origin which was used by the rural population and by a large segment of the urban dwellers for daily transactions, correspondence, etc. This system created chaos in a centralized state. The date which we know as March 21, 1957, would be called Chaitra 7 in Bengal, Chaitra 8 in Orissa, and Panguni (Phalguna) 8 in the South. By the Indian lunar calendar it would be called Chaitra Vadi 6 or Phalguna Vadi 6, depending upon the convention followed.

All the calendars of India are, from a standpoint of solar measurement, based on the Kali Yuga and are, from the Kali Yuga on down, based solidly on astronomical measurements made in accordance with and interpreted by astrological methods. The India astrologers used the same symbols and many of the same principals as do astrologers of the Western world today; the Indian solar year, like the Western year, consists of 12 months, each month having assigned to it one of the 12 signs of the zodiac. Each sign contains 30 degrees; the sign begins at 0° and runs through to 29°59′59″ before entering the next sign. A major difference between the two systems is that the western zodiac is based on the tropical year, while the Hindu and Buddhist zodiaks are based on the sidereal year, which is about 24 minutes longer. The Indian solar year begins with the month of Chaitra, or around April 13/14 by the western calendar. This year is divided into 6 seasons of 2 months each, which are named as follows: (1) Vasanta = ♓ and ♈ (2) Grishma = ♉ and ♊ (3) Varsha = ♋ and ♌ (4) Saruda = ♍ and ♎ (5) Hemanta = ♏ and ♐ (6) Sisira = ♑ and ♒.

The length of the solar month depends on the length of the apparent motion of the sun through each sign; this ranges from as few as 27 days during the shortest winter month to as many as 32 days during the longest summer month. Unlike our months, these solar months correspond exactly to the signs of the zodiac. A new month cannot begin until the sun or moon actually enters the next sign, which can happen any time during the 24 hours period we call a day. The names for the zodiacal signs remain the same throughout India and the Indo-Chinese Peninsula, while the names of the months vary according to the dialect spoken. The names for the months and signs are set forth in the following table:

Signs			Months		
English	Sanskrit	Hindi	Bengali	Urdu	Tamil
Aries	Mesha	Vyshak	Vaisakha	Baisakh	Chaitram
Taurus	Vrisha	Jyest	Jyestha	Jeth	Vyassie
Gemini	Mithuna	Ashadh	Ashadh	Asarh	Auni
Cancer	Karkata	Shrawun	Sravana	Sawan	Audi

Signs English	Sanskrit	Hindi	Months Bengali	Urdu	Tamil
Leo	Sinha	Bhadurpud	Bhadra	Bhadon	Auvani
Virgo	Kanya	Ashwin	Aswina	Asan	Paratasi
Libra	Tula	Kartick	Kartiku	Kartik	Arpesi
Scorpio	Vrishiga	Margashirs	Margasirsha or Agrahayana	Aghan	Kartiga
Sagittarius	Dhanus	Poush	Pousha	Pus	Margali
Capricorn	Makara	Maugh	Magha	Magh	Tye
Aquarius	Kumbha	Phalgoon	Phalgoona	Phagun	Maussi
Pisces	Mina	Chytr	Chaitra	Chait	Punguni

Note that the Tamil name their month one sign later than the others. Between 1876 and 1895, however, the months listed here under the sign of Mina, or Pisces, were changed so that Chytr, Chaitra and Chait fell under the sign of Mesha, or Aries, thus bringing the Sanskrit, Bengali and Urdu months into line with the Tamil.

As in the west, there are seven days in a week, each day having assigned to it a planet, excluding Earth but including the Sun and Moon, from which the name is derived. These occur in exactly the same order as they do in the west, as illustrated by the following table:

English	Hindu	Indian	Singhalee	Tibetan	Burmese
Sunday	Ravi-var	Etwar	Eri-da	Gyah-nyi-ma	Tanang-ganve
Monday	Som-var	Peer or Somwar	Sa-du-da	Gyah-zla-va	Tanang-la
Tuesday	Mangal-var	Mungul	Ang-ga-ha-nuva-da	Gyah-mig-amar	Ang-gar
Wednesday	Budh-var	Boodh	Ba-da-da	Gyah-thag-pa	Buddha-hu
Thursday	Vrihaspat-var or Guru-var	Jumerat	Bra-has-pa-ting-da	Gyah-phur-bu	Kyasa-pade
Friday	Sukra-var	Juma	Si-ku-ra-da	Gyah-pa-sangs	Sok-kya
Saturday	Sanichar or Sani-var	Sunneecher	Sina-su-ra-da	Gyah-spen-pa	Cha-na

The solar day can be measured by the time from sunrise to sunrise or by the time it takes for the sun's apparent motion to cover 1° on the ecliptic. In either case, this time period is subdivided according to sexagesimal system, which is set forth below, beginning with the two-month season:

60 Kshanas	= 1 Lava	
60 Lavas	= 1 Nimesha	
60 Nimeshas	= 1 Kastha	
60 Kasthas	= 1 Atipala	
60 Atipala	= 1 Vipala	= 0.4″ (western)
60 Vipala	= 1 Pala	= 24″ (")
60 Palas	= 1 Danda	= 24′ (")
60 Dandas	= 1 Dina	= 24 hours (")
60 Dinas	= 1 Ritu	= 2 months season

In addition to these solar measurements, there are parallel lunar measurements which overlap the solar ones. The Indian lunar year consists of 12 lunar months, with an intercalary month, called *adhika*, which occurs approximately every 3 years. The beginning of the lunar year can be calculated in two ways, depending upon which system of calculating the lunar months is used.

A lunar month may be calculated from new moon to new moon or from full moon to full moon. There are 30 lunar days in a lunar month. In the south of India, they consider the new moon to be the beginning of the month. They divide the month into two parts of 15 days each, called *sucha* or *sukla-paksha* and *krishna* or *bahula-paksha*, or the waxing and waning of the moon.

In other areas the month begins with the full, rather than the new, moon. By this system, the lunar year begins in the middle of the month Chaitra, with the waning, rather than the waxing, of the moon.

The lunar months are named for the solar months in which the new moons occur. The system of intercalation mentioned above is used in order to bring the lunar years into line with the solar ones. When 2 new moons occur within one solar month, the year is intercalary and the name of that month is repeated for the next lunar month. In most areas, the word *nija,* or ordinary, is added to the name of the month the first time it occurs, *adhika* is added to it the second time. Among the Tamils this is reversed, and the first month, rather than the second, is considered the intercalated one.

Approximately every 160 years, the reverse situation occurs; during the second half of the year, there will be a solar month during which no new moon occurs. When this happens, the lunar month named for that solar month will be dropped from the calendar; however, this always happens in a year during which two new moons occur in one of the first 6 solar months, and the extra intercalation balances this out. A common intercalary year is called *adhika-samvat-sara,* and the double intercalary year with the dropped lunar month is called *ksyhaya-samvat-sara.*

The calculation of lunar days is similar to that of lunar months. As stated, there are 30 lunar days, called *tithis,* in every lunar month. A tithi is equal to about .984 of a day, so that 64 tithis are about equal to 63 days. A tithi which begins at or before sunrise is considered to belong to that day. If it begins after sunrise it will end on the following day and in that case is omitted from the calendar. When two tithis end on the same solar day, the intermediate one is called *kyshaya-tithi,* and is dropped from the calendar; when no tithi begins or ends a solar day, the tithi is repeated on two successive solar days, and the first one is called *adhika.* A tithi is dropped approximately every 64 days, so that the lunar days are brought into line with the solar ones.

In addition to the solar and lunar days, there are 27 lunar mansions, called *nakshatra.* These are calculated by the time between 2 consecutive risings of the moon at the same point or degree of the ecliptic on the horizon. This is considered the true sideral day. These are equal for the whole year and are used in all astrological computations. The names of these lunar mansions are as follows:

1. Aswini	10. Magha	19. Mula
2. Bharani	11. Purva-phalguni	20. Purva-shadha
3. Krittika	12. Uttara-phalguni	21. Uttara-shadha
4. Rohini	13. Hasta	22. Sravana
5. Mriga	14. Chitra	23. Dhanishtha
6. Ardra	15. Swati	24. Satataraka
7. Punarvasu	16. Visakha	25. Purva-bhadrapada
8. Pushya	17. Anuradha	26. Uttara-bhadrapada
9. Ashlesha	18. Jyeshtha	27. Revati

There are 3 cycles used in conjunction with the Kali Yuga. One is a 60-year cycle, called the Jupiter cycle, the origin of which is unknown. It is based on the time it takes for the planet Jupiter to orbit the sun 5 times. Another cycle, called the Grahaparavritti Cycle, is a 90-year cycle based on the apparent average motion of each of the following: 15 cycles of Mars, 22 of Mercury, 11 of Jupiter, 5 of Venus, 29 of Saturn, and one of the sun.

About 1192 B.C. it was discovered that every 247 years and one month completed a series of cycles of the lunar measurement of the zodiac. This meant that at the end of 247 years and 1 month, the beginning of the year would shift to the next month in succession. Over a period of 1800 years the cycle looks like this:

Periods	New Year began	Name of New Year Month
1	20/21 August 1192 B.C.	Aswina
2	20/21 September 945 B.C.	Kartika
3	18/19 October 698 B.C.	Agrahayana
4	16/17 November 451 B.C.	Pausha
5	14/15 December 204 B.C.	Magha
6	12/13 January 44 A.D.	Phalguna
7	10/11 February 291 A.D.	Chaitra
8	11/12 March 538 A.D.	Vaisakha

At this point, 538 A.D., the shift arrived at the vernal equinox, and it was decided to leave it there. This brought the solar year into line with the lunar one and made the first month of the year Vaisakha, equal to 0° Aries, or Mesha. These are no longer synonymous today, as the sidereal year has shifted to a point where 0° Mesha now arrives on the 13/14 April.

Some of the major eras which have sprung from the Kali Yuga are as follows:

Jain	569 B.C.	Aji Saka	74 A.D.
Buddhist	544 B.C.	Saka	78 A.D.
Parasurama	176 B.C.	Newar	78 A.D.
Vikrama (Bikrama)	57 B.C.	Burmese Prome	79 A.D.
Grahaparivritti	24 B.C.	Bali	81 A.D.
		Balabhi	318 A.D.

The one chosen by the Indian Government as the basis for the standardized official calendar was the Saka era. It had been introduced in India by the Saka ruling powers, and had been used exclusively by the Sakadvipi Brahmins, the astrologer caste, since the 1st century A.D., on the basis of *siddhantic,* or scientific astronomy, combined with astronomical conceptions prevalent in the West.

The unified national calendar of India, therefore, is 78 years behind the Christian era; the Saka year 1902 corresponds to the western year 1980-81. The tropical year of 365.2422 days was adopted for the purpose of calendar-making; as in the west, a normal year has 365 days, and a leap year has 366. A leap year is determined by adding 78 to the Saka era; if that sum is divisible by 4 it is a leap year. When the sum is divisible by 100, the year is only a leap year if it as also divisible by 400.

The extra day of the leap year falls in the month of Chaitra, the first month of the year, which begins on the day following the vernal equinox. The five months following Chaitra each have 31 days, and the last 6 months of the year each have 30. Chaitra itself has 30 days in a normal year and 31 in a leap year. Thus the dates of the reformed India calendar have a permanent correspondence with the dates of the present Gregorian calendar, as illustrated below:

Chaitra 1	March 22 in normal year, March 21 in leap year
Vaisakha 1	April 21
Jaistha 1	May 22
Asadha 1	June 22
Sravana 1	July 23
Bhadra 1	August 23
Asvina 1	September 23
Kartika 1	October 23
Agrahayana 1	November 22
Pausa 1	December 22
Magha 1	January 21
Phalguna 1	February 20

The Indian seasons are fixed with respect to the reformed calendar as follows:

Grisma (Summer) = Vaisakha and Jyaistha
Varsa (Rains) = Asadha and Sravana
Sarat (Autumn) = Bhadra and Asvina
Hemanta (Late Autumn) = Kartika and Agrahayana
Sisira (Winter) = Pausa and Magha
Vasanta (Spring) = Phalguna and Chaitra

The Indian day now begins and ends at midnight. All calculations are made from a Central Station at 82½° E. Longitude and 23°11′ N. Latitude.

The requirements for the religious calendar are slightly different, in order to avoid a sharp break with the established religious practices. The calculation of solar months necessary to determining the lunar months begins 23°15′ ahead of the vernal equinox, rather than the day following it. Thus solar Vaisakha begins when the sun reaches a longitude of 23°15′; with each succeeding month the longitude advances 30°, and reaches 353°15′ by the beginning of Chaitra.

The lunar months begin with the new moon by the reformed calendar and are named, as before, after the corresponding solar months. They are subject to the same rules of intercalation as previously described. The day, for religious purposes, is reckoned from sunrise to sunrise, rather than from midnight to midnight.

The Indian festivals fall into 2 categories: solar festivals, which are mostly, but not entirely, civil ones, and lunar festivals, which are religious. We list here only those solar festivals which are celebrated throughout most of India:

22 March (21 leap year)	Indian New Year
13 April	Vaisakhi, called Vishu in Kerala, Mesa Samkranti in W. Bengal and Tripura, Bahag Bihu in Assam, Cheiraoba in Manipur
15 August	Independence Day
2 October	Mahatma Gandhi's Birthday
1 January	English New Year
26 January	Republich Day

21 March	End of the year, or the vernal equinox

These solar festivals follow astronomically correct seasons according to the reformed calendar. The lunar ones are still observed according to the old customs; however, the corrections which were introduced regarding the year length prevent their shifting in relation to the seasons. No dates can be given for these lunar festivals because they depend upon the position of the moon and the method of calculation. The names of these festivals are as follows:

Ramanavami
Buddha Purnima
Janmashtami
Dussera
Diwali
Guru Nanak's Birthday
Mahasivaratri
Holi (2 days)

Below are modern versions of three of the calendars in use in India at the time of the reform, and the Saka calendar chosen by the Indian government.

SAKA CALENDAR

Saka Year	Western Date of New Year (Julian)		Saka Year	Western Date of New Year (Julian)		Saka Year	Western Date of New Year (Julian)		Saka Year	Western Date of New Year (Julian)	
1	79	18 Feb*	33	111	25 Feb	65	143	3 Mar	97	175	9 Mar
2	80*	9 Mar	34	112*	14 Feb*	66	144*	20 Feb*	98	176*	26 Feb
3	81	26 Feb	35	113	5 Mar	67	145	11 Mar	99	177	15 Feb*
4	82	15 Feb*	36	114	21 Feb*	68	146	28 Feb	100	178	6 Mar
5	83	6 Mar	37	115	12 Mar	69	147	17 Feb*	101	179	23 Feb*
6	84*	23 Feb	38	116*	1 Mar	70	148*	8 Mar	102	180*	14 Mar
7	85	12 Feb*	39	117	18 Feb*	71	149	25 Feb*	103	181	3 Mar
8	86	3 Mar	40	118	9 Mar	72	150	14 Feb*	104	182	20 Feb*
9	87	20 Feb*	41	119	26 Feb	73	151	5 Mar	105	183	11 Mar
10	88*	11 Mar	42	120*	15 Feb*	74	152*	21 Feb*	106	184*	28 Feb
11	89	28 Feb	43	121	6 Mar	75	153	12 Mar	107	185	17 Feb*
12	90	17 Feb*	44	122	23 Feb	76	154	1 Mar	108	186	8 Mar
13	91	8 Mar	45	123	12 Feb*	77	155	18 Feb*	109	187	25 Feb
14	92*	25 Feb	46	124*	3 Mar	78	156*	9 Mar	110	188*	14 Feb*
15	93	14 Feb*	47	125	20 Feb*	79	157	26 Feb	111	189	5 Mar
16	94	5 Mar	48	126	11 Mar	80	158	15 Feb*	112	190	21 Feb*
17	95	21 Feb*	49	127	28 Feb	81	159	6 Mar	113	191	12 Mar
18	96*	12 Mar	50	128*	17 Feb*	82	160*	23 Feb*	114	192*	1 Mar
19	97	1 Mar	51	129	8 Mar	83	161	14 Mar	115	193	18 Feb*
20	98	18 Feb*	52	130	25 Feb	84	162	3 Mar	116	194	9 Mar
21	99	9 Mar	53	131	14 Feb*	85	163	20 Feb*	117	195	26 Feb
22	100*	26 Feb	54	132*	5 Mar	86	164*	11 Mar	118	196*	15 Feb*
23	101	15 Feb*	55	133	21 Feb*	87	165	28 Feb	119	197	6 Mar
24	102	6 Mar	56	134	12 Mar	88	166	17 Feb*	120	198	23 Feb*
25	103	23 Feb	57	135	1 Mar	89	167	8 Mar	121	199	14 Mar
26	104*	12 Feb*	58	136*	18 Feb*	90	168*	25 Feb	122	200*	3 Mar
27	105	3 Mar	59	137	9 Mar	91	169	14 Feb*	123	201	20 Feb*
28	106	20 Feb*	60	138	26 Feb	92	170	5 Mar	124	202	11 Mar
29	107	11 Mar	61	139	15 Feb*	93	171	21 Feb*	125	203	28 Feb
30	108*	28 Feb	62	140*	6 Mar	94	172*	12 Mar	126	204*	17 Feb*
31	109	17 Feb*	63	141	23 Feb	95	173	1 Mar	127	205	8 Mar
32	110	8 Mar	64	142	12 Feb	96	174	18 Feb*	128	206	25 Feb

Saka Year	Western Date of New Year (Julian)	Saka Year	Western Date of New Year (Julian)	Saka Year	Western Date of New Year (Julian)	Saka Year	Western Date of New Year (Julian)
129	207 14 Feb*	180	258 20 Feb*	231	309 26 Feb	282	360* 5 Mar
130	208* 5 Mar	181	259 11 Mar	232	310 15 Feb*	283	361 21 Feb*
131	209 21 Feb*	182	260* 28 Feb	233	311 6 Mar	284	362 12 Mar
132	210 12 Mar	183	261 17 Feb*	234	312* 23 Feb*	285	363 1 Mar
133	211 1 Mar	184	262 8 Mar	235	313 14 Mar	286	364* 18 Feb*
134	212* 18 Feb*	185	263 25 Feb	236	314 3 Mar	287	365 9 Mar
135	213 9 Mar	186	264* 14 Feb*	237	315 20 Feb*	288	366 26 Feb*
136	214 26 Feb	187	265 5 Mar	238	316* 11 Mar	289	367 17 Mar
137	215 15 Feb*	188	266 21 Feb*	239	317 28 Feb	290	368* 6 Mar*
138	216* 6 Mar	189	267 12 Mar	240	318 17 Feb*	291	369 23 Feb
139	217 23 Feb*	190	268* 1 Mar	241	319 8 Mar	292	370 14 Mar
140	218 14 Mar	191	269 18 Feb*	242	320* 25 Feb*	293	371 3 Mar
141	219 3 Mar	192	270 9 Mar	243	321 16 Mar	294	372* 20 Feb*
142	220* 20 Feb*	193	271 26 Feb	244	322 5 Mar	295	373 11 Mar
143	221 11 Mar	194	272* 15 Feb*	245	323 21 Feb*	296	374 28 Feb
144	222 28 Feb	195	273 6 Mar	246	324* 12 Mar	297	375 17 Feb*
145	223 17 Feb*	196	274 23 Feb*	247	325 1 Mar	298	376* 8 Mar
146	224* 8 Mar	197	275 14 Mar	248	326 18 Feb*	299	377 25 Feb*
147	225 25 Feb	198	276* 3 Mar	249	327 9 May	300	378 16 Mar
148	226 14 Feb*	199	277 20 Feb*	250	328* 26 Feb	301	379 5 Mar
149	227 5 Mar	200	278 11 Mar	251	329 15 Feb*	302	380* 21 Feb*
150	228* 21 Feb*	201	279 28 Feb	252	330 6 Mar	303	381 12 Mar
151	229 12 Mar	202	280* 17 Feb*	253	331 23 Feb*	304	382 1 Mar
152	230 1 Mar	203	281 8 Mar	254	332* 14 Mar	305	383 18 Feb*
153	231 18 Feb*	204	282 25 Feb	255	333 3 Mar	306	384* 9 Mar
154	232* 9 Mar	205	283 14 Feb*	256	334 20 Feb*	307	385 26 Feb*
155	233 26 Feb	206	284* 5 Mar	257	335 11 Mar	308	386 17 Mar
156	234 15 Feb*	207	285 21 Feb*	258	336* 28 Feb	309	387 6 Mar
157	235 6 Mar	208	286 12 Mar	259	337 17 Feb*	310	388* 23 Feb*
158	236* 23 Feb*	209	287 1 Mar	260	338 8 Mar	311	389 14 Mar
159	237 14 Mar	210	288* 18 Feb*	261	339 25 Feb*	312	390 3 Mar
160	238 3 Mar	211	289 9 Mar	262	340* 16 Mar	313	391 20 Feb*
161	239 20 Feb*	212	290 26 Feb	263	341 5 Mar	314	392* 11 Mar
162	240* 11 Mar	213	291 15 Feb*	264	342 21 Feb*	315	393 28 Feb
163	241 28 Feb	214	292* 6 Mar	265	343 12 Mar	316	394 17 Feb*
164	242 17 Feb*	215	293 23 Feb*	266	344* 1 Mar	317	395 8 Mar
165	243 8 Mar	216	294 14 Mar	267	345 18 Feb*	318	396* 25 Feb*
166	244* 25 Feb	217	295 3 Mar	268	346 9 Mar	319	397 16 Mar
167	245 14 Feb*	218	296* 20 Feb*	269	347 26 Feb	320	398 5 Mar
168	246 5 Mar	219	297 11 Mar	270	348* 15 Feb*	321	399 21 Feb*
169	247 21 Feb*	220	298 28 Feb	271	349 6 Mar	322	400* 12 Mar
170	248* 12 Mar	221	299 17 Feb*	272	350 23 Feb*	323	401 1 Mar
171	249 1 Mar	222	300* 8 Mar	273	351 14 Mar	324	402 18 Feb*
172	250 18 Feb*	223	301 25 Feb*	274	352* 3 Mar	325	403 9 Mar
173	251 9 Mar	224	302 16 Mar	275	353 20 Feb*	326	404* 26 Feb
174	252* 26 Feb	225	303 5 Mar	276	354 11 Mar	327	405 15 Feb*
175	253 15 Feb*	226	304* 21 Feb*	277	355 28 Feb	328	406 6 Mar
176	254 6 Mar	227	305 12 Mar	278	356* 17 Feb*	329	407 23 Feb*
177	255 23 Feb*	228	306 1 Mar	279	357 8 Mar	330	408* 14 Mar
178	256* 14 Mar	229	307 18 Feb*	280	358 25 Feb*	331	409 3 Mar
179	257 3 Mar	230	308* 9 Mar	281	359 16 Mar	332	410 20 Feb*

Saka Year	Western Date of New Year (Julian)	Saka Year	Western Date of New Year (Julian)	Saka Year	Western Date of New Year (Julian)	Saka Year	Western Date of New Year (Julian)
333	411 11 Mar	384	462 16 Mar	435	513 21 Feb*	486	564* 28 Feb*
334	412* 28 Feb	385	463 6 Mar	436	514 12 Mar	487	565 19 Mar
335	413 17 Feb*	386	464* 23 Feb*	437	515 1 Mar	488	566 8 Mar
336	414 8 Mar	387	465 14 Mar	438	516* 18 Feb*	489	567 25 Feb*
337	415 25 Feb*	388	466 3 Mar	439	517 9 Mar	490	568* 16 Mar
338	416* 16 Mar	389	467 20 Feb*	440	518 26 Feb*	491	569 5 Mar
339	417 5 Mar	390	468* 11 Mar	441	519 17 Mar	492	570 21 Feb*
340	418 21 Feb*	391	469 28 Feb	442	520* 6 Mar	493	571 12 Mar
341	419 12 Mar	392	470 17 Feb*	443	521 23 Feb*	494	572* 1 Mar
342	420* 1 Mar	393	471 8 Mar	444	522 14 Mar	495	573 18 Feb*
343	421 18 Feb*	394	472* 25 Feb*	445	523 3 Mar	496	574 9 Mar
344	422 9 Mar	395	473 16 Mar	446	524* 20 Feb*	497	575 26 Feb*
345	423 26 Feb	396	474 5 Mar	447	525 11 Mar	498	576* 17 Mar
346	424* 15 Feb*	397	475 21 Feb*	448	526 28 Feb*	499	577 6 Mar
347	425 6 Mar	398	476* 12 Mar	449	527 19 Mar	500	578 23 Feb*
348	426 23 Feb*	399	477 1 Mar	450	528* 8 Mar	501	579 14 Mar
349	427 14 Mar	400	478 18 Feb*	451	529 25 Feb*	502	580* 3 Mar
350	428* 3 Mar	401	479 9 Mar	452	530 16 Mar	503	581 20 Feb*
351	429 20 Feb*	402	480* 26 Feb*	453	531 5 Mar	504	582 11 Mar
352	430 11 Mar	403	481 17 Mar	454	532* 21 Feb*	505	583 28 Feb*
353	431 28 Feb	404	482 6 Mar	455	533 12 Mar	506	584* 19 Mar
354	432* 17 Feb*	405	483 23 Feb*	456	534 1 Mar	507	585 8 Mar
355	433 8 Mar	406	484* 14 Mar	457	535 18 Feb*	508	586 25 Feb*
356	434 25 Feb*	407	485 3 Mar	458	536* 9 Mar	509	587 16 Mar
357	435 16 Mar	408	486 20 Feb*	459	537 26 Feb*	510	588* 5 Mar
358	436* 5 Mar	409	487 11 Mar	460	538 17 Mar	511	589 21 Feb*
359	437 2 Feb*	410	488* 28 Feb	461	539 6 Mar	512	590 12 Mar
360	438 12 Mar	411	489 17 Feb*	462	540* 23 Feb*	513	591 1 Mar
361	439 1 Mar	412	490 8 Mar	463	541 14 Mar	514	592* 18 Feb*
362	440* 18 Feb*	413	491 25 Feb*	464	542 3 Mar	515	593 9 Mar
363	441 9 Mar	414	492* 16 Mar	465	543 20 Feb	516	594 26 Feb*
364	442 26 Feb*	415	493 5 Mar	466	544* 11 Mar	517	595 17 Mar
365	443 17 Mar	416	494 21 Feb*	467	545 28 Feb*	518	596* 6 Mar
366	444* 6 Mar	417	495 12 Mar	468	546 19 Mar	519	597 23 Feb*
367	445 23 Feb*	418	496* 1 Mar	469	547 8 Mar	520	598 14 Mar
368	446 14 Mar	419	497 18 Feb	470	548* 25 Feb*	521	599 3 Mar
369	447 3 Mar	420	498 9 Mar	471	549 16 Mar	522	600* 20 Feb*
370	448* 20 Feb*	421	499 26 Feb*	472	550 5 Mar	523	601 11 Mar
371	449 11 Mar	422	500* 17 Mar	473	551 21 Feb*	524	602 28 Feb*
372	450 28 Feb	423	501 6 Mar	474	552* 12 Mar	525	603 19 Mar
373	451 17 Feb*	424	502 23 Feb*	475	553 1 Mar	526	604* 8 Mar
374	452* 8 Mar	425	503 14 Mar	476	554 18 Feb*	527	605 25 Feb*
375	453 25 Feb*	426	504* 3 Mar	477	555 9 Mar	528	606 16 Mar
376	454 16 Mar	427	505 20 Feb*	478	556* 26 Feb*	529	607 5 Mar
377	455 5 Mar	428	506 11 Mar	479	557 17 Mar	530	608* 21 Feb*
378	456* 21 Feb*	429	507 28 Feb*	480	558 6 Mar	531	609 12 Mar
379	457 12 Mar	430	508* 19 Mar	481	559 23 Feb*	532	610 1 Mar
380	458 1 Mar	431	509 8 Mar	482	560* 14 Mar	533	611 18 Feb*
381	459 18 Feb*	432	510 25 Feb*	483	561 3 Mar	534	612* 9 Mar
382	460* 9 Mar	433	511 16 Mar	484	562 20 Feb*	535	613 26 Feb*
383	461 26 Feb*	434	512* 5 Mar	485	563 11 Mar	536	614 17 Mar

Saka Year	Western Date of New Year (Julian)	Saka Year	Western Date of New Year (Julian)	Saka Year	Western Date of New Year (Julian)	Saka Year	Western Date of New Year (Julian)
537	615 6 Mar	588	666 12 Mar	639	717 19 Mar	690	768* 24 Feb*
538	616* 23 Feb*	589	667 2 Mar*	640	718 8 Mar	691	769 13 Mar
539	617 14 Mar	590	668* 20 Mar	641	719 25 Feb*	692	770 3 Mar
540	618 3 Mar	591	669 10 Mar	642	720* 15 Mar	693	771 20 Feb*
541	619 20 Feb*	592	670 27 Feb*	643	721 4 Mar	694	772* 10 Mar
542	620* 11 Mar	593	671 17 Mar	644	722 21 Feb*	695	773 28 Feb*
543	621 28 Feb*	594	672* 6 Mar	645	723 13 Mar	696	774 18 Mar
544	622 19 Mar	595	673 23 Feb*	646	724* 1 Mar*	697	775 8 Mar
545	623 8 Mar	596	674 14 Mar	647	725 19 Mar	698	776* 25 Feb*
546	624* 25 Feb*	597	675 4 Mar	648	726 9 Mar	699	777 15 Mar
547	625 16 Mar	598	676* 21 Feb*	649	727 26 Feb*	700	778 5 Mar
548	626 5 Mar	599	677 11 Mar	650	728* 17 Mar	701	779 22 Feb*
549	627 22 Feb*	600	678 28 Feb*	651	729 6 Mar	702	780* 11 Mar
550	628* 12 Mar	601	679 19 Mar	652	730 23 Feb*	703	781 1 Mar*
551	629 1 Mar	602	680* 8 Mar	653	731 14 Mar	704	782 20 Mar
552	630 19 Feb*	603	681 25 Feb*	654	732* 2 Mar	705	783 9 Mar
553	631 10 Mar	604	682 15 Mar	655	733 20 Feb*	706	784* 27 Feb*
554	632* 27 Feb*	605	683 5 Mar	656	734 11 Mar	707	785 16 Mar
555	633 17 Mar	606	684* 22 Feb*	657	735 1 Mar*	708	786 6 Mar
556	634 6 Mar	607	685 12 Mar	658	736* 18 Mar	709	787 23 Feb*
557	635 24 Feb*	608	686 2 Mar*	659	737 7 Mar	710	788* 13 Mar
558	636* 14 Mar	609	687 20 Mar	660	738 25 Feb*	711	789 3 Mar*
559	637 3 Mar	610	688* 9 Mar	661	739 16 Mar	712	790 21 Mar
560	638 21 Feb*	611	689 26 Feb*	662	740* 4 Mar	713	791 10 Mar
561	639 11 Mar	612	690 17 Mar	663	741 22 Feb*	714	792* 28 Feb*
562	640* 29 Feb*	613	691 7 Mar	664	742 12 Mar	715	793 18 Mar
563	641 19 Mar	614	692* 24 Feb*	665	743 1 Mar*	716	794 8 Mar
564	642 8 Mar	615	693 13 Mar	666	744* 20 Mar	717	795 25 Feb*
565	643 26 Feb*	616	694 3 Mar	667	745 9 Mar	718	796* 15 Mar
566	644* 15 Mar	617	695 20 Feb*	668	746 27 Feb*	719	797 4 Mar
567	645 4 Mar	618	696* 10 Mar	669	747 17 Mar	720	798 21 Feb*
568	646 22 Feb*	619	697 28 Feb*	670	748* 5 Mar	721	799 13 Mar
569	647 13 Mar	620	698 19 Mar	671	749 23 Feb*	722	800* 1 Mar*
570	648* 2 Mar*	621	699 8 Mar	672	750 14 Mar	723	801 19 Mar
571	649 20 Mar	622	700* 25 Feb*	673	751 3 Mar	724	802 9 Mar
572	650 9 Mar	623	701 16 Mar	674	752* 21 Feb*	725	803 26 Feb*
573	651 27 Feb*	624	702 5 Mar	675	753 10 Mar	726	804* 17 Mar
574	652* 17 Mar	625	703 22 Feb*	676	754 27 Feb*	727	805 6 Mar
575	653 6 Mar	626	704* 12 Mar	677	755 19 Mar	728	806 23 Feb*
576	654 24 Feb*	627	705 1 Mar*	678	756* 7 Mar	729	807 14 Mar
577	655 14 Mar	628	706 21 Mar	679	757 25 Feb*	730	808* 2 Mar*
578	656* 2 Mar	629	707 10 Mar	680	758 15 Mar	731	809 21 Mar
579	657 20 Feb*	630	708* 27 Feb*	681	759 4 Mar	732	810 11 Mar
580	658 11 Mar	631	709 17 Mar	682	760* 22 Feb*	733	811 28 Feb*
581	659 1 Mar*	632	710 6 Mar	683	761 12 Mar	734	812* 17 Mar
582	660* 18 Mar*	633	711 23 Feb*	684	762 1 Mar*	735	813 7 Mar
583	661 7 Mar	634	712* 15 Mar	685	763 20 Mar	736	814 24 Feb*
584	662 25 Feb*	635	713 3 Mar	686	764* 9 Mar	737	815 16 Mar
585	663 16 Mar	636	714 20 Feb*	687	765 26 Feb*	738	816* 4 Mar
586	664* 4 Mar	637	715 11 Mar	688	766 17 Mar	739	817 21 Feb*
587	665 22 Feb*	638	716* 28 Feb*	689	767 7 Mar	740	818 12 Mar

Saka Year	Western Date of New Year (Julian)	Saka Year	Western Date of New Year (Julian).	Saka Year	Western Date of New Year (Julian)	Saka Year	Western Date of New Year (Julian)
741	819 1 Mar*	792	870 8 Mar	843	921 13 Mar	894	972* 19 Mar
742	820* 19 Mar	793	871 25 Feb*	844	922 2 Mar*	895	973 8 Mar
743	821 9 Mar	794	872* 14 Mar	845	923 21 Mar	896	974 26 Feb*
744	822 26 Feb*	795	873 4 Mar	846	924* 10 Mar	897	975 16 Mar
745	823 17 Mar	796	874 21 Feb*	847	925 27 Feb*	898	976* 4 Mar
746	824* 5 Mar	797	875 12 Mar	848	926 18 Mar	899	977 22 Feb*
747	825 22 Feb*	798	876* 1 Mar*	849	927 7 Mar	900	978 13 Mar
748	826 14 Mar	799	877 19 Mar	850	928* 24 Feb*	901	979 3 Mar*
749	827 3 Mar*	800	878 8 Mar	851	929 15 Mar	902	980* 20 Mar
750	828* 21 Mar	801	879 26 Feb*	852	930 4 Mar*	903	981 9 Mar
751	829 10 Mar	802	880* 16 Mar	853	931 23 Mar	904	982 27 Feb*
752	830 27 Feb*	803	881 6 Mar	854	932* 11 Mar	905	983 18 Mar
753	831 19 Mar	804	882 23 Feb*	855	933 1 Mar*	906	984* 6 Mar
754	832* 7 Mar	805	883 13 Mar	856	934 20 Mar	907	985 24 Feb*
755	833 25 Feb*	806	884* 2 Mar*	857	935 9 Mar	908	986 14 Mar
756	834 15 Mar	807	885 21 Mar	858	936* 26 Feb*	909	987 3 Mar*
757	835 4 Mar	808	886 10 Mar	859	937 16 Mar	910	988* 22 Mar
758	836* 22 Feb*	809	887 28 Feb*	860	938 5 Mar	911	989 11 Mar
759	837 12 Mar	810	888* 18 Mar	861	939 23 Feb*	912	990 1 Mar*
760	838 1 Mar*	811	889 6 Mar	862	940* 13 Mar	913	991 19 Mar
761	839 20 Mar	812	890 24 Feb*	863	941 2 Mar*	914	992* 8 Mar
762	840* 8 Mar	813	891 15 Mar	864	942 21 Mar	915	993 25 Feb*
763	841 25 Feb*	814	892* 4 Mar	865	943 10 Mar	916	994 16 Mar
764	842 17 Mar	815	893 21 Feb*	866	944* 27 Feb*	917	995 6 Mar
765	843 6 Mar	816	894 12 Mar	867	945 18 Mar	918	996* 23 Feb*
766	844* 24 Feb*	817	895 1 Mar*	868	946 7 Mar	919	997 13 Mar
767	845 13 Mar	818	896* 19 Mar	869	947 24 Feb*	920	998 2 Mar*
768	846 2 Mar*	819	897 9 Mar	870	948* 14 Mar	921	999 19 Mar
769	847 22 Mar	820	898 26 Feb*	871	949 3 Mar*	922	1000* 10 Mar
770	848* 10 Mar	821	899 16 Mar	872	950 23 Mar	923	1001 27 Feb*
771	849 27 Feb*	822	900* 5 Mar	873	951 12 Mar	924	1002 17 Mar
772	850 18 Mar	823	901 22 Feb*	874	952* 29 Feb*	925	1003 7 Mar
773	851 7 Mar	824	902 14 Mar	875	953 19 Mar	926	1004* 26 Feb*
774	852* 25 Feb*	825	903 3 Mar*	876	954 8 Mar	927	1005 14 Mar
775	853 15 Mar	826	904* 20 Mar	877	955 25 Feb*	928	1006 4 Mar*
776	854 4 Mar	827	905 10 Mar	878	956* 16 Mar	929	1007 22 Mar
777	855 22 Feb*	828	906 27 Feb*	879	957 5 Mar	930	1008* 11 Mar
778	856* 11 Mar	829	907 17 Mar	880	958 22 Feb*	931	1009 28 Feb*
779	857 28 Feb*	830	908* 7 Mar	881	959 13 Mar	932	1010 19 Mar
780	858 20 Mar	831	909 24 Feb*	882	960* 2 Mar*	933	1011 9 Mar
781	859 9 Mar	832	910 15 Mar	883	961 21 Mar	934	1012* 26 Feb*
782	860* 26 Feb*	833	911 4 Mar	884	962 10 Mar	935	1013 15 Mar
783	861 16 Mar	834	912* 21 Feb*	885	963 28 Feb*	936	1014 5 Mar
784	862 6 Mar	835	913 12 Mar	886	964* 17 Mar	937	1015 22 Feb*
785	863 23 Feb*	836	914 1 Mar*	887	965 6 Mar	938	1016* 12 Mar
786	864* 13 Mar	837	915 19 Mar	888	966 24 Feb*	939	1017 2 Mar*
787	865 3 Mar*	838	916* 8 Mar	889	967 15 Mar	940	1018 26 Mar
788	866 21 Mar	839	917 25 Feb*	890	968* 4 Mar*	941	1019 10 Mar
789	867 10 Mar	840	918 16 Mar	891	969 22 Mar	942	1020* 27 Feb*
790	868* 28 Feb*	841	919 6 Mar	892	970 11 Mar	943	1021 17 Mar
791	869 18 Mar	842	920* 23 Feb*	893	971 1 Mar*	944	1022 7 Mar

Saka Year	Western Date of New Year (Julian)	Saka Year	Western Date of New Year (Julian)	Saka Year	Western Date of New Year (Julian)	Saka Year	Western Date of New Year (Julian)
945	1023 24 Feb*	996	1074 1 Mar*	1047	1125 8 Mar	1098	1176* 13 Mar
946	1024* 14 Mar	997	1075 21 Mar	1048	1126 25 Feb*	1099	1177 2 Mar*
947	1025 3 Mar*	998	1076* 9 Mar	1049	1127 16 Mar	1100	1178 22 Mar
948	1026 23 Mar	999	1077 27 Feb*	1050	1128* 4 Mar*	1101	1179 11 Mar
949	1027 12 Mar	1000	1078 17 Mar	1051	1129 23 Mar	1102	1180* 28 Feb*
950	1028* 29 Feb*	1001	1079 6 Mar	1052	1130 13 Mar	1103	1181 17 Mar
951	1029 19 Mar	1002	1080* 24 Feb*	1053	1131 2 Mar*	1104	1182 7 Mar
952	1030 8 Mar	1003	1081 14 Mar	1054	1132* 19 Mar	1105	1183 25 Feb*
953	1031 25 Feb*	1004	1082 3 Mar*	1055	1133 9 Mar	1106	1184* 15 Mar
954	1032* 16 Mar	1005	1083 22 Mar	1056	1134 26 Feb*	1107	1185 4 Mar*
955	1033 5 Mar	1006	1084* 10 Mar	1057	1135 18 Mar	1108	1186 23 Mar
956	1034 22 Feb*	1007	1085 28 Feb*	1058	1136* 6 Mar	1109	1187 12 Mar
957	1035 13 Mar	1008	1086 19 Mar	1059	1137 23 Feb*	1110	1188* 1 Mar*
958	1036* 1 Mar*	1009	1087 8 Mar	1060	1138 14 Mar	1111	1189 20 Mar
959	1037 21 Mar	1010	1088* 26 Feb*	1061	1139 3 Mar*	1112	1190 9 Mar
960	1038 10 Mar	1011	1089 15 Mar	1062	1140* 21 Mar	1113	1191 27 Feb*
961	1039 27 Feb*	1012	1090 5 Mar*	1063	1141 11 Mar	1114	1192* 16 Mar
962	1040* 17 Mar	1013	1091 24 Mar	1064	1142 28 Feb*	1115	1193 6 Mar
963	1041 6 Mar	1014	1092* 12 Mar	1065	1143 19 Mar	1116	1194 23 Feb*
964	1042 23 Feb*	1015	1093 2 Mar*	1066	1144* 7 Mar	1117	1195 14 Mar
965	1043 15 Mar	1016	1094 20 Mar	1067	1145 24 Feb*	1118	1196* 3 Mar*
966	1044* 3 Mar*	1017	1095 10 Mar	1068	1146 16 Mar	1119	1197 21 Mar
967	1045 21 Mar	1018	1096* 27 Feb*	1069	1147 5 Mar*	1120	1198 10 Mar
968	1046 11 Mar	1019	1097 17 Mar	1070	1148* 22 Mar	1121	1199 28 Feb*
969	1047 28 Feb*	1020	1098 7 Mar	1071	1149 12 Mar	1122	1200* 18 Mar
970	1048* 19 Mar	1021	1099 24 Feb*	1072	1150 1 Mar*	1123	1201 8 Mar
971	1049 8 Mar	1022	1100* 13 Mar	1073	1151 20 Mar	1124	1202 25 Feb*
972	1050 25 Feb*	1023	1101 3 Mar*	1074	1152* 9 Mar	1125	1203 15 Mar
973	1051 16 Mar	1024	1102 22 Mar	1075	1153 26 Feb*	1126	1204* 4 Mar*
974	1052* 4 Mar	1025	1103 11 Mar	1076	1154 17 Mar	1127	1205 23 Mar
975	1053 21 Feb*	1026	1104* 29 Feb*	1077	1155 6 Mar	1128	1206 12 Mar
976	1054 13 Mar	1027	1105 18 Mar	1078	1156* 24 Feb*	1129	1207 2 Mar*
977	1055 2 Mar*	1028	1106 8 Mar	1079	1157 14 Mar	1130	1208* 19 Mar
978	1056* 20 Mar	1029	1107 25 Feb*	1080	1158 3 Mar*	1131	1209 8 Mar
979	1057 9 Mar	1030	1108* 15 Mar	1081	1159 22 Mar	1132	1210 26 Feb*
980	1058 27 Feb*	1031	1109 5 Mar*	1082	1160* 10 Mar	1133	1211 17 Mar
981	1059 18 Mar	1032	1110 24 Mar	1083	1161 27 Feb*	1134	1212* 6 Mar*
982	1060* 6 Mar	1033	1111 12 Mar	1084	1162 19 Mar	1135	1213 24 Mar
983	1061 24 Feb*	1034	1112* 1 Mar*	1085	1163 8 Mar	1136	1214 13 Mar
984	1062 14 Mar	1035	1113 20 Mar	1086	1164* 26 Feb*	1137	1215 3 Mar*
985	1063 3 Mar*	1036	1114 10 Mar	1087	1165 15 Mar	1138	1216* 21 Mar
986	1064* 22 Mar	1037	1115 27 Feb*	1088	1166 4 Mar*	1139	1217 10 Mar
987	1065 11 Mar	1038	1116* 16 Mar	1089	1167 24 Mar	1140	1218 28 Feb*
988	1066 1 Mar*	1039	1117 6 Mar	1090	1168* 15 Mar	1141	1219 18 Mar
989	1067 19 Mar	1040	1118 23 Feb*	1091	1169 4 Mar*	1142	1220* 7 Mar
990	1068* 7 Mar	1041	1119 14 Mar	1092	1170 20 Mar	1143	1221 24 Feb*
991	1069 25 Feb*	1042	1120* 3 Mar*	1093	1171 9 Mar	1144	1222 16 Mar
992	1070 16 Mar	1043	1121 21 Mar	1094	1172* 27 Feb*	1145	1223 5 Mar*
993	1071 5 Mar*	1044	1122 11 Mar	1095	1173 17 Mar	1146	1224* 22 Mar
984	1072* 23 Mar	1045	1123 28 Feb*	1096	1174 6 Mar	1147	1225 12 Mar
995	1073 12 Mar	1046	1124* 19 Mar	1097	1175 24 Feb*	1148	1226 1 Mar*

Saka Year	Western Date of New Year (Julian)	Saka Year	Western Date of New Year (Julian)	Saka Year	Western Date of New Year (Julian)	Saka Year	Western Date of New Year (Julian)
1149	1227 20 Mar	1200	1278 25 Mar	1251	1329 2 Mar*	1302	1380* 8 Mar
1150	1228* 10 Mar	1201	1279 15 Mar	1252	1330 21 Mar	1303	1381 25 Feb*
1151	1229 26 Feb*	1202	1280* 4 Mar*	1253	1331 11 Mar	1304	1382 16 Mar
1152	1230 17 Mar	1203	1281 23 Mar	1254	1332* 28 Feb*	1305	1383 5 Mar*
1153	1231 6 Mar*	1204	1282 12 Mar	1255	1333 17 Mar	1306	1384* 24 Mar
1154	1232* 24 Mar	1205	1283 1 Mar*	1256	1334 7 Mar*	1307	1385 13 Mar
1155	1233 14 Mar	1206	1284* 19 Mar	1257	1335 26 Mar	1308	1386 3 Mar*
1156	1234 3 Mar*	1207	1285 8 Mar	1258	1336* 14 Mar	1309	1387 21 Mar
1157	1235 21 Mar	1208	1286 26 Feb*	1259	1337 4 Mar*	1310	1388* 9 Mar
1158	1236* 10 Mar	1209	1287 17 Mar	1260	1338 22 Mar	1311	1389 27 Feb*
1159	1237 27 Feb*	1210	1288* 6 Mar*	1261	1339 12 Mar	1312	1390 18 Mar
1160	1238 18 Mar	1211	1289 24 Mar	1262	1340* 29 Feb*	1313	1391 7 Mar*
1161	1239 8 Mar	1212	1290 13 Mar	1263	1341 19 Mar	1314	1392* 25 Mar
1162	1240* 25 Feb*	1213	1291 3 Mar*	1264	1342 9 Mar	1315	1393 14 Mar
1163	1241 15 Mar	1214	1292* 21 Mar	1265	1343 26 Feb*	1316	1394 3 Mar*
1164	1242 4 Mar*	1215	1293 10 Mar	1266	1344* 15 Mar	1317	1395 23 Mar
1165	1243 23 Mar	1216	1294 28 Feb*	1267	1345 5 Mar*	1318	1396* 11 Mar
1166	1244* 12 Mar	1217	1295 18 Mar	1268	1346 24 Mar	1319	1397 1 Mar*
1167	1245 1 Mar*	1218	1296* 6 Mar*	1269	1347 14 Mar	1320	1398 19 Mar
1168	1246 19 Mar	1219	1297 26 Mar	1270	1348* 2 Mar*	1321	1399 8 Mar
1169	1247 9 Mar	1220	1298 15 Mar	1271	1349 21 Mar	1322	1400* 25 Feb*
1170	1248* 26 Feb*	1221	1299 5 Mar*	1272	1350 10 Mar	1323	1401 16 Mar
1171	1249 16 Mar	1222	1300* 22 Mar	1273	1351 27 Feb*	1324	1402 5 Mar*
1172	1250 6 Mar*	1223	1301 11 Mar	1274	1352* 18 Mar	1325	1403 24 Mar
1173	1251 25 Mar	1224	1302 1 Mar*	1275	1353 7 Mar*	1326	1404* 12 Mar
1174	1252* 13 Mar	1225	1303 20 Mar	1276	1354 25 Mar	1327	1405 2 Mar*
1175	1253 2 Mar*	1226	1304* 8 Mar	1277	1355 15 Mar	1328	1406 21 Mar
1176	1254 22 Mar	1227	1305 26 Feb*	1278	1356* 3 Mar*	1329	1407 10 Mar
1177	1255 11 Mar	1228	1306 16 Mar	1279	1357 23 Mar	1330	1408* 28 Feb*
1178	1256* 28 Feb*	1229	1307 5 Mar*	1280	1358 12 Mar	1331	1409 17 Mar
1179	1257 18 Mar	1230	1308* 24 Mar	1281	1359 1 Mar*	1332	1410 6 Mar*
1180	1258 7 Mar	1231	1309 13 Mar	1282	1360* 19 Mar	1333	1411 26 Mar
1181	1259 25 Feb*	1232	1310 3 Mar*	1283	1361 8 Mar	1334	1412* 14 Mar
1182	1260* 15 Mar	1223	1311 21 Mar	1284	1362 26 Feb*	1335	1413 3 Mar*
1183	1261 4 Mar*	1234	1312* 9 Mar	1285	1363 17 Mar	1336	1414 22 Mar
1184	1262 23 Mar	1235	1313 27 Feb*	1286	1364* 5 Mar*	1337	1415 12 Mar
1185	1263 12 Mar	1236	1314 18 Mar	1287	1365 23 Mar	1338	1416* 29 Feb*
1186	1264* 29 Feb*	1237	1315 7 Mar*	1288	1366 13 Mar	1339	1417 19 Mar
1187	1265 20 Mar	1238	1316* 26 Mar	1289	1367 2 Mar*	1340	1418 9 Mar*
1188	1266 9 Mar	1239	1317 15 Mar	1290	1368* 21 Mar	1341	1419 27 Mar
1189	1267 26 Feb*	1240	1318 4 Mar*	1291	1369 10 Mar	1342	1420* 15 Mar
1190	1268* 16 Mar	1241	1319 23 Mar	1292	1370 27 Feb*	1343	1421 5 Mar*
1191	1269 5 Mar*	1242	1320* 12 Mar	1293	1371 18 Mar	1344	1422 24 Mar
1192	1270 25 Mar	1243	1321 1 Mar*	1294	1372* 6 Mar*	1345	1423 13 Mar
1193	1271 12 Mar	1244	1322 19 Mar	1295	1373 25 Mar	1346	1424* 2 Mar*
1194	1272* 2 Mar*	1245	1323 9 Mar	1296	1374 15 Mar	1347	1425 19 Mar
1195	1273 21 Mar	1246	1324* 26 Feb*	1297	1375 4 Mar*	1348	1426 10 Mar
1196	1274 10 Mar	1247	1325 16 Mar	1298	1376* 22 Mar	1349	1427 27 Feb*
1197	1275 27 Feb*	1248	1326 6 Mar*	1299	1377 11 Mar	1350	1428* 17 Mar
1198	1276* 18 Mar	1249	1327 24 Mar	1300	1378 28 Feb*	1351	1429 7 Mar*
1199	1277 7 Mar*	1250	1328* 13 Mar	1301	1379 20 Mar	1352	1430 25 Mar

Saka Year	Western Date of New Year (Julian)	Saka Year	Western Date of New Year (Julian)	Saka Year	Western Date of New Year (Julian)	Saka Year	Western Date of New Year (Julian)
1353	1431 14 Mar	1391	1469 14 Mar	1429	1507 14 Mar	1467	1545 14 Mar
1354	1432* 3 Mar*	1392	1470 3 Mar*	1430	1508* 2 Mar*	1468	1546 3 Mar*
1355	1433 22 Mar	1393	1471 22 Mar	1431	1509 22 Mar	1469	1547 22 Mar
1356	1434 12 Mar	1394	1472* 11 Mar	1432	1510 11 Mar	1470	1548* 11 Mar
1357	1435 1 Mar*	1395	1473 28 Feb*	1433	1511 28 Feb*	1471	1549 28 Feb*
1358	1436* 18 Mar	1396	1474 19 Mar	1434	1512* 18 Mar	1472	1550 19 Mar
1359	1437 8 Mar*	1397	1475 8 Mar*	1435	1513 8 Mar*	1473	1551 8 Mar*
1360	1438 27 Mar	1398	1476* 26 Mar	1436	1514 27 Mar	1474	1552* 26 Mar
1361	1439 16 Mar	1399	1477 16 Mar	1437	1515 16 Mar	1475	1553 16 Mar
1362	1440* 5 Mar*	1400	1478 5 Mar*	1438	1516* 5 Mar*	1476	1554 5 Mar*
1363	1441 23 Mar	1401	1479 24 Mar	1439	1517 23 Mar	1477	1555 23 Mar
1364	1442 12 Mar	1402	1480* 12 Mar	1440	1518 12 Mar	1478	1556* 12 Mar
1365	1443 2 Mar*	1403	1481 1 Mar*	1441	1519 2 Mar*	1479	1557 1 Mar*
1366	1444* 20 Mar	1404	1482 21 Mar	1442	1520* 20 Mar	1480	1558 20 Mar
1367	1445 10 Mar	1405	1483 10 Mar	1443	1521 10 Mar	1481	1559 10 Mar*
1368	1446 27 Feb*	1406	1484* 28 Feb*	1444	1522 27 Feb*	1482	1560* 27 Mar
1369	1447 18 Mar	1407	1485 17 Mar	1445	1523 17 Mar	1483	1561 17 Mar
1370	1448* 6 Mar*	1408	1486 6 Mar*	1446	1524* 6 Mar*	1484	1562 6 Mar*
1371	1449 25 Mar	1409	1487 26 Mar	1447	1525 25 Mar	1485	1563 25 Mar
1372	1450 15 Mar	1410	1488* 14 Mar	1448	1526 14 Mar	1486	1564* 14 Mar
1373	1451 4 Mar*	1411	1489 3 Mar*	1449	1527 4 Mar*	1487	1565 3 Mar*
1374	1452* 21 Mar	1412	1490 22 Mar	1450	1528* 21 Mar	1488	1566 21 Mar
1375	1453 11 Mar	1413	1491 11 Mar	1451	1529 10 Mar	1489	1567 11 Mar
1376	1454 28 Feb*	1414	1492* 29 Feb*	1452	1530 26 Feb*	1490	1568* 28 Feb*
1377	1455 20 Mar	1415	1493 19 Mar	1453	1531 19 Mar	1491	1569 18 Mar
1378	1456* 8 Mar*	1416	1494 8 Mar*	1454	1532* 8 Mar*	1492	1570 8 Mar*
1379	1457 26 Mar	1417	1495 26 Mar	1455	1533 26 Mar	1493	1571 26 Mar
1380	1458 16 Mar	1418	1496* 15 Mar	1456	1534 15 Mar	1494	1572* 15 Mar
1381	1459 5 Mar*	1419	1497 4 Mar*	1457	1535 5 Mar*	1495	1573 4 Mar*
1382	1460* 23 Mar	1420	1498 24 Mar	1458	1536* 23 Mar	1496	1574 23 Mar
1383	1461 13 Mar	1421	1499 13 Mar	1459	1537 12 Mar	1497	1575 13 Mar
1384	1462 2 Mar*	1422	1500* 1 Mar*	1460	1538 2 Mar*	1498	1576* 1 Mar*
1385	1463 21 Mar	1423	1501 20 Mar	1461	1539 20 Mar	1499	1577 20 Mar
1386	1464* 9 Mar	1424	1502 9 Mar	1462	1540* 8 Mar	1500	1578 9 Mar*
1387	1465 26 Feb*	1425	1503 27 Feb*	1463	1541 26 Feb*	1501	1579 29 Mar
1388	1466 18 Mar	1426	1504* 17 Mar	1464	1542 17 Mar	1502	1580* 17 Mar
1389	1467 7 Mar*	1427	1505 6 Mar*	1465	1543 7 Mar*	1503	1581 6 Mar*
1390	1468* 24 Mar	1428	1506 25 Mar	1466	1544* 24 Mar	1504	1582 25 Mar

Saka Year	Western Date of New Year (Julian)		(Gregorian)	Saka Year	Western Date of New Year (Julian)		(Gregorian)	Saka Year	Western Date of New Year (Julian)		(Gregorian)
1505	1583	14 Mar	24 Mar	1512	1590	27 Mar	6 Apr	1519	1597	7 Apr*	17 Apr
1506	1584*	2 Mar*	12 Mar	1513	1591	16 Mar	26 Mar	1520	1598	27 Mar	6 Apr
1507	1585	22 Mar	1 Apr	1514	1592*	4 Mar*	14 Mar	1521	1599	17 Mar	27 Mar
1508	1586	11 Mar	21 Mar	1515	1593	23 Mar	3 Apr	1522	1600*	5 Mar*	15 Mar
1509	1587	28 Feb*	10 Mar	1516	1594	12 Mar	22 Mar	1523	1601	25 Mar	4 Apr
1510	1588*	18 Mar	28 Mar	1517	1595	1 Mar*	11 Mar	1524	1602	14 Mar	24 Mar
1511	1589	7 Mar*	17 Mar	1518	1596*	20 Mar	30 Mar	1525	1603	3 Mar*	13 Mar

Saka Year	Western Date of New Year (Julian)		(Gregorian)
1526	1604*	21 Mar	31 Mar
1527	1605	10 Mar	20 Mar
1528	1606	27 Feb*	9 Mar
1529	1607	19 Mar	29 Mar
1530	1608*	7 Mar*	17 Mar
1531	1609	26 Mar	5 Apr
1532	1610	15 Mar	25 Mar
1533	1611	5 Mar*	15 Mar
1534	1612*	23 Mar	2 Apr
1535	1613	12 Mar	22 Mar
1536	1614	2 Mar*	12 Mar
1537	1615	20 Mar	30 Mar
1538	1616*	8 Mar*	18 Mar
1539	1617	28 Mar	7 Apr
1540	1618	17 Mar	27 Mar
1541	1619	7 Mar*	17 Mar
1542	1620*	24 Mar	3 Apr
1543	1621	13 Mar	23 Mar
1544	1622	3 Mar*	13 Mar
1545	1623	22 Mar	1 Apr
1546	1624*	10 Mar	20 Mar
1547	1625	28 Feb*	10 Mar
1548	1626	18 Mar	28 Mar
1549	1627	7 Mar*	17 Mar
1550	1628*	26 Mar	5 Apr
1551	1629	15 Mar	25 Mar
1552	1630	5 Mar*	15 Mar
1553	1631	23 Mar	2 Apr
1554	1632*	11 Mar	21 Mar
1555	1633	1 Mar*	11 Mar
1556	1634	20 Mar	30 Mar
1557	1635	9 Mar*	19 Mar
1558	1636*	27 Mar	6 Apr
1559	1637	16 Mar	26 Mar
1560	1638	6 Mar*	16 Mar
1561	1639	25 Mar	4 Apr
1562	1640*	13 Mar	23 Mar
1563	1641	3 Mar*	13 Mar
1564	1642	21 Mar	31 Mar
1565	1643	11 Mar	21 Mar
1566	1644*	28 Feb*	9 Mar
1567	1645	18 Mar	28 Mar
1568	1646	8 Mar*	18 Mar
1569	1647	26 Mar	5 Apr
1570	1648*	15 Mar	25 Mar
1571	1649	4 Mar*	14 Mar
1572	1650	23 Mar	2 Apr
1573	1651	13 Mar	23 Mar
1574	1652*	1 Mar*	11 Mar
1575	1653	19 Mar	29 Mar
1576	1654	9 Mar*	19 Mar
1577	1655	26 Feb	8 Mar
1578	1656*	16 Mar	26 Mar
1579	1657	6 Mar*	16 Mar
1580	1658	24 Mar	3 Apr
1581	1659	14 Mar	24 Mar
1582	1660*	2 Mar*	12 Mar
1583	1661	21 Mar	31 Mar
1584	1662	11 Mar	21 Mar
1585	1663	28 Feb*	9 Mar
1586	1664*	17 Mar	27 Mar
1587	1665	7 Mar*	17 Mar
1588	1666	26 Mar	5 Apr
1589	1667	16 Mar	26 Mar
1590	1668*	4 Mar*	14 Mar
1591	1669	22 Mar	1 Apr
1592	1670	12 Mar	22 Mar
1593	1671	1 Mar*	11 Mar
1594	1672*	19 Mar	29 Mar
1595	1673	9 Mar*	19 Mar
1596	1674	27 Mar	6 Apr
1597	1675	17 Mar	27 Mar
1598	1676*	5 Mar*	15 Mar
1599	1677	25 Mar	4 Apr
1600	1678	14 Mar	24 Mar
1601	1679	3 Mar*	13 Mar
1602	1680*	21 Mar	31 Mar
1603	1681	10 Mar*	20 Mar
1604	1682	29 Mar	8 Apr
1605	1683	19 Mar	29 Mar
1606	1684*	7 Mar*	17 Mar
1607	1685	25 Mar	4 Apr
1608	1686	15 Mar	25 Mar
1609	1687	4 Mar*	14 Mar
1610	1688*	23 Mar	2 Apr
1611	1689	12 Mar	22 Mar
1612	1690	1 Mar*	11 Mar
1613	1691	20 Mar	30 Mar
1614	1692*	8 Mar*	18 Mar
1615	1693	27 Mar	6 Apr
1616	1694	17 Mar	27 Mar
1617	1695	6 Mar*	16 Mar
1618	1696*	24 Mar	3 Apr
1619	1697	13 Mar	23 Mar
1620	1698	2 Mar*	12 Mar
1621	1699	22 Mar	1 Apr
1622	1700	10 Mar*	21 Mar
1623	1701	28 Mar	8 Apr
1624	1702	18 Mar	29 Mar
1625	1703	7 Mar*	18 Mar
1626	1704*	25 Mar	5 Apr
1627	1705	15 Mar	26 Mar
1628	1706	4 Mar*	15 Mar
1629	1707	23 Mar	3 Apr
1630	1708*	11 Mar	22 Mar
1631	1709	1 Mar*	12 Mar
1632	1710	20 Mar	31 Mar
1633	1711	9 Mar*	20 Mar
1634	1712*	27 Mar	7 Apr
1635	1713	16 Mar	27 Mar
1636	1714	5 Mar*	16 Mar
1637	1715	25 Mar	5 Apr
1638	1716*	13 Mar	24 Mar
1639	1717	3 Mar*	14 Mar
1640	1718	21 Mar	1 Apr
1641	1719	10 Mar*	21 Mar
1642	1720*	29 Mar	9 Apr
1643	1721	18 Mar	29 Mar
1644	1722	7 Mar*	18 Mar
1645	1723	26 Mar	6 Apr
1646	1724*	14 Mar	25 Mar
1647	1725	4 Mar*	15 Mar
1648	1726	23 Mar	3 Apr
1649	1727	12 Mar	23 Mar
1650	1728*	1 Mar*	12 Mar
1651	1729	19 Mar	30 Mar
1652	1730	8 Mar*	19 Mar
1653	1731	27 Mar	7 Apr
1654	1732*	16 Mar	27 Mar
1655	1733	5 Mar*	16 Mar
1656	1734	24 Mar	4 Apr
1657	1735	13 Mar	24 Mar
1658	1736*	2 Mar*	13 Mar
1659	1737	21 Mar	1 Apr
1660	1738	10 Mar*	21 Mar
1661	1739	29 Mar	9 Apr
1662	1740*	17 Mar	28 Mar
1663	1741	7 Mar*	18 Mar
1664	1742	26 Mar	6 Apr
1665	1743	15 Mar	26 Mar
1666	1744*	4 Mar*	15 Mar
1667	1745	22 Mar	2 Apr
1668	1746	12 Mar	23 Mar
1669	1747	1 Mar*	12 Mar
1670	1748*	19 Mar	30 Mar
1671	1749	9 Mar*	20 Mar
1672	1750	27 Mar	7 Apr
1673	1751	16 Mar	27 Mar
1674	1752*	5 Mar*	16 Mar
1675	1753	25 Mar	5 Apr

Saka Year	Western Date of New Year (Julian)	Saka Year	Western Date of New Year (Julian)	Saka Year	Western Date of New Year (Julian)	Saka Year	Western Date of New Year (Julian)
1676	1754 24 Mar	1727	1805 31 Mar	1778	1856* 6 Apr	1829	1907 15 Mar*
1677	1755 13 Mar*	1728	1806 21 Mar*	1779	1857 26 Mar	1830	1908* 2 Apr
1678	1756* 31 Mar	1729	1807 9 Apr	1780	1858 16 Mar*	1831	1909 22 Mar*
1679	1757 20 Mar*	1730	1808* 28 Mar	1781	1859 4 Apr	1832	1910 11 Apr
1680	1758 8 Apr	1731	1809 17 Mar*	1782	1860* 23 Mar*	1833	1911 31 Mar
1681	1759 29 Mar	1732	1810 5 Apr	1783	1861 11 Apr	1834	1912* 19 Mar*
1682	1760* 18 Mar*	1733	1811 25 Mar	1784	1862 31 Mar	1835	1913 7 Apr
1683	1761 6 Apr	1734	1812* 14 Mar*	1785	1863 20 Mar*	1836	1914 27 Mar
1684	1762 26 Mar	1735	1813 2 Apr	1786	1864* 7 Apr	1837	1915 16 Mar*
1685	1763 15 Mar*	1736	1814 22 Mar	1787	1865 27 Mar	1838	1916* 4 Apr
1686	1764* 2 Apr	1737	1815 10 Apr*	1788	1866 16 Mar*	1839	1917 24 Mar*
1687	1765 22 Mar	1738	1816* 29 Mar	1789	1867 4 Apr	1840	1918 13 Apr
1688	1766 11 Mar*	1739	1817 18 Mar*	1790	1868* 24 Mar	1841	1919 1 Apr
1689	1767 30 Mar	1740	1818 6 Apr	1791	1869 14 Mar*	1842	1920* 20 Mar*
1690	1768* 19 Mar*	1741	1819 26 Mar	1792	1870 1 Apr	1843	1921 9 Apr
1691	1769 7 Apr	1742	1820* 15 Mar*	1793	1871 22 Mar*	1844	1922 29 Mar
1692	1770 28 Mar	1743	1821 3 Apr	1794	1872* 9 Apr	1845	1923 18 Mar*
1693	1771 17 Mar*	1744	1822 24 Mar	1795	1873 30 Mar	1846	1924* 5 Apr
1694	1772* 4 Apr	1745	1823 13 Mar*	1796	1874 18 Mar*	1847	1925 25 Mar
1695	1773 24 Mar	1746	1824* 31 Mar	1797	1875 6 Apr	1848	1926 14 Mar*
1696	1774 13 Mar*	1747	1825 20 Mar*	1798	1876* 26 Mar	1849	1927 3 Apr
1697	1775 1 Apr	1748	1826 8 Apr	1799	1877 16 Mar*	1850	1928* 22 Mar*
1698	1776* 20 Mar*	1749	1827 28 Mar	1800	1878 3 Apr	1851	1929 10 Apr
1699	1777 8 Apr	1750	1828* 16 Mar*	1801	1879 23 Mar*	1852	1930 30 Mar
1700	1778 29 Mar	1751	1829 4 Apr	1802	1880* 10 Apr	1853	1931 19 Mar*
1701	1779 19 Mar*	1752	1830 25 Mar	1803	1881 31 Mar	1854	1932* 7 Apr
1702	1780* 5 Apr	1753	1831 15 Mar*	1804	1882 19 Mar*	1855	1933 26 Mar
1703	1781 25 Mar	1754	1832* 2 Apr	1805	1883 7 Apr	1856	1934 16 Mar*
1704	1782 14 Mar*	1755	1833 22 Mar*	1806	1884* 28 Mar	1857	1935 4 Apr
1705	1783 2 Apr	1756	1834 10 Apr	1807	1885 16 Mar*	1858	1936* 23 Mar*
1706	1784* 22 Mar	1757	1835 30 Mar	1808	1886 4 Apr	1859	1937 12 Apr
1707	1785 11 Mar*	1758	1836* 18 Mar*	1809	1887 25 Mar	1860	1938 1 Apr
1708	1786 30 Mar	1759	1837 6 Apr	1810	1888* 13 Mar*	1861	1939 22 Mar*
1709	1787 20 Mar*	1760	1838 26 Mar	1811	1889 1 Apr	1862	1940* 8 Apr
1710	1788* 7 Apr	1761	1839 16 Mar*	1812	1890 22 Mar*	1863	1941 28 Mar
1711	1789 27 Mar	1762	1840* 3 Apr	1813	1891 9 Apr	1864	1942 18 Mar*
1712	1790 16 Mar*	1763	1841 24 Mar*	1814	1892* 29 Mar	1865	1943 6 Apr
1713	1791 4 Apr	1764	1842 11 Apr	1815	1893 18 Mar*	1866	1944* 25 Mar
1714	1792* 23 Mar	1765	1843 31 Mar	1816	1894 6 Apr	1867	1945 15 Mar*
1715	1793 13 Mar*	1766	1844* 19 Mar*	1817	1895 26 Mar	1868	1946 2 Apr
1716	1794 1 Apr	1767	1845 7 Apr	1818	1896* 15 Mar*	1869	1947 22 Mar*
1717	1795 21 Mar*	1768	1846 28 Mar	1819	1897 2 Apr	1870	1948* 10 Apr
1718	1796* 8 Apr	1769	1847 17 Mar*	1820	1898 23 Mar*	1871	1949 30 Mar
1719	1797 29 Mar	1770	1848* 4 Apr	1821	1899 1 Apr	1872	1950 20 Mar*
1720	1798 18 Mar*	1771	1849 25 Mar	1822	1900 31 Mar	1873	1951 7 Apr
1721	1799 6 Apr	1772	1850 14 Mar*	1823	1901 20 Mar*	1874	1952* 26 Mar
1722	1800 26 Mar	1773	1851 2 Apr	1824	1902 9 Apr	1875	1953 16 Mar*
1723	1801 15 Mar*	1774	1852* 21 Mar*	1825	1903 28 Mar	1876	1954 4 Apr
1724	1802 3 Apr	1775	1853 10 Apr	1826	1904* 17 Mar*	1877	1955 24 Mar*
1725	1803 24 Mar	1776	1854 29 Mar	1827	1905 6 Apr	1878	1956* 11 Apr
1726	1804* 12 Mar*	1777	1855 19 Mar*	1828	1906 26 Mar	1879	1957 30 Mar

Saka Year	Western Date of New Year (Julian)		Saka Year	Western Date of New Year (Julian)		Saka Year	Western Date of New Year (Julian)		Saka Year	Western Date of New Year (Julian)	
1880	1958	20 Mar*	1891	1969	19 Mar*	1902	1980*	17 Mar*	1913	1991	16 Mar*
1881	1959	9 Apr	1892	1970	7 Apr	1903	1981	5 Apr	1914	1992*	3 Apr
1882	1960*	28 Mar	1893	1971	28 Mar	1904	1982	26 Mar*	1915	1993	24 Mar*
1883	1961	18 Mar*	1894	1972*	16 Mar*	1905	1983	15 Apr	1916	1994	13 Apr
1884	1962	5 Apr	1895	1973	3 Apr	1906	1984*	1 Apr	1917	1995	1 Apr
1885	1963	25 Mar	1896	1974	24 Mar*	1907	1985	22 Mar*	1918	1996*	20 Mar*
1886	1964*	14 Mar*	1897	1975	12 Apr	1908	1986	10 Apr	1919	1997	8 Apr
1887	1965	2 Apr	1898	1976*	31 Mar	1909	1987	31 Mar	1920	1998	29 Mar
1888	1966	22 Mar*	1899	1977	21 Mar*	1910	1988*	19 Mar*	1921	1999	18 Mar*
1889	1967	10 Apr	1900	1978	8 Apr	1911	1989	6 Apr	1922	2000*	5 Apr
1890	1968*	30 Mar	1901	1979	29 Mar	1912	1990	27 Mar			

SOUTHEAST ASIA

SOUTHEAST ASIA

Asia has been the site of numerous civilizations throughout its long history. Nations have risen only to be conquered by outside invaders. Indigeneous cultures and religions have developed and been influenced by outside forces. This great panorama is reflected in the calendars of the region.

Early in history, this area consisted of a series of independent principalities which based their time reckonings on the ancient Kali Yuga, an era dating back to January 21, 3102 B.C., which in turn is said to be based on a much older time scale. In the 11th century, Islam began to spread to the East, and within a short time, Southeast Asia was almost entirely controlled by Muslim governments. Local observatories were destroyed and the use of indigenous calendars officially prohibited. In the 16th century European influence began to penetrate the area, and, as colonization progressed, the Western calendar was imposed. In the 20th century, when these countries regained their independence, the local calendars were often revived and used in conjunction with the Gregorian. In addition to these dominant calendars, a number of others were employed, including the Zoroastrian.

During the 16th and 17th centuries, Akabar, Mogul emperor of India from 1556 to 1605, imposed his calendar on the empire. Akbar had become disillusioned with orthodox Islam and promulgated an eclectic creed of his own, derived from Islam, Zoroastrianism, Hinduism and Christianity. In 1582 he outlawed the Islamic calendar and instituted a solar tropical one which had its epoch at the year of his ascension to the throne, February 19, 1556. His creed died out soon after his death, but the calendar is still used in some areas. The Gregorian form of this calendar is given below. for dates prior to 1582 subtract 10 days.

During the reign of the Emperor Shah Jehan, Islam was restored as the official religion of the Mogul Empire, and in 1636, another calendar was instituted, the Fasli Deccan. It is probably a variant of the Kali Yuga, although there is a two week discrepancy in the zodiacal patterns. In the 19th century the Madras government declared its epoch to be July 12, 590 A.D.

The Parasurama calendar was also used in portions of the region. It is a strictly solar calendar based on the Kali Yuga. In addition to the 60 year cycle of the Kali Yuga, it uses a cycle of 1000 years. At the end of this cycle, the calculations begin over again. Its epoch is the year 1176 B.C., so the first year of the second cycle was the year 176 B.C.; the first year of the third cycle was 825 A.D. The fourth cycle began in 1825 A.D.. The year 2000 will be the 175th year of the fifth cycle. Another peculiarity of this calendar is that the new year begins with the entry of the sun into the sign of Virgo by the sidereal year, rather than at one of the solstices or equinoxes.

BUDDHIST CALENDAR

The Buddhist calendar is used extensively in Southeast Asia. Originating in India, it is a lunar calendar that uses intercalations to bring the lunar year in line with the sidereal solar year. It differs from the Saka calendar in that the year is considered to begin with the full moon in the zodiacal month of Taurus (May). It is used in India as well as in the following areas:

SRI LANKA

Although Ceylon officially utilized the Western calendar since the colonial period, the Buddhist population always used the Buddhist calendar for religious purposes and holidays. After Sri Lanka gained its independence in 1966, the government attempted to make this the official calendar. It was employed officially from 1966 until 1971, when it was again replaced by the Western calendar because of the difficulties of using the Buddhist calendar in international commerce.

THAILAND

Thailand, a largely Buddhist country, uses that calendar except for international commerce and political purposes.

CAMBODIA, LAOS AND VIETNAM

Prior to the Communist takeover of these nations, the Buddhist calendar was used for religious purposes with the Gregorian calendar employed for political and commercial purposes. In Vietnam, with its large Chinese population, the Chinese calendar was also used for religious purposes.

BURMA

While the old Buddhist calendar is observed and the religious New Year is celebrated with the full moon in May, the Burmese also follow the system of the solar sidereal year, and the official New Year is celebrated with the entry of the Sun into the sign of Aries according to the sidereal zodiac. This New Year is called Thingyan Tet, and except in the section of Burma called Arakan, the New Year cannot begin until the hour, minute and second at which the Sun enters Aries. In Arakan only the day is observed. The calendar is given below.

AKBAR CALENDAR

Akbar Year	Western Date (Gregorian) of New Year	Akbar Year	Western Date (Gregorian) of New Year	Akbar Year	Western Date (Gregorian) of New Year	Akbar Year	Western Date (Gregorian) of New Year
1	1556* 19 Feb	12	1567 20 Feb	23	1578 20 Feb	34	1589 21 Feb
2	1557 20 Feb	13	1568* 19 Feb	24	1579 20 Feb	35	1590 21 Feb
3	1558 20 Feb	14	1569 20 Feb	25	1580* 20 Feb	36	1591 21 Feb
4	1559 20 Feb	15	1570 20 Feb	26	1581 21 Feb	37	1592* 20 Feb
5	1560* 19 Feb	16	1571 20 Feb	27	1582 21 Feb	38	1593 21 Feb
6	1561 20 Feb	17	1572* 19 Feb	28	1583 21 Feb	39	1594 21 Feb
7	1562 20 Feb	18	1573 20 Feb	29	1584* 20 Feb	40	1595 21 Feb
8	1563 20 Feb	19	1574 20 Feb	30	1585 21 Feb	41	1596* 20 Feb
9	1564* 19 Feb	20	1575 20 Feb	31	1586 21 Feb	42	1597 21 Feb
10	1565 20 Feb	21	1576* 19 Feb	32	1587 21 Feb	43	1598 21 Feb
11	1566 20 Feb	22	1577 20 Feb	33	1588* 20 Feb	44	1599 21 Feb

Akbar Year	Western Date (Gregorian) of New Year	Akbar Year	Western Date (Gregorian) of New Year	Akbar Year	Western Date (Gregorian) of New Year	Akbar Year	Western Date (Gregorian) of New Year
45	1600* 20 Feb	96	1651 22 Feb	147	1702 23 Feb	198	1753 23 Feb
46	1601 21 Feb	97	1652* 21 Feb	148	1703 23 Feb	199	1754 23 Feb
47	1602 21 Feb	98	1653 22 Feb	149	1704* 22 Feb	200	1755 23 Feb
48	1603 21 Feb	99	1654 22 Feb	150	1705 23 Feb	201	1756* 22 Feb
49	1604* 20 Feb	100	1655 22 Feb	151	1706 23 Feb	202	1757 23 Feb
50	1605 21 Feb	101	1656* 21 Feb	152	1707 23 Feb	203	1758 23 Feb
51	1606 21 Feb	102	1657 22 Feb	153	1708* 22 Feb	204	1759 23 Feb
52	1607 21 Feb	103	1658 22 Feb	154	1709 23 Feb	205	1760* 23 Feb
53	1608* 20 Feb	104	1659 22 Feb	155	1710 23 Feb	206	1761 24 Feb
54	1609 21 Feb	105	1660* 21 Feb	156	1711 23 Feb	207	1762 24 Feb
55	1610 21 Feb	106	1661 22 Feb	157	1712* 22 Feb	208	1763 24 Feb
56	1611 21 Feb	107	1662 22 Feb	158	1713 23 Feb	209	1764* 23 Feb
57	1612* 20 Feb	108	1663 22 Feb	159	1714 23 Feb	210	1765 24 Feb
58	1613 21 Feb	109	1664* 21 Feb	160	1715 23 Feb	211	1766 24 Feb
59	1614 21 Feb	110	1665 22 Feb	161	1716* 22 Feb	212	1767 24 Feb
60	1615 21 Feb	111	1666 22 Feb	162	1717 23 Feb	213	1768* 23 Feb
61	1616* 20 Feb	112	1667 22 Feb	163	1718 23 Feb	214	1769 24 Feb
62	1617 21 Feb	113	1668* 21 Feb	164	1719 23 Feb	215	1770 24 Feb
63	1618 21 Feb	114	1669 22 Feb	165	1720* 22 Feb	216	1771 24 Feb
64	1619 21 Feb	115	1670 22 Feb	166	1721 23 Feb	217	1772* 23 Feb
65	1620* 20 Feb	116	1671 22 Feb	167	1722 23 Feb	218	1773 24 Feb
66	1621 21 Feb	117	1672* 21 Feb	168	1723 23 Feb	219	1774 24 Feb
67	1622 21 Feb	118	1673 22 Feb	169	1724* 22 Feb	220	1775 24 Feb
68	1623 21 Feb	119	1674 22 Feb	170	1725 23 Feb	221	1776* 23 Feb
69	1624* 20 Feb	120	1675 22 Feb	171	1726 23 Feb	222	1777 24 Feb
70	1625 21 Feb	121	1676* 21 Feb	172	1727 23 Feb	223	1778 24 Feb
71	1626 21 Feb	122	1677 22 Feb	173	1728* 22 Feb	224	1779 24 Feb
72	1627 21 Feb	123	1678 22 Feb	174	1729 23 Feb	225	1780* 23 Feb
73	1628* 20 Feb	124	1679 22 Feb	175	1730 23 Feb	226	1781 24 Feb
74	1629 21 Feb	125	1680* 21 Feb	176	1731 23 Feb	227	1782 24 Feb
75	1630 21 Feb	126	1681 22 Feb	177	1732* 22 Feb	228	1783 24 Feb
76	1631 21 Feb	127	1682 22 Feb	178	1733 23 Feb	229	1784* 23 Feb
77	1632* 20 Feb	128	1683 22 Feb	179	1734 23 Feb	230	1785 24 Feb
78	1633 21 Feb	129	1684* 21 Feb	180	1735 23 Feb	231	1786 24 Feb
79	1634 21 Feb	130	1685 22 Feb	181	1736* 22 Feb	232	1787 24 Feb
80	1635 21 Feb	131	1686 22 Feb	182	1737 23 Feb	233	1788* 23 Feb
81	1636* 20 Feb	132	1687 22 Feb	183	1738 23 Feb	234	1789 24 Feb
82	1637 21 Feb	133	1688* 21 Feb	184	1739 23 Feb	235	1790 24 Feb
83	1638 21 Feb	134	1689 22 Feb	185	1740* 22 Feb	236	1791 24 Feb
84	1639 21 Feb	135	1690 22 Feb	186	1741 23 Feb	237	1792* 23 Feb
85	1640* 21 Feb	136	1691 22 Feb	187	1742 23 Feb	238	1793 24 Feb
86	1641 22 Feb	137	1692* 21 Feb	188	1743 23 Feb	239	1794 24 Feb
87	1642 22 Feb	138	1693 22 Feb	189	1744* 22 Feb	240	1795 24 Feb
88	1643 22 Feb	139	1694 22 Feb	190	1745 23 Feb	241	1796* 23 Feb
89	1644* 21 Feb	140	1695 22 Feb	191	1746 23 Feb	242	1797 24 Feb
90	1645 22 Feb	141	1696* 21 Feb	192	1747 23 Feb	243	1798 24 Feb
91	1646 22 Feb	142	1697 22 Feb	193	1748* 22 Feb	244	1799 24 Feb
92	1647 22 Feb	143	1698 22 Feb	194	1749 23 Feb	245	1800 23 Feb
93	1648* 21 Feb	144	1699 22 Feb	195	1750 23 Feb	246	1801 24 Feb
94	1649 22 Feb	145	1700 22 Feb	196	1751 23 Feb	247	1802 24 Feb
95	1650 22 Feb	146	1701 23 Feb	197	1752* 22 Feb	248	1803 24 Feb

Akbar Year	Western Date (Gregorian) of New Year	Akbar Year	Western Date (Gregorian) of New Year	Akbar Year	Western Date (Gregorian) of New Year	Akbar Year	Western Date (Gregorian) of New Year
249	1804* 23 Feb	298	1853 25 Feb	347	1902 26 Feb	395	1950 27 Feb
250	1805 24 Feb	299	1854 25 Feb	348	1903 26 Feb	396	1951 27 Feb
251	1806 24 Feb	300	1855 25 Feb	349	1904* 25 Feb	397	1952* 26 Feb
252	1807 24 Feb	301	1856* 24 Feb	350	1905 26 Feb	398	1953 27 Feb
253	1808* 23 Feb	302	1857 25 Feb	351	1906 26 Feb	399	1954 27 Feb
254	1809 24 Feb	303	1858 25 Feb	352	1907 26 Feb	400	1955 27 Feb
255	1810 24 Feb	304	1859 25 Feb	353	1908* 25 Feb	401	1956* 26 Feb
256	1811 24 Feb	305	1860* 24 Feb	354	1909 26 Feb	402	1957 27 Feb
257	1812* 23 Feb	306	1861 25 Feb	355	1910 26 Feb	403	1958 27 Feb
258	1813 24 Feb	307	1862 25 Feb	356	1911 26 Feb	404	1959 27 Feb
259	1814 24 Feb	308	1863 25 Feb	357	1912* 25 Feb	405	1960* 26 Feb
260	1815 24 Feb	309	1864* 24 Feb	358	1913 26 Feb	406	1961 27 Feb
261	1816* 23 Feb	310	1865 25 Feb	359	1914 26 Feb	407	1962 27 Feb
262	1817 24 Feb	311	1866 25 Feb	360	1915 26 Feb	408	1963 27 Feb
263	1818 24 Feb	312	1867 25 Feb	361	1916* 25 Feb	409	1964* 26 Feb
264	1819 24 Feb	313	1868* 24 Feb	362	1917 26 Feb	410	1965 27 Feb
265	1820* 24 Feb	314	1869 25 Feb	363	1918 26 Feb	411	1966 27 Feb
266	1821 25 Feb	315	1870 25 Feb	364	1919 26 Feb	412	1967 27 Feb
267	1822 25 Feb	316	1871 25 Feb	365	1920* 25 Feb	413	1968* 26 Feb
268	1823 25 Feb	317	1872* 24 Feb	366	1921 26 Feb	414	1969 27 Feb
269	1824* 24 Feb	318	1873 25 Feb	367	1922 26 Feb	415	1970 27 Feb
270	1825 25 Feb	319	1874 25 Feb	368	1923 26 Feb	416	1971 27 Feb
271	1826 25 Feb	320	1875 25 Feb	369	1924* 25 Feb	417	1972* 26 Feb
272	1827 25 Feb	321	1876* 24 Feb	370	1925 26 Feb	418	1973 27 Feb
273	1828* 24 Feb	322	1877 25 Feb	371	1926 26 Feb	419	1974 27 Feb
274	1829 25 Feb	323	1878 25 Feb	372	1927 26 Feb	420	1975 27 Feb
275	1830 25 Feb	324	1879 25 Feb	373	1928* 25 Feb	421	1976* 26 Feb
276	1831 25 Feb	325	1880* 25 Feb	374	1929 26 Feb	422	1977 27 Feb
277	1832* 24 Feb	326	1881 26 Feb	375	1930 26 Feb	423	1978 27 Feb
278	1833 25 Feb	327	1882 26 Feb	376	1931 26 Feb	424	1979 27 Feb
279	1834 25 Feb	328	1883 26 Feb	377	1932* 25 Feb	425	1980* 26 Feb
280	1835 25 Feb	329	1884* 25 Feb	378	1933 26 Feb	426	1981 27 Feb
281	1836* 24 Feb	330	1885 26 Feb	379	1934 26 Feb	427	1982 27 Feb
282	1837 25 Feb	331	1886 26 Feb	380	1935 26 Feb	428	1983 27 Feb
283	1838 25 Feb	332	1887 26 Feb	381	1936* 25 Feb	429	1984* 26 Feb
284	1839 25 Feb	333	1888* 25 Feb	382	1937 26 Feb	430	1985 27 Feb
285	1840* 24 Feb	334	1889 26 Feb	383	1938 26 Feb	431	1986 27 Feb
286	1841 25 Feb	335	1890 26 Feb	384	1939 26 Feb	432	1987 27 Feb
287	1842 25 Feb	336	1891 26 Feb	385	1940* 26 Feb	433	1988* 26 Feb
288	1843 25 Feb	337	1892* 25 Feb	386	1941 27 Feb	434	1989 27 Feb
289	1844* 24 Feb	338	1893 26 Feb	387	1942 27 Feb	435	1990 27 Feb
290	1845 25 Feb	339	1894 26 Feb	388	1943 27 Feb	436	1991 27 Feb
291	1846 25 Feb	340	1895 26 Feb	389	1944* 26 Feb	437	1992* 26 Feb
292	1847 25 Feb	341	1896* 25 Feb	390	1945 27 Feb	438	1993 27 Feb
293	1848* 24 Feb	342	1897 26 Feb	391	1946 27 Feb	439	1994 27 Feb
294	1849 25 Feb	343	1898 26 Feb	392	1947 27 Feb	440	1995 27 Feb
295	1850 25 Feb	344	1899 26 Feb	393	1948* 26 Feb	441	1996* 26 Feb
296	1851 25 Feb	345	1900 25 Feb	394	1949 27 Feb	442	1997 27 Feb
297	1852* 24 Feb	346	1901 26 Feb				

FASLI DECCAN CALENDAR

Fasli Deccan Year	Western Date (Gregorian) of New Year	Fasli Deccan Year	Western Date (Gregorian) of New Year	Fasli Deccan Year	Western Date (Gregorian) of New Year	Fasli Deccan Year	Western Date (Gregorian) of New Year
1	590 12 Jul	50	639 13 Jul	99	688* 14 Jul	148	737 13 Jul
2	591 12 Jul	51	640* 13 Jul	100	689 13 Jul	149	738 14 Jul
3	592* 12 Jul	52	641 12 Jul	101	690 14 Jul	150	739 14 Jul
4	593 11 Jul	53	642 13 Jul	102	691 14 Jul	151	740* 14 Jul
5	594 12 Jul	54	643 13 Jul	103	692* 14 Jul	152	741 14 Jul
6	595 12 Jul	55	644* 13 Jul	104	693 13 Jul	153	742 15 Jul
7	596* 12 Jul	56	645 12 Jul	105	694 14 Jul	154	743 15 Jul
8	597 11 Jul	57	646 13 Jul	106	695 14 Jul	155	744* 15 Jul
9	598 12 Jul	58	647 13 Jul	107	696* 14 Jul	156	745 14 Jul
10	599 12 Jul	59	648* 13 Jul	108	697 13 Jul	157	746 15 Jul
11	600* 12 Jul	60	649 12 Jul	109	698 14 Jul	158	747 15 Jul
12	601 11 Jul	61	650 13 Jul	110	699 14 Jul	159	748* 15 Jul
13	602 12 Jul	62	651 13 Jul	111	700* 14 Jul	160	749 14 Jul
14	603 12 Jul	63	652* 13 Jul	112	701 13 Jul	161	750 15 Jul
15	604* 12 Jul	64	653 12 Jul	113	702 14 Jul	162	751 15 Jul
16	605 11 Jul	65	654 13 Jul	114	703 14 Jul	163	752* 15 Jul
17	606 12 Jul	66	655 13 Jul	115	704* 14 Jul	164	753 14 Jul
18	607 12 Jul	67	656* 13 Jul	116	705 13 Jul	165	754 15 Jul
19	608* 12 Jul	68	657 12 Jul	117	706 14 Jul	166	755 15 Jul
20	609 11 Jul	69	658 13 Jul	118	707 14 Jul	167	756* 15 Jul
21	610 12 Jul	70	659 13 Jul	119	708* 14 Jul	168	757 14 Jul
22	611 12 Jul	71	660* 13 Jul	120	709 13 Jul	169	758 15 Jul
23	612* 12 Jul	72	661 12 Jul	121	710 14 Jul	170	759 15 Jul
24	613 11 Jul	73	662 13 Jul	122	711 14 Jul	171	760* 15 Jul
25	614 12 Jul	74	663 13 Jul	123	712* 14 Jul	172	761 14 Jul
26	615 12 Jul	75	664* 13 Jul	124	713 13 Jul	173	762 15 Jul
27	616* 12 Jul	76	665 12 Jul	125	714 14 Jul	174	763 15 Jul
28	617 12 Jul	77	666 13 Jul	126	715 14 Jul	175	764* 15 Jul
29	618 13 Jul	78	667 13 Jul	127	716* 14 Jul	176	765 14 Jul
30	619 13 Jul	79	668* 13 Jul	128	717 13 Jul	177	766 15 Jul
31	620* 13 Jul	80	669 12 Jul	129	718 14 Jul	178	767 15 Jul
32	621 12 Jui	81	670 13 Jul	130	719 14 Jul	179	768* 15 Jul
33	622 13 Jul	82	671 13 Jul	131	720* 14 Jul	180	769 14 Jul
34	623 13 Jul	83	672* 13 Jul	132	721 13 Jul	181	770 15 Jul
35	624* 13 Jul	84	673 12 Jul	133	722 14 Jul	182	771 15 Jul
36	625 12 Jul	85	674 13 Jul	134	723 14 Jul	183	772* 15 Jul
37	626 13 Jul	86	675 13 Jul	135	724* 14 Jul	184	773 14 Jul
38	627 13 Jul	87	676* 13 Jul	136	725 13 Jul	185	774 15 Jul
39	628* 13 Jul	88	677 12 Jul	137	726 14 Jul	186	775 15 Jul
40	629 12 Jul	89	678 13 Jul	138	727 14 Jul	187	776* 15 Jul
41	630 13 Jul	90	679 13 Jul	139	728* 14 Jul	188	777 14 Jul
42	631 13 Jul	91	680* 13 Jul	140	729 13 Jul	189	778 15 Jul
43	632* 13 Jul	92	681 13 Jul	141	730 14 Jul	190	779 15 Jul
44	633 12 Jul	93	682 14 Jul	142	731 14 Jul	191	780* 15 Jul
45	634 13 Jul	94	683 14 Jul	143	732* 14 Jul	192	781 14 Jul
46	635 13 Jul	95	684* 14 Jul	144	733 13 Jul	193	782 15 Jul
47	636* 13 Jul	96	685 13 Jul	145	734 14 Jul	194	783 15 Jul
48	637 12 Jul	97	686 14 Jul	146	735 14 Jul	195	784* 15 Jul
49	638 13 Jul	98	687 14 Jul	147	736* 14 Jul	196	785 14 Jul

Fasli Deccan Year	Western Date (Gregorian) of New Year	Fasli Deccan Year	Western Date (Gregorian) of New Year	Fasli Deccan Year	Western Date (Gregorian) of New Year	Fasli Deccan Year	Western Date (Gregorian) of New Year
197	786 15 Jul	248	837 14 Jul	299	888* 16 Jul	350	939 17 Jul
198	787 15 Jul	249	838 15 Jul	300	889 15 Jul	351	940* 17 Jul
199	788* 15 Jul	250	839 15 Jul	301	890 16 Jul	352	941 16 Jul
200	789 14 Jul	251	840* 15 Jul	302	891 16 Jul	353	942 17 Jul
201	790 15 Jul	252	841 14 Jul	303	892* 16 Jul	354	943 17 Jul
202	791 15 Jul	253	842 15 Jul	304	893 15 Jul	355	944* 17 Jul
203	792* 15 Jul	254	843 15 Jul	305	894 16 Jul	356	945 16 Jul
204	793 14 Jul	255	844* 15 Jul	306	895 16 Jul	357	946 17 Jul
205	794 15 Jul	256	845 14 Jul	307	896* 16 Jul	358	947 17 Jul
206	795 15 Jul	257	846 15 Jul	308	897 15 Jul	359	948* 17 Jul
207	796* 15 Jul	258	847 15 Jul	309	898 16 Jul	360	949 16 Jul
208	797 14 Jul	259	848* 15 Jul	310	899 16 Jul	361	950 17 Jul
209	798 15 Jul	260	849 14 Jul	311	900* 16 Jul	362	951 17 Jul
210	799 15 Jul	261	850 15 Jul	312	901 15 Jul	363	952* 17 Jul
211	800* 15 Jul	262	851 15 Jul	313	902 16 Jul	364	953 16 Jul
212	801 14 Jul	263	852* 15 Jul	314	903 16 Jul	365	954 17 Jul
213	802 15 Jul	264	853 14 Jul	315	904* 16 Jul	366	955 17 Jul
214	803 15 Jul	265	854 15 Jul	316	905 15 Jul	367	956* 17 Jul
215	804* 15 Jul	266	855 15 Jul	317	906 16 Jul	368	957 16 Jul
216	805 14 Jul	267	856* 15 Jul	318	907 16 Jul	369	958 17 Jul
217	806 15 Jul	268	857 14 Jul	319	908* 16 Jul	370	959 17 Jul
218	807 15 Jul	269	858 15 Jul	320	909 15 Jul	371	960* 17 Jul
219	808* 15 Jul	270	859 15 Jul	321	910 16 Jul	372	961 16 Jul
220	809 14 Jul	271	860* 15 Jul	322	911 16 Jul	373	962 17 Jul
221	810 15 Jul	272	861 15 Jul	323	912* 16 Jul	374	963 17 Jul
222	811 15 Jul	273	862 16 Jul	324	913 15 Jul	375	964* 17 Jul
223	812* 15 Jul	274	863 16 Jul	325	914 16 Jul	376	965 16 Jul
224	813 14 Jul	275	864* 16 Jul	326	915 16 Jul	377	966 17 Jul
225	814 15 Jul	276	865 15 Jul	327	916* 16 Jul	378	967 17 Jul
226	815 15 Jul	277	866 16 Jul	328	917 15 Jul	379	968* 17 Jul
227	816* 15 Jul	278	867 16 Jul	329	918 16 Jul	380	969 16 Jul
228	817 14 Jul	279	868* 16 Jul	330	919 16 Jul	381	970 17 Jul
229	818 15 Jul	280	869 15 Jul	331	920* 16 Jul	382	971 17 Jul
230	819 15 Jul	281	870 16 Jul	332	921 16 Jul	383	972* 17 Jul
231	820* 15 Jul	282	871 16 Jul	333	922 17 Jul	384	973 16 Jul
232	821 14 Jul	283	872* 16 Jul	334	923 17 Jul	385	974 17 Jul
233	822 15 Jul	284	873 15 Jul	335	924* 17 Jul	386	975 17 Jul
234	823 15 Jul	285	874 16 Jul	336	925 16 Jul	387	976* 17 Jul
235	824* 15 Jul	286	875 16 Jul	337	926 17 Jul	388	977 16 Jul
236	825 14 Jul	287	876* 16 Jul	338	927 17 Jul	389	978 17 Jul
237	826 15 Jul	288	877 15 Jul	339	928* 17 Jul	390	979 17 Jul
238	827 15 Jul	289	878 16 Jul	340	929 16 Jul	391	980* 17 Jul
239	828* 15 Jul	290	879 16 Jul	341	930 17 Jul	392	981 17 Jul
240	829 14 Jul	291	880* 16 Jul	342	931 17 Jul	393	982 18 Jul
241	830 15 Jul	292	881 15 Jul	343	932* 17 Jul	394	983 18 Jul
242	831 15 Jul	293	882 16 Jul	344	933 16 Jul	395	984* 18 Jul
243	832* 15 Jul	294	883 16 Jul	345	934 17 Jul	396	985 17 Jul
244	833 14 Jul	295	884* 16 Jul	346	935 17 Jul	397	986 18 Jul
245	834 15 Jul	296	885 15 Jul	347	936* 17 Jul	398	987 18 Jul
246	835 15 Jul	297	886 16 Jul	348	937 16 Jul	399	988* 18 Jul
247	836* 15 Jul	298	887 16 Jul	349	938 17 Jul	400	989 17 Jul

Fasli Deccan Year	Western Date (Gregorian) of New Year	Fasli Deccan Year	Western Date (Gregorian) of New Year	Fasli Deccan Year	Western Date (Gregorian) of New Year	Fasli Deccan Year	Western Date (Gregorian) of New Year
401	990 18 Jul	452	1041 18 Jul	503	1092* 19 Jul	554	1143 20 Jul
402	991 18 Jul	453	1042 19 Jul	504	1093 18 Jul	555	1144* 20 Jul
403	992* 18 Jul	454	1043 19 Jul	505	1094 19 Jul	556	1145 19 Jul
404	993 17 Jul	455	1044* 19 Jul	506	1095 19 Jul	557	1146 20 Jul
405	994 18 Jul	456	1045 18 Jul	507	1096* 19 Jul	558	1147 20 Jul
406	995 18 Jul	457	1046 19 Jul	508	1097 18 Jul	559	1148* 20 Jul
407	996* 18 Jul	458	1047 19 Jul	509	1098 19 Jul	560	1149 19 Jul
408	997 17 Jul	459	1048* 19 Jul	510	1099 19 Jul	561	1150 20 Jul
409	998 18 Jul	460	1049 18 Jul	511	1100* 19 Jul	562	1151 20 Jul
410	999 18 Jul	461	1050 19 Jul	512	1101 19 Jul	563	1152* 20 Jul
411	1000* 18 Jul	462	1051 19 Jul	513	1102 20 Jul	564	1153 19 Jul
412	1001 17 Jul	463	1052* 19 Jul	514	1103 20 Jul	565	1154 20 Jul
413	1002 18 Jul	464	1053 18 Jul	515	1104* 20 Jul	566	1155 20 Jul
414	1003 18 Jul	465	1054 19 Jul	516	1105 19 Jul	567	1156* 20 Jul
415	1004* 18 Jul	466	1055 19 Jul	517	1106 20 Jul	568	1157 19 Jul
416	1005 17 Jul	467	1056* 19 Jul	518	1107 20 Jul	569	1158 20 Jul
417	1006 18 Jul	468	1057 18 Jul	519	1108* 20 Jul	570	1159 20 Jul
418	1007 18 Jul	469	1058 19 Jul	520	1109 19 Jul	571	1160* 20 Jul
419	1008* 18 Jul	470	1059 19 Jul	521	1110 20 Jul	572	1161 20 Jul
420	1009 17 Jul	471	1060* 19 Jul	522	1111 20 Jul	573	1162 21 Jul
421	1010 18 Jul	472	1061 18 Jul	523	1112* 20 Jul	574	1163 21 Jul
422	1011 18 Jul	473	1062 19 Jul	524	1113 19 Jul	575	1164* 21 Jul
423	1012* 18 Jul	474	1063 19 Jul	525	1114 20 Jul	576	1165 20 Jul
424	1013 17 Jul	475	1064* 19 Jul	526	1115 20 Jul	577	1166 21 Jul
425	1014 18 Jul	476	1065 18 Jul	527	1116* 20 Jul	578	1167 21 Jul
426	1015 18 Jul	477	1066 19 Jul	528	1117 19 Jul	579	1168* 21 Jul
427	1016* 18 Jul	478	1067 19 Jul	529	1118 20 Jul	580	1169 20 Jul
428	1017 17 Jul	479	1068* 19 Jul	530	1119 20 Jul	581	1170 21 Jul
429	1018 18 Jul	480	1069 18 Jul	531	1120* 20 Jul	582	1171 21 Jul
430	1019 18 Jul	481	1070 19 Jul	532	1121 19 Jul	583	1172* 21 Jul
431	1020* 18 Jul	482	1071 19 Jul	533	1122 20 Jul	584	1173 20 Jul
432	1021 17 Jul	483	1072* 19 Jul	534	1123 20 Jul	585	1174 21 Jul
433	1022 18 Jul	484	1073 18 Jul	535	1124* 20 Jul	586	1175 21 Jul
434	1023 18 Jul	485	1074 19 Jul	536	1125 19 Jul	587	1176* 21 Jul
435	1024* 18 Jul	486	1075 19 Jul	537	1126 20 Jul	588	1177 20 Jul
436	1025 17 Jul	487	1076* 19 Jul	538	1127 20 Jul	589	1178 21 Jul
437	1026 18 Jul	488	1077 18 Jul	539	1128* 20 Jul	590	1179 21 Jul
438	1027 18 Jul	489	1078 19 Jul	540	1129 19 Jul	591	1180* 21 Jul
439	1028* 18 Jul	490	1079 19 Jul	541	1130 20 Jul	592	1181 20 Jul
440	1029 17 Jul	491	1080* 19 Jul	542	1131 20 Jul	593	1182 21 Jul
441	1030 18 Jul	492	1081 18 Jul	543	1132* 20 Jul	594	1183 21 Jul
442	1031 18 Jul	493	1082 19 Jul	544	1133 19 Jul	595	1184* 21 Jul
443	1032* 18 Jul	494	1083 19 Jul	545	1134 20 Jul	596	1185 20 Jul
444	1033 17 Jul	495	1084* 19 Jul	546	1135 20 Jul	597	1186 21 Jul
445	1034 18 Jul	496	1085 18 Jul	547	1136* 20 Jul	598	1187 21 Jul
446	1035 18 Jul	497	1086 19 Jul	548	1137 19 Jul	599	1188* 21 Jul
447	1036* 18 Jul	498	1087 19 Jul	549	1138 20 Jul	600	1189 20 Jul
448	1037 17 Jul	499	1088* 19 Jul	550	1139 20 Jul	601	1190 21 Jul
449	1038 18 Jul	500	1089 18 Jul	551	1140* 20 Jul	602	1191 21 Jul
450	1039 18 Jul	501	1090 19 Jul	552	1141 19 Jul	603	1192* 21 Jul
451	1040* 18 Jul	502	1091 19 Jul	553	1142 20 Jul	604	1193 20 Jul

Fasli Deccan Year	Western Date (Gregorian) of New Year	Fasli Deccan Year	Western Date (Gregorian) of New Year	Fasli Deccan Year	Western Date (Gregorian) of New Year	Fasli Deccan Year	Western Date (Gregorian) of New Year
605	1194 21 Jul	656	1245 21 Jul	707	1296* 23 Jul	758	1347 24 Jul
606	1195 21 Jul	657	1246 22 Jul	708	1297 22 Jul	759	1348* 24 Jul
607	1196* 21 Jul	658	1247 22 Jul	709	1298 23 Jul	760	1349 23 Jul
608	1197 20 Jul	659	1248* 22 Jul	710	1299 23 Jul	761	1350 24 Jul
609	1198 21 Jul	660	1249 21 Jul	711	1300* 23 Jul	762	1351 24 Jul
610	1199 21 Jul	661	1250 22 Jul	712	1301 22 Jul	763	1352* 24 Jul
611	1200* 21 Jul	662	1251 22 Jul	713	1302 23 Jul	764	1353 23 Jul
612	1201 20 Jul	663	1252* 22 Jul	714	1303 23 Jul	765	1354 24 Jul
613	1202 21 Jul	664	1253 21 Jul	715	1304* 23 Jul	766	1355 24 Jul
614	1203 21 Jul	665	1254 22 Jul	716	1305 22 Jul	767	1356* 24 Jul
615	1204* 21 Jul	666	1255 22 Jul	717	1306 23 Jul	768	1357 23 Jul
616	1205 20 Jul	667	1256* 22 Jul	718	1307 23 Jul	769	1358 24 Jul
617	1206 21 Jul	668	1257 21 Jul	719	1308* 23 Jul	770	1359 24 Jul
618	1207 21 Jul	669	1258 22 Jul	720	1309 22 Jul	771	1360* 24 Jul
619	1208* 21 Jul	670	1259 22 Jul	721	1310 23 Jul	772	1361 23 Jul
620	1209 20 Jul	671	1260* 22 Jul	722	1311 23 Jul	773	1362 24 Jul
621	1210 21 Jul	672	1261 21 Jul	723	1312* 23 Jul	774	1363 24 Jul
622	1211 21 Jul	673	1262 22 Jul	724	1313 22 Jul	775	1364* 24 Jul
623	1212* 21 Jul	674	1263 22 Jul	725	1314 23 Jul	776	1365 23 Jul
624	1213 20 Jul	675	1264* 22 Jul	726	1315 23 Jul	777	1366 24 Jul
625	1214 21 Jul	676	1265 21 Jul	727	1316* 23 Jul	778	1367 24 Jul
626	1215 21 Jul	677	1266 22 Jul	728	1317 22 Jul	779	1368* 24 Jul
627	1216* 21 Jul	678	1267 22 Jul	729	1318 23 Jul	780	1369 23 Jul
628	1217 20 Jul	679	1268* 22 Jul	730	1319 23 Jul	781	1370 24 Jul
629	1218 21 Jul	680	1269 21 Jul	731	1320* 23 Jul	782	1371 24 Jul
630	1219 21 Jul	681	1270 22 Jul	732	1321 22 Jul	783	1372* 24 Jul
631	1220* 21 Jul	682	1271 22 Jul	733	1322 23 Jul	784	1373 23 Jul
632	1221 21 Jul	683	1272* 22 Jul	734	1323 23 Jul	785	1374 24 Jul
633	1222 22 Jul	684	1273 21 Jul	735	1324* 23 Jul	786	1375 24 Jul
634	1223 22 Jul	685	1274 22 Jul	736	1325 22 Jul	787	1376* 24 Jul
635	1224* 22 Jul	686	1275 22 Jul	737	1326 23 Jul	788	1377 23 Jul
636	1225 21 Jul	687	1276* 22 Jul	738	1327 23 Jul	789	1378 24 Jul
637	1226 22 Jul	688	1277 21 Jul	739	1328* 23 Jul	790	1379 24 Jul
638	1227 22 Jul	689	1278 22 Jul	740	1329 22 Jul	791	1380* 24 Jul
639	1228* 22 Jul	690	1279 22 Jul	741	1330 23 Jul	792	1381 23 Jul
640	1229 21 Jul	691	1280* 22 Jul	742	1331 23 Jul	793	1382 24 Jul
641	1230 22 Jul	692	1281 22 Jul	743	1332* 23 Jul	794	1383 24 Jul
642	1231 22 Jul	693	1282 23 Jul	744	1333 22 Jul	795	1384* 24 Jul
643	1232* 22 Jul	694	1283 23 Jul	745	1334 23 Jul	796	1385 23 Jul
644	1233 21 Jul	695	1284* 23 Jul	746	1335 23 Jul	797	1386 24 Jul
645	1234 22 Jul	696	1285 22 Jul	747	1336* 23 Jul	798	1387 24 Jul
646	1235 22 Jul	697	1286 23 Jul	748	1337 22 Jul	799	1388* 24 Jul
647	1236* 22 Jul	698	1287 23 Jul	749	1338 23 Jul	800	1389 23 Jul
648	1237 21 Jul	699	1288* 23 Jul	750	1339 23 Jul	801	1390 24 Jul
649	1238 22 Jul	700	1289 22 Jul	751	1340* 23 Jul	802	1391 24 Jul
650	1239 22 Jul	701	1290 23 Jul	752	1341 23 Jul	803	1392* 24 Jul
651	1240* 22 Jul	702	1291 23 Jul	753	1342 24 Jul	804	1393 24 Jul
652	1241 21 Jul	703	1292* 23 Jul	754	1343 24 Jul	805	1394 25 Jul
653	1242 22 Jul	704	1293 22 Jul	755	1344* 24 Jul	806	1395 25 Jul
654	1243 22 Jul	705	1294 23 Jul	756	1345 23 Jul	807	1396* 25 Jul
655	1244* 22 Ju'	706	1295 23 Jul	757	1346 24 Jul	808	1397 24 Jul

Fasli Deccan Year	Western Date (Gregorian) of New Year	Fasli Deccan Year	Western Date (Gregorian) of New Year	Fasli Deccan Year	Western Date (Gregorian) of New Year	Fasli Deccan Year	Western Date (Gregorian) of New Year
809	1398 25 Jul	860	1449 24 Jul	911	1500* 26 Jul	962	1551 27 Jul
810	1399 25 Jul	861	1450 25 Jul	912	1501 25 Jul	963	1552* 27 Jul
811	1400* 25 Jul	862	1451 25 Jul	913	1502 26 Jul	964	1553 26 Jul
812	1401 24 Jul	863	1452* 25 Jul	914	1503 26 Jul	965	1554 27 Jul
813	1402 25 Jul	864	1453 24 Jul	915	1504* 26 Jul	966	1555 27 Jul
814	1403 25 Jul	865	1454 25 Jul	916	1505 25 Jul	967	1556* 27 Jul
815	1404* 25 Jul	866	1455 25 Jul	917	1506 26 Jul	968	1557 26 Jul
816	1405 24 Jul	867	1456* 25 Jul	918	1507 26 Jul	969	1558 27 Jul
817	1406 25 Jul	868	1457 24 Jul	919	1508* 26 Jul	970	1559 27 Jul
818	1407 25 Jul	869	1458 25 Jul	920	1509 25 Jul	971	1560* 27 Jul
819	1408* 25 Jul	870	1459 25 Jul	921	1510 26 Jul	972	1561 26 Jul
820	1409 24 Jul	871	1460* 25 Jul	922	1511 26 Jul	973	1562 27 Jul
821	1410 25 Jul	872	1461 25 Jul	923	1512* 26 Jul	974	1563 27 Jul
822	1411 25 Jul	873	1462 26 Jul	924	1513 25 Jul	975	1564* 27 Jul
823	1412* 25 Jul	874	1463 26 Jul	925	1514 26 Jul	976	1565 26 Jul
824	1413 24 Jul	875	1464* 26 Jul	926	1515 26 Jul	977	1566 27 Jul
825	1414 25 Jul	876	1465 25 Jul	927	1516* 26 Jul	978	1567 27 Jul
826	1415 25 Jul	877	1466 26 Jul	928	1517 25 Jul	979	1568* 27 Jul
827	1416* 25 Jul	878	1467 26 Jul	929	1518 26 Jul	980	1569 26 Jul
828	1417 24 Jul	879	1468* 26 Jul	930	1519 26 Jul	981	1570 27 Jul
829	1418 25 Jul	880	1469 25 Jul	931	1520* 26 Jul	982	1571 27 Jul
830	1419 25 Jul	881	1470 26 Jul	932	1521 26 Jul	983	1572* 27 Jul
831	1420* 25 Jul	882	1471 26 Jul	933	1522 27 Jul	984	1573 26 Jul
832	1421 24 Jul	883	1472* 26 Jul	934	1523 27 Jul	985	1574 27 Jul
833	1422 25 Jul	884	1473 25 Jul	935	1524* 27 Jul	986	1575 27 Jul
834	1423 25 Jul	885	1474 26 Jul	936	1525 26 Jul	987	1576* 27 Jul
835	1424* 25 Jul	886	1475 26 Jul	937	1526 27 Jul	988	1577 26 Jul
836	1425 24 Jul	887	1476* 26 Jul	938	1527 27 Jul	989	1578 27 Jul
837	1426 25 Jul	888	1477 25 Jul	939	1528* 27 Jul	990	1579 27 Jul
838	1427 25 Jul	889	1478 26 Jul	940	1529 26 Jul	991	1580* 27 Jul
839	1428* 25 Jul	890	1479 26 Jul	941	1530 27 Jul	992	1581 27 Jul
840	1429 24 Jul	891	1480* 26 Jul	942	1531 27 Jul	993	1582 28 Jul
841	1430 25 Jul	892	1481 25 Jul	943	1532* 27 Jul	994	1583 28 Jul
842	1431 25 Jul	893	1482 26 Jul	944	1533 26 Jul	995	1584* 28 Jul
843	1432* 25 Jul	894	1483 26 Jul	945	1534 27 Jul	996	1585 27 Jul
844	1433 24 Jul	895	1484* 26 Jul	946	1535 27 Jul	997	1586 28 Jul
845	1434 25 Jul	896	1485 25 Jul	947	1536* 27 Jul	998	1587 28 Jul
846	1435 25 Jul	897	1486 26 Jul	948	1537 26 Jul	999	1588* 28 Jul
847	1436* 25 Jul	898	1487 26 Jul	949	1538 27 Jul	1000	1589 27 Jul
848	1437 24 Jul	899	1488* 26 Jul	950	1539 27 Jul	1001	1590 28 Jul
849	1438 25 Jul	900	1489 25 Jul	951	1540* 27 Jul	1002	1591 28 Jul
850	1439 25 Jul	901	1490 26 Jul	952	1541 26 Jul	1003	1592* 28 Jul
851	1440* 25 Jul	902	1491 26 Jul	953	1542 27 Jul	1004	1593 27 Jul
852	1441 24 Jul	903	1492* 26 Jul	954	1543 27 Jul	1005	1594 28 Jul
853	1442 25 Jul	904	1493 25 Jul	955	1544* 27 Jul	1006	1595 28 Jul
854	1443 25 Jul	905	1494 26 Jul	956	1545 26 Jul	1007	1596* 28 Jul
855	1444* 25 Jul	906	1495 26 Jul	957	1546 27 Jul	1008	1597 27 Jul
856	1445 24 Jul	907	1496* 26 Jul	958	1547 27 Jul	1009	1598 28 Jul
857	1446 25 Jul	908	1497 25 Jul	959	1548* 27 Jul	1010	1599 28 Jul
858	1447 25 Jul	909	1498 26 Jul	960	1549 26 Jul	1011	1600* 28 Jul
859	1448* 25 Jul	910	1499 26 Jul	961	1550 27 Jul	1012	1601 27 Jul

Fasli Deccan Year	Western Date (Gregorian) of New Year	Fasli Deccan Year	Western Date (Gregorian) of New Year	Fasli Deccan Year	Western Date (Gregorian) of New Year	Fasli Deccan Year	Western Date (Gregorian) of New Year
1013	1602 28 Jul	1064	1653 28 Jul	1115	1704* 30 Jul	1166	1755 30 Jul
1014	1603 28 Jul	1065	1654 29 Jul	1116	1705 29 Jul	1167	1756* 30 Jul
1015	1604* 28 Jul	1066	1655 29 Jul	1117	1706 30 Jul	1168	1757 29 Jul
1016	1605 27 Jul	1067	1656* 29 Jul	1118	1707 30 Jul	1169	1758 30 Jul
1017	1606 28 Jul	1068	1657 28 Jul	1119	1708* 30 Jul	1170	1759 30 Jul
1018	1607 28 Jul	1069	1658 29 Jul	1120	1709 29 Jul	1171	1760* 30 Jul
1019	1608* 28 Jul	1070	1659 29 Jul	1121	1710 30 Jul	1172	1761 30 Jul
1020	1609 27 Jul	1071	1660* 29 Jul	1122	1711 30 Jul	1173	1762 31 Jul
1021	1610 28 Jul	1072	1661 28 Jul	1123	1712* 30 Jul	1174	1763 31 Jul
1022	1611 28 Jul	1073	1662 29 Jul	1124	1713 29 Jul	1175	1764* 31 Jul
1023	1612* 28 Jul	1074	1663 29 Jul	1125	1714 30 Jul	1176	1765 30 Jul
1024	1613 27 Jul	1075	1664* 29 Jul	1126	1715 30 Jul	1177	1766 31 Jul
1025	1614 28 Jul	1076	1665 28 Jul	1127	1716* 30 Jul	1178	1767 31 Jul
1026	1615 28 Jul	1077	1666 29 Jul	1128	1717 29 Jul	1179	1768* 31 Jul
1027	1616* 28 Jul	1078	1667 29 Jul	1129	1718 30 Jul	1180	1769 30 Jul
1028	1617 27 Jul	1079	1668* 29 Jul	1130	1719 30 Jul	1181	1770 31 Jul
1029	1618 28 Jul	1080	1669 28 Jul	1131	1720* 30 Jul	1182	1771 31 Jul
1030	1619 28 Jul	1081	1670 29 Jul	1132	1721 29 Jul	1183	1772* 31 Jul
1031	1620* 28 Jul	1082	1671 29 Jul	1133	1722 30 Jul	1184	1773 30 Jul
1032	1621 27 Jul	1083	1672* 29 Jul	1134	1723 30 Jul	1185	1774 31 Jul
1033	1622 28 Jul	1084	1673 28 Jul	1135	1724* 30 Jul	1186	1775 31 Jul
1034	1623 28 Jul	1085	1674 29 Jul	1136	1725 29 Jul	1187	1776* 31 Jul
1035	1624* 28 Jul	1086	1675 29 Jul	1137	1726 30 Jul	1188	1777 30 Jul
1036	1625 27 Jul	1087	1676* 29 Jul	1138	1727 30 Jul	1189	1778 31 Jul
1037	1626 28 Jul	1088	1677 28 Jul	1139	1728* 30 Jul	1190	1779 31 Jul
1038	1627 28 Jul	1089	1678 29 Jul	1140	1729 29 Jul	1191	1780* 31 Jul
1039	1628* 28 Jul	1090	1679 29 Jul	1141	1730 30 Jul	1192	1781 30 Jul
1040	1629 27 Jul	1091	1680* 29 Jul	1142	1731 30 Jul	1193	1782 31 Jul
1041	1630 28 Jul	1092	1681 28 Jul	1143	1732* 30 Jul	1194	1783 31 Jul
1042	1631 28 Jul	1093	1682 29 Jul	1144	1733 29 Jul	1195	1784* 31 Jul
1043	1632* 28 Jul	1094	1683 29 Jul	1145	1734 30 Jul	1196	1785 30 Jul
1044	1633 27 Jul	1095	1684* 29 Jul	1146	1735 30 Jul	1197	1786 31 Jul
1045	1634 28 Jul	1096	1685 28 Jul	1147	1736* 30 Jul	1198	1787 31 Jul
1046	1635 28 Jul	1097	1686 29 Jul	1148	1737 29 Jul	1199	1788* 31 Jul
1047	1636* 28 Jul	1098	1687 29 Jul	1149	1738 30 Jul	1200	1789 30 Jul
1048	1637 27 Jul	1099	1688* 29 Jul	1150	1739 30 Jul	1201	1790 31 Jul
1049	1638 28 Jul	1100	1689 28 Jul	1151	1740* 30 Jul	1202	1791 31 Jul
1050	1639 28 Jul	1101	1690 29 Jul	1152	1741 29 Jul	1203	1792* 31 Jul
1051	1640* 28 Jul	1102	1691 29 Jul	1153	1742 30 Jul	1204	1793 30 Jul
1052	1641 28 Jul	1103	1692* 29 Jul	1154	1743 30 Jul	1205	1794 31 Jul
1053	1642 28 Jul	1104	1693 28 Jul	1155	1744* 30 Jul	1206	1795 31 Jul
1054	1643 29 Jul	1105	1694 29 Jul	1156	1745 29 Jul	1207	1796* 31 Jul
1055	1644* 29 Jul	1106	1695 29 Jul	1157	1746 30 Jul	1208	1797 30 Jul
1056	1645 28 Jul	1107	1696* 29 Jul	1158	1747 30 Jul	1209	1798 31 Jul
1057	1646 29 Jul	1108	1697 28 Jul	1159	1748* 30 Jul	1210	1799 31 Jul
1058	1647 29 Jul	1109	1698 29 Jul	1160	1749 29 Jul	1211	1800* 31 Jul
1059	1648* 29 Jul	1110	1699 29 Jul	1161	1750 30 Jul	1212	1801 30 Jul
1060	1649 28 Jul	1111	1700* 29 Jul	1162	1751 30 Jul	1213	1802 31 Jul
1061	1650 29 Jul	1112	1701 29 Jul	1163	1752* 30 Jul	1214	1803 31 Jul
1062	1651 29 Jul	1113	1702 30 Jul	1164	1753 29 Jul	1215	1804* 31 Jul
1063	1652* 29 Jul	1114	1703 30 Jul	1165	1754 30 Jul	1216	1805 30 Jul

Fasli Deccan Year	Western Date (Gregorian) of New Year	Fasli Deccan Year	Western Date (Gregorian) of New Year	Fasli Deccan Year	Western Date (Gregorian) of New Year	Fasli Deccan Year	Western Date (Gregorian) of New Year
1217	1806 31 Jul	1265	1854 1 Aug	1313	1902 2 Aug	1361	1950 3 Aug
1218	1807 31 Jul	1266	1855 1 Aug	1314	1903 2 Aug	1362	1951 3 Aug
1219	1808* 31 Jul	1267	1856* 1 Aug	1315	1904* 2 Aug	1363	1952* 3 Aug
1220	1809 30 Jul	1268	1857 31 Jul	1316	1905 1 Aug	1364	1953 2 Aug
1221	1810 31 Jul	1269	1858 1 Aug	1317	1906 2 Aug	1365	1954 3 Aug
1222	1811 31 Jul	1270	1859 1 Aug	1318	1907 2 Aug	1366	1955 3 Aug
1223	1812* 31 Jul	1271	1860* 1 Aug	1319	1908* 2 Aug	1367	1956* 3 Aug
1224	1813 30 Jul	1272	1861 31 Jul	1320	1909 1 Aug	1368	1957 2 Aug
1225	1814 31 Jul	1273	1862 1 Aug	1321	1910 2 Aug	1369	1958 3 Aug
1226	1815 31 Jul	1274	1863 1 Aug	1322	1911 2 Aug	1370	1959 3 Aug
1227	1816* 31 Jul	1275	1864* 1 Aug	1323	1912* 2 Aug	1371	1960* 3 Aug
1228	1817 30 Jul	1276	1865 31 Jul	1324	1913 1 Aug	1372	1961 2 Aug
1229	1818 31 Jul	1277	1866 1 Aug	1325	1914 2 Aug	1373	1962 3 Aug
1230	1819 31 Jul	1278	1867 1 Aug	1326	1915 2 Aug	1374	1963 3 Aug
1231	1820* 31 Jul	1279	1868* 1 Aug	1327	1916* 2 Aug	1375	1964* 3 Aug
1232	1821 31 Jul	1280	1869 31 Jul	1328	1917 1 Aug	1376	1965 2 Aug
1233	1822 1 Aug	1281	1870 1 Aug	1329	1918 2 Aug	1377	1966 3 Aug
1234	1823 1 Aug	1282	1871 1 Aug	1330	1919 2 Aug	1378	1967 3 Aug
1235	1824* 1 Aug	1283	1872* 1 Aug	1331	1920* 2 Aug	1379	1968* 3 Aug
1236	1825 31 Jul	1284	1873 31 Jul	1332	1921 1 Aug	1380	1969 2 Aug
1237	1826 1 Aug	1285	1874 1 Aug	1333	1922 2 Aug	1381	1970 3 Aug
1238	1827 1 Aug	1286	1875 1 Aug	1334	1923 2 Aug	1382	1971 3 Aug
1239	1828* 1 Aug	1287	1876* 1 Aug	1335	1924* 2 Aug	1383	1972* 3 Aug
1240	1829 31 Jul	1288	1877 31 Jul	1336	1925 1 Aug	1384	1973 2 Aug
1241	1830 1 Aug	1289	1878 1 Aug	1337	1926 2 Aug	1385	1974 3 Aug
1242	1831 1 Aug	1290	1879 1 Aug	1338	1927 2 Aug	1386	1975 3 Aug
1243	1832* 1 Aug	1291	1880* 1 Aug	1339	1928* 2 Aug	1387	1976* 3 Aug
1244	1833 31 Jul	1292	1881 1 Aug	1340	1929 1 Aug	1388	1977 2 Aug
1245	1834 1 Aug	1293	1882 2 Aug	1341	1930 2 Aug	1389	1978 3 Aug
1246	1835 1 Aug	1294	1883 2 Aug	1342	1931 2 Aug	1390	1979 3 Aug
1247	1836* 1 Aug	1295	1884* 2 Aug	1343	1932* 2 Aug	1391	1980* 3 Aug
1248	1837 31 Jul	1296	1885 1 Aug	1344	1933 1 Aug	1392	1981 2 Aug
1249	1838 1 Aug	1297	1886 2 Aug	1345	1934 2 Aug	1393	1982 3 Aug
1250	1839 1 Aug	1298	1887 2 Aug	1346	1935 2 Aug	1394	1983 3 Aug
1251	1840* 1 Aug	1299	1888* 2 Aug	1347	1936* 2 Aug	1395	1984* 3 Aug
1252	1841 31 Jul	1300	1889 1 Aug	1348	1937 1 Aug	1396	1985 2 Aug
1253	1842 1 Aug	1301	1890 2 Aug	1349	1938 2 Aug	1397	1986 3 Aug
1254	1843 1 Aug	1302	1891 2 Aug	1350	1939 2 Aug	1398	1987 3 Aug
1255	1844* 1 Aug	1303	1892* 2 Aug	1351	1940* 2 Aug	1399	1988* 3 Aug
1256	1845 31 Jul	1304	1893 1 Aug	1352	1941 2 Aug	1400	1989 2 Aug
1257	1846 1 Aug	1305	1894 2 Aug	1353	1942 3 Aug	1401	1990 3 Aug
1258	1847 1 Aug	1306	1895 2 Aug	1354	1943 3 Aug	1402	1991 3 Aug
1259	1848* 1 Aug	1307	1896* 2 Aug	1355	1944* 3 Aug	1403	1992* 3 Aug
1260	1849 31 Jul	1308	1897 1 Aug	1356	1945 2 Aug	1404	1993 2 Aug
1261	1850 1 Aug	1309	1898 2 Aug	1357	1946 3 Aug	1405	1994 3 Aug
1262	1851 1 Aug	1310	1899 2 Aug	1358	1947 3 Aug	1406	1995 3 Aug
1263	1852* 1 Aug	1311	1900* 2 Aug	1359	1948* 3 Aug	1407	1996* 3 Aug
1264	1853 31 Jul	1312	1901 1 Aug	1360	1949 2 Aug	1408	1997 3 Aug

PARASURAM CALENDAR

Western Date of New Year		Parasurám Year of Malayála
1	Aug 14	177
2	Aug 15	178
3	Aug 15	179
4*	Aug 14	180
5	Aug 15	181
6	Aug 15	182
7	Aug 15	183
8*	Aug 14	184
9	Aug 15	185
10	Aug 15	186
11	Aug 15	187
12*	Aug 14	188
13	Aug 15	189
14	Aug 15	190
15	Aug 15	191
16*	Aug 14	192
17	Aug 15	193
18	Aug 15	194
19	Aug 15	195
20*	Aug 14	196
21	Aug 15	197
22	Aug 15	198
23	Aug 15	199
24*	Aug 14	200
25	Aug 15	201
26	Aug 15	202
27	Aug 15	203
28*	Aug 15	204
29	Aug 16	205
30	Aug 16	206
31	Aug 16	207
32*	Aug 15	208
33	Aug 16	209
34	Aug 16	210
35	Aug 16	211
36*	Aug 15	212
37	Aug 16	213
38	Aug 16	214
39	Aug 16	215
40*	Aug 15	216
41	Aug 16	217
42	Aug 16	218
43	Aug 16	219
44*	Aug 15	220
45	Aug 16	221
46	Aug 16	222
47	Aug 16	223
48*	Aug 15	224
49	Aug 16	225
50	Aug 16	226
51	Aug 16	227
52*	Aug 15	228
53	Aug 16	229
54	Aug 16	230
55	Aug 16	231
56*	Aug 15	232
57	Aug 16	233
58	Aug 16	234
59	Aug 16	235
60*	Aug 15	236
61	Aug 16	237
62	Aug 16	238
63	Aug 16	239
64*	Aug 15	240
65	Aug 16	241
66	Aug 16	242
67	Aug 16	243
68*	Aug 15	244
69	Aug 16	245
70	Aug 16	246
71	Aug 16	247
72*	Aug 15	248
73	Aug 16	249
74	Aug 16	250
75	Aug 16	251
76*	Aug 15	252
77	Aug 16	253
78	Aug 16	254
79	Aug 16	255
80*	Aug 15	256
81	Aug 16	257
82	Aug 16	258
83	Aug 16	259
84*	Aug 15	260
85	Aug 16	261
86	Aug 16	262
87	Aug 16	263
88*	Aug 16	264
89	Aug 17	265
90	Aug 17	266
91	Aug 7	267
92*	Aug 6	268
93	Aug 7	269
94	Aug 7	270
95	Aug 7	271
96*	Aug 6	272
97	Aug 7	273
98	Aug 7	274
99	Aug 7	275
100*	Aug 6	276
101	Aug 7	277
102	Aug 7	278
103	Aug 7	279
104*	Aug 6	280
105	Aug 7	281
106	Aug 7	282
107	Aug 7	283
108*	Aug 6	284
109	Aug 7	285
110	Aug 7	286
111	Aug 7	287
112*	Aug 6	288
113	Aug 7	289
114	Aug 7	290
115	Aug 7	291
116*	Aug 6	292
117	Aug 7	293
118	Aug 7	294
119	Aug 7	295
120*	Aug 6	296
121	Aug 7	297
122	Aug 7	298
123	Aug 7	299
124*	Aug 6	300
125	Aug 7	301
126	Aug 7	302
127	Aug 7	303
128*	Aug 6	304
129	Aug 7	305
130	Aug 7	306
131	Aug 7	307
132*	Aug 6	308
133	Aug 7	309
134	Aug 7	310
135	Aug 7	311
136*	Aug 6	312
137	Aug 7	313
138	Aug 7	314
139	Aug 7	315
140*	Aug 6	316
141	Aug 7	317
142	Aug 7	318
143	Aug 7	319
144*	Aug 6	320
145	Aug 7	321
146	Aug 7	322
147	Aug 7	323
148*	Aug 7	324
149	Aug 8	325
150	Aug 8	326
151	Aug 7	327
152*	Aug 7	328
153	Aug 8	329
154	Aug 8	330
155	Aug 8	331
156*	Aug 7	332
157	Aug 8	333
158	Aug 8	334
159	Aug 8	335
160*	Aug 7	336
161	Aug 8	337
162	Aug 8	338
163	Aug 8	339
164*	Aug 7	340
165	Aug 8	341
166	Aug 8	342
167	Aug 8	343
168*	Aug 7	344
169	Aug 8	345
170	Aug 8	346
171	Aug 8	347
172*	Aug 7	348
173	Aug 8	349
174	Aug 8	350
175	Aug 8	351
176*	Aug 7	352
177	Aug 8	353
178	Aug 8	354
179	Aug 8	355
180*	Aug 7	356
181	Aug 18	357
182	Aug 18	358
183	Aug 18	359
184*	Aug 17	360
185	Aug 18	361
186	Aug 18	362
187	Aug 18	363
188*	Aug 17	364
189	Aug 18	365
190	Aug 18	366
191	Aug 18	367
192*	Aug 17	368
193	Aug 18	369
194	Aug 18	370
195	Aug 18	371
196*	Aug 17	372

Western Date of New Year		Parasurám Year of Malayála	Western Date of New Year		Parasurám Year of Malayála	Western Date of New Year		Parasurám Year of Malayála	Western Date of New Year		Parasurám Year of Malayála
197	Aug 18	373	248*	Aug 18	424	299	Aug 20	475	350	Aug 21	526
198	Aug 18	374	249	Aug 19	425	300*	Aug 19	476	351	Aug 21	527
199	Aug 18	375	250	Aug 19	426	301	Aug 20	477	352*	Aug 20	528
200*	Aug 17	376	251	Aug 19	427	302	Aug 20	478	353	Aug 21	529
201	Aug 18	377	252*	Aug 18	428	303	Aug 20	479	354	Aug 21	530
202	Aug 18	378	253	Aug 19	429	304*	Aug 19	480	355	Aug 21	531
203	Aug 18	379	254	Aug 19	430	305	Aug 20	481	356*	Aug 20	532
204*	Aug 17	380	255	Aug 19	431	306	Aug 20	482	357	Aug 21	533
205	Aug 18	381	256*	Aug 18	432	307	Aug 20	483	358	Aug 21	534
206	Aug 18	382	257	Aug 19	433	308*	Aug 19	484	359	Aug 21	535
207	Aug 18	383	258	Aug 19	434	309	Aug 20	485	360*	Aug 20	536
208*	Aug 17	384	259	Aug 19	435	310	Aug 20	486	361	Aug 21	537
209	Aug 18	385	260*	Aug 18	436	311	Aug 20	487	362	Aug 21	538
210	Aug 18	386	261	Aug 19	437	312*	Aug 19	488	363	Aug 21	539
211	Aug 18	387	262	Aug 19	438	313	Aug 20	489	364*	Aug 20	540
212*	Aug 18	388	263	Aug 19	439	314	Aug 20	490	365	Aug 21	541
213	Aug 19	389	264*	Aug 19	440	315	Aug 20	491	366	Aug 21	542
214	Aug 19	390	265	Aug 20	441	316*	Aug 19	492	367	Aug 21	543
215	Aug 19	391	266	Aug 20	442	317	Aug 20	493	368*	Aug 20	544
216*	Aug 18	392	267	Aug 20	443	318	Aug 20	494	369	Aug 21	545
217	Aug 19	393	268*	Aug 19	444	319	Aug 20	495	370	Aug 21	546
218	Aug 19	394	269	Aug 20	445	320*	Aug 19	496	371	Aug 21	547
219	Aug 19	395	270	Aug 20	446	321	Aug 20	497	372*	Aug 20	548
220*	Aug 18	396	271	Aug 20	447	322	Aug 20	498	373	Aug 21	549
221	Aug 19	397	272*	Aug 19	448	323	Aug 20	499	374	Aug 21	550
222	Aug 19	398	273	Aug 20	449	324*	Aug 20	500	375	Aug 21	551
223	Aug 19	399	274	Aug 20	450	325	Aug 21	501	376*	Aug 20	552
224*	Aug 18	400	275	Aug 20	451	326	Aug 21	502	377	Aug 21	553
225	Aug 19	401	276*	Aug 19	452	327	Aug 21	503	378	Aug 21	554
226	Aug 19	402	277	Aug 20	453	328*	Aug 20	504	379	Aug 21	555
227	Aug 19	403	278	Aug 20	454	329	Aug 21	505	380*	Aug 20	556
228*	Aug 18	404	279	Aug 20	455	330	Aug 21	506	381	Aug 21	557
229	Aug 19	405	280*	Aug 19	456	331	Aug 21	507	382	Aug 21	558
230	Aug 19	406	281	Aug 20	457	332*	Aug 20	508	383	Aug 21	559
231	Aug 19	407	282	Aug 20	458	333	Aug 21	509	384*	Aug 21	560
232*	Aug 18	408	283	Aug 20	459	334	Aug 21	510	385	Aug 22	561
233	Aug 19	409	284*	Aug 19	460	335	Aug 21	511	386	Aug 22	562
234	Aug 19	410	285	Aug 20	461	336*	Aug 20	512	387	Aug 22	563
235	Aug 19	411	286	Aug 20	462	337	Aug 21	513	388*	Aug 21	564
236*	Aug 18	412	287	Aug 20	463	338	Aug 21	514	389	Aug 22	565
237	Aug 19	413	288*	Aug 19	464	339	Aug 21	515	390	Aug 22	566
238	Aug 19	414	289	Aug 20	465	340*	Aug 20	516	391	Aug 22	567
239	Aug 19	415	290	Aug 20	466	341	Aug 21	517	392*	Aug 21	568
240*	Aug 18	416	291	Aug 20	467	342	Aug 21	518	393	Aug 22	569
241	Aug 19	417	292*	Aug 19	468	343	Aug 21	519	394	Aug 22	570
242	Aug 19	418	293	Aug 20	469	344*	Aug 20	520	395	Aug 22	571
243	Aug 19	419	294	Aug 20	470	345	Aug 21	521	396*	Aug 21	572
244*	Aug 18	420	295	Aug 20	471	346	Aug 21	522	397	Aug 22	573
245	Aug 19	421	296*	Aug 19	472	347	Aug 21	523	398	Aug 22	574
246	Aug 19	422	297	Aug 20	473	348*	Aug 20	524	399	Aug 22	575
247	Aug 19	423	298	Aug 20	474	349	Aug 21	525	400*	Aug 21	576

Western Date of New Year		Parasurám Year of Malayála	Western Date of New Year		Parasurám Year of Malayála	Western Date of New Year		Parasurám Year of Malayála	Western Date of New Year		Parasurám Year of Malayála
401	Aug 22	577	452*	Aug 22	628	503	Aug 24	679	554	Aug 24	730
402	Aug 22	578	453	Aug 23	629	504*	Aug 23	680	555	Aug 24	731
403	Aug 22	579	454	Aug 23	630	505	Aug 24	681	556*	Aug 23	732
404*	Aug 21	580	455	Aug 23	631	506	Aug 24	682	557	Aug 24	733
405	Aug 22	581	456*	Aug 22	632	507	Aug 24	683	558	Aug 24	734
406	Aug 22	582	457	Aug 23	633	508*	Aug 23	684	559	Aug 24	735
407	Aug 22	583	458	Aug 23	634	509	Aug 24	685	560*	Aug 23	736
408*	Aug 21	584	459	Aug 23	635	510	Aug 24	686	561	Aug 24	737
409	Aug 22	585	460*	Aug 22	636	511	Aug 24	687	562	Aug 24	738
410	Aug 22	586	461	Aug 23	637	512*	Aug 23	688	563	Aug 24	739
411	Aug 22	587	462	Aug 23	638	513	Aug 24	689	564*	Aug 23	740
412*	Aug 21	588	463	Aug 23	639	514	Aug 24	690	565	Aug 24	741
413	Aug 22	589	464*	Aug 22	640	515	Aug 24	691	566	Aug 24	742
414	Aug 22	590	465	Aug 23	641	516*	Aug 23	692	567	Aug 24	743
415	Aug 22	591	466	Aug 23	642	517	Aug 24	693	568*	Aug 23	744
416*	Aug 21	592	467	Aug 23	643	518	Aug 24	694	569	Aug 24	745
417	Aug 22	593	468*	Aug 22	644	519	Aug 24	695	570	Aug 24	746
418	Aug 22	594	469	Aug 23	645	520*	Aug 23	696	571	Aug 24	747
419	Aug 22	595	470	Aug 23	646	521	Aug 24	697	572*	Aug 23	748
420*	Aug 21	596	471	Aug 23	647	522	Aug 24	698	573	Aug 24	749
421	Aug 22	597	472*	Aug 22	648	523	Aug 24	699	574	Aug 24	750
422	Aug 22	598	473	Aug 23	649	524*	Aug 23	700	575	Aug 24	751
423	Aug 22	599	474	Aug 23	650	525	Aug 24	701	576*	Aug 23	752
424*	Aug 21	600	475	Aug 23	651	526	Aug 24	702	577	Aug 24	753
425	Aug 22	601	476*	Aug 22	652	527	Aug 24	703	578	Aug 24	754
426	Aug 22	602	477	Aug 23	653	528*	Aug 23	704	579	Aug 24	755
427	Aug 22	603	478	Aug 23	654	529	Aug 24	705	580*	Aug 23	756
428*	Aug 21	604	479	Aug 23	655	530	Aug 24	706	581	Aug 24	757
429	Aug 22	605	480*	Aug 22	656	531	Aug 24	707	582	Aug 24	758
430	Aug 22	606	481	Aug 23	657	532*	Aug 23	708	583	Aug 24	759
431	Aug 22	607	482	Aug 23	658	533	Aug 24	709	584*	Aug 23	760
432*	Aug 21	608	483	Aug 23	659	534	Aug 24	710	585	Aug 24	761
433	Aug 22	609	484*	Aug 22	660	535	Aug 24	711	586	Aug 24	762
434	Aug 22	610	485	Aug 23	661	536*	Aug 23	712	587	Aug 24	763
435	Aug 22	611	486	Aug 23	662	537	Aug 24	713	588*	Aug 23	764
436*	Aug 21	612	487	Aug 23	663	538	Aug 24	714	589	Aug 24	765
437	Aug 22	613	488*	Aug 22	664	539	Aug 24	715	590	Aug 24	766
438	Aug 22	614	489	Aug 23	665	540*	Aug 23	716	591	Aug 24	767
439	Aug 22	615	490	Aug 23	666	541	Aug 24	717	592*	Aug 23	768
440*	Aug 22	616	491	Aug 23	667	542	Aug 24	718	593	Aug 24	769
441	Aug 23	617	492*	Aug 22	668	543	Aug 24	719	594	Aug 24	770
442	Aug 23	618	493	Aug 23	669	544*	Aug 23	720	595	Aug 24	771
443	Aug 23	619	494	Aug 23	670	545	Aug 24	721	596*	Aug 23	772
444*	Aug 22	620	495	Aug 23	671	546	Aug 24	722	597	Aug 24	773
445	Aug 23	621	496*	Aug 22	672	547	Aug 24	723	598	Aug 24	774
446	Aug 23	622	497	Aug 23	673	548*	Aug 23	724	599	Aug 24	775
447	Aug 23	623	498	Aug 23	674	549	Aug 24	725	600*	Aug 24	776
448*	Aug 22	624	499	Aug 23	675	550	Aug 24	726	601	Aug 25	777
449	Aug 23	625	500*	Aug 23	676	551	Aug 24	727	602	Aug 25	778
450	Aug 23	626	501	Aug 24	677	552*	Aug 23	728	603	Aug 25	779
451	Aug 23	627	502	Aug 24	678	553	Aug 24	729	604*	Aug 24	780

Western Date of New Year		Parasurám Year of Malayála	Western Date of New Year		Parasurám Year of Malayála	Western Date of New Year		Parasurám Year of Malayála	Western Date of New Year		Parasurám Year of Malayála
605	Aug 25	781	656*	Aug 25	832	707	Aug 27	883	758	Aug 28	934
606	Aug 25	782	657	Aug 26	833	708*	Aug 26	884	759	Aug 28	935
607	Aug 25	783	658	Aug 26	834	709	Aug 27	885	760*	Aug 27	936
608*	Aug 24	784	659	Aug 26	835	710	Aug 27	886	761	Aug 28	937
609	Aug 25	785	660*	Aug 25	836	711	Aug 27	887	762	Aug 28	938
610	Aug 25	786	661	Aug 26	837	712*	Aug 26	888	763	Aug 28	939
611	Aug 25	787	662	Aug 26	838	713	Aug 27	889	764*	Aug 27	940
612*	Aug 24	788	663	Aug 26	839	714	Aug 27	890	765	Aug 28	941
613	Aug 25	789	664*	Aug 25	840	715	Aug 27	891	766	Aug 28	942
614	Aug 25	790	665	Aug 26	841	716*	Aug 26	892	767	Aug 28	943
615	Aug 25	791	666	Aug 26	842	717	Aug 27	893	768*	Aug 27	944
616*	Aug 24	792	667	Aug 26	843	718	Aug 27	894	769	Aug 28	945
617	Aug 25	793	668*	Aug 25	844	719	Aug 27	895	770	Aug 28	946
618	Aug 25	794	669	Aug 26	845	720*	Aug 26	896	771	Aug 28	947
619	Aug 25	795	670	Aug 26	846	721	Aug 27	897	772*	Aug 27	948
620*	Aug 25	796	671	Aug 26	847	722	Aug 27	898	773	Aug 28	949
621	Aug 26	797	672*	Aug 25	848	723	Aug 27	899	774	Aug 28	950
622	Aug 26	798	673	Aug 26	849	724*	Aug 26	900	775	Aug 28	951
623	Aug 26	799	674	Aug 26	850	725	Aug 27	901	776*	Aug 27	952
624*	Aug 25	800	675	Aug 26	851	726	Aug 27	902	777	Aug 28	953
625	Aug 26	801	676*	Aug 26	852	727	Aug 27	903	778	Aug 28	954
626	Aug 26	802	677	Aug 27	853	728*	Aug 26	904	779	Aug 28	955
627	Aug 26	803	678	Aug 27	854	729	Aug 27	905	780*	Aug 27	956
628*	Aug 25	804	679	Aug 27	855	730	Aug 27	906	781	Aug 28	957
629	Aug 26	805	680*	Aug 26	856	731	Aug 27	907	782	Aug 28	958
630	Aug 26	806	681	Aug 27	857	732*	Aug 26	908	783	Aug 28	959
631	Aug 26	807	682	Aug 27	858	733	Aug 27	909	784*	Aug 27	960
632*	Aug 25	808	683	Aug 27	859	734	Aug 27	910	785	Aug 28	961
633	Aug 26	809	684*	Aug 26	860	735	Aug 27	911	786	Aug 28	962
634	Aug 26	810	685	Aug 27	861	736*	Aug 27	912	787	Aug 28	963
635	Aug 26	811	686	Aug 27	862	737	Aug 28	913	788*	Aug 27	964
636*	Aug 25	812	687	Aug 27	863	738	Aug 28	914	789	Aug 28	965
637	Aug 26	813	688*	Aug 26	864	739	Aug 28	915	790	Aug 28	966
638	Aug 26	814	689	Aug 27	865	740*	Aug 27	916	791	Aug 28	967
639	Aug 26	815	690	Aug 27	866	741	Aug 28	917	792*	Aug 27	968
640*	Aug 25	816	691	Aug 27	867	742	Aug 28	918	793	Aug 28	969
641	Aug 26	817	692*	Aug 26	868	743	Aug 28	919	794	Aug 28	970
642	Aug 26	818	693	Aug 27	869	744*	Aug 27	920	795	Aug 28	971
643	Aug 26	819	694	Aug 27	870	745	Aug 28	921	796*	Aug 28	972
644*	Aug 25	820	695	Aug 27	871	746	Aug 28	922	797	Aug 29	973
645	Aug 26	821	696*	Aug 26	872	747	Aug 28	923	798	Aug 29	974
646	Aug 26	822	697	Aug 27	873	748*	Aug 27	924	799	Aug 29	975
647	Aug 26	823	698	Aug 27	874	749	Aug 28	925	800*	Aug 28	976
648*	Aug 25	824	699	Aug 27	875	750	Aug 28	926	801	Aug 29	977
649	Aug 26	825	700*	Aug 26	876	751	Aug 28	927	802	Aug 29	978
650	Aug 26	826	701	Aug 27	877	752*	Aug 27	928	803	Aug 29	979
651	Aug 26	827	702	Aug 27	878	753	Aug 28	929	804*	Aug 28	980
652*	Aug 25	828	703	Aug 27	879	754	Aug 28	930	805	Aug 29	981
653	Aug 26	829	704*	Aug 26	880	755	Aug 28	931	806	Aug 29	982
654	Aug 26	830	705	Aug 27	881	756*	Aug 27	932	807	Aug 29	983
655	Aug 26	831	706	Aug 27	882	757	Aug 28	933	808*	Aug 28	984

Western Date of New Year		Parasurám Year of Malayála	Western Date of New Year		Parasurám Year of Malayála	Western Date of New Year		Parasurám Year of Malayála	Western Date of New Year		Parasurám Year of Malayála
809	Aug 29	985	859	Aug 30	1035	909	Aug 30	1085	959	Aug 31	1135
810	Aug 29	986	860*	Aug 29	1036	910	Aug 30	1086	960*	Aug 31	1136
811	Aug 29	987	861	Aug 30	1037	911	Aug 30	1087	961	Aug 31	1137
812*	Aug 28	988	862	Aug 30	1038	912*	Aug 31	1088	962	Aug 31	1138
813	Aug 29	989	863	Aug 30	1039	913	Aug 31	1089	963	Aug 31	1139
814	Aug 29	990	864*	Aug 29	1040	914	Aug 31	1090	964*	Aug 31	1140
815	Aug 29	991	865	Aug 30	1041	915	Aug 31	1091	965	Aug 31	1141
816*	Aug 28	992	866	Aug 30	1042	916*	Aug 31	1092	966	Aug 31	1142
817	Aug 29	993	867	Aug 30	1043	917	Aug 31	1093	967	Aug 31	1143
818	Aug 29	994	868*	Aug 29	1044	918	Aug 31	1094	968*	Aug 31	1144
819	Aug 29	995	869	Aug 30	1045	919	Aug 31	1095	969	Aug 31	1145
820*	Aug 28	996	870	Aug 30	1046	920*	Aug 31	1096	970	Aug 31	1146
821	Aug 29	997	871	Aug 30	1047	921	Aug 31	1097	971	Aug 31	1147
822	Aug 29	998	872*	Aug 29	1048	922	Aug 31	1098	972*	Aug 31	1148
823	Aug 29	999	873	Aug 30	1049	923	Aug 31	1099	973	Sep 1	1149
824*	Aug 28	1000	874	Aug 30	1050	924*	Aug 31	1100	974	Sep 1	1150
825	Aug 29	1001	875	Aug 30	1051	925	Aug 31	1101	975	Sep 1	1151
826	Aug 29	1002	876*	Aug 29	1052	926	Aug 31	1102	976*	Aug 31	1152
827	Aug 29	1003	877	Aug 30	1053	927	Aug 31	1103	977	Sep 1	1153
828*	Aug 28	1004	878	Aug 30	1054	928*	Aug 31	1104	978	Sep 1	1154
829	Aug 29	1005	879	Aug 30	1055	929	Aug 31	1105	979	Sep 1	1155
830	Aug 29	1006	880*	Aug 29	1056	930	Aug 31	1106	980*	Aug 31	1156
831	Aug 29	1007	881	Aug 30	1057	931	Aug 31	1107	981	Sep 1	1157
832*	Aug 28	1008	882	Aug 30	1058	932*	Aug 31	1108	982	Sep 1	1158
833	Aug 29	1009	883	Aug 30	1059	933	Aug 31	1109	983	Sep 1	1159
834	Aug 29	1010	884*	Aug 29	1060	934	Aug 31	1110	984*	Aug 31	1160
835	Aug 29	1011	885	Aug 30	1061	935	Aug 31	1111	985	Sep 1	1161
836*	Aug 28	1012	886	Aug 30	1062	936*	Aug 31	1112	986	Sep 1	1162
837	Aug 29	1013	887	Aug 30	1063	937	Aug 31	1113	987	Sep 1	1163
838	Aug 29	1014	888*	Aug 29	1064	938	Aug 31	1114	988*	Aug 31	1164
839	Aug 29	1015	889	Aug 30	1065	939	Aug 31	1115	989	Sep 1	1165
840*	Aug 28	1016	890	Aug 30	1066	940*	Aug 31	1116	990	Sep 1	1166
841	Aug 29	1017	891	Aug 30	1067	941	Aug 31	1117	991	Sep 1	1167
842	Aug 29	1018	892*	Aug 29	1068	942	Aug 31	1118	992*	Aug 31	1168
843	Aug 29	1019	893	Aug 30	1069	943	Aug 31	1119	993	Sep 1	1169
844*	Aug 28	1020	894	Aug 30	1070	944*	Aug 31	1120	994	Sep 1	1170
845	Aug 29	1021	895	Aug 30	1071	945	Aug 31	1121	995	Sep 1	1171
846	Aug 29	1022	896*	Aug 29	1072	946	Aug 31	1122	996*	Aug 31	1172
847	Aug 29	1023	897	Aug 30	1073	947	Aug 31	1123	997	Sep 1	1173
848*	Aug 28	1024	898	Aug 30	1074	948*	Aug 31	1124	998	Sep 1	1174
849	Aug 29	1025	899	Aug 30	1075	949	Aug 31	1125	999	Sep 1	1175
850	Aug 29	1026	900*	Aug 29	1076	950	Aug 31	1126	1000*	Aug 31	1176
851	Aug 29	1027	901	Aug 30	1077	951	Aug 31	1127	1001	Sep 1	1177
852*	Aug 28	1028	902	Aug 30	1078	952*	Aug 31	1128	1002	Sep 1	1178
853	Aug 29	1029	903	Aug 30	1079	953	Aug 31	1129	1003	Sep 1	1179
854	Aug 29	1030	904*	Aug 29	1080	954	Aug 31	1130	1004*	Aug 31	1180
855	Aug 29	1031	905	Aug 30	1081	955	Aug 31	1131	1005	Sep 1	1181
856*	Aug 29	1032	906	Aug 30	1082	956*	Aug 31	1132	1006	Sep 1	1182
857	Aug 30	1033	907	Aug 30	1083	957	Aug 31	1133	1007	Sep 1	1183
858	Aug 30	1034	908*	Aug 29	1084	958	Aug 31	1134	1008*	Aug 31	1184

Western Date of New Year			Parasurám Year of Malayála	Western Date of New Year			Parasurám Year of Malayála	Western Date of New Year			Parasurám Year of Malayála	Western Date of New Year			Parasurám Year of Malayála
1009	Sep	1	1185	1059	Sep	2	1235	1109	Sep	3	1285	1159	Sep	4	1335
1010	Sep	1	1186	1060*	Sep	1	1236	1110	Sep	3	1286	1160*	Sep	3	1336
1011	Sep	1	1187	1061	Sep	2	1237	1111	Sep	3	1287	1161	Sep	4	1337
1012*	Aug	31	1188	1062	Sep	2	1238	1112*	Sep	2	1288	1162	Sep	4	1338
1013	Sep	1	1189	1063	Sep	2	1239	1113	Sep	3	1289	1163	Sep	4	1339
1014	Sep	1	1190	1064*	Sep	1	1240	1114	Sep	3	1290	1164*	Sep	3	1340
1015	Sep	1	1191	1065	Sep	2	1241	1115	Sep	3	1291	1165	Sep	4	1341
1016*	Aug	31	1192	1066	Sep	2	1242	1116*	Sep	2	1292	1166	Sep	4	1342
1017	Sep	1	1193	1067	Sep	2	1243	1117	Sep	3	1293	1167	Sep	4	1343
1018	Sep	1	1194	1068*	Sep	1	1244	1118	Sep	3	1194	1168*	Sep	3	1344
1019	Sep	1	1195	1069	Sep	2	1245	1119	Sep	3	1295	1169	Sep	4	1345
1020*	Aug	31	1196	1070	Sep	2	1246	1120*	Sep	2	1296	1170	Sep	4	1346
1021	Sep	1	1197	1071	Sep	2	1247	1121	Sep	3	1297	1171	Sep	4	1347
1022	Sep	1	1198	1072*	Sep	1	1248	1122	Sep	3	1298	1172*	Sep	3	1348
1023	Sep	1	1199	1073	Sep	2	1249	1123	Sep	3	1299	1173	Sep	4	1349
1024*	Aug	31	1200	1074	Sep	2	1250	1124*	Sep	2	1300	1174	Sep	4	1350
1025	Sep	1	1201	1075	Sep	2	1251	1125	Sep	3	1301	1175	Sep	4	1351
1026	Sep	1	1202	1076*	Sep	1	1252	1126	Sep	3	1302	1176*	Sep	3	1352
1027	Sep	1	1203	1077	Sep	2	1253	1127	Sep	3	1303	1177	Sep	4	1353
1028*	Aug	31	1204	1078	Sep	2	1254	1128*	Sep	2	1304	1178	Sep	4	1354
1029	Sep	1	1205	1079	Sep	2	1255	1129	Sep	3	1305	1179	Sep	4	1355
1030	Sep	1	1206	1080*	Sep	1	1256	1130	Sep	3	1306	1180*	Sep	3	1356
1031	Sep	1	1207	1081	Sep	2	1257	1131	Sep	3	1307	1181	Sep	4	1357
1032*	Sep	1	1208	1082	Sep	2	1258	1132*	Sep	2	1308	1182	Sep	4	1358
1033	Sep	2	1209	1083	Sep	2	1259	1133	Sep	3	1309	1183	Sep	4	1359
1034	Sep	2	1210	1084*	Sep	1	1260	1134	Sep	3	1310	1184*	Sep	3	1360
1035	Sep	2	1211	1085	Sep	2	1261	1135	Sep	3	1311	1185	Sep	4	1361
1036*	Sep	1	1212	1086	Sep	2	1262	1136*	Sep	2	1312	1186	Sep	4	1362
1037	Sep	2	1213	1087	Sep	2	1263	1137	Sep	3	1313	1187	Sep	4	1363
1038	Sep	2	1214	1088*	Sep	1	1264	1138	Sep	3	1314	1188*	Sep	3	1364
1039	Sep	2	1215	1089	Sep	2	1265	1139	Sep	3	1315	1189	Sep	4	1365
1040*	Sep	1	1216	1090	Sep	2	1266	1140*	Sep	2	1316	1190	Sep	4	1366
1041	Sep	2	1217	1091	Sep	2	1267	1141	Sep	3	1317	1191	Sep	4	1367
1042	Sep	2	1218	1092*	Sep	2	1268	1142	Sep	3	1318	1192*	Sep	3	1368
1043	Sep	2	1219	1093	Sep	3	1269	1143	Sep	3	1319	1193	Sep	4	1369
1044*	Sep	1	1220	1094	Sep	3	1270	1144*	Sep	2	1320	1194	Sep	4	1370
1045	Sep	2	1221	1095	Sep	3	1271	1145	Sep	3	1321	1195	Sep	4	1371
1046	Sep	2	1222	1096*	Sep	2	1272	1146	Sep	3	1322	1196*	Sep	3	1372
1047	Sep	2	1223	1097	Sep	3	1273	1147	Sep	3	1323	1197	Sep	4	1373
1048*	Sep	1	1224	1098	Sep	3	1274	1148*	Sep	2	1324	1198	Sep	4	1374
1049	Sep	2	1225	1099	Sep	3	1275	1149	Sep	3	1325	1199	Sep	4	1375
1050	Sep	2	1226	1100*	Sep	2	1276	1150	Sep	3	1326	1200*	Sep	3	1376
1051	Sep	2	1227	1101	Sep	3	1277	1151	Sep	3	1327	1201	Sep	4	1377
1052*	Sep	1	1228	1102	Sep	3	1278	1152*	Sep	3	1328	1202	Sep	4	1378
1053	Sep	2	1229	1103	Sep	3	1279	1153	Sep	4	1329	1203	Sep	4	1379
1054	Sep	2	1230	1104*	Sep	2	1280	1154	Sep	4	1330	1204*	Sep	3	1380
1055	Sep	2	1231	1105	Sep	3	1281	1155	Sep	4	1331	1205	Sep	4	1381
1056*	Sep	1	1232	1106	Sep	3	1282	1156*	Sep	3	1332	1206	Sep	4	1382
1057	Sep	2	1233	1107	Sep	3	1283	1157	Sep	4	1333	1207	Sep	4	1383
1058	Sep	2	1234	1108*	Sep	2	1284	1158	Sep	4	1334	1208*	Sep	3	1384

Western Date of New Year			Parasurám Year of Malayála	Western Date of New Year			Parasurám Year of Malayála	Western Date of New Year			Parasurám Year of Malayála	Western Date of New Year			Parasurám Year of Malayála
1209	Sep	4	1385	1259	Sep	5	1435	1309	Sep	6	1485	1359	Sep	7	1535
1210	Sep	4	1386	1260*	Sep	4	1436	1310	Sep	6	1486	1360*	Sep	6	1536
1211	Sep	4	1387	1261	Sep	5	1437	1311	Sep	6	1487	1361	Sep	7	1537
1212*	Sep	4	1388	1262	Sep	5	1438	1312*	Sep	5	1488	1362	Sep	7	1538
1213	Sep	5	1389	1263	Sep	5	1439	1313	Sep	6	1489	1363	Sep	7	1539
1214	Sep	5	1390	1264*	Sep	4	1440	1314	Sep	6	1490	1364*	Sep	6	1540
1215	Sep	5	1391	1265	Sep	5	1441	1315	Sep	6	1491	1365	Sep	7	1541
1216*	Sep	4	1392	1266	Sep	5	1442	1316*	Sep	5	1492	1366	Sep	7	1542
1217	Sep	5	1393	1267	Sep	5	1443	1317	Sep	6	1493	1367	Sep	7	1543
1218	Sep	5	1394	1268*	Sep	4	1444	1318	Sep	6	1494	1368*	Sep	6	1544
1219	Sep	5	1395	1269	Sep	5	1445	1319	Sep	6	1495	1369	Sep	7	1545
1220*	Sep	4	1396	1270	Sep	5	1446	1320*	Sep	5	1496	1370	Sep	7	1546
1221	Sep	5	1397	1271	Sep	5	1447	1321	Sep	6	1497	1371	Sep	7	1547
1222	Sep	5	1398	1272*	Sep	5	1448	1322	Sep	6	1498	1372*	Sep	6	1548
1223	Sep	5	1399	1273	Sep	6	1449	1323	Sep	6	1499	1373	Sep	7	1549
1224*	Sep	4	1400	1274	Sep	6	1450	1324*	Sep	5	1500	1374	Sep	7	1550
1225	Sep	5	1401	1275	Sep	6	1451	1325	Sep	6	1501	1375	Sep	7	1551
1226	Sep	5	1402	1276*	Sep	5	1452	1326	Sep	6	1502	1376*	Sep	6	1552
1227	Sep	5	1403	1277	Sep	6	1453	1327	Sep	6	1503	1377	Sep	7	1553
1228*	Sep	4	1404	1278	Sep	6	1454	1328*	Sep	6	1504	1378	Sep	7	1554
1229	Sep	5	1405	1279	Sep	6	1455	1329	Sep	7	1505	1379	Sep	7	1555
1230	Sep	5	1406	1280*	Sep	5	1456	1330	Sep	7	1506	1380*	Sep	6	1556
1231	Sep	5	1407	1281	Sep	6	1457	1331	Sep	7	1507	1381	Sep	7	1557
1232*	Sep	4	1408	1282	Sep	6	1458	1332*	Sep	6	1508	1382	Sep	7	1558
1233	Sep	5	1409	1283	Sep	6	1459	1333	Sep	7	1509	1383	Sep	7	1559
1234	Sep	5	1410	1284*	Sep	5	1460	1334	Sep	7	1510	1384*	Sep	6	1560
1235	Sep	5	1411	1285	Sep	6	1461	1335	Sep	7	1511	1385	Sep	7	1561
1236*	Sep	4	1412	1286	Sep	6	1462	1336*	Sep	6	1512	1386	Sep	7	1562
1237	Sep	5	1413	1287	Sep	6	1463	1337	Sep	7	1513	1387	Sep	7	1563
1238	Sep	5	1414	1288*	Sep	5	1464	1338	Sep	7	1514	1388*	Sep	7	1564
1239	Sep	5	1415	1289	Sep	6	1465	1339	Sep	7	1515	1389	Sep	8	1565
1240*	Sep	4	1416	1290	Sep	6	1466	1340*	Sep	6	1516	1390	Sep	8	1566
1241	Sep	5	1417	1291	Sep	6	1467	1341	Sep	7	1517	1391	Sep	8	1567
1242	Sep	5	1418	1292*	Sep	5	1468	1342	Sep	7	1518	1392*	Sep	7	1568
1243	Sep	5	1419	1293	Sep	6	1469	1343	Sep	7	1519	1393	Sep	8	1569
1244*	Sep	4	1420	1294	Sep	6	1470	1344*	Sep	6	1520	1394	Sep	8	1570
1245	Sep	5	1421	1295	Sep	6	1471	1345	Sep	7	1521	1395	Sep	8	1571
1246	Sep	5	1422	1296*	Sep	5	1472	1346	Sep	7	1522	1396*	Sep	7	1572
1247	Sep	5	1423	1297	Sep	6	1473	1347	Sep	7	1523	1397	Sep	8	1573
1248*	Sep	4	1424	1298	Sep	6	1474	1348*	Sep	6	1524	1398	Sep	8	1574
1249	Sep	5	1425	1299	Sep	6	1475	1349	Sep	7	1525	1399	Sep	8	1575
1250	Sep	5	1426	1300*	Sep	5	1476	1350	Sep	7	1526	1400*	Sep	7	1576
1251	Sep	5	1427	1301	Sep	6	1477	1351	Sep	7	1527	1401	Sep	8	1577
1252*	Sep	4	1428	1302	Sep	6	1478	1352*	Sep	6	1528	1402	Sep	8	1578
1253	Sep	5	1429	1303	Sep	6	1479	1353	Sep	7	1529	1403	Sep	8	1579
1254	Sep	5	1430	1304*	Sep	5	1480	1354	Sep	7	1530	1404*	Sep	7	1580
1255	Sep	5	1431	1305	Sep	6	1481	1355	Sep	7	1531	1405	Sep	8	1581
1256*	Sep	4	1432	1306	Sep	6	1482	1356*	Sep	6	1532	1406	Sep	8	1582
1257	Sep	5	1433	1307	Sep	6	1483	1357	Sep	7	1533	1407	Sep	8	1583
1258	Sep	5	1434	1308*	Sep	5	1484	1358	Sep	7	1534	1408*	Sep	7	1584

Western Date of New Year			Parasurám Year of Malayála
1409	Sep	8	1585
1410	Sep	8	1586
1411	Sep	8	1587
1412*	Sep	7	1588
1413	Sep	8	1589
1414	Sep	8	1590
1415	Sep	8	1591
1416*	Sep	7	1592
1417	Sep	8	1593
1418	Sep	8	1594
1419	Sep	8	1595
1420*	Sep	7	1596
1421	Sep	8	1597
1422	Sep	8	1598
1423	Sep	8	1599
1424*	Sep	7	1600
1425	Sep	8	1601
1426	Sep	8	1602
1427	Sep	8	1603
1428*	Sep	7	1604
1429	Sep	8	1605
1430	Sep	8	1606
1431	Sep	8	1607
1432*	Sep	7	1608
1433	Sep	8	1609
1434	Sep	8	1610
1435	Sep	8	1611
1436*	Sep	7	1612
1437	Sep	8	1613
1438	Sep	8	1614
1439	Sep	8	1615
1440*	Sep	7	1616
1441	Sep	8	1617
1442	Sep	8	1618
1443	Sep	8	1619
1444*	Sep	8	1620
1445	Sep	9	1621
1446	Sep	9	1622
1447	Sep	9	1623
1448*	Sep	8	1624
1449	Sep	9	1625
1450	Sep	9	1626
1451	Sep	9	1627
1452*	Sep	8	1628
1453	Sep	9	1629
1454	Sep	9	1630
1455	Sep	9	1631
1456*	Sep	8	1632
1457	Sep	9	1633
1458	Sep	9	1634

Western Date of New Year			Parasurám Year of Malayála
1459	Sep	9	1635
1460*	Sep	8	1636
1461	Sep	9	1637
1462	Sep	9	1638
1463	Sep	9	1639
1464*	Sep	8	1640
1465	Sep	9	1641
1466	Sep	9	1642
1467	Sep	9	1643
1468*	Sep	8	1644
1469	Sep	9	1645
1470	Sep	9	1646
1471	Sep	9	1647
1472*	Sep	8	1648
1473	Sep	9	1649
1474	Sep	9	1650
1475	Sep	9	1651
1476*	Sep	8	1652
1477	Sep	9	1653
1478	Sep	9	1654
1479	Sep	9	1655
1480*	Sep	8	1656
1481	Sep	9	1657
1482	Sep	9	1658
1483	Sep	9	1659
1484*	Sep	8	1660
1485	Sep	9	1661
1486	Sep	9	1662
1487	Sep	9	1663
1488*	Sep	8	1664
1489	Sep	9	1665
1490	Sep	9	1666
1491	Sep	9	1667
1492*	Sep	8	1668
1493	Sep	9	1669
1494	Sep	9	1670
1495	Sep	9	1671
1496*	Sep	8	1672
1497	Sep	9	1673
1498	Sep	9	1674
1499	Sep	9	1675
1500*	Sep	8	1676
1501	Sep	9	1677
1502	Sep	9	1678
1503	Sep	9	1679
1504*	Sep	9	1680
1505	Sep	10	1681
1506	Sep	10	1682
1507	Sep	10	1683
1508*	Sep	9	1684

Western Date of New Year			Parasurám Year of Malayála
1509	Sep	10	1685
1510	Sep	10	1686
1511	Sep	10	1687
1512*	Sep	9	1688
1513	Sep	10	1689
1514	Sep	10	1690
1515	Sep	10	1691
1516*	Sep	9	1692
1517	Sep	10	1693
1518	Sep	10	1694
1519	Sep	10	1695
1520*	Sep	9	1696
1521	Sep	10	1697
1522	Sep	10	1698
1523	Sep	10	1699
1524*	Sep	9	1700
1525	Sep	10	1701
1526	Sep	10	1702
1527	Sep	10	1703
1528*	Sep	9	1704
1529	Sep	10	1705
1530	Sep	10	1706
1531	Sep	10	1707
1532*	Sep	9	1708
1533	Sep	10	1709
1534	Sep	10	1710
1535	Sep	10	1711
1536*	Sep	9	1712
1537	Sep	10	1713
1538	Sep	10	1714
1539	Sep	10	1715
1540*	Sep	9	1716
1541	Sep	10	1717
1542	Sep	10	1718
1543	Sep	10	1719
1544*	Sep	9	1720
1545	Sep	10	1721
1546	Sep	10	1722
1547	Sep	10	1723
1548*	Sep	9	1724
1549	Sep	10	1725
1550	Sep	10	1726
1551	Sep	10	1727
1552*	Sep	9	1728
1553	Sep	10	1729
1554	Sep	10	1730
1555	Sep	10	1731
1556*	Sep	9	1732
1557	Sep	10	1733
1558	Sep	10	1734

Western Date of New Year			Parasurám Year of Malayála
1559	Sep	10	1735
1560*	Sep	9	1736
1561	Sep	10	1737
1562	Sep	10	1738
1563	Sep	10	1739
1564*	Sep	10	1740
1565	Sep	11	1741
1566	Sep	11	1742
1567	Sep	11	1743
1568*	Sep	10	1744
1569	Sep	11	1745
1570	Sep	11	1746
1571	Sep	11	1747
1572*	Sep	10	1748
1573	Sep	11	1749
1574	Sep	11	1750
1575	Sep	11	1751
1576*	Sep	10	1752
1577	Sep	11	1753
1578	Sep	11	1754
1579	Sep	11	1755
1580*	Sep	10	1756
1581	Sep	11	1757
1582	Sep	11	1758
1583	Sep	11	1759
1584*	Sep	10	1760
1585	Sep	11	1761
1586	Sep	11	1762
1587	Sep	11	1763
1588*	Sep	10	1764
1589	Sep	11	1765
1590	Sep	11	1766
1591	Sep	11	1767
1592*	Sep	10	1768
1593	Sep	11	1769
1594	Sep	11	1770
1595	Sep	11	1771
1596*	Sep	10	1772
1597	Sep	11	1773
1598	Sep	11	1774
1599	Sep	11	1775
1600*	Sep	10	1776
1601	Sep	11	1777
1602	Sep	11	1778
1603	Sep	11	1779
1604*	Sep	10	1780
1605	Sep	11	1781
1606	Sep	11	1782
1607	Sep	11	1783
1608*	Sep	10	1784

Western Date of New Year		Parasurám Year of Malayála
1609	Sep 11	1785
1610	Sep 11	1786
1611	Sep 11	1787
1612*	Sep 10	1788
1613	Sep 11	1789
1614	Sep 11	1790
1615	Sep 11	1791
1616*	Sep 10	1792
1617	Sep 11	1793
1618	Sep 11	1794
1619	Sep 11	1795
1620*	Sep 10	1796
1621	Sep 11	1797
1622	Sep 11	1798
1623	Sep 11	1799
1624*	Sep 11	1800
1625	Sep 12	1801
1626	Sep 12	1802
1627	Sep 12	1803
1628*	Sep 11	1804
1629	Sep 12	1805
1630	Sep 12	1806
1631	Sep 12	1807
1632*	Sep 11	1808
1633	Sep 12	1809
1634	Sep 12	1810
1635	Sep 12	1811
1636*	Sep 11	1812
1637	Sep 12	1813
1638	Sep 12	1814
1639	Sep 12	1815
1640*	Sep 11	1816
1641	Sep 12	1817
1642	Sep 12	1818
1643	Sep 12	1819
1644*	Sep 11	1820
1645	Sep 12	1821
1646	Sep 12	1822
1647	Sep 12	1823
1648*	Sep 11	1824
1649	Sep 12	1825
1650	Sep 12	1826
1651	Sep 12	1827
1652*	Sep 11	1828
1653	Sep 12	1829
1654	Sep 12	1830
1655	Sep 12	1831
1656*	Sep 11	1832
1657	Sep 12	1833
1658	Sep 12	1834
1659	Sep 12	1835
1660*	Sep 11	1836
1661	Sep 12	1837
1662	Sep 12	1838
1663	Sep 12	1839
1664*	Sep 11	1840
1665	Sep 12	1841
1666	Sep 12	1842
1667	Sep 12	1843
1668*	Sep 11	1844
1669	Sep 12	1845
1670	Sep 12	1846
1671	Sep 12	1847
1672*	Sep 11	1848
1673	Sep 12	1849
1674	Sep 12	1850
1675	Sep 12	1851
1676*	Sep 11	1852
1677	Sep 12	1853
1678	Sep 12	1854
1679	Sep 12	1855
1680*	Sep 11	1856
1681	Sep 12	1857
1682	Sep 12	1858
1683	Sep 12	1859
1684*	Sep 11	1860
1685	Sep 12	1861
1686	Sep 12	1862
1687	Sep 12	1863
1688*	Sep 12	1864
1689	Sep 13	1865
1690	Sep 13	1866
1691	Sep 13	1867
1692*	Sep 12	1868
1693	Sep 13	1869
1694	Sep 13	1870
1695	Sep 13	1871
1696*	Sep 12	1872
1697	Sep 13	1873
1698	Sep 13	1874
1699	Sep 13	1875
1700*	Sep 12	1876
1701	Sep 13	1877
1702	Sep 13	1878
1703	Sep 13	1879
1704*	Sep 12	1880
1705	Sep 13	1881
1706	Sep 13	1882
1707	Sep 13	1883
1708*	Sep 12	1884
1709	Sep 13	1885
1710	Sep 13	1886
1711	Sep 13	1887
1712*	Sep 12	1888
1713	Sep 13	1889
1714	Sep 13	1890
1715	Sep 13	1891
1716*	Sep 12	1892
1717	Sep 13	1893
1718	Sep 13	1894
1719	Sep 13	1895
1720*	Sep 12	1896
1721	Sep 13	1897
1722	Sep 13	1898
1723	Sep 13	1899
1724*	Sep 12	1900
1725	Sep 13	1901
1726	Sep 13	1902
1727	Sep 13	1903
1728*	Sep 12	1904
1729	Sep 13	1905
1730	Sep 13	1906
1731	Sep 13	1907
1732*	Sep 12	1908
1733	Sep 13	1909
1734	Sep 13	1910
1735	Sep 13	1911
1736*	Sep 12	1912
1737	Sep 13	1913
1738	Sep 13	1914
1739	Sep 13	1915
1740*	Sep 13	1916
1741	Sep 14	1917
1742	Sep 14	1918
1743	Sep 14	1919
1744*	Sep 13	1920
1745	Sep 14	1921
1746	Sep 14	1922
1747	Sep 14	1923
1748*	Sep 13	1924
1749	Sep 14	1925
1750	Sep 14	1926
1751	Sep 14	1927
1752*	Sep 13	1928
1753	Sep 14	1929
1754	Sep 14	1930
1755	Sep 14	1931
1756*	Sep 13	1932
1757	Sep 14	1933
1758	Sep 14	1934
1759	Sep 14	1935
1760*	Sep 13	1936
1761	Sep 14	1937
1762	Sep 14	1938
1763	Sep 14	1939
1764*	Sep 13	1940
1765	Sep 14	1941
1766	Sep 14	1942
1767	Sep 14	1943
1768*	Sep 13	1944
1769	Sep 14	1945
1770	Sep 14	1946
1771	Sep 14	1947
1772*	Sep 13	1948
1773	Sep 14	1949
1774	Sep 14	1950
1775	Sep 14	1951
1776*	Sep 13	1952
1777	Sep 14	1953
1778	Sep 14	1954
1779	Sep 14	1955
1780*	Sep 13	1956
1781	Sep 14	1957
1782	Sep 14	1958
1783	Sep 14	1959
1784*	Sep 13	1960
1785	Sep 14	1961
1786	Sep 14	1962
1787	Sep 14	1963
1788*	Sep 13	1964
1789	Sep 14	1965
1790	Sep 14	1966
1791	Sep 14	1967
1792*	Sep 13	1968
1793	Sep 14	1969
1794	Sep 14	1970
1795	Sep 14	1971
1796*	Sep 13	1972
1797	Sep 14	1973
1798	Sep 14	1974
1799	Sep 14	1975
1800*	Sep 14	1976
1801	Sep 15	1977
1802	Sep 15	1978
1803	Sep 15	1979
1804*	Sep 14	1980
1805	Sep 15	1981
1806	Sep 15	1982
1807	Sep 15	1983
1808*	Sep 14	1984

Western Date of New Year			Parasurám Year of Malayála	Western Date of New Year			Parasurám Year of Malayála	Western Date of New Year			Parasurám Year of Malayála	Western Date of New Year			Parasurám Year of Malayála
1809	Sep	15	1985	1857	Sep	16	2033	1905	Sep	16	2081	1953	Sep	17	2129
1810	Sep	15	1986	1858	Sep	16	2034	1906	Sep	16	2082	1954	Sep	17	2130
1811	Sep	15	1987	1859	Sep	16	2035	1907	Sep	16	2083	1955	Sep	17	2131
1812*	Sep	14	1988	1860*	Sep	15	2036	1908*	Sep	15	2084	1956*	Sep	16	2132
1813	Sep	15	1989	1861	Sep	16	2037	1909	Sep	16	2085	1957	Sep	17	2133
1814	Sep	15	1990	1862	Sep	16	2038	1910	Sep	16	2086	1958	Sep	17	2134
1815	Sep	15	1991	1863	Sep	16	2039	1911	Sep	16	2087	1959	Sep	17	2135
1816*	Sep	14	1992	1864*	Sep	15	2040	1912*	Sep	15	2088	1960*	Sep	16	2136
1817	Sep	15	1993	1865	Sep	16	2041	1913	Sep	16	2089	1961	Sep	17	2137
1818	Sep	15	1994	1866	Sep	16	2042	1914	Sep	16	2090	1962	Sep	17	2138
1819	Sep	15	1995	1867	Sep	16	2043	1915	Sep	16	2091	1963	Sep	17	2139
1820*	Sep	14	1996	1868*	Sep	15	2044	1916*	Sep	16	2092	1964*	Sep	16	2140
1821	Sep	15	1997	1869	Sep	16	2045	1917	Sep	17	2093	1965	Sep	17	2141
1822	Sep	15	1998	1870	Sep	16	2046	1918	Sep	17	2094	1966	Sep	17	2142
1823	Sep	15	1999	1871	Sep	16	2047	1919	Sep	17	2095	1967	Sep	17	2143
1824*	Sep	14	2000	1872*	Sep	15	2048	1920*	Sep	16	2096	1968*	Sep	16	2144
1825	Sep	15	2001	1873	Sep	16	2049	1921	Sep	17	2097	1969	Sep	17	2145
1826	Sep	15	2002	1874	Sep	16	2050	1922	Sep	17	2098	1970	Sep	17	2146
1827	Sep	15	2003	1875	Sep	16	2051	1923	Sep	17	2099	1971	Sep	17	2147
1828*	Sep	14	2004	1876*	Sep	15	2052	1924*	Sep	16	2100	1972*	Sep	16	2148
1829	Sep	15	2005	1877	Sep	16	2053	1925	Sep	17	2101	1973	Sep	17	2149
1830	Sep	15	2006	1878	Sep	16	2054	1926	Sep	17	2102	1974	Sep	17	2150
1831	Sep	15	2007	1879	Sep	16	2055	1927	Sep	17	2103	1975	Sep	17	2151
1832*	Sep	14	2008	1880*	Sep	15	2056	1928*	Sep	16	2104	1976*	Sep	17	2152
1833	Sep	15	2009	1881	Sep	16	2057	1929	Sep	17	2105	1977	Sep	18	2153
1834	Sep	15	2010	1882	Sep	16	2058	1930	Sep	17	2106	1978	Sep	18	2154
1835	Sep	15	2011	1883	Sep	16	2059	1931	Sep	17	2107	1979	Sep	18	2155
1836*	Sep	14	2012	1884*	Sep	15	2060	1932*	Sep	16	2108	1980*	Sep	17	2156
1837	Sep	15	2013	1885	Sep	16	2061	1933	Sep	17	2109	1981	Sep	18	2157
1838	Sep	15	2014	1886	Sep	16	2062	1934	Sep	17	2110	1982	Sep	18	2158
1839	Sep	15	2015	1887	Sep	16	2063	1935	Sep	17	2111	1983	Sep	18	2159
1840*	Sep	14	2016	1888*	Sep	15	2064	1936*	Sep	16	2112	1984*	Sep	17	2160
1841	Sep	15	2017	1889	Sep	16	2065	1937	Sep	17	2113	1985	Sep	18	2161
1842	Sep	15	2018	1890	Sep	16	2066	1938	Sep	17	2114	1986	Sep	18	2162
1843	Sep	15	2019	1891	Sep	16	2067	1939	Sep	17	2115	1987	Sep	18	2163
1844*	Sep	14	2020	1892*	Sep	15	2068	1940*	Sep	16	2116	1988*	Sep	17	2164
1845	Sep	15	2021	1893	Sep	16	2069	1941	Sep	17	2117	1989	Sep	18	2165
1846	Sep	15	2022	1894	Sep	16	2070	1942	Sep	17	2118	1990	Sep	18	2166
1847	Sep	15	2023	1895	Sep	16	2071	1943	Sep	17	2119	1991	Sep	18	2167
1848*	Sep	14	2024	1896*	Sep	15	2072	1944*	Sep	16	2120	1992*	Sep	17	2168
1849	Sep	15	2025	1897	Sep	16	2073	1945	Sep	17	2121	1993	Sep	18	2169
1850	Sep	15	2026	1898	Sep	16	2074	1946	Sep	17	2122	1994	Sep	18	2170
1851	Sep	15	2027	1899	Sep	16	2075	1947	Sep	17	2123	1995	Sep	18	2171
1852*	Sep	14	2028	1900*	Sep	15	2076	1948*	Sep	16	2124	1996*	Sep	17	2172
1853	Sep	15	2029	1901	Sep	16	2077	1949	Sep	17	2125	1997	Sep	18	2173
1854	Sep	15	2030	1902	Sep	16	2078	1950	Sep	17	2126	1998	Sep	18	2174
1855	Sep	15	2031	1903	Sep	16	2079	1951	Sep	17	2127	1999	Sep	18	2175
1856*	Sep	15	2032	1904*	Sep	15	2080	1952*	Sep	16	2128	2000*	Sep	17	2176

BURMESE AND ARAKANSE CALENDARS

Western Date (Gregorian)		Burmese Thingyan Tet Hour	Minute	Second	Year
1739	12 Apr	10	28	12	1101
1740*	11 Apr	16	40	48	1102
1741	11 Apr	22	53	24	1103
1742	12 Apr	5	6	0	1104
1743	12 Apr	11	18	36	1105
1744*	11 Apr	17	31	12	1106
1745	11 Apr	23	43	48	1107
1746	12 Apr	5	56	24	1108
1747	12 Apr	12	9	0	1109
1748*	11 Apr	18	21	36	1110
1749	12 Apr	0	34	12	1111
1750	12 Apr	6	46	48	1112
1751	12 Apr	12	59	24	1113
1752*	11 Apr	19	12	0	1114
1753	12 Apr	1	24	36	1115
1754	12 Apr	7	37	12	1116
1755	12 Apr	13	49	48	1117
1756*	11 Apr	20	2	24	1118
1757	12 Apr	2	15	0	1119
1758	12 Apr	8	27	36	1120
1759	12 Apr	14	40	12	1121
1760*	11 Apr	20	52	48	1122
1761	12 Apr	3	5	24	1123
1762	12 Apr	9	18	0	1124
1763	12 Apr	15	30	36	1125
1764*	11 Apr	21	43	12	1126
1765	12 Apr	3	55	48	1127
1766	12 Apr	10	8	24	1128
1767	12 Apr	16	21	0	1129
1768*	11 Apr	22	33	36	1130
1769	12 Apr	4	46	12	1131
1770	12 Apr	10	58	48	1132
1771	12 Apr	17	11	24	1133
1772*	11 Apr	23	24	0	1134
1773	12 Apr	5	36	36	1135
1774	12 Apr	11	49	12	1136
1775	12 Apr	18	1	48	1137
1776*	12 Apr	0	14	24	1138
1777	12 Apr	6	27	0	1139
1778	12 Apr	12	39	36	1140
1779	12 Apr	18	52	12	1141
1780*	12 Apr	1	4	48	1142
1781	12 Apr	7	17	24	1143
1782	12 Apr	13	30	0	1144
1783	12 Apr	19	42	36	1145

Western Date (Gregorian)		Burmese Thingyan Tet Hour	Minute	Second	Year
1784*	12 Apr	1	55	12	1146
1785	12 Apr	8	7	48	1147
1786	12 Apr	14	20	24	1148
1787	12 Apr	20	33	0	1149
1788*	12 Apr	2	45	36	1150
1789*	12 Apr	8	58	12	1151
1790	12 Apr	15	10	48	1152
1791	12 Apr	21	23	24	1153
1792	12 Apr	3	36	0	1154
1793*	12 Apr	9	48	36	1155
1794	12 Apr	16	1	12	1156
1795	12 Apr	22	13	48	1157
1796*	12 Apr	4	26	24	1158
1797*	12 Apr	10	39	0	1159
1798	12 Apr	16	51	36	1160
1799	12 Apr	23	4	12	1161
1800*	13 Apr	5	16	48	1162
1801	13 Apr	11	29	24	1163
1802	13 Apr	17	42	0	1164
1803	13 Apr	23	54	36	1165
1804*	13 Apr	6	7	12	1166
1805	13 Apr	12	19	48	1167
1806	13 Apr	18	32	24	1168
1807	14 Apr	0	45	0	1169
1808*	13 Apr	6	57	36	1170
1809	13 Apr	13	10	12	1171
1810	13 Apr	19	22	48	1172
1811	14 Apr	1	35	24	1173
1812*	13 Apr	7	48	0	1174
1813	13 Apr	15	0	36	1175
1814	13 Apr	20	13	12	1176
1815	14 Apr	2	25	48	1177
1816*	13 Apr	8	38	24	1178
1817	13 Apr	14	51	0	1179
1818	13 Apr	21	3	36	1180
1819	14 Apr	3	16	12	1181
1820*	13 Apr	9	28	48	1182
1821	13 Apr	15	41	24	1183
1822	13 Apr	21	54	0	1184
1823	14 Apr	4	6	36	1185
1824*	13 Apr	10	19	12	1186
1825	13 Apr	16	31	48	1187
1826	13 Apr	22	44	24	1188
1827	14 Apr	4	57	0	1189
1828*	13 Apr	11	9	36	1190

Western Date (Gregorian)		Burmese Thingyan Tet Hour	Minute	Second	Year
1829	13 Apr	17	22	12	1191
1830	13 Apr	23	34	48	1192
1831	14 Apr	5	47	24	1193
1832*	13 Apr	12	0	0	1194
1833	13 Apr	18	12	36	1195
1834	14 Apr	0	25	12	1196
1835	14 Apr	6	37	48	1197
1836*	13 Apr	12	50	24	1198
1837	13 Apr	19	3	0	1199
1838	14 Apr	1	15	36	1200
1839	14 Apr	7	28	12	1201
1840*	13 Apr	13	40	48	1202
1841	13 Apr	19	53	24	1203
1842	14 Apr	2	6	0	1204
1843	14 Apr	8	18	36	1205
1844*	13 Apr	14	31	12	1206
1845	13 Apr	20	43	48	1207
1846	14 Apr	2	56	24	1208
1847	14 Apr	9	9	0	1209
1848*	13 Apr	15	21	36	1210
1849	13 Apr	21	34	12	1211
1850	14 Apr	3	46	48	1212
1851	14 Apr	9	59	24	1213
1852*	13 Apr	16	12	0	1214
1853	13 Apr	22	24	36	1215
1854	14 Apr	4	37	12	1216
1855	14 Apr	10	49	48	1217
1856*	13 Apr	17	2	24	1218
1857	13 Apr	23	15	0	1219
1858	14 Apr	5	27	36	1220
1859	14 Apr	11	40	12	1221
1860*	13 Apr	17	52	48	1222
1861	14 Apr	0	5	24	1223
1862	14 Apr	6	18	0	1224
1863	14 Apr	12	30	36	1225
1864*	13 Apr	18	43	12	1226
1865	14 Apr	0	55	48	1227
1866	14 Apr	7	8	24	1228
1867	14 Apr	12	21	0	1229
1868*	13 Apr	19	33	36	1230
1869	14 Apr	1	46	12	1231
1870	14 Apr	7	58	48	1232
1871	14 Apr	14	11	24	1233
1872*	13 Apr	20	24	0	1234
1873	14 Apr	2	36	36	1235
1874	14 Apr	8	49	12	1236
1875	14 Apr	15	1	48	1237
1876*	13 Apr	21	14	24	1238

Western Date (Gregorian)		Burmese Thingyan Tet Hour	Minute	Second	Year
1877	14 Apr	3	27	0	1239
1878	14 Apr	9	39	36	1240
1879	14 Apr	15	52	12	1241
1880*	13 Apr	22	4	48	1242
1881	14 Apr	4	17	24	1243
1882	14 Apr	10	30	0	1244
1883	14 Apr	16	42	36	1245
1884*	13 Apr	22	55	12	1246
1885	14 Apr	5	7	48	1247
1886	14 Apr	11	20	24	1248
1887	14 Apr	17	33	0	1249
1888*	13 Apr	23	45	36	1250
1889	14 Apr	5	58	12	1251
1890	14 Apr	12	10	48	1252
1891	14 Apr	18	23	24	1253
1892*	13 Apr	0	36	0	1254
1893	14 Apr	6	48	36	1255
1894	14 Apr	13	1	12	1256
1895	14 Apr	19	13	48	1257
1896*	13 Apr	1	26	24	1258
1897	14 Apr	7	39	0	1259
1898	14 Apr	13	51	36	1260
1899	14 Apr	20	4	12	1261
1900	15 Apr	2	16	48	1262
1901	15 Apr	8	29	24	1263
1902	15 Apr	14	42	0	1264
1903	15 Apr	20	54	36	1265
1904*	15 Apr	3	7	12	1266
1905	15 Apr	9	19	48	1267
1906	15 Apr	15	32	24	1268
1907	15 Apr	21	45	0	1269
1908*	15 Apr	3	57	36	1270
1909	15 Apr	10	10	12	1271
1910	15 Apr	16	22	48	1272
1911	15 Apr	22	35	24	1273
1912*	15 Apr	4	48	0	1274
1913	15 Apr	11	0	36	1275
1914	15 Apr	17	13	12	1276
1915	15 Apr	23	25	48	1277
1916*	15 Apr	5	38	24	1278
1917	15 Apr	11	51	0	1279
1918	15 Apr	18	3	36	1280
1919	16 Apr	0	16	12	1281
1920*	15 Apr	6	28	48	1282
1921	15 Apr	12	41	24	1283
1922	15 Apr	18	54	0	1284
1923	16 Apr	1	6	36	1285
1924*	15 Apr	7	19	12	1286

Western Date (Gregorian)		Burmese Thingyan Tet Hour	Minute	Second	Year
1925	15 Apr	13	31	48	1287
1926	15 Apr	19	44	24	1288
1927	16 Apr	1	56	0	1289
1928*	15 Apr	8	9	36	1290
1929	15 Apr	14	22	12	1291
1930	15 Apr	20	34	48	1292
1931	16 Apr	2	49	12	1293
1932*	15 Apr	9	1	48	1294
1933	15 Apr	15	14	24	1295
1934	15 Apr	21	27	0	1296
1935	16 Apr	3	39	36	1297
1936*	15 Apr	9	52	12	1298
1937	15 Apr	16	4	48	1299
1938	15 Apr	22	17	24	1300
1939	16 Apr	4	29	0	1301
1940*	15 Apr	10	42	36	1302
1941	15 Apr	16	55	12	1303
1942	15 Apr	23	7	48	1304
1943	16 Apr	5	20	24	1305
1944*	15 Apr	11	33	0	1306
1945	15 Apr	17	45	36	1307
1946	15 Apr	23	58	12	1308
1947	16 Apr	6	10	48	1309
1948*	15 Apr	12	22	24	1310
1949	15 Apr	18	36	0	1311
1950	16 Apr	0	48	36	1312
1951	16 Apr	7	1	12	1313
1952*	15 Apr	13	13	48	1314
1953	15 Apr	19	25	24	1315
1954	16 Apr	1	39	0	1316
1955	16 Apr	7	51	36	1317
1956*	15 Apr	14	4	12	1318
1957	15 Apr	20	16	48	1319
1958	16 Apr	2	29	4	1320
1959	16 Apr	8	42	0	1321
1960*	15 Apr	14	54	36	1322
1961	15 Apr	21	7	12	1323
1962	16 Apr	3	19	48	1324

Western Date (Gregorian)		Burmese Thingyan Tet Hour	Minute	Second	Year
1963	16 Apr	9	32	24	1325
1964*	15 Apr	15	45	0	1326
1965	15 Apr	21	57	36	1327
1966	16 Apr	4	10	12	1328
1967	16 Apr	10	22	48	1329
1968*	15 Apr	16	35	24	1330
1969	15 Apr	22	48	0	1331
1970	16 Apr	5	0	36	1332
1971	16 Apr	11	13	12	1333
1972*	15 Apr	17	25	48	1334
1973	15 Apr	23	38	24	1335
1974	16 Apr	5	51	0	1336
1975	16 Apr	12	3	36	1337
1976*	15 Apr	18	16	12	1338
1977	16 Apr	0	28	48	1339
1978	16 Apr	6	41	24	1340
1979	16 Apr	12	54	0	1341
1980*	15 Apr	19	6	36	1342
1981	16 Apr	1	19	12	1343
1982	16 Apr	7	31	48	1344
1983	16 Apr	13	44	24	1345
1984*	15 Apr	19	57	0	1346
1985	16 Apr	2	9	36	1347
1986	16 Apr	8	22	12	1348
1987	16 Apr	14	34	48	1349
1988*	15 Apr	20	47	24	1350
1989	16 Apr	3	0	0	1351
1990	16 Apr	9	12	36	1352
1991	16 Apr	15	25	12	1353
1992*	15 Apr	21	37	48	1354
1993	16 Apr	3	50	24	1355
1994	16 Apr	10	3	0	1356
1995	16 Apr	16	15	36	1357
1996*	15 Apr	22	28	12	1358
1997	16 Apr	4	40	48	1359
1998	16 Apr	10	53	24	1360
1999	16 Apr	17	6	0	1361
2000*	15 Apr	23	18	36	1362

FAR EAST

THE CHINESE CALENDAR

The Chinese calendar is the longest unbroken sequence of time measurement in history. Its epoch is said to be 2953 B.C. As Chinese culture spread, the calendar was adopted by a large number of people including the Koreans and the Japanese. Time measurement was taken very seriously by the ancient Chinese. The calendar was considered a sacred document. Each year the new calendar was presented in an elaborate ceremony held on the first day of the tenth month. Copies were given first to the emperor and his family, then to the regional governors and other dignitaries. Falsification of the calendar was a capital crime. The Chinese calendar was not subject to the local variations which occurred in India. From time to time the Chinese modified their methods of astronomical calculation in an effort to make them more accurate, particularly with regard to predicting eclipses; however, the basic structure of the calendar remained unchanged.

Like all other calendars, the Chinese one is based on the apparent motion of the sun, moon and planets which is expressed by the Chinese concept of three roads through the heavens. The first of these is the Red Road, or what we would call the equator. It is along this path that the 28 Chinese lunar mansions are placed. The second is called the Yellow Road, which we call the ecliptic, or the path travelled by the sun. The third is called the White Road, or the path of the moon, which travels up and down over the ecliptic at an angle just short of 6°. The Zodiac, or the Twelve Branches as the Chinese call it, was developed from the twelve places to which the seven stars of the Big Dipper point during the twelve months of the year. The calendar itself is luni-solar, and is intercalated whenever two new months fall within a zodiacal sign.

Some time during the very early period in Chinese astronomy/astrology, two systems were developed, both of which covered a 60 year cycle. The first system combines 10 signs related to the Chinese constellations with the 12 animals of the Chinese zodiac. The 12 zodiacal signs are given below with their English translations. The 10 signs of the Chinese constellations are also given, but without translation, as there is no equivalent in English.

12 animals of the Zodiac		10 celestial signs
1. Tse	the Rat	1. Kiah
2. Chau	the Ox	2. Yih
3. Yin	the Tiger	3. Ping
4. Mau	the Hare	4. Ting
5. Shin	the Dragon	5. Wu
6. Se	the Snake	6. Ki
7. Wu	the Horse	7. Kang
8. Wi	the Sheep	8. Sin
9. Shin	the Monkey	9. Jin
10. Yu	the Rooster	10. Kwei
11. Siuh	the Dog	
12. Hai	the Pig	

The first sign in each series is combined to form the name of the first year in the 60 year cycle, Kia-tsu. The second sign in each series combines to form the name of the 2nd year, I-chaw and so on through the tenth sign. The eleventh sign in the 1st series then combines with the 1st sign in the second series to form the name of the eleventh year, Kiah-siuh and so on until the last signs in each series coincide, forming the name of the 60th year, Kwei-hai.

The second system for obtaining the 60 year cycle (less frequently used and never part of the other calendar) works exactly the same way, but instead of using the ten signs relating to the Chinese constellations, it uses the five "elements," wood, fire, earth, metal and water, each repeated twice.

Terrestrial Sign		Western Year	Element
Chinese	English		
Tzu	Rat	1924	Wood
Chou	Ox	1925	Wood
Yin	Tiger	1926	Fire
Mao	Hare	1927	Fire
Shin	Dragon	1928	Earth
Ssu	Snake	1929	Earth
Wu	Horse	1930	Metal

Terrestrail Sign Chinese	Terrestrail Sign English	Western Year	Element
We	Sheep	1931	Metal
Shin	Monkey	1932	Water
Yu	Rooster	1933	Water
Hsu	Dog	1934	Wood
Hai	Pig	1935	Wood
Tzu	Rat	1936	Fire
Chou	Ox	1937	Fire
Yin	Tiger	1938	Earth
Mao	Hare	1939	Earth
Shin	Dragon	1940	Metal
Ssu	Snake	1941	Metal
Wu	Horse	1942	Water
We	Sheep	1943	Water
Shin	Monkey	1944	Wood
Yu	Rooster	1945	Wood
Hsu	Dog	1946	Fire
Hai	Pig	1947	Fire
Tzu	Rat	1948	Metal
Chou	Ox	1949	Metal
Yin	Tiger	1950	Water
Mao	Hare	1951	Water
Shin	Dragon	1952	Wood
Ssu	Snake	1953	Wood
Wu	Horse	1954	Fire
We	Sheep	1955	Fire
Shin	Monkey	1956	Earth
Yu	Rooster	1957	Earth
Hsu	Dog	1958	Metal
Hai	Pig	1959	Metal
Tzu	Rat	1960	Earth
Chou	Ox	1961	Earth
Yin	Tiger	1962	Metal
Mao	Hare	1963	Metal
Shin	Dragon	1964	Water
Ssu	Snake	1965	Water
Wu	Horse	1966	Wood
We	Sheep	1967	Wood

Terrestrail Sign Chinese	Terrestrail Sign English	Western Year	Element
Shin	Monkey	1968	Fire
Yu	Rooster	1969	Fire
Hsu	Dog	1970	Earth
Hai	Pig	1971	Earth
Tzu	Rat	1972	Water
Chou	Ox	1973	Water
Yin	Tiger	1974	Wood
Mao	Hare	1975	Wood
Shin	Dragon	1976	Fire
Ssu	Snake	1977	Fire
Wu	Horse	1978	Earth
We	Sheep	1979	Earth
Shin	Monkey	1980	Metal
Yu	Rooster	1981	Metal
Hsu	Dog	1982	Water
Hai	Pig	1983	Water

The Chinese, like most other peoples, use a zodiac based on 360°. But they do not use the 12 signs known in the west and other parts of the world. Instead, they use 28 lunar mansions which represent constellations along the ecliptic through which the moon passes. These mansions are unequal—ranging from 1° of the sky to 34°. There are two possible translations for the names of the mansions and two calculations for the size of each. The English translations from the 11th century Soochow astronomical charts and the common Chinese names with English translations are given in the table below. The number of degrees in each tables does not add up to 360 because in the 4th century B.C. the Chinese astrologers suddenly changed the division of the circle from 360° to 365°15′.

THE LUNAR MANSIONS—CHINESE

	Common Translation		Soochow Astronomical Chart	
Chinese Name	English Name	Degrees	English Name	Degrees
Keo	Crocodile	11°	The Horn	12°
Kang	Dragon	11	Neck of the Dragon	9
Te	Badger	18	Root or Base	16
Fang	Fox	5	House	6
Sin	Dog	7	Dragon's Heart	6
Wei	Wolf	16	Dragon's Tail	19
Ke	Hare	9	Sieve	11
Tow	Porcupine	24	Measure (or bushel)	25
New	Rat	8	Ox	7
Neu	Leopard	12	Virgin	11
Heu	Griffon	10	Emptiness	9
Wei	Bat	20	Danger (Fate)	16
Shih	Pheasant	15	Room	17
Peih	Gibbon	12	Wall	9
Kwei	Cock	12	Sandal	16
Lew	Crow	13	Reapers	12
Wei	Horse	13	Stomach (Grain Store)	15
Maou	Earthworm	8	Setting Sun	11
Peih	Deer	15	End	17
Tsuy	Monkey	1	Bird's Bill	1
Tsan	Serpent	11	Military Chieftan	10
Tsing	Stag	31	Well	34
Kwei	Sheep	4	Spirits of Dead	2
Lew	Tapir	17	Willow	14
Sing	Swallow	9	Star	7
Chang	Ox	18	Drawn Bow	17
Yen	Tiger	17	Wing of Red Bird	19
Chin	Pig	13	Crossbar of Chariot	17

The Chinese use a 60 day cycle which works the same way as the 60 year cycle and uses the same system of 12 and 10 signs. For example, the name of the first day in the 60-day cycle is Kia-tzu. The name of the second day is I-Chou, and so on. Because of the 60-day cycle, the day on which each year begins moves 5 (or in leap year 6) days forward.

The Chinese New Year falls on the new moon nearest to the 15th degree of Aquarius. In modern times this corresponds to about the 4th or the 5th of February so that the new moon could be 15 days on either side of that date. The year is divided into 24 periods of about 2 weeks each (each covers 15° on the 360° circle). The names of these periods with approximate dates are given below:

Feb.	5	1. Spring begins	Aug.	7	13. The Autumn Begins
	19	2. The Rain Water		23	14. The Limit of Heat
Mar.	5	3. The Excited Insects	Sept.	8	15. The White Dew
	20	4. The Vernal Equinox		23	16. The Autumnal Equinox
April	5	5. The Clear and Bright	Oct.	8	17. The Cold Dew
	20	6. The Grain Rains		23	18. The Hoar Frost Descends
May	5	7. The Summer Begins	Nov	7	19. The Winter Begins
	21	8. The Grain Fills		22	20. The Little Snow

June	6	9. The Grain in Ear
	21	10. The Summer Solstice
July	7	11. The Slight Heat
	23	12. The Great Heat
Dec.	7	21. The Heavy Snow
	21	22. The Winter Solstice
Jan.	6	23. The Little Cold
	21	24. The Severe Cold

The Chinese adopted the Gregorian calendar in 1911 for official purposes, but the ancient lunar calendar is still in general use.

In the 2000-year conversion table below, we give the Western year, the Western date of the Chinese New Year, the Chinese cycle number, the year name, its place in the cycle, and the Japanese name of the year and the year number. There is an asterisk next to those years in which there is an intercalary month.

CHINESE AND JAPANESE CALENDARS

Western Date of New Year (Julian)			Cycle No.	Chinese Year Name & Cycle		Intercalculary Month	Japanese Name of Year Cycle and Year Number	
1 A.D.	Feb	10	44	Sin-yu	58		Kanno-to-torri	661
2	Jan	31		Jin-siuh	59		Midsno-je-in	662
3	Jan	20		Kwei-hai	60	*	Midsno-to-y	663
4*	Feb	7	45	Kiah-tse	1		Kino-je-ne	664
5	Jan	28		Yih-chau	2		Kino-to-oos	665
6	Jan	17		Ping-yin	3	*	Fino-je-torra	666
7	Feb	4		Ting-mau	4		Fino-to-ov	667
8*	Jan	25		Wu-shin	5		Tsutsno-je-tats	668
9	Jan	14		Ki-se	6	*	Tsutsno-to-mi	669
10	Feb	2		Kang-wu	7		Kanno-je-ooma	670
11	Jan	22		Sin-wi	8	*	Kanno-to-tsitsuse	671
12*	Feb	9		Jin-shin	9		Midsno-ie-sar	672
13	Jan	30		Kwei-yu	10		Midsno-to-torri	673
14	Jan	19		Kiah-siuh	11	*	Kino-je-in	674
15	Feb	6		Yih-hai	12		Kino-to-y	675
16*	Jan	27		Ping-tse	13		Fino-je-ne	676
17	Jan	16		Ting-chau	14	*	Fino-to-oos	677
18	Feb	3		Wuyin	15		Tsutsno-je-torra	678
19	Jan	23		Ki-mau	16		Tsutsno-to-ov	679
20*	Feb	10		Kang-shin	17	*	Kanno-je-tats	680
21	Jan	31		Sin-se	18		Kanno-to-mi	681
22	Jan	20		Jin-wu	19	*	Midsno-je-ooma	682
23	Feb	7		Kwei-wi	20		Midsno-totsitsuse	683
24*	Jan	28		Kiah-shin	21		Kino-je-sar	684
25	Jan	17		Yih-yu	22	*	Kino-to-torri	685
26	Feb	4		Ping-siuh	23		Fino-je-in	686
27	Jan	25		Ting-hai	24		Fino-to-y	687
28*	Jan	14		Wutse	25	*	Tsutsno-je-ne	688
29	Feb	2		Ki-chau	26		Tsutsno-to-oos	689
30	Jan	22		Kang-yin	27	*	Kanno-je-torra	690

Western Date of New Year (Julian)			Cycle No.	Chinese Year Name & Cycle		Intercalculary Month	Japanese Name of Year Cycle and Year Number	
31	Feb	9		Sin-mau	28		Kanno-to-ov	691
32*	Jan	30		Jin-shin	29	*	Midsno-je-tats	692
33	Jan	19		Kwei-se	30		Midsno-to-mi	693
34	Feb	6		Kiah-wu	31		Kino-je-ooma	694
35	Jan	27		Yih-wi	32		Kino-to-tsitsuse	695
36*	Jan	16		Ping-shin	33	*	Fino-je-sar	696
37	Feb	3		Ting-yu	34		Fino-to-torri	697
38	Jan	23		Wu-siuh	35	*	Tsutsno-je-in	698
39	Feb	10		Ki-hai	36		Tsutsno-to-y	699
40*	Jan	31		Kang-tse	37		Kanno-je-ne	700
41	Jan	20		Sin-chau	38	*	Kanno-to-oos	701
42	Feb	7		Jin-yin	39		Midsno-je-torra	702
43	Jan	28		Kwei-mau	40		Midsno-to-ov	703
44*	Jan	17		Kiah-shin	41	*	Kino-je-tats	704
45	Feb	4		Yih-se	42		Kino-to-mi	705
46	Jan	25		Ping-wu	43		Fino-je-ooma	706
47	Jan	14		Ting-wi	44	*	Fino-to-tsitsuse	707
48*	Feb	2		Wu-shin	45		Tsutsno-je-sar	708
49	Jan	22		Ki-vu	46	*	Tsutsno-to-torri	709
50	Feb	9		Kang-siuh	47		Kanno-je-in	710
51	Jan	30		Sin-hai	48		Kanno-to-y	711
52*	Jan	19		Jin-tse	49	*	Midsno-je-ne	712
53	Feb	6		Kwei-chau	50		Midsno-to-os	713
54	Jan	27		Kiah-yin	51		Kino-je-torra	714
55	Jan	16		Yih-man	52	*	Kino-to-ov	715
56*	Feb	3		Ping-shin	53		Fino-je-tats	716
57	Jan	23		Ting-wu	54	*	Fino-to-mi	717
58	Feb	10		Wu-wu	55		Tsutsno-je-ooma	718
59	Jan	31		Ki-wi	56		Tsutsno-to-tsitsuse	719
60*	Jan	20		Kang-shin	57	*	Kanno-je-sar	720
61	Feb	7		Sin-yu	58		Kanno-to-torri	721
62	Jan	28		Jin-siuh	59		Midsno-je-in	722
63	Jan	17		Kwei-hai	60	*	Midsno-to-y	723
64*	Feb	4	46	Kiah-tse	1		Kino-je-ne	724
65	Jan	25		Yih-chau	2		Kino-to-oos	725
66	Jan	14		Ping-yin	3	*	Fino-je-torra	726
67	Feb	2		Ting-mau	4		Fino-to-ov	727
68*	Jan	22		Wu-shin	5	*	Tsutsno-je-tats	728
69	Feb	9		Ki-se	6		Tsutsno-tomi	729
70	Jan	30		Kang-wu	7		Kanno-je-ooma	730
71	Jan	19		Sin-wi	8	*	Kanno-to-tsituse	731
72*	Feb	6		Jin-shin	9		Midsno-je-sar	732
73	Jan	27		Kwei-yu	10	*	Midsno-to-torri	733
74	Jan	16		Kiah-siuh	11		Kino-je-in	734

Western Date of New Year (Julian)			Cycle No.	Chinese Year Name & Cycle		Intercalculary Month	Japanese Name of Year Cycle and Year Number	
75	Feb	3		Yih-hai	12		Kino-to-y	735
76*	Jan	23		Ping-tse	13	*	Fino-je-ne	736
77	Feb	10		Ting-chau	14		Fino-to-oos	737
78	Jan	31		Wu-yin	15	*	Tsutsno-je-torra	738
79	Jan	20		Ki-mau	16		Tsutsno-to-ov	739
80*	Feb	7		Kang-shin	17		Kanno-je-tats	740
81	Jan	28		Sin-se	18		Kanno-to-mi	741
82	Jan	17		Jin-wu	19	*	Midsno-je-ooma	742
83	Feb	4		Kwei-wi	20		Midsno-to-tsitsuse	743
84*	Jan	15		Kiah-shin	21		Kino-je-sar	744
85	Jan	25		Yih-yu	22	*	Kino-to-torri	745
86	Jan	14		Ping-siuh	23		Fino-je-in	746
87	Feb	2		Ting-hai	24	*	Fino-to-y	747
88*	Jan	22		Wu-tse	25		Tsutsno-je-ne	748
89	Feb	9		Ki-chau	26		Tsutsno-to-oos	749
90	Jan	30		Kang-yin	27	*	Kanno-je-torra	750
91	Jan	19		Sin-mau	28		Kanno-to-ov	751
92*	Feb	6		Jin-shin	29		Midsno-je-tats	752
93	Jan	27		Kwei-so	30	*	Midsno-to-mi	753
94	Jan	16		Kiah-wu	31		Kno-je-ooma	754
95	Feb	3		Yih-wi	32	*	Kino-to-tsitsuse	755
96*	Jan	23		Ping-shin	33		Fino-jo-sar	756
97	Feb	10		Ting-yu	34		Fino-to-torri	757
98	Jan	31		Wu-siuh	35	*	Tsutsno-je-in	758
99	Jan	20		Ki-hai	36		Tsutsno-to-v	759
100*	Feb	7		Kang-tse	37		Kanno-je-ne	760
101	Jan	28		Sin-chau	38	*	Kanno-to-oos	761
102	Jan	17		Jin-yin	39		Midsno-je-torra	762
103	Feb	4		Kwei-mau	40		Midsno-to-ov	763
104*	Jan	25		Kiah-shin	41	*	Kino-je-tats	764
105	Jan	14		Yih-se	42		Kino-to-mi	765
106	Feb	2		Ping-wu	43	*	Fino-je-ooma	766
107	Jan	22		Ting-wi	44		Fino-to-tsitsuse	767
108*	Feb	9		Wu-shin	45		Tsutsno-je-sar	768
109	Jan	30		Ki-yo	46	*	Tsutsno-to-torri	769
110	Jan	19		Kang-siuh	47		Kanno-je-in	770
111	Feb	6		Sin-hai	48		Kanno-to-v	771
112*	Jan	27		Jin-tse	49	*	Midsno-je-ne	772
113	Jan	16		Kwei-chau	50		Midsno-to-oos	773
114	Feb	3		Kiah-yin	51	*	Kino-je-torra	774
115	Jan	23		Yin-mau	52		Kino-to-ov	775
116*	Feb	10		Ping-shin	53		Fino-je-tats	776
117	Jan	31		Ting-wu	54	*	Fino-to-mi	777
118	Jan	20		Wu-wu	55		Tsutsno-je-ooma	778

Western Date of New Year (Julian)			Cycle No.	Chinese Year Name & Cycle		Intercalculary Month	Japanese Name of Year Cycle and Year Number	
119	Feb	7		Ki-wi	56		Tsutsno-to-tsituse	779
120*	Jan	28		Kang-shin	57	*	Kanno-je-sar	780
121	Jan	17		Sin-yu	58		Kanno-to-torri	781
122	Feb	4		Jin-siuh	59		Midsno-je-in	782
123	Jan	25		Kwei-hai	60	*	Midsno-to-y	783
124*	Jan	14	47	Kiah-tse	1		Kino-je-ne	784
125	Feb	2		Yih-chau	2		Kino-to-oos	785
126	Jan	22		Ping-yin	3		Fino-je-torra	786
127	Feb	9		Ting-mau	4		Fino-to-ov	787
128*	Jan	30		Wu-shin	5	*	Tsutsno-je-tats	788
129	Jan	19		Ki-se	6		Tsutsno-to-mi	789
130	Jan	27		Kang-wu	7		Kanno-je-ooma	790
131	Jan	16		Sin-wi	8	*	Kanno-to-tsitsuse	791
132*	Feb	3		Jin-shin	9		Midsno-je-sar	792
133	Jan	23		Kwei-vu	10	*	Midsno-to-torri	793
134	Feb	10		Kiah-siuh	11		Kino-je-in	794
135	Jan	31		Yih-hai	12		Kino-to-y	795
136*	Jan	20		Ping-tse	13	*	Fino-je-ne	796
137	Feb	7		Ting-chau	14		Fino-to-oos	797
138	Jan	28		Wu-yin	15		Tsutsno-je-torra	798
139	Jan	17		Ki-mau	16	*	Tsutsno-to-ov	799
140*	Feb	4		Kang-shin	17		Kanno-je-tats	800
141	Jan	25		Sin-se	18		Kanno-to-mi	801
142	Jan	14		Jin-wu	19	*	Midsno-je-ooma	802
143	Feb	2		Kwei-wi	20		Midsno-to-tsitsuse	803
144*	Jan	22		Kiah-shin	21	*	Kino-je-sar	804
145	Feb	9		Yih-yu	22		Kino-to-torri	805
146	Jan	30		Ping-siuh	23		Fino-je-in	806
147	Jan	19		Ting-hai	24	*	Fino-to-y	807
148*	Feb	6		Wutse	25		Tsutsno-je-ne	808
149	Jan	27		Ki-chau	26		Tsutsno-to-oos	809
150	Jan	16		Kang-yin	27	*	Kanno-je-torra	810
151	Feb	3		Sin-mau	28		Kanno-to-ov	811
152*	Jan	23		Jin-shin	29	*	Midsno-je-tats	812
153	Feb	10		Kwei-se	30		Midsno-to-mi	813
154	Jan	31		Kiah-wu	31		Kino-je-ooma	814
155	Jan	20		Yih-wi	32	*	Kino-to-tsitsuse	815
156*	Feb	7		Ping-shin	33		Fino-je-sar	816
157	Jan	28		Ting-yu	34		Fino-to-torri	817
158	Jan	17		Wu-siuh	35	*	Tsutsno-je-in	818
159	Feb	4		Ki-hai	36		Tsutsno-to-y	819
160*	Jan	25		Kang-tse	37		Kanno-je-ne	820
161	Jan	14		Sin-chau	38	*	Kanno-to-oos	821
162	Feb	2		Jin-yin	39		Midsno-je-torra	822

Western Date of New Year (Julian)			Cycle No.	Chinese Year Name & Cycle		Intercalculary Month	Japanese Name of Year Cycle and Year Number	
163	Jan	22		Kwei-mau	40	*	Midsno-to-ov	823
164*	Feb	9		Kiah-shin	41		Kino-je-tats	824
165	Jan	13		Yih-se	42		Kino-to-mi	825
166	Jan	19		Ping-wu	43	*	Fino-je-ooma	826
167	Feb	6		Ting-wi	44		Fino-to-tsitsuse	827
168*	Jan	27		Wu-shin	45		Tsutsno-je-sar	828
169	Jan	16		Ki-yu	46	*	Tsutsno-to-torri	829
170	Feb	3		Kang-siuh	47		Kanno-je-in	830
171	Jan	23		Sin-hai	48	*	Kanno-to-y	831
172*	Feb	10		Jin-tse	49		Midsno-je-ne	832
173	Jan	31		Kwei-chau	50		Midsno-to-oos	833
174	Jan	20		Kiah-yin	51	*	Kino-je-torra	834
175	Feb	7		Yih-mau	52		Kino-to-ov	835
176*	Jan	28		Ping-shin	53		Fino-je-tats	836
177	Jan	17		Ting-wu	54	*	Fino-je-mi	837
178	Feb	4		Wu-wu	55		Tsutsno-je-ooma	838
179	Jan	25		Ki-wi	56		Tsutsno-to-tsitsuse	839
180*	Jan	14		Kang-shiu	57	*	Kanno-je-sar	840
181	Feb	2		Sin-yu	58		Kanno-to-torri	841
182	Jan	22		Jin-siuh	59	*	Midsno-je-in	842
183	Feb	9		Kwei-hai	60		Midsno-to-y	843
184*	Jan	30	48	Kiah-tse	1		Kino-je-ne	844
185	Jan	19		Yih-chau	2	*	Kino-to-oos	845
186	Feb	6		Ping-yin	3		Fino-je-torra	846
187	Jan	27		Ting-mau	4	*	Fino-to-ov	847
188*	Jan	16		Wu-shin	5		Tsutsno-je-tats	848
189	Feb	3		Ki-se	6		Tsutsno-to-mi	849
190	Jan	23		Kang-wu	7	*	Kanno-je-ooma	850
191	Feb	10		Sin-wi	8		Kanno-to-tsitsuse	851
192*	Jan	31		Jin-shin	9		Midsno-je-sar	852
193	Jan	20		Kwei-yu	10	*	Midsno-to-torri	853
194	Feb	7		Kiah-siuh	11		Kino-je-in	854
195	Jan	28		Yih-hai	12		Kino-to-y	855
196*	Jan	17		Ping-tse	13	*	Fino-je-ne	856
197	Feb	4		Ting-chau	14		Fino-to-oos	857
198	Jan	25		Wu-yin	15		Tsutsno-je-torra	858
199	Jan	14		Ki-mau	16	*	Tsutsno-to-ov	859
200*	Feb	2		Kang-shin	17		Kanno-je-tats	860
201	Jan	22		Sin-se	18	*	Kanno-to-mi	861
202	Feb	9		Jin-wu	19		Midsno-je-ooma	862
203	Jan	30		Kwei-wi	20		Midsno-to-tsitsuse	863
204*	Jan	19		Kiah-shin	21	*	Kino-je-sar	864
205	Feb	6		Yih-yu	22		Kino-to-torri	865
206	Jan	27		Ping-siuh	23		Fino-je-in	866

Western Date of New Year (Julian)			Cycle No.	Chinese Year Name & Cycle		Intercalculary Month	Japanese Name of Year Cycle and Year Number	
207	Jan	16		Ting-hai	24	*	Fino-to-y	867
208*	Feb	3		Wu-tse	25		Tsutsno-je-ne	868
209	Jan	23		Ki-chau	26	*	Tsutsno-to-oos	869
210	Feb	10		Kang-yin	27		Kanno-je-torra	870
211	Jan	31		Sin-mau	28		Kanno-to-ov	871
212*	Jan	20		Jin-shin	29	*	Midsno-je-tats	872
213	Feb	7		Kwei-se	30		Midsno-to-mi	873
214	Jan	28		Kiah-wu	31		Kino-je-ooma	874
215	Jan	17		Yih-wi	32	*	Kino-to-tsitsuse	875
216*	Feb	4		Ping-shin	33		Fino-je-sar	876
217	Jan	25		Ting-yu	34		Fino-to-torri	877
218	Feb	14		Wu-siuh	35	*	Tsutsno-je-in	878
219	Feb	2		Ki-hai	36		Tsutsno-to-y	879
220*	Jan	22		Kang-tse	37	*	Kanno-je-ne	880
221	Feb	9		Sin-chau	38		Kanno-to-oos	881
222	Jan	30		Jin-yin	39		Midsno-je-torra	882
223	Jan	19		Kwei-mau	40	*	Midsno-to-ov	883
224*	Feb	6		Kiah-shin	41		Kino-je-tats	884
225	Jan	27		Yih-se	42		Kino-to-mi	885
226	Jan	16		Ping-wu	43	*	Fino-je-ooma	886
227	Feb	3		Ting-wi	44		Fino-to-tsitsuse	887
228*	Jan	23		Wu-shin	45	*	Tsutsno-je-sar	888
229	Feb	10		Ki-yu	46		Tsutsno-to-torri	889
230	Jan	31		Kang-siuh	47		Kanno-je-in	890
231	Jan	20		Sin-hai	48	*	Kanno-to-y	891
232*	Feb	7		Jin-tse	49		Midsno-je-ne	892
233	Jan	28		Kwei-chau	50		Midsno-to-oos	893
234	Jan	17		Kiah-yin	51	*	Kino-je-torra	894
235	Feb	4		Yih-mau	52		Kino-to-ov	895
236*	Jan	25		Ping-shin	53		Fino-je-tats	896
237	Jan	14		Ting-wu	54	*	Fino-to-mi	897
238	Feb	2		Wu-wu	55		Tsutsno-je-ooma	898
239	Jan	22		Ki-wi	56	*	Tsutsno-to-tsitsuse	899
240*	Feb	9		Kang-shin	57		Kanno-je-sar	900
241	Jan	30		Sin-yu	58		Kanno-to-torri	901
242	Jan	19		Jin-siuh	59	*	Midsno-je-in	902
243	Feb	6		Kwei-hai	60		Midsno-to-y	903
244*	Jan	27	49	Kiah-tse	1		Kino-je-ne	904
245	Jan	16		Yih-chau	2	*	Kino-to-oos	905
246	Feb	3		Ping-yin	3		Fino-je-torra	906
247	Jan	23		Ting-mau	4	*	Fino-to-ov	907
248*	Feb	10		Wu-shin	5		Tsutsno-je-tats	908
249	Jan	31		Ki-se	6		Tsutsno-to-mi	909
250	Jan	20		Kang-wu	7	*	Kanno-je-ooma	910

Western Date of New Year (Julian)			Cycle No.	Chinese Year Name & Cycle		Intercalculary Month	Japanese Name of Year Cycle and Year Number	
251	Feb	7		Sin-wi	8		Kanno-to-tsitsuse	911
252*	Jan	28		Jin-shin	9		Midsno-je-sar	912
253	Jan	17		Kwei-yu	10	*	Midsno-to-torri	913
254	Feb	4		Kiah-siuh	11		Kino-je-in	914
255	Jan	25		Yih-hai	12		Kino-to-y	915
256*	Jan	14		Ping-tse	13	*	Fino-je-ne	916
257	Feb	2		Ting-chau	14		Fino-to-oos	917
258	Jan	22		Wu-yin	15	*	Tsutsno-je-torra	918
259	Feb	9		Ki-mau	16		Tsutsno-to-ov	919
260*	Jan	13		Kang-shin	17		Kanno-je-tats	920
261	Jan	19		Sin-se	18	*	Kanno-to-mi	921
262	Feb	6		Jin-wu	19		Midsno-je-ooma	922
263	Jan	27		Kwei-wi	20		Midsno-to-tsitsuse	923
264*	Jan	16		Kiah-shin	21	*	Kino-je-sar	924
265	Feb	3		Yih-yu	22		Kino-to-torri	925
266	Jan	23		Ping-siuh	23	*	Fino-je-in	926
267	Feb	10		Ting-hai	24		Fino-to-y	927
268*	Jan	31		Wu-tse	25		Tsutsno-je-ne	928
269	Jan	20		Ki-chau	26	*	Tsutsno-to-oos	929
270	Feb	7		Kang-yin	27		Kanno-je-torra	930
271	Jan	28		Sin-mau	28		Kanno-to-ov	931
272*	Jan	17		Jin-shin	29	*	Midsno-je-tats	932
273	Feb	4		Kwei-se	30		Midsno-to-mi	933
274	Jan	25		Kiah-wu	31		Kino-je-ooma	934
275	Jan	14		Yih-wi	32	*	Kino-to-tsitsuse	935
276*	Feb	2		Ping-shin	33		Fino-je-sar	936
277	Jan	23		Ting-yu	34	*	Fino-to-torri	937
278	Feb	9		Wu-siuh	35		Tsutsno-je-in	938
279	Jan	30		Ki-hai	36		Tsutsno-to-y	939
280*	Jan	19		Kang-tse	37	*	Kanno-je-ne	940
281	Feb	6		Sin-chau	38		Kanno-to-oos	941
282	Jan	27		Jin-yin	39		Midsno-je-torra	942
283	Jan	16		Kwei-mau	40	*	Midsno-to-ov	943
284*	Feb	3		Kiah-shin	41		Kino-je-tats	944
285	Jan	23		Yih-se	42	*	Kino-to-mi	945
286	Feb	10		Ping-wu	43		Fino-je-ooma	946
287	Jan	31		Ting-wi	44		Fino-to-tsitsuse	947
288*	Jan	20		Wu-shin	45	*	Tsutsno-je-sar	948
289	Feb	7		Ki-yu	46		Tsutsno-to-torri	949
290	Jan	28		Kang-siuh	47		Kanno-je-in	950
291	Jan	17		Sin-hai	48	*	Kanno-to-y	951
292*	Feb	4		Jin-tse	49		Midsno-je-ne	952
293	Jan	25		Kwei-chau	50		Midsno-to-oos	953
294	Jan	14		Kiah-yin	51	*	Kino-je-torra	954

Western Date of New Year (Julian)			Cycle No.	Chinese Year Name & Cycle		Intercalculary Month	Japanese Name of Year Cycle and Year Number	
295	Feb	2		Yih-mau	52		Kino-to-ov	955
296*	Jan	22		Ping-shin	53	*	Fino-je-tats	956
297	Feb	9		Ting-wu	54		Fino-to-mi	957
298	Jan	30		Wu-wu	55		Tsutsno-je-ooma	958
299	Jan	19		Ki-wi	56	*	Tsutsno-to-tsitsuse	959
300*	Feb	6		Kang-shin	57		Kanno-je-sar	960
301	Jan	27		Sin-yu	58		Kanno-to-torri	961
302	Jan	16		Jin-siuh	59	*	Midsno-je-in	962
303	Feb	3		Kwei-hai	60		Midsno-to-y	963
304*	Jan	23	50	Kiah-tse	1	*	Kino-je-ne	964
305	Feb	10		Yih-chau	2		Kino-to-oos	965
306	Jan	31		Ping-yin	3		Fino-je-torra	966
307	Jan	20		Ting-mau	4	*	Fino-to-ov	967
308*	Feb	7		Wu-shin	5		Tsutsno-je-tats	968
309	Jan	28		Ki-se	6		Tsutsno-to-mi	969
310	Jan	17		Kang-wu	7	*	Kanno-je-ooma	970
311	Feb	4		Sin-wi	8		Kanno-to-tsitsuse	971
312*	Jan	25		Jin-shin	9		Midsno-je-sar	972
313	Jan	14		Kwei-yu	10		Midsno-to-torri	973
314	Feb	2		Kiah-siuh	11		Kino-je-in	974
315	Jan	22		Yih-hai	12	*	Kino-to-y	975
316*	Feb	9		Ping-tse	13		Fino-je-ne	976
317	Jan	30		Ting-chau	14		Fino-to-oos	977
318	Jan	19		Wu-yin	15	*	Tsutsno-je-torra	978
319	Feb	6		Ki-mau	16		Tsutsno-to-ov	979
320*	Jan	27		Kang-shin	17		Kanno-je-tats	980
321	Jan	16		Sin-se	18	*	Kanno-to-mi	981
322	Feb	3		Jin-wu	19		Midsno-je-ooma	982
323	Jan	23		Kwei-wi	20	*	Midsno-to-tsitsuse	983
324*	Feb	10		Kiah-shin	21		Kino-je-sar	984
325	Jan	31		Yih-yu	22		Kino-to-torri	985
326	Jan	20		Ping-siuh	23	*	Fino-je-in	986
327	Feb	7		Ting-hai	24		Fino-to-y	987
328*	Jan	28		Wu-tse	25		Tsutsno-je-ne	988
329	Jan	17		Ki-chau	26	*	Tsutsno-to-oos	989
330	Feb	4		Kang-yin	27		Kanno-je-torra	990
331	Jan	25		Sin-mau	28		Kanno-to-ov	991
332*	Jan	14		Jin-shin	29	*	Midsno-je-tats	992
333	Feb	2		Kwei-se	30		Midsno-to-mi	993
334	Jan	22		Kiah-wu	31	*	Kino-je-ooma	994
335	Feb	9		Yih-wi	32		Kino-to-tsitsuse	995
336*	Jan	30		Ping-shin	33		Fino-je-sar	996
337	Jan	19		Ting-yu	34	*	Fino-to-torri	997
338	Feb	6		Wu-siuh	35		Tsutsno-je-in	998

Western Date of New Year (Julian)			Cycle No.	Chinese Year Name & Cycle		Intercalculary Month	Japanese Name of Year Cycle and Year Number	
339	Jan	27		Ki-hai	36		Tsutsno-to-y	999
340*	Jan	16		Kang-tse	37	*	Kanno-je-ne	1000
341	Feb	3		Sin-chau	38		Kanno-to-oos	1001
342	Jan	23		Jin-yin	39	*	Midsno-je-torra	1002
343	Feb	10		Kwei-mau	40		Midsno-to-ov	1003
344*	Jan	31		Kiah-shin	41		Kino-je-tats	1004
345	Jan	20		Yih-se	42	*	Kino-to-mi	1005
346	Feb	7		Ping-wu	43		Fino-je-ooma	1006
347	Jan	28		Ting-wi	44		Fino-to-tsitsuse	1007
348*	Jan	17		Wu-shin	45	*	Tsutsno-je-sar	1008
349	Feb	4		Ki-yu	46		Tsutsno-to-torri	1009
350	Jan	25		Kang-siuh	47		Kanno-je-in	1010
351	Jan	14		Sin-hai	48	*	Kanno-to-y	1011
352*	Feb	2		Jin-tse	49		Midsno-je-ne	1012
353	Jan	22		Kwei-chau	50	*	Midsno-to-oos	1013
354	Feb	9		Kiah-yin	51		Kino-je-torra	1014
355	Jan	30		Yih-mau	52		Kino-to-ov	1015
356*	Jan	19		Ping-shin	53	*	Fino-je-tats	1016
357	Feb	6		Ting-wu	54		Fino-to-mi	1017
358	Jan	27		Wu-wu	55		Tsutsno-je-ooma	1018
359	Jan	16		Ki-wi	56	*	Tsutsno-to-tsitsuse	1019
360*	Feb	3		Kang-shin	57		Kanno-je-sar	1020
361	Jan	23		Sin-yu	58	*	Kanno-to-torri	1021
362	Feb	10		Jin-siuh	59		Midsno-je-in	1022
363	Jan	31		Kwei-hai	60	*	Midsno-to-y	1023
364*	Jan	20	51	Kiah-tse	1		Kino-je-ne	1024
365	Feb	7		Yih-chau	2		Kino-to-oos	1025
366	Jan	28		Ping-yin	3		Fino-je-torra	1026
367	Jan	17		Ting-mau	4	*	Fino-to-ov	1027
368*	Feb	4		Wu-shin	5		Tsutsno-je-tats	1028
369	Jan	25		Ki-se	6	*	Tsutsno-to-mi	1029
370	Jan	14		Kang-wu	7		Kanno-je-ooma	1030
371	Feb	2		Sin-wi	8		Kanno-to-tsitsuse	1031
372*	Jan	22		Jin-shin	9	*	Midsno-je-sar	1032
373	Feb	9		Kwei-yu	10		Midsno-to-torri	1033
374	Jan	30		Kiah-siuh	11		Kino-je-in	1034
375	Jan	19		Yih-hai	12	*	Kino-to-y	1035
376*	Feb	6		Ping-tse	13		Fino-je-ne	1036
377	Jan	27		Ting-chau	14		Fino-to-oos	1037
378	Jan	15		Wu-yin	15		Tsutsno-je-torra	1038
379	Feb	3		Ki-mau	16		Tsutsno-to-ov	1039
380*	Jan	23		Kang-shin	17	*	Kanno-je-tats	1040
381	Feb	10		Sin-se	18		Kanno-to-mi	1041
382	Jan	31		Jin-wu	19		Midsno-je-ooma	1042

Western Date of New Year (Julian)			Cycle No.	Chinese Year Name & Cycle		Intercalculary Month	Japanese Name of Year Cycle and Year Number	
383	Jan	20		Kwei-wi	20	*	Midsno-to-tsitsuse	1043
384*	Feb	7		Kiah-shin	21		Kino-je-sar	1044
385	Jan	28		Yih-yu	22		Kino-to-torri	1045
386	Jan	17		Ping-siuh	23	*	Fino-je-in	1046
387	Feb	4		Ting-hai	24		Fino-to-y	1047
388*	Jan	25		Wu-tse	25		Tsutsno-je-ne	1048
389	Jan	14		Ki-chau	26	*	Tsutsno-to-oos	1049
390	Feb	2		Kang-yin	27		Kanno-je-torra	1050
391	Jan	22		Sin-mau	28	*	Kanno-to-ov	1051
392*	Feb	9		Jin-shin	29		Midsno-je-tats	1052
393	Jan	30		Kwei-se	30		Midsno-to-mi	1053
394	Jan	19		Kiah-wu	31	*	Kino-je-ooma	1054
395	Feb	6		Yih-wi	32		Kino-to-tsitsuse	1055
396*	Jan	27		Ping-shin	33		Fino-je-sar	1056
397	Jan	16		Ting-yu	34	*	Fino-to-torri	1057
398	Feb	3		Wu-siuh	35		Tsutsno-je-in	1058
399	Jan	23		Ki-hai	36	*	Tsutsno-to-y	1059
400*	Feb	10		Kang-tse	37		Kanno-je-ne	1060
401	Jan	31		Sin-chau	38		Kanno-to-oos	1061
402	Jan	20		Jin-yin	39	*	Midsno-je-torra	1062
403	Feb	7		Kwei-mau	40		Midsno-to-ov	1063
404*	Jan	28		Kiah-shin	41		Kino-je-tats	1064
405	Jan	17		Yih-se	42	*	Kino-to-mi	1065
406	Feb	4		Ping-wu	43		Fino-je-ooma	1066
407	Jan	25		Ting-wi	44		Fino-to-tsitsuse	1067
408*	Jan	14		Wu-shin	45	*	Tsutsno-je-sar	1068
409	Feb	2		Ki-yu	46		Tsutsno-to-torri	1069
410	Jan	22		Kang-siuh	47	*	Kanno-je-in	1070
411	Feb	9		Sin-hai	48		Kanno-to-y	1071
412*	Jan	30		Jin-tse	49		Midsno-je-ne	1072
413	Jan	19		Kwei-chau	50	*	Midsno-to-oos	1073
414	Feb	6		Kiah-yin	51		Kino-je-torra	1074
415	Jan	27		Yih-mau	52		Kino-to-ov	1075
416*	Jan	16		Ping-shin	53	*	Fino-je-tats	1076
417	Feb	3		Ting-wu	54		Fino-to-mi	1077
418	Jan	23		Wu-wu	55	*	Tsutsno-je-ooma	1078
419	Feb	10		Ki-wi	56		Tsutsno-to-tsitsuse	1079
420*	Jan	31		Kang-shin	57		Kanno-je-sar	1080
421	Jan	20		Sin-yu	58	*	Kanno-to-torri	1081
422	Feb	7		Jin-siuh	59		Midsno-je-in	1082
423	Jan	28		Kwei-hai	60		Midsno-to-y	1083
424*	Jan	17	52	Kiah-tse	1	*	Kino-je-ne	1084
425	Feb	4		Yih-chau	2		Kino-to-oos	1085
426	Jan	25		Ping-yin	3		Fino-je-torra	1086

Western Date of New Year (Julian)			Cycle No.	Chinese Year Name & Cycle		Intercalculary Month	Japanese Name of Year Cycle and Year Number	
427	Jan	14		Ting-mau	4	*	Fino-to-ov	1087
428*	Feb	2		Wu-shin	5		Tsutsno-je-tats	1088
429	Jan	22		Ki-se	6	*	Tsutsno-to-mi	1089
430	Feb	9		Kang-wu	7		Kanno-je-ooma	1090
431	Jan	30		Sin-wi	8		Kanno-to-tsitsuse	1091
432*	Jan	19		Jin-shin	9	*	Midsno-je-sar	1092
433	Feb	6		Kwei-yu	10		Midsno-to-torri	1093
434	Jan	27		Kiah-siuh	11		Kino-je-in	1094
435	Jan	16		Yih-hai	12	*	Kino-to-y	1095
436*	Feb	3		Ping-tse	13		Fino-je-ne	1096
437	Jan	23		Ting-chau	14	*	Fino-to-oos	1097
438	Feb	10		Wu-yin	15		Tsutsno-je-torra	1098
439	Jan	31		Ki-mau	16		Tsutsno-to-ov	1099
440*	Jan	20		Kang-shin	17	*	Kanno-je-tats	1100
441	Feb	7		Sin-se	18		Kanno-to-mi	1101
442	Jan	28		Jin-wu	19		Midsno-je-ooma	1102
443	Jan	17		Kwei-wi	20	*	Midsno-to-tsitsuse	1103
444*	Feb	4		Kiah-shin	21		Kino-je-sar	1104
445	Jan	25		Yih-yu	22		Kino-to-torri	1105
446	Jan	14		Ping-siuh	23	*	Fino-je-in	1106
447	Feb	2		Ting-hai	24		Fino-to-y	1107
448*	Jan	20		Wu-tse	25	*	Tsutsno-je-ne	1108
449	Feb	9		Ki-chau	26		Tsutsno-to-oos	1109
450	Jan	30		Kang-yin	27		Kanno-je-torra	1110
451	Jan	19		Sin-mau	28	*	Kanno-to-ov	1111
452*	Feb	6		Jin-shin	29		Midsno-je-tats	1112
453	Jan	27		Kwei-se	30		Midsno-to-mi	1113
454	Jan	16		Kiah-wu	31	*	Kino-je-ooma	1114
455	Feb	3		Yih-wi	32		Kino-to-tsitsuse	1115
456*	Jan	23		Ping-shin	33	*	Fino-je-sar	1116
447	Feb	10		Ting-yu	34		Fino-to-torri	1117
448	Jan	31		Wu-siuh	35		Tsutsno-je-in	1118
459	Jan	20		Ki-hai	36	*	Tsutsno-to-y	1119
460*	Feb	7		Kang-tse	37		Kanno-je-ne	1120
461	Jan	28		Sin-chau	38		Kanno-to-oos	1121
462	Jan	17		Jin-yin	39	*	Midsno-je-torra	1122
463	Feb	4		Kwei-mau	40		Midsno-to-ov	1123
464*	Jan	25		Kiah-shin	41		Kino-je-tats	1124
465	Jan	14		Yih-se	42	*	Kino-to-mi	1125
466	Feb	2		Ping-wu	43		Fino-je-ooma	1126
467	Jan	22		Ting-wi	44	*	Fino-to-tsitsuse	1127
468*	Feb	9		Wu-shin	45		Tsutsno-je-sar	1128
469	Jan	30		Ki-yu	46		Tsutsno-to-torri	1129
470	Jan	19		Kang-siuh	47	*	Kanno-je-in	1130

Western Date of New Year (Julian)			Cycle No.	Chinese Year Name & Cycle		Intercalculary Month	Japanese Name of Year Cycle and Year Number	
471	Feb	6		Sin-hai	48		Kanno-to-y	1131
472*	Jan	27		Jin-tse	49		Midsno-je-ne	1132
473	Jan	16		Kwei-chau	50	*	Midsno-to-oos	1133
474	Feb	3		Kiah-yin	51		Kino-je-torra	1134
475	Jan	23		Yih-mau	52	*	Kino-to-ov	1135
476*	Feb	10		Ping-shin	53		Fino-je-tats	1136
477	Jan	31		Ting-wu	54		Fino-to-mi	1137
478	Jan	20		Wu-wu	55	*	Tsutsno-je-ooma	1138
479	Feb	7		Ki-wi	56		Tsutsno-to-tsitsuse	1139
480*	Jan	27		Kang-shin	57		Kanno-je-sar	1140
481	Jan	17		Sin-yu	58	*	Kanno-to-torri	1141
482	Feb	4		Jin-siuh	59		Midsno-je-in	1142
483	Jan	25		Kwei-hai	60		Midsno-to-y	1143
484*	Jan	14	53	Kiah-tse	1	*	Kino-je-ne	1144
485	Feb	2		Yih-chau	2		Kino-to-oos	1145
486	Jan	22		Ping-yin	3	*	Fino-je-torra	1146
487	Feb	9		Ting-mau	4		Fino-to-ov	1147
488*	Jan	30		Wu-shin	5		Tsutsno-je-tats	1148
489	Jan	19		Ki-se	6	*	Tsutsno-to-mi	1149
490	Feb	6		Kang-wu	7		Kanno-je-ooma	1150
491	Jan	27		Sin-wi	8		Kanno-to-tsitsuse	1151
492*	Jan	16		Jin-shin	9	*	Midsno-je-sar	1152
493	Feb	3		Kwei-yu	10		Midsno-to-torri	1153
494	Jan	23		Kiah-siuh	11	*	Kino-je-in	1154
495	Feb	10		Yih-hai	12		Kino-to-y	1155
496*	Jan	31		Ping-tse	13		Fino-je-ne	1156
497	Jan	20		Ting-chau	14	*	Fino-to-oos	1157
498	Feb	7		Wu-yin	15		Tsutsno-je-torra	1158
499	Jan	28		Kimau	16		Tsutsno-to-ov	1159
500*	Jan	17		Kang-shin	17	*	Kanno-je-tats	1160
501	Feb	4		Sin-se	18		Kanno-to-mi	1161
502	Jan	25		Jin-wu	19		Midsno-je-ooma	1162
503	Jan	14		Kwei-wi	20	*	Midsno-to-tsitsuse	1163
504*	Feb	2		Kiah-shin	21		Kino-de-sar	1164
505	Jan	22		Yih-yu	22	*	Kino-to-torri	1165
506	Feb	9		Ping-siuh	23		Fino-je-in	1166
507	Jan	30		Ting-hai	24		Fino-to-y	1167
508*	Jan	19		Wu-tse	25	*	Tsutsno-je-ne	1168
509	Feb	6		Ki-chau	26		Tsutsno-to-oos	1169
510	Jan	27		Kang-yin	27		Kanno-je-torra	1170
511	Jan	16		Sin-mau	28	*	Kanno-to-ov	1171
512*	Feb	3		Jin-shin	29		Midsno-je-tats	1172
513	Jan	23		Kwei-se	30	*	Midsno-to-mi	1173
514	Feb	10		Kiah-wu	31		Kino-je-ooma	1174

Western Date of New Year (Julian)			Cycle No.	Chinese Year Name & Cycle		Intercalculary Month	Japanese Name of Year Cycle and Year Number	
515	Jan	31		Yih-wi	32		Kino-to-tsitsuse	1175
516*	Jan	20		Ping-shin	33	*	Fino-je-sar	1176
517	Feb	7		Ting-yu	34		Fino-to-torri	1177
518	Jan	28		Wu-siuh	35		Tsutsno-je-in	1178
519	Jan	17		Ki-hai	36	*	Tsutsno-to-y	1179
520*	Feb	4		Kang-tse	37		Kanno-je-ne	1180
521	Jan	25		Sin-chau	38		Kanno-to-oos	1181
522	Jan	14		Jin-yin	39	*	Midsno-je-torra	1182
523	Feb	2		Kwei-mau	40		Midsno-to-ov	1183
524*	Jan	22		Kiah-shin	41	*	Kino-je-tats	1184
525	Feb	9		Yih-se	42		Kino-to-mi	1185
526	Jan	30		Ping-wu	43		Fino-je-ooma	1186
527	Jan	19		Ting-wi	44	*	Fino-to-tsitsuse	1187
528*	Feb	6		Wu-shin	45		Tsutsno-je-sar	1188
529	Jan	27		Ki-yu	46		Tsutsno-to-torri	1189
530	Jan	16		Kang-siuh	47	*	Kanno-je-in	1190
531	Feb	3		Sin-hai	48		Kanno-to-y	1191
532*	Jan	23		Jin-tse	49	*	Midsno-je-ne	1192
533	Feb	10		Kwei-chau	50		Midsno-to-oos	1193
534	Jan	31		Kiah-yin	51		Kino-je-torra	1194
535	Jan	20		Yih-mau	52	*	Kino-to-ov	1195
536*	Feb	7		Ping-shin	53		Fino-je-tats	1196
537	Jan	28		Ting-wu	54		Fino-to-mi	1197
538	Jan	17		Wu-wu	55	*	Tsutsno-je-ooma	1198
539	Feb	4		Ki-wi	56		Tsutsno-to-tsitsuse	1199
540*	Jan	25		Kang-shin	57		Kanno-je-sar	1200
541	Jan	14		Sin-yu	58	*	Kanno-to-torri	12012
542	Feb	2		Jin-siuh	59		Midsno-je-in	1202
543	Jan	22		Kwei-hai	60	*	Midsno-to-y	1203
544*	Feb	9	54	Kiah-tse	1		Kino-je-ne	1204
545	Jan	30		Yih-chau	2		Kino-to-oos	1205
546	Jan	19		Ping-yin	3	*	Fino-je-torra	1206
547	Feb	6		Ting-mau	4		Fino-to-ov	1207
548*	Jan	27		Wu-shin	5		Tsutsno-je-tats	1208
549	Jan	16		Ki-se	6	*	Tsutsno-to-mi	1209
550	Feb	3		Kang-wu	7		Kanno-je-ooma	1210
551	Jan	23		Sin-wi	8	*	Kanno-to-tsitsuse	1211
552*	Feb	10		Jin-shin	9		Midsno-je-sar	1212
553	Jan	31		Kwei-yu	10		Midsno-to-torri	1213
554	Jan	20		Kiah-siuh	11	*	Kino-je-in	1214
555	Feb	7		Yih-hai	12		Kino-to-y	1215
556*	Jan	28		Ping-tse	13		Fino-je-ne	1216
557	Jan	17		Ting-chau	14	*	Fino-to-oos	1217
558	Feb	4		Wu-yin	15		Tsutsno-je-torra	1218

Western Date of New Year (Julian)			Cycle No.	Chinese Year Name & Cycle		Intercalculary Month	Japanese Name of Year Cycle and Year Number	
559	Jan	25		Ki-mau	16		Tsutsno-to-ov	1219
560*	Jan	14		Kang-shin	17	*	Kanno-je-tats	1220
561	Feb	2		Sin-se	18		Kanno-to-mi	1221
562	Jan	22		Jin-wu	19	*	Midsno-je-ooma	1222
563	Feb	9		Kwei-wi	20		Midsno-to-tsitsuse	1223
564*	Jan	30		Kiah-shin	21		Kino-je-sar	1224
565	Jan	19		Yih-yu	22	*	Kino-to-torri	1225
566	Feb	6		Ping-siuh	23		Fino-je-in	1226
567	Jan	27		Ting-hai	24		Fino-to-y	1227
568*	Jan	16		Wu-tse	25	*	Tsutsno-je-ne	1228
569	Feb	3		Ki-chau	26		Tsutsno-to-oos	1229
570	Jan	23		Kang-yin	27	*	Kanno-je-torra	1230
571	Feb	10		Sin-mau	28		Kanno-to-ov	1231
572*	Jan	31		Jin-shin	29		Midsno-je-tats	1232
573	Jan	20		Kwei-se	30	*	Midsno-to-mi	1233
574	Feb	7		Kiah-wu	31		Kino-je-ooma	1234
575	Jan	28		Yih-wi	32		Kino-to-tsitsuse	1235
576*	Jan	17		Ping-shin	33	*	Fino-je-sar	1236
577	Feb	4		Ting-yu	34		Fino-to-torri	1237
578	Jan	25		Wu-siuh	35		Tsutsno-je-in	1238
579	Jan	14		Ki-hai	36	*	Tsutsno-to-y	1239
580*	Feb	2		Kang-tse	37		Kanno-je-ne	1240
581	Jan	22		Sin-chau	38	*	Kanno-to-oos	1241
582	Feb	9		Jin-yin	39		Midsno-je-torra	1242
583	Jan	30		Kwei-mau	40		Midsno-to-ov	1243
584*	Jan	19		Kiah-shin	41	*	Kino-je-tats	1244
585	Feb	6		Yih-se	42		Kino-to-me	1245
586	Jan	27		Ping-wu	43		Fino-je-ooma	1246
587	Jan	16		Ting-wi	44	*	Fino-to-tsitsuse	1247
588*	Feb	3		Wushin	45		Tsutsno-je-sar	1248
589	Jan	23		Ki-yu	46	*	Tsutsno-to-torri	1249
590	Feb	10		Kang-siuh	47		Kanno-je-in	1250
591	Jan	31		Sin-hai	48		Kanno-to-y	1251
592*	Jan	20		Jin-tse	49	*	Midsno-je-ne	1252
593	Feb	7		Kwei-chau	50		Midsno-to-oos	1253
594	Jan	28		Kiah-yin	51		Kino-je-torra	1254
595	Jan	17		Yih-mau	52	*	Kino-to-ov	1255
596*	Feb	4		Ping-shin	53		Fino-je-tats	1256
597	Jan	25		Ting-wu	54		Fino-to-mi	1257
598	Jan	14		Wu-wu	55	*	Tsutsno-je-ooma	1258
599	Feb	2		Ki-wi	56		Tsutsno-to-tsitsuse	1259
600*	Jan	22		Kang-shin	57	*	Kanno-je-sar	1260
601	Feb	9		Sin-yu	58		Kanno-to-torri	1261
602	Jan	30		Jin-siuh	59		Midsno-je-in	1262

Western Date of New Year (Julian)			Cycle No.	Chinese Year Name & Cycle		Intercalculary Month	Japanese Name of Year Cycle and Year Number	
603	Jan	19		Kwei-hai	60	*	Midsno-to-y	1263
604*	Feb	6	55	Kiah-tse	1		Kino-je-ne	1264
605	Jan	27		Yih-chau	2		Kino-to-oos	1265
606	Jan	16		Ping-yin	3	*	Fino-je-torra	1266
607	Feb	3		Ting-mau	4		Fino-to-ov	1267
608	Jan	23		Wu-shin	5	*	Tsutsno-je-tats	1268
609	Feb	10		Ki-se	6		Tsutsno-to-mi	1269
610	Jan	31		Kang-wu	7		Kanno-je-ooma	1270
611	Jan	20		Sin-wi	8	*	Kanno-to-tsitsuse	1271
612*	Feb	7		Jin-shin	9		Midsno-je-sar	1272
613	Jan	28		Kwei-yu	10		Midsno-to-torri	1273
614	Jan	17		Kiah-siuh	11	*	Kino-je-in	1274
615	Feb	4		Yih-hai	12		Kino-to-y	1275
616*	Jan	25		Ping-tse	13		Fino-je-ne	1276
617	Jan	14		Ting-chau	14	*	Fino-to-oos	1277
618	Feb	2		Wu-yin	15		Tsutsno-je-torra	1278
619	Jan	22		Ki-mau	16	*	Tsutsno-to-ov	1279
620*	Feb	9		Kang-shin	17		Kanno-je-tats	1280
621	Jan	30		Sin-se	18		Kanno-to-mi	1281
622	Jan	19		Jin-wu	19	*	Midsno-je-ooma	1282
623	Feb	7		Kwei-wi	20		Midsno-to-tsitsuse	1283
624*	Jan	27		Kiah-shin	21		Kino-je-sar	1284
625	Jan	16		Yih-yu	22	*	Kino-to-torri	1285
626	Feb	3		Ping-siuh	23		Fino-je-in	1286
627	Jan	23		Ting-hai	24	*	Fino-to-y	1287
628*	Feb	12		Wu-tse	25		Tsutsno-je-ne	1288
629	Jan	31		Ki-chau	26		Tsutsno-to-oos	1289
630	Jan	21		Kang-yin	27	*	Kanno-je-torra	1290
631	Feb	8		Sin-mau	28		Kanno-to-ov	1291
632*	Jan	28		Jin-shin	29		Midsno-je-tats	1292
633	Jan	17		Kwei-se	30	*	Midsno-to-mi	1293
634	Feb	5		Kiah-wu	31		Kino-je-ooma	1294
635	Jan	25		Yih-wi	32		Kino-to-tsitsuse	1295
636*	Jan	15		Ping-shin	33	*	Fino-je-sar	1296
637	Feb	1		Ting-yu	34		Fino-to-torri	1297
638	Jan	22		Wu-siuh	35	*	Tsutsno-je-in	1298
639	Feb	10		Ki-hai	36		Tsutsno-to-y	1299
640*	Jan	31		Kang-tse	37		Kanno-je-ne	1300
641	Jan	19		Sin-chau	38	*	Kanno-to-oos	1301
642	Feb	6		Jin-yin	39		Midsno-je-torra	1302
643	Jan	27		Kwei-mau	40		Midsno-to-ov	1303
644*	Jan	16		Kiah-shin	41	*	Kino-je-tats	1304
645	Feb	3		Yih-se	42		Kino-to-mi	1305
646	Jan	24		Ping-wu	43	*	Fino-je-ooma	1306

Western Date of New Year (Julian)			Cycle No.	Chinese Year Name & Cycle		Intercalculary Month	Japanese Name of Year Cycle and Year Number	
647	Feb	11		Ting-wi	44		Fino-to-tsitsuse	1307
648*	Feb	1		Wu-shin	45		Tsutsno-je-sar	1308
649	Jan	20		Ki-yu	46	*	Tsutsno-to-torri	1309
650	Feb	8		Kang-siuh	47		Kanno-je-in	1310
651	Jan	29		Sin-hai	48		Kanno-to-y	1311
652*	Jan	18		Jin-tse	49	*	Midsno-je-ne	1312
653	Feb	4		Kwei-chau	50		Midsno-to-oos	1313
654	Jan	25		Kiah-yin	51		Kino-je-torra	1314
655	Jan	14		Yih-mau	52	*	Kino-to-ov	1315
656*	Feb	2		Ping-shin	53		Fino-je-tats	1316
657	Jan	22		Ting-wu	54	*	Fino-to-mi	1317
658	Feb	9		Wu-wu	55		Tsutsno-je-ooma	1318
659	Jan	30		Ki-wi	56		Tsutsno-to-tsitsuse	1319
660*	Jan	19		Kang-shin	57	*	Kanno-je-sar	1320
661	Feb	6		Sin-yu	58		Kanno-to-torri	1321
662	Jan	27		Jin-siuh	59		Midsno-je-in	1322
663	Jan	16		Kwei-hai	60	*	Midsno-to-y	1323
664*	Feb	3	56	Kiah-tse	1		Kino-je-ne	1324
665	Jan	23		Yih-chau	2	*	Kino-to-oos	1325
666	Feb	11		Ping-yin	3		Fino-je-torra	1326
667	Jan	31		Ting-mau	4		Fino-to-ov	1327
668*	Jan	21		Wu-shin	5	*	Tsutsno-je-tats	1328
669	Feb	6		Ki-se	6		Tsutsno-to-mi	1329
670	Jan	28		Kang-wu	7		Kanno-je-ooma	1330
671	Jan	17		Sin-wi	8	*	Kanno-to-tsitsuse	1331
672*	Feb	6		Jin-shin	9		Midsno-je-sar	1332
673	Jan	25		Kwei-yu	10		Midsno-to-torri	1333
674	Jan	14		Kiah-siuh	11	*	Kino-je-ne	1334
675	Feb	2		Yih-hai	12		Kino-to-y	1335
676*	Jan	22		Ping-tse	13	*	Fino-je-ne	1336
677	Feb	10		Ting-chau	14		Fino-to-oos	1337
678	Jan	30		Wu-yin	15		Tsutsno-je-torra	1338
679	Jan	19		Ki-mau	16	*	Tsutsno-to-ov	1339
680*	Feb	7		Kang-shin	17		Kanno-je-tats	1340
681	Jan	26		Sin-se	18		Kanno-to-mi	1341
682	Jan	15		Jin-wu	19	*	Midsno-je-ooma	1342
683	Feb	4		Kwei-wi	20		Midsno-to-tsitsuse	1343
684*	Jan	24		Kiah-shin	21	*	Kino-je-sar	1344
685	Feb	10		Yih-yu	22		Kino-to-torri	1345
686	Jan	31		Ping-siuh	23		Fino-je-in	1346
687	Jan	20		Ting-hai	24	*	Fino-to-y	1347
688*	Feb	9		Wu-tse	25		Tsutsno-je-ne	1348
689	Jan	28		Ki-chau	26		Tsutsno-to-oos	1349
690	Jan	17		Kang-yin	27	*	Kanno-je-torra	1350

Western Date of New Year (Julian)			Cycle No.	Chinese Year Name & Cycle		Intercalculary Month	Japanese Name of Year Cycle and Year Number	
691	Feb	5		Sin-mau	28		Kanno-to-ov	1351
692*	Jan	25		Jin-shin	29		Midsno-je-tats	1352
693	Jan	13		Kwei-se	30	*	Midsno-to-mi	1353
694	Feb	2		Kiah-wu	31		Kino-je-ooma	1354
695	Jan	22		Yih-wi	32	*	Kino-to-tsitsuse	1355
696*	Feb	9		Ping-shin	33		Fino-je-sar	1356
697	Jan	29		Ting-yu	34		Fino-to-torri	1357
698	Jan	18		Wu-siuh	35	*	Tsutsno-je-in	1358
699	Feb	7		Ki-hai	36		Tsutsno-to-y	1359
700*	Jan	27		Kang-tse	37		Kanno-je-ne	1360
701	Jan	15		Sin-chau	38	*	Kanno-to-oox	1361
702	Feb	3		Jin-yin	39		Midsno-je-torra	1362
703	Jan	23		Kwei-mau	40	*	Midsno-to-ov	1363
704*	Feb	12		Kiah-shin	41		Kino-je-tats	1364
705	Jan	31		Yih-se	42		Kino-to-mi	1365
706	Jan	21		Ping-wu	43	*	Fino-je-ooma	1366
707	Feb	8		Tin-wi	44		Fino-to-tsitsuse	1367
708*	Jan	28		Wu-shin	45		Tsutsno-je-sar	1368
709	Jan	17		Ki-yu	46	*	Tsutsno-to-torri	1369
710	Feb	5		Kang-siuh	47		Kanno-je-in	1370
711	Jan	25		Sin-hai	48		Kanno-to-y	1371
712*	Jan	15		Jin-tse	49	*	Midsno-je-ne	1372
713	Feb	1		Kwei-chau	50		Midsno-to-oos	1373
714	Jan	21		Kiah-yin	51	*	Kino-je-torra	1374
715	Feb	10		Yih-mau	52		Kino-to-ov	1375
716*	Jan	30		Ping-shin	53		Fino-je-tats	1376
717	Jan	19		Ting-wu	54	*	Fino-to-mi	1377
718	Feb	6		Wu-wu	55		Tsutsno-je-ooma	1378
719	Jan	26		Ki-wi	56		Tsutsno-to-tsitsuse	1379
720*	Jan	16		Kang-shin	57	*	Kanno-je-sar	1380
721	Feb	3		Sin-yu	58		Kanno-to-torri	1381
722	Jan	23		Jin-siuh	59	*	Midsno-je-in	1382
723	Feb	11		Kwei-hai	60		Midsno-to-y	1383
724*	Jan	31	57	Kiah-tse	1		Kino-je-ne	1384
725	Jan	19		Yih-chau	2	*	Kino-to-oos	1385
726	Feb	8		Ping-yin	3		Fino-je-torra	1386
727	Jan	28		Ting-mau	4		Fino-to-ov	1387
728*	Jan	18		Wu-shin	5	*	Tsutsno-je-tats	1388
729	Feb	4		Ki-se	6		Tsutsno-to-mi	1389
730	Jan	24		Kang-wu	7		Kanno-je-ooma	1390
731	Jan	14		Sin-wi	8	*	Kanno-to-tsitsuse	1391
732*	Feb	2		Jin-shin	9		Midsno-je-sar	1392
733	Jan	21		Kwei-yu	10	*	Midsno-to-torri	1393
734	Feb	9		Kiah-siuh	11		Kino-je-in	1394

Western Date of New Year (Julian)			Cycle No.	Chinese Year Name & Cycle		Intercalculary Month	Japanese Name of Year Cycle and Year Number	
735	Jan	30		Yih-hai	12		Kino-to-y	1395
736*	Jan	19		Ping-tse	13	*	Fino-je-ne	1396
737	Feb	6		Ting-chau	14		Fino-to-oos	1397
738	Jan	27		Wu-yin	15		Tsutsno-je-torra	1398
739	Jan	16		Ki-mau	16	*	Tsutsno-to-ov	1399
740*	Feb	3		Kang-shin	17		Kanno-je-tats	1400
741	Jan	23		Sin-se	18	*	Kanno-to-mi	1401
742	Feb	11		Jin-wu	19		Midsno-je-ooma	1402
743	Jan	31		Kwei-wi	20		Midsno-to-tsitsuse	1403
744*	Jan	21		Kiah-shin	21	*	Kino-je-sar	1404
745	Feb	7		Yih-yu	22		Kino-to-torri	1405
746	Jan	28		Ping-siuh	23		Fino-je-in	1406
747	Jan	17		Ting-hai	24	*	Fino-to-y	1407
748*	Feb	5		Wu-tse	25		Tsutsno-je-ne	1408
749	Jan	25		Ki-chau	26	*	Tsutsno-to-oos	1409
750	Jan	14		Kang-yin	27		Kanno-je-torra	1410
751	Feb	1		Sin-mau	28		Kanno-to-ov	1411
752*	Jan	22		Jin-shin	29	*	Midsno-je-tats	1412
753	Feb	9		Kwei-se	30		Midsno-to-mi	1413
754	Jan	29		Kiah-wu	31		Kino-je-ooma	1414
755	Jan	19		Yih-wi	32	*	Kino-to-tsitsuse	1415
756*	Feb	6		Ping-shin	33		Fino-je-sar	1416
757	Jan	26		Ting-yu	34		Fino-to-torri	1417
758	Jan	16		Wu-siuh	35	*	Tsutsno-je-in	1418
759	Feb	3		Ki-hai	36		Tsutsno-to-y	1419
760*	Jan	24		Kang-tse	37	*	Kanno-je-ne	1420
761	Feb	10		Sin-chau	38		Kanno-to-oos	1421
762	Jan	30		Jin-yin	39		Midsno-je-torra	1422
763	Jan	20		Kwei-mau	40	*	Midsno-to-ov	1423
764*	Feb	8		Kiah-shin	41		Kino-je-tats	1424
765	Jan	28		Yih-se	42		Kino-to-mi	1425
766	Jan	17		Ping-wu	43	*	Fino-je-ooma	1426
767	Feb	5		Ting-wi	44		Fino-to-tsitsuse	1427
768*	Jan	25		Wu-shin	45		Tsutsno-je-sar	1428
769	Jan	13		Ki-yu	46	*	Tsutsno-to-torri	1429
770	Feb	2		Kang-siuh	47		Kanno-je-in	1430
771	Jan	22		Sin-hai	48	*	Kanno-to-y	1431
772*	Feb	9		Jin-tse	49		Midsno-je-ne	1432
773	Jan	29		Kwei-chau	50		Midsno-to-oos	1433
774	Jan	18		Kiah-yin	51	*	Kino-je-torra	1434
775	Feb	7		Yih-mau	52		Kino-to-ov	1435
776*	Jan	27		Ping-shin	53		Fino-je-tats	1436
777	Jan	15		Ting-wu	54	*	Fino-to-mi	1437
778	Feb	3		Wu-wu	55		Tsutsno-je-ooma	1438

Western Date of New Year (Julian)			Cycle No.	Chinese Year Name & Cycle		Intercalculary Month	Japanese Name of Year Cycle and Year Number	
779	Jan	23		Ki-wi	56	*	Tsutsno-to-tsitsuse	1439
780*	Feb	11		Kang-shin	57		Kanno-je-sar	1440
781	Jan	31		Sin-yu	58		Kanno-to-torri	1441
782	Jan	20		Jin-siuh	59	*	Midsno-je-in	1442
783	Feb	7		Kwei-hai	60		Midsno-to-y	1443
784*	Jan	28	58	Kiah-tse	1		Kino-je-ne	1444
785	Jan	16		Yih-chau	2	*	Kino-to-oos	1445
786	Feb	5		Ping-yin	3		Fino-je-torra	1446
787	Jan	25		Ting-mau	4	*	Fino-to-ov	1447
788*	Feb	12		Wu-shin	5		Tsutsno-je-tats	1448
789	Feb	1		Ki-se	6		Tsutsno-to-mi	1449
790	Jan	21		Kang-wu	7	*	Kanno-je-ooma	1450
791	Feb	9		Sin-wi	8		Kanno-to-tsitsuse	1451
792*	Jan	30		Jin-shin	9		Midsno-je-sar	1452
793	Jan	18		Kwei-yu	10	*	Midsno-to-torri	1453
794	Feb	6		Kiah-siuh	11		Kino-je-in	1454
795	Jan	26		Yih-hai	12		Kino-to-y	1455
796*	Jan	15		Ping-tse	13	*	Fino-je-ne	1456
797	Feb	3		Ting-chau	14		Fino-to-oos	1457
798	Jan	23		Wu-yin	15	*	Tsutsno-je-torra	1458
799	Feb	10		Ki-mau	16		Tsutsno-to-ov	1459
800*	Jan	31		Kang-shin	17		Kanno-je-tats	1460
801	Jan	19		Sin-se	18	*	Kanno-to-mi	1461
802	Feb	8		Jin-wu	19		Midsno-je-ooma	1462
803	Jan	28		Kwei-wi	20		Midsno-to-tsitsuse	1463
804*	Jan	18		Kiah-shin	21	*	Kino-je-sar	1464
805	Feb	4		Yih-yu	22		Kino-to-torri	1465
806	Jan	24		Ping-siuh	23	*	Fino-je-in	1466
807	Feb	13		Ting-hai	24		Fino-to-y	1467
808*	Feb	2		Wu-tse	25		Tsutsno-je-ni	1468
809	Jan	21		Ki-chau	26	*	Tsutsno-to-oos	1469
810	Feb	9		Kang-yin	27		Kanno-je-torra	1470
811	Jan	29		Sin-mau	28		Kanno-to-ov	1471
812*	Jan	18		Jin-shin	29	*	Midsno-je-tats	1472
813	Feb	6		Kwei-se	30		Midsno-to-mi	1473
814	Jan	26		Kiah-wu	31		Kino-je-ooma	1474
815	Jan	16		Yih-wi	32	*	Kino-to-tsitsuse	1475
816*	Feb	3		Ping-shin	33		Fino-je-sar	1476
817	Jan	22		Ting-yu	34	*	Fino-to-torri	1477
818	Feb	11		Wu-siuh	35		Tsutsno-je-in	1478
819	Jan	31		Ki-hai	36		Tsutsno-to-y	1479
820*	Jan	20		Kang-tse	37	*	Kanno-je-ne	1480
821	Feb	7		Sin-chau	38		Kanno-to-oos	1481
822	Jan	27		Jin-yin	39		Midsno-je-torra	1482

Western Date of New Year (Julian)			Cycle No.	Chinese Year Name & Cycle		Intercalculary Month	Japanese Name of Year Cycle and Year Number	
823	Jan	17		Kwei-mau	40	*	Midsno-to-ov	1483
824*	Feb	5		Kiah-shin	41		Kino-je-tats	1484
825	Jan	24		Yih-se	42	*	Kino-to-mi	1485
826	Feb	12		Ping-wu	43		Fino-je-ooma	1486
827	Feb	1		Ting-wi	44		Fino-to-tsitsuse	1487
828*	Jan	21		Wu-shin	45	*	Tsutsno-je-sar	1488
829	Feb	9		Ki-yu	46		Tsutsno-to-torri	1489
830	Jan	29		Kang-siuh	47		Kanno-je-in	1490
831	Jan	18		Sin-hai	48	*	Kanno-to-y	1491
832*	Feb	6		Jin-tse	49		Midsno-je-ne	1492
833	Jan	26		Kwei-chau	50		Midsno-to-oos	1493
834	Jan	15		Kiah-yin	51	*	Kino-je-torra	1494
835	Feb	3		Yih-mau	52		Kino-to-ov	1495
836*	Jan	24		Ping-shin	53	*	Fino-je-tats	1496
837	Feb	10		Ting-wu	54		Fino-to-mi	1497
838	Jan	30		Wu-wu	55		Tsutsno-je-ooma	1498
839	Jan	20		Ki-wi	56	*	Tsutsno-to-tsitsuse	1499
840*	Feb	8		Kang-shin	57		Kanno-je-sar	1500
841	Jan	27		Sin-yu	58		Kanno-to-torri	1501
842	Jan	17		Jin-siuh	59	*	Midsno-je-in	1502
843	Feb	4		Kwei-hai	60		Midsno-to-y	1503
844*	Jan	25	59	Kiah-tse	1	*	Kino-je-ne	1504
845	Feb	12		Yih-chau	2		Kino-to-oos	1505
846	Feb	1		Ping-yin	3		Fino-je-torra	1506
847	Jan	22		Ting-mau	4	*	Fino-to-ov	1507
848*	Feb	9		Wu-shin	5		Tsutsno-je-tats	1508
849	Jan	28		Ki-se	6		Tsutsno-to-mi	1509
850	Jan	18		Kang-wu	7	*	Kanno-je-ooma	1510
851	Feb	6		Sin-wi	8		Kanno-to-tsitsuse	1511
852*	Jan	27		Jin-shin	9		Midsno-je-sar	1512
853	Jan	15		Kwei-yu	10	*	Midsno-to-torri	1513
854	Feb	2		Kiah-siuh	11		Kino-je-in	1514
855	Jan	23		Yih-hai	12	*	Kino-to-y	1515
856*	Feb	11		Ping-tse	13		Fino-je-ne	1516
857	Jan	30		Ting-chau	14		Fino-to-oos	1517
858	Jan	20		Wu-yin	15	*	Tsutsno-je-torra	1518
859	Feb	7		Ki-mau	16		Tsutsno-to-ov	1519
860*	Jan	27		Kang-shin	17		Kanno-je-tats	1520
861	Jan	16		Sin-se	18	*	Kanno-to-mi	1521
862	Feb	4		Jin-wu	19		Midsno-je-ooma	1522
863	Jan	25		Kwei-wi	20	*	Midsno-to-tsitsuse	1523
864*	Feb	12		Kiah-shin	21		Kino-je-sar	1524
865	Feb	1		Yih-yu	22		Kino-to-torri	1525
866	Jan	21		Ping-siuh	23	*	Fino-je-in	1526

Western Date of New Year (Gregorian)			Cycle No.	Chinese Year Name & Cycle		Intercalculary Month	Japanese Name of Year Cycle and Year Number	
867	Feb	9		Ting-hai	24		Fino-to-y	1527
868*	Jan	30		Wu-tse	25		Tsutsno-je-ne	1528
869	Jan	18		Ki-chau	26		Tsutsno-to-oos	1529
870	Feb	6		Kang-yin	27		Kanno-je-torra	1530
871	Jan	26		Sin-mau	28		Kanno-to-ov	1531
872*	Jan	15		Jin-shin	29	*	Midsno-je-tats	1532
873	Feb	3		Kwei-se	30		Midsno-to-mi	1533
874	Jan	23		Kiah-wu	31	*	Kino-je-ooma	1534
875	Feb	10		Yih-wi	32		Kino-to-tsitsuse	1535
876*	Jan	31		Ping-shin	33		Fino-je-sar	1536
877	Jan	19		Ting-yu	34	*	Fino-to-torri	1537
878	Feb	7		Wu-siuh	35		Tsutsno-je-in	1538
879	Jan	28		Ki-hai	36		Tsutsno-to-y	1539
880*	Jan	17		Kang-tse	37	*	Kanno-je-ne	1540
881	Feb	4		Sin-chau	38		Kanno-to-oos	1541
882	Jan	24		Jin-yin	39	*	Midsno-je-torra	1542
883	Feb	12		Kwei-mau	40		Midsno-to-ov	1543
884*	Feb	2		Kiah-shin	41		Kino-je-tats	1544
885	Jan	21		Yih-se	42	*	Kino-to-mi	1545
886	Feb	8		Ping-wu	43		Fino-je-ooma	1546
887	Jan	29		Ting-wi	44		Fino-to-tsitsuse	1547
888*	Jan	19		Wu-shin	45	*	Tsutsno-je-sar	1548
889	Feb	5		Ki-yu	46		Tsutsno-to-torri	1549
890	Jan	26		Kang-siuh	47		Kanno-je-in	1550
891	Jan	15		Sin-hai	48	*	Kanno-to-y	1551
892*	Feb	3		Jin-tse	49		Midsno-je-ne	1552
893	Jan	22		Kwei-chau	50	*	Midsno-to-oos	1553
894	Feb	10		Kiah-yin	51		Kino-je-torra	1554
895	Jan	31		Yih-mau	52		Kino-to-ov	1555
896*	Jan	20		Ping-shin	53	*	Fino-je-tats	1556
897	Feb	7		Ting-wu	54		Fino-to-mi	1557
898	Jan	27		Wu-wu	55		Tsutsno-je-ooma	1558
899	Jan	16		Ki-wi	56	*	Tsutsno-to-tsitsuse	1559
900*	Feb	5		Kang-shin	57		Kanno-je-sar	1560
901	Jan	24		Sin-yu	58	*	Kanno-to-torri	1561
902	Feb	12		Jin-siuh	59		Midsno-je-ne	1562
903	Feb	1		Kwei-hai	60		Midsno-to-y	1563
904*	Jan	21	60	Kiah-tse	1	*	Kino-je-ne	1564
905	Feb	9		Yih-chau	2		Kino-to-oos	1565
906	Jan	29		Ping-yin	3		Fino-je-torra	1566
907	Jan	18		Ting-mau	4	*	Fino-to-ov	1567
908*	Feb	6		Wu-shin	5		Tsutsno-je-tats	1568
909	Jan	25		Ki-se	6		Tsutsno-to-mi	1569
910	Jan	15		Kang-wu	7	*	Kanno-je-ooma	1570

Western Date of New Year (Julian)			Cycle No.	Chinese Year Name & Cycle		Intercalculary Month	Japanese Name of Year Cycle and Year Number	
911	Feb	3		Sin-wi	8		Kanno-to-tsitsuse	1571
912*	Jan	23		Jin-shin	9	*	Midsno-je-sar	1572
913	Feb	10		Kwei-yu	10		Midsno-to-torri	1573
914	Jan	30		Kiah-siuh	11		Kino-je-in	1574
915	Jan	19		Yih-hai	12	*	Kino-to-y	1575
916*	Feb	8		Ping-tse	13		Fino-je-ne	1576
917	Jan	27		Ting-chau	14		Fino-to-oos	1577
918	Jan	16		Wu-yin	15	*	Tsutsno-je-torra	1578
919	Feb	4		Ki-mau	16		Tsutsno-to-ov	1579
920*	Jan	24		Kang-shin	17	*	Kanno-je-tats	1580
921	Feb	12		Sin-se	18		Kanno-to-mi	1581
922	Feb	1		Jin-wu	19	*	Midsno-je-ooma	1582
923	Jan	21		Kwei-wi	20		Midsno-to-tsitsuse	1583
924*	Feb	9		Kiah-shin	21		Kino-je-sar	1584
925	Jan	28		Yih-yu	22		Kino-to-torri	1585
926	Jan	17		Ping-siuh	23	*	Fino-je-in	1586
927	Feb	6		Ting-hai	24		Fino-to-y	1587
928*	Jan	26		Wu-tse	25	*	Tsutsno-je-ne	1588
929	Feb	13		Ki-chau	26		Tsutsno-to-oos	1589
930	Feb	2		Kang-yin	27		Kanno-je-torra	1590
931	Jan	23		Sin-mau	28	*	Kanno-to-ov	1591
932*	Feb	11		Jin-shin	29		Midsno-je-tats	1592
933	Jan	31		Kwei-se	30		Midsno-to-mi	1593
934	Jan	20		Kiah-wu	31	*	Kino-je-ooma	1594
935	Feb	7		Yih-wi	32		Kino-to-tsitsuse	1595
936*	Jan	27		Ping-shin	33		Fino-je-sar	1596
937	Jan	16		Ting-yu	34	*	Fino-to-torri	1597
938	Feb	4		Wu-siuh	35		Tsutsno-je-in	1598
939	Jan	25		Ki-hai	36	*	Tsutsno-to-y	1599
940*	Feb	12		Kang-tse	37		Kanno-je-ne	1600
941	Jan	31		Sin-chau	38		Kanno-to-oos	1601
942	Jan	21		Jin-yin	39	*	Midsno-je-torra	1602
943	Feb	9		Kwei-mau	40		Midsno-to-ov	1603
944*	Jan	29		Kiah-shin	41		Kino-je-tats	1604
945	Jan	18		Yih-se	42	*	Kino-to-mi	1605
946	Feb	5		Ping-wu	43		Fino-je-ooma	1606
947	Jan	25		Ting-wi	44		Fino-to-tsitsuse	1607
948*	Jan	15		Wu-shin	45	*	Tsutsno-je-sar	1608
949	Feb	2		Ki-yu	46		Tsutsno-to-torri	1609
950	Jan	23		Kang-siuh	47	*	Kanno-je-in	1610
951	Feb	10		Sin-hai	48		Kanno-to-y	1611
952*	Jan	30		Jin-tse	49		Midsno-je-ne	1612
953	Jan	19		Kwei-chau	50	*	Midsno-to-oos	1613
954	Feb	7		Kiah-yin	51		Kino-je-torra	1614

Western Date of New Year (Julian)			Cycle No.	Chinese Year Name & Cycle		Intercalculary Month	Japanese Name of Year Cycle and Year Number	
955	Jan	27		Yih-mau	52		Kino-to-ov	1615
956*	Jan	17		Ping-shin	53	*	Fino-je-tats	1616
957	Feb	3		Ting-wu	54		Fino-to-mi	1617
958	Jan	23		Wu-wu	55	*	Tsutsno-je-ooma	1618
959	Feb	12		Ki-wi	56		Tsutsno-to-tsitsuse	1619
960*	Feb	1		Kang-shin	57		Kanno-je-sar	1620
961	Jan	21		Sin-yu	58	*	Kanno-to-torri	1621
962	Feb	8		Jin-siuh	59		Midsno-je-in	1622
963	Jan	29		Kwei-hai	60		Midsno-to-y	1623
964*	Jan	18	61	Kiah-tse	1	*	Kino-je-ne	1624
965	Feb	5		Yih-chau	2		Kino-to-oos	1625
966	Jan	26		Ping-yin	3	*	Fino-je-torra	1626
967	Feb	13		Ting-mau	4		Fino-to-ov	1627
968*	Feb	3		Wu-shin	5		Tsutsno-je-tats	1628
969	Jan	22		Ki-se	6	*	Tsutsno-to-mi	1629
970	Feb	10		Kang-wu	7		Kanno-je-ooma	1630
971	Jan	31		Sin-wi	8		Kanno-to-tsitsuse	1631
972*	Jan	20		Jin-shin	9	*	Midsno-je-sar	1632
973	Feb	6		Kwei-yu	10		Midsno-to-torri	1633
974	Jan	27		Kiah-siuh	11		Kino-je-in	1634
975	Jan	16		Yih-hai	12	*	Kino-to-y	1635
976*	Feb	4		Ping-tse	13		Fino-je-ne	1636
977	Jan	24		Ting-chau	14	*	Fino-to-oos	1637
978	Feb	11		Wu-yin	15		Tsutsno-je-torra	1638
979	Feb	1		Ki-mau	16		Tsutsno-to-ov	1639
980*	Jan	21		Kang-shin	17	*	Kanno-je-tats	1640
981	Feb	8		Sin-se	18		Kanno-to-mi	1641
982	Jan	29		Jin-wu	19		Midsno-je-ooma	1642
983	Jan	18		Kwei-wi	20	*	Midsno-to-tsitsuse	1643
984*	Feb	5		Kiah-shin	21		Kino-je-sar	1644
985	Jan	25		Yih-yu	22	*	Kino-to-torri	1645
986	Feb	13		Ping-siuh	23		Fino-je-in	1646
987	Feb	2		Ting-hai	24		Fino-to-y	1647
988*	Jan	23		Wu-tse	25	*	Tsutsno-je-ne	1648
989	Feb	9		Ki-chau	26		Tsutsno-to-oos	1649
990	Jan	30		Kang-yin	27		Kanno-je-torra	1650
991	Jan	19		Sin-mau	28		Kanno-to-ov	1651*
992*	Feb	7		Jin-shin	29		Midsno-je-tats	1652
993	Jan	27		Kwei-se	30		Midsno-to-mi	1653
994	Jan	16		Kiah-wu	31	*	Kino-je-ooma	1654
995	Feb	4		Yih-wi	32		Kino-to-tsitsuse	1655
996*	Jan	24		Ping-shin	33	*	Fino-je-sar	1656
997	Feb	12		Ting-yu	34		Fino-to-torri	1657
998	Feb	1		Wu-siuh	35		Tsutsno-je-in	1658

Western Date of New Year (Julian)			Cycle No.	Chinese Year Name & Cycle		Intercalculary Month	Japanese Name of Year Cycle and Year Number	
999	Jan	21		Ki-hai	36	*	Tsutsno-to-y	1659
1000*	Feb	9		Kang-tse	37		Kanno-je-ne	1660
1001	Jan	28		Sin-chau	38		Kanno-to-oos	1661
1002	Jan	17		Jin-yin	39	*	Midsno-je-torra	1662
1003	Feb	6		Kwei-mau	40		Midsno-to-ov	1663
1004*	Jan	26		Kiah-shin	41	*	Kino-je-tats	1664
1005	Feb	12		Yih-se	42		Kino-to-mi	1665
1006	Feb	2		Ping-wu	43		Fino-je-ooma	1666
1007	Jan	22		Ting-wi	44	*	Fino-to-tsitsuse	1667
1008*	Feb	11		Wu-shin	45		Tsutsno-je-sar	1668
1009	Jan	30		Ki-yu	46		Tsutsno-to-torri	1669
1010	Jan	19		Kang-siuh	47	*	Kanno-je-in	1670
1011	Feb	7		Sin-hai	48		Kanno-to-y	1671
1012*	Jan	27		Jin-tse	49		Midsno-je-ni	1672
1013	Jan	15		Kwei-chau	50	*	Midsno-to-oos	1673
1014	Feb	4		Kiah-yin	51		Kino-je-torra	1674
1015	Jan	24		Yih-mau	52	*	Kino-to-ov	1675
1016*	Feb	11		Ping-shin	53		Fino-je-tats	1676
1017	Jan	31		Ting-wu	54		Fino-to-mi	1677
1018	Jan	20		Wu-wu	55	*	Tsutsno-je-ooma	1678
1019	Feb	9		Ki-wi	56		Tsutsno-to-tsitsuse	1679
1020*	Jan	29		Kang-shin	57		Kanno-je-sar	1680
1021	Jan	17		Sin-yu	58	*	Kanno-to-torri	1681
1022	Feb	5		Jin-siuh	59		Midsno-je-in	1682
1023	Jan	25		Kwei-hai	60	*	Midsno-to-y	1683
1024*	Feb	13	62	Kiah-tse	1		Kino-je-ne	1684
1025	Feb	2		Yih-chau	2		Kino-to-oos	1685
1026	Jan	22		Ping-yin	3	*	Fino-je-torra	1686
1027	Feb	10		Ting-mau	4		Fino-to-ov	1687
1028*	Jan	30		Wu-shin	5		Tsutsno-je-tats	1688
1029	Jan	19		Ki-se	6	*	Tsutsno-to-mi	1689
1030	Feb	7		Kang-wu	7		Kanno-je-ooma	1690
1031	Jan	27		Sin-wi	8		Kanno-to-tsitsuse	1691
1032*	Jan	17		Jin-shin	9	*	Midsno-je-sar	1692
1033	Feb	3		Kwei-yu	10		Midsno-to-torri	1693
1034	Jan	23		Kiah-siuh	11	*	Kino-je-ne·	1694
1035	Feb	12		Yih-hai	12		Kino-to-y	1695
1036*	Feb	1		Ping-tse	13		Fino-je-ne	1696
1037	Jan	21		Ting-chau	14	*	Fino-to-oos	1697
1038	Feb	8		Wu-yin	15		Tsutsno-je-torra	1698
1039	Jan	28		Ki-mau	16		Tsutsno-to-ov	1699
1040*	Jan	18		Kang-shin	17	*	Kanno-je-tats	1700
1041	Feb	5		Sin-se	18		Kanno-to-mi	1701
1042	Jan	25		Jin-wu	19	*	Midsno-je-ooma	1702

Western Date of New Year (Julian)			Cycle No.	Chinese Year Name & Cycle		Intercalculary Month	Japanese Name of Year Cycle and Year Number	
1043	Feb	13		Kwei-wi	20		Midsno-to-tsitsuse	1703
1044*	Feb	2		Kiah-shin	21		Kino-je-sar	1704
1045	Jan	21		Yih-yu	22	*	Kino-to-torri	1705
1046	Feb	10		Ping-siuh	23		Fino-je-in	1706
1047	Jan	30		Ting-hai	24		Fino-to-y	1707
1048*	Jan	20		Wu-tse	25	*	Tsutsno-je-ne	1708
1049	Feb	6		Ki-chau	26		Tsutsno-to-oos	1709
1050	Jan	26		Kang-yin	27		Kanno-je-torra	1710
1051	Jan	16		Sin-mau	28	*	Kanno-to-ov	1711
1052*	Feb	4		Jin-shin	29		Midsno-je-tats	1712
1053	Jan	23		Kwei-se	30	*	Midsno-to-mi	1713
1054	Feb	11		Kiah-wu	31		Kino-je-ooma	1714
1055	Jan	31		Yih-wi	32		Kino-to-tsitsuse	1715
1056*	Jan	21		Ping-shin	33	*	Fino-je-sar	1716
1057	Feb	8		Ting-yu	34		Fino-to-torri	1717
1058	Jan	28		Wu-siuh	35		Tsutsno-je-in	1718
1059	Jan	18		Ki-hai	36	*	Tsutsno-to-y	1719
1060*	Feb	5		Kang-tse	37		Kanno-je-ne	1720
1061	Jan	25		Sin-chau	38	*	Kanno-to-oos	1721
1062	Feb	13		Jin-yin	39		Midsno-je-torra	1722
1063	Feb	2		Kwei-mau	40		Midsno-to-ov	1723
1064*	Jan	23		Kiah-shin	41	*	Kino-je-tats	1724
1065	Feb	9		Yih-se	42		Kino-to-mi	1725
1066	Jan	30		Ping-wu	43		Fino-je-ooma	1726
1067	Jan	19		Ting-wi	44	*	Fino-to-tsitsuse	1727
1068*	Feb	7		Wu-shin	45		Tsutsno-je-sar	1728
1069	Jan	27		Ki-yu	46		Tsutsno-to-torri	1729
1070	Jan	16		Kang-siuh	47	*	Kanno-je-in	1730
1071	Feb	3		Sin-hai	48		Kanno-to-y	1731
1072*	Jan	24		Jin-tse	49	*	Midsno-je-ne	1732
1073	Feb	11		Kwei-chau	50		Midsno-to-oos	1733
1074	Jan	31		Kiah-yin	51		Kino-je-torra	1734
1075	Jan	21		Yih-mau	52	*	Kino-to-ov	1735
1076*	Feb	8		Ping-shin	53		Fino-je-tats	1736
1077	Jan	28		Ting-wu	54		Fino-to-mi	1737
1078	Jan	17		Wu-wu	55	*	Tsutsno-je-ooma	1738
1079	Feb	5		Ki-wi	56		Tsutsno-to-tsitsuse	1739
1080*	Jan	26		Kang-shin	57	*	Kanno-je-sar	1740
1081	Feb	12		Sin-yu	58		Kanno-to-torri	1741
1082	Feb	1		Jin-siuh	59		Midsno-je-ne	1742
1083	Jan	22		Kwei-hai	60	*	Midsno-to-y	1743
1084*	Feb	10	63	Kiah-tse	1		Kino-je-ne	1744
1085	Jan	30		Yih-chau	2		Kino-to-oos	1745
1086	Jan	19		Ping-yin	3	*	Fino-je-torra	1746

Western Date of New Year (Julian)			Cycle No.	Chinese Year Name & Cycle		Intercalculary Month	Japanese Name of Year Cycle and Year Number	
1087	Feb	6		Ting-mau	4		Fino-to-ov	1747
1088*	Jan	27		Wu-shin	5		Tsutsno-je-tats	1748
1089	Jan	15		Ki-se	6	*	Tsutsno-to-mi	1749
1090	Feb	3		Kang-wu	7		Kanno-je-ooma	1750
1091	Jan	24		Sin-wi	8	*	Kanno-to-tsitsuse	1751
1092*	Feb	11		Jin-shin	9		Midsno-je-sar	1752
1093	Jan	31		Kwei-yu	10		Midsno-to-torri	1753
1094	Jan	20		Kiah-siuh	11	*	Kino-je-in	1754
1095	Feb	9		Yih-ahi	12		Kino-to-y	1755
1096*	Jan	29		Ping-tse	13		Fino-je-ne	1756
1097	Jan	17		Ting-chau	14	*	Fino-to-oos	1757
1098	Feb	5		Wu-yin	15		Tsutsno-je-torra	1758
1099	Jan	25		Ki-mau	16	*	Tsutsno-to-ov	1759
1100*	Feb	13		Kang-shin	17		Kanno-je-tats	1760
1101	Feb	2		Sin-se	18		Kanno-to-mi	1761
1102	Jan	22		Jin-wu	19	*	Midsno-je-ooma	1762
1103	Feb	9		Kwei-wi	20		Midsno-to-tsitsuse	1763
1104*	Jan	30		Kiah-shin	21		Kino-je-sar	1764
1105	Jan	18		Yih-yu	22	*	Kino-to-torri	1765
1106	Feb	7		Ping-siuh	23		Fino-je-in	1766
1107	Jan	27		Ting-hai	24		Fino-to-y	1767
1108*	Jan	16		Wu-tse	25	*	Tsutsno-je-ne	1768
1109	Feb	3		Ki-chau	26		Tsutsno-to-oos	1769
1110	Jan	24		Kang-yin	27	*	Kanno-je-torra	1770
1111	Feb	11		Sin-mau	28		Kanno-to-ov	1771
1112*	Feb	1		Jin-shin	34		Midsno-je-tats	1772
1113	Jan	20		Kwei-se	30	*	Midsno-to-mi	1773
1114	Feb	8		Kiah-wu	31		Kino-je-ooma	1774
1115	Jan	28		Yih-wi	32		Kino-to-tsitsuse	1775
1116*	Jan	17		Ping-shin	33	*	Fino-je-sar	1776
1117	Feb	5		Ting-yu	39		Fino-to-torri	1777
1118	Jan	25		Wu-siuh	35	*	Tsutsno-je-in	1778
1119	Feb	12		Ki-hai	36		Tsutsno-to-y	1779
1120*	Feb	2		Kang-tse	37		Kanno-je-ne	1780
1121	Jan	21		Sin-chau	38	*	Kanno-to-oos	1781
1122	Feb	9		Jin-yin	39		Midsno-je-torra	1782
1123	Jan	30		Kwei-mau	40		Midsno-to-ov	1783
1124*	Jan	19		Kiah-shin	41	*	Kino-je-tats	1784
1125	Feb	6		Yih-se	42		Kino-to-mi	1785
1126	Jan	26		Ping-wu	43		Fino-je-ooma	1786
1127	Jan	16		Ting-wi	44		Fino-to-tsitsuse	1787
1128*	Feb	4		Wu-shin	45		Tsutsno-je-sar	1788
1129	Jan	23		Ki-yu	46	*	Tsutsno-to-torri	1789
1130	Feb	11		Kang-siuh	47		Kanno-je-in	1790

Western Date of New Year (Julian)			Cycle No.	Chinese Year Name & Cycle		Intercalculary Month	Japanese Name of Year Cycle and Year Number	
1131	Jan	31		Sin-hai	48		Kanno-to-y	1791
1132*	Jan	20		Jin-tse	49	*	Midsno-je-ne	1792
1133	Feb	8		Kwei-chau	50		Midsno-to-oos	1793
1134	Jan	28		Kiah-yin	51		Kino-je-torra	1794
1135	Jan	18		Yih-mau	52	*	Kino-to-ov	1795
1136*	Feb	5		Ping-shin	53		Fino-je-tats	1796
1137	Jan	24		Ting-wu	54	*	Fino-to-mi	1797
1138	Feb	13		Wu-wu	55		Tsutsno-je-ooma	1798
1139	Feb	2		Ki-wi	56		Tsutsno-to-tsitsuse	1799
1140*	Jan	22		Kang-shin	57	*	Kanno-je-sar	1800
1141	Feb	9		Sin-yu	58		Kanno-to-torri	1801
1142	Jan	29		Jin-siuh	59		Midsno-je-in	1802
1143	Jan	19		Kwei-hai	60	*	Midsno-to-y	1803
1144*	Feb	7	64	Kiah-tse	1		Kino-je-ne	1804
1145	Jan	26		Yih-chau	2		Kino-to-oos	1805
1146	Jan	16		Ping-yin	3	*	Fino-je-torra	1806
1147	Feb	3		Ting-mau	4		Fino-to-ov	1807
1148*	Jan	23		Wu-shin	5	*	Tsutsno-je-tats	1808
1149	Feb	11		Ki-se	6		Tsutsno-to-mi	1809
1150	Jan	31		Kang-wu	7		Kanno-je-ooma	1810
1151	Jan	20		Sin-wi	8	*	Kanno-to-tsitsuse	1811
1152*	Feb	8		Jin-shin	9		Midsno-je-sar	1812
1153	Jan	27		Kwei-yu	10		Midsno-to-torri	1813
1154	Jan	17		Kiah-siuh	11	*	Kino-je-in	1814
1155	Feb	5		Yih-hai	12		Kino-to-y	1815
1156*	Jan	25		Ping-tse	13	*	Fino-je-ne	1816
1157	Feb	12		Ting-chau	14		Fino-to-oos	1817
1158	Feb	1		Wu-yin	15		Tsutsno-je-torra	1818
1159	Jan	22		Ki-mau	16	*	Tsutsno-to-ov	1819
1160*	Feb	10		Kang-shin	17		Kanno-je-tats	1820
1161	Jan	29		Sin-se	18		Kanno-to-mi	1821
1162	Jan	19		Jin-wu	19	*	Midsno-je-ooma	1822
1163	Feb	6		Kwei-wi	20		Midsno-to-tsituse	1823
1164*	Jan	27		Kiah-shin	21		Kino-je-sar	1824
1165	Jan	15		Yih-yu	22	*	Kino-to-torri	1825
1166	Feb	3		Ping-siuh	23		Fino-je-in	1826
1167	Jan	24		Ting-hai	24	*	Fino-to-y	1827
1168*	Feb	11		Wu-tse	25		Tsutsno-je-ne	1828
1169	Jan	30		Ki-chau	26		Tsutsno-to-oos	1829
1170	Jan	20		Kang-yin	27	*	Kanno-je-torra	1830
1171	Feb	8		Sin-mau	28		Kanno-to-ov	1831
1172*	Jan	29		Jin-shin	29		Midsno-je-tats	1832
1173	Jan	17		Kwei-se	30	*	Midsno-to-mi	1833
1174	Feb	4		Kiah-wu	31		Kino-je-ooma	1834

Western Date of New Year (Julian)		Cycle No.	Chinese Year Name & Cycle		Intercalculary Month	Japanese Name of Year Cycle and Year Number	
1175	Jan 25		Yih-wi	32	*	Kino-to-tsitsuse	1835
1176*	Feb 13		Ping-shin	33		Fino-je-sar	1836
1177	Feb 1		Ting-yu	34		Fino-to-torri	1837
1178	Jan 22		Wu-siuh	35	*	Tsutsno-je-in	1838
1179	Feb 9		Ki-hai	36		Tsutsno-to-y	1839
1180*	Jan 29		Kang-tse	37		Kanno-je-ne	1840
1181	Jan 17		Sin-chau	38	*	Kanno-to-oos	1841
1182	Feb 6		Jin-yin	39		Midsno-je-torra	1842
1183	Jan 27		Kwei-mau	40		Midsno-to-ov	1843
1184*	Jan 16		Kiah-shin	41	*	Kino-je-tats	1844
1185	Feb 2		Yih-se	42		Kino-to-mi	1845
1186	Jan 23		Ping-wu	43	*	Fino-je-ooma	1846
1187	Feb 11		Ting-wi	44		Fino-to-tsitsuse	1847
1188*	Jan 30		Wu-shin	45		Tsutsno-je-sar	1848
1189	Jan 20		Ki-yu	46	*	Tsutsno-to-torri	1849
1190	Feb 7		Kang-siuh	47		Kanno-je-in	1850
1191	Jan 28		Sin-hai	48		Kanno-to-y	1851
1192*	Jan 17		Jin-tse	49	*	Midsno-je-ne	1852
1193	Feb 5		Kwei-chau	50		Midsno-to-oos	1853
1194	Jan 25		Kiah-yin	51		Kino-je-torra	1854
1195	Jan 14		Yih-mau	52	*	Kino-to-ov	1855
1196*	Feb 2		Ping-shin	53		Fino-je-tats	1856
1197	Jan 21		Ting-wu	54	*	Fino-to-mi	1857
1198	Feb 9		Wu-wu	55		Tsutsno-je-ooma	1858
1199	Jan 30		Ki-wi	56		Tsutsno-to-tsitsuse	1859
1200*	Jan 19		Kang-shin	57	*	Kanno-je-sar	1860
1201	Feb 6		Sin-yu	58		Kanno-to-torri	1861
1202	Jan 26		Jin-siuh	59		Midsno-je-in	1862
1203	Jan 15		Kwei-hai	60	*	Midsno-to-y	1863
1204*	Feb 4	65	Kiah-tse	1		Kino-je-ne	1864
1205	Jan 23		Yih-chau	2	*	Kino-to-oos	1865
1206	Feb 10		Ping-yin	3		Fino-je-torra	1866
1207	Jan 31		Ting-mau	4		Fino-to-ov	1867
1208*	Jan 20		Wu-shin	5	*	Tsutsno-je-tats	1868
1209	Feb 7		Ki-se	6		Tsutsno-to-mi	1869
1210	Jan 28		Kang-wu	7		Kanno-je-ooma	1870
1211	Jan 17		Sin-wi	8	*	Kanno-to-tsituse	1871
1212*	Feb 5		Jin-shin	9		Midsno-je-sar	1872
1213	Jan 24		Kwei-yu	10		Midsno-to-torri	1873
1214	Jan 13		Kiah-siuh	11	*	Kino-je-in	1874
1215	Feb 2		Yih-hai	12		Kino-to-y	1875
1216*	Jan 22		Ping-tse	13	*	Fino-je-ne	1876
1217	Feb 8		Ting-chau	14		Fino-to-oos	1877
1218	Jan 29		Wu-yin	15		Tsutsno-je-torra	1878

Western Date of New Year (Julian)			Cycle No.	Chinese Year Name & Cycle		Intercalculary Month	Japanese Name of Year Cycle and Year Number	
1219	Jan	18		Ki-mau	16	*	Tsutsno-to-ov	1879
1220*	Feb	6		Kang-shin	17		Kanno-je-tats	1880
1221	Jan	26		Sin-se	18		Kanno-to-mi	1881
1222	Jan	15		Jin-wu	19	*	Midsno-je-ooma	1882
1223	Feb	3		Kwei-wi	20		Midsno-to-tsitsuse	1883
1224*	Jan	23		Kiah-shin	21	*	Kino-je-sar	1884
1225	Feb	11		Yih-yu	22		Kino-to-torri	1885
1226	Jan	31		Ping-siuh	23		Fino-je-in	1886
1227	Jan	20		Ting-hai	24	*	Fino-to-y	1887
1228*	Feb	9		Wu-tse	25		Tsutsno-je-ne	1888
1229	Jan	27		Ki-chau	26		Tsutsno-to-oos	1889
1230	Jan	17		Kang-yin	27	*	Kanno-je-torra	1890
1231	Feb	5		Sin-mau	28		Kanno-to-ov	1891
1232*	Jan	25		Jin-shin	29		Midsno-je-tats	1892
1233	Jan	14		Kwei-se	30	*	Midsno-to-mi	1893
1234	Feb	1		Kiah-wu	31		Kino-je-ooma	1894
1235	Jan	21		Yih-wi	32	*	Kino-to-tsitsuse	1895
1236*	Feb	10		Ping-shin	33		Fino-je-sar	1896
1237	Jan	29		Ting-yu	34		Fino-to-torri	1897
1238	Jan	18		Wu-siuh	35		Tsutsno-je-in	1898
1239	Feb	6		Ki-hai	36		Tsutsno-to-y	1899
1240*	Jan	26		Kang-tse	37		Kanno-je-ne	1900
1241	Jan	15		Sin-chau	38	*	Kanno-to-oos	1901
1242	Feb	3		Jin-yin	39		Midsno-je-torra	1902
1243	Jan	23		Kwei-mau	40	*	Midsno-to-ov	1903
1244*	Feb	11		Kiah-shin	41		Kino-je-tats	1904
1245	Jan	30		Yih-se	42		Kino-to-mi	1905
1246	Jan	19		Ping-wu	43	*	Fino-je-ooma	1906
1247	Feb	8		Ting-wi	44		Fino-to-tsitsuse	1907
1248*	Jan	28		Wu-shin	45		Tsutsno-je-sar	1908
1249	Jan	16		Ki-yu	46	*	Tsutsno-to-torri	1909
1250	Feb	4		Kang-siuh	47		Kanno-je-in	1910
1251	Jan	24		Sin-hai	48		Kanno-to-y	1911
1252*	Jan	13		Jin-tse	49	*	Midsno-jc-ne	1912
1253	Feb	1		Kwei-chau	50		Midsno-to-oos	1913
1254	Jan	21		Kiah-yin	51	*	Kino-je-torra	1914
1255	Feb	9		Yih-mau	52		Kino-to-ov	1915
1256*	Jan	29		Ping-shin	53		Fino-je-tats	1916
1257	Jan	18		Ting-wu	54	*	Fino-to-mi	1917
1258	Feb	6		Wu-wu	55		Tsutsno-je-ooma	1918
1259	Jan	27		Ki-wi	56		Tsutsno-to-tsitsuse	1919
1260*	Jan	16		Kang-shin	57	*	Kanno-je-sar	1920
1261	Feb	2		Sin-yu	58		Kanno-to-torri	1921
1262	Jan	23		Jin-siuh	59	*	Midsno-je-in	1922

Western Date of New Year (Gregorian)			Cycle No.	Chinese Year Name & Cycle		Intercalculary Month	Japanese Name of Year Cycle and Year Number	
1263	Feb	11		Kwei-hai	60		Midsno-to-y	1923
1264*	Jan	31	66	Kiah-tse	1		Kino-je-ne	1924
1265	Jan	20		Yih-chau	2	*	Kino-to-oos	1925
1266	Feb	7		Ping-yin	3		Fino-je-torra	1926
1267	Jan	27		Ting-mau	4		Fino-to-ov	1927
1268*	Jan	17		Wu-shin	5	*	Tsutsno-je-tats	1928
1269	Feb	4		Ki-se	6		Tsutsno-to-mi	1929
1270	Jan	25		Kang-wu	7		Kanno-je-ooma	1930
1271	Jan	14		Sin-wi	8	*	Kanno-to-tsitsuse	1931
1272*	Feb	1		Jin-shin	9		Midsno-je-sar	1932
1273	Jan	21		Kwei-yu	10	*	Midsno-to-torri	1933
1274	Feb	9		Kiah-siuh	11		Kino-je-in	1934
1275	Jan	29		Yih-hai	12		Kino-to-y	1935
1276*	Jan	19		Ping-tse	13	*	Fino-je-ne	1936
1277	Feb	5		Ting-chau	14		Fino-to-oos	1937
1278	Jan	25		Wu-yin	15		Tsutsno-je-torra	1938
1279	Jan	15		Ki-mau	16	*	Tsutsno-to-ov	1939
1280*	Feb	3		Kaug-shin	17		Kanno-je-tats	1940
1281	Jan	23		Sin-se	18	*	Kanno-to-mi	1941
1282	Feb	11		Jin-wu	19		Midsno-je-ooma	1942
1283	Jan	30		Kwei-wi	20		Midsno-to-tsitsuse	1943
1284*	Jan	20		Kiah-shin	21	*	Kino-je-sar	1944
1285	Feb	7		Yih-yu	22		Kino-to-torri	1945
1286	Jan	27		Ping-siuh	23		Fino-je-in	1946
1287	Jan	17		Ting-hai	24	*	Fino-to-y	1947
1288*	Feb	5		Wu-tse	25		Tsutsno-je-ne	1948
1289	Jan	24		Ki-chau	26		Tsutsno-to-oos	1949
1290	Jan	13		Kang-yin	27	*	Kanno-je-torra	1950
1291	Feb	2		Sin-mau	28		Kanno-to-ov	1951
1292*	Jan	22		Jin-shin	29	*	Midsno-je-tats	1952
1293	Feb	8		Kwei-se	30		Midsno-to-mi	1953
1294	Jan	29		Kiah-wu	31		Kino-je-ooma	1954
1295	Jan	18		Yih-wi	32	*	Kino-to-tsitsuse	1955
1296*	Feb	6		Ping-shin	33		Fino-je-sar	1956
1297	Jan	26		Ting-yu	34		Fino-to-torri	1957
1298	Jan	15		Wu-siuh	35	*	Tsutsno-je-in	1958
1299	Feb	3		Ki-hai	36		Tsutsno-to-y	1959
1300*	Jan	23		Kang-tse	37	*	Kanno-je-ne	1960
1301	Feb	10		Sin-chau	38		Kanno-to-oos	1961
1302	Jan	31		Jin-yin	39		Midsno-je-torra	1962
1303	Jan	20		Kwei-mau	40	*	Midsno-to-ov	1963
1304*	Feb	7		Kiah-shin	41		Kino-je-tats	1964
1305	Jan	27		Yih-se	42		Kino-to-mi	1965
1306	Jan	16		Ping-wu	43	*	Fino-je-ooma	1966

Western Date of New Year (Julian)			Cycle No.	Chinese Year Name & Cycle		Intercalculary Month	Japanese Name of Year Cycle and Year Number	
1307	Feb	4		Ting-wi	44		Fino-to-tsitsuse	1967
1308*	Jan	25		Wu-shin	45	*	Tsutsno-je-sar	1968
1309	Feb	11		Ki-yu	46		Tsutsno-to-torri	1969
1310	Feb	1		Kang-siuh	47		Kanno-je-in	1970
1311	Jan	21		Sin-hai	48	*	Kanno-to-y	1971
1312*	Feb	9		Jin-tse	49		Midsno-je-ne	1972
1313	Jan	29		Kwei-chau	50		Midsno-to-oos	1973
1314	Jan	18		Kiah-yin	51	*	Kino-je-torra	1974
1315	Feb	5		Yih-mau	52		Kino-to-ov	1975
1316*	Jan	26		Ping-shin	53		Fino-je-tats	1976
1317	Jan	14		Ting-wu	54	*	Fino-to-mi	1977
1318	Feb	3		Wu-wu	55		Tsutsno-je-ooma	1978
1319	Jan	23		Ki-wi	56		Tsutsno-to-tsitsuse	1979
1320*	Feb	11		Kang-shin	57		Kanno-je-sar	1980
1321	Jan	30		Sin-yu	58		Kanno-to-torri	1981
1322	Jan	19		Jin-siuh	59	*	Midsno-je-in	1982
1323	Feb	8		Kwei-hai	60		Midsno-to-y	1983
1324*	Jan	28	67	Kiah-tse	1		Kino-je-ne	1984
1325	Jan	16		Yih-chau	2	*	Kino-to-oos	1985
1326	Feb	4		Ping-yin	3		Fino-je-torra	1986
1327	Jan	24		Ting-mau	4	*	Fino-to-ov	1987
1328*	Feb	13		Wu-shin	5		Tsutsno-je-tats	1988
1329	Feb	1		Ki-se	6		Tsutsno-to-mi	1989
1330	Jan	21		Kang-wu	7	*	Kanno-je-ooma	1990
1331	Feb	9		Sin-wi	8		Kanno-to-tsitsuse	1991
1332*	Jan	29		Jin-shin	9		Midsno-je-sar	1992
1333	Jan	17		Kwei-yu	10	*	Midsno-to-torri	1993
1334	Feb	6		Kiah-siuh	11		Kino-je-in	1994
1335	Jan	26		Yih-ahi	12		Kino-to-y	1995
1336*	Jan	15		Ping-tse	13	*	Fino-je-ne	1996
1337	Feb	2		Ting-chau	14		Fino-to-oos	1997
1338	Jan	22		Wu-yin	15	*	Tsutsno-je-torra	1998
1339	Feb	11		Ki-mau	16		Tsutsno-to-ov	1999
1340*	Jan	31		Kang-shin	17		Kanno-je-tats	2000
1341	Jan	19		Sin-se	18	*	Kanno-to-mi	2001
1342	Feb	7		Jin-wu	19		Midsno-je-ooma	2002
1343	Jan	27		Kwei-wi	20		Midsno-to-tsitsuse	2003
1344*	Jan	16		Kiah-shin	21	*	Kino-je-sar	2004
1345	Feb	4		Yih-yu	22		Kino-to-torri	2005
1346	Jan	24		Ping-siuh	23	*	Fino-je-in	2006
1347	Feb	12		Ting-hai	24		Fino-to-y	2007
1348*	Feb	1		Wu-tse	25		Tsutsno-je-ne	2008
1349	Jan	20		Ki-chau	26	*	Tsutsno-to-oos	2009
1350	Feb	9		Kang-yin	27		Kanno-je-torra	2010

Western Date of New Year (Julian)			Cycle No.	Chinese Year Name & Cycle		Intercalculary Month	Japanese Name of Year Cycle and Year Number	
1351	Jan	29		Sin-mau	28		Kanno-to-ov	2011
1352*	Jan	18		Jin-shin	29	*	Midsno-je-tats	2012
1353	Feb	5		Kwei-se	30		Midsno-to-mi	2013
1354	Jan	25		Kiah-wu	31		Kino-je-ooma	2014
1355	Jan	15		Yih-wi	32	*	Kino-to-tsitsuse	2015
1356*	Feb	3		Ping-shin	33		Fino-je-sar	2016
1357	Jan	23		Ting-yu	34	*	Fino-to-torri	2017
1358	Feb	10		Wu-siuh	35		Tsutsno-je-in	2018
1359	Jan	30		Ki-hai	36		Tsutsno-to-y	2019
1360*	Jan	20		Kang-tse	37	*	Kanno-je-ne	2020
1361	Feb	7		Sin-chau	38		Kanno-to-oos	2021
1362	Jan	27		Jin-yin	39		Midsno-je-torra	2022
1363	Jan	17		Kwei-mau	40	*	Midsno-to-ov	2023
1364*	Feb	4		Kiah-shin	41		Kino-je-tats	2024
1365	Jan	23		Yih-se	42	*	Kino-to-mi	2025
1366	Feb	12		Ping-wu	43		Fino-je-ooma	2026
1367	Feb	1		Ting-wi	44		Fino-to-tsitsuse	2027
1368*	Jan	22		Wu-shin	45	*	Tsutsno-je-sar	2028
1369	Feb	8		Ki-yu	46		Tsutsno-to-torri	2029
1370	Jan	28		Kang-siuh	47		Kanno-je-in	2030
1371	Jan	18		Sin-hai	48	*	Kanno-to-y	2031
1372*	Feb	6		Jin-tse	49		Midsno-je-ne	2032
1373	Jan	25		Kwei-chau	50		Midsno-to-oos	2033
1374	Jan	15		Kiah-yin	51	*	Kino-je-torra	2034
1375	Feb	2		Yih-mau	52		Kino-to-ov	2035
1376*	Jan	23		Ping-shin	53	*	Fino-je-tats	2036
1377	Feb	10		Ting-wu	54		Fino-to-mi	2037
1378	Jan	30		Wu-wu	55		Tsutsno-je-ooma	2038
1379	Jan	20		Ki-wi	56	*	Tsutsno-to-tsitsuse	2039
1380*	Feb	7		Kang-shin	57		Kanno-je-sar	2040
1381	Jan	26		Sin-yu	58		Kanno-to-torri	2041
1382	Jan	16		Jin-siuh	59	*	Midsno-je-in	2042
1383	Feb	4		Kwei-hai	60		Midsno-to-y	2043
1384*	Jan	24	68	Kiah-tse	1	*	Kino-je-ne	2044
1385	Feb	11		Yih-chau	2		Kino-to-oos	2045
1386	Feb	1		Ping-yin	3		Fino-je-torra	2046
1387	Jan	21		Ting-mau	4	*	Fino-to-ov	2047
1388*	Feb	9		Wu-shin	5		Tsutsno-je-tats	2048
1389	Jan	29		Ki-se	6		Tsutsno-to-mi	2049
1390	Jan	18		Kang-wu	7	*	Kanno-je-ooma	2050
1391	Feb	5		Sin-wi	8		Kanno-to-tsitsuse	2051
1392*	Jan	26		Jin-shin	9		Midsno-je-sar	2052
1393	Jan	14		Kwei-yu	10	*	Midsno-to-torri	2053
1394	Feb	2		Kiah-siuh	11		Kino-je-in	2054

Western Date of New Year (Julian)			Cycle No.	Chinese Year Name & Cycle		Intercalculary Month	Japanese Name of Year Cycle and Year Number	
1395	Jan	23		Yih-hai	12	*	Kino-to-y	2055
1396*	Feb	10		Ping-tse	13		Fino-je-ne	2056
1397	Jan	30		Ting-chau	14		Fino-to-oos	2057
1398	Jan	19		Wu-yin	15	*	Tustsno-je-torra	2058
1399	Feb	7		Ki-mau	16		Tsutsno-to-ov	2059
1400*	Jan	27		Kang-shin	17		Kanno-je-tats	2060
1401	Jan	16		Sin-se	18	*	Kanno-to-mi	2061
1402	Feb	3		Jin-wu	19		Midsno-je-ooma	2062
1403	Jan	24		Kwei-wi	20	*	Midsno-to-tsitsuse	2063
1404*	Feb	12		Kiah-shin	21		Kino-je-sar	2064
1405	Feb	1		Yih-yu	22		Kino-to-torri	2065
1406	Jan	21		Ping-siuh	23	*	Fino-je-in	2066
1407	Feb	8		Ting-hai	24		Fino-to-y	2067
1408*	Jan	29		Wu-tse	25		Tsutsno-je-ne	2068
1409	Jan	17		Ki-chau	26	*	Tsutsno-to-oos	2069
1410	Feb	5		Kang-yin	27		Kanno-je-torra	2070
1411	Jan	26		Sin-mau	28		Kanno-to-ov	2071
1412*	Jan	15		Jin-shin	29	*	Midsno-je-tats	2072
1413	Feb	1		Kwei-se	30		Midsno-to-mi	2073
1414	Jan	22		Kiah-wu	31	*	Kino-je-ooma	2074
1415	Feb	10		Yih-wi	32		Kino-to-tsitsuse	2075
1416*	Jan	31		Ping-shin	33		Fino-je-sar	2076
1417	Jan	19		Ting-yu	34	*	Fino-to-torri	2077
1418	Feb	7		Wu-siuh	35		Tsutsno-je-in	2078
1419	Jan	27		Ki-hai	36		Tsutsno-to-y	2079
1420*	Jan	16		Kang-tse	37	*	Kanno-je-ne	2080
1421	Feb	4		Sin-chau	38		Kanno-to-oos	2081
1422	Jan	24		Jin-yin	39	*	Midsno-je-torra	2082
1423	Feb	11		Kwei-mau	40		Midsno-to-ov	2083
1424*	Feb	1		Kiah-shin	41		Kino-je-tats	2084
1425	Jan	20		Yih-se	42	*	Kino-to-mi	2085
1426	Feb	9		Ping-wu	43		Fino-je-ooma	2086
1427	Jan	29		Ting-wi	44		Fino-to-tsitsuse	2087
1428*	Jan	18		Wu-shin	45	*	Tsutsno-je-sar	2088
1429	Feb	5		Ki-yu	46		Tsutsno-to-torri	2089
1430	Jan	25		Kang-siuh	47		Kanno-je-in	2090
1431	Jan	14		Sin-hai	48	*	Kanno-to-y	2091
1432*	Feb	3		Jin-tse	49		Midsno-je-ne	2092
1433	Jan	22		Kwei-chau	50	*	Midsno-to-oos	2093
1434	Feb	10		Kiah-yin	51		Kino-je-torra	2094
1435	Jan	30		Yih-mau	52		Kino-to-ov	2095
1436*	Jan	19		Ping-shin	53	*	Fino-je-tats	2096
1437	Feb	7		Ting-wu	54		Fino-to-mi	2097
1438	Jan	27		Wu-wu	55		Tsutsno-je-ooma	2098

Western Date of New Year (Julian)			Cycle No.	Chinese Year Name & Cycle		Intercalculary Month	Japanese Name of Year Cycle and Year Number	
1439	Jan	16		Ki-wi	56	*	Tsutsno-o-tsitsuse	2099
1440*	Feb	4		Kang-shin	57		Kanno-je-sar	2100
1441	Jan	23		Sin-yu	58	*	Kanno-to-torri	2101
1442	Feb	11		Jin-siuh	59		Midsno-je-in	2102
1443	Feb	1		Kwei-hai	60		Midsno-to-y	2103
1444*	Jan	21	69	Kiah-tse	1	*	Kino-je-ne	2104
1445	Feb	8		Yih-chau	2		Kino-to-oos	2105
1446	Jan	28		Ping-yin	3		Fino-je-torra	2106
1447	Jan	17		Ting-mau	4	*	Fino-to-ov	2107
1448*	Feb	16		Wu-shin	5		Tsutsno-je-tats	2108
1449	Jan	25		Ki-se	6		Tsutsno-to-mi	2109
1450	Jan	14		Kang-wu	7	*	Kanno-je-ooma	2110
1451	Feb	2		Sin-wi	8		Kanno-to-tsitsuse	2111
1452*	Jan	22		Jin-shin	9	*	Midsno-je-sar	2112
1453	Feb	10		Kwei-yu	10		Midsno-to-torri	2113
1454	Jan	30		Kiah-siuh	11		Kino-je-in	2114
1455	Jan	20		Yih-hai	12	*	Kino-to-y	2115
1456*	Feb	7		Ping-tse	13		Fino-je-ne	2116
1457	Jan	26		Ting-chau	14		Fino-to-oos	2117
1458	Jan	16		Wu-yin	15	*	Tsutsno-je-torra	2118
1459	Feb	4		Ki-mau	16		Tsutsno-to-ov	2119
1460*	Jan	24		Kang-shin	17	*	Kanno-je-tats	2120
1461	Feb	11		Sin-se	18		Kanno-to-mi	2121
1462	Jan	31		Jin-wu	19		Midsno-je-ooma	2122
1463	Jan	21		Kwei-wi	20	*	Midsno-to-tsitsuse	2123
1464*	Feb	9		Kiah-shin	21		Kino-je-sar	2124
1465	Jan	28		Yih-yu	22		Kino-to-torri	2125
1466	Jan	18		Ping-siuh	23	*	Fino-je-in	2126
1467	Feb	5		Ting-hai	24		Fino-to-y	2127
1468*	Jan	25		Wu-tse	25		Tsutsno-je-ne	2128
1469	Jan	14		Ki-chau	26	*	Tsutsno-to-oos	2129
1470	Feb	2		Kang-yin	27		Kanno-je-torra	2130
1471	Jan	22		Sin-mau	28	*	Kanno-to-ov	2131
1472*	Feb	10		Jin-shin	29		Midsno-je-tats	2132
1473	Jan	29		Kwei-se	30		Midsno-to-mi	2133
1474	Jan	19		Kiah-wu	31	*	Kino-je-ooma	2134
1475	Feb	7		Yih-wi	32		Kino-to-tsitsuse	2135
1476*	Jan	27		Ping-shin	33		Fino-je-sar	2136
1477	Jan	16		Ting-yu	34	*	Fino-to-torri	2137
1478	Feb	3		Wu-siuh	35		Tsutsno-je-in	2138
1479	Jan	23		Ki-hai	36	*	Tsutsno-to-y	2139
1480*	Feb	12		Kang-tse	37		Kanno-je-ne	2140
1481	Jan	31		Sin-chau	38		Kanno-to-oos	2141
1482	Jan	20		Jin-yin	39	*	Midsno-je-torra	2142

Western Date of New Year (Julian)			Cycle No.	Chinese Year Name & Cycle		Intercalculary Month	Japanese Name of Year Cycle and Year Number	
1483	Feb	8		Kwei-mau	40		Midsno-to-ov	2143
1484*	Jan	29		Kiah-shin	41		Kino-je-tats	2144
1485	Jan	17		Yih-se	42	*	Kino-to-mi	2145
1486	Feb	5		Ping-wu	43		Fino-je-ooma	2146
1487	Jan	26		Ting-wi	44		Fino-to-tsitsuse	2147
1488*	Jan	15		Wu-shin	45	*	Tsutsno-je-sar	2148
1489	Feb	1		Ki-yu	46		Tsutsno-to-torri	2149
1490	Jan	22		Kang-siuh	47	*	Kanno-je-in	2150
1491	Feb	11		Sin-hai	48		Kanno-to-y	2151
1492*	Jan	31		Jin-tse	49		Midsno-je-ne	2152
1493	Jan	19		Kwei-chau	50	*	Midsno-to-oos	2153
1494	Feb	6		Kiah-yin	51		Kino-je-torra	2154
1495	Jan	27		Yih-mau	52		Kino-to-ov	2155
1496*	Jan	16		Ping-shin	53	*	Fino-je-tats	2156
1497	Feb	3		Ting-wu	54		Fino-to-mi	2157
1498	Jan	24		Wu-wu	55	*	Tsutsno-je-ooma	2158
1499	Feb	4		Ki-wi	56		Tsutsno-to-tsitsuse	2159
1500*	Jan	31		Kang-shin	57		Kanno-je-sar	2160
1501	Jan	20		Sin-yu	58	*	Kanno-to-torri	2161
1502	Feb	8		Jin-siuh	59		Midsno-je-in	2162
1503	Jan	29		Kwei-hai	60		Midsno-to-y	2163
1504*	Jan	18	70	Kiah-tse	1	*	Kino-je-ne	2164
1505	Feb	4		Yih-chau	2		Kino-to-oos	2165
1506	Jan	25		Ping-yin	3		Fino-je-torra	2166
1507	Jan	14		Ting-mau	4	*	Fino-to-ov	2167
1508*	Feb	2		Wu-shin	6		Tsutsno-je-tats	2168
1509	Jan	22		Ki-se	6	*	Tsutsno-to-mi	2169
1510	Feb	9		Kang-wu	7		Kanno-je-ooma	2170
1511	Jan	29		Sin-wi	8		Kanno-to-tsitsuse	2171
1512*	Jan	19		Jin-shin	9	*	Midsno-je-sar	2172
1513	Feb	6		Kwei-yu	10		Midsno-to-torri	2173
1514	Jan	27		Kiah-siuh	11		Kino-je-in	2174
1515	Jan	16		Yih-hai	12	*	Kino-to-y	2175
1516*	Feb	4		Ping-tse	13		Fino-je-ne	2176
1517	Jan	23		Ting-chau	14	*	Fino-to-oos	2177
1518	Feb	11		Wu-yin	15		Tsutsno-je-torra	2178
1519	Feb	1		Ki-mau	16		Tsutsno-to-ov	2179
1520*	Jan	21		Kang-shin	17	*	Kanno-je-tats	2180
1521	Feb	8		Sin-se	18		Kanno-to-mi	2181
1522	Jan	28		Jin-wu	19		Midsno-je-ooma	2182
1523	Jan	17		Kwei-wi	20	*	Midsno-to-tsitsuse	2183
1524*	Feb	6		Kiah-shin	21		Kino-je-sar	2184
1525	Jan	25		Yih-yu	22		Kino-to-torri	2185
1526	Jan	14		Ping-siuh	23	*	Fino-je-in	2186

Western Date of New Year (Julian)			Cycle No.	Chinese Year Name & Cycle		Intercalculary Month	Japanese Name of Year Cycle and Year Number	
1527	Feb	2		Ting-hai	24		Fino-to-y	2187
1528*	Jan	22		Wu-tse	25	*	Tsutsno-je-ne	2188
1529	Feb	9		Ki-chau	26		Tsutsno-to-oos	2189
1530	Jan	27		Kang-yin	27		Kanno-je-torra	2190
1531	Jan	17		Sin-mau	28	*	Kanno-to-ov	2191
1532*	Feb	7		Jin-shin	29		Midsno-je-tats	2192
1533	Jan	26		Kwei-se	30		Midsno-to-mi	2193
1534	Jan	15		Kiah-wu	31	*	Kino-je-ooma	2194
1535	Feb	4		Yih-wi	32		Kino-to-tsitsuse	2195
1536*	Jan	24		Ping-shin	33	*	Fino-je-sar	2196
1537	Feb	10		Ting-yu	34		Fino-to-torri	2197
1538	Jan	31		Wu-siuh	35		Tsutsno-je-in	2198
1539	Jan	20		Ki-hai	36	*	Tsutsno-to-y	2199
1540*	Feb	8		Kang-tse	37		Kanno-je-ne	2200
1541	Jan	28		Sin-chau	38		Kanno-to-oos	2201
1542	Jan	17		Jin-yin	39	*	Midsno-je-torra	2202
1543	Feb	5		Kewi-mau	40		Midsno-to-ov	2203
1544*	Jan	25		Kiah-shin	41		Kino-je-tats	2204
1545	Jan	13		Yih-se	42	*	Kino-to-mi	2205
1546	Feb	2		Ping-wu	43		Fino-je-ooma	2206
1547	Jan	22		Ting-wi	44	*	Fino-to-tsitsuse	2207
1548*	Feb	10		Wu-shin	45		Tsutsno-je-sar	2208
1549	Jan	29		Ki-yu	46		Tsutsno-to-torri	2209
1550	Jan	19		Kang-siuh	47	*	Kanno-je-in	2210
1551	Feb	7		Sin-hai	48		Kanno-to-y	2211
1552*	Jan	27		Jin-tse	49		Midsno-je-ne	2212
1553	Jan	16		Kwei-chau	50	*	Midsno-to-oos	2213
1554	Feb	3		Kiah-yin	51		Kino-je-torra	2214
1555	Jan	23		Yih-mau	52	*	Kino-to-ov	2215
1556*	Feb	12		Ping-shin	53		Fino-je-tats	2216
1557	Jan	31		Ting-wu	54		Fino-to-mi	2217
1558	Jan	20		Wu-wu	55	*	Tsutsno-je-ooma	2218
1559	Feb	8		Ki-wi	56		Tsutsno-to-tsitsuse	2219
1560*	Jan	28		Kang-shin	57		Kanno-je-sar	2220
1561	Jan	17		Sin-yu	58	*	Kanno-to-torri	2221
1562	Feb	5		Jin-siuh	59		Midsno-je-in	2222
1563	Jan	25		Kwei-hai	60		Midsno-to-y	2223
1564*	Jan	15	71	Kiah-tse	1	*	Kino-je-ne	2224
1565	Feb	1		Yih-chau	2		Kino-to-oos	2225
1566	Jan	21		Ping-yin	3	*	Fino-je-torra	2226
1567	Feb	10		Ting-mau	4		Fino-to-ov	2227
1568*	Jan	30		Wu-shin	5		Tsutsno-je-tats	2228
1569	Jan	18		Ki-se	6	*	Tsutsno-to-mi	2229
1570	Feb	6		Kang-wu	7		Kanno-je-ooma	2230

Western Date of New Year (Julian)			Cycle No.	Chinese Year Name & Cycle		Intercalculary Month	Japanese Name of Year Cycle and Year Number	
1571	Jan	26		Sin-wi	8		Kanno-to-tsitsuse	2231
1572*	Jan	16		Jin-shin	9	*	Midsno-je-sar	2232
1573	Feb	3		Kwei-yu	10		Midsno-to-torri	2233
1574	Jan	23		Kiah-siuh	11	*	Kino-je-in	2234
1575	Feb	11		Yih-hai	12		Kino-to-y	2235
1576*	Jan	31		Ping-tse	13		Fino-je-ne	2236
1577	Jan	19		Ting-chau	14	*	Fino-to-oos	2237
1578	Feb	8		Wu-yin	15		Tsutsno-je-torra	2238
1579	Jan	28		Ki-mau	16		Tsutsno-to-ov	2239
1580*	Jan	18		Kang-shin	17	*	Kanno-je-tats	2240
1581	Feb	4		Sin-se	18		Kanno-to-mi	2241
1582	Jan	25		Jin-wu	19		Midsno-je-ooma	2242

	Western Date of New Year (Gregorian)		(Julian)		Cycle No.	Chinese Year Name & Cycle		Intercalculary Month	Japanese Name of Year Cycle and Year Number	
1583	Jan	26	Jan	14		Kwei-wi	20	*	Midsno-to-tsitsuse	2243
1485*	Feb	12	Feb	2		Kiah-shin	21		Kino-je-sar	2244
1585	Feb	1	Jan	22		Yih-yu	22		Kino-to-torri	2245
1586	Feb	19	Feb	9		Ping-siuh	23	*	Fino-je-in	2246
1587	Feb	8	Jan	29		Ting-hai	24		Fino-to-y	2247
1588*	Jan	29	Jan	19		Wu-tse	25	*	Tsutsno-je-ne	2248
1589	Feb	16	Feb	6		Ki-chau	26		Tsutsno-to-oos	2249
1590	Feb	6	Jan	27		Kang-yin	27		Kanno-je-torra	2250
1591	Jan	26	Jan	16		Sin-mau	28	*	Kanno-to-ov	2251
1592*	Feb	13	Feb	3		Jin-shin	29		Midsno-je-tats	2252
1593	Feb	2	Jan	23		Kwei-se	30		Midsno-to-mi	2253
1594	Feb	21	Feb	11		Kiah-wu	31	*	Kino-je-ooma	2254
1595	Feb	10	Jan	31		Yih-wi	32		Kino-to-tsitsuse	2255
1596*	Jan	31	Jan	21		Ping-shin	33	*	Fino-je-sar	2256
1597	Feb	17	Feb	7		Ting-yu	34		Fino-to-torri	2257
1598	Feb	6	Jan	27		Wu-siuh	35		Tsutsno-je-in	2258
1599	Jan	27	Jan	17		Ki-hai	36	*	Tsutsno-to-y	2259
1600*	Feb	15	Feb	5		Kang-tse	37		Kanno-je-ne	2260
1601	Feb	4	Jan	25		Sin-chau	38		Kanno-to-oos	2261
1602	Jan	24	Jan	14		Jin-yin	39	*	Midsno-je-torra	2262
1603	Feb	11	Feb	1		Kwei-mau	40		Midsno-to-ov	2263
1604*	Feb	1	Jan	22		Kiah-hsin	41		Kino-je-tats	2264
1605	Feb	19	Feb	9		Yih-se	42	*	Kino-to-mi	2265
1606	Feb	8	Jan	29		Ping-wu	43		Fino-je-ooma	2266
1607	Jan	29	Jan	19		Ting-wi	44	*	Fino-to-tsitsuse	2267
1608*	Feb	16	Feb	6		Wu-shin	45		Tsutsno-je-sar	2268

	Western Date of New Year (Gregorian)		(Julian)		Cycle No.	Chinese Year Name & Cycle		Intercalculary Month	Japanese Name of Year Cycle and Year Number	
1609	Feb	5	Jan	26		Ki-yu	46		Tsutsno-to-torri	2269
1610	Jan	25	Jan	15		Kang-siuh	47	*	Kanno-je-in	2270
1611	Feb	13	Feb	3		Sin-hai	48		Kanno-to-y	2271
1612*	Feb	3	Jan	24		Jin-tse	49		Midsno-je-ne	2272
1613	Feb	20	Feb	10		Kwei-chau	50	*	Midsno-to-oos	2273
1614	Feb	10	Jan	31		Kiah-yin	51		Kino-je-torra	2274
1615	Jan	30	Jan	20		Yih-mau	52	*	Kino-to-ov	2275
1616*	Feb	18	Feb	8		Ping-shin	53		Fino-je-tats	2276
1617	Feb	7	Jan	28		Ting-wu	54		Fino-to-mi	2277
1618	Jan	27	Jan	17		Wu-wu	55	*	Tsutsno-je-ooma	2278
1619	Feb	15	Feb	5		Ki-wi	56		Tsutsno-to-tsitsuse	2279
1620*	Feb	4	Jan	25		Kang-shin	57		Kanno-je-sar	2280
1621	Feb	22	Feb	12		Sin-yu	58	*	Kanno-to-torri	2281
1622	Feb	12	Feb	2		Jin-siuh	59		Midsno-je-in	2282
1623	Feb	1	Jan	22		Kwei-hai	60		Midsno-to-y	2283
1624*	Feb	19	Feb	9	72	Kiah-tse	1	*	Kino-je-ne	2284
1625	Feb	8	Jan	29		Yih-chau	2		Kino-to-oos	2285
1626	Jan	28	Jan	18		Ping-yin	3	*	Fino-je-torra	2286
1627	Feb	16	Feb	6		Ting-mau	4		Fino-to-ov	2287
1628*	Feb	6	Jan	27		Wu-shin	5		Tsutsno-je-tats	2288
1629	Jan	25	Jan	15		Ki-se	6	*	Tsutsno-to-mi	2289
1630	Feb	13	Feb	3		Kang-wu	7		Kanno-je-ooma	2290
1631	Feb	2	Jan	23		Sin-wu	8		Kanno-to-tsitsuse	2291
1632*	Feb	21	Feb	11		Jin-shin	9	*	Midsno-je-sar	2292
1633	Feb	10	Jan	31		Kwei-yu	10		Midsno-to-torri	2293
1634	Jan	30	Jan	20		Kiah-siuh	11	*	Kino-je-in	2294
1635	Feb	17	Feb	7		Yih-hai	12		Kino-to-y	2295
1636*	Feb	7	Jan	28		Ping-tse	13		Fino-je-ne	2296
1637	Jan	26	Jan	16		Ting-chau	14	*	Fino-to-oos	2297
1638	Feb	15	Feb	5		Wu-yin	15		Tsutsno-je-torra	2298
1639	Feb	4	Jan	25		Ki-mau	16		Tsutsno-to-ov	2299
1640*	Jan	24	Jan	14		Kang-shin	17	*	Kanno-je-tats	2300
1641	Feb	11	Feb	1		Sin-se	18		Kanno-to-mi	2301
1642	Jan	31	Jan	21		Jin-wu	19		Midsno-je-ooma	2302
1643	Feb	19	Feb	9		Kwei-wi	20	*	Midsno-to-tsitsuse	2303
1644*	Feb	9	Jan	30		Kiah-shin	21		Kino-je-sar	2304
1645	Jan	28	Jan	18		Yih-yu	22	*	Kino-to-torri	2305
1646	Feb	16	Feb	6		Ping-siuh	23		Fino-je-in	2306
1647	Feb	5	Jan	26		Ting-hai	24		Fino-to-y	2307
1648*	Jan	26	Jan	16		Wu-tse	25	*	Tsutsno-je-ne	2308
1649	Feb	13	Feb	3		Ki-chau	26		Tsutsno-to-oos	2309
1650	Feb	2	Jan	23		Kang-yin	27		Kanno-je-torra	2310
1651	Feb	21	Feb	11		Sin-mau	28	*	Kanno-to-ov	2311
1652*	Feb	10	Jan	31		Jin-shin	29		Midsno-je-tats	2312

Western Date of New Year (Gregorian)			(Julian)		Cycle No.	Chinese Year Name & Cycle		Intercalculary Month	Japanese Name of Year Cycle and Year Number	
1653	Jan	29	Jan	19		Kwei-se	30	*	Midsno-to-mi	2313
1654	Feb	18	Feb	8		Kiah-wu	31		Kino-je-ooma	2314
1655	Feb	7	Jan	28		Yih-wi	32		Kino-to-tsitsuse	2315
1656*	Jan	27	Jan	17		Ping-shin	33	*	Fino-je-sar	2316
1657	Feb	14	Feb	4		Ting-yu	34		Fino-to-torri	2317
1658	Feb	3	Jan	24		Wu-siuh	35		Tsutsno-je-in	2318
1659	Jan	24	Jan	14		Ki-hai	36	*	Tsutsno-to-y	2319
1660*	Feb	12	Feb	2		Kang-tse	37		Kanno-je-ne	2320
1661	Jan	31	Jan	21		Sin-chau	38		Kanno-to-oos	2321
1662	Feb	19	Feb	9		Jin-yin	39	*	Midsno-je-torra	2322
1663	Feb	8	Jan	29		Kwei-mau	40		Midsno-to-ov	2323
1664*	Jan	28	Jan	18		Kiah-shin	41	*	Kino-je-tats	2324
1665	Feb	16	Feb	6		Yih-se	42		Kino-to-mi	2325
1666	Feb	5	Jan	26		Ping-wu	43		Fino-je-ooma	2326
1667	Jan	26	Jan	16		Ting-wi	44	*	Fino-to-tsitsuse	2327
1668*	Feb	13	Feb	3		Wu-shin	45		Tsutsno-je-sar	2328
1669	Feb	1	Jan	22		Ki-yu	46	*	Tsutsno-to-torri	2329
1670	Feb	21	Feb	11		Kang-siuh	47		Kanno-je-in	2330
1671	Feb	10	Jan	31		Sin-hai	48		Kanno-to-y	2331
1672*	Jan	30	Jan	20		Jin-tse	49	*	Midsno-je-ne	2332
1673	Feb	17	Feb	7		Kwei-chau	50		Midsno-to-oos	2333
1674	Feb	6	Jan	27		Kiah-yin	51		Kino-je-torra	2334
1675	Jan	26	Jan	16		Yih-mau	52	*	Kino-to-ov	2335
1676*	Feb	15	Feb	5		Ping-shin	53		Fino-je-tats	2336
1677	Feb	3	Jan	24		Ting-wu	54		Fino-to-mi	2337
1678	Jan	24	Jan	14		Wu-wu	55	*	Tsutsno-je-ooma	2338
1679	Feb	11	Feb	1		Ki-wi	56		Tsustsno-to-tsitsuse	2339
1680*	Feb	1	Jan	22		Kang-shin	57		Kanno-je-sar	2340
1681	Feb	19	Feb	9		Sin-yu	58	*	Kanno-to-torri	2341
1682	Feb	8	Jan	29		Jin-siuh	59		Midsno-je-in	2342
1683	Jan	29	Jan	19		Kwei-hai	60	*	Midsno-to-y	2343
1684*	Feb	16	Feb	6	73	Kiah-tse	1		Kino-je-ne	2344
1685	Feb	4	Jan	25		Yih-chau	2		Kino-to-oos	2345
1686	Jan	25	Jan	15		Ping-yin	3	*	Fino-je-torra	2346
1687	Feb	13	Feb	3		Ting-mau	4		Fino-to-ov	2347
1688*	Feb	3	Jan	24		Wu-shin	5		Tsutsno-je-tats	2348
1689	Feb	20	Feb	10		Ki-se	6	*	Tsutsno-to-mi	2349
1690	Feb	9	Jan	30		Kang-wu	7		Kanno-je-ooma	2350
1691	Jan	30	Jan	20		Sin-wi	8	*	Kanno-to-tsitsuse	2351
1692*	Feb	18	Feb	8		Jin-shin	9		Midsno-je-sar	2352
1693	Feb	6	Jan	27		Kwei-yu	10		Midsno-to-torri	2353
1694	Jan	27	Jan	17		Kiah-siuh	11	*	Kino-je-in	2354
1695	Feb	14	Feb	4		Yih-hai	12		Kino-to-y	2355
1696*	Feb	4	Jan	25		Ping-tse	13		Fino-je-ne	2356

Western Date of New Year (Gregorian)		(Julian)	Cycle No.	Chinese Year Name & Cycle		Intercalculary Month	Japanese Name of Year Cycle and Year Number	
1697	Feb 22	Feb 12		Ting-chau	14	*	Fino-to-oos	2357
1698	Feb 11	Feb 1		Wu-yin	15		Tsutsno-je-torra	2358
1699	Feb 1	Jan 22		Ki-mau	16		Tsutsno-to-ov	2359
1700	Feb 20	Feb 9		Kang-shin	17	*	Kanno-je-tats	2360
1701	Feb 8	Jan 28		Sin-se	18		Kanno-to-mi	2361
1702	Jan 29	Jan 18		Jin-wu	19	*	Midsno-je-ooma	2362
1703	Feb 17	Feb 6		Kwei-wi	20		Midsno-to-tsitsuse	2363
1704*	Feb 6	Jan 26		Kiah-shin	21		Kino-je-sar	2364
1705	Jan 26	Jan 15		Yih-yu	22	*	Kino-to-torri	2365
1706	Feb 13	Feb 2		Ping-siuh	23		Fino-je-in	2366
1707	Feb 3	Jan 23		Ting-hai	24		Fino-to-y	2367
1708*	Feb 22	Feb 11		Wu-tse	25	*	Tsutsno-je-ne	2368
1709	Feb 10	Jan 30		Ki-chau	26		Tsutsno-to-oos	2369
1710	Jan 31	Jan 20		Kang-yin	27	*	Kanno-je-torra	2370
1711	Feb 18	Feb 7		Sin-mau	28		Kanno-to-ov	2371
1712*	Feb 8	Jan 28		Jin-shin	29		Midsno-je-tats	2372
1713	Jan 27	Jan 16		Kwei-se	30	*	Midsno-to-mi	2373
1714	Feb 15	Feb 4		Kiah-wu	31		Kino-je-ooma	2374
1715	Feb 5	Jan 25		Yih-wi	32		Kino-to-tsitsuse	2375
1716*	Jan 25	Jan 14		Ping-shin	33	*	Fino-je-sar	2376
1717	Feb 12	Feb 1		Ting-yu	34		Fino-to-torri	2377
1718	Feb 1	Jan 21		Wu-siuh	35		Tsutsno-je-in	2378
1719	Feb 20	Feb 9		Ki-ahi	36	*	Tsutsno-to-y	2379
1720*	Feb 10	Jan 30		Kang-tse	37		Kanno-je-ne	2380
1721	Jan 29	Jan 18		Sin-chau	38	*	Kanno-to-oos	2381
1722	Feb 16	Feb 5		Jin-yin	39		Midsno-je-torra	2382
1723	Feb 6	Jan 26		Kwei-mau	40		Midsno-to-ov	2383
1724*	Jan 26	Jan 15		Kiah-shin	41	*	Kino-je-tats	2384
1725	Feb 14	Feb 3		Yih-se	42		Kino-to-mi	2385
1726	Feb 3	Jan 23		Ping-wu	43		Fino-je-ooma	2386
1727	Jan 23	Jan 12		Ting-wi	44	*	Fino-to-tsitsuse	2387
1728*	Feb 11	Jan 31		Wu-shin	45		Tsutsno-je-sar	2388
1729	Jan 30	Jan 19		Ki-yu	46	*	Tsutsno-to-torri	2389
1730	Feb 18	Feb 7		Kang-siuh	47		Kanno-je-in	2390
1731	Feb 7	Jan 27		Sin-hai	48		Kanno-to-y	2391
1732*	Jan 28	Jan 17		Jin-tse	49	*	Midsno-je-ne	2392
1734	Feb 14	Feb 3		Kwei-chau	50		Midsno-to-oos	2393
1735	Feb 4	Jan 24		Kiah-yin	51		Kino-je-tora	2394
1735	Jan 24	Jan 13		Yih-mau	52	*	Kino-to-ov	2395
1736*	Feb 13	Feb 2		Ping-shin	53		Fino-je-tats	2396
1737	Feb 1	Jan 21		Ting-wu	54		Fino-to-mi	2397
1738	Feb 19	Feb 8		Wu-wu	55	*	Tsutsno-je-ooma	2398
1739	Feb 9	Jan 29		Ki-wi	56		Tsutsno-to-tsitsuse	2399
1740*	Jan 29	Jan 18		Kang-shin	57	*	Kanno-je-sar	2400

Western Date of New Year (Gregorian)			(Julian)		Cycle No.	Chinese Year Name & Cycle		Intercalculary Month	Japanese Name of Year Cycle and Year Number	
1741	Feb	16	Feb	5		Sin-yu	58		Kanno-to-torri	2401
1742	Feb	6	Jan	26		Jin-siuh	59		Midsno-je-in	2402
1743	Feb	24	Feb	13		Kwei-hai	60	*	Midsno-to-y	2403
1744*	Feb	14	Feb	3	74	Kiah-tse	1		Kino-je-ne	2404
1745	Feb	2	Jan	22		Yih-chau	2		Kino-to-oos	2405
1746	Jan	23	Jan	12		Ping-yin	3	*	Fino-je-torra	2406
1747	Feb	11	Jan	31		Ting-mau	4		Fino-to-ov	2407
1748*	Jan	31	Jan	20		Wu-shin	5	*	Tsutsno-je-tats	2408
1749	Feb	18	Feb	7		Ki-se	6		Tsutsno-to-mi	2409
1750	Feb	7	Jan	27		Kang-wu	7		Kanno-je-ooma	2410
1751	Jan	27	Jan	15		Sin-wi	8	*	Kanno-to-tsitsuse	2411
1752*	Feb	16	Feb	5		Jin-shin	9		Midsno-je-sar	2412

Western Date of New Year (Gregorian)			Cycle No.	Chinese Year Name & Cycle		Intercalculary Month	Japanese Name of Year Cycle and Year Number	
1753	Feb	4		Kwei-yu	10		Midsno-to-torri	2413
1754	Jan	24		Kiah-siuh	11	*	Kino-je-in	2414
1755	Feb	12		Yih-hai	12		Kino-to-y	2415
1756*	Feb	1		Ping-tse	13		Fino-je-ne	2416
1757	Jan	20		Ting-chau	14	*	Fino-to-oos	2417
1758	Feb	9		Wu-yin	15		Tsutsno-je-torra	2418
1759	Jan	29		Ki-mau	16	*	Tsutsno-to-ov	2419
1760*	Feb	17		Kang-shin	17		Kanno-je-tats	2420
1761	Feb	6		Sin-se	18		Kanno-to-mi	2421
1762	Jan	26		Jin-wu	19	*	Midsno-je-ooma	2422
1763	Feb	13		Kwei-wi	20		Midsno-to-tsitsuse	2423
1764*	Feb	2		Kiah-shin	21		Kino-je-sar	2424
1765	Jan	22		Yih-yu	22	*	Kino-to-torri	2425
1766	Feb	10		Ping-siuh	23		Fino-je-in	2426
1767	Jan	31		Ting-hai	24	*	Fino-to-y	2427
1768*	Feb	19		Wu-tse	25		Tsutsno-je-ne	2428
1769	Feb	7		Ki-chau	26		Tsutsno-to-oos	2429
1770	Jan	27		Kang yin	27	*	Kanno-je-torra	2430
1771	Feb	15		Sin-mau	28		Kanno-to-ov	2431
1772*	Feb	4		Jin-shin	29		Midsno-je-tats	2432
1773	Jan	23		Kwei-se	30	*	Midsno-to-mi	2433
1774	Feb	11		Kiah-wu	31		Kino-je-ooma	2434
1775	Jan	31		Yih-wi	32	*	Kino-to-tsitsuse	2435
1776*	Feb	20		Ping-shin	33		Fino-je-sar	2436
1777	Feb	9		Ting-yu	34		Fino-to-torri	2437
1778	Jan	29		Wu-siuh	35	*	Tsutsno-je-in	2438
1779	Feb	17		Ki-hai	36		Tsutsno-to-y	2439
1780*	Feb	6		Kang-tse	37		Kanno-je-ne	2440

Western Date of New Year (Gregorian)			Cycle No.	Chinese Year Name & Cycle		Intercalculary Month	Japanese Name of Year Cycle and Year Number	
1781	Jan	25		Sin-chau	38	*	Kanno-to-oos	2441
1782	Feb	13		Jin-yin	39		Midsno-je-torra	2442
1783	Feb	2		Kwei-mau	40		Midsno-to-ov	2443
1784*	Jan	23		Kiah-shin	41	*	Kino-je-tats	2444
1785	Feb	10		Yih-se	42		Kino-to-mi	2445
1786	Jan	31		Ping-wu	43	*	Fino-je-ooma	2446
1787	Feb	19		Ting-wi	44		Fino-to-tsitsuse	2447
1788*	Feb	8		Wu-shin	45		Tsutsno-je-sar	2448
1789	Jan	27		Ki-yu	46	*	Tsutsno-to-torri	2449
1790	Feb	14		Kang-siuh	47		Kanno-je-in	2450
1791	Feb	4		Sin-hai	48		Kanno-to-y	2451
1792*	Jan	24		Jin-tse	49	*	Midsno-je-ne	2452
1793	Feb	11		Kwei-chau	50		Midsno-to-oos	2453
1794	Feb	1		Kiah-yin	51		Kino-je-torra	2454
1795	Jan	21		Yih-mau	52	*	Kino-to-ov	2455
1796*	Feb	9		Ping-shin	53		Fino-je-tats	2456
1797	Jan	28		Ting-wu	54	*	Fino-to-mi	2457
1798	Feb	16		Wu-wu	55		Tsutsno-je-ooma	2458
1799	Feb	5		Ki-wi	56		Tsutsno-to-tsitsuse	2459
1800	Jan	26		Kang-shin	57	*	Kanno-je-sar	2460
1801	Feb	14		Sin-yu	58		Kanno-to-torri	2461
1802	Feb	3		Jin-siuh	59		Midsno-je-in	2462
1803	Jan	24		Kwei-hai	60	*	Midsno-to-y	2463
1804*	Feb	12	75	Kiah-tse	1		Kino-je-ne	2464
1805	Jan	31		Yih-chau	2	*	Kino-to-oos	2465
1806	Feb	19		Ping-yin	3		Fino-je-torra	2466
1807	Feb	8		Ting-mau	4		Fino-to-ov	2467
1808*	Jan	28		Wu-shin	5	*	Tsutsno-je-tats	2468
1809	Feb	15		Ki-se	6		Tsutsno-to-mi	2469
1810	Feb	4		Kang-wu	7		Kanno-je-ooma	2470
1811	Jan	25		Sin-wi	8	*	Kanno-to-tsitsuse	2471
1812*	Feb	14		Jin-shin	9		Midsno-je-sar	2472
1813	Feb	2		Kwei-yu	10		Midsno-to-torri	2473
1814	Jan	22		Kiah-siuh	11	*	Kino-je-in	2474
1815	Feb	10		Yih-hai	12		Kino-to-y	2475
1816*	Jan	30		Ping-tse	13	*	Fino-je-ne	2476
1817	Feb	15		Ting-chau	14		Fino-to-oos	2477
1818	Feb	6		Wu-yin	15		Tsutsno-je-torra	2478
1819	Jan	27		Ki-mau	16	*	Tsutsno-to-ov	2479
1820*	Feb	14		Kang-shin	17		Kanno-je-tats	2480
1821	Feb	3		Sin-se	18		Kanno-to-mi	2481
1822	Jan	24		Jin-wu	19	*	Midsno-je-ooma	2482
1823	Feb	12		Kwei-wi	20		Midsno-to-tsitsuse	2483
1824*	Feb	1		Kiah-shin	21	*	Kino-je-sar	2484

Western Date of New Year (Gregorian)			Cycle No.	Chinese Year Name & Cycle		Intercalculary Month	Japanese Name of Year Cycle and Year Number	
1825	Feb	18		Yih-yu	22		Kino-to-torri	2485
1826	Feb	7		Ping-siuh	23		Fino-je-in	2486
1827	Jan	28		Ting-hai	24	*	Fino-to-y	2487
1828*	Feb	16		Wu-tse	25		Tsutsno-je-ne	2488
1829	Feb	5		Ki-chau	26		Tsutsno-to-oos	2489
1830	Jan	25		Kang-yin	27	*	Kanno-je-torra	2490
1831	Feb	13		Sin-mau	28		Kanno-to-ov	2491
1832*	Feb	2		Jin-shin	29		Midsno-je-tats	2492
1833	Jan	20		Kwei-se	30	*	Midsno-to-mi	2493
1834	Feb	9		Kiah-wu	31		Kino-je-ooma	2494
1835	Jan	29		Yih-wi	32	*	Kino-to-tsitsuse	2495
1836*	Feb	17		Ping-shin	33		Fino-je-sar	2496
1837	Feb	6		Ting-yu	34		Fino-to-torri	2497
1838	Jan	27		Wu-siuh	35	*	Tsutsno-je-in	2498
1839	Feb	15		Ki-ahi	36		Tsutsno-to-y	2499
1840*	Feb	4		Kang-tse	37		Kanno-je-ne	2500
1841	Feb	24		Sin-chau	38	*	Kanno-to-oos	2501
1842	Feb	11		Jin-yin	39		Midsno-je-torra	2502
1843	Jan	31		Kwei-mau	40	*	Midsno-to-ov	2503
1844*	Feb	19		Kiah-shin	41		Kino-je-tats	2504
1845	Feb	7		Yih-se	42		Kino-to-mi	2505
1846	Jan	28		Ping-wu	43	*	Fino-je-ooma	2506
1847	Feb	16		Ting-wi	44		Fino-to-tsitsuse	2507
1848*	Feb	6		Wu-shin	45		Tsutsno-je-sar	2508
1849	Jan	24		Ki-yu	46		Tsutsno-to-torri	2509
1850	Feb	13		Kang-siuh	47		Kanno-je-in	2510
1851	Feb	1		Sin-hai	48	*	Kanno-to-y	2511
1852*	Feb	20		Jin-tse	49		Midsno-je-ne	2512
1853	Feb	8		Kwei-chau	50		Midsno-to-oos	2513
1854	Jan	31		Kiah-yin	51	*	Kino-je-torra	2514
1855	Feb	17		Yih-mau	52		Kino-to-ov	2515
1856*	Feb	7		Ping-shin	53		Fino-je-tats	2516
1857	Jan	26		Ting-wu	54	*	Fino-to-mi	2517
1858	Feb	13		Wu-wu	55		Tsutsno-je-ooma	2518
1859	Feb	3		Ki-wi	56		Tsutsno-to-tsitsuse	2519
1860*	Jan	23		Kang-shin	57	*	Kanno-je-sar	2520
1861	Feb	10		Sin-yu	58		Kanno-to-torri	2521
1862	Jan	30		Jin-siuh	59	*	Midsno-je-in	2522
1863	Feb	18		Kwei-hai	60		Midsno-to-y	2523
1864*	Feb	7	76	Kiah-tse	1		Kino-je-ne	2524
1865	Jan	27		Yih-chau	2	*	Kino-to-oos	2525
1866	Feb	15		Ping-yin	3		Fino-je-torra	2526
1867	Feb	4		Ting-mau	4		Fino-to-ov	2527
1868*	Jan	24		Wu-shin	5		Tsutsno-je-tats	2528

Western Date of New Year (Gregorian)			Cycle No.	Chinese Year Name & Cycle		Intercalculary Month	Japanese Name of Year Cycle and Year Number	
1869	Feb	11		Ki-se	6		Tsutsno-to-mi	2529
1870	Feb	1		Kang-wu	7	*	Kanno-je-ooma	2530
1871	Feb	20		Sin-wi	8		Kanno-to-tsitsuse	2531
1872*	Feb	10		Jin-shin	9		Midsno-je-sar	2532
1873	Jan	28		Kwei-yu	10	*	Midsno-to-torri	2533
1874	Feb	16		Kiah-siuh	11		Kino-je-in	2534
1875	Feb	6		Yih-hai	12		Kino-to-y	2535
1876*	Jan	26		Ping-tse	13	*	Fino-je-ne	2536
1877	Feb	13		Ting-chau	14		Fino-to-oos	2537
1878	Feb	2		Wu-yin	15		Tsutsno-je-torra	2538
1879	Jan	23		Ki-mau	16	*	Tsutsno-to-ov	2539
1880*	Feb	11		Kang-shin	17		Kanno-je-tats	2540
1881	Jan	30		Sin-se	18	*	Kanno-to-mi	2541
1882	Feb	18		Jin-wu	19		Midsno-je-ooma	2542
1883	Feb	7		Kwei-wi	20		Midsno-to-tsitsuse	2543
1884*	Jan	28		Kiah-shin	21	*	Kino-je-sar	2544
1885	Feb	14		Yih-yu	22		Kino-to-torri	2545
1886	Feb	4		Ping-siuh	23		Fino-je-in	2546
1887	Jan	24		Ting-hai	24	*	Fino-to-y	2547
1888*	Feb	13		Wu-tse	25		Tsutsno-je-ne	2548
1889	Jan	31		Ki-chau	26	*	Tsutsno-to-oos	2549
1890	Jan	19		Kang-yin	27		Kanno-je-torra	2550
1891	Feb	9		Sin-mau	28		Kanno-to-ov	2551
1892*	Jan	29		Jin-shin	29	*	Midsno-je-tats	2552
1893	Feb	16		Kwei-se	30		Midsno-to-mi	2553
1894	Feb	5		Kiah-wu	31		Kino-je-ooma	2554
1895	Jan	26		Yih-wi	32	*	Kino-to-tsitsuse	2555
1896*	Feb	13		Ping-shin	33		Fino-je-sar	2556
1897	Feb	2		Ting-yu	34		Fino-to-torri	2557
1898	Jan	22		Wu-siuh	35	*	Tsutsno-je-in	2558
1899	Feb	10		Ki-ahi	36		Tsutsno-to-y	2559
1900	Feb	1		Kang-tse	37	*	Kanno-je-ne	2560
1901	Feb	18		Sin-chau	38		Kanno-to-oos	2561
1902	Feb	7		Jin-yin	39		Midsno-je-torra	2562
1903	Jan	28		Kwei-mau	40	*	Midsno-to-ov	2563
1904*	Feb	16		Kiah-shin	41		Kino-je-tats	2564
1905	Feb	4		Yih-se	42		Kino-to-mi	2565
1906	Jan	26		Ping-wu	43	*	Fino-je-ooma	2566
1907	Feb	13		Ting-wi	44		Fino-to-tsitsuse	2567
1908*	Feb	2		Wu-shin	45	*	Tsutsno-je-sar	2568
1909	Feb	20		Ki-yu	46		Tsutsno-to-torri	2569
1910	Feb	10		Kang-siuh	47		Kanno-je-in	2570
1911	Jan	30		Sin-hai	48	*	Kanno-to-y	2571
1912*	Feb	17		Jin-tse	49		Midsno-je-ne	2572

Western Date of New Year (Gregorian)			Cycle No.	Chinese Year Name & Cycle		Intercalculary Month	Japanese Name of Year Cycle and Year Number	
1913	Feb	6		Kwei-chau	50		Midsno-to-oos	2573
1914	Jan	27		Kiah-yin	51	*	Kino-je-torra	2574
1915	Feb	14		Yih-mau	52		Kino-to-ov	2575
1916*	Feb	4		Ping-shin	53		Fino-je-tats	2576
1917	Jan	24		Ting-wu	54	*	Fino-to-mi	2577
1918	Feb	11		Wu-wu	55		Tsutsno-je-ooma	2578
1919	Feb	1		Ki-wi	56	*	Tsutsno-to-tsitsuse	2579
1920*	Feb	19		Kang-shin	57		Kanno-je-sar	2580
1921	Feb	8		Sin-yu	58		Kanno-to-torri	2581
1922	Jan	28		Jin-siuh	59	*	Midsno-je-in	2582
1923	Feb	15		Kwei-hai	60		Midsno-to-y	2583
1924*	Feb	5	77	Kiah-tse	1		Kino-je-ne	2584
1925	Jan	25		Yih-chau	2	*	Kino-to-oos	2585
1926	Feb	13		Ping-yin	3		Fino-je-torra	2586
1927	Feb	2		Ting-mau	4		Fino-to-ov	2587
1928*	Jan	22		Wu-shin	5	*	Tsutsno-je-tats	2588
1929	Feb	9		Ki-se	6		Tsutsno-to-mi	2589
1930	Jan	30		Kang-wu	7	*	Kanno-je-ooma	2590
1931	Feb	17		Sin-wi	8	*	Kanno-to-tsitsuse	2591
1932*	Feb	7		Jin-shin	9		Midsno-je-sar	2592
1933	Jan	26		Kwei-yu	10	*	Midsno-to-torri	2593
1934	Feb	14		Kiah-siuh	11		Kino-je-in	2594
1935	Feb	3		Yih-hai	12		Kino-to-y	2595
1936*	Jan	24		Ping-tse	13	*	Fino-je-ne	2596
1937	Feb	11		Ting-chau	14		Fino-to-oos	2597
1938	Feb	1		Wu-yin	15	*	Tsutsno-je-torra	2598
1939	Feb	19		Ki-amu	16		Tsutsno-to-ov	2599
1940*	Feb	8		Kang-shin	17		Kanno-je-tats	2600
1941	Jan	28		Sin-se	18	*	Kanno-to-mi	2601
1942	Feb	16		Jin-wu	19		Midsno-je-ooma	2602
1943	Feb	5		Kwei-wi	20		Midsno-to-tsitsuse	2603
1944*	Jan	25		Kiah-shin	21	*	Kino-je-sar	2604
1945	Feb	12		Yih-yu	22		Kino-to-torri	2605
1946	Feb	2		Ping-siuh	23		Fino-je-in	2606
1947	Jan	22		Ting-hai	24	*	Fino-to-y	2607
1948*	Feb	10		Wu-tse	25		Tsutsno-je-ne	2608
1949	Jan	30		Ki-chau	26	*	Tsutsno-to-oos	2609
1950	Feb	17		Kang-yin	27		Kanno-je-torra	2610
1951	Feb	6		Sin-mau	28		Kanno-to-ov	2611
1952*	Jan	27		Jin-shin	29	*	Midsno-je-tats	2612
1953	Feb	14		Kwei-se	30		Midsno-to-mi	2613
1954	Feb	1		Kiah-wu	31		Kino-je-ooma	2614
1955	Jan	24		Yih-wi	32	*	Kino-to-tsitsuse	2615
1956*	Feb	11		Ping-shin	33		Fino-je-sar	2616

Western Date of New Year (Gregorian)			Cycle No.	Chinese Year Name & Cycle		Intercalculary Month	Japanese Name of Year Cycle and Year Number	
1957	Jan	31		Ting-yu	34	*	Fino-to-torri	2617
1958	Feb	19		Wu-siuh	35		Tsutsno-je-in	2618
1959	Feb	8		Ki-hai	36		Tsutsno-to-y	2619
1960*	Jan	28		Kang-tse	37	*	Kanno-je-ne	2620
1961	Feb	16		Sin-chau	38		Kanno-to-oos	2621
1962	Feb	4		Jin-yin	39		Midsno-je-torra	2622
1963	Jan	25		Kwei-mau	40	*	Midsno-to-ov	2623
1964*	Feb	13		Kiah-shin	41		Kino-je-tats	2624
1965	Feb	2		Yih-se	42		Kino-to-mi	2625
1966	Jan	22		Ping-wu	43	*	Fino-je-ooma	2626
1967	Feb	9		Ting-wi	44		Fino-to-tsitsuse	2627
1968*	Jan	30		Wu-shin	45	*	Tsutsno-je-sar	2628
1969	Feb	17		Ki-yu	46		Tsutsno-to-torri	2629
1970	Feb	6		Kang-siuh	47		Kanno-je-in	2630
1971	Jan	27		Sin-hai	48	*	Kanno-to-y	2631
1972*	Feb	14		Jin-tse	49		Midsno-je-ne	2632
1973	Feb	4		Kwei-chau	50		Midsno-to-oos	2633
1974	Jan	24		Kiah-yin	51	*	Kino-je-torra	2634
1975	Feb	11		Yih-mau	52		Kino-to-ov	2635
1976*	Jan	31		Ping-shin	53	*	Fino-je-tats	2636
1977	Feb	18		Ting-wu	54		Fino-to-mi	2637
1978	Feb	7		Wu-wu	55		Tsutsno-je-ooma	2638
1979	Jan	28		Ki-wi	56	*	Tsutsno-to-tsitsuse	2639
1980*	Feb	16		Kang-shin	57		Kanno-je-sar	2640
1981	Feb	4		Sin-yu	58		Kanno-to-torri	2641
1982	Jan	25		Jin-siuh	59	*	Midsno-je-in	2642
1983	Feb	12		Kwei-hai	60		Midsno-to-y	2643
1984*	Feb	2	78	Kiah-tse	1		Kino-je-ne	2644
1985	Jan	22		Yih-chau	2	*	Kino-to-oos	2645
1986	Feb	9		Ping-yin	3		Fino-je-torra	2646
1987	Jan	30		Ting-amu	4	*	Fino-to-ov	2647
1988*	Feb	17		Wu-shin	5		Tsutsno-je-tats	2648
1989	Feb	6		Ki-se	6		Tsutsno-to-mi	2649
1990	Jan	27		Kang-wu	7	*	Kanno-je-ooma	2650
1991	Feb	14		Sin-wi	8		Kanno-to-tsitsuse	2651
1992*	Feb	4		Jin-shin	9		Midsno-je-sar	2652
1993	Jan	24		Kwei-yu	10	*	Midsno-to-torri	2653
1994	Feb	11		Kiah-siuh	11		Kino-je-in	2654
1995	Jan	31		Yih-ahi	12	*	Kino-to-y	2655
1996*	Feb	19		Ping-tse	13		Fino-je-ne	2656
1997	Feb	7		Ting-chau	14		Fino-to-oos	2657
1998	Jan	28		Wu-yin	15	*	Tsutsno-je-torra	2658
1999	Feb	15		Ki-mau	16		Tsutsno-to-ov	2659
1200*	Feb	4		Kang-shin	17		Kanno-je-tats	2660

TIBET

In the former Buddhist stronghold of Tibet, a somewhat different form of the Buddhist calendar is used. The Tibetan form is also used by Buddhists in central China and to some degree by the people of Bhutan and Nepal. In the latter two areas, the old Buddhist calendar is also used.

The Buddhists moved into Tibet some time during the 8th century A.D. The Himalayas limited communication with India, and the Tibetans came into increasing contact with the Chinese. As a result, the Tibetans adopted the tropical solar year in the same manner as it is used by the Chinese and like the Chinese, established a lunar calendar, using the tropical solar motion for intercalations. The Tibetan New Year, however, unlike the Chinese, falls on the full moon, rather than the new moon, nearest to the 15° of Aquarius.

The Tibetans calculate a 60-year cycle on the same basis as the Chinese cycle, and, in addition, use a second 60 year cycle called the Grahaparivritti, which was brought from India. These cycles are distinct from each other: there is a two year difference in their application.

CENTRAL AMERICA

CENTRAL AMERICA

The many ancient civilizations of Central America—the Mayan, Aztec, Inca, etc.—employed calendars which were closely related to each other, differing chiefly in the exact dating of the New Year and in the epoch.

Evidently the original system of time measurement used a 60-year cycle and a year of 12 30-day months plus 5 extra days, but at some point this system was abandoned and a very different, very complex calendar was constructed.

What we refer to as the Mayan calendar uses a 365-day year with 18 months to a year, 20 days to each month, and one short month of 5 days. This short month was called Uayeb; its five days were considered extremely unlucky. They were used in what is known as the "long count" of the calendar, but were eliminated from the "short county", and not considered part of the year calculation. Thus the long count was based on a year of 365 days, ignoring the extra fraction of a day of the true year. There is some evidence that the Maya were aware of this and periodically adjusted, not their calendar, but their festivals, to correspond to the correct seasons. The short count was the one used for longer periods of time and was based on a year of 360 days, ignoring the 5-day month. The names of the known periods of the short count are as follows:

		1 Kin	=	1 Day
20 Kin	=	1 Uinal	=	20 Days
18 Uinal	=	1 Tun	=	360 Days
20 Tun	=	1 Katun	=	7,200 Days
20 Katun	=	1 Baktun	=	144,000 Days
20 Baktun	=	1 Pictun	=	2,880,000 Days
20 Pictun	=	1 Cabaltun	=	57,600,000 Days
20 Cabaltun	=	1 Kinchiltun	=	1,152,000,000 Days
20 Kinchiltun	=	1 Alautun	=	23,040,000,000 Days
20 Alautun	=	1 Hablatun	=	460,800,000,000 Days

These are the glyphs which represent the time periods of the short count:

Kin

Uinal

Tun

Katun

Baktun

Pictun

Calabtun

Kinchiltun

Alatun

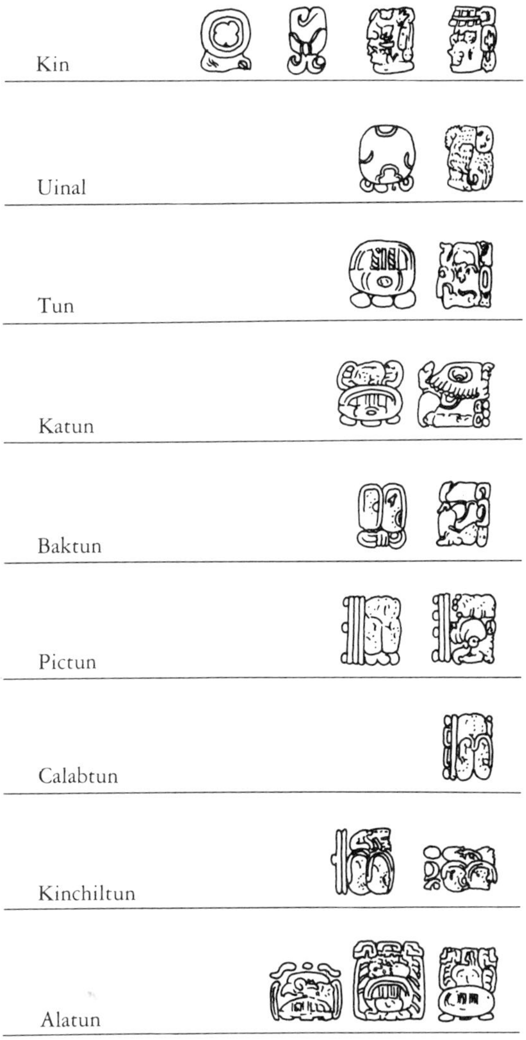

The nine known time periods

The Maya used special glyphs for each month, including the short month Uayeb.

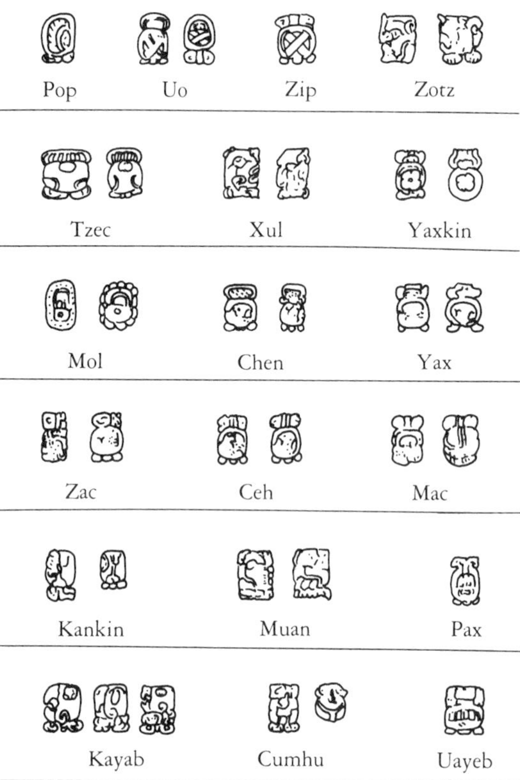

The Mayan Month Glyphs

The following are the glyphs for the 20 days of the Mayan month:

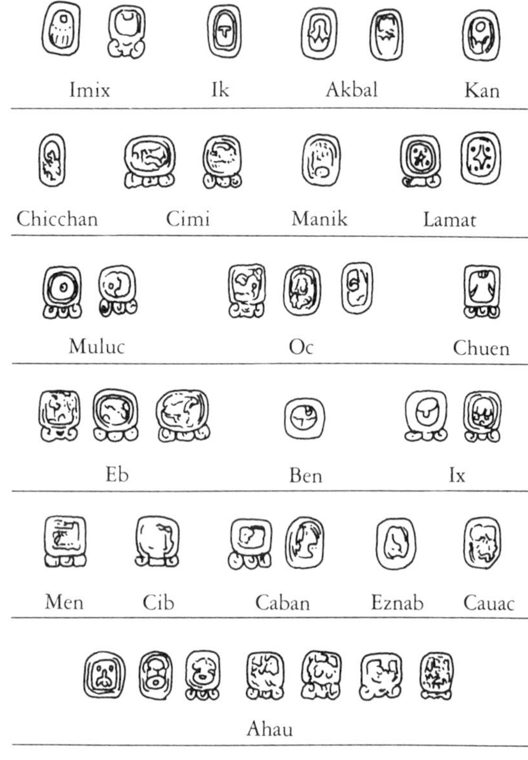

Mayan Day Glyphs

The Maya used an inner cycle of 260 days, called the "Tzolkin". To produce this cycle, the 20 day-names were used in combination with 13 day-numbers. The following table shows how this was done:

THE TZOLKIN

Day Names and Sequence of Months	Numbers												
	1	2	3	4	5	6	7	8	9	10	11	12	13
1 Imix	1	8	2	9	3	10	4	11	5	12	6	13	7
2 Ik	2	9	3	10	4	11	5	12	6	13	7	1	8
3 Akbal	3	10	4	11	5	12	6	13	7	1	8	2	9
4 Kan	4	11	5	12	6	13	7	1	8	2	9	3	10
5 Chicchan	5	12	6	13	7	1	8	2	9	3	10	4	11
6 Cimi	6	13	7	1	8	2	9	3	10	4	11	5	12
7 Manik	7	1	8	2	9	3	10	4	11	5	12	6	13

Day Names and Sequence of Months	Numbers												
	1	2	3	4	5	6	7	8	9	10	11	12	13
8 Lamat	8	2	9	3	10	4	11	5	12	6	13	7	1
9 Muluc	9	3	10	4	11	5	12	6	13	7	1	8	2
10 Oc	10	4	11	5	12	6	13	7	1	8	2	9	3
11 Chuen	11	5	12	6	13	7	1	8	2	9	3	10	4
12 Eb	12	6	13	7	1	8	2	9	3	10	4	11	5
13 Ben	13	7	1	8	2	9	3	10	4	11	5	12	6
14 Ix	1	8	2	9	3	10	4	11	5	12	6	13	7
15 Men	2	9	3	10	4	11	5	12	6	13	7	1	8
16 Cib	3	10	4	11	5	12	6	13	7	1	8	2	9
17 Caban	4	11	5	12	6	13	7	1	8	2	9	3	10
18 Eznab	5	12	6	13	7	1	8	2	9	3	10	4	11
19 Cauac	6	13	7	1	8	2	9	3	10	4	11	5	12
20 Ahau	7	1	8	2	9	3	10	4	11	5	12	6	13

There is no agreement regarding the epoch, or beginning, of this calendar. Two noted archaeologists of the 1920's, Sylvanus G. Morley and Herbert J. Spinden, both studied this matter extensively and found themselves in disagreement over the epoch, and hence over the Gregorian conversion of the calendar. This disagreement remains some 60 years later. They did agree that the epoch and the date when the calendar first became effective are two different things, and that some drastic alterations in the counting system occurred between the 6th and 4th centuries B.C., and some minor ones later on, at about the time when our own calendar came into existence. They also agreed that the eclipse cycle was known and used, and that it may have been the reason for the drastic changes during the B.C. period. The day-by-day count of the Maya resulted in their ability not only to calculate solar and lunar cycles more accurately even than we do today, but it also enabled them to include the planetary cycles of the solar system in their calendar.

In the accompanying tables we give Spinden's count in even baktuns, and a count in tuns, kins, uinals and again tuns, calculated by Pavon Abreu, who followed through on Morley's investigations. As these latter tables are extensive, we have used samples to show the manner of the count between 3113 B.C. and 339 A.D., and the complete tun count from 435 A.D. on.

PAVON ABREU'S COUNT IN UINALS

Gregorian Date								
322	6 Aug	8.	14.	5.	0.	0	13 Ahau	18 Zotz
322	26 Aug	8.	14.	5.	1.	0	7 Ahau	18 Tzec
322	15 Sep	8.	14.	5.	2.	0	1 Ahau	18 Xul
322	5 Oct	8.	14.	5.	3.	0	8 Ahau	18 Yaxkin
322	25 Oct	8.	14.	5.	4.	0	2 Ahau	18 Mol
322	14 Nov	8.	14.	5.	5.	0	9 Ahau	18 Chen
322	4 Dec	8.	14.	5.	6.	0	3 Ahau	18 Yax
322	24 Dec	8.	14.	5.	7.	0	10 Ahau	18 Zac
323	13 Jan	8.	14.	5.	8.	0	4 Ahau	18 Ceh
323	2 Feb	8.	14.	5.	9.	0	11 Ahau	18 Mac
323	22 Mar	8.	14.	5.	10.	0	5 Ahau	18 Kankin

Gregorian Date								
323	14 Mar	8.	14.	5.	11.	0	12 Ahau	18 Muan
323	3 Apr	8.	14.	5.	12.	0	6 Ahau	18 Pax
323	23 Apr	8.	14.	5.	13.	0	13 Ahau	18 Kayab
323	13 May	8.	14.	5.	14.	0	7 Ahau	18 Cumhú
323	2 Jun	8.	14.	5.	15.	0	1 Ahau	13 Pop
323	22 Jun	8.	14.	5.	16.	0	8 Ahau	13 Uo
323	12 Jul	8.	14.	5.	17.	0	2 Ahau	13 Zip
323	1 Aug	8.	14.	6.	0.	0	9 Ahau	13 Zotz
323	21 Aug	8.	14.	6.	1.	0	3 Ahau	13 Tzec
323	10 Sep	8.	14.	6.	2.	0	10 Ahau	13 Xul
323	30 Sep	8.	14.	6.	3.	0	4 Ahau	13 Yaxkin
323	20 Oct	8.	14.	6.	4.	0	11 Ahau	13 Mol
323	9 Nov	8.	14.	6.	5.	0	5 Ahau	13 Chen
323	29 Nov	8.	14.	6.	6.	0	12 Ahau	13 Yax
323	19 Dec	8.	14.	6.	7.	0	6 Ahau	13 Zac
324	8 Jan	8.	14.	6.	8.	0	13 Ahau	13 Ceh
324	28 Jan	8.	14.	6.	9.	0	7 Ahau	13 Mac
324	17 Feb	8.	14.	6.	10.	0	1 Ahau	13 Kankin
324	8 Mar	8.	14.	6.	11.	0	8 Ahau	13 Muan
324	28 Mar	8.	14.	6.	12.	0	2 Ahau	13 Pax
324	17 Apr	8.	14.	6.	13.	0	9 Ahau	13 Kayab
324	7 May	8.	14.	6.	14.	0	3 Ahau	13 Cumhú
324	27 May	8.	14.	6.	15.	0	10 Ah[illegible]	8 Pop
324	16 Jun	8.	14.	6.	16.	0	4 A[illegible]	8 Uo
324	6 Jul	8.	14.	6.	17.	0	11 Ahau	8 Zip
324	26 Jul	8.	14.	7.	0.	0	5 Ahau	8 Zotz
324	15 Aug	8.	14.	7.	1.	0	12 Ahau	8 Tzec
324	4 Sep	8.	14.	7.	2.	0	6 Ahau	8 Xul
324	24 Sep	8.	14.	7.	3.	0	13 Ahau	8 Yaxkin
324	14 Oct	8.	14.	7.	4.	0	7 Ahau	8 Mol
324	3 Nov	8.	14.	7.	5.	0	1 Ahau	8 Chen
324	23 Nov	8.	14.	7.	6.	0	8 Ahau	8 Yax
324	13 Dec	8.	14.	7.	7.	0	2 Ahau	8 Zac
325	2 Jan	8.	14.	7.	8.	0	9 Ahau	8 Ceh
325	22 Jan	8.	14.	7.	9.	0	3 Ahau	8 Mac
325	11 Feb	8.	14.	7.	10.	0	10 Ahau	8 Kankin
325	3 Mar	8.	14.	7.	11.	0	4 Ahau	8 Muan
325	23 Mar	8.	14.	7.	12.	0	11 Ahau	8 Pax
325	12 Apr	8.	14.	7.	13.	0	5 Ahau	8 Kayab
325	2 May	8.	14.	7.	14.	0	12 Ahau	8 Cumhú
325	22 May	8.	14.	7.	15.	0	6 Ahau	3 Pop
325	11 Jun	8.	14.	7.	16.	0	13 Ahau	3 Uo
325	1 Jul	8.	14.	7.	17.	0	7 Ahau	3 Zip
325	21 Jul	8.	14.	8.	0.	0	1 Ahau	3 Zotz
325	10 Aug	8.	14.	8.	1.	0	8 Ahau	3 Tzec
325	30 Aug	8.	14.	8.	2.	0	2 Ahau	3 Xul
325	19 Sep	8.	14.	8.	3.	0	9 Ahau	3 Yaxkin
325	9 Oct	8.	14.	8.	4.	0	3 Ahau	3 Mol
325	29 Oct	8.	14.	8.	5.	0	10 Ahau	3 Chen
325	18 Nov	8.	14.	8.	6.	0	4 Ahau	3 Yax

Gregorian Date								
325	8 Dec	8.	14.	8.	7.	0	11 Ahau	3 Zac
325	28 Dec	8.	14.	8.	8.	0	5 Ahau	3 Ceh
326	17 Jan	8.	14.	8.	9.	0	12 Ahau	3 Mac
326	6 Feb	8.	14.	8.	10.	0	6 Ahau	3 Kankin
326	26 Feb	8.	14.	8.	11.	0	13 Ahau	3 Muan
326	18 Mar	8.	14.	8.	12.	0	7 Ahau	3 Pax
326	7 Apr	8.	14.	8.	13.	0	1 Ahau	3 Kayab
326	27 Apr	8.	14.	8.	14.	0	8 Ahau	3 Cumhú
326	17 May	8.	14.	8.	15.	0	2 Ahau	3 Uayeb
326	6 Jun	8.	14.	8.	16.	0	9 Ahau	18 Pop
326	26 Jun	8.	14.	8.	17.	0	3 Ahau	18 Uo
326	16 Jul	8.	14.	9.	0.	0	10 Ahau	18 Zip
326	5 Aug	8.	14.	9.	1.	0	4 Ahau	18 Zotz
326	25 Aug	8.	14.	9.	2.	0	11 Ahau	18 Tzec
326	14 Sep	8.	14.	9.	3.	0	5 Ahau	18 Xul
326	4 Oct	8.	14.	9.	4.	0	12 Ahau	18 Yaxkin
326	24 Oct	8.	14.	9.	5.	0	6 Ahau	18 Mol
326	13 Nov	8.	14.	9.	6.	0	13 Ahau	18 Chen
326	3 Dec	8.	14.	9.	7.	0	7 Ahau	18 Yax
326	23 Dec	8.	14.	9.	8.	0	1 Ahau	18 Zac
327	12 Jan	8.	14.	9.	9.	0	8 Ahau	18 Ceh
327	1 Feb	8.	14.	9.	10.	0	2 Ahau	18 Mac
327	21 Feb	8.	14.	9.	11.	0	9 Ahau	18 Kankin
327	13 Mar	8.	14.	9.	12.	0	3 Ahau	18 Muan
327	2 Apr	8.	14.	9.	13.	0	10 Ahau	18 Pax
327	22 Apr	8.	14.	9.	14.	0	4 Ahau	18 Kayab
327	12 May	8.	14.	9.	15.	0	11 Ahau	18 Cumhú
327	1 Jun	8.	14.	9.	16.	0	5 Ahau	13 Pop
327	21 Jun	8.	14.	9.	17.	0	12 Ahau	13 Uo
327	11 Jul	8.	14.	10.	0.	0	6 Ahau	13 Zip
327	31 Jul	8.	14.	10.	1.	0	13 Ahau	13 Zotz
327	20 Aug	8.	14.	10.	2.	0	7 Ahau	13 Tzec
327	9 Sep	8.	14.	10.	3.	0	1 Ahau	13 Xul
327	29 Sep	8.	14.	10.	4.	0	8 Ahau	13 Yaxkin
327	19 Oct	8.	14.	10.	5.	0	2 Ahau	13 Mol
327	8 Nov	8.	14.	10.	6.	0	9 Ahau	13 Chen
327	28 Nov	8.	14.	10.	7.	0	3 Ahau	13 Yax
327	18 Dec	8.	14.	10.	8.	0	10 Ahau	13 Zac
328	7 Jan	8.	14.	10.	9.	0	4 Ahau	13 Ceh
328	27 Jan	8.	14.	10.	10.	0	11 Ahau	13 Mac
328	16 Feb	8.	14.	10.	11.	0	5 Ahau	13 Kankin
328	7 Mar	8.	14.	10.	12.	0	12 Ahau	13 Muan
328	27 Mar	8.	14.	10.	13.	0	6 Ahau	13 Pax
328	16 Apr	8.	14.	10.	14.	0	13 Ahau	13 Kayab
328	6 May	8.	14.	10.	15.	0	7 Ahau	13 Cumhú
328	26 May	8.	14.	10.	16.	0	1 Ahau	8 Pop
328	15 Jun	8.	14.	10.	17.	0	8 Ahau	8 Up
328	5 Jul	8.	14.	11.	0.	0	2 Ahau	8 Zip
328	25 Jul	8.	14.	11.	1.	0	9 Ahau	8 Zotz
328	14 Aug	8.	14.	11.	2.	0	3 Ahau	8 Tzec

Gregorian Date								
328	3 Sep	8.	14.	11.	3.	0	10 Ahau	8 Xul
328	23 Sep	8.	14.	11.	4.	0	4 Ahau	8 Yaxkin
328	13 Oct	8.	14.	11.	5.	0	11 Ahau	8 Mol
328	2 Nov	8.	14.	11.	6.	0	5 Ahau	8 Chen
328	22 Nov	8.	14.	11.	7.	0	12 Ahau	8 Yax
328	12 Dec	8.	14.	11.	8.	0	6 Ahau	8 Zac
329	1 Jan	8.	14.	11.	9.	0	13 Ahau	8 Ceh
329	21 Jan	8.	14.	11.	10.	0	7 Ahau	8 Mac
329	10 Feb	8.	14.	11.	11.	0	1 Ahau	8 Kankin
329	2 Mar	8.	14.	11.	12.	0	8 Ahau	8 Muan
329	22 Mar	8.	14.	11.	13.	0	2 Ahau	8 Pax
329	11 Apr	8.	14.	11.	14.	0	9 Ahau	8 Kayab
329	1 May	8.	14.	11.	15.	0	3 Ahau	8 Cumhú
329	21 May	8.	14.	11.	16.	0	10 Ahau	3 Pop
329	10 Jun	8.	14.	11.	17.	0	4 Ahau	3 Uo
329	30 Jun	8.	14.	12.	0.	0	11 Ahau	3 Zip
329	20 Jul	8.	14.	12.	1.	0	5 Ahau	3 Zotz
329	9 Aug	8.	14.	12.	2.	0	12 Ahau	3 Tzec
329	29 Aug	8.	14.	12.	3.	0	6 Ahau	3 Xul
329	18 Sep	8.	14.	12.	4.	0	13 Ahau	3 Yaxkin
329	8 Oct	8.	14.	12.	5.	0	7 Ahau	3 Mol
329	28 Oct	8.	14.	12.	6.	0	1 Ahau	3 Chen
329	17 Nov	8.	14.	12.	7.	0	8 Ahau	3 Yax
329	7 Dec	8.	14.	12.	8.	0	2 Ahau	3 Zac
329	27 Dec	8.	14.	12.	9.	0	9 Ahau	3 Ceh
330	16 Jan	8.	14.	12.	10.	0	3 Ahau	3 Mac
330	5 Feb	8.	14.	12.	11.	0	10 Ahau	3 Kankin
330	25 Feb	8.	14.	12.	12.	0	4 Ahau	3 Muan
330	17 Mar	8.	14.	12.	13.	0	11 Ahau	3 Pax
330	6 Apr	8.	14.	12.	14.	0	5 Ahau	3 Kayab
330	26 Apr	8.	14.	12.	15.	0	12 Ahau	3 Cumhú
330	16 May	8.	14.	12.	16.	0	6 Ahau	3 Uayeb
330	5 Jun	8.	14.	12.	17.	0	13 Ahau	18 Pop
330	25 Jun	8.	14.	13.	0.	0	7 Ahau	18 Uo
330	15 Jul	8.	14.	13.	1.	0	1 Ahau	18 Zip
330	4 Aug	8.	14.	13.	2.	0	8 Ahau	18 Zotz
330	24 Aug	8.	14.	13.	3.	0	2 Ahau	18 Tzec
330	13 Sep	8.	14.	13.	4.	0	9 Ahau	18 Xul
330	3 Oct	8.	14.	13.	5.	0	3 Ahau	18 Yaxkin
330	23 Oct	8.	14.	13.	6.	0	10 Ahau	18 Mol
330	12 Nov	8.	14.	13.	7.	0	4 Ahau	18 Chen
330	2 Dec	8.	14.	13.	8.	0	11 Ahau	18 Yax
330	22 Dec	8.	14.	13.	9.	0	5 Ahau	18 Zac
331	11 Jan	8.	14.	13.	10.	0	12 Ahau	18 Ceh
331	31 Jan	8.	14.	13.	11.	0	6 Ahau	18 Mac
331	20 Feb	8.	14.	13.	12.	0	13 Ahau	18 Kankin
331	12 Mar	8.	14.	13.	13.	0	7 Ahau	18 Muan
331	1 Apr	8.	14.	13.	14.	0	1 Ahau	18 Pax
331	21 Apr	8.	14.	13.	15.	0	8 Ahau	18 Kayab
331	11 May	8.	14.	13.	16.	0	2 Ahau	18 Cumhú
331	31 May	8.	14.	13.	17.	0	9 Ahau	13 Pop

Gregorian Date								
331	20 Jun	8.	14.	14.	0.	0	3 Ahau	13 Uo
331	10 Jul	8.	14.	14.	1.	0	10 Ahau	13 Zip
331	30 Jul	8.	14.	14.	2.	0	4 Ahau	13 Zotz
331	19 Aug	8.	14.	14.	3.	0	11 Ahau	13 Tzec
331	8 Sep	8.	14.	14.	4.	0	5 Ahau	13 Xul
331	28 Sep	8.	14.	14.	5.	0	12 Ahau	13 Yaxkin
331	18 Oct	8.	14.	14.	6.	0	6 Ahau	13 Mol
331	7 Nov	8.	14.	14.	7.	0	13 Ahau	13 Chen
331	27 Nov	8.	14.	14.	8.	0	7 Ahau	13 Yax
331	17 Dec	8.	14.	14.	9.	0	1 Ahau	13 Zac
332	6 Jan	8.	14.	14.	10.	0	8 Ahau	13 Ceh
332	26 Jan	8.	14.	14.	11.	0	2 Ahau	13 Mac
332	15 Feb	8.	14.	14.	12.	0	9 Ahau	13 Kankin
332	6 Mar	8.	14.	14.	13.	0	3 Ahau	13 Muan
332	26 Mar	8.	14.	14.	14.	0	10 Ahau	13 Pax
332	15 Apr	8.	14.	14.	15.	0	4 Ahau	13 Kayab
332	5 May	8.	14.	14.	16.	0	11 Ahau	13 Cumhú
332	25 May	8.	14.	14.	17.	0	5 Ahau	8 Pop
332	14 Jun	8.	14.	15.	0.	0	12 Ahau	8 Uo
332	4 Jul	8.	14.	15.	1.	0	6 Ahau	8 Zip
332	24 Jul	8.	14.	15.	2.	0	13 Ahau	8 Zotz
332	13 Aug	8.	14.	15.	3.	0	7 Ahau	8 Tzec
332	2 Sep	8.	14.	15.	4.	0	1 Ahau	8 Xul
332	22 Sep	8.	14.	15.	5.	0	8 Ahau	8 Yaxkin
332	12 Oct	8.	14.	15.	6.	0	2 Ahau	8 Mol
332	1 Nov	8.	14.	15.	7.	0	9 Ahau	8 Chen
332	21 Nov	8.	14.	15.	8.	0	3 Ahau	8 Yax
332	11 Dec	8.	14.	15.	9.	0	10 Ahau	8 Zac
332	31 Dec	8.	14.	15.	10.	0	4 Ahau	8 Ceh
333	20 Jan	8.	14.	15.	11.	0	11 Ahau	8 Mac
333	9 Feb	8.	14.	15.	12.	0	5 Ahau	8 Kankin
333	1 Mar	8.	14.	15.	13.	0	12 Ahau	8 Muan
333	21 Mar	8.	14.	15.	14.	0	6 Ahau	8 Pax
333	10 Apr	8.	14.	15.	15.	0	13 Ahau	8 Kayab
333	30 Apr	8.	14.	15.	16.	0	7 Ahau	8 Cumhú
333	20 May	8.	14.	15.	17.	0	1 Ahau	8 Pop
333	9 Jun	8.	14.	16.	0.	0	8 Ahau	3 Uo
333	29 Jun	8.	14.	16.	1.	0	2 Ahau	3 Zip
333	19 Jul	8.	14.	16.	2.	0	9 Ahau	3 Zotz
333	8 Aug	8.	14.	16.	3.	0	3 Ahau	3 Tzec
333	28 Aug	8.	14.	16.	4.	0	10 Ahau	3 Xul
333	17 Sep	8.	14.	16.	5.	0	4 Ahau	3 Yaxkin
333	7 Oct	8.	14.	16.	6.	0	11 Ahau	3 Mol
333	27 Oct	8.	14.	16.	7.	0	5 Ahau	3 Chen
333	16 Nov	8.	14.	16.	8.	0	12 Ahau	3 Yax
333	6 Dec	8.	14.	16.	9.	0	6 Ahau	3 Zac
333	26 Dec	8.	14.	16.	10.	0	13 Ahau	3 Ceh
334	15 Jan	8.	14.	16.	11.	0	7 Ahau	3 Mac
334	4 Feb	8.	14.	16.	12.	0	1 Ahau	3 Kankin
334	24 Feb	8.	14.	16.	13.	0	8 Ahau	3 Muan
334	16 Mar	8.	14.	16.	14.	0	2 Ahau	3 Pax

Gregorian Date

334	5 Apr	8.	14.	16.	15.	0	9 Ahau	3 Kayab
334	25 Apr	8.	14.	16.	16.	0	3 Ahau	3 Cumhú
334	15 May	8.	14.	16.	17.	0	10 Ahau	3 Uayeb
334	4 Jun	8.	14.	17.	0.	0	4 Ahau	18 Pop
334	24 Jun	8.	14.	17.	1.	0	11 Ahau	18 Uo
334	14 Jul	8.	14.	17.	2.	0	5 Ahau	18 Zip
334	3 Aug	8.	14.	17.	3.	0	12 Ahau	18 Zotz
334	23 Aug	8.	14.	17.	4.	0	6 Ahau	18 Tzec
334	12 Sep	8.	14.	17.	5.	0	13 Ahau	18 Xul
334	2 Oct	8.	14.	17.	6.	0	7 Ahau	18 Yaxkin
334	22 Oct	8.	14.	17.	7.	0	1 Ahau	18 Mol
334	11 Nov	8.	14.	17.	8.	0	8 Ahau	18 Chen
334	1 Dec	8.	14.	17.	9.	0	2 Ahau	18 Yax
334	21 Dec	8.	14.	17.	10.	0	9 Ahau	18 Zac
335	10 Jan	8.	14.	17.	11.	0	3 Ahau	18 Ceh
335	30 Jan	8.	14.	17.	12.	0	10 Ahau	18 Mac
335	19 Feb	8.	14.	17.	13.	0	4 Ahau	18 Kankin
335	11 Mar	8.	14.	17.	14.	0	11 Ahau	18 Muan
335	31 Mar	8.	14.	17.	15.	0	5 Ahau	18 Pax
335	20 Apr	8.	14.	17.	16.	0	12 Ahau	18 Kayab
335	10 May	8.	14.	17.	17.	0	6 Ahau	18 Cumhú
335	30 May	8.	14.	18.	0.	0	13 Ahau	13 Pop
335	19 Jun	8.	14.	18.	1.	0	7 Ahau	13 Uo
335	9 Jul	8.	14.	18.	2.	0	1 Ahau	13 Zip
335	29 Jul	8.	14.	18.	3.	0	8 Ahau	13 Zotz
335	18 Aug	8.	14.	18.	4.	0	2 Ahau	13 Tzec
335	7 Sep	8.	14.	18.	5.	0	9 Ahau	13 Xul
335	27 Sep	8.	14.	18.	6.	0	3 Ahau	13 Yaxkin
335	17 Oct	8.	14.	18.	7.	0	10 Ahau	13 Mol
335	6 Nov	8.	14.	18.	8.	0	4 Ahau	13 Chen
335	26 Nov	8.	14.	18.	9.	0	11 Ahau	13 Yax
335	16 Dec	8.	14.	18.	10.	0	5 Ahau	13 Zac
336	5 Jan	8.	14.	18.	11.	0	12 Ahau	13 Ceh
336	25 Jan	8.	14.	18.	12.	0	6 Ahau	13 Mac
336	14 Feb	8.	14.	18.	13.	0	13 Ahau	13 Kankin
336	5 Mar	8.	14.	18.	14.	0	7 Ahau	13 Muan
336	25 Mar	8.	14.	18.	15.	0	1 Ahau	13 Pax
336	14 Apr	8.	14.	18.	16.	0	8 Ahau	13 Kayab
336	4 May	8.	14.	18.	17.	0	2 Ahau	13 Cumhú
336	24 May	8.	14.	19.	0.	0	9 Ahau	8 Pop
336	13 Jun	8.	14.	19.	1.	0	3 Ahau	8 Uo
336	3 Jul	8.	14.	19.	2.	0	10 Ahau	8 Zip
336	23 Jul	8.	14.	19.	3.	0	4 Ahau	8 Zotz
336	12 Aug	8.	14.	19.	4.	0	11 Ahau	8 Tzec
336	1 Sep	8.	14.	19.	5.	0	5 Ahau	8 Xul
336	21 Sep	8.	14.	19.	6.	0	12 Ahau	8 Yaxkin
336	11 Oct	8.	14.	19.	7.	0	6 Ahau	8 Mol
336	31 Oct	8.	14.	19.	8.	0	13 Ahau	8 Chen
336	20 Nov	8.	14.	19.	9.	0	7 Ahau	8 Yax
336	10 Dec	8.	14.	19.	10.	0	1 Ahau	8 Zac

Gregorian Date								
336	30 Dec	8.	14.	19.	11.	0	8 Ahau	8 Ceh
337	19 Jan	8.	14.	19.	12.	0	2 Ahau	8 Mac
337	8 Feb	8.	14.	19.	13.	0	9 Ahau	8 Kankin
337	28 Feb	8.	14.	19.	14.	0	3 Ahau	8 Muan
337	20 Mar	8.	14.	19.	15.	0	10 Ahau	8 Pax
337	9 Apr	8.	14.	19.	16.	0	4 Ahau	8 Kayab
337	29 Apr	8.	14.	19.	17.	0	11 Ahau	8 Cumhú
337	19 May	8.	14.	0.	0.	0	5 Ahau	3 Pop
337	8 Jun	8.	14.	0.	1.	0	12 Ahau	3 Uo
337	28 Jun	8.	14.	0.	2.	0	6 Ahau	3 Zip
337	18 Jul	8.	14.	0.	3.	0	13 Ahau	3 Zotz
337	7 Aug	8.	14.	0.	4.	0	7 Ahau	3 Tzec
337	27 Aug	8.	14.	0.	5.	0	1 Ahau	3 Xul
337	16 Sep	8.	14.	0.	6.	0	8 Ahau	3 Yaxkin
337	6 Oct	8.	14.	0.	7.	0	2 Ahau	3 Mol
337	26 Oct	8.	14.	0.	8.	0	9 Ahau	3 Chen
337	15 Nov	8.	14.	0.	9.	0	3 Ahau	3 Yax
337	5 Dec	8.	14.	0.	10.	0	10 Ahau	3 Zac
337	25 Dec	8.	14.	0.	11.	0	4 Ahau	3 Ceh
338	14 Jan	8.	14.	0.	12.	0	11 Ahau	3 Mac
338	3 Feb	8.	14.	0.	13.	0	5 Ahau	3 Kankin
338	23 Feb	8.	14.	0.	14.	0	12 Ahau	3 Muan
338	15 Mar	8.	14.	0.	15.	0	6 Ahau	3 Pax
338	4 Apr	8.	14.	0.	16.	0	13 Ahau	3 Kayab
338	24 Apr	8.	14.	0.	17.	0	7 Ahau	3 Cumhú

PAVON ABREU'S COUNT IN KINS

Gregorian Date								
321	9 Dec	8.	14.	4.	6.	0	7 Ahau	3 Zac
321	10 Dec	8.	14.	4.	6.	1	8 Imix	4 Zac
321	11 Dec	8.	14.	4.	6.	2	9 Ik	5 Zac
321	12 Dec	8.	14.	4.	6.	3	10 Akbal	6 Zac
321	13 Dec	8.	14.	4.	6.	4	11 Kan	7 Zac
321	14 Dec	8.	14.	4.	6.	5	12 Chicchan	8 Zac
321	15 Dec	8.	14.	4.	6.	6	13 Cimi	9 Zac
321	16 Dec	8.	14.	4.	6.	7	1 Manik	10 Zac
321	17 Dec	8.	14.	4.	6.	8	2 Lamat	11 Zac
321	18 Dec	8.	14.	4.	6.	9	3 Muluc	12 Zac
321	19 Dec	8.	14.	4.	6.	10	4 Oc	13 Zac
321	20 Dec	8.	14.	4.	6.	11	5 Chuen	14 Zac
321	21 Dec	8.	14.	4.	6.	12	6 Eb	15 Zac
321	22 Dec	8.	14.	4.	6.	13	7 Ben	16 Zac
321	23 Dec	8.	14.	4.	6.	14	8 Ix	17 Zac
321	24 Dec	8.	14.	4.	6.	15	9 Men	18 Zac
321	25 Dec	8.	14.	4.	6.	16	10 Cib	19 Zac
321	26 Dec	8.	14.	4.	6.	17	11 Caban	0 Ceh
321	27 Dec	8.	14.	4.	6.	18	12 Eznab	1 Ceh
321	28 Dec	8.	14.	4.	6.	19	13 Cauac	2 Ceh

Gregorian Date								
321	29 Dec	8.	14.	4.	7.	0	1 Ahau	3 Ceh
321	30 Dec	8.	14.	4.	7.	1	2 Imix	4 Ceh
321	31 Dec	8.	14.	4.	7.	2	3 Ik	5 Ceh
322	1 Jan	8.	14.	4.	7.	3	4 Akbal	6 Ceh
322	2 Jan	8.	14.	4.	7.	4	5 Kan	7 Ceh
322	3 Jan	8.	14.	4.	7.	5	6 Chicchan	8 Ceh
322	4 Jan	8.	14.	4.	7.	6	7 Cimi	9 Ceh
322	5 Jan	8.	14.	4.	7.	7	8 Manik	10 Ceh
322	6 Jan	8.	14.	4.	7.	8	9 Lamat	11 Ceh
322	7 Jan	8.	14.	4.	7.	9	10 Muluc	12 Ceh
322	8 Jan	8.	14.	4.	7.	10	11 Oc	13 Ceh
322	9 Jan	8.	14.	4.	7.	11	12 Chuen	14 Ceh
322	10 Jan	8.	14.	4.	7.	12	13 Eb	15 Ceh
322	11 Jan	8.	14.	4.	7.	13	1 Ben	16 Ceh
322	12 Jan	8.	14.	4.	7.	14	2 Ix	17 Ceh
322	13 Jan	8.	14.	4.	7.	15	3 Men	18 Ceh
322	14 Jan	8.	14.	4.	7.	16	4 Cib	19 Ceh
322	15 Jan	8.	14.	4.	7.	17	5 Caban	0 Mac
322	16 Jan	8.	14.	4.	7.	18	6 Eznab	1 Mac
322	17 Jan	8.	14.	4.	7.	19	7 Cauac	2 Mac
322	18 Jan	8.	14.	4.	8.	0	8 Ahau	3 Mac
322	19 Jan	8.	14.	4.	8.	1	9 Imix	4 Mac
322	20 Jan	8.	14.	4.	8.	2	10 Ik	5 Mac
322	21 Jan	8.	14.	4.	8.	3	11 Akbal	6 Mac
322	22 Jan	8.	14.	4.	8.	4	12 Kan	7 Mac
322	23 Jan	8.	14.	4.	8.	5	13 Chicchan	8 Mac
322	24 Jan	8.	14.	4.	8.	6	1 Cimi	9 Mac
322	25 Jan	8.	14.	4.	8.	7	2 Manik	10 Mac
322	26 Jan	8.	14.	4.	8.	8	3 Lamat	11 Mac
322	27 Jan	8.	14.	4.	8.	9	4 Muluc	12 Mac
322	28 Jan	8.	14.	4.	8.	10	5 Oc	13 Mac
322	29 Jan	8.	14.	4.	8.	11	6 Chuen	14 Mac
322	30 Jan	8.	14.	4.	8.	12	7 Eb	15 Mac
322	31 Jan	8.	14.	4.	8.	13	8 Ben	16 Mac
322	1 Feb	8.	14.	4.	8.	14	9 Ix	17 Mac
322	2 Feb	8.	14.	4.	8.	15	10 Men	18 Mac
322	3 Feb	8.	14.	4.	8.	16	11 Cib	19 Mac
322	4 Feb	8.	14.	4.	8.	17	12 Caban	0 Kankin
322	5 Feb	8.	14.	4.	8.	18	13 Eznab	1 Kankin
322	6 Feb	8.	14.	4.	8.	19	1 Cauac	2 Kankin
322	7 Feb	8.	14.	4.	9.	0	2 Ahau	3 Kankin
322	8 Feb	8.	14.	4.	9.	1	3 Imix	4 Kankin
322	9 Feb	8.	14.	4.	9.	2	4 Ik	5 Kankin
322	10 Feb	8.	14.	4.	9.	3	5 Akbal	6 Kankin
322	11 Feb	8.	14.	4.	9.	4	6 Kan	7 Kankin
322	12 Feb	8.	14.	4.	9.	5	7 Chicchan	8 Kankin
322	13 Feb	8.	14.	4.	9.	6	8 Cimi	9 Kankin
322	14 Feb	8.	14.	4.	9.	7	9 Manik	10 Kankin
322	15 Feb	8.	14.	4.	9.	8	10 Lamat	11 Kankin
322	16 Feb	8.	14.	4.	9.	9	11 Muluc	12 Kankin
322	17 Feb	8.	14.	4.	9.	10	12 Oc	13 Kankin

Gregorian Date								
322	18 Feb	8.	14.	4.	9.	11	13 Chuen	14 Kankin
322	19 Feb	8.	14.	4.	9.	12	1 Eb	15 Kankin
322	20 Feb	8.	14.	4.	9.	13	2 Ben	16 Kankin
322	21 Feb	8.	14.	4.	9.	14	3 Ix	17 Kankin
322	22 Feb	8.	14.	4.	9.	15	4 Men	18 Kankin
322	23 Feb	8.	14.	4.	9.	16	5 Cib	19 Kankin
322	24 Feb	8.	14.	4.	9.	17	6 Caban	0 Muan
322	25 Feb	8.	14.	4.	9.	18	7 Eznab	1 Muan
322	26 Feb	8.	14.	4.	9.	19	8 Cauac	2 Muan
322	27 Feb	8.	14.	4.	10.	0	9 Ahau	3 Muan
322	28 Feb	8.	14.	4.	10.	1	10 Imix	4 Muan
322	1 Mar	8.	14.	4.	10.	2	11 Ik	5 Muan
322	2 Mar	8.	14.	4.	10.	3	12 Akbal	6 Muan
322	3 Mar	8.	14.	4.	10.	4	13 Kan	7 Muan
322	4 Mar	8.	14.	4.	10.	5	1 Chicchan	8 Muan
322	5 Mar	8.	14.	4.	10.	6	2 Cimi	9 Muan
322	6 Mar	8.	14.	4.	10.	7	3 Manik	10 Muan
322	7 Mar	8.	14.	4.	10.	8	4 Lamat	11 Muan
322	8 Mar	8.	14.	4.	10.	9	5 Muluc	12 Muan
322	9 Mar	8.	14.	4.	10.	10	6 Oc	13 Muan
322	10 Mar	8.	14.	4.	10.	11	7 Chuen	14 Muan
322	11 Mar	8.	14.	4.	10.	12	8 Eb	15 Muan
322	12 Mar	8.	14.	4.	10.	13	9 Ben	16 Muan
322	13 Mar	8.	14.	4.	10.	14	10 Ix	17 Muan
322	14 Mar	8.	14.	4.	10.	15	11 Men	18 Muan
322	15 Mar	8.	14.	4.	10.	16	12 Cib	19 Muan
322	16 Mar	8.	14.	4.	10.	17	13 Caban	0 Pax
322	17 Mar	8.	14.	4.	10.	18	1 Eznab	1 Pax
322	18 Mar	8.	14.	4.	10.	19	2 Cauac	2 Pax
322	19 Mar	8.	14.	4.	11.	0	3 Ahau	3 Pax
322	20 Mar	8.	14.	4.	11.	1	4 Imix	4 Pax
322	21 Mar	8.	14.	4.	11.	2	5 Ik	5 Pax
322	22 Mar	8.	14.	4.	11.	3	6 Akbal	6 Pax
322	23 Mar	8.	14.	4.	11.	4	7 Kan	7 Pax
322	24 Mar	8.	14.	4.	11.	5	8 Chicchan	8 Pax
322	25 Mar	8.	14.	4.	11.	6	9 Cimi	9 Pax
322	26 Mar	8.	14.	4.	11.	7	10 Manik	10 Pax
322	27 Mar	8.	14.	4.	11.	8	11 Lamat	11 Pax
322	28 Mar	8.	14.	4.	11.	9	12 Muluc	12 Pax
322	29 Mar	8.	14.	4.	11.	10	13 Oc	13 Pax
322	30 Mar	8.	14.	4.	11.	11	1 Chuen	14 Pax
322	31 Mar	8.	14.	4.	11.	12	2 Eb	15 Pax
322	1 Apr	8.	14.	4.	11.	13	3 Ben	16 Pax
322	2 Apr	8.	14.	4.	11.	14	4 Ix	17 Pax
322	3 Apr	8.	14.	4.	11.	15	5 Men	18 Pax
322	4 Apr	8.	14.	4.	11.	16	6 Cib	19 Pax
322	5 Apr	8.	14.	4.	11.	17	7 Caban	0 Kayab
322	6 Apr	8.	14.	4.	11.	18	8 Eznab	1 Kayab
322	7 Apr	8.	14.	4.	11.	19	9 Cauac	2 Kayab
322	8 Apr	8.	14.	4.	12.	0	10 Ahau	3 Kayab
322	9 Apr	8.	14.	4.	12.	1	11 Imix	4 Kayab

Gregorian Date								
322	10 Apr	8.	14.	4.	12.	2	12 Ik	5 Kayab
322	11 Apr	8.	14.	4.	12.	3	13 Akbal	6 Kayab
322	12 Apr	8.	14.	4.	12.	4	1 Kan	7 Kayab
322	13 Apr	8.	14.	4.	12.	5	2 Chicchan	8 Kayab
322	14 Apr	8.	14.	4.	12.	6	3 Cimi	9 Kayab
322	15 Apr	8.	14.	4.	12.	7	4 Manik	10 Kayab
322	16 Apr	8.	14.	4.	12.	8	5 Lamat	11 Kayab
322	17 Apr	8.	14.	4.	12.	9	6 Muluc	12 Kayab
322	18 Apr	8.	14.	4.	12.	10	7 Oc	13 Kayab
322	19 Apr	8.	14.	4.	12.	11	8 Chuen	14 Kayab
322	20 Apr	8.	14.	4.	12.	12	9 Eb	15 Kayab
322	21 Apr	8.	14.	4.	12.	13	10 Ben	16 Kayab
322	22 Apr	8.	14.	4.	12.	14	11 Ix	17 Kayab
322	23 Apr	8.	14.	4.	12.	15	12 Men	18 Kayab
322	24 Apr	8.	14.	4.	12.	16	13 Cib	19 Kayab
322	25 Apr	8.	14.	4.	12.	17	1 Caban	0 Cumhú
322	26 Apr	8.	14.	4.	12.	18	2 Eznab	1 Cumhú
322	27 Apr	8.	14.	4.	12.	19	3 Cauac	2 Cumhú
322	28 Apr	8.	14.	4.	13.	0	4 Ahau	3 Cumhú
322	29 Apr	8.	14.	4.	13.	1	5 Imix	4 Cumhú
322	30 Apr	8.	14.	4.	13.	2	6 Ik	5 Cumhú
322	1 May	8.	14.	4.	13.	3	7 Akbal	6 Cumhú
322	2 May	8.	14.	4.	13.	4	8 Kan	7 Cumhú
322	3 May	8.	14.	4.	13.	5	9 Chicchan	8 Cumhú
322	4 May	8.	14.	4.	13.	6	10 Cimi	9 Cumhú
322	5 May	8.	14.	4.	13.	7	11 Manik	10 Cumhú
322	6 May	8.	14.	4.	13.	8	12 Lamat	11 Cumhú
322	7 May	8.	14.	4.	13.	9	13 Muluc	12 Cumhú
322	8 May	8.	14.	4.	13.	10	1 Oc	13 Cumhú
322	9 May	8.	14.	4.	13.	11	2 Chuen	14 Cumhú
322	10 May	8.	14.	4.	13.	12	3 Eb	15 Cumhú
322	11 May	8.	14.	4.	13.	13	4 Ben	16 Cumhú
322	12 May	8.	14.	4.	13.	14	5 Ix	17 Cumhú
322	13 May	8.	14.	4.	13.	15	6 Men	18 Cumhú
322	14 May	8.	14.	4.	13.	16	7 Cib	19 Cumhú
322	15 May	8.	14.	4.	13.	17	8 Caban	0 Uayeb
322	16 May	8.	14.	4.	13.	18	9 Eznab	1 Uayeb
322	17 May	8.	14.	4.	13.	19	10 Cauac	2 Uayeb

SPINDEN'S COUNT IN EVEN BAKTUNS

Gregorian Date								
3373	14 Oct	13.	0.	0.	0.	0	4 Ahau	8 Cumhu
3353	1 Jul	13.	1.	0.	0.	0	2 Ahau	8 Mac
3333	18 Mar	13.	2.	0.	0.	0	13 Ahau	8 Mol
3314	3 Dec	13.	3.	0.	0.	0	11 Ahau	8 Zip
3294	21 Aug	13.	4.	0.	0.	0	9 Ahau	13 Pax
3274	8 May	13.	5.	0.	0.	0	7 Ahau	13 Zac
3254	23 Jan	13.	6.	0.	0.	0	5 Ahau	13 Xul
3235	10 Oct	13.	7.	0.	0.	0	3 Ahau	13 Pop

Gregorian Date								
3215	27 Jun	13.	8.	0.	0.	0	1 Ahau	18 Kankin
3195	14 Mar	13.	9.	0.	0.	0	12 Ahau	18 Chen
3176	29 Nov	13.	10.	0.	0.	0	10 Ahau	18 Zotz
3156	16 Aug	13.	11.	0.	0.	0	8 Ahau	3 Cumhu
3136	3 May	13.	12.	0.	0.	0	6 Ahau	3 Mac
3116	18 Jan	13.	13.	0.	0.	0	4 Ahau	3 Mol
3097	7 Oct	13.	14.	0.	0.	0	2 Ahau	3 Zip
3077	24 Jun	13.	15.	0.	0.	0	13 Ahau	8 Pax
3057	11 Mar	13.	16.	0.	0.	0	11 Ahau	8 Zac
3038	26 Nov	13.	17.	0.	0.	0	9 Ahau	8 Xul
3018	13 Aug	13.	18.	0.	0.	0	7 Ahau	8 Pop
2998	1 May	13.	19.	0.	0.	0	5 Ahau	13 Kankin
2978	16 Jan	1.	0.	0.	0.	0	3 Ahau	13 Chen
2959	3 Oct	1.	1.	0.	0.	0	1 Ahau	13 Zotz
2939	20 Jun	1.	2.	0.	0.	0	12 Ahau	18 Kayab
2919	7 Mar	1.	3.	0.	0.	0	10 Ahau	18 Ceh
2900	23 Nov	1.	4.	0.	0.	0	8 Ahau	18 Yaxkin
2880	10 Aug	1.	5.	0.	0.	0	6 Ahau	18 Uo
2860	27 Apr	1.	6.	0.	0.	0	4 Ahau	3 Pax
2840	12 Jan	1.	7.	0.	0.	0	3 Ahau	3 Zac
2821	30 Sep	1.	8.	0.	0.	0	13 Ahau	3 Xul
2801	17 Jun	1.	9.	0.	0.	0	11 Ahau	3 Pop
2781	4 Mar	1.	10.	0.	0.	0	9 Ahau	8 Kankin
2762	19 Nov	1.	11.	0.	0.	0	7 Ahau	8 Chen
2742	6 Aug	1.	12.	0.	0.	0	5 Ahau	8 Zotz
2722	23 Apr	1.	13.	0.	0.	0	3 Ahau	13 Kayab
2702	8 Jan	1.	14.	0.	0.	0	1 Ahau	13 Ceh
2683	26 Sep	1.	15.	0.	0.	0	12 Ahau	13 Yaxkin
2663	13 Jun	1.	16.	0.	0.	0	10 Ahau	13 Uo
2643	28 Feb	1.	17.	0.	0.	0	8 Ahau	18 Muan
2624	15 Nov	1.	18.	0.	0.	0	6 Ahau	18 Yax
2604	2 Aug	1.	19.	0.	0.	0	4 Ahau	18 Tzec
2584	20 Apr	2.	0.	0.	0.	0	2 Ahau	3 Uayeb
2564	5 Jan	2.	1.	0.	0.	0	13 Ahau	3 Kankin
2545	23 Sep	2.	2.	0.	0.	0	11 Ahau	3 Chen
2525	10 Jun	2.	3.	0.	0.	0	9 Ahau	3 Zotz
2505	25 Feb	2.	4.	0.	0.	0	7 Ahau	8 Kayab
2486	13 Nov	2.	5.	0.	0.	0	5 Ahau	8 Ceh
2466	31 Jul	2.	6.	0.	0.	0	3 Ahau	8 Yaxkin
2446	17 Apr	2.	7.	0.	0.	0	1 Ahau	8 Uo
2426	2 Jan	2.	8.	0.	0.	0	12 Ahau	13 Muan
2407	19 Sep	2.	9.	0.	0.	0	10 Ahau	13 Yax
2387	6 Jun	2.	10.	0.	0.	0	8 Ahau	13 Tzec
2367	21 Feb	2.	11.	0.	0.	0	6 Ahau	18 Cumhu
2348	8 Nov	2.	12.	0.	0.	0	4 Ahau	18 Mac
2328	26 Jul	2.	13.	0.	0.	0	2 Ahau	18 Mol
2308	12 Apr	2.	14.	0.	0.	0	13 Ahau	18 Zip
2289	30 Dec	2.	15.	0.	0.	0	11 Ahau	3 Kayab
2269	16 Sep	2.	16.	0.	0.	0	9 Ahau	3 Ceh
2249	3 Jun	2.	17.	0.	0.	0	7 Ahau	3 Yaxkin
2229	18 Feb	2.	18.	0.	0.	0	5 Ahau	3 Uo
2210	6 Nov	2.	19.	0.	0.	0	3 Ahau	8 Muan

Gregorian Date								
2190	24 Jul	3.	0.	0.	0.	0	1 Ahau	8 Yax
2170	10 Apr	3.	1.	0.	0.	0	12 Ahau	8 Tzec
2151	26 Dec	3.	2.	0.	0.	0	10 Ahau	13 Cumhu
2131	12 Sep	3.	3.	0.	0.	0	8 Ahau	13 Mac
2111	30 May	3.	4.	0.	0.	0	6 Ahau	13 Mol
2091	15 Feb	3.	5.	0.	0.	0	4 Ahau	13 Zip
2072	2 Nov	3.	6.	0.	0.	0	2 Ahau	18 Pax
2052	20 Jul	3.	7.	0.	0.	0	13 Ahau	18 Zac
2032	6 Apr	3.	8.	0.	0.	0	11 Ahau	18 Xul
2013	23 Dec	3.	9.	0.	0.	0	9 Ahau	18 Pop
1993	10 Sep	3.	10.	0.	0.	0	7 Ahau	3 Muon
1973	28 May	3.	11.	0.	0.	0	5 Ahau	3 Yax
1953	12 Feb	3.	12.	0.	0.	0	3 Ahau	3 Zac
1934	30 Oct	3.	13.	0.	0.	0	1 Ahau	8 Cumhu
1914	17 Jul	3.	14.	0.	0.	0	12 Ahau	8 Mac
1894	4 Apr	3.	15.	0.	0.	0	10 Ahau	8 Mol
1875	20 Dec	3.	16.	0.	0.	0	8 Ahau	8 Zip
1855	6 Sep	3.	17.	0.	0.	0	6 Ahau	13 Pax
1835	24 May	3.	18.	0.	0.	0	4 Ahau	13 Zac
1815	8 Feb	3.	19.	0.	0.	0	2 Ahau	13 Xul
1796	26 Oct	4.	0.	0.	0.	0	13 Ahau	13 Pop
1776	14 Jul	4.	1.	0.	0.	0	11 Ahau	18 Kankin
1756	31 Mar	4.	2.	0.	0.	0	9 Ahau	18 Chen
1737	17 Dec	4.	3.	0.	0.	0	7 Ahau	18 Zotz
1717	3 Sep	4.	4.	0.	0.	0	5 Ahau	3 Cumhu
1697	22 May	4.	5.	0.	0.	0	3 Ahau	3 Mac
1677	6 Feb	4.	6.	0.	0.	0	1 Ahau	3 Mol
1658	24 Oct	4.	7.	0.	0.	0	12 Ahau	3 Zip
1638	11 Jul	4.	8.	0.	0.	0	10 Ahau	8 Pax
1618	28 Mar	4.	9.	0.	0.	0	8 Ahau	8 Zac
1599	13 Dec	4.	10.	0.	0.	0	6 Ahau	8 Xul
1579	30 Aug	4.	11.	0.	0.	0	4 Ahau	8 Pop
1559	17 May	4.	12.	0.	0.	0	2 Ahau	13 Kankin
1539	1 Feb	4.	13.	0.	0.	0	13 Ahau	13 Chen
1520	19 Oct	4.	14.	0.	0.	0	11 Ahau	13 Zotz
1500	6 Jul	4.	15.	0.	0.	0	9 Ahau	18 Kayab
1480	24 Mar	4.	16.	0.	0.	0	7 Ahau	18 Ceh
1461	10 Dec	4.	17.	0.	0.	0	5 Ahau	18 Yaxkin
1441	27 Aug	4.	18.	0.	0.	0	3 Ahau	18 Uo
1421	14 May	4.	19.	0.	0.	0	1 Ahau	3 Pax
1401	29 Jan	5.	0.	0.	0.	0	12 Ahau	3 Zac
1382	17 Oct	5.	1.	0.	0.	0	10 Ahau	3 Xul
1362	4 Jul	5.	2.	0.	0.	0	8 Ahau	3 Pop
1342	20 Mar	5.	3.	0.	0.	0	6 Ahau	8 Kankin
1323	6 Dec	5.	4.	0.	0.	0	4 Ahau	8 Chen
1303	23 Aug	5.	5.	0.	0.	0	2 Ahau	8 Zotz
1283	11 May	5.	6.	0.	0.	0	13 Ahau	13 Kayab
1263	26 Jan	5.	7.	0.	0.	0	11 Ahau	13 Ceh
1244	13 Oct	5.	8.	0.	0.	0	9 Ahau	13 Yaxkin
1224	1 Jul	5.	9.	0.	0.	0	7 Ahau	13 Uo
1204	17 Mar	5.	10.	0.	0.	0	5 Ahau	18 Muan

Gregorian Date								
1185	3 Dec	5.	11.	0.	0.	0	3 Ahau	18 Yax
1165	20 Aug	5.	12.	0.	0.	0	1 Ahau	18 Tzec
1145	7 May	5.	13.	0.	0.	0	12 Ahau	3 Uayeb
1125	22 Jan	5.	14.	0.	0.	0	10 Ahau	3 Kankin
1106	9 Oct	5.	15.	0.	0.	0	8 Ahau	3 Chen
1086	27 Jun	5.	16.	0.	0.	0	6 Ahau	3 Zotz
1066	14 Mar	5.	17.	0.	0.	0	4 Ahau	8 Kayab
1047	29 Nov	5.	18.	0.	0.	0	2 Ahau	8 Ceh
1027	16 Aug	5.	19.	0.	0.	0	13 Ahau	8 Yaxkin
1007	3 May	6.	0.	0.	0.	0	11 Ahau	8 Uo
987	19 Jan	6.	1.	0.	0.	0	9 Ahau	13 Muan
968	6 Oct	6.	2.	0.	0.	0	7 Ahau	13 Yax
948	23 Jun	6.	3.	0.	0.	0	5 Ahau	13 Tzec
928	10 Mar	6.	4.	0.	0.	0	3 Ahau	18 Cumhu
909	26 Nov	6.	5.	0.	0.	0	1 Ahau	18 Mac
889	14 Aug	6.	6.	0.	0.	0	12 Ahau	18 Mol
869	1 May	6.	7.	0.	0.	0	10 Ahau	18 Zip
849	16 Jan	6.	8.	0.	0.	0	8 Ahau	3 Kayab
830	3 Oct	6.	9.	0.	0.	0	6 Ahau	3 Ceh
810	20 Jun	6.	10.	0.	0.	0	4 Ahau	3 Yax
790	7 Mar	6.	11.	0.	0.	0	2 Ahau	3 Uo
771	22 Nov	6.	12.	0.	0.	0	13 Ahau	8 Muan
751	9 Aug	6.	13.	0.	0.	0	11 Ahau	8 Yax
731	26 Apr	6.	14.	0.	0.	0	9 Ahau	8 Tzec
711	13 Jan	6.	15.	0.	0.	0	7 Ahau	13 Cumhu
692	29 Sep	6.	16.	0.	0.	0	5 Ahau	13 Mac
672	16 Jun	6.	17.	0.	0.	0	3 Ahau	13 Mol
652	3 Mar	6.	18.	0.	0.	0	1 Ahau	13 Zip
633	19 Nov	6.	19.	0.	0.	0	12 Ahau	18 Pax
613	6 Aug	7.	0.	0.	0.	0	10 Ahau	18 Zac
593	24 Apr	7.	1.	0.	0.	0	8 Ahau	18 Xul
573	9 Jan	7.	2.	0.	0.	0	6 Ahau	18 Pop
554	26 Sep	7.	3.	0.	0.	0	4 Ahau	3 Muan
534	13 Jun	7.	4.	0.	0.	0	2 Ahau	3 Yax
514	28 Feb	7.	5.	0.	0.	0	13 Ahau	3 Tzec
495	16 Nov	7.	6.	0.	0.	0	11 Ahau	8 Cumhu
475	3 Aug	7.	7.	0.	0.	0	9 Ahau	8 Mac
455	20 Apr	7.	8.	0.	0.	0	7 Ahau	8 Mol
435	5 Jan	7.	9.	0.	0.	0	5 Ahau	8 Zip
416	22 Sep	7.	10.	0.	0.	0	3 Ahau	13 Pax
396	9 Jun	7.	11.	0.	0.	0	1 Ahau	13 Zac
376	24 Feb	7.	12.	0.	0.	0	12 Ahau	13 Xul
357	12 Nov	7.	13.	0.	0.	0	10 Ahau	13 Pop
337	30 Jul	7.	14.	0.	0.	0	8 Ahau	18 Kankin
317	16 Apr	7.	15.	0.	0.	0	6 Ahau	18 Chen
297	2 Jan	7.	16.	0.	0.	0	4 Ahau	18 Zotz
278	19 Sep	7.	17.	0.	0.	0	2 Ahau	3 Cumhu
258	6 Jun	7.	18.	0.	0.	0	13 Ahau	3 Mac
238	21 Feb	7.	19.	0.	0.	0	11 Ahau	3 Mol

Gregorian Date								
219	7 Nov	8.	0.	0.	0.	0	9 Ahau	3 Zip
199	26 Jul	8.	1.	0.	0.	0	7 Ahau	8 Pax
179	13 Apr	8.	2.	0.	0.	0	5 Ahau	8 Zac
160	29 Dec	8.	3.	0.	0.	0	3 Ahau	8 Xul
140	15 Sep	8.	4.	0.	0.	0	1 Ahau	8 Pop
120	2 Jun	8.	5.	0.	0.	0	12 Ahau	13 Kankin
100	17 Feb	8.	6.	0.	0.	0	10 Ahau	13 Chen
81	5 Nov	8.	7.	0.	0.	0	8 Ahau	13 Zotz
61	23 Jul	8.	8.	0.	0.	0	6 Ahau	18 Kayab
41	9 Apr	8.	9.	0.	0.	0	4 Ahau	18 Ceh
22	25 Dec	8.	10.	0.	0.	0	2 Ahau	18 Yaxkin
2	12 Sep	8.	11.	0.	0.	0	13 Ahau	18 Uo
18	30 May	8.	12.	0.	0.	0	11 Ahau	3 Pax
37	14 Feb	8.	13.	0.	0.	0	9 Ahau	3 Zac
57	1 Nov	8.	14.	0.	0.	0	7 Ahau	3 Xul
77	19 Jul	8.	15.	0.	0.	0	5 Ahau	3 Pop
97	5 Apr	8.	16.	0.	0.	0	3 Ahau	8 Kankin
116*	22 Dec	8.	17.	0.	0.	0	1 Ahau	8 Chen
136*	8 Sep	8.	18.	0.	0.	0	12 Ahau	8 Zotz
156*	26 May	8.	19.	0.	0.	0	10 Ahau	13 Kayab
176*	10 Feb	9.	0.	0.	0.	0	8 Ahau	13 Ceh
195	29 Oct	9.	1.	0.	0.	0	6 Ahau	13 Yaxkin
215	17 Jul	9.	2.	0.	0.	0	4 Ahau	13 Uo
235	3 Apr	9.	3.	0.	0.	0	2 Ahau	18 Muan
254	18 Dec	9.	4.	0.	0.	0	13 Ahau	18 Yax
274	5 Sep	9.	5.	0.	0.	0	11 Ahau	18 Tzec
294	23 May	9.	6.	0.	0.	0	9 Ahau	3 Uayeb
314	8 Feb	9.	7.	0.	0.	0	7 Ahau	3 Kankin
333	26 Oct	9.	8.	0.	0.	0	5 Ahau	3 Chen
353	13 Jul	9.	9.	0.	0.	0	3 Ahau	3 Zotz
373	30 Mar	9.	10.	0.	0.	0	1 Ahau	8 Kayab
392*	15 Dec	9.	11.	0.	0.	0	12 Ahau	8 Ceh
412*	1 Sep	9.	12.	0.	0.	0	10 Ahau	8 Yaxkin
432*	19 May	9.	13.	0.	0.	0	8 Ahau	8 Uo
452*	3 Feb	9.	14.	0.	0.	0	6 Ahau	13 Muan
471	22 Oct	9.	15.	0.	0.	0	4 Ahau	13 Yax
491	9 Jul	9.	16.	0.	0.	0	2 Ahau	13 Tzec
511	27 Mar	9.	17.	0.	0.	0	13 Ahau	18 Cumhu
530	12 Dec	9.	18.	0.	0.	0	11 Ahau	18 Mac
550	29 Aug	9.	19.	0.	0.	0	9 Ahau	18 Mol
570	17 May	10.	0.	0.	0.	0	7 Ahau	18 Zip
590	31 Jan	10.	1.	0.	0.	0	5 Ahau	3 Kayab
609	19 Oct	10.	2.	0.	0.	0	3 Ahau	3 Ceh
629	6 Jul	10.	3.	0.	0.	0	1 Ahau	3 Yaxkin
649	23 Mar	10.	4.	0.	0.	0	12 Ahau	3 Uo
668*	8 Dec	10.	5.	0.	0.	0	10 Ahau	8 Muan
688*	25 Aug	10.	6.	0.	0.	0	8 Ahau	8 Yax
708*	13 May	10.	7.	0.	0.	0	6 Ahau	8 Tzec
728*	28 Jan	10.	8.	0.	0.	0	4 Ahau	13 Cumhu
747	16 Oct	10.	9.	0.	0.	0	2 Ahau	13 Mac

Gregorian Date									
767	3 Jul	10.	10.	0.	0.	0	13 Ahau	13 Mol
787	20 Mar	10.	11.	0.	0.	0	11 Ahau	13 Zip
806	5 Dec	10.	12.	0.	0.	0	9 Ahau	18 Pax
826	22 Aug	10.	13.	0.	0.	0	7 Ahau	18 Zac
846	9 May	10.	14.	0.	0.	0	5 Ahau	18 Xul
866	24 Jan	10.	15.	0.	0.	0	3 Ahau	18 Pop
885	11 Oct	10.	16.	0.	0.	0	1 Ahau	3 Muan
905	29 Jun	10.	17.	0.	0.	0	12 Ahau	3 Yax
925	16 Mar	10.	18.	0.	0.	0	10 Ahau	3 Tzec
944*	1 Dec	10.	19.	0.	0.	0	8 Ahau	8 Cumhu
964*	18 Aug	11.	0.	0.	0.	0	6 Ahau	8 Mac
984*	5 May	11.	1.	0.	0.	0	4 Ahau	8 Mol
1004*	22 Jan	11.	2.	0.	0.	0	2 Ahau	8 Zip
1023	9 Oct	11.	3.	0.	0.	0	13 Ahau	13 Pax
1043	26 Jun	11.	4.	0.	0.	0	11 Ahau	13 Zac
1063	13 Mar	11.	5.	0.	0.	0	9 Ahau	13 Xul
1082	28 Nov	11.	6.	0.	0.	0	7 Ahau	13 Pop
1102	16 Aug	11.	7.	0.	0.	0	5 Ahau	18 Kankin
1122	3 May	11.	8.	0.	0.	0	3 Ahau	18 Chen
1142	18 Jan	11.	9.	0.	0.	0	1 Ahau	18 Zotz
1161	5 Oct	11.	10.	0.	0.	0	12 Ahau	3 Cumhu
1181	22 Jun	11.	11.	0.	0.	0	10 Ahau	3 Mac
1201	9 Mar	11.	12.	0.	0.	0	8 Ahau	3 Mol
1220*	24 Nov	11.	13.	0.	0.	0	6 Ahau	3 Zip
1240*	11 Aug	11.	14.	0.	0.	0	4 Ahau	8 Pax
1260*	28 Apr	11.	15.	0.	0.	0	2 Ahau	8 Zac
1280*	14 Jan	11.	16.	0.	0.	0	13 Ahau	8 Xul
1299	1 Oct	11.	17.	0.	0.	0	11 Ahau	8 Pop
1319	18 Jun	11.	18.	0.	0.	0	9 Ahau	13 Kankin
1339	5 Mar	11.	19.	0.	0.	0	7 Ahau	13 Chen
1358	21 Nov	12.	0.	0.	0.	0	5 Ahau	13 Zotz
1378	8 Aug	12.	1.	0.	0.	0	3 Ahau	18 Kayab
1398	25 Apr	12.	2.	0.	0.	0	1 Ahau	18 Ceh
1418	11 Jan	12.	3.	0.	0.	0	12 Ahau	18 Yaxkin
1437	28 Sep	12.	4.	0.	0.	0	10 Ahau	18 Uo
1457	15 Jun	12.	5.	0.	0.	0	8 Ahau	3 Pax
1477	2 Mar	12.	6.	0.	0.	0	6 Ahau	3 Zac
1496*	17 Nov	12.	7.	0.	0.	0	4 Ahau	3 Xul
1516*	5 Aug	12.	8.	0.	0.	0	2 Ahau	3 Pop
1536*	22 Apr	12.	9.	0.	0.	0	13 Ahau	8 Kankin
1556*	7 Jan	12.	10.	0.	0.	0	11 Ahau	8 Chen
1575	25 Sep	12.	11.	0.	0.	0	9 Ahau	8 Zotz
1595	12 Jun	12.	12.	0.	0.	0	7 Ahau	13 Kayab
1615	27 Feb	12.	13.	0.	0.	0	5 Ahau	13 Ceh
1634	14 Nov	12.	14.	0.	0.	0	3 Ahau	13 Yaxkin
1654	1 Aug	12.	15.	0.	0.	0	1 Ahau	13 Uo
1674	18 Apr	12.	16.	0.	0.	0	12 Ahau	18 Muan
1694	3 Jan	12.	17.	0.	0.	0	10 Ahau	18 Yax
1713	21 Sep	12.	18.	0.	0.	0	8 Ahau	18 Tzec
1733	8 Jun	12.	19.	0.	0.	0	6 Ahau	3 Uayeb

Gregorian Date								
1753	23 Feb	13.	0.	0.	0.	0	4 Ahau	3 Kankin
1772*	10 Nov	13.	1.	0.	0.	0	2 Ahau	3 Chen
1792*	28 Jul	13.	2.	0.	0.	0	13 Ahau	3 Zotz
1812*	15 Apr	13.	3.	0.	0.	0	11 Ahau	8 Kayab
1832*	1 Jan	13.	4.	0.	0.	0	9 Ahau	8 Ceh
1851	18 Sep	13.	5.	0.	0.	0	7 Ahau	8 Yaxkin
1871	5 Jun	13.	6.	0.	0.	0	5 Ahau	8 Uo
1891	20 Feb	13.	7.	0.	0.	0	3 Ahau	13 Muan
1910	8 Nov	13.	8.	0.	0.	0	1 Ahau	13 Yax
1930	26 Jul	13.	9.	0.	0.	0	12 Ahau	13 Tzec
1950	12 Apr	13.	10.	0.	0.	0	10 Ahau	18 Cumhu
1969	28 Dec	13.	11.	0.	0.	0	8 Ahau	18 Mac
1989	14 Sep	13.	12.	0.	0.	0	6 Ahau	18 Mol
2009	1 Jun	13.	13.	0.	0.	0	4 Ahau	18 Zip

PAVON ABREU'S COUNT IN TUNS

Gregorian Date								
3113	12 Aug	13.	0.	0.	0.	0	4 Ahau	8 Cumhú
3112	6 Aug	13.	0.	1.	0.	0	13 Ahau	3 Chmhú
3111	1 Aug	13.	0.	2.	0.	0	9 Ahau	18 Kayab
3110	27 Jul	13.	0.	3.	0.	0	5 Ahau	13 Kayab
3109	22 Jul	13.	0.	4.	0.	0	1 Ahau	8 Kayab
3108	16 Jul	13.	0.	5.	0.	0	10 Ahau	3 Kayab
3107	11 Jul	13.	0.	6.	0.	0	6 Ahau	18 Pax
3106	6 Jul	13.	0.	7.	0.	0	2 Ahau	13 Pax
3105	1 Jul	13.	0.	8.	0.	0	11 Ahau	8 Pax
3104	25 Jun	13.	0.	9.	0.	0	7 Ahau	3 Pax
3103	20 Jun	13.	0.	10.	0.	0	3 Ahau	18 Muan
3102	15 Jun	13.	0.	11.	0.	0	12 Ahau	13 Muan
3101	10 Jun	13.	0.	12.	0.	0	8 Ahau	8 Muan
3100	5 Jun	13.	0.	13.	0.	0	4 Ahau	3 Muan
3099	31 May	13.	0.	14.	0.	0	13 Ahau	18 Kankin
3098	26 May	13.	0.	15.	0.	0	9 Ahau	13 Kankin
3097	21 May	13.	0.	16.	0.	0	5 Ahau	8 Kankin
3096	15 May	13.	0.	17.	0.	0	1 Ahau	3 Kankin
3095	10 May	13.	0.	18.	0.	0	10 Ahau	18 Mac
3094	5 May	13.	0.	19.	0.	0	6 Ahau	13 Mac
3093	30 Apr	13.	1.	0	0.	0	2 Ahau	8 Mac
3092	24 Apr	13.	1.	1.	0.	0	11 Ahau	3 Mac
3091	19 Apr	13.	1.	2.	0.	0	7 Ahau	18 Ceh
3090	14 Apr	13.	1.	3.	0.	0	3 Ahau	13 Ceh
3089	9 Apr	13.	1.	4.	0.	0	12 Ahau	8 Ceh
3088	3 Apr	13.	1.	5.	0.	0	8 Ahau	3 Ceh
3087	29 Mar	13.	1.	6.	0.	0	4 Ahau	18 Zac
3086	24 Mar	13.	1.	7.	0.	0	13 Ahau	13 Zac
3085	19 Mar	13.	1.	8.	0.	0	9 Ahau	8 Zac
3084	13 Mar	13.	1.	9.	0.	0	5 Ahau	3 Zac
3083	8 Mar	13.	1.	10.	0.	0	1 Ahau	18 Yax
3082	3 Mar	13.	1.	11.	0.	0	10 Ahau	13 Yax
3081	26 Feb	13.	1.	12.	0.	0	6 Ahau	8 Yax

Gregorian Date								
3080	20 Feb	13.	1.	13.	0.	0	2 Ahau	3 Yax
3079	15 Feb	13.	1.	14.	0.	0	11 Ahau	18 Chen
3078	10 Feb	13.	1.	15.	0.	0	7 Ahau	13 Chen
3077	5 Feb	13.	1.	16.	0.	0	3 Ahau	8 Chen
3076	30 Jan	13.	1.	17.	0.	0	12 Ahau	3 Chen
3075	25 Jan	13.	1.	18.	0.	0	8 Ahau	18 Mol
3074	20 Jan	13.	1.	19.	0.	0	4 Ahau	13 Mol
3073	15 Jan	13.	2.	0.	0.	0	13 Ahau	8 Mol
3072	9 Jan	13.	2.	1.	0.	0	9 Ahau	3 Mol
3071)	4 Jan	13.	2.	2.	0.	0	5 Ahau	18 Yaxkin
3071)	30 Dec	13.	2.	3.	0.	0	1 Ahau	13 Yaxkin
3070	25 Dec	13.	2.	4.	0.	0	10 Ahau	8 Yaxkin
3069	20 Dec	13.	2.	5.	0.	0	6 Ahau	3 Yaxkin
3068	14 Dec	13.	2.	6.	0.	0	2 Ahau	18 Xul
3067	9 Dec	13.	2.	7.	0.	0	11 Ahau	13 Xul
3066	4 Dec	13.	2.	8.	0.	0	7 Ahau	8 Xul
3065	29 Nov	13.	2.	9.	0.	0	3 Ahau	3 Xul
3064	23 Nov	13.	2.	10.	0.	0	12 Ahau	18 Tzec
3063	18 Nov	13.	2.	11.	0.	0	8 Ahau	13 Tzec
3062	13 Nov	13.	2.	12.	0.	0	4 Ahau	8 Tzec
3061	8 Nov	13.	2.	13.	0.	0	13 Ahau	3 Tzec
3060	2 Nov	13.	2.	14.	0.	0	9 Ahau	18 Zotz
3059	28 Oct	13.	2.	15.	0.	0	5 Ahau	13 Zotz
3058	23 Oct	13.	2.	16.	0.	0	1 Ahau	8 Zotz
3057	18 Oct	13.	2.	17.	0.	0	10 Ahau	3 Zotz
3056	12 Oct	13.	2.	18.	0.	0	6 Ahau	18 Zip
3055	7 Oct	13.	2.	19.	0.	0	2 Ahau	13 Zip
3054	2 Oct	13.	3.	0.	0.	0	11 Ahau	8 Zip
3053	27 Sep	13.	3.	1.	0.	0	7 Ahau	3 Zip
3052	21 Sep	13.	3.	2.	0.	0	3 Ahau	18 Uo
3051	16 Sep	13.	3.	3.	0.	0	12 Ahau	13 Uo
3050	11 Sep	13.	3.	4.	0.	0	8 Ahau	8 Uo
3049	6 Sep	13.	3.	5.	0.	0	4 Ahau	3 Uo
3048	31 Aug	13.	3.	6.	0.	0	13 Ahau	18 Pop
3047	26 Aug	13.	3.	7.	0.	0	9 Ahau	13 Pop
3046	21 Aug	13.	3.	8.	0.	0	5 Ahau	8 Pop
3045	16 Aug	13.	3.	9.	0.	0	1 Ahau	3 Pop
3044	10 Aug	13.	3.	10.	0.	0	10 Ahau	3 Uayeb
3043	5 Aug	13.	3.	11.	0.	0	6 Ahau	18 Cumhú
3042	31 Jul	13.	3.	12.	0.	0	2 Ahau	13 Cumhú
3041	26 Jul	13.	3.	13.	0.	0	11 Ahau	8 Cumhú
3040	20 Jul	13.	3.	14.	0.	0	7 Ahau	3 Cumhú
3039	15 Jul	13.	3.	15.	0.	0	3 Ahau	18 Kayab
3038	10 Jul	13.	3.	16.	0.	0	12 Ahau	13 Kayab
3037	5 Jul	13.	3.	17.	0.	0	8 Ahau	8 Kayab
3036	29 Jul	13.	3.	18.	0.	0	4 Ahau	3 Kayab
3035	24 Jun	13.	3.	19.	0.	0	13 Ahau	18 Pax
629	11 Jun	6.	6.	0.	0.	0	12 Ahau	18 Mol
628	5 Jun	6.	6.	1.	0.	0	8 Ahau	13 Mol
627	31 May	6.	6.	2.	0.	0	4 Ahau	8 Mol

Gregorian Date								
626	26 May	6.	6.	3.	0.	0	13 Ahau	3 Mol
625	21 May	6.	6.	4.	0.	0	9 Ahau	18 Yaxkin
624	15 May	6.	6.	5.	0.	0	5 Ahau	13 Yaxkin
623	10 May	6.	6.	6.	0.	0	1 Ahau	8 Yaxkin
622	5 May	6.	6.	7.	0.	0	10 Ahau	3 Yaxkin
621	30 Apr	6.	6.	8.	0.	0	6 Ahau	18 Xul
620	24 Apr	6.	6.	9.	0.	0	2 Ahau	13 Xul
619	19 Apr	6.	6.	10.	0.	0	11 Ahau	8 Xul
618	14 Apr	6.	6.	11.	0.	0	7 Ahau	3 Xul
617	9 Apr	6.	6.	12.	0.	0	3 Ahau	18 Tzec
616	3 Apr	6.	6.	13.	0.	0	12 Ahau	13 Tzec
615	29 Mar	6.	6.	14.	0.	0	8 Ahau	8 Tzec
614	24 Mar	6.	6.	15.	0.	0	4 Ahau	3 Tzec
613	19 Mar	6.	6.	16.	0.	0	13 Ahau	18 Zotz
612	13 Mar	6.	6.	17.	0.	0	9 Ahau	13 Zotz
611	8 Mar	6.	6.	18.	0.	0	5 Ahau	8 Zotz
610	3 Mar	6.	6.	19.	0.	0	1 Ahau	3 Zotz
609	26 Feb	6.	7.	0.	0.	0	10 Ahau	18 Zip
608	20 Feb	6.	7.	1.	0.	0	6 Ahau	13 Zip
607	15 Feb	6.	7.	2.	0.	0	2 Ahau	8 Zip
606	10 Feb	6.	7.	3.	0.	0	11 Ahau	3 Zip
605	5 Feb	6.	7.	4.	0.	0	7 Ahau	18 Uo
604	30 Jan	6.	7.	5.	0.	0	3 Ahau	13 Uo
603	25 Jan	6.	7.	6.	0.	0	12 Ahau	8 Uo
602	20 Jan	6.	7.	7.	0.	0	8 Ahau	3 Uo
601	15 Jan	6.	7.	8.	0.	0	4 Ahau	18 Pop
600	10 Jan	6.	7.	9.	0.	0	13 Ahau	13 Pop
599)	5 Jan	6.	7.	10.	0.	0	9 Ahau	8 Pop
599)	31 Dec	6.	7.	11.	0.	0	5 Ahau	3 Pop
598	26 Dec	6.	7.	12.	0.	0	1 Ahau	3 Uayeb
597	21 Dec	6.	7.	13.	0.	0	10 Ahau	18 Cumhú
596	15 Dec	6.	7.	14.	0.	0	6 Ahau	13 Cumhú
595	10 Dec	6.	7.	15.	0.	0	2 Ahau	8 Cumhú
594	5 Dec	6.	7.	16.	0.	0	11 Ahau	3 Cumhú
593	30 Nov	6.	7.	17.	0.	0	7 Ahau	18 Kayab
592	24 Nov	6.	7.	18.	0.	0	3 Ahau	13 Kayab
591	19 Nov	6.	7.	19.	0.	0	12 Ahau	8 Kayab
590	14 Nov	6.	8.	0.	0.	0	8 Ahau	3 Kayab
589	9 Nov	6.	8.	1.	0.	0	4 Ahau	18 Pax
588	3 Nov	6.	8.	2.	0.	0	13 Ahau	13 Pax
587	29 Oct	6.	8.	3.	0.	0	9 Ahau	8 Pax
586	24 Oct	6.	8.	4.	0.	0	5 Ahau	3 Pax
585	19 Oct	6.	8.	5.	0.	0	1 Ahau	18 Muan
584	13 Oct	6.	8.	6.	0.	0	10 Ahau	13 Muan
583	8 Oct	6.	8.	7.	0.	0	6 Ahau	8 Muan
582	3 Oct	6.	8.	8.	0.	0	2 Ahau	3 Muan
581	28 Sep	6.	8.	9.	0.	0	11 Ahau	18 Kankin
580	22 Sep	6.	8.	10.	0.	0	7 Ahau	13 Kankin
579	17 Sep	6.	8.	11.	0.	0	3 Ahau	8 Kankin
578	12 Sep	6.	8.	12.	0.	0	12 Ahau	3 Kankin
577	7 Sep	6.	8.	13.	0.	0	8 Ahau	18 Mac

Gregorian Date								
576	1 Sep	6.	8.	14.	0.	0	4 Ahau	13 Mac
575	27 Aug	6.	8.	15.	0.	0	13 Ahau	8 Mac
574	22 Aug	6.	8.	16.	0.	0	9 Ahau	3 Mac
573	17 Aug	6.	8.	17.	0.	0	5 Ahau	18 Ceh
572	11 Aug	6.	8.	18.	0.	0	1 Ahau	13 Ceh
571	6 Aug	6.	8.	19.	0.	0	10 Ahau	8 Ceh
570	1 Aug	6.	9.	0.	0.	0	6 Ahau	3 Ceh
569	27 Jul	6.	9.	1.	0.	0	2 Ahau	18 Zac
568	21 Jul	6.	9.	2.	0.	0	11 Ahau	13 Zac
567	16 Jul	6.	9.	3.	0.	0	7 Ahau	8 Zac
566	11 Jul	6.	9.	4.	0.	0	3 Ahau	3 Zac
565	6 Jul	6.	9.	5.	0.	0	12 Ahau	18 Yax
564	30 Jun	6.	9.	6.	0.	0	8 Ahau	13 Yax
563	25 Jun	6.	9.	7.	0.	0	4 Ahau	8 Yax
562	20 Jun	6.	9.	8.	0.	0	13 Ahau	3 Yax
561	15 Jun	6.	9.	9.	0.	0	9 Ahau	18 Chen
560	9 Jun	6.	9.	10.	0.	0	5 Ahau	13 Chen
559	4 Jun	6.	9.	11.	0.	0	1 Ahau	8 Chen
558	30 May	6.	9.	12.	0.	0	10 Ahau	3 Chen
557	25 May	6.	9.	13.	0.	0	6 Ahau	18 Mol
556	19 May	6.	9.	14.	0.	0	2 Ahau	13 Mol
555	14 May	6.	9.	15.	0.	0	11 Ahau	8 Mol
554	9 May	6.	9.	16.	0.	0	7 Ahau	3 Mol
553	4 May	6.	9.	17.	0.	0	3 Ahau	18 Yaxkin
552	28 Apr	6.	9.	18.	0.	0	12 Ahau	13 Yaxkin
551	23 Apr	6.	9.	19.	0.	0	8 Ahau	8 Yaxkin
77	29 May	7.	14.	0.	0.	0	8 Ahau	18 Kankin
76	23 May	7.	14.	1.	0.	0	4 Ahau	13 Kankin
75	18 May	7.	14.	2.	0.	0	13 Ahau	8 Kankin
74	13 May	7.	14.	3.	0.	0	9 Ahau	3 Kankin
73	8 May	7.	14.	4.	0.	0	5 Ahau	18 Mac
72	2 May	7.	14.	5.	0.	0	1 Ahau	13 Mac
71	27 Apr	7.	14.	6.	0.	0	10 Ahau	8 Mac
70	22 Apr	7.	14.	7.	0.	0	6 Ahau	3 Mac
69	17 Apr	7.	14.	8.	0.	0	2 Ahau	18 Ceh
68	11 Apr	7.	14.	9.	0.	0	11 Ahau	13 Ceh
67	6 Apr	7.	14.	10.	0.	0	7 Ahau	8 Ceh
66	1 Apr	7.	14.	11.	0.	0	3 Ahau	3 Ceh
65	27 Mar	7.	14.	12.	0.	0	12 Ahau	18 Zac
64	21 Mar	7.	14.	13.	0.	0	8 Ahau	13 Zac
63	16 Mar	7.	14.	14.	0.	0	4 Ahau	8 Zac
62	11 Mar	7.	14.	15.	0.	0	13 Ahau	3 Zac
61	6 Mar	7.	14.	16.	0.	0	9 Ahau	18 Yax
60	28 Feb	7.	14.	17.	0.	0	5 Ahau	13 Yax
59	23 Feb	7.	14.	18.	0.	0	1 Ahau	8 Yax
58	18 Feb	7.	14.	19.	0.	0	10 Ahau	3 Yax
57	13 Feb	7.	15.	0.	0.	0	6 Ahau	18 Chen
56	7 Feb	7.	15.	1.	0.	0	2 Ahau	13 Chen
55	2 Feb	7.	15.	2.	0.	0	11 Ahau	8 Chen
54	28 Jan	7.	15.	3.	0.	0	7 Ahau	3 Chen

Gregorian Date								
53	23 Jan	7.	15.	4.	0.	0	3 Ahau	18 Mol
52	17 Jan	7.	15.	5.	0.	0	12 Ahau	13 Mol
51	12 Jan	7.	15.	6.	0.	0	8 Ahau	8 Mol
50	7 Jan	7.	15.	7.	0.	0	4 Ahau	3 Mol
49)	2 Jan	7.	15.	8.	0.	0	13 Ahau	18 Yaxkin
49)	28 Dec	7.	15.	9.	0.	0	9 Ahau	13 Yaxkin
48	22 Dec	7.	15.	10.	0.	0	5 Ahau	8 Yaxkin
47	17 Dec	7.	15.	11.	0.	0	1 Ahau	3 Yaxkin
46	12 Dec	7.	15.	12.	0.	0	10 Ahau	18 Xul
45	7 Dec	7.	15.	13.	0.	0	6 Ahau	13 Xul
44	1 Dec	7.	15.	14.	0.	0	2 Ahau	8 Xul
43	26 Nov	7.	15.	15.	0.	0	11 Ahau	3 Xul
42	21 Nov	7.	15.	16.	0.	0	7 Ahau	18 Tzec
41	16 Nov	7.	15.	17.	0.	0	3 Ahau	13 Tzec
40	10 Nov	7.	15.	18.	0.	0	12 Ahau	8 Tzec
39	5 Nov	7.	15.	19.	0.	0	8 Ahau	3 Tzec
38	31 Oct	7.	16.	0.	0.	0	4 Ahau	18 Zotz
37	26 Oct	7.	16.	1.	0.	0	13 Ahau	13 Zotz
36	20 Oct	7.	16.	2.	0.	0	9 Ahau	8 Zotz
35	15 Oct	7.	16.	3.	0.	0	5 Ahau	3 Zotz
34	10 Oct	7.	16.	4.	0.	0	1 Ahau	18 Zip
33	5 Oct	7.	16.	5.	0.	0	10 Ahau	13 Zip
32	29 Sep	7.	16.	6.	0.	0	6 Ahau	8 Zip
31	24 Sep	7.	16.	7.	0.	0	2 Ahau	3 Zip
30	19 Sep	7.	16.	8.	0.	0	11 Ahau	18 Uo
29	14 Sep	7.	16.	9.	0.	0	7 Ahau	13 Uo
28	8 Sep	7.	16.	10.	0.	0	3 Ahau	8 Uo
27	3 Sep	7.	16.	11.	0.	0	12 Ahau	3 Uo
26	29 Aug	7.	16.	12.	0.	0	8 Ahau	18 Pop
25	24 Aug	7.	16.	13.	0.	0	4 Ahau	13 Pop
24	18 Aug	7.	16.	14.	0.	0	13 Ahau	8 Pop
23	13 Aug	7.	16.	15.	0.	0	9 Ahau	3 Pop
22	8 Aug	7.	16.	16.	0.	0	5 Ahau	3 Uayeb
21	3 Aug	7.	16.	17.	0.	0	1 Ahau	18 Cumhú
20	28 Jul	7.	16.	18.	0.	0	10 Ahau	13 Cumhú
19	23 Jul	7.	16.	19.	0.	0	6 Ahau	8 Cumhú
18	18 Jul	7.	17.	0.	0.	0	2 Ahau	3 Cumhú
17	13 Jul	7.	17.	1.	0.	0	11 Ahau	18 Kayab
16	7 Jul	7.	17.	2.	0.	0	7 Ahau	13 Kayab
15	2 Jul	7.	17.	3.	0.	0	3 Ahau	8 Kayab
14	27 Jun	7.	17.	4.	0.	0	12 Ahau	3 Kayab
13	22 Jun	7.	17.	5.	0.	0	8 Ahau	18 Pax
12	16 Jun	7.	17.	6.	0.	0	4 Ahau	13 Pax
11	11 Jun	7.	17.	7.	0.	0	13 Ahau	8 Pax
10	6 Jun	7.	17.	8.	0.	0	9 Ahau	3 Pax
9	1 Jun	7.	17.	9.	0.	0	5 Ahau	18 Muan
8	26 May	7.	17.	10.	0.	0	1 Ahau	13 Muan
7	21 May	7.	17.	11.	0.	0	10 Ahau	8 Muan
6	16 May	7.	17.	12.	0.	0	6 Ahau	3 Muan
5	11 May	7.	17.	13.	0.	0	2 Ahau	18 Kankin
4	5 May	7.	17.	14.	0.	0	11 Ahau	13 Kankin

Gregorian Date								
3	30 Apr	7.	17.	15.	0.	0	7 Ahau	8 Kankin
2	25 Apr	7.	17.	16.	0.	0	3 Ahau	3 Kankin
1	20 Apr	7.	17.	17.	0.	0	12 Ahau	18 Mac
0	15 Apr	7.	17.	18.	0.	0	8 Ahau	13 Mac
1	10 Apr	7.	17.	19.	0.	0	4 Ahau	8 Mac
2	5 Apr	7.	18.	0.	0.	0	13 Ahau	3 Mac
3	31 Mar	7.	18.	1.	0.	0	9 Ahau	18 Ceh
4*	25 Mar	7.	18.	2.	0.	0	5 Ahau	13 Ceh
5	20 Mar	7.	18.	3.	0.	0	1 Ahau	8 Ceh
6	15 Mar	7.	18.	4.	0.	0	10 Ahau	3 Ceh
7	10 Mar	7.	18.	5.	0.	0	6 Ahau	18 Zac
8*	4 Mar	7.	18.	6.	0.	0	2 Ahau	13 Zac
9	27 Feb	7.	18.	7.	0.	0	11 Ahau	8 Zac
10	22 Feb	7.	18.	8.	0.	0	7 Ahau	3 Zac
11	17 Feb	7.	18.	9.	0.	0	3 Ahau	18 Yax
12*	11 Feb	7.	18.	10.	0.	0	12 Ahau	13 Yax
13	6 Feb	7.	18.	11.	0.	0	8 Ahau	8 Yax
14	1 Feb	7.	18.	12.	0.	0	4 Ahau	3 Yax
15	27 Jan	7.	18.	13.	0.	0	13 Ahau	18 Chen
16*	21 Jan	7.	18.	14.	0.	0	9 Ahau	13 Chen
17	16 Jan	7.	18.	15.	0.	0	5 Ahau	8 Chen
18	11 Jan	7.	18.	16.	0.	0	1 Ahau	3 Chen
19	6 Jan	7.	18.	17.	0.	0	10 Ahau	18 Mol
20*)	1 Jan	7.	18.	18.	0.	0	6 Ahau	13 Mol
20*)	26 Dec	7.	18.	19.	0.	0	2 Ahau	8 Mol
21	21 Dec	7.	19.	0.	0.	0	11 Ahau	3 Mol
22	16 Dec	7.	19.	1.	0.	0	7 Ahau	18 Yaxkin
23	11 Dec	7.	19.	2.	0.	0	3 Ahau	13 Yaxkin
24*	5 Dec	7.	19.	3.	0.	0	12 Ahau	8 Yaxkin
25	30 Nov	7.	19.	4.	0.	0	8 Ahau	3 Yaxkin
26	25 Nov	7.	19.	5.	0.	0	4 Ahau	18 Xul
27	20 Nov	7.	19.	6.	0.	0	13 Ahau	13 Xul
28*	14 Nov	7.	19.	7.	0.	0	9 Ahau	8 Xul
29	9 Nov	7.	19.	8.	0.	0	5 Ahau	3 Xul
30	4 Nov	7.	19.	9.	0.	0	1 Ahau	18 Tzec
31	30 Oct	7.	19.	10.	0.	0	10 Ahau	13 Tzec
32*	24 Oct	7.	19.	11.	0.	0	6 Ahau	8 Tzec
33	19 Oct	7.	19.	12.	0.	0	2 Ahau	3 Tzec
34	14 Oct	7.	19.	13.	0.	0	11 Ahau	18 Zotz
35	9 Oct	7.	19.	14.	0.	0	7 Ahau	13 Zotz
36*	3 Oct	7.	19.	15.	0.	0	3 Ahau	8 Zotz
37	28 Sep	7.	19.	16.	0.	0	12 Ahau	3 Zotz
38	23 Sep	7.	19.	17.	0.	0	8 Ahau	18 Zip
39	18 Sep	7.	19.	18.	0.	0	4 Ahau	13 Zip
40*	12 Sep	7.	19.	19.	0.	0	13 Ahau	8 Zip
41	7 Sep	8.	0.	0.	0.	0	9 Ahau	3 Zip
42	2 Sep	8.	0.	1.	0.	0	5 Ahau	18 Uo
43	28 Aug	8.	0.	2.	0.	0	1 Ahau	13 Uo
44*	22 Aug	8.	0.	3.	0.	0	10 Ahau	8 Uo

	Gregorian Date							
45	17 Aug	8.	0.	4.	0.	0	6 Ahau	3 Uo
46	12 Aug	8.	0.	5.	0.	0	2 Ahau	18 Pop
47	7 Aug	8.	0.	6.	0.	0	11 Ahau	13 Pop
48*	1 Aug	8.	0.	7.	0.	0	7 Ahau	8 Pop
49	27 Jul	8.	0.	8.	0.	0	3 Ahau	3 Pop
50	22 Jul	8.	0.	9.	0.	0	12 Ahau	3 Uayeb
51	17 Jul	8.	0.	10.	0.	0	8 Ahau	18 Cumhú
52*	11 Jul	8.	0.	11.	0.	0	4 Ahau	13 Cumhú
53	6 Jul	8.	0.	12.	0.	0	13 Ahau	8 Cumhú
54	1 Jul	8.	0.	13.	0.	0	9 Ahau	3 Cumhú
55	26 Jun	8.	0.	14.	0.	0	5 Ahau	18 Kayab
56*	20 Jun	8.	0.	15.	0.	0	1 Ahau	13 Kayab
57	15 Jun	8.	0.	16.	0.	0	10 Ahau	8 Kayab
58	10 Jun	8.	0.	17.	0.	0	6 Ahau	3 Kayab
59	5 Jun	8.	0.	18.	0.	0	2 Ahau	18 Pax
60*	30 May	8.	0.	19.	0.	0	11 Ahau	13 Pax
61	25 May	8.	1.	0.	0.	0	7 Ahau	8 Pax
62	20 May	8.	1.	1.	0.	0	3 Ahau	3 Pax
63	15 May	8.	1.	2.	0.	0	12 Ahau	18 Muan
64*	9 May	8.	1.	3.	0.	0	8 Ahau	13 Muan
65	4 May	8.	1.	4.	0.	0	4 Ahau	8 Muan
66	29 Apr	8.	1.	5.	0.	0	13 Ahau	3 Muan
67	24 Apr	8.	1.	6.	0.	0	9 Ahau	18 Kankin
68*	18 Apr	8.	1.	7.	0.	0	5 Ahau	13 Kankin
69	13 Apr	8.	1.	8.	0.	0	1 Ahau	8 Kankin
70	8 Apr	8.	1.	9.	0.	0	10 Ahau	3 Kankin
71	3 Apr	8.	1.	10.	0.	0	6 Ahau	18 Mac
72*	28 Mar	8.	1.	11.	0.	0	2 Ahau	13 Mac
73	23 Mar	8.	1.	12.	0.	0	11 Ahau	8 Mac
74	18 Mar	8.	1.	13.	0.	0	7 Ahau	3 Mac
75	13 Mar	8.	1.	14.	0.	0	3 Ahau	18 Ceh
76*	7 Mar	8.	1.	15.	0.	0	12 Ahau	13 Ceh
77	2 Mar	8.	1.	16.	0.	0	8 Ahau	8 Ceh
78	25 Feb	8.	1.	17.	0.	0	4 Ahau	3 Ceh
79	20 Feb	8.	1.	18.	0.	0	13 Ahau	18 Zac
80*	14 Feb	8.	1.	19.	0.	0	9 Ahau	13 Zac

WESTERN CALENDARS

EARLY NORTHERN EUROPEAN CALENDARS

During the seventh and eighth centuries, England and other areas conquered by the Scandinavians and other "barbarian" tribes employed a unique calendar. The calendar had a peculiar construction known as a "week-year." It consisted of 52 weeks of seven days, approximately 1¼ days less than the tropical year. In northern Europe the year was divided into two sections of 26 weeks each, one called winter and the other summer. These sections were reckoned as occurring about 13 weeks on either side of the solstices. In the south, where the climate was milder and the winter season shorter, only 22 weeks were considered winter and the balance of 30 weeks was called summer. The odd 1¼ days were intercalated from time to time as a extra week. In both the north and south, this period was added to the summer half of the year. The major festivals occurred at the beginning of the winter season, at the Winter Solstice and at the beginning of the summer season at the Summer Solstice. Most festivals were celebrated for a week. The year began with the start of summer.

The Celts developed another form of this calendar. They divided their year into quarters of 13 weeks each, with approximately seven weeks before each of the solstices and equinoxes and approximately six weeks after them. They considered the first day of each quarter a holiday and celebrated the New Year about the first of November. The major holidays were celebrated for about two weeks before and two weeks after August 1.

Although the moon does not figure prominently in most versions of this calendar, except as a timekeeper of shorter periods, the Celts apparently ran another time count simultaneously with the solar one. In France a bronze plate believed to be of Celtic origin was recently found. It shows a 62 month lunar reckoning with two intercalations to adjust it to the solar year. The authorities who found it suspect that it may be indicative of the use of the 19-year eclipse cycle. The plate divides each lunation, or month into halves, the waxing or light half of the full moon, and the waning or dark half. The plate also contains notations indicating which days were auspicious and which were inauspicious, suggesting such a calendar may have been used in conjunction with a set of astronomical tables of solar, lunar and planetary motion. However, researchers have found no traces of these tables.

These early calendars were gradually replaced by the Julian calendar as Christianity expanded throughout Europe. However, it remained in use for long periods in remote areas such as Lappland and Iceland. Although the Lapps had been converted to Christianity and had accepted, in theory at least, the Julian calendar, they clung to a 8-day week well into the 17th century. In Iceland the old calendar remained in use into the 20th century. Officially Iceland adopted the Gregorian calendar in 1700 but it was well into the 19th century before that country ceased using the old reckoning of a 364-day "week-year." And, in isolated areas, reckoning by the old style calendar only died out after World War II.

JULIAN AND GREGORIAN CALENDARS

In 46 B.C. Julius Caesar reformed the Roman calendar once more. On the advice of the astronomer Sosigenes, he discarded the concept of a lunar calendar with its intercalated months and established a completely solar calendar of 365 and ¼ days with the extra day added every four years. Caesar added 90 days to the year 46 B.C. (between November and February). Spring therefore began in March in 45 B.C. In order to maintain this seasonal position, he rearranged the number of days in each month. January, March, May, July, September and November were all to have 31 days. All other months except February would contain 30 days. February was to have 29 days in common years and 30 days in leap year. The year began on January 1.

After Caesar's death, the number of days in each month was rearranged. February was reduced to 28 days in common years and August was given an extra day. In order to avoid three successive months of 31 days, September and November were reduced to 30 days and October and December were given 31 days. The calendar was again changed during the reign of Augustus. Around 10 B.C. it was discovered that the priests who had charge of the calendar had added the leap day every third year rather than every fourth. In order to correct this no further leap years were added until 4 A.D.

In 325 A.D. the Council of Nicaea adopted the Julian Calendar as the official calendar of the church. Prior to that local calendars had been used in Christian areas not under Roman control. The Council, however, changed the era to the birth of Christ, 1 A.D. Because the Julian year contained 365 days and six hours, the surplus time gradually moved the vernal equinox from March 21 to March 11 by 1582. That year Pope Gregory XIII reformed the calendar to rectify the error. He surpressed 10 days in 1582 (October 5 became October 15) and decreed that no year ending in 00 should be a leap year unless divisible by 400. Thus 1700, 1800 and 1900 were not leap years but 2000 will be. The Gregorian calendar was accepted quickly by Roman Catholic countries. It was adopted by Spain, Portugal and some areas of Italy the same day it was in Rome. France adopted it in December 1582 and the Catholic states in Germany began using it the following year. The Protestant countries were slower to accept it. Protestant areas in Germany instituted it in 1700 as did most sections of Scandinavia. Sweden, however, decided to act cautiously. Instead of dropping the 10 days at once, it preferred to eliminate them gradually, beginning with the year 1700, which was made a common year. For an unknown reason, however, this process was not continued, so that for some years the calendar was a day ahead of the Julian calendar and 9 days behind the Gregorian one. To resolve the situation it reverted to the Old Style calendar, making 1712 a leap year by adding the day that had been omitted in 1700; this day was intercalated between February 29 and March 1, and named February 30. Although the New Style was successfully introduced in 1753 for the computation of Easter and the other movable feasts, it was not until 1844 that the Gregorian calendar was fully adopted. Consequently for several years Sweden celebrated Easter on a different date than the other Christian countries.

Great Britain waited until 1750 to adopt the Gregorian calendar and put it into effect in 1752. At the same time the beginning of the legal year was changed from March 25 to January 1. Scotland had done this in 1600. consequently year dates between these two areas vary for the period 1600 to 1752.

Russia continued to use the Julian calendar until the Revolution. Currently the Gregorian calendar is used in most areas of the world either as the primary calendar or in conjunction with local calendars. It is the primary calendar for international business and diplomacy.

JULIAN AND GREGORIAN CALENDAR CONVERSIONS

The following four tables can be used for converting the Julian (OS) calendar to the Gregorian (NS) calendar from October 4, 1582 (OS) through January 14, 1918 (NS). It can also be used to find the complete Julian calendar and Gregorian calendar for any year up to 2000.

In order to convert a date from Old Style to New Style, first find the country or area you are interested in on Table 1. The table gives the date the Gregorian calendar was instituted and the corresponding date of the Julian or other calendar. Then locate that year in Table 2. Beside the year you will find references to two of the 14 calendars in the Perpetual Calendar (Table 4). By referring to these calendars in the Perpetual Calendar, you will find the complete calendar for the year.

In order to use the Perpetual calendar to survey a year from 1918 to 2000 proceed immediately to Table 2. To find the complete Julian calendar for a year from 1 A.D. to 2000 procede to Table 3.

Note that the years 1600, 1700, 1800 and 1900 were leap years in the Julian calendar. In the Gregorian calendar the year 1600 was a leap year, but the years 1700,1800, and 1900 were not. The year 2000 wil be. The century ends with 00 not 99. The new century begins with the year 01.

TABLE 1

Country	Province	Year	Date	Day
ALASKA	as Russia until	1867	1 day less for meridian	
	U.S.A.	1867	18 Oct.	(5 Oct OS until)
		1900	20 Aug	7 Aug
ALSACE		1682	16 Feb	5 Feb
AUSTRIA	Tyrol	1583	16 Oct	6 Oct
	Carinthia		25 Dec	5 Dec
	Styria			
	Bohemia	1584	17 Jan	7 Jan
BELGIUM		1583	1 Jan	22 Dec (1582)
BULGARIA	Part	1915	13 Nov	1 Nov
	Part	1920	17 Sep	4 Sep
CANADA	English colonies	1752	14 Sep	3 Sep
		also New Year from 25 Mar to 1 Jan.		
	French colonies	As France		
CHINA		1912	12 Feb Chinese calendar	
DENMARK		1700	1 Mar	19 Feb
ENGLAND		1752	14 Sep	3 Sep
		also New Year from 25 Mar to 1 Jan		
ESTONIA		1918	15 Feb	2 Feb
FINLAND		1918	14 Jan	1 Jan
FRANCE		1582	20 Dec	10 Dec
	Revolution Calendar	1793	26 Nov through	
		1805	31 Dec	
		1806	1 Jan	

Country	Province	Year	Date	Day
GERMANY	*Catholic*			
	some Provinces	1583	14 Nov	4 Nov
	rest, except	1584	17 Jan	7 Jan
	Bavaria	1583	16 Oct	6 Oct
	Strassburg	1682	1 Mar	19 Feb
	Protestant			
	Saxony	1699	15 Nov	4 Nov
	Brandenberg			
	Hesse			
	Nuremburg	1699	3 Oct	22 Sep
	Ulm			
	Augsburg			
	Rhenish Palatinate			
	Utrecht (part)	1700	12 Dec	1 Dec
GREECE	Adopted Julian (O.S.) calendar 1846			
	part	1916	28 Jul	15 Jul
	rest	1920	18 Mar	5 Mar
	(except where Orthodox church is still O.S.)			
HOLLAND	Flanders	1583	1 Jan	22 Dec
	S. Provinces			
	Gelderland	1700	12 Jul	1 Jul
	Utrecht (part)			
	Overyssel			
	Friesland	1701	12 Jan	31 Dec
	Groningen			(1700)
HUNGARY		1582	1 Nov	22 Oct
ITALY	Church	1582	15 Oct	5 Oct
	Genoa			
	Savona			
	(The following changed to N.S. but New Year 25 Mar after 1 Jan until 1750.)			
	Treviso	1582	15 Oct	5 Oct
	Tuscany, including Florence			
	Venice			
ITALY	(the following changed to N.S., but New Year 25 Mar year before 1 Jan. until 1 Jan. 1745)			
	Pisa	1582	15 Oct	5 Oct
	Lucca			
	Sienna			
	Lodi			
	(the following changed to N.S. and to New Year 1 Jan for the civil and common year, but for notorial documents, 25 Mar. of the current year until the mid XVII Century)			
	Sicily	1582	15 Oct	5 Oct
IRELAND (EIRE)		1752	14 Sep	3 Sep
		Also New Year from 25 Mar to 1 Jan		
JAPAN		1893	1 Jan Japanese Calendar	
LATVIA		1918	15 Feb	2 Feb
LITHUANIA		1918	15 Feb	2 Feb
LORRAINE		1760	28 Feb	17 Feb
NORWAY		1700	1 Mar	19 Feb
POLAND	Austrian & German	1582	15 Oct	5 Oct
	Russian	1918	14 Jan	1 Jan
PORTUGAL		1582	15 Oct	5 Oct
RUMANIA	Catholic	1919	18 Mar	5 Mar

Country	Province	Year	Date	Day
	Gr. Orthodox	1920	18 Mar	5 Mar
RUSSIA	Western	1918	14 Jan	1Jan
	Eastern	1920	18 Mar	5 Mar
	All	1929	(end) instituted a 5 day week and altered calendar accordingly.	
		1932	instituted a 6 day week and again changed calendar.	
		1940	27 Jun returned to N.S.	
SCOTLAND		1600	Changed New year from 25 Mar to 1 Jan, but O.S. calendar.	
		1752	14 Sep	3 Sep
SPAIN		1582	15 Oct	5 Oct
SWEDEN		1700	Was Leap Year O.S. 29 Feb dropped from calendar making 1 day earlier than O.S.	
		1712	Went back to O.S. calendar by adding 30 Feb (1712 Leap Year)	
		1753	1 Mar	18 Feb
SWITZERLAND	*Catholic*			
	Fribourg	1584	22 Jan	12 Jan
	Lucern			
	Schwyz			
	Solothurn			
	Unterwalden			
	Uri			
	Zug			
	Appenzell	1597	17 Jan	7 Jan
	Valais (3/10ths)	1622	1 Jan	22 Dec
	Valais (rest)	1656	1 Mar	19 Feb
	Protestant			
	Basle	1701	12 Jan	1 Jan
	Bern			
	Biel			
	Cargous			
	Geneva			
	Neuchatel			
	Schaffhausen			
	Thurgan			
	Zurich			
	Appenzell	1724	1 Jan	20 Dec (1723)
	Glorus			
	St Galen			
	Grisons	1812	1 Mar	17 Feb
TURKEY	European	1908		
	Asian	1914		
UNITED STATES	As England			
WALES	As England			
YUGOSLAVIA	1919	18 Mar	5 Mar	

TABLE 2

Year	Calendar Number (O.S.)	(N.S.)	Year	Calendar Number (O.S.)	(N.S.)	Year	Calendar Number (O.S.)	(N.S.)	Year	Calendar Number (O.S.)	(N.S.)
1582	2 O.S. through 4		1628	10*	14*	1676	14*	11*	1724	11*	14*
Oct. 6 N.S. October on.			1629	5	2	1677	2	6	1725	6	2
1583	3	7	1630	6	3	1678	3	7	1726	7	3
1584	11*	8*	1631	7	4	1679	4	1	1727	1	4
1585	6	3	1632	8*	12*	1680	12*	9*	1728	9*	12*
1586	7	4	1633	3	7	1681	7	4	1729	4	7
1587	1	5	1634	4	1	1682	1	5	1730	5	1
1588	9*	13*	1635	5	2	1683	2	6	1731	6	2
1589	4	1	1636	13*	10*	1684	10*	14*	1732	14*	10*
1590	5	2	1637	1	5	1685	5	2	1733	2	5
1591	6	3	1638	2	6	1686	6	3	1734	3	6
1592	14*	11*	1639	3	7	1687	7	4	1735	4	7
1593	2	6	1640	11*	8*	1688	8*	12*	1736	12*	8*
1594	3	7	1641	6	3	1689	3	7	1737	7	3
1595	4	1	1642	7	4	1690	4	1	1738	1	4
1596	12*	9*	1643	1	5	1691	5	2	1739	2	5
1597	7	4	1644	9*	13*	1692	13*	10*	1740	10*	13*
1598	1	5	1645	4	1	1693	1	5	1741	5	1
1599	2	6	1646	5	2	1694	2	6	1742	6	2
1600	10*	14*	1647	6	3	1695	3	7	1743	7	3
1601	5	2	1648	14*	11*	1696	11*	8*	1744	8*	11*
1602	6	3	1649	2	6	1697	6	3	1745	3	6
1603	7	4	1650	3	7	1698	7	4	1746	4	7
1604	8*	12*	1651	4	1	1699	1	5	1747	5	1
1605	3	7	1652	12*	9*	1700	9*	6*	1748	13*	9*
1606	4	1	1653	7	4	1701	4	7	1749	1	4
1607	5	2	1654	1	5	1702	5	1	1750	2	5
1608	13*	10*	1655	2	6	1703	6	2	1751	3	6
1609	1	5	1656	10*	14*	1704	14*	10*	1752	11*	14*
1610	2	6	1657	5	2	1705	2	5	1753	6	2
1611	3	7	1658	6	3	1706	3	6	1754	7	3
1612	11*	8*	1659	7	4	1707	4	7	1755	1	4
1612	11*	8*	1660	8*	12*	1708	12*	8*	1756	9*	12*
1613	6	3	1661	3	7	1709	7	3	1757	4	7
1614	7	4	1662	4	1	1710	1	4	1758	5	1
1615	1	5	1663	5	2	1711	2	5	1759	6	2
1616	9*	13*	1664	13*	10*	1712	10*	13*	1760	14*	10*
1617	4	1	1665	1	5	1713	5	1	1761	2	5
1618	5	2	1666	2	6	1714	6	2	1762	3	6
1619	6	3	1667	3	7	1715	7	3	1763	4	7
1620	14*	11*	1668	11*	8*	1716	8*	11*	1764	12*	8*
1621	2	6	1669	6	3	1717	3	6	1765	7	3
1622	3	7	1670	7	4	1718	4	7	1766	1	4
1623	4	1	1671	1	5	1719	5	1	1767	2	5
1624	12*	9*	1672	9*	13*	1720	13*	9*	1768	10*	13*
1625	7	4	1673	4	1	1721	1	4	1769	5	1
1626	1	5	1674	5	2	1722	2	5	1770	6	2
1627	2	6	1675	6	3	1723	3	6	1771	7	3

*Leap year

Year	Calendar (O.S.)	Number (N.S.)
1772	8*	11*
1773	3	6
1774	4	7
1775	5	1
1776	13*	9*
1777	1	4
1778	2	5
1779	3	6
1780	11*	14*
1781	6	2
1782	7	3
1783	1	4
1784	9*	12*
1785	4	7
1786	5	1
1787	6	2
1788	14*	10*
1789	2	5
1790	3	6
1791	4	7
1792	12*	8*
1793	7	3
1794	1	4
1795	2	5
1796	10*	13*
1797	5	1
1798	6	2
1799	7	3
1800	8*	4
1801	3	5
1802	4	6
1803	5	7
1804	13*	8*
1805	1	3
1806	2	4
1807	3	5
1808	11*	13*
1809	6	1

Year	Calendar (O.S.)	Number (N.S.)
1810	7	2
1811	1	3
1812	9*	11*
1813	4	6
1814	5	7
1815	6	1
1816	14*	9*
1817	2	4
1818	3	5
1819	4	6
1820	12*	14*
1821	7	2
1822	1	3
1823	2	4
1824	10*	12*
1825	5	7
1826	6	1
1827	7	2
1828	8*	10*
1829	3	5
1830	4	6
1831	5	7
1832	13*	8*
1833	1	3
1834	2	4
1835	3	5
1836	11*	13*
1837	6	1
1838	7	2
1839	1	3
1840	9*	11*
1841	4	6
1842	5	7
1843	6	1
1844	14*	9*
1845	2	4
1846	3	5
1847	4	6

Year	Calendar (O.S.)	Number (N.S.)
1848	12*	14*
1849	7	2
1850	1	3
1851	2	4
1852	10*	12*
1853	5	7
1854	6	1
1855	7	2
1856	8*	10*
1857	3	5
1858	4	6
1859	5	7
1860	13*	8*
1861	1	3
1862	2	4
1863	3	5
1864	11*	13*
1865	6	1
1866	7	2
1867	1	3
1868	9*	11*
1869	4	6
1870	5	7
1871	6	1
1872	14*	9*
1873	2	4
1874	3	5
1875	4	6
1876	12*	14*
1877	7	2
1878	1	3
1879	2	4
1880	10*	12*
1881	5	7
1882	6	1
1883	7	2
1884	8*	10*
1885	3	5

Year	Calendar (O.S.)	Number (N.S.)
1886	4	6
1887	5	7
1888	13*	8*
1889	1	3
1890	2	4
1891	3	5
1892	11*	13*
1893	6	1
1894	7	2
1895	1	3
1896	9*	11*
1897	4	6
1898	5	7
1899	6	1
1900	14*	2
1901	2	3
1902	3	4
1903	4	5
1904	12*	13*
1905	7	1
1906	1	2
1907	2	3
1908	10*	11*
1909	5	6
1910	6	7
1911	7	1
1912	8*	9*
1913	3	4
1914	4	5
1915	5	6
1916	13*	14*
1917	1	2
1918	2	3

1918 The U.S.S.R. began the year on 14th January.

TABLE 3
THE O.S. CALENDAR ACCORDING TO OUR RECKONING

Year								Calendar Number
1	29	57	85	113	141	169	197	7
2	30	58	86	114	142	170	198	1
3	31	59	87	115	143	171	199	2
4	32	60	88	116	144	172	200	10*

*Leap year

Year								Calendar Year
5	33	61	89	117	145	173	201	5
6	34	62	90	118	146	174	202	6
7	35	63	91	119	147	175	203	7
8	36	64	92	120	148	176	204	8*
9	37	65	93	121	149	177	205	3
10	38	66	94	122	150	178	206	4
11	39	67	95	123	151	179	207	5
12	40	68	96	124	152	180	208	13*
13	41	69	97	125	153	181	209	1
14	42	70	98	126	154	182	210	2
15	43	71	99	127	155	183	211	3
16	44	72	100	128	156	184	212	11*
17	45	73	101	129	157	185	213	6
18	46	74	102	130	158	186	214	7
19	47	75	103	131	159	187	215	1
20	48	76	104	132	160	188	216	9*
21	49	77	105	133	161	189	217	4
22	50	78	106	134	162	190	218	5
23	51	79	107	135	163	191	219	6
24	52	80	108	136	164	192	220	14*
25	53	81	109	137	165	193	221	2
26	54	82	110	138	166	194	222	3
27	55	83	111	139	167	195	223	4
28	56	84	112	140	168	196	224	12*
225	253	281	309	337	365	393	421	7
226	254	282	310	338	366	394	422	1
227	255	283	311	339	367	395	423	2
228	256	284	312	340	368	396	424	10*
229	257	285	313	341	369	397	425	5
230	258	286	314	342	370	398	426	6
231	259	287	315	343	371	399	427	7
232	260	288	316	344	372	400	428	8*
233	261	289	317	345	373	401	429	3
234	262	290	318	346	374	402	430	4
235	263	291	319	347	375	403	431	5
236	264	292	320	348	376	404	432	13*
237	265	293	321	349	377	405	433	1
238	266	294	322	350	378	406	434	2
239	267	295	323	351	379	407	435	3
240	268	296	324	352	380	408	436	11*
241	269	297	325	353	381	409	437	6
242	270	298	326	354	382	410	438	7
243	271	299	327	355	383	411	439	1
244	272	300	328	356	384	412	440	9*
245	273	301	329	357	385	413	441	4
246	274	302	330	358	386	414	442	5
247	275	303	331	359	387	415	443	6

*Leap year

Year								Calendar Year
248	276	304	332	360	388	416	444	14*
249	277	305	333	361	389	417	445	2
250	278	306	334	362	390	418	446	3
251	279	307	335	363	391	419	447	4
252	280	308	336	364	392	420	448	12*
449	477	505	533	561	589	617	645	7
450	478	506	534	562	590	618	646	1
451	479	507	535	563	591	619	647	2
452	480	508	536	564	592	620	648	10*
453	481	509	537	565	593	621	649	5
454	482	510	538	566	594	622	650	6
455	483	511	539	567	595	623	651	7
456	484	512	540	568	596	624	652	8*
457	485	513	541	569	597	625	653	3
458	486	514	542	570	598	626	654	4
459	487	515	543	571	599	627	655	5
460	488	516	544	572	600	628	656	13*
461	489	517	545	573	601	629	657	1
462	490	518	546	574	602	630	658	2
463	491	519	547	575	603	631	659	3
464	492	520	548	576	604	632	660	11*
465	493	521	549	577	605	633	661	6
466	494	522	550	578	606	634	662	7
467	495	523	551	579	607	635	663	1
468	496	524	552	580	608	636	664	9*
469	497	525	553	581	609	637	665	4
470	498	526	554	582	610	638	666	5
471	499	527	555	583	611	639	667	4
472	500	528	556	584	612	640	668	14*
473	501	529	557	585	613	641	669	2
474	502	530	558	586	614	642	670	3
475	503	531	559	587	615	643	671	4
476	504	532	560	588	616	644	672	12*
673	701	729	757	785	813	841	869	7
674	702	730	758	786	814	842	870	1
675	703	731	759	787	815	843	871	2
676	704	732	760	788	816	844	872	10*
677	705	733	761	789	817	845	873	5
678	706	734	762	790	818	846	874	6
679	707	735	763	791	819	847	875	7
680	708	736	764	792	820	848	876	8*
681	709	737	765	793	821	849	877	3
682	710	738	766	794	822	850	878	4
683	711	739	767	795	823	851	879	5
684	712	740	768	796	824	852	880	13*
685	713	741	769	797	825	853	881	1

*Leap year

Year								Calendar Year
686	714	742	770	798	826	854	882	2
687	715	743	771	799	827	855	883	3
688	716	744	772	800	828	856	884	11*
689	717	745	773	801	829	857	885	6
690	718	746	774	802	830	858	886	7
691	719	747	775	803	831	859	887	1
692	720	748	776	804	832	860	888	9*
693	721	749	777	805	833	861	889	4
694	722	750	778	806	834	862	890	5
695	723	751	779	807	835	863	891	4
696	724	752	780	808	836	864	892	14*
697	725	753	781	809	837	865	893	2
698	726	754	782	810	838	866	894	3
699	727	755	783	811	839	867	895	4
700	728	756	784	812	840	868	896	12*
897	925	953	981	1009	1037	1065	1093	7
898	926	954	982	1010	1038	1066	1094	1
899	927	955	983	1011	1039	1067	1095	2
900	928	956	984	1012	1040	1068	1096	10*
901	929	957	985	1013	1041	1069	1097	5
902	930	958	986	1014	1042	1070	1098	6
903	931	959	987	1015	1043	1071	1099	7
904	932	960	988	1016	1044	1072	1100	8*
905	933	961	989	1017	1045	1073	1101	3
906	934	962	990	1018	1046	1074	1102	4
907	935	963	991	1019	1047	1075	1103	5
908	936	964	992	1020	1048	1076	1104	13*
909	937	965	993	1021	1049	1077	1105	1
910	938	966	994	1022	1050	1078	1106	2
911	939	967	995	1023	1051	1079	1107	3
912	940	968	996	1024	1052	1080	1108	11*
913	941	969	997	1025	1053	1081	1109	6
914	942	970	998	1026	1054	1082	1110	7
915	943	971	999	1027	1055	1083	1111	1
916	944	972	1000	1028	1056	1084	1112	9*
917	945	973	1001	1029	1057	1085	1113	4
918	946	974	1002	1030	1058	1086	1114	5
910	947	975	1003	1031	1059	1087	1115	6
920	948	976	1004	1032	1060	1088	1116	14*
921	949	977	1005	1033	1061	1089	1117	2
922	950	978	1006	1034	1062	1090	1118	3
923	951	979	1007	1035	1063	1091	1119	4
924	952	980	1008	1036	1064	1092	1120	12*
1121	1149	1177	1205	1233	1261	1289	1317	7
1122	1150	1178	1206	1234	1262	1290	1318	1
1123	1151	1179	1207	1235	1263	1291	1319	2

*Leap year

Year								Calendar Year
1124	1152	1180	1208	1236	1264	1292	1320	10*
1125	1153	1181	1209	1237	1265	1293	1321	5
1126	1154	1182	1210	1238	1266	1294	1322	6
1127	1155	1183	1211	1239	1267	1295	1323	7
1128	1156	1184	1212	1240	1268	1296	1324	8*
1129	1157	1185	1213	1241	1269	1297	1325	3
1130	1158	1186	1214	1242	1270	1298	1326	4
1131	1159	1187	1215	1243	1271	1299	1327	5
1132	1160	1188	1216	1244	1272	1300	1328	13*
1133	1161	1189	1217	1245	1273	1301	1329	1
1134	1162	1190	1218	1246	1274	1302	1330	2
1135	1163	1191	1219	1247	1275	1303	1331	3
1136	1164	1192	1220	1248	1276	1304	1332	11*
1137	1165	1193	1221	1249	1277	1305	1333	6
1138	1166	1194	1222	1250	1278	1306	1334	7
1139	1167	1195	1223	1251	1279	1307	1335	1
1140	1168	1196	1224	1252	1280	1308	1336	9*
1141	1169	1197	1225	1253	1281	1309	1337	4
1142	1170	1198	1226	1254	1282	1310	1338	5
1143	1171	1199	1227	1255	1283	1311	1339	6
1144	1172	1200	1228	1256	1284	1312	1340	14*
1145	1173	1201	1229	1257	1285	1313	1341	2
1146	1174	1202	1230	1258	1286	1314	1342	3
1147	1175	1203	1231	1259	1287	1315	1343	4
1148	1176	1204	1232	1260	1288	1316	1344	12*
1345	1373	1401	1429	1457	1485	1513	1541	7
1346	1374	1402	1430	1458	1486	1514	1542	1
1347	1375	1403	1431	1459	1487	1515	1543	2
1348	1376	1404	1432	1460	1488	1516	1544	10*
1349	1377	1405	1433	1461	1489	1517	1545	5
1350	1378	1406	1434	1462	1490	1518	1546	6
1351	1379	1407	1435	1463	1491	1519	1547	7
1352	1380	1408	1436	1464	1492	1520	1548	8*
1353	1381	1409	1437	1465	1493	1521	1549	3
1354	1382	1410	1438	1466	1494	1522	1550	4
1355	1383	1411	1439	1467	1495	1523	1551	5
1356	1384	1412	1440	1468	1496	1524	1552	13*
1357	1385	1413	1441	1469	1497	1525	1553	1
1358	1386	1414	1442	1470	1498	1526	1554	2
1359	1387	1415	1443	1471	1499	1527	1555	3
1360	1388	1416	1444	1472	1500	1528	1556	11*
1361	1389	1417	1445	1473	1501	1529	1557	6
1362	1390	1418	1446	1474	1502	1530	1558	7
1363	1391	1419	1447	1475	1503	1531	1559	1
1364	1392	1420	1448	1476	1504	1532	1560	9*
1365	1393	1421	1449	1477	1505	1533	1561	4
1366	1394	1422	1450	1478	1506	1534	1562	5

*Leap year

Year								Calendar Year
1367	1395	1423	1451	1479	1507	1535	1563	6
1368	1396	1424	1452	1480	1508	1536	1564	14*
1369	1397	1425	1453	1481	1509	1537	1565	2
1370	1398	1426	1454	1482	1510	1538	1566	3
1371	1399	1427	1455	1483	1511	1539	1567	4
1372	1400	1428	1456	1484	1512	1540	1568	12*
1569	1597	1625	1653	1681	1709	1737	1765	7
1570	1598	1626	1654	1682	1710	1738	1766	1
1571	1599	1627	1655	1683	1711	1739	1767	2
1572	1600	1628	1656	1684	1712	1740	1768	10*
1573	1601	1629	1657	1685	1713	1741	1769	5
1574	1602	1630	1658	1686	1714	1742	1770	6
1575	1603	1631	1659	1687	1715	1743	1771	7
1576	1604	1632	1660	1688	1716	1744	1772	8*
1577	1605	1633	1661	1689	1717	1745	1773	3
1578	1606	1634	1662	1690	1718	1746	1774	4
1579	1607	1635	1663	1691	1719	1747	1775	5
1580	1608	1636	1664	1692	1720	1748	1776	13*
1581	1609	1637	1665	1693	1721	1749	1777	1
1582	1610	1638	1666	1694	1722	1750	1778	2
1583	1611	1639	1667	1695	1723	1751	1779	3
1584	1612	1640	1668	1696	1724	1752	1780	11*
1585	1613	1641	1669	1697	1725	1753	1781	6
1586	1614	1642	1670	1698	1726	1754	1782	7
1587	1615	1643	1671	1699	1727	1755	1783	1
1588	1616	1644	1672	1700	1728	1756	1784	9*
1589	1617	1645	1673	1701	1729	1757	1785	4
1590	1618	1646	1674	1702	1730	1758	1786	5
1591	1619	1647	1675	1703	1731	1759	1787	6
1592	1620	1648	1676	1704	1732	1760	1788	14*
1593	1621	1649	1677	1705	1733	1761	1789	2
1594	1622	1650	1678	1706	1734	1762	1790	3
1595	1623	1651	1679	1707	1735	1763	1791	4
1596	1624	1652	1680	1708	1736	1764	1792	12*
1793	1821	1849	1877	1905	1933	1961	1989	7
1794	1822	1850	1878	1906	1934	1962	1990	1
1795	1823	1851	1879	1907	1935	1963	1991	2
1796	1824	1852	1880	1908	1936	1964	1992	10*
1797	1825	1853	1881	1909	1937	1965	1993	5
1798	1826	1854	1882	1910	1938	1966	1994	6
1799	1827	1855	1883	1911	1939	1967	1995	7
1800	1828	1856	1884	1912	1940	1968	1996	8*
1801	1829	1857	1885	1913	1941	1969	1997	3
1802	1830	1858	1886	1914	1942	1970	1998	4
1803	1831	1859	1887	1915	1943	1971	1999	5
1804	1832	1860	1888	1916	1944	1972	2000	13*

*Leap year

Year							Calendar Year
1805	1833	1861	1889	1917	1945	1973	1
1806	1834	1862	1890	1918	1946	1974	2
1807	1835	1863	1891	1919	1947	1975	3
1808	1836	1864	1892	1920	1948	1976	11*
1809	1837	1865	1893	1921	1949	1977	6
1810	1838	1866	1894	1922	1950	1978	7
1811	1839	1867	1895	1923	1951	1979	1
1812	1840	1868	1896	1924	1952	1980	9*
1813	1841	1869	1897	1925	1953	1981	4
1814	1842	1870	1898	1926	1954	1982	5
1815	1843	1871	1899	1927	1955	1983	6
1816	1844	1872	1900	1928	1956	1984	14*
1817	1845	1873	1901	1929	1957	1985	2
1818	1846	1874	1902	1930	1958	1986	3
1819	1847	1875	1903	1931	1959	1987	4
1820	1848	1876	1904	1932	1960	1988	12*

*Leap year

14 POSSIBLE CALENDARS FOR THE JULIAN AND GREGORIAN CALENDAR

Calendar 1

JANUARY

1	2	3	4	5	6	7
8	9	10	11	12	13	14
15	16	17	18	19	20	21
22	23	24	25	26	27	28
29	30	31				

FEBRUARY

			1	2	3	4
5	6	7	8	9	10	11
12	13	14	15	16	17	18
19	20	21	22	23	24	25
26	27	28				

MARCH

			1	2	3	4
5	6	7	8	9	10	11
12	13	14	15	16	17	18
19	20	21	22	23	24	25
26	27	28	29	30	31	

JULY

						1
2	3	4	5	6	7	8
9	10	11	12	13	14	15
16	17	18	19	20	21	22
23	24	25	26	27	28	29
30	31					

AUGUST

		1	2	3	4	5
6	7	8	9	10	11	12
13	14	15	16	17	18	19
20	21	22	23	24	25	26
27	28	29	30	31		

SEPTEMBER

					1	2
3	4	5	6	7	8	9
10	11	12	13	14	15	16
17	18	19	20	21	22	23
24	25	26	27	28	29	30

APRIL

						1
2	3	4	5	6	7	8
9	10	11	12	13	14	15
16	17	18	19	20	21	22
23	24	25	26	27	28	29
30						

MAY

	1	2	3	4	5	6
7	8	9	10	11	12	13
14	15	16	17	18	19	20
21	22	23	24	25	26	27
28	29	30	31			

JUNE

				1	2	3
4	5	6	7	8	9	10
11	12	13	14	15	16	17
18	19	20	21	22	23	24
25	26	27	28	29	30	

OCTOBER

1	2	3	4	5	6	7
8	9	10	11	12	13	14
15	16	17	18	19	20	21
22	23	24	25	26	27	28
29	30	31				

NOVEMBER

			1	2	3	4
5	6	7	8	9	10	11
12	13	14	15	16	17	18
19	20	21	22	23	24	25
26	27	28	29	30		

DECEMBER

					1	2
3	4	5	6	7	8	9
10	11	12	13	14	15	16
17	18	19	20	21	22	23
24	25	26	27	28	29	30
31						

Calendar 2

JANUARY

	1	2	3	4	5	6
7	8	9	10	11	12	13
14	15	16	17	18	19	20
21	22	23	24	25	26	27
28	29	30	31			

FEBRUARY

				1	2	3
4	5	6	7	8	9	10
11	12	13	14	15	16	17
18	19	20	21	22	23	24
25	26	27	28			

MARCH

				1	2	3
4	5	6	7	8	9	10
11	12	13	14	15	16	17
18	19	20	21	22	23	24
25	26	27	28	29	30	31

APRIL

1	2	3	4	5	6	7
8	9	10	11	12	13	14
15	16	17	18	19	20	21
22	23	24	25	26	27	28
29	30					

JULY

1	2	3	4	5	6	7
8	9	10	11	12	13	14
15	16	17	18	19	20	21
22	23	24	25	26	27	28
29	30	31				

AUGUST

			1	2	3	4
5	6	7	8	9	10	11
12	13	14	15	16	17	18
19	20	21	22	23	24	25
26	27	28	29	30	31	

SEPTEMBER

						1
2	3	4	5	6	7	8
9	10	11	12	13	14	15
16	17	18	19	20	21	22
23	24	25	26	27	28	29
30						

OCTOBER

	1	2	3	4	5	6
7	8	9	10	11	12	13
14	15	16	17	18	19	20
21	22	23	24	25	26	27
28	29	30	31			

MAY

		1	2	3	4	5
6	7	8	9	10	11	12
13	14	15	16	17	18	19
20	21	22	23	24	25	26
27	28	29	30	31		

JUNE

					1	2
3	4	5	6	7	8	9
10	11	12	13	14	15	16
17	18	19	20	21	22	23
24	25	26	27	28	29	30

NOVEMBER

				1	2	3
4	5	6	7	8	9	10
11	12	13	14	15	16	17
18	19	20	21	22	23	24
25	26	27	28	29	30	

DECEMBER

						1
2	3	4	5	6	7	8
9	10	11	12	13	14	15
16	17	18	19	20	21	22
23	24	25	26	27	28	29
30	31					

Calendar 3

JANUARY

		1	2	3	4	5
6	7	8	9	10	11	12
13	14	15	16	17	18	19
20	21	22	23	24	25	26
27	28	29	30	31		

FEBRUARY

					1	2
3	4	5	6	7	8	9
10	11	12	13	14	15	16
17	18	19	20	21	22	23
24	25	26	27	28		

MARCH

					1	2
3	4	5	6	7	8	9
10	11	12	13	14	15	16
17	18	19	20	21	22	23
24	25	26	27	28	29	30
31						

APRIL

	1	2	3	4	5	6
7	8	9	10	11	12	13
14	15	16	17	18	19	20
21	22	23	24	25	26	27
28	29	30				

MAY

			1	2	3	4
5	6	7	8	9	10	11
12	13	14	15	16	17	18
19	20	21	22	23	24	25
26	27	28	29	30	31	

JULY

	1	2	3	4	5	6
7	8	9	10	11	12	13
14	15	16	17	18	19	20
21	22	23	24	25	26	27
28	29	30	31			

AUGUST

				1	2	3
4	5	6	7	8	9	10
11	12	13	14	15	16	17
18	19	20	21	22	23	24
25	26	27	28	29	30	31

SEPTEMBER

1	2	3	4	5	6	7
8	9	10	11	12	13	14
15	16	17	18	19	20	21
22	23	24	25	26	27	28
29	30					

OCTOBER

		1	2	3	4	5
6	7	8	9	10	11	12
13	14	15	16	17	18	19
20	21	22	23	24	25	26
27	28	29	30	31		

NOVEMBER

					1	2
3	4	5	6	7	8	9
10	11	12	13	14	15	16
17	18	19	20	21	22	23
24	25	26	27	28	29	30

JUNE

						1
2	3	4	5	6	7	8
9	10	11	12	13	14	15
16	17	18	19	20	21	22
23	24	25	26	27	28	29
30						

DECEMBER

1	2	3	4	5	6	7
8	9	10	11	12	13	14
15	16	17	18	19	20	21
22	23	24	25	26	27	28
29	30	31				

Calendar 4

JANUARY

			1	2	3	4
5	6	7	8	9	10	11
12	13	14	15	16	17	18
19	20	21	22	23	24	25
26	27	28	29	30	31	

FEBRUARY

						1
2	3	4	5	6	7	8
9	10	11	12	13	14	15
16	17	18	19	20	21	22
23	24	25	26	27	28	

MARCH

						1
2	3	4	5	6	7	8
9	10	11	12	13	14	15
16	17	18	19	20	21	22
23	24	25	26	27	28	29
30	31					

APRIL

		1	2	3	4	5
6	7	8	9	10	11	12
13	14	15	16	17	18	19
20	21	22	23	24	25	26
27	28	29	30			

MAY

				1	2	3
4	5	6	7	8	9	10
11	12	13	14	15	16	17
18	19	20	21	22	23	24
25	26	27	28	29	30	31

JUNE

1	2	3	4	5	6	7
8	9	10	11	12	13	14
15	16	17	18	19	20	21
22	23	24	25	26	27	28
29	30					

JULY

		1	2	3	4	5
6	7	8	9	10	11	12
13	14	15	16	17	18	19
20	21	22	23	24	25	26
27	28	29	30	31		

AUGUST

					1	2
3	4	5	6	7	8	9
10	11	12	13	14	15	16
17	18	19	20	21	22	23
24	25	26	27	28	29	30
31						

SEPTEMBER

	1	2	3	4	5	6
7	8	9	10	11	12	13
14	15	16	17	18	19	20
21	22	23	24	25	26	27
28	29	30				

OCTOBER

			1	2	3	4
5	6	7	8	9	10	11
12	13	14	15	16	17	18
19	20	21	22	23	24	25
26	27	28	29	30	31	

NOVEMBER

						1
2	3	4	5	6	7	8
9	10	11	12	13	14	15
16	17	18	19	20	21	22
23	24	25	26	27	28	29
30						

DECEMBER

	1	2	3	4	5	6
7	8	9	10	11	12	13
14	15	16	17	18	19	20
21	22	23	24	25	26	27
28	29	30	31			

Calendar 5

JANUARY

				1	2	3
4	5	6	7	8	9	10
11	12	13	14	15	16	17
18	19	20	21	22	23	24
25	26	27	28	29	30	31

FEBRUARY

1	2	3	4	5	6	7
8	9	10	11	12	13	14
15	16	17	18	19	20	21
22	23	24	25	26	27	28

MARCH

1	2	3	4	5	6	7
8	9	10	11	12	13	14
15	16	17	18	19	20	21
22	23	24	25	26	27	28
29	30	31				

APRIL

			1	2	3	4
5	6	7	8	9	10	11
12	13	14	15	16	17	18
19	20	21	22	23	24	25
26	27	28	29	30		

MAY

					1	2
3	4	5	6	7	8	9
10	11	12	13	14	15	16
17	18	19	20	21	22	23
24	25	26	27	28	29	30
31						

JUNE

	1	2	3	4	5	6
7	8	9	10	11	12	13
14	15	16	17	18	19	20
21	22	23	24	25	26	27
28	29	30				

JULY

			1	2	3	4
5	6	7	8	9	10	11
12	13	14	15	16	17	18
19	20	21	22	23	24	25
26	27	28	29	30	31	

AUGUST

						1
2	3	4	5	6	7	8
9	10	11	12	13	14	15
16	17	18	19	20	21	22
23	24	25	26	27	28	29
30	31					

SEPTEMBER

		1	2	3	4	5
6	7	8	9	10	11	12
13	14	15	16	17	18	19
20	21	22	23	24	25	26
27	28	29	30			

OCTOBER

				1	2	3
4	5	6	7	8	9	10
11	12	13	14	15	16	17
18	19	20	21	22	23	24
25	26	27	28	29	30	31

NOVEMBER

1	2	3	4	5	6	7
8	9	10	11	12	13	14
15	16	17	18	19	20	21
22	23	24	25	26	27	28
29	30					

DECEMBER

		1	2	3	4	5
6	7	8	9	10	11	12
13	14	15	16	17	18	19
20	21	22	23	24	25	26
27	28	29	30	31		

Calendar 6

JANUARY

					1	2
3	4	5	6	7	8	9
10	11	12	13	14	15	16
17	18	19	20	21	22	23
24	25	26	27	28	29	30
31						

JULY

				1	2	3
4	5	6	7	8	9	10
11	12	13	14	15	16	17
18	19	20	21	22	23	24
25	26	27	28	29	30	31

FEBRUARY

	1	2	3	4	5	6
7	8	9	10	11	12	13
14	15	16	17	18	19	20
21	22	23	24	25	26	27
28						

MARCH

	1	2	3	4	5	6
7	8	9	10	11	12	13
14	15	16	17	18	19	20
21	22	23	24	25	26	27
28	29	30	31			

APRIL

				1	2	3
4	5	6	7	8	9	10
11	12	13	14	15	16	17
18	19	20	21	22	23	24
25	26	27	28	29	30	

MAY

						1
2	3	4	5	6	7	8
9	10	11	12	13	14	15
16	17	18	19	20	21	22
23	24	25	26	27	28	29
30	31					

JUNE

		1	2	3	4	5
6	7	8	9	10	11	12
13	14	15	16	17	18	19
20	21	22	23	24	25	26
27	28	29	30			

AUGUST

1	2	3	4	5	6	7
8	9	10	11	12	13	14
15	16	17	18	19	20	21
22	23	24	25	26	27	28
29	30	31				

SEPTEMBER

			1	2	3	4
5	6	7	8	9	10	11
12	13	14	15	16	17	18
19	20	21	22	23	24	25
26	27	28	29	30		

OCTOBER

					1	2
3	4	5	6	7	8	9
10	11	12	13	14	15	16
17	18	19	20	21	22	23
24	25	26	27	28	29	30
31						

NOVEMBER

	1	2	3	4	5	6
7	8	9	10	11	12	13
14	15	16	17	18	19	20
21	22	23	24	25	26	27
28	29	30				

DECEMBER

			1	2	3	4
5	6	7	8	9	10	11
12	13	14	15	16	17	18
19	20	21	22	23	24	25
26	27	28	29	30	31	

Calendar 7

JANUARY

						1
2	3	4	5	6	7	8
9	10	11	12	13	14	15
16	17	18	19	20	21	22
23	24	25	26	27	28	29
30	31					

FEBRUARY

		1	2	3	4	5
6	7	8	9	10	11	12
13	14	15	16	17	18	19
20	21	22	23	24	25	26
27	28					

JULY

					1	2
3	4	5	6	7	8	9
10	11	12	13	14	15	16
17	18	19	20	21	22	23
24	25	26	27	28	29	30
31						

AUGUST

	1	2	3	4	5	6
7	8	9	10	11	12	13
14	15	16	17	18	19	20
21	22	23	24	25	26	27
28	29	30	31			

MARCH

		1	2	3	4	5
6	7	8	9	10	11	12
13	14	15	16	17	18	19
20	21	22	23	24	25	26
27	28	29	30	31		

APRIL

					1	2
3	4	5	6	7	8	9
10	11	12	13	14	15	16
17	18	19	20	21	22	23
24	25	26	27	28	29	30

MAY

1	2	3	4	5	6	7
8	9	10	11	12	13	14
15	16	17	18	19	20	21
22	23	24	25	26	27	28
29	30	31				

JUNE

			1	2	3	4
5	6	7	8	9	10	11
12	13	14	15	16	17	18
19	20	21	22	23	24	25
26	27	28	29	30		

SEPTEMBER

				1	2	3
4	5	6	7	8	9	10
11	12	13	14	15	16	17
18	19	20	21	22	23	24
25	26	27	28	29	30	

OCTOBER

						1
2	3	4	5	6	7	8
9	10	11	12	13	14	15
16	17	18	19	20	21	22
23	24	25	26	27	28	29
30	31					

NOVEMBER

		1	2	3	4	5
6	7	8	9	10	11	12
13	14	15	16	17	18	19
20	21	22	23	24	25	26
27	28	29	30			

DECEMBER

				1	2	3
4	5	6	7	8	9	10
11	12	13	14	15	16	17
18	19	20	21	22	23	24
25	26	27	28	29	30	31

Calendar 8

JANUARY

1	2	3	4	5	6	7
8	9	10	11	12	13	14
15	16	17	18	19	20	21
22	23	24	25	26	27	28
29	30	31				

FEBRUARY

			1	2	3	4
5	6	7	8	9	10	11
12	13	14	15	16	17	18
19	20	21	22	23	24	25
26	27	28	29			

MARCH

				1	2	3
4	5	6	7	8	9	10
11	12	13	14	15	16	17
18	19	20	21	22	23	24
25	26	27	28	29	30	31

JULY

1	2	3	4	5	6	7
8	9	10	11	12	13	14
15	16	17	18	19	20	21
22	23	24	25	26	27	28
29	30	31				

AUGUST

			1	2	3	4
5	6	7	8	9	10	11
12	13	14	15	16	17	18
19	20	21	22	23	24	25
26	27	28	29	30	31	

SEPTEMBER

						1
2	3	4	5	6	7	8
9	10	11	12	13	14	15
16	17	18	19	20	21	22
23	24	25	26	27	28	29
30						

APRIL

1	2	3	4	5	6	7
8	9	10	11	12	13	14
15	16	17	18	19	20	21
22	23	24	25	26	27	28
29	30					

MAY

		1	2	3	4	5
6	7	8	9	10	11	12
13	14	15	16	17	18	19
20	21	22	23	24	25	26
27	28	29	30	31		

JUNE

					1	2
3	4	5	6	7	8	9
10	11	12	13	14	15	16
17	18	19	20	21	22	23
24	25	26	27	28	29	30

OCTOBER

	1	2	3	4	5	6
7	8	9	10	11	12	13
14	15	16	17	18	19	20
21	22	23	24	25	26	27
28	29	30	31			

NOVEMBER

				1	2	3
4	5	6	7	8	9	10
11	12	13	14	15	16	17
18	19	20	21	22	23	24
25	26	27	28	29	30	

DECEMBER

						1
2	3	4	5	6	7	8
9	10	11	12	13	14	15
16	17	18	19	20	21	22
23	24	25	26	27	28	29
30	31					

Calendar 9

JANUARY

	1	2	3	4	5	6
7	8	9	10	11	12	13
14	15	16	17	18	19	20
21	22	23	24	25	26	27
28	29	30	31			

FEBRUARY

				1	2	3
4	5	6	7	8	9	10
11	12	13	14	15	16	17
18	19	20	21	22	23	24
25	26	27	28	29		

MARCH

					1	2
3	4	5	6	7	8	9
10	11	12	13	14	15	16
17	18	19	20	21	22	23
24	25	26	27	28	29	30
31						

APRIL

	1	2	3	4	5	6
7	8	9	10	11	12	13
14	15	16	17	18	19	20
21	22	23	24	25	26	27
28	29	30				

JULY

	1	2	3	4	5	6
7	8	9	10	11	12	13
14	15	16	17	18	19	20
21	22	23	24	25	26	27
28	29	30	31			

AUGUST

				1	2	3
4	5	6	7	8	9	10
11	12	13	14	15	16	17
18	19	20	21	22	23	24
25	26	27	28	29	30	31

SEPTEMBER

1	2	3	4	5	6	7
8	9	10	11	12	13	14
15	16	17	18	19	20	21
22	23	24	25	26	27	28
29	30					

OCTOBER

		1	2	3	4	5
6	7	8	9	10	11	12
13	14	15	16	17	18	19
20	21	22	23	24	25	26
27	28	29	30	31		

MAY

			1	2	3	4
5	6	7	8	9	10	11
12	13	14	15	16	17	18
19	20	21	22	23	24	25
26	27	28	29	30	31	

JUNE

						1
2	3	4	5	6	7	8
9	10	11	12	13	14	15
16	17	18	19	20	21	22
23	24	25	26	27	28	29
30						

NOVEMBER

					1	2
3	4	5	6	7	8	9
10	11	12	13	14	15	16
17	18	19	20	21	22	23
24	25	26	27	28	29	30

DECEMBER

1	2	3	4	5	6	7
8	9	10	11	12	13	14
15	16	17	18	19	20	21
22	23	24	25	26	27	28
29	30	31				

Calendar 10

JANUARY

		1	2	3	4	5
6	7	8	9	10	11	12
13	14	15	16	17	18	19
20	21	22	23	24	25	26
27	28	29	30	31		

FEBRUARY

					1	2
3	4	5	6	7	8	9
10	11	12	13	14	15	16
17	18	19	20	21	22	23
24	25	26	27	28	29	

MARCH

						1
2	3	4	5	6	7	8
9	10	11	12	13	14	15
16	17	18	19	20	21	22
23	24	25	26	27	28	29
30	31					

APRIL

		1	2	3	4	5
6	7	8	9	10	11	12
13	14	15	16	17	18	19
20	21	22	23	24	25	26
27	28	29	30			

MAY

				1	2	3
4	5	6	7	8	9	10
11	12	13	14	15	16	17
18	19	20	21	22	23	24
25	26	27	28	29	30	31

JULY

		1	2	3	4	5
6	7	8	9	10	11	12
13	14	15	16	17	18	19
20	21	22	23	24	25	26
27	28	29	30	31		

AUGUST

					1	2
3	4	5	6	7	8	9
10	11	12	13	14	15	16
17	18	19	20	21	22	23
24	25	26	27	28	29	30
31						

SEPTEMBER

	1	2	3	4	5	6
7	8	9	10	11	12	13
14	15	16	17	18	19	20
21	22	23	24	25	26	27
28	29	30				

OCTOBER

			1	2	3	4
5	6	7	8	9	10	11
12	13	14	15	16	17	18
19	20	21	22	23	24	25
26	27	28	29	30	31	

NOVEMBER

						1
2	3	4	5	6	7	8
9	10	11	12	13	14	15
16	17	18	19	20	21	22
23	24	25	26	27	28	29
30						

JUNE

1	2	3	4	5	6	7
8	9	10	11	12	13	14
15	16	17	18	10	20	21
22	23	24	25	26	27	28
29	30					

DECEMBER

	1	2	3	4	5	6
7	8	9	10	11	12	13
14	15	16	17	18	19	20
21	22	23	24	25	26	27
28	29	30	31			

Calendar 11

JANUARY

			1	2	3	4
5	6	7	8	9	10	11
12	13	14	15	16	17	18
19	20	21	22	23	24	25
26	27	28	29	30	31	

FEBRUARY

						1
2	3	4	5	6	7	8
9	10	11	12	13	14	15
16	17	18	19	20	21	22
23	24	25	26	27	28	29

MARCH

1	2	3	4	5	6	7
8	9	10	11	12	13	14
15	16	17	18	19	20	21
22	23	24	25	26	27	28
29	30	31				

APRIL

			1	2	3	4
5	6	7	8	9	10	11
12	13	14	15	16	17	18
19	20	21	22	23	24	25
26	27	28	29	30		

MAY

					1	2
3	4	5	6	7	8	9
10	11	12	13	14	15	16
17	18	19	20	21	22	23
24	25	26	27	28	29	30
31						

JUNE

	1	2	3	4	5	6
7	8	9	10	11	12	13
14	15	16	17	18	19	20
21	22	23	24	25	26	27
28	29	30				

JULY

			1	2	3	4
5	6	7	8	9	10	11
12	13	14	15	16	17	18
19	20	21	22	23	24	25
26	27	28	29	30	31	

AUGUST

						1
2	3	4	5	6	7	8
9	10	11	12	13	14	15
16	17	18	19	20	21	22
23	24	25	26	27	28	29
30	31					

SEPTEMBER

		1	2	3	4	5
6	7	8	9	10	11	12
13	14	15	16	17	18	19
20	21	22	23	24	25	26
27	28	29	30			

OCTOBER

				1	2	3
4	5	6	7	8	9	10
11	12	13	14	15	16	17
18	19	20	21	22	23	24
25	26	27	28	29	30	31

NOVEMBER

1	2	3	4	5	6	7
8	9	10	11	12	13	14
15	16	17	18	19	20	21
22	23	24	25	26	27	28
29	30					

DECEMBER

		1	2	3	4	5
6	7	8	9	10	11	12
13	14	15	16	17	18	19
20	21	22	23	24	25	26
27	28	29	30	31		

Calendar 12

JANUARY

				1	2	3
4	5	6	7	8	9	10
11	12	13	14	15	16	17
18	19	20	21	22	23	24
25	26	27	28	29	30	31

FEBRUARY

1	2	3	4	5	6	7
8	9	10	11	12	13	14
15	16	17	18	19	20	21
22	23	24	25	26	27	28
29						

MARCH

	1	2	3	4	5	6
7	8	9	10	11	12	13
14	15	16	17	18	19	20
21	22	23	24	25	26	27
28	29	30	31			

APRIL

				1	2	3
4	5	6	7	8	9	10
11	12	13	14	15	16	17
18	19	20	21	22	23	24
25	26	27	28	29	30	

MAY

						1
2	3	4	5	6	7	8
9	10	11	12	13	14	15
16	17	18	19	20	21	22
23	24	25	26	27	28	29
30	31					

JUNE

		1	2	3	4	5
6	7	8	9	10	11	12
13	14	15	16	17	18	19
20	21	22	23	24	25	26
27	28	29	30			

JULY

				1	2	3
4	5	6	7	8	9	10
11	12	13	14	15	16	17
18	19	20	21	22	23	24
25	26	27	28	29	30	31

AUGUST

1	2	3	4	5	6	7
8	9	10	11	12	13	14
15	16	17	18	19	20	21
22	23	24	25	26	27	28
29	30	31				

SEPTEMBER

			1	2	3	4
5	6	7	8	9	10	11
12	13	14	15	16	17	18
19	20	21	22	23	24	25
26	27	28	29	30		

OCTOBER

					1	2
3	4	5	6	7	8	9
10	11	12	13	14	15	15
17	18	19	20	21	22	23
24	25	26	27	28	29	30
31						

NOVEMBER

	1	2	3	4	5	6
7	8	9	10	11	12	13
14	15	16	17	18	19	20
21	22	23	24	25	26	27
28	29	30				

DECEMBER

			1	2	3	4
5	6	7	8	9	10	11
12	13	14	15	16	17	18
19	20	21	22	23	24	25
26	27	28	29	30	31	

Calendar 13

JANUARY

					1	2
3	4	5	6	7	8	9
10	11	12	13	14	15	16
17	18	19	20	21	22	23
24	25	26	27	28	29	30
31						

JULY

					1	2
3	4	5	6	7	8	9
10	11	12	13	14	15	16
17	18	19	20	21	22	23
24	25	26	27	28	29	30
31						

FEBRUARY

	1	2	3	4	5	6
7	8	9	10	11	12	13
14	15	16	17	18	19	20
21	22	23	24	25	26	27
28	29					

MARCH

		1	2	3	4	5
6	7	8	9	10	11	12
13	14	15	16	17	18	19
20	21	22	23	24	25	26
27	28	29	30	31		

APRIL

					1	2
3	4	5	6	7	8	9
10	11	12	13	14	15	16
17	18	19	20	21	22	23
24	25	26	27	28	29	30

MAY

1	2	3	4	5	6	7
8	9	10	11	12	13	14
15	16	17	18	19	20	21
22	23	24	25	26	27	28
29	30	31				

JUNE

			1	2	3	4
5	6	7	8	9	10	11
12	13	14	15	16	17	18
19	20	21	22	23	24	25
26	27	28	29	30		

AUGUST

	1	2	3	4	5	6
7	8	9	10	11	12	13
14	15	16	17	18	19	20
21	22	23	24	25	26	27
28	29	30	31			

SEPTEMBER

				1	2	3
4	5	6	7	8	9	10
11	12	13	14	15	16	17
18	19	20	21	22	23	24
25	26	27	28	29	30	

OCTOBER

						1
2	3	4	5	6	7	8
9	10	11	12	13	14	15
16	17	18	19	20	21	22
23	24	25	26	27	28	29
30	31					

NOVEMBER

		1	2	3	4	5
6	7	8	9	10	11	12
13	14	15	16	17	18	19
20	21	22	23	24	25	26
27	28	29	30			

DECEMBER

				1	2	3
4	5	6	7	8	9	10
11	12	13	14	15	16	17
18	19	20	21	22	23	24
25	26	27	28	29	30	31

Calendar 14

JANUARY

						1
2	3	4	5	6	7	8
9	10	11	12	13	14	15
16	17	18	19	20	21	22
23	24	25	26	27	28	29
30	31					

FEBRUARY

		1	2	3	4	5
6	7	8	9	10	11	12
13	14	15	16	17	18	19
20	21	22	23	24	25	26
27	28	29				

JULY

						1
2	3	4	5	6	7	8
9	10	11	12	13	14	15
16	17	18	19	20	21	22
23	24	25	26	27	28	29
30	31					

AUGUST

		1	2	3	4	5
6	7	8	9	10	11	12
13	14	15	16	17	18	19
20	21	22	23	24	25	26
27	28	29	30	31		

MARCH

			1	2	3	4
5	6	7	8	9	10	11
12	13	14	15	16	17	18
19	20	21	22	23	24	25
26	27	28	29	30	31	

APRIL

						1
2	3	4	5	6	7	8
9	10	11	12	13	14	15
16	17	18	19	20	21	22
23	24	25	26	27	28	29
30						

MAY

	1	2	3	4	5	6
7	8	9	10	11	12	13
14	15	16	17	18	19	20
21	22	23	24	25	26	27
28	29	30	31			

JUNE

				1	2	3
4	5	6	7	8	9	10
11	12	13	14	15	16	17
18	19	20	21	22	23	24
25	26	27	28	29	30	

SEPTEMBER

					1	2
3	4	5	6	7	8	9
10	11	12	13	14	15	16
17	18	19	20	21	22	23
24	25	26	27	28	29	30

OCTOBER

1	2	3	4	5	6	7
8	9	10	11	12	13	14
15	16	17	18	19	20	21
22	23	24	25	26	27	28
29	30	31				

NOVEMBER

			1	2	3	4
5	6	7	8	9	10	11
12	13	14	15	16	17	18
19	20	21	22	23	24	25
26	27	28	29	30		

DECEMBER

					1	2
3	4	5	6	7	8	9
10	11	12	13	14	15	16
17	18	19	20	21	22	23
24	25	26	27	28	29	30
31						

CHRISTIAN ECCLESIASTICAL CALENDAR

The ecclesiastical calendar, used by Roman Catholics and any Protestant groups, relates the year to various events in the life of Christ and the history of the Church. It is highlighted by a series of movable and immovable feasts and seasons either preparatory to these festivals or continuing the celebration of them. The year begins not on any fixed calendar date but four Sundays before Christmas with the season of Advent, a penitential period that prepares the church for Christmas. The season of Epiphany, commemorating the coming of the Maji, follows Christmas.

The calendar culminates in the celebration of Easter, the major feast of the year. Like Christmas, it is preceded by a penetential season, Lent, which lasts 40 days. The Easter Sequence lasts 123 days from the Septuagesima Sunday, nine weeks before Easter to Trinity Sunday, eight weeks after Easter. The length of the Sequence is fixed. It must be 123 days. This fact dictates the remainder of the calendar. Because the date of Easter varies, from March 22 to April 25, the calendar must be adjusted yearly so that there can be four Sundays in Advent. This is done by varying the length of the Epiphany and Trinity seasons. Epiphany can have from one to six Sundays while Trinity can have from 22 to 27, depending on when Easter falls.

The ecclesiastical calendar is luni-solar, regulated in part by the solar and partly by the lunar year. It is based on the calculation of Easter. Prior to the Fourth Century Christians disputed the date for celebrating the feast. Most agreed that it should occur on a Sunday, the day that Christ rose according to the Scriptures. The Quartodecimans, however, celebrated Easter on Passover (which occurs on the 14th Nisan) since the Crucifixion and Resurrection occurred around that period.

In 325 A.D. the Council of Nicaea decreed that Easter should be observed on the Sunday following the full moon occurring after the vernal equinox, which they determined to be March 21. Should the 14th of Nisan fall on that Sunday, Easter would be celebrated on the following Sunday to avoid Passover and the date celebrated by the Quartodecimans, who were considered heretics.

These rules made it necessary to reconcile the three periods of the calendar, the week, the lunar month and the solar year. In order to connect the lunar month with the solar year, the Church adopted a lunar cycle. The lunations consisted of 29 and 30 days alternately in a year of 354 days. When six intercalary months of 30 days and one of 29 days are added to this cycle it equals exactly 19 years in the Julian calendar. This lunar cycle was used to indicate new moons in the calendar prior to the Reformation. Each year was given a number—called the Golden Number, either because it was denoted so by the Greeks or because it was specially noted in the calendar. Thus an individual could predict when new moons would occur if he knew the year of the cycle. The Golden number was introduced around 530 A.D., but was used as if it had begun in 325 A.D., at the Council of Nicaea. The new moons determined by the cycle of the Golden Number differ from astronomical new moons by as much as two days. This factor led to serious problems with the calendar.

In addition to the Golden Number, the church used a Solar Cycle of 28 years called the Domenical Letter. The Domenical Letter connects the week with the year. It identifies on which date the first Sunday of the year will fall. Each of the first seven days of the year is given a letter, A to G. If January 1 is a Sunday, the letter A is used and the year would be A. If the first Sunday occurred on January 2, the letter B would be used and the year would be B. Since there are seven days in the week and four years in an intercalary cycle, it takes 28 years to go through the cycle.

Still another cycle was used in the calendar, the 15 year cycle of Indiction. This was utilized primarily by chronologists. This cycle began on January 1, 313 A.D.

During the 16th century, Joseph Scaliger suggested a universal measure of chronology. It was formed by taking the product of the number of each of the three cycles discussed above. Scaliger called this the Julian Period after his father Julius Scaliger.

The ancient church calendar was based on two suppositions: that the year was 365¼ days long and that 235 lunations would equal 19 years. Both were wrong. Over the centuries, astronomers and monks concerned with calculating the date of Easter observed that the Sun was days behind the cycles. Before the Eighth Century calculations were so confused that as many as three different Sundays were celebrated for Easter in the Christian world. Yet despite demands for reform and growing knowledge of more accurate means of calculations in the Muslim world and among the Jews, the Popes refused to intervene.

The hierarchy finally became interested in reform during the 15th century. But it was not until 1582 that Pope Gregory XIII reformed the calendar. Ironically in so doing he chose to ignore the problem of calculating Easter. In 1582 he dropped 10 days from October beginning with October 5, which became October 15. He also ordered that full centuries not divisible by four be common rather than leap years.

In order to correct the problem of predicting lunations with astronomical facts, the Golden Number was replaced with Epacts which indicated the moon's age at the beginning of the New Year. Over the course of centuries, the values will range from 1 to 30, the days of a full lunar month. The Epact is calculated by adding 11 to the day of the new moon in January and then, each succeeding year, adding an additional 11. In the third year of the cycle, 11 is added and then 30 is subtracted to allow for one period from full moon to full moon. The process is repeated with each succeeding year until the year when 30 is subtracted with the result of 0. Then the cycle begins again. A modification was made in this system. In the 19th year of the cycle, always occurring with epact 29, 12 was added instead of 11.

The Christian Church over the centuries denoted each day a feast of a given saint. Either the birth or death in the case of martyrdom of the saint is celebrated. There may be more than one saint venerated on a given day, but the day is commonly remembered for the major religious festival that occurs or for the important saint.

The ecclesiastical day developed from the Roman division of the day which began at sunrise. The day was divided into four three hour vigils as was the night. The vigils were

1st vigil,	6 A.M. or 6 P.M.
2nd vigil,	9 A.M. or 9 P.M.
3rd vigil,	12 noon or midnight
4th vigil,	3 A.M. or 3 P.M.

The cannonical hours were patterned on these. They are:

Prime	— about 6 A.M.
Tierce	— about 9 A.M.
Sext	— about 12 noon
Nones	— about 2 or 3 P.M.
Vespers	— about 4 P.M. or later
Compline	— about 7 P.M.
Matin & Lauds at midnight	

EASTER DATES

Year	Western	Churches Using Different Date Eastern	Egypt	Alexandria
211			A 21	
248				A 21
251			M 30	
252			A 18	
306	A 21			
326	A 10	A 10		A 10
346	M 30			
349	M 26			
360	M 26			
368	M 23	(some Western only)		
387	A 18	(some Western)		
	M 21	(others, against Nicean Council)		
397	M 29			
401	A 21			
406	M 25	(some Latins)		
414		M 29	(St. Cyril)	
417	M 25	(some Western only)		
421	A 10	A 10		A 10

Year	Western	Churches Using Different Date Eastern	Egypt	Alexandria
424			M 23	
425	M 22	(some Western only)		
441		M 30		M 30
444	M 26	(some Latins)		
455	A 17	(some Western only)		
475		A 13		
482	A 18	(some Latins)		
	M 21	(other Latins)		
495	A 2			
496	A 21			
499	A 18	(most Western)		
501	M 25			
516	A 10			
520	M 22	(some Latins)		
536	M 30	(some Western)		
550	A 17			
570	A 13	(Latins)		
577	A 18	(Gauls and others)		
	M 21	(Spaniards)		
590	A 2			
594	A 18			
645	A 17			
665	A 13			
672	A 18	(some Western)		
	M 21	(some Western)		
682	A 2			
689	A 18			
729	English and Roman churches joined			
740	A 17	(Latins)		
743	A 21			
748	M 24	(Latins)		
760	A 13			
763	A 10			
780	A 2			
783	M 30			
784	A 18			

DATES OF EASTER
A.D. 1-1999

Year	Easter	Year	Easter	Year	Easter	Year	Easter	Year	Easter
1	M 27	48	A 21	95	A 12	142	A 2	189	A 20
2	A 16	49	A 6	96	M 27	143	A 22	190	A 12
3	A 8	50	M 29	97	A 16	144	A 6	191	M 28
4	M 23	51	A 18	98	A 8	145	M 29	192	A 16
5	A 12	52	A 2	99	M 24	146	A 18	193	A 8
6	A 4	53	M 25	100	A 12	147	A 3	194	M 24
7	A 24	54	A 14	101	A 4	148	M 25	195	A 13
8	A 8	55	M 30	102	A 24	149	A 14	196	A 4
9	M 31	56	A 18	103	A 9	150	M 30	197	A 24
10	A 20	57	A 10	104	M 31	151	A 19	198	A 9
11	A 5	58	M 26	105	A 20	152	A 10	199	A 1
12	M 27	59	A 15	106	A 5	153	M 56	200	A 20
13	A 16	60	A 6	107	M 28	154	A 15	201	A 5
14	A 8	61	M 29	108	A 16	155	A 7	202	M 28
15	M 24	62	A 11	109	A 8	156	M 29	203	A 17
16	A 12	63	A 3	110	M 24	157	A 11	204	A 8
17	A 4	64	A 22	111	A 13	158	A 3	205	M 24
18	A 24	65	A 14	112	A 4	159	A 23	206	A 10
19	A 9	66	M 30	113	A 24	160	A 14	207	A 5
20	M 31	67	A 19	114	A 9	161	M 30	208	A 24
21	A 20	68	A 10	115	A 1	162	A 19	209	A 9
22	A 5	69	M 26	116	A 20	163	A 11	210	A 1
23	M 28	70	A 15	117	A 5	164	M 26	211*	A 14*
24	A 16	71	A 7	118	M 28	165	A 15	212	A 5
25	A 1	72	M 22	119	A 17	166	A 7	213	M 28
26	A 21	73	A 11	120	A 1	167	M 23	214	A 17
27	A 13	74	A 3	121	A 21	168	A 11	215	A 2
28	M 28	75	A 23	122	A 13	169	A 3	216	A 21
29	A 17	76	A 7	123	M 29	170	A 23	217	A 13
30	A 9	77	M 30	124	A 17	171	A 8	218	M 29
31	M 25	78	A 19	125	A 9	172	M 30	219	A 18
32	A 13	79	A 4	126	M 25	173	A 19	220	A 9
33	A 5	80	M 26	127	A 14	174	A 4	221	M 25
34	M 28	81	A 15	128	A 5	175	M 27	222	A 14
35	A 10	82	M 31	129	M 28	176	A 15	223	A 6
36	A 1	83	A 20	130	A 10	177	M 31	224	M 28
37	A 21	84	A 11	131	A 2	178	A 20	225	A 10
38	A 6	85	A 3	132	A 21	179	A 12	226	A 2
39	M 29	86	A 16	133	A 6	180	A 3	227	A 22
40	A 17	87	A 8	134	M 29	181	A 16	228	A 6
41	A 9	88	M 30	135	A 18	182	A 8	229	M 29
42	M 25	89	A 19	136	A 9	183	M 31	230	A 18
43	A 14	90	A 4	137	M 25	184	A 19	231	A 3
44	A 5	91	M 27	138	A 14	185	A 4	232	A 25
45	A 25	92	A 15	139	A 6	186	M 27	233	A 14
46	A 10	93	M 31	140	A 25	187	A 16	234	A 6
47	A 2	94	A 20	141	A 10	188	M 31	235	A 19

M-March A-April
*Confused Dates

Year	Easter	Year	Easter	Year	Easter	Year	Easter	Year	Easter
236	A 10	286	M 28	336	A 18	386	A 5	436	A 19
237	A 2	287	A 17	337	A 3	387*	A 25*	437	A 11
238	A 22	288	A 8	338	M 26	388	A 9	438	M 27
239	A 7	289	M 24	339	A 15	389	A 1	439	A 16
240	M 29	290	A 13	340	M 30	390	A 21	440	A 7
241	A 18	291	A 5	341	A 19	391	A 6	441*	M 23
242	A 3	292	A 24	342	A 11	392	M 28	442	A 12
243	M 26	293	A 9	343	M 27	393	A 17	443	A 4
244	A 14	294	A 1	344	A 15	394	A 2	444*	A 23*
245	M 30	295	A 21	345	A 7	395	M 25	445	A 8
246	A 19	296	A 5	346*	M 23*	396	A 13	446	M 31
247	A 11	297	M 28	347	A 12	397*	A 5*	447	A 20
248*	M 26*	298	A 17	348	A 3	398	A 18	448	M 31
249	A 15	299	A 2	349*	A 23*	399	A 10	449	M 27
250	A 7	300	M 24	350	A 8	400	A 1	450	A 16
251*	M 23*	301	A 13	351	M 31	401*	A 14*	451	A 8
252*	A 11*	302	A 5	352	A 19	402	A 6	452	M 23
253	A 3	303	A 18	353	A 11	403	M 29	453	A 12
254	A 23	304	A 9	354	M 27	404	A 17	454	A 4
255	A 8	305	A 1	355	A 16	405	A 2	455*	A 24*
256	M 30	306*	A 14	356	A 7	406*	A 22*	456	A 8
257	A 19	307	A 6	357	M 23	407	A 14	457	M 31
258	A 11	308	M 28	358	A 12	408	M 29	458	A 20
259	M 27	309	A 17	359	A 4	409	A 17	459	A 5
260	A 15	310	A 2	360	A 23	410	A 2	460	M 27
261	A 7	311	A 22	361	A 8	411	M 26	461	A 16
262	M 23	312	A 13	362	M 31	412	A 14	462	A 1
263	A 12	313	M 29	363	A 20	413	A 6	463	A 21
264	A 3	314	A 18	364	A 4	414*	M 22*	464	A 12
265	A 23	315	A 10	365	M 27	415	A 11	465	M 28
266	A 8	316	M 26	366	A 16	416	A 2	466	A 17
267	M 31	317	A 14	367	A 1	417*	A 22*	467	A 9
268	A 19	318	A 6	368*	A 20*	418	A 7	468	M 31
269	A 4	319	M 22	369	A 12	419	M 30	469	A 13
270	M 27	320	A 10	370	M 28	420	A 18	470	A 5
271	A 16	321	A 2	371	A 17	421*	A 3*	471	M 28
272	M 31	322	A 22	372	A 8	422	M 26	472	A 16
273	A 20	323	A 7	373	M 31	423	A 15	473	A 1
274	A 12	324	M 29	374	A 13	424*	A 6*	474	A 21
275	M 28	325	A 18	375	A 5	425*	A 19*	475*	A 6*
276	A 16	326*	A 3*	376	M 27	426	A 11	476	M 28
277	A 8	327	M 26	377	A 16	427	A 3	477	A 17
278	M 31	328	A 14	378	A 1	428	A 22	478	A 9
279	A 13	329	A 6	379	A 21	429	A 7	479	M 25
280	A 4	330	A 19	380	A 12	430	M 30	480	A 13
281	M 27	331	A 11	381	M 28	431	A 19	481	A 5
282	A 16	332	A 2	382	A 17	432	A 3	482*	A 25*
283	A 1	333	A 22	383	A 9	433	M 26	483	A 10
284	A 20	334	A 7	384	M 24	434	A 15	484	A 1
285	A 12	335	M 30	385	A 13	435	M 31	485	A 21

M-March A-April
*Confused Dates

Year	Easter	Year	Easter	Year	Easter	Year	Easter	Year	Easter
486	A 6	536*	M 23*	586	A 14	636	M 31	686	A 15
487	M 29	537	A 12	587	M 30	637	A 20	687	A 7
488	A 17	538	A 4	588	A 18	638	A 5	688	M 29
489	A 2	539	A 24	589	A 10	639	M 28	689*	A 11*
490	M 25	540	A 8	590*	M 26*	640	A 16	690	A 3
491	A 14	541	M 31	591	A 15	641	A 8	691	A 23
492	A 5	542	A 20	592	A 6	642	M 24	692	A 14
493	A 18	543	A 5	593	M 29	643	A 13	693	M 20
494	A 10	544	M 27	594*	A 11*	644	A 4	694	A 19
495*	M 26*	545	A 16	595	A 3	645*	A 24*	695	A 11
496*	A 14*	546	A 8	596	A 22	646	A 9	696	M 26
497	A 6	547	M 24	597	A 14	647	A 1	697	A 15
498	M 29	548	A 12	598	M 30	648	A 20	698	A 7
499*	A 11*	549	A 4	599	A 19	649	A 5	699	M 23
500	A 2	550*	A 24*	600	A 10	650	M 28	700	A 11
501*	A 22*	551	A 9	601	M 26	651	A 17	701	A 3
502	A 14	552	M 31	602	A 15	652	A 1	702	A 23
503	M 30	553	A 20	603	A 7	653	A 21	703	A 8
504	A 18	554	A 5	604	M 22	654	A 13	704	M 30
505	A 10	555	M 28	605	A 11	655	M 29	705	A 19
506	M 26	556	A 16	606	A 3	656	A 17	706	A 4
507	A 15	557	A 1	607	A 23	657	A 9	707	M 27
508	A 6	558	A 21	608	A 7	658	M 25	708	A 15
509	M 22	559	A 13	609	M 30	659	A 14	709	M 31
510	A 11	560	M 28	610	A 19	660	A 5	710	A 20
511	A 3	561	A 17	611	A 4	661	M 28	711	A 12
512	A 22	562	A 9	612	M 26	662	A 10	712	A 3
513	A 7	563	M 25	613	A 15	663	A 2	713	A 16
514	M 30	564	A 13	614	M 31	664	A 21	714	A 8
515	A 19	565	A 5	615	A 20	665*	A 6*	715	M 31
516*	A 3*	566	M 28	616	A 11	666	M 29	716	A 19
517	M 26	567	A 10	617	A 3	667	A 18	717	A 4
518	A 15	568	A 1	618	A 16	668	A 9	718	M 27
519	M 31	569	A 21	619	A 8	669	M 25	719	A 16
520*	A 19*	570*	A 6*	620	M 30	670	A 14	720	M 31
521	A 11	571	M 29	621	A 19	671	A 6	721	A 20
522	A 3	572	A 17	622	A 4	672*	A 25*	722	A 12
523	A 16	573	A 9	623	A 2	673	A 10	723	M 28
524	A 7	574	M 25	624	A 15	674	A 2	724	A 16
525	M 30	575	A 14	625	M 31	675	A 22	725	A 8
526	A 19	576	A 5	626	A 20	676	A 6	726	M 24
527	A 4	577*	A 25*	627	A 12	677	M 29	727	A 13
528	M 26	578	A 10	628	M 27	678	A 18	728	A 4
529	A 15	579	A 2	629	A 16	679	A 3	729*	A 24*
530	M 31	580	A 21	630	A 8	680	M 25	730	A 9
531	A 20	581	A 6	631	M 24	681	A 14	731	A 1
532	A 11	582	M 29	632	A 12	682	M 30	732	A 20
533	M 27	583	A 18	633	A 4	683	A 19	733	A 5
534	A 16	584	A 2	634	A 24	684	A 10	734	M 28
535	A 8	585	M 25	635	A 9	685*	M 26*	735	A 17

M-March A-April
*Confused Dates

Year	Easter	Year	Easter	Year	Easter	Year	Easter	Year	Easter
736	A 8	786	A 23	836	A 9	886	M 27	936	A 17
737	M 24	787	A 8	837	A 1	887	A 16	937	A 2
738	A 13	788	M 30	838	A 14	888	A 7	938	A 22
739	A 5	789	A 19	839	A 6	889	M 23	939	A 14
740*	A 24*	790	A 11	840	M 28	890	A 12	940	A 6
741	A 9	791	M 27	841	A 17	891	A 4	941	A 18
742	A 1	792	A 15	842	A 2	892	A 23	942	A 10
743*	A 14*	793	A 7	843	A 22	893	A 8	943	M 26
744	A 5	794	M 23	844	A 13	894	M 31	944	A 14
745	M 28	795	A 12	845	M 29	895	A 20	945	A 6
746	A 17	796	A 3	846	A 18	896	A 4	946	M 22
747	A 2	797	A 23	847	A 10	897	M 27	947	A 11
748*	A 21*	798	A 8	848	M 25	898	A 16	948	A 2
749	A 13	799	M 31	849	A 14	899	A 1	949	A 22
750	M 29	800	A 19	850	A 6	900	A 20	950	A 7
751	A 18	801	A 4	851	M 22	901	A 12	951	M 30
752	A 9	802	M 27	852	A 10	902	M 28	952	A 18
753	M 25	803	A 16	853	A 2	903	A 17	953	A 3
754	A 14	804	M 31	854	A 22	904	A 8	954	M 26
755	A 6	805	A 20	855	A 7	905	M 31	955	A 15
756	M 28	806	A 12	856	M 29	906	A 13	956	A 6
757	A 10	807	M 28	857	A 18	907	A 5	957	A 19
758	A 2	808	A 16	858	A 3	908	M 27	958	A 11
759	A 22	809	A 8	859	M 26	909	A 16	959	A 3
760*	A 6*	810	M 31	860	A 14	910	A 1	960	A 22
761	M 29	811	A 13	861	A 6	911	A 21	961	A 7
762	A 18	812	A 4	862	A 19	912	A 12	962	M 30
763*	A 3*	813	M 27	863	A 11	913	M 28	963	A 19
764	M 25	814	A 16	864	A 2	914	A 17	964	A 3
765	A 14	815	A 1	865	A 22	915	A 9	965	M 26
766	A 6	816	A 20	866	A 7	916	M 24	966	A 15
767	A 19	817	A 12	867	M 30	917	A 13	967	M 31
768	A 10	818	M 28	868	A 18	918	A 5	968	A 19
769	A 2	819	A 17	869	A 3	919	A 25	969	A 11
770	A 22	820	A 8	870	M 26	920	A 9	970	M 27
771	A 7	821	M 24	871	A 15	921	A 1	971	A 16
772	M 29	822	A 13	872	M 30	922	A 21	972	A 7
773	A 18	823	A 5	873	A 19	923	A 6	973	M 23
774	A 3	824	A 24	874	A 11	924	M 28	974	A 12
775	M 26	825	A 9	875	M 27	925	A 17	975	A 4
776	A 14	826	A 1	876	A 15	926	A 2	976	A 23
777	M 30	827	A 21	877	A 7	927	M 25	977	A 8
778	A 19	828	A 5	878	M 23	928	A 13	978	M 31
779	A 11	829	M 28	879	A 12	929	A 5	979	A 20
780*	M 26*	830	A 17	880	A 3	930	A 18	980	A 11
781	A 15	831	A 2	881	A 23	931	A 10	981	M 27
782	A 7	832	M 24	882	A 8	932	A 1	982	A 16
783*	M 23*	833	A 13	883	M 31	933	A 14	983	A 8
784*	A 11*	834	A 5	884	A 19	934	A 6	984	M 23
785	A 3	835	A 18	885	A 11	935	M 29	985	A 12

M-March A-April
*Confused Dates

Year	Easter	Year	Easter	Year	Easter	Year	Easter	Year	Easter
986	A 4	1036	A 18	1086	A 5	1136	M 22	1186	A 13
987	A 24	1037	A 10	1087	M 28	1137	A 11	1187	M 29
988	A 8	1038	M 26	1088	A 16	1138	A 3	1188	A 17
989	M 31	1039	A 15	1089	A 1	1139	A 23	1189	A 9
990	A 20	1040	A 6	1090	A 21	1140	A 7	1190	M 25
991	A 5	1041	M 22	1091	A 13	1141	M 30	1191	A 14
992	M 27	1042	A 11	1092	M 28	1142	A 19	1192	A 5
993	A 16	1043	A 3	1093	A 17	1143	A 4	1193	M 28
994	A 1	1044	A 22	1094	A 9	1144	M 26	1194	A 10
995	A 21	1045	A 7	1095	M 25	1145	A 15	1195	A 2
996	A 12	1046	M 30	1096	A 13	1146	M 31	1196	A 21
997	M 28	1047	A 19	1097	A 5	1147	A 20	1197	A 6
998	A 17	1048	A 3	1098	M 28	1148	A 11	1198	M 29
999	A 9	1049	M 26	1099	A 10	1149	A 3	1199	A 18
1000	M 31	1050	A 15	1100	A 1	1150	A 16	1200	A 9
1001	A 13	1051	M 31	1101	A 21	1151	A 8	1201	M 25
1002	A 5	1052	A 19	1102	A 6	1152	M 31	1202	A 14
1003	M 28	1053	A 11	1103	M 29	1153	A 19	1203	A 6
1004	A 16	1054	A 3	1104	A 17	1154	A 4	1204	A 25
1005	A 1	1055	A 16	1105	A 9	1155	M 27	1205	A 10
1006	A 21	1056	A 7	1106	M 25	1156	A 15	1206	A 2
1007	A 6	1057	M 30	1107	A 14	1157	M 31	1207	A 22
1008	M 28	1058	A 19	1108	A 5	1158	A 20	1208	A 6
1009	A 17	1059	A 4	1109	A 25	1159	A 12	1209	M 29
1010	A 9	1060	M 26	1110	A 10	1160	M 27	1210	A 18
1011	A 2	1061	A 15	1111	A 2	1161	A 16	1211	A 3
1012	A 13	1062	M 31	1112	A 21	1162	A 8	1212	M 25
1013	A 6	1063	A 20	1113	A 6	1163	M 24	1213	A 14
1014	A 25	1064	A 11	1114	M 29	1164	A 12	1214	M 30
1015	A 10	1065	M 27	1115	A 18	1165	A 4	1215	A 19
1016	A 1	1066	A 16	1116	A 1	1166	A 24	1216	A 10
1017	A 21	1067	A 8	1117	M 25	1167	A 9	1217	M 26
1018	A 6	1068	M 23	1118	A 14	1168	M 31	1218	A 15
1019	M 29	1069	A 12	1119	M 30	1169	A 20	1219	A 7
1020	A 17	1070	A 4	1120	A 18	1170	A 5	1220	M 29
1021	A 2	1071	A 24	1121	A 10	1171	M 28	1221	A 11
1022	M 25	1072	A 8	1122	M 26	1172	A 16	1222	A 3
1023	A 14	1073	M 31	1123	A 15	1173	A 8	1223	A 23
1024	A 5	1074	A 20	1124	A 6	1174	M 24	1224	A 14
1025	A 18	1075	A 5	1125	M 29	1175	A 13	1225	M 30
1026	A 10	1076	M 27	1126	A 11	1176	A 4	1226	A 19
1027	M 26	1077	A 16	1127	A 3	1177	A 24	1227	A 11
1028	A 14	1078	A 8	1128	A 22	1178	A 9	1228	M 26
1029	A 6	1079	M 24	1129	A 14	1179	A 1	1229	A 15
1030	M 29	1080	A 12	1130	M 30	1180	A 20	1230	A 7
1031	A 11	1081	A 4	1131	A 19	1181	A 5	1231	M 23
1032	A 2	1082	A 24	1132	A 10	1182	M 28	1232	A 11
1033	A 22	1083	A 9	1133	M 26	1183	A 17	1233	A 3
1034	A 14	1084	M 31	1134	A 15	1184	A 1	1234	A 23
1035	M 30	1085	A 20	1135	A 7	1185	A 21	1235	A 8

M-March A-April
*Confused Dates

Year	Easter	Year	Easter	Year	Easter	Year	Easter	Year	Easter
1236	M 30	1286	A 14	1336	M 31	1386	A 22	1436	A 8
1237	A 19	1287	A 6	1337	A 20	1387	A 7	1437	M 31
1238	A 4	1288	M 28	1338	A 12	1388	M 29	1438	A 13
1239	M 27	1289	A 10	1339	M 28	1389	A 18	1439	A 5
1240	A 15	1290	A 2	1340	A 16	1390	A 3	1440	M 27
1241	M 31	1291	A 22	1341	A 8	1391	M 26	1441	A 16
1242	A 20	1292	A 6	1342	M 31	1392	A 14	1442	A 1
1243	A 12	1293	M 29	1343	A 13	1393	A 6	1443	A 21
1244	A 3	1294	A 18	1344	A 4	1394	A 19	1444	A 12
1245	A 16	1295	A 3	1345	M 27	1395	A 11	1445	M 28
1246	A 8	1296	M 25	1346	A 16	1396	A 2	1446	A 17
1247	M 31	1297	A 14	1347	A 1	1397	A 22	1447	A 9
1248	A 19	1298	A 6	1348	A 20	1398	A 7	1448	M 24
1249	A 4	1299	A 19	1349	A 12	1399	M 30	1449	A 13
1250	M 27	1300	A 10	1350	M 28	1400	A 18	1450	A 5
1251	A 16	1301	A 2	1351	A 17	1401	A 3	1451	A 25
1252	M 31	1302	A 22	1352	A 8	1402	M 26	1452	A 9
1253	A 20	1303	A 7	1353	M 24	1403	A 15	1453	A 1
1254	A 12	1304	M 29	1354	A 13	1404	M 30	1454	A 21
1255	M 28	1305	A 18	1355	A 5	1405	A 19	1455	A 6
1256	A 16	1306	A 3	1356	A 24	1406	A 11	1456	M 28
1257	A 8	1307	M 26	1357	A 9	1407	M 27	1457	A 17
1258	M 24	1308	A 14	1358	A 1	1408	A 15	1458	A 2
1259	A 13	1309	M 30	1359	A 21	1409	A 7	1459	M 25
1260	A 4	1310	A 19	1360	A 5	1410	M 23	1460	A 13
1261	A 24	1311	A 11	1361	M 28	1411	A 12	1461	A 5
1262	A 9	1312	M 26	1362	A 17	1412	A 3	1462	A 18
1263	A 1	1313	A 15	1363	A 2	1413	A 23	1463	A 10
1264	A 20	1314	A 7	1364	M 24	1414	A 8	1464	A 1
1265	A 5	1315	M 23	1365	A 13	1415	M 31	1465	A 14
1266	M 28	1316	A 11	1366	A 5	1416	A 19	1466	A 6
1267	A 17	1317	A 3	1367	A 18	1417	A 11	1467	M 29
1268	A 8	1318	A 23	1368	A 9	1418	M 27	1468	A 17
1269	M 24	1319	A 8	1369	A 1	1419	A 16	1469	A 2
1270	A 13	1320	M 30	1370	A 14	1420	A 7	1470	A 22
1271	A 5	1321	A 19	1371	A 6	1421	M 23	1471	A 14
1272	A 24	1322	A 11	1372	M 28	1422	A 12	1472	M 29
1273	A 9	1323	M 27	1373	A 17	1423	A 4	1473	A 18
1274	A 1	1324	A 15	1374	A 2	1424	A 23	1474	A 10
1275	A 14	1325	A 7	1375	A 22	1425	A 8	1475	M 26
1276	A 5	1326	M 23	1376	A 13	1426	M 31	1476	A 14
1277	M 28	1327	A 12	1377	M 29	1427	A 20	1477	A 6
1278	A 17	1328	A 3	1378	A 18	1428	A 4	1478	M 22
1279	A 2	1329	A 23	1379	A 10	1429	M 27	1479	A 11
1280	A 21	1330	A 8	1380	M 25	1430	A 16	1480	A 2
1281	A 13	1331	M 31	1381	A 14	1431	A 1	1481	A 22
1282	M 29	1332	A 19	1382	A 6	1432	A 20	1482	A 7
1283	A 18	1333	A 4	1383	M 22	1433	A 12	1483	M 30
1284	A 9	1334	M 27	1384	A 10	1434	M 28	1484	A 18
1285	M 25	1335	A 16	1385	A 2	1435	A 17	1485	A 3

M-March A-April
*Confused Dates

Year	Easter	Year	Easter	Year	Easter	Year	Easter	Year	Easter
1486	M 26	1506	A 12	1526	A 1	1546	A 25	1566	A 14
1487	A 15	1507	A 4	1527	A 21	1547	A 10	1567	M 30
1488	A 6	1508	A 23	1528	A 12	1548	A 1	1568	A 18
1489	A 19	1509	A 8	1529	M 28	1549	A 21	1569	A 10
1490	A 11	1510	M 31	1530	A 17	1550	A 6	1570	M 26
1491	A 3	1511	A 20	1531	A 9	1551	M 29	1571	A 15
1492	A 22	1512	A 11	1532	M 31	1552	A 17	1572	A 6
1493	A 7	1513	M 27	1533	A 13	1553	A 2	1573	M 22
1494	M 30	1514	A 16	1534	A 5	1554	M 25	1574	A 11
1495	A 19	1515	A 8	1535	M 28	1555	A 14	1575	A 3
1496	A 3	1516	M 23	1536	A 16	1556	A 5	1576	A 22
1497	M 26	1517	A 12	1537	A 1	1557	A 18	1577	A 7
1498	A 15	1518	A 4	1538	A 21	1558	A 10	1578	M 30
1499	M 31	1519	A 24	1539	A 6	1559	M 26	1579	A 19
1500	A 19	1520	A 8	1540	M 28	1560	A 14	1580	A 3
1501	A 11	1521	M 31	1541	A 17	1561	A 6	1581	M 26
1502	M 27	1522	A 20	1542	A 9	1562	M 29	1582	A 13
1503	A 16	1523	A 5	1543	M 25	1563	A 11		
1504	A 7	1524	M 27	1544	A 13	1564	A 2		
1505	M 23	1525	A 16	1545	A 5	1565	A 22		

	Easter			Easter			Easter			Easter	
Year	O.S.	N.S.	Year	O.S.	N.S.	Year	O.S.	N.S.	Year	O.S.	N.S.
1583	M 31	A 10	1608	M 27	A 6	1633	A 21	M 27	1658	A 11	A 21
1584	A 19	A 1	1609	A 16	A 19	1634	A 6	A 16	1659	A 3	A 13
1585	A 11	A 21	1610	A 8	A 11	1635	M 29	M 8	1660	A 22	M 28
1586	A 3	A 6	1611	M 24	A 3	1636	A 17	M 23	1661	A 14	A 17
1587	A 16	M 29	1612	A 12	A 22	1637	A 9	A 12	1662	M 30	A 9
1588	A 7	A 17	1613	A 4	A 7	1638	M 25	A 4	1663	A 19	M 25
1589	M 30	A 2	1614	A 24	M 30	1639	A 14	A 24	1664	A 10	A 13
1590	A 19	A 22	1615	A 9	A 19	1640	A 5	A 8	1665	M 26	A 5
1591	A 4	A 14	1616	M 31	A 3	1641	A 25	M 31	1666	A 15	A 25
1592	M 26	M 29	1617	A 20	M 26	1642	A 10	A 20	1667	A 7	A 10
1593	A 15	A 18	1618	A 5	A 15	1643	A 2	A 5	1668	M 22	A 1
1594	M 31	A 10	1619	M 28	M 31	1644	A 21	M 27	1669	A 11	A 21
1595	A 20	M 26	1620	A 16	A 19	1645	A 6	A 16	1670	A 3	A 6
1596	A 11	A 14	1621	A 1	A 11	1646	M 29	A 1	1671	A 23	M 29
1597	M 27	A 6	1622	A 21	M 27	1647	A 18	A 21	1672	A 7	A 17
1598	A 16	M 22	1623	A 13	A 16	1648	A 2	A 12	1673	M 30	A 2
1599	A 8	A 18	1624	M 28	A 7	1649	M 25	A 4	1674	A 19	M 25
1600	M 23	A 2	1625	A 17	M 30	1650	A 14	A 17	1675	A 4	A 14
1601	A 12	A 22	1626	A 9	A 12	1651	M 30	A 9	1676	M 26	A 5
1602	A 4	A 7	1627	M 25	A 4	1652	A 18	M 31	1677	A 15	A 18
1603	A 244	M 30	1628	A 13	A 23	1653	A 10	A 13	1678	M 31	A 10
1604	A 8	A 18	1629	A 5	A 15	1654	M 26	A 5	1679	A 20	A 2
1605	M 31	A 10	1630	M 28	M 31	1655	A 15	M 28	1680	A 11	A 21
1606	A 20	M 26	1631	A 10	A 20	1656	A 6	A 16	1681	A 3	A 6
1607	A 5	A 15	1632	A 1	A 11	1657	M 29	A 1	1682	A 16	M 29

M-March A-April
*Confused Dates

Year	Easter O.S.		Easter N.S.	
1683	A	8	A	18
1684	M	30	A	2
1685	A	19	A	22
1686	A	4	A	14
1687	M	27	M	30
1688	A	15	A	18
1689	M	31	A	10
1690	A	20	M	26
1691	A	12	A	15
1692	M	27	A	6
1693	A	16	M	22
1694	A	8	A	11
1695	M	24	A	3
1696	A	12	A	22
1697	A	4	A	7
1698	A	24	M	30
1699	A	9	A	19
1700	M	31	A	11
1701	A	20	M	27
1702	A	5	A	16
1703	M	28	A	8
1704	A	16	M	23
1705	A	8	A	2
1706	M	24	A	4
1707	A	13	A	24
1708	A	4	A	8
1709	A	24	M	31
1710	A	9	A	20
1711	A	1	A	5
1712	A	20	M	27
1713	A	5	A	16
1714	M	28	A	1
1715	A	17	A	21
1716	A	1	A	12
1717	A	21	M	28
1718	A	13	A	17
1719	M	29	A	9
1720	A	17	M	31
1721	A	9	A	13
1722	M	25	A	5
1723	A	14	M	28
1724	A	5	M	16
1725	M	28	A	1
1726	A	10	A	21
1727	A	2	A	13
1728	A	21	M	28
1729	A	6	A	17
1730	M	29	A	9
1731	A	18	M	25
1732	A	9	A	13

Year	Easter O.S.		Easter N.S.	
1733	M	25	A	5
1734	A	14	A	25
1735	A	6	A	10
1736	A	25	A	1
1737	A	10	A	21
1738	A	2	A	6
1739	A	22	M	29
1740	A	6	A	17
1741	M	29	A	2
1742	A	18	M	25
1743	A	3	A	14
1744	M	25	A	5
1745	A	14	A	18
1746	M	30	A	10
1747	A	19	A	2
1748	A	10	A	14
1749	M	26	A	6
1750	A	15	M	29
1751	A	7	A	11
1752	M	29	A	2
1753	A	11	A	22
1754	A	3	A	14
1755	A	23	M	30
1756	A	14	A	18
1757	M	30	A	10
1758	A	19	M	26
1759	A	11	A	15
1760	M	26	A	6
1761	A	15	M	22
1762	A	7	A	11
1763	M	23	A	3
1764	A	11	A	22
1765	A	3	A	7
1766	A	23	M	30
1767	A	8	A	19
1768	M	30	A	3
1769	A	19	M	26
1770	A	4	A	15
1771	M	27	M	31
1772	A	15	A	19
1773	M	31	A	11
1774	A	20	A	3
1775	A	12	A	16
1776	A	3	A	7
1777	A	16	M	30
1778	A	8	A	19
1779	M	31	A	4
1780	A	19	M	26
1781	A	4	A	15
1782	M	27	M	31

Year	Easter O.S.		Easter N.S.	
1783	A	16	A	20
1784	M	31	A	11
1785	A	20	M	27
1786	A	12	A	16
1787	M	28	A	8
1788	A	16	M	23
1789	A	8	A	12
1790	M	24	A	4
1791	A	13	A	24
1792	A	4	A	8
1793	A	24	M	31
1794	A	9	A	20
1795	A	1	A	5
1796	A	20	M	27
1797	A	5	A	16
1798	M	28	A	8
1799	A	17	M	24
1800	A	8	A	13
1801	M	24	A	5
1802	A	13	A	18
1803	A	5	A	10
1804	A	24	A	1
1805	A	9	A	14
1806	A	1	A	6
1807	A	13	M	29
1808	A	5	A	17
1809	M	28	A	2
1810	A	17	A	22
1811	A	2	A	14
1812	A	21	M	29
1813	A	13	A	18
1814	M	29	A	10
1815	A	18	M	26
1816	A	9	A	14
1817	M	25	A	6
1818	A	14	M	22
1819	A	6	A	11
1820	M	28	A	2
1821	A	10	A	22
1822	A	2	A	7
1823	A	22	M	30
1824	A	7	A	18
1825	M	29	A	3
1826	A	18	M	26
1827	A	3	A	15
1828	M	25	A	6
1829	A	14	A	19
1830	A	6	A	11
1831	A	19	A	3
1832	A	10	A	22

Year	Easter O.S.		Easter N.S.	
1833	A	2	A	7
1834	A	22	M	30
1835	A	7	A	19
1836	M	29	A	3
1837	A	18	M	26
1838	A	3	A	15
1839	M	26	M	31
1840	A	14	A	19
1841	M	30	A	11
1842	A	19	M	27
1843	A	11	A	16
1844	M	26	A	7
1845	A	15	M	23
1846	A	7	A	12
1847	M	23	A	4
1848	A	11	A	23
1849	A	3	A	8
1850	A	23	M	31
1851	A	8	A	20
1852	M	30	A	11
1853	A	19	M	27
1854	A	11	A	16
1855	M	27	A	8
1856	A	15	M	23
1857	A	7	A	12
1858	M	23	A	4
1859	A	12	A	24
1860	A	3	A	8
1861	A	23	M	31
1862	A	8	A	20
1863	M	31	A	5
1864	A	19	M	27
1865	A	4	A	16
1866	M	27	A	1
1867	A	16	A	21
1868	A	31	A	12
1869	A	20	M	28
1870	A	12	A	17
1871	M	28	A	9
1872	A	16	M	31
1873	A	8	A	13
1874	M	31	A	5
1875	A	13	M	28
1876	A	4	A	16
1877	M	27	A	1
1878	A	16	A	21
1879	A	1	A	13
1880	A	20	M	28
1881	A	12	A	17
1882	M	28	A	9

M-March A-April
*Confused Dates

Year	Easter O.S.		Easter N.S.		Year	Easter O.S.		Easter N.S.		Year	Easter O.S.		Easter N.S.		Year	Easter O.S.		Easter N.S.	
1883	A	17	M	25	1913	A	14	M	23	1943	A	12	A	25	1973	A	16	A	22
1884	A	8	A	13	1914	M	6	A	12	1944	A	3	A	9	1974	A	1	A	14
1885	M	24	A	5	1915	A	22	A	4	1945	A	23	A	1	1975	A	21	M	30
1886	A	13	A	25	1916	A	10	A	23	1946	A	8	A	21	1976	A	12	A	18
1887	A	5	A	10	1917	A	2	A	8	1947	M	31	A	6	1977	M	28	A	10
1888	A	24	A	1	1918	A	22	M	31	1948	A	19	M	28	1978	A	17	M	26
1889	A	9	A	21	1919	A	7	A	20	1949	A	11	A	17	1979	A	9	A	15
1890	A	1	A	6	1920	M	29	A	4	1950	M	27	A	9	1980	M	24	A	6
1891	A	21	M	29	1921	A	18	M	27	1951	A	16	M	25	1981	A	13	A	19
1892	A	5	A	17	1922	A	3	A	16	1952	A	7	A	13	1982	A	5	A	11
1893	M	28	A	2	1923	M	26	A	1	1953	M	23	A	5	1983	A	25	A	3
1894	A	17	M	25	1924	A	14	A	20	1954	A	12	A	18	1984	A	9	A	22
1895	A	2	A	14	1925	A	6	A	12	1955	A	4	A	10	1985	A	1	A	7
1896	M	24	A	5	1926	A	19	A	4	1956	A	23	A	1	1986	A	21	M	30
1897	A	13	A	18	1927	A	11	A	17	1957	A	8	A	21	1987	A	6	A	19
1898	A	5	A	10	1928	A	2	A	8	1958	M	31	A	6	1988	M	28	A	3
1899	A	18	A	2	1929	A	22	M	31	1959	A	20	M	29	1989	A	17	M	26
1900	A	9	A	15	1930	A	7	A	20	1960	A	4	A	17	1990	A	2	A	15
1901	A	1	A	7	1931	M	30	A	5	1961	M	27	A	2	1991	M	25	M	31
1902	A	14	M	30	1932	A	18	M	27	1962	A	16	A	22	1992	A	13	A	19
1903	A	6	A	12	1933	A	3	A	16	1963	A	1	A	14	1993	A	5	A	11
1904	M	28	A	3	1934	M	26	A	1	1964	A	20	M	29	1994	A	18	A	3
1905	A	17	A	23	1935	A	15	A	21	1965	A	12	A	18	1995	A	10	A	16
1906	A	2	A	15	1936	M	30	A	12	1966	M	28	A	10	1996	A	1	A	7
1907	A	22	M	31	1937	A	19	M	28	1967	A	17	M	26	1997	A	14	M	30
1908	A	13	A	19	1938	A	11	A	17	1968	A	8	A	14	1998	A	6	A	12
1909	M	29	A	11	1939	M	27	A	9	1969	M	31	A	6	1999	M	29	A	4
1910	A	18	M	27	1940	A	15	M	24	1970	A	13	M	29					
1911	A	10	A	16	1941	A	7	A	13	1971	A	5	A	11					
1912	M	25	A	7	1942	M	23	A	5	1972	M	27	A	2					

M-March A-April
*Confused Dates

THE ECCLESIASTICAL CALENDAR

Advent	4 Sundays
Christmas	December 25
The Feast of the Epiphany	January 6
Epiphany Season	1-6 Sundays
Septuagesima Sunday	9 weeks before Easter
Sexagesima Sunday	8 weeks before Easter
Quinquagesima	7 weeks before Easter
Ash Wednesday	46 days before Easter
Invocavit Sunday	6 weeks before Easter
Reminiscere Sunday	5 weeks before Easter
Oculi Sunday	4 weeks before Easter
Laetare Sunday	3 weeks before Easter
Judica or Passion Sunday	2 weeks before Easter
Palmarum Sunday	1 week before Easter
Maundy Thursday	3 days before Easter
Good Friday	2 days before Easter
Easter	
Quasimodogeneti	1 week after Easter
Misericordia Sunday	2 weeks after Easter
Jubilate Sunday	3 weeks after Easter
Cantate Sunday	4 weeks after Easter
Vocem Juncunditatis	5 weeks after Easter
The Feast of the Ascension	40 days after Easter
Exaudi Sunday	6 weeks after Easter
The Feast of Pentecost	50 days after Easter
The Feast of the Holy Trinity	8 weeks after Easter
Trinity Season	22-27 Sundays

WESTERN ERA

Western Era Julian

Year	Month	Golden Number	Epact	Solar Cycle	Domenical Letter	Roman Indiction	Julian Period
1	Jan	2	22	10	B	4	4714
2	Jan	3	3	11	A	5	4715
3	Jan	4	14	12	G	6	4716
4*	Jan	5	25	13	FE	7	4717
5	Jan	6	8	14	D	8	4718
6	Jan	7	17	15	C	9	4719
7	Jan	8	28	16	B	10	4720
8*	Jan	9	9	17	AG	11	4721
9	Jan	10	20	18	F	12	4722
10	Jan	11	1	19	E	13	4723
11	Jan	12	12	20	D	14	4724
12*	Jan	13	23	21	CB	15	4725
13	Jan	14	4	22	A	1	4726
14	Jan	15	15	23	G	2	4727
15	Jan	16	26	24	F	3	4728
16*	Jan	17	7	25	ED	4	4729
17	Jan	18	18	26	C	5	4730
18	Jan	19	9	27	B	6	4731
19	Jan	1	11	28	A	7	4732
20*	Jan	2	22	1	GF	8	4733
21	Jan	3	3	2	E	9	4734
22	Jan	4	14	3	D	10	4735
23	Jan	5	25	4	C	11	4736
24*	Jan	6	6	5	BA	12	4737
25	Jan	7	17	6	G	13	4738
26	Jan	8	28	7	F	14	4739
27	Jan	9	9	8	E	15	4740
28*	Jan	10	20	9	DC	1	4741
29	Jan	11	1	10	B	2	4742
30	Jan	12	12	11	A	3	4743
31	Jan	13	23	12	G	4	4744
32*	Jan	14	4	13	FE	5	4745
33	Jan	15	15	14	D	6	4746
34	Jan	16	26	15	C	7	4747
35	Jan	17	7	16	B	8	4748
36*	Jan	18	18	17	AG	9	4749
37	Jan	19	9	18	F	10	4750
38	Jan	1	11	19	E	11	4751
39	Jan	2	22	20	D	12	4752
40*	Jan	3	3	21	CB	13	4753
41	Jan	4	14	22	A	14	4754
42	Jan	5	25	23	G	15	4755

Western Era Julian

Year	Month	Golden Number	Epact	Solar Cycle	Domenical Letter	Roman Indiction	Julian Period
43	Jan	6	6	24	F	1	4756
44*	Jan	7	17	25	ED	2	4757
45	Jan	8	28	26	C	3	4758
46	Jan	9	9	27	B	4	4759
47	Jan	10	20	28	A	5	4760
48*	Jan	11	1	1	GF	6	4761
49	Jan	12	12	2	E	7	4762
50	Jan	13	23	3	D	8	4763
51	Jan	14	4	4	C	9	4764
52*	Jan	15	15	5	BA	10	4765
53	Jan	16	26	6	G	11	4766
54	Jan	17	7	7	F	12	4767
55	Jan	18	18	8	E	13	4768
56*	Jan	19	9	9	DC	14	4769
57	Jan	1	11	10	B	15	4770
58	Jan	2	22	11	A	1	4771
59	Jan	3	3	12	G	2	4772
60*	Jan	4	14	13	FE	3	4773
61	Jan	5	25	14	D	4	4774
62	Jan	6	6	15	C	5	4775
63	Jan	7	17	16	B	6	4776
64*	Jan	8	28	17	AG	7	4777
65	Jan	9	9	18	F	8	4778
66	Jan	10	20	19	E	9	4779
67	Jan	11	1	20	D	10	4780
68*	Jan	12	12	21	CB	11	4781
69	Jan	13	23	22	A	12	4782
70	Jan	14	4	23	G	13	4783
71	Jan	15	15	24	F	14	4784
72*	Jan	16	26	25	ED	15	4785
73	Jan	17	7	26	C	1	4786
74	Jan	18	18	27	B	2	4787
75	Jan	19	9	28	A	3	4788
76*	Jan	1	11	1	GF	4	4789
77	Jan	2	22	2	E	5	4790
78	Jan	3	3	3	D	6	4791
79	Jan	4	14	4	C	7	4792
80*	Jan	5	25	5	BA	8	4793
81	Jan	6	6	6	G	9	4794
82	Jan	7	17	7	F	10	4795
83	Jan	8	28	8	E	11	4796
84*	Jan	9	9	9	DC	12	4797

Western Era Julian Year	Month	Golden Number	Epact	Solar Cycle	Domenical Letter	Roman Indiction	Julian Period
85	Jan	10	20	10	B	13	4798
86	Jan	11	1	11	A	14	4799
87	Jan	12	12	12	G	15	4800
88*	Jan	13	23	13	FE	1	4801
89	Jan	14	4	14	D	2	4802
90	Jan	15	15	15	C	3	4803
91	Jan	16	26	16	B	4	4804
92*	Jan	17	7	17	AG	5	4805
93	Jan	18	18	18	F	6	4806
94	Jan	19	9	19	E	7	4807
95	Jan	1	11	20	D	8	4808
96*	Jan	2	22	21	CB	9	4809
97	Jan	3	3	22	A	10	4810
98	Jan	4	14	23	G	11	4811
99	Jan	5	25	24	F	12	4812
100*	Jan	6	6	25	ED	13	4813
101	Jan	7	17	26	C	14	4814
102	Jan	8	28	27	B	15	4815
103	Jan	9	9	28	A	1	4816
104*	Jan	10	20	1	GF	2	4817
105	Jan	11	1	2	E	3	4818
106	Jan	12	12	3	D	4	4819
107	Jan	13	23	4	C	5	4820
108*	Jan	14	4	5	BA	6	4821
109	Jan	15	15	6	G	7	4822
110	Jan	16	26	7	F	8	4823
111	Jan	17	7	8	E	9	4824
112*	Jan	18	18	9	DC	10	4825
113	Jan	19	9	10	B	11	4826
114	Jan	1	11	11	A	12	4827
115	Jan	2	22	12	G	13	4828
116*	Jan	3	3	13	FE	14	4829
117	Jan	4	14	14	D	15	4830
118	Jan	5	25	15	C	1	4831
119	Jan	6	6	16	B	2	4832
120*	Jan	7	17	17	AG	3	4833
121	Jan	8	28	18	F	4	4834
122	Jan	9	9	19	E	5	4835
123	Jan	10	20	20	D	6	4836
124*	Jan	11	1	21	CB	7	4837
125	Jan	12	12	22	A	8	4838
126	Jan	13	23	23	G	9	4839
127	Jan	14	4	24	F	10	4840
128*	Jan	15	15	25	ED	11	4841

Western Era Julian Year	Month	Golden Number	Epact	Solar Cycle	Domenical Letter	Roman Indiction	Julian Period
129	Jan	16	26	26	C	12	4842
130	Jan	17	7	27	B	13	4843
131	Jan	18	18	28	A	14	4844
132*	Jan	19	9	1	GF	15	4845
133	Jan	1	11	2	E	1	4846
134	Jan	2	22	3	D	2	4847
135	Jan	3	3	4	C	3	4848
136*	Jan	4	14	5	BA	4	4849
137	Jan	5	25	6	G	5	4850
138	Jan	6	6	7	F	6	4851
139	Jan	7	17	8	E	7	4852
140*	Jan	8	28	9	DC	8	4853
141	Jan	9	9	10	B	9	4854
142	Jan	10	20	11	A	10	4855
143	Jan	11	1	12	G	11	4856
144*	Jan	12	12	13	FE	12	4857
145	Jan	13	23	14	D	13	4858
146	Jan	14	4	15	C	14	4859
147	Jan	15	15	16	B	15	4860
148*	Jan	16	26	17	AG	1	4861
149	Jan	17	7	18	F	2	4862
150	Jan	18	18	19	E	3	4863
151	Jan	19	9	20	D	4	4864
152*	Jan	1	11	21	CB	5	4865
153	Jan	2	22	22	A	6	4866
154	Jan	3	3	23	G	7	4867
155	Jan	4	14	24	F	8	4868
156*	Jan	5	25	25	ED	9	4869
157	Jan	6	6	26	C	10	4870
158	Jan	7	17	27	B	11	4871
159	Jan	8	28	28	A	12	4872
160*	Jan	9	9	1	GF	13	4873
161	Jan	10	20	2	E	14	4874
162	Jan	11	1	3	D	15	4875
163	Jan	12	12	4	C	1	4876
164*	Jan	13	23	5	BA	2	4877
165	Jan	14	4	6	G	3	4878
166	Jan	15	15	7	F	4	4879
167	Jan	16	26	8	E	5	4880
168*	Jan	17	7	9	DC	6	4881
169	Jan	18	18	10	B	7	4882
170	Jan	19	9	11	A	8	4883
171	Jan	1	11	12	G	9	4884
172*	Jan	2	22	13	FE	10	4885

Western Era
Julian

Year	Month	Golden Number	Epact	Solar Cycle	Domenical Letter	Roman Indiction	Julian Period
173	Jan	3	3	14	D	11	4886
174	Jan	4	14	15	C	12	4887
175	Jan	5	25	16	B	13	4888
176*	Jan	6	6	17	AG	14	4889
177	Jan	7	17	18	F	15	4890
178	Jan	8	28	19	E	1	4891
179	Jan	9	9	20	D	2	4892
180*	Jan	10	20	21	CB	3	4893
181	Jan	11	1	22	A	4	4894
182	Jan	12	12	23	G	5	4895
183	Jan	13	23	24	F	6	4896
184*	Jan	14	4	25	ED	7	4897
185	Jan	15	15	26	C	8	4898
186	Jan	16	26	27	B	9	4899
187	Jan	17	7	28	A	10	4900
188*	Jan	18	18	1	GF	11	4901
189	Jan	19	9	2	E	12	4902
190	Jan	1	11	3	D	13	4903
191	Jan	2	22	4	C	14	4904
192*	Jan	3	3	5	BA	15	4905
193	Jan	4	14	6	G	1	4906
194	Jan	5	25	7	F	2	4907
195	Jan	6	6	8	E	3	4908
196*	Jan	7	17	9	DC	4	4909
197	Jan	8	28	10	B	5	4910
198	Jan	9	9	11	A	6	4911
199	Jan	10	20	12	G	7	4912
200*	Jan	11	1	13	FE	8	4913
201	Jan	12	12	14	D	9	4914
202	Jan	13	23	15	C	10	4915
203	Jan	14	4	16	B	11	4916
204*	Jan	15	15	17	AG	12	4917
205	Jan	16	26	18	F	13	4918
206	Jan	17	7	19	E	14	4919
207	Jan	18	18	20	D	15	4920
208*	Jan	19	9	21	CB	1	4921
209	Jan	1	11	22	A	2	4922
210	Jan	2	22	23	G	3	4923
211	Jan	3	3	24	F	4	4924
212*	Jan	4	14	25	ED	5	4925
213	Jan	5	25	26	C	6	4926
214	Jan	6	6	27	B	7	4927
215	Jan	7	17	28	A	8	4928
216*	Jan	8	28	1	GF	9	4929

Western Era
Julian

Year	Month	Golden Number	Epact	Solar Cycle	Domenical Letter	Roman Indiction	Julian Period
217	Jan	9	9	2	E	10	4930
218	Jan	10	20	3	D	11	4931
219	Jan	11	1	4	C	12	4932
220*	Jan	12	12	5	BA	13	4933
221	Jan	13	23	6	G	14	4934
222	Jan	14	4	7	F	15	4935
223	Jan	15	15	8	E	1	4936
224*	Jan	16	26	9	DC	2	4937
225	Jan	17	7	10	B	3	4938
226	Jan	18	18	11	A	4	4939
227	Jan	19	9	12	G	5	4940
228*	Jan	1	11	13	FE	6	4941
229	Jan	2	22	14	D	7	4942
230	Jan	3	3	15	C	8	4943
231	Jan	4	14	16	B	9	4944
232*	Jan	5	25	17	AG	10	4945
233	Jan	6	6	18	F	11	4946
234	Jan	7	17	19	E	12	4947
235	Jan	8	28	20	D	13	4948
236*	Jan	9	9	21	CB	14	4949
237	Jan	10	20	22	A	15	4950
238	Jan	11	1	23	G	1	4951
239	Jan	12	12	24	F	2	4952
240*	Jan	13	23	25	ED	3	4953
241	Jan	14	4	26	C	4	4954
242	Jan	15	15	27	B	5	4955
243	Jan	16	26	28	A	6	4956
244*	Jan	17	7	1	GF	7	4957
245	Jan	18	18	2	E	8	4958
246	Jan	19	9	3	D	9	4959
247	Jan	1	11	4	C	10	4960
248*	Jan	2	22	5	BA	11	4961
249	Jan	3	3	6	G	12	4962
250	Jan	4	14	7	F	13	4963
251	Jan	5	25	8	E	14	4964
252*	Jan	6	6	9	DC	15	4965
253	Jan	7	17	10	B	1	4966
254	Jan	8	28	11	A	2	4967
255	Jan	9	9	12	G	3	4968
256*	Jan	10	20	13	FE	4	4969
257	Jan	11	1	14	D	5	4970
258	Jan	12	12	15	C	6	4971
259	Jan	13	23	16	B	7	4972
260*	Jan	14	4	17	AG	8	4973

Western Era
Julian

Year	Month	Golden Number	Epact	Solar Cycle	Domenical Letter	Roman Indiction	Julian Period
261	Jan	15	15	18	F	9	4974
262	Jan	16	26	19	E	10	4975
263	Jan	17	7	20	D	11	4976
264*	Jan	18	18	21	CB	12	4977
265	Jan	19	9	22	A	13	4978
266	Jan	1	11	23	G	14	4979
267	Jan	2	22	24	F	15	4980
268*	Jan	3	3	25	ED	1	4981
269	Jan	4	14	26	C	2	4982
270	Jan	5	25	27	B	3	4983
271	Jan	6	6	28	A	4	4984
272*	Jan	7	17	1	GF	5	4985
273	Jan	8	28	2	E	6	4986
274	Jan	9	9	3	D	7	4987
275	Jan	10	20	4	C	8	4988
276*	Jan	11	1	5	BA	9	4989
277	Jan	12	12	6	G	10	4990
278	Jan	13	23	7	F	11	4991
279	Jan	14	4	8	E	12	4992
280*	Jan	15	15	9	DC	13	4993
281	Jan	16	26	10	B	14	4994
282	Jan	17	7	11	A	15	4995
283	Jan	18	18	12	G	1	4996
284*	Jan	19	9	13	FE	2	4997
285	Jan	1	11	14	D	3	4998
286	Jan	2	22	15	C	4	4999
287	Jan	3	3	16	B	5	5000
288*	Jan	4	14	17	AG	6	5001
289	Jan	5	25	18	F	7	5002
290	Jan	6	6	19	E	8	5003
291	Jan	7	17	20	D	8	5004
292*	Jan	8	28	21	CB	10	5005
293	Jan	9	9	22	A	11	5006
294	Jan	10	20	23	G	12	5007
295	Jan	11	1	24	F	13	5008
296*	Jan	12	12	25	ED	14	5009
297	Jan	13	23	26	C	15	5010
298	Jan	14	4	27	B	1	5011
299	Jan	15	15	28	A	2	5012
300*	Jan	16	26	1	GF	3	5013
301	Jan	17	7	2	E	4	5014
302	Jan	18	18	3	D	5	5015
303	Jan	19	9	4	C	6	5016
304*	Jan	1	11	5	BA	7	5017

Western Era
Julian

Year	Month	Golden Number	Epact	Solar Cycle	Domenical Letter	Roman Indiction	Julian Period
305	Jan	2	22	6	G	8	5018
306	Jan	3	3	7	F	9	5019
307	Jan	4	14	8	E	10	5020
308*	Jan	5	25	9	DC	11	5021
309	Jan	6	6	10	B	12	5022
310	Jan	7	17	11	A	13	5023
311	Jan	8	28	12	G	14	5024
312*	Jan	9	9	13	FE	15	5025
313	Jan	10	20	14	D	1	5026
314	Jan	11	1	15	C	2	5027
315	Jan	12	12	16	B	3	5028
316*	Jan	13	23	17	AG	4	5029
317	Jan	14	4	18	F	5	5030
318	Jan	15	15	19	E	6	5031
319	Jan	16	26	20	D	7	5032
320*	Jan	17	7	21	CB	8	5033
321	Jan	18	18	22	A	9	5034
322	Jan	19	9	23	G	10	5035
323	Jan	1	11	24	F	11	5036
324*	Jan	2	22	25	ED	12	5037
325	Jan	3	3	26	C	13	5038
326	Jan	4	14	27	B	14	5039
327	Jan	5	25	28	A	15	5040
328*	Jan	6	6	1	GF	1	5041
329	Jan	7	17	2	E	2	5042
330	Jan	8	28	3	D	3	5043
331	Jan	9	9	4	C	4	5044
332*	Jan	10	20	5	BA	5	5045
333	Jan	11	1	6	G	6	5046
334	Jan	12	12	7	F	7	5047
335	Jan	13	23	8	E	8	5048
336*	Jan	14	4	9	DC	9	5049
337	Jan	15	15	10	B	10	5050
338	Jan	16	26	11	A	11	5051
339	Jan	17	7	12	G	12	5052
340*	Jan	18	18	13	FE	13	5053
341	Jan	19	9	14	D	14	5054
342	Jan	1	11	15	C	15	5055
343	Jan	2	22	16	B	1	5056
344*	Jan	3	3	17	AG	2	5057
345	Jan	4	14	18	F	3	5058
346	Jan	5	25	19	E	4	5059
347	Jan	6	6	20	D	5	5060
348*	Jan	7	17	21	CB	6	5061

Western Era
Julian

Year	Month	Golden Number	Epact	Solar Cycle	Domenical Letter	Roman Indiction	Julian Period
349	Jan	8	28	22	A	7	5062
350	Jan	9	9	23	G	8	5063
351	Jan	10	20	24	F	9	5064
352*	Jan	11	1	25	ED	10	5065
353	Jan	12	12	26	C	11	5066
354	Jan	13	23	27	B	12	5067
355	Jan	14	4	28	A	13	5068
356*	Jan	15	15	1	GF	14	5069
357	Jan	16	26	2	E	15	5070
358	Jan	17	7	3	D	1	5071
359	Jan	18	18	4	C	2	5072
360*	Jan	19	9	5	BA	3	5073
361	Jan	1	11	6	G	4	5074
362	Jan	2	22	7	F	5	5075
363	Jan	3	3	8	E	6	5076
364*	Jan	4	14	9	DC	7	5077
365	Jan	5	25	10	B	8	5078
366	Jan	6	6	11	A	9	5079
367	Jan	7	17	12	G	10	5080
368*	Jan	8	28	13	FE	11	5081
369	Jan	9	9	14	D	12	5082
370	Jan	10	20	15	C	13	5083
371	Jan	11	1	26	B	14	5084
372*	Jan	12	12	17	AG	15	5085
373	Jan	13	23	18	F	1	5086
374	Jan	14	4	19	E	2	5087
375	Jan	15	15	20	D	3	5088
376*	Jan	16	26	21	CB	4	5089
377	Jan	17	7	22	A	5	5090
378	Jan	18	18	23	G	6	5091
379	Jan	19	9	24	F	7	5092
380*	Jan	1	11	25	ED	8	5093
381	Jan	2	22	26	C	9	5094
382	Jan	3	3	27	B	10	5095
383	Jan	4	14	28	A	11	5096
384*	Jan	5	25	1	GF	12	5097
385	Jan	6	6	2	E	18	5098
386	Jan	7	17	3	D	14	5099
387	Jan	8	28	4	C	15	5100
388*	Jan	9	9	5	BA	1	5101
389	Jan	10	20	6	G	2	5102
390	Jan	11	1	7	F	3	5103
391	Jan	12	12	8	E	4	5104
392*	Jan	13	23	9	DC	5	5105

Western Era
Julian

Year	Month	Golden Number	Epact	Solar Cycle	Domenical Letter	Roman Indiction	Julian Period
393	Jan	14	4	10	B	6	5106
394	Jan	15	15	11	A	7	5107
395	Jan	16	26	12	G	8	5108
396*	Jan	17	7	13	FE	9	5109
397	Jan	18	18	14	D	10	5110
398	Jan	19	9	15	C	11	5111
399	Jan	1	11	16	B	12	5112
400*	Jan	2	22	17	AG	13	5113
401	Jan	3	3	18	F	14	5114
402	Jan	4	14	19	E	15	5115
403	Jan	5	25	20	D	1	5116
404*	Jan	6	6	21	CB	2	5117
405	Jan	7	17	22	A	3	5118
406	Jan	8	28	23	G	4	5119
407	Jan	9	9	24	F	5	5120
408*	Jan	10	20	25	ED	6	5121
409	Jan	11	1	26	C	7	5122
410	Jan	12	12	27	B	8	5123
411	Jan	13	23	28	A	9	5124
412*	Jan	14	4	1	GF	10	5125
413	Jan	15	15	2	E	11	5126
414	Jan	16	26	3	D	12	5127
415	Jan	17	7	4	C	13	5128
416*	Jan	18	18	5	BA	14	5129
417	Jan	19	9	6	G	15	5130
418	Jan	1	11	7	F	1	5131
419	Jan	2	22	8	E	2	5132
420*	Jan	3	3	9	DC	3	5133
421	Jan	4	14	10	B	4	5134
422	Jan	5	25	11	A	5	5135
423	Jan	6	6	12	G	6	5136
424*	Jan	7	17	13	FE	7	5137
425	Jan	8	28	14	D	8	5138
426	Jan	9	9	15	C	9	5139
427	Jan	10	20	16	B	10	5140
428*	Jan	11	1	17	AG	11	5141
429	Jan	12	12	18	F	12	5142
430	Jan	13	23	19	E	13	5143
431	Jan	14	4	20	D	14	5144
432*	Jan	15	15	21	CB	15	5145
433	Jan	16	26	22	A	1	5146
434	Jan	17	7	23	G	2	5147
435	Jan	18	18	24	F	3	5148
436*	Jan	19	9	25	ED	4	5149

Western Era
Julian

Year	Month	Golden Number	Epact	Solar Cycle	Domenical Letter	Roman Indiction	Julian Period
437	Jan	1	11	26	C	5	5150
438	Jan	2	22	27	B	6	5151
439	Jan	3	3	28	A	7	5152
440*	Jan	4	14	1	GF	8	5153
441	Jan	5	25	2	E	9	5154
442	Jan	6	6	3	D	10	5155
443	Jan	7	17	4	C	11	5156
444*	Jan	8	28	5	BA	12	5157
445	Jan	9	9	6	G	13	5158
446	Jan	10	20	7	F	14	5159
447	Jan	11	1	8	E	15	5160
448*	Jan	12	12	9	DC	1	5161
449	Jan	13	23	10	B	2	5162
450	Jan	14	4	11	A	3	5163
451	Jan	15	15	12	G	4	5164
452*	Jan	16	26	13	FE	5	5165
453	Jan	17	7	14	D	6	5166
454	Jan	18	18	15	C	7	5167
455	Jan	19	9	16	B	8	5168
456*	Jan	1	11	17	AG	9	5169
457	Jan	2	22	18	F	10	5170
458	Jan	3	3	19	E	11	5171
459	Jan	4	14	20	D	12	5172
460*	Jan	5	25	21	CB	13	5173
461	Jan	6	6	22	A	14	5174
462	Jan	7	17	23	G	15	5175
463	Jan	8	28	24	F	1	5176
464*	Jan	9	9	25	ED	2	5177
465	Jan	10	20	26	C	3	5178
466	Jan	11	1	27	B	4	5179
467	Jan	12	12	28	A	5	5180
468*	Jan	12	23	1	GF	6	5181
469	Jan	14	4	2	E	7	5182
470	Jan	15	15	3	D	8	5183
471	Jan	16	26	4	C	9	5184
472*	Jan	17	7	5	BA	10	5185
473	Jan	18	18	6	G	11	5186
474	Jan	19	9	7	F	12	5187
475	Jan	1	11	8	E	13	5188
476*	Jan	2	22	9	DC	14	5189
477	Jan	3	3	10	B	15	5190
478	Jan	4	14	11	A	1	5191
479	Jan	5	25	12	G	2	5192
480*	Jan	6	6	13	FE	3	5193

Western Era
Julian

Year	Month	Golden Number	Epact	Solar Cycle	Domenical Letter	Roman Indiction	Julian Period
481	Jan	7	17	14	D	4	5194
482	Jan	8	28	15	C	5	5195
483	Jan	9	9	16	B	6	5196
484*	Jan	10	20	17	AG	7	5197
485	Jan	11	1	18	F	8	5198
486	Jan	12	12	19	E	9	5199
487	Jan	13	23	20	D	10	5200
488*	Jan	14	4	21	CB	11	5201
489	Jan	15	15	22	A	12	5202
490	Jan	16	26	23	G	13	5203
491	Jan	17	7	24	F	14	5204
492*	Jan	18	18	25	ED	15	5205
493	Jan	19	9	26	C	1	5206
494	Jan	1	11	27	B	2	5207
495	Jan	2	22	28	A	3	5208
496*	Jan	3	3	1	GF	4	5209
497	Jan	4	14	2	E	5	5210
498	Jan	5	25	3	D	6	5211
499	Jan	6	6	4	C	7	5212
500*	Jan	7	17	5	BA	8	5213
501	Jan	8	28	6	G	9	5214
502	Jan	9	9	7	F	10	5215
503	Jan	10	20	8	E	11	5216
504*	Jan	11	1	9	DC	12	5217
505	Jan	12	12	10	B	13	5218
506	Jan	13	23	11	A	14	5219
507	Jan	14	4	12	G	15	5220
508*	Jan	15	15	13	FE	1	5221
509	Jan	16	26	14	D	2	5222
510	Jan	17	7	15	C	3	5223
511	Jan	18	18	16	B	4	5224
512*	Jan	19	9	17	AG	5	5225
513	Jan	1	11	18	F	6	5226
514	Jan	2	22	19	E	7	5227
515	Jan	3	3	20	D	8	5228
516*	Jan	4	14	21	CB	9	5229
517	Jan	5	25	22	A	10	5230
518	Jan	6	6	23	G	11	5231
519	Jan	7	17	24	F	12	5232
520*	Jan	8	28	25	ED	13	5233
521	Jan	9	9	26	C	14	5234
522	Jan	10	20	27	B	15	5235
523	Jan	11	1	28	A	1	5236
524*	Jan	12	12	1	GF	2	5237

Western Era
Julian

Year	Month	Golden Number	Epact	Solar Cycle	Domenical Letter	Roman Indiction	Julian Period
525	Jan	13	23	2	E	3	5238
526	Jan	14	4	3	D	4	5239
527	Jan	15	15	4	C	5	5240
528*	Jan	16	26	5	BA	6	5241
529	Jan	17	7	6	G	7	5242
530	Jan	18	18	7	F	8	5243
531	Jan	19	9	8	E	9	5244
532*	Jan	1	11	9	DC	10	5245
533	Jan	2	22	10	B	11	5246
534	Jan	3	3	11	A	12	5247
535	Jan	4	14	12	G	13	5248
536*	Jan	5	25	13	FE	14	5249
537	Jan	6	6	14	D	15	5250
538	Jan	7	17	15	C	1	5251
539	Jan	8	28	16	B	2	5252
540*	Jan	9	9	17	AG	3	5253
541	Jan	10	20	18	F	4	5254
542	Jan	11	1	19	E	5	5255
543	Jan	12	12	20	D	6	5256
544*	Jan	13	23	21	CB	7	5257
545	Jan	14	4	22	A	8	5258
546	Jan	15	15	23	G	9	5259
547	Jan	16	26	24	F	10	5260
548*	Jan	17	7	25	ED	11	5261
549	Jan	18	18	26	C	12	5262
550	Jan	19	9	27	B	13	5263
551	Jan	1	11	28	A	14	5264
552*	Jan	2	22	1	GF	15	5265
553	Jan	3	3	2	E	1	5266
554	Jan	4	14	3	D	2	5267
555	Jan	5	25	4	C	3	5268
556*	Jan	6	6	5	BA	4	5269
557	Jan	7	17	6	G	5	5270
558	Jan	8	28	7	F	6	5271
559	Jan	9	9	8	E	7	5272
560*	Jan	10	20	9	DC	8	5273
561	Jan	11	1	10	B	9	5274
562	Jan	12	12	11	A	10	5275
563	Jan	13	23	12	G	11	5276
564*	Jan	14	4	13	FE	12	5277
565	Jan	15	15	14	D	13	5278
566	Jan	16	26	15	C	14	5279
567	Jan	17	7	16	B	15	5280
568*	Jan	18	18	17	AG	1	5281

Western Era
Julian

Year	Month	Golden Number	Epact	Solar Cycle	Domenical Letter	Roman Indiction	Julian Period
569	Jan	19	9	18	F	2	5282
570	Jan	1	11	19	E	3	5283
571	Jan	2	22	20	D	4	5284
572*	Jan	3	3	21	CB	5	5285
573	Jan	4	14	22	A	6	5286
574	Jan	5	25	23	G	7	5287
575	Jan	6	6	24	F	8	5288
576*	Jan	7	17	25	ED	9	5289
577	Jan	8	28	26	C	10	5290
578	Jan	9	9	27	B	11	5291
579	Jan	10	20	28	A	12	5292
580*	Jan	11	1	1	GF	13	5293
581	Jan	12	12	2	E	14	5294
582	Jan	13	23	3	D	15	5295
583	Jan	14	4	4	C	1	5296
584*	Jan	15	15	5	BA	2	5297
585	Jan	16	26	6	G	3	5298
586	Jan	17	7	7	F	4	5299
587	Jan	18	18	8	E	5	5300
588*	Jan	19	9	9	DC	6	5301
589	Jan	1	11	10	B	7	5302
590	Jan	2	22	11	A	8	5303
591	Jan	3	3	12	G	9	5304
592*	Jan	4	14	13	FE	10	5305
593	Jan	5	25	14	D	11	5306
594	Jan	6	6	15	C	12	5307
595	Jan	7	17	16	B	13	5308
596*	Jan	8	28	17	AG	14	5309
597	Jan	9	9	18	F	15	5310
598	Jan	10	20	19	E	1	5311
599	Jan	11	1	20	D	2	5312
600*	Jan	12	12	21	CB	3	5313
601	Jan	13	23	22	A	4	5314
602	Jan	14	4	23	G	5	5315
603	Jan	15	15	24	F	6	5316
604*	Jan	16	26	25	ED	7	5317
605	Jan	17	7	26	C	8	5318
606	Jan	18	18	27	B	9	5319
607	Jan	19	9	28	A	10	5320
608*	Jan	1	11	1	GF	11	5321
609	Jan	2	22	2	E	12	5322
610	Jan	3	3	3	D	13	5323
611	Jan	4	14	4	C	14	5324
612*	Jan	5	25	5	BA	15	5325

Western Era Julian Year	Month	Golden Number	Epact	Solar Cycle	Domenical Letter	Roman Indiction	Julian Period
613	Jan	6	6	6	G	1	5326
614	Jan	7	17	7	F	2	5327
615	Jan	8	28	8	E	3	5328
616*	Jan	9	9	9	DC	4	5329
617	Jan	10	20	10	B	5	5330
618	Jan	11	1	11	A	6	5331
619	Jan	12	12	12	G	7	5332
620*	Jan	13	23	13	FE	8	5333
621	Jan	14	4	14	D	9	5334
622	Jan	15	15	15	C	10	5335
623	Jan	16	26	16	B	11	5336
624*	Jan	17	7	17	AG	12	5337
625	Jan	18	18	18	F	13	5338
626	Jan	19	9	19	E	14	5339
627	Jan	1	11	20	D	15	5340
628*	Jan	2	22	21	CB	1	5341
629	Jan	3	3	22	A	2	5342
630	Jan	4	14	23	G	3	5343
631	Jan	5	25	24	F	4	5344
632*	Jan	6	6	25	ED	5	5345
633	Jan	7	17	26	C	6	5346
634	Jan	8	28	27	B	7	5347
635	Jan	9	9	28	A	8	5348
636*	Jan	10	20	1	GF	9	5349
637	Jan	11	1	2	E	10	5350
638	Jan	12	12	3	D	11	5351
639	Jan	13	23	4	C	12	5352
640*	Jan	14	4	5	BA	13	5353
641	Jan	15	15	6	G	14	5354
642	Jan	16	26	7	F	15	5355
643	Jan	17	7	8	E	1	5356
644*	Jan	18	18	9	DC	2	5357
645	Jan	19	9	10	B	3	5358
646	Jan	1	11	11	A	4	5359
647	Jan	2	22	12	G	5	5360
648*	Jan	3	3	13	FE	6	5361
649	Jan	4	14	14	D	7	5362
650	Jan	5	25	15	C	8	5363
651	Jan	6	6	16	B	9	5364
652*	Jan	7	17	17	AG	10	5365
653	Jan	8	28	18	F	11	5366
654	Jan	9	9	19	E	12	5367
655	Jan	10	20	20	D	13	5368
656*	Jan	11	1	21	CB	14	5369

Western Era Julian Year	Month	Golden Number	Epact	Solar Cycle	Domenical Letter	Roman Indiction	Julian Period
657	Jan	12	12	22	A	15	5370
658	Jan	13	23	23	G	1	5371
659	Jan	14	4	24	F	2	5372
660*	Jan	15	15	25	ED	3	5373
661	Jan	16	26	26	C	4	5374
662	Jan	17	7	27	B	5	5375
663	Jan	18	18	28	A	6	5376
664*	Jan	19	9	1	GF	7	5377
665	Jan	1	11	2	E	8	5378
666	Jan	2	22	3	D	9	5379
667	Jan	3	3	4	C	10	5380
668*	Jan	4	14	5	BA	11	5381
669	Jan	5	25	6	G	12	5382
670	Jan	6	6	7	F	13	5383
671	Jan	7	17	8	E	14	5384
672*	Jan	8	28	9	DC	15	5385
673	Jan	9	9	10	B	1	5386
674	Jan	10	20	11	A	2	5387
675	Jan	11	1	12	G	3	5388
676*	Jan	12	12	13	FE	4	5389
677	Jan	13	23	14	D	5	5390
678	Jan	14	4	15	C	6	5391
679	Jan	15	15	16	B	7	5392
680*	Jan	16	23	17	AG	8	5393
681	Jan	17	7	18	F	9	5394
682	Jan	18	18	19	E	10	5395
683	Jan	19	9	20	D	11	5396
684*	Jan	1	11	21	CB	12	5397
685	Jan	2	22	22	A	13	5398
686	Jan	3	3	23	G	14	5399
687	Jan	4	14	24	F	15	5400
688*	Jan	5	25	25	ED	1	5401
689	Jan	6	6	26	C	2	5402
690	Jan	7	17	27	B	3	5403
691	Jan	8	28	28	A	4	5404
692*	Jan	9	9	1	GF	5	5405
693	Jan	10	20	2	E	6	5406
694	Jan	11	1	3	D	7	5407
695	Jan	12	12	4	C	8	5408
696*	Jan	13	23	5	BA	9	5409
697	Jan	14	4	6	G	10	5410
698	Jan	15	15	7	F	11	5411
699	Jan	16	26	8	E	12	5412
700*	Jan	17	7	9	DC	13	5413

Western Era Julian

Year	Month	Golden Number	Epact	Solar Cycle	Domenical Letter	Roman Indiction	Julian Period
701	Jan	18	18	10	B	14	5414
702	Jan	19	9	11	A	15	5415
703	Jan	1	11	12	G	1	5416
704*	Jan	2	22	13	FE	2	5417
705	Jan	3	3	14	D	3	5418
706	Jan	4	14	15	C	4	5419
707	Jan	5	25	16	B	5	5420
708*	Jan	6	6	17	AG	6	5421
709	Jan	7	17	18	F	7	5422
710	Jan	8	28	19	E	8	5423
711	Jan	9	9	20	D	9	5424
712*	Jan	10	20	21	CB	10	5425
713	Jan	11	1	22	A	11	5426
714	Jan	12	12	23	G	12	5427
715	Jan	13	23	24	F	13	5428
716*	Jan	14	4	25	ED	14	5429
717	Jan	15	15	26	C	15	5430
718	Jan	16	26	27	B	1	5431
719	Jan	17	7	28	A	2	5432
720*	Jan	18	18	1	GF	3	5433
721	Jan	19	9	2	E	4	5434
722	Jan	1	11	3	D	5	5435
723	Jan	2	22	4	C	6	5436
724*	Jan	3	3	5	BA	7	5437
725	Jan	4	14	6	G	8	5438
726	Jan	5	25	7	F	9	5439
727	Jan	6	6	8	E	10	5440
728*	Jan	7	17	9	DC	11	5441
729	Jan	8	28	10	B	12	5442
730	Jan	9	9	11	A	13	5443
731	Jan	10	20	12	G	14	5444
732*	Jan	11	1	13	FE	15	5445
733	Jan	12	12	14	D	1	5446
734	Jan	13	23	15	C	2	5447
735	Jan	14	4	16	B	3	5448
736*	Jan	15	15	17	AG	4	5449
737	Jan	16	26	18	F	5	5450
738	Jan	17	7	19	E	6	5451
739	Jan	18	18	20	D	7	5452
740*	Jan	19	9	21	CB	8	5453
741	Jan	1	11	22	A	9	5454
742	Jan	2	22	23	G	10	5455
743	Jan	3	3	24	F	11	5456
744*	Jan	4	14	25	ED	12	5457

Western Era Julian

Year	Month	Golden Number	Epact	Solar Cycle	Domenical Letter	Roman Indiction	Julian Period
745	Jan	5	25	26	C	13	5458
746	Jan	6	6	27	B	14	5459
747	Jan	7	17	28	A	15	5460
748*	Jan	8	28	1	GF	1	5461
749	Jan	9	9	2	E	2	5462
750	Jan	10	20	3	D	3	5463
751	Jan	11	1	4	C	4	5464
752*	Jan	12	12	5	BA	5	5465
753	Jan	13	23	6	G	6	5466
754	Jan	14	4	7	F	7	5467
755	Jan	15	15	8	E	8	5468
756*	Jan	16	26	9	DC	9	5469
757	Jan	17	7	10	B	10	5470
758	Jan	18	18	11	A	11	5471
759	Jan	19	9	12	G	12	5472
760*	Jan	1	11	13	FE	13	5473
761	Jan	2	22	14	D	14	5474
762	Jan	3	3	15	C	15	5475
763	Jan	4	14	16	B	1	5476
764*	Jan	5	25	17	AG	2	5477
765	Jan	6	6	18	F	3	5478
766	Jan	7	17	19	E	4	5479
767	Jan	8	28	20	D	5	5480
768*	Jan	9	9	21	CB	6	5481
769	Jan	10	20	22	A	7	5482
770	Jan	11	1	23	G	8	5483
771	Jan	12	12	24	F	9	5484
772*	Jan	13	23	25	ED	10	5485
773	Jan	14	4	26	C	11	5486
774	Jan	15	15	27	B	12	5487
775	Jan	16	26	28	A	13	5488
776*	Jan	17	7	1	GF	14	5489
777	Jan	18	18	2	E	15	5490
778	Jan	19	9	3	D	1	5491
779	Jan	1	11	4	C	2	5492
780*	Jan	2	22	5	BA	3	5493
781	Jan	3	3	6	G	4	5494
782	Jan	4	14	7	F	5	5495
783	Jan	5	25	8	E	6	5496
784*	Jan	6	6	9	DC	7	5497
785	Jan	7	17	10	B	8	5498
786	Jan	8	28	11	A	9	5499
787	Jan	9	9	12	G	10	5500
788*	Jan	10	20	13	FE	11	5501

Western Era
Julian

Year	Month	Golden Number	Epact	Solar Cycle	Domenical Letter	Roman Indiction	Julian Period
789	Jan	11	1	14	D	12	5502
790	Jan	12	12	15	C	13	5503
791	Jan	13	23	16	B	14	5504
792*	Jan	14	4	17	AG	15	5505
793	Jan	15	15	18	F	1	5506
794	Jan	16	26	19	E	2	5507
795	Jan	17	7	20	D	3	5508
796*	Jan	18	18	21	CB	4	5509
797	Jan	19	9	22	A	5	5510
798	Jan	1	11	23	G	6	5511
799	Jan	2	22	24	F	7	5512
800*	Jan	3	3	25	ED	8	5513
801	Jan	4	14	26	C	9	5514
802	Jan	5	25	27	B	10	5515
803	Jan	6	6	28	A	11	5516
804*	Jan	7	17	1	GF	12	5517
805	Jan	8	28	2	E	13	5518
806	Jan	9	9	3	D	14	5519
807	Jan	10	20	4	C	15	5520
808*	Jan	11	1	5	BA	1	5521
809	Jan	12	12	6	G	2	5522
810	Jan	13	23	7	F	3	5523
811	Jan	14	4	8	E	4	5524
812*	Jan	15	15	9	DC	5	5525
813	Jan	16	26	10	B	6	5526
814	Jan	17	7	11	A	7	5527
815	Jan	18	18	12	G	8	5528
816*	Jan	19	9	13	FE	9	5529
817	Jan	1	11	14	D	10	5530
818	Jan	2	22	15	C	11	5531
819	Jan	3	3	16	B	12	5532
820*	Jan	4	14	17	AG	13	5533
821	Jan	5	25	18	F	14	5534
822	Jan	6	6	19	E	15	5535
823	Jan	7	17	20	D	1	5536
824*	Jan	8	28	21	CB	2	5537
825	Jan	9	9	22	A	3	5538
826	Jan	10	20	23	G	4	5539
827	Jan	11	1	24	F	5	5540
828*	Jan	12	12	25	ED	6	5541
829	Jan	13	23	26	C	7	5542
830	Jan	14	4	27	B	8	5543
831	Jan	15	15	28	A	9	5544
832*	Jan	16	26	1	GF	10	5545

Western Era
Julian

Year	Month	Golden Number	Epact	Solar Cycle	Domenical Letter	Roman Indiction	Julian Period
833	Jan	17	7	2	E	11	5546
834	Jan	18	18	3	D	12	5547
835	Jan	19	9	4	C	13	5548
836*	Jan	1	11	5	BA	14	5549
837	Jan	2	22	6	G	15	5550
838	Jan	3	3	7	F	1	5551
839	Jan	4	14	8	E	2	5552
840*	Jan	5	25	9	DC	3	5553
841	Jan	6	6	10	B	4	5554
842	Jan	7	17	11	A	5	5555
843	Jan	8	28	12	G	6	5556
844*	Jan	9	9	13	FE	7	5557
845	Jan	10	20	14	D	8	5558
846	Jan	11	1	15	C	9	5559
847	Jan	12	12	16	B	10	5560
848*	Jan	13	23	17	AG	11	5561
849	Jan	14	4	18	F	12	5562
850	Jan	15	15	19	E	13	5563
851	Jan	16	26	20	D	14	5564
852*	Jan	17	7	21	CB	15	5565
853	Jan	18	18	22	A	1	5566
854	Jan	19	9	23	G	2	5567
855	Jan	1	11	24	F	3	5568
856*	Jan	2	22	25	ED	4	5569
857	Jan	3	3	26	C	5	5570
858	Jan	4	14	27	B	6	5571
859	Jan	5	25	28	A	7	5572
860*	Jan	6	6	1	GF	8	5573
861	Jan	7	17	2	E	9	5574
862	Jan	8	28	3	D	10	5575
863	Jan	9	9	4	C	11	5576
864*	Jan	10	20	5	BA	12	5577
865	Jan	11	4	6	G	13	5578
866	Jan	12	12	7	F	14	5579
867	Jan	13	23	8	E	15	5580
868*	Jan	14	4	9	DC	1	5581
869	Jan	15	15	10	B	2	5582
870	Jan	16	26	11	A	3	5583
871	Jan	17	7	12	G	4	5584
872*	Jan	18	18	13	FE	5	5585
873	Jan	19	9	14	D	6	5586
874	Jan	1	11	15	C	7	5587
875	Jan	2	22	16	B	8	5588
876*	Jan	3	3	17	AG	9	5589

Western Era Julian Year	Month	Golden Number	Epact	Solar Cycle	Domenical Letter	Roman Indiction	Julian Period
877	Jan	4	14	18	F	10	5590
878	Jan	5	25	19	E	11	5591
879	Jan	6	6	20	D	12	5592
880*	Jan	7	17	21	CB	13	5593
881	Jan	8	28	22	A	14	5594
882	Jan	9	9	23	G	15	5595
883	Jan	10	20	24	F	1	5596
884*	Jan	11	1	25	ED	2	5597
885	Jan	12	12	26	C	3	5598
886	Jan	13	23	27	B	4	5599
887	Jan	14	4	28	A	5	5600
888*	Jan	15	15	1	GF	6	5601
889	Jan	16	26	2	E	7	5602
890	Jan	17	7	3	D	8	5603
891	Jan	18	18	4	C	9	5604
892*	Jan	19	9	5	BA	10	5605
893	Jan	1	11	6	G	11	5606
894	Jan	2	22	7	F	12	5607
895	Jan	3	3	8	E	13	5608
896*	Jan	4	14	9	DC	14	5609
897	Jan	5	25	10	B	15	5610
898	Jan	6	6	11	A	1	5611
899	Jan	7	17	12	G	2	5612
900*	Jan	8	28	13	FE	3	5613
901	Jan	9	9	14	D	4	5614
902	Jan	10	20	15	C	5	5615
903	Jan	11	1	16	B	6	5616
904*	Jan	12	12	17	AG	7	5617
905	Jan	13	23	18	F	8	5618
906	Jan	14	4	19	E	9	5619
907	Jan	15	15	20	D	10	5620
908*	Jan	16	26	21	CB	11	5621
909	Jan	17	7	22	A	12	5622
910	Jan	18	18	23	G	13	5623
911	Jan	19	9	24	F	14	5624
912*	Jan	1	11	25	ED	15	5625
913	Jan	2	22	26	C	1	5626
914	Jan	3	3	27	B	2	5627
915	Jan	4	14	28	A	3	5628
916*	Jan	5	25	1	GF	4	5629
917	Jan	6	6	2	E	5	5630
918	Jan	7	17	3	D	6	5631
919	Jan	8	28	4	C	7	5632
920*	Jan	9	9	5	BA	8	5633

Western Era Julian Year	Month	Golden Number	Epact	Solar Cycle	Domenical Letter	Roman Indiction	Julian Period
921	Jan	10	20	6	G	9	5634
922	Jan	11	1	7	F	10	5635
923	Jan	12	12	8	E	11	5636
924*	Jan	13	22	9	DC	12	5637
925	Jan	14	4	10	B	13	5638
926	Jan	15	15	11	A	14	5639
927	Jan	16	26	12	G	15	5640
928*	Jan	17	7	13	FE	1	5641
929	Jan	18	18	14	D	2	5642
930	Jan	19	9	15	C	3	5643
931	Jan	1	11	16	B	4	5644
932*	Jan	2	22	17	AG	5	5645
933	Jan	3	3	18	F	6	5646
934	Jan	4	14	19	E	7	5647
935	Jan	5	25	20	D	8	5648
936*	Jan	6	6	21	CB	9	5649
937	Jan	7	17	22	A	10	5650
938	Jan	8	28	23	G	11	5651
939	Jan	9	9	24	F	12	5652
940*	Jan	10	20	25	ED	13	5653
941	Jan	11	1	26	C	14	5654
942	Jan	12	12	27	B	15	5655
943	Jan	13	23	28	A	1	5656
944*	Jan	14	4	1	GF	2	5657
945	Jan	15	15	2	E	3	5658
946	Jan	16	26	3	D	4	5659
947	Jan	17	7	4	C	5	5660
948*	Jan	18	18	5	BA	6	5661
949	Jan	19	9	6	G	7	5662
950	Jan	1	11	7	F	8	5663
951	Jan	2	22	8	E	9	5664
952*	Jan	3	3	9	DC	10	5665
953	Jan	4	14	10	B	11	5666
954	Jan	5	25	11	A	12	5667
955	Jan	6	6	12	G	13	5668
956*	Jan	7	17	13	FE	14	5669
957	Jan	8	28	14	D	15	5670
958	Jan	9	9	15	C	1	5671
959	Jan	10	20	16	B	2	5672
960*	Jan	11	1	17	AG	3	5673
961	Jan	12	12	18	F	4	5674
962	Jan	13	23	19	E	5	5675
963	Jan	14	4	20	D	6	5676
964*	Jan	15	15	21	CB	7	5677

Western Era
Julian

Year	Month	Golden Number	Epact	Solar Cycle	Domenical Letter	Roman Indiction	Julian Period
965	Jan	16	26	22	A	8	5678
966	Jan	17	7	23	G	9	5679
967	Jan	18	18	24	F	10	5680
968*	Jan	19	9	25	ED	11	5681
969	Jan	1	11	26	C	12	5682
970	Jan	2	22	27	B	13	5683
971	Jan	3	3	28	A	14	5684
972*	Jan	4	14	1	GF	15	5685
973	Jan	5	25	2	E	1	5686
974	Jan	6	6	3	D	2	5687
975	Jan	7	17	4	C	3	5688
976*	Jan	8	28	5	BA	4	5689
977	Jan	9	9	6	C	5	5690
978	Jan	10	20	7	F	6	5691
979	Jan	11	1	8	E	7	5692
980*	Jan	12	12	9	DC	8	5693
981	Jan	13	23	10	B	9	5694
982	Jan	14	4	11	A	10	5695
983	Jan	15	15	12	G	11	5696
984*	Jan	16	26	13	FE	12	5697
985	Jan	17	7	14	D	13	5698
986	Jan	18	18	15	C	14	5699
987	Jan	19	9	16	B	15	5700
988*	Jan	1	11	17	AG	1	5701
989	Jan	2	22	18	F	2	5702
990	Jan	3	3	19	E	3	5703
991	Jan	4	14	20	D	4	5704
992*	Jan	5	25	21	CB	5	5705
993	Jan	6	6	22	A	6	5706
994	Jan	7	17	23	G	7	5707
995	Jan	8	28	24	F	8	5708
996*	Jan	9	9	25	ED	9	5709
997	Jan	10	20	26	C	10	5710
998	Jan	11	1	27	B	11	5711
999	Jan	12	12	28	A	12	5712
1000*	Jan	13	23	1	GF	13	5713
1001	Jan	14	4	2	E	14	5714
1002	Jan	15	15	3	D	15	5715
1003	Jan	16	26	4	C	1	5716
1004*	Jan	17	7	5	BA	2	5717
1005	Jan	18	18	6	G	3	5718
1006	Jan	19	9	7	F	4	5719
1007	Jan	1	11	8	E	5	5720
1008*	Jan	2	22	9	DC	6	5721

Western Era
Julian

Year	Month	Golden Number	Epact	Solar Cycle	Domenical Letter	Roman Indiction	Julian Period
1009	Jan	3	3	10	B	7	5722
1010	Jan	4	14	11	A	8	5723
1011	Jan	5	25	12	G	9	5724
1012*	Jan	6	6	13	FE	10	5725
1013	Jan	7	17	14	D	11	5726
1014	Jan	8	28	15	C	12	5727
1015	Jan	9	9	16	B	13	5728
1016*	Jan	10	20	17	AG	14	5729
1017	Jan	11	1	18	F	15	5730
1018	Jan	12	12	19	E	1	5731
1019	Jan	13	23	20	D	2	5732
1020*	Jan	14	4	21	CB	3	5733
1021	Jan	15	15	22	A	4	5734
1022	Jan	16	26	23	G	5	5735
1023	Jan	17	7	24	F	6	5736
1024*	Jan	18	18	25	ED	7	5737
1025	Jan	19	9	26	C	8	5738
1026	Jan	1	11	27	B	9	5739
1027	Jan	2	22	28	A	10	5740
1028*	Jan	3	3	1	GF	11	5741
1029	Jan	4	14	2	E	12	5742
1030	Jan	5	25	3	D	13	5743
1031	Jan	6	6	4	C	14	5744
1032*	Jan	7	17	5	BA	15	5745
1033	Jan	8	28	6	G	1	5746
1034	Jan	9	9	7	F	2	5747
1035	Jan	10	20	8	E	3	5748
1036*	Jan	11	1	9	DC	4	5749
1037	Jan	12	12	10	B	5	5750
1038	Jan	13	23	11	A	6	5751
1039	Jan	14	4	12	G	7	5752
1040*	Jan	15	15	13	FE	8	5753
1041	Jan	16	26	14	D	9	5754
1042	Jan	17	7	15	C	10	5755
1043	Jan	18	18	16	B	11	5756
1044*	Jan	19	9	17	AG	12	5757
1045	Jan	1	11	18	F	13	5758
1046	Jan	2	22	19	E	14	5759
1047	Jan	3	3	20	D	15	5760
1048*	Jan	4	14	21	CB	1	5761
1049	Jan	5	25	22	A	2	5762
1050	Jan	6	6	23	G	3	5763
1051	Jan	7	17	24	F	4	5764
1052*	Jan	8	28	25	ED	5	5765

Western Era Julian Year	Month	Golden Number	Epact	Solar Cycle	Domenical Letter	Roman Indiction	Julian Period
1053	Jan	9	9	26	C	6	5766
1054	Jan	10	20	27	B	7	5767
1055	Jan	11	1	28	A	8	5768
1056*	Jan	12	12	1	GF	9	5769
1057	Jan	13	23	2	E	10	5770
1058	Jan	14	4	3	D	11	5771
1059	Jan	15	15	4	C	12	5772
1060*	Jan	16	26	5	BA	13	5773
1061	Jan	17	7	6	G	14	5774
1062	Jan	18	18	7	F	15	5775
1063	Jan	19	9	8	E	1	5776
1064*	Jan	1	11	9	DC	2	5777
1065	Jan	2	22	10	B	3	5778
1066	Jan	3	3	11	A	4	5779
1067	Jan	4	14	12	G	5	5780
1068*	Jan	5	25	13	FE	6	5781
1069	Jan	6	6	14	D	7	5782
1070	Jan	7	17	15	C	8	5783
1071	Jan	8	28	16	B	9	5784
1072*	Jan	9	9	17	AG	10	5785
1073	Jan	10	20	18	F	11	5786
1074	Jan	11	1	19	E	12	5787
1075	Jan	12	12	20	D	13	5788
1076*	Jan	13	23	21	CB	14	5789
1077	Jan	14	4	22	A	15	5790
1078	Jan	15	15	23	G	1	5791
1079	Jan	16	6	24	F	2	5792
1080*	Jan	17	7	25	ED	3	5793
1081	Jan	18	18	26	C	4	5794
1082	Jan	19	9	27	B	5	5795
1083	Jan	1	11	28	A	6	5796
1084*	Jan	2	22	1	GF	7	5797
1085	Jan	3	3	2	E	8	5798
1086	Jan	4	14	3	D	9	5799
1087	Jan	5	25	4	C	10	5800
1088*	Jan	6	6	5	BA	11	5801
1089	Jan	7	17	6	G	12	5802
1090	Jan	8	28	7	F	13	5803
1091	Jan	9	9	8	E	14	5804
1092*	Jan	10	20	9	DC	15	5805
1093	Jan	11	1	10	B	1	5806
1094	Jan	12	12	11	A	2	5807
1095	Jan	13	23	12	G	3	5808
1096*	Jan	14	4	13	FE	4	5809

Western Era Julian Year	Month	Golden Number	Epact	Solar Cycle	Domenical Letter	Roman Indiction	Julian Period
1097	Jan	15	15	14	D	5	5810
1098	Jan	16	26	15	C	6	5811
1099	Jan	17	7	16	B	7	5812
1100*	Jan	18	18	17	AG	8	5813
1101	Jan	19	9	18	F	9	5814
1102	Jan	1	11	19	E	10	5815
1103	Jan	2	22	20	D	11	5816
1104*	Jan	3	3	21	CB	12	5817
1105	Jan	4	14	22	A	13	5818
1106	Jan	5	25	23	G	14	5819
1107	Jan	6	6	24	F	15	5820
1108*	Jan	7	17	25	ED	1	5821
1109	Jan	8	28	26	C	2	5822
1110	Jan	9	9	27	B	3	5823
1111	Jan	10	20	28	A	4	5824
1112*	Jan	11	1	1	GF	5	5825
1113	Jan	12	12	2	E	6	5826
1114	Jan	13	23	3	D	7	5827
1115	Jan	14	4	4	C	8	5828
1116*	Jan	15	15	5	BA	9	5829
1117	Jan	16	26	6	G	10	5830
1118	Jan	17	7	7	F	11	5831
1119	Jan	18	18	8	E	12	5832
1120*	Jan	19	9	9	DC	13	5833
1121	Jan	1	11	10	B	14	5834
1122	Jan	2	22	11	A	15	5835
1123	Jan	3	3	12	G	1	5836
1124*	Jan	4	14	13	FE	2	5837
1125	Jan	5	25	14	D	3	5838
1126	Jan	6	6	15	C	4	5839
1127	Jan	7	17	16	B	5	5840
1128*	Jan	8	28	17	AG	6	5841
1129	Jan	9	9	18	F	7	5842
1130	Jan	10	20	19	E	8	5843
1131	Jan	11	1	20	D	9	5844
1132*	Jan	12	12	21	CB	10	5845
1133	Jan	13	23	22	A	11	5846
1134	Jan	14	4	23	G	12	5847
1135	Jan	15	15	24	F	13	5848
1136*	Jan	16	26	25	ED	14	5849
1137	Jan	17	7	26	C	15	5850
1138	Jan	18	18	27	B	1	5851
1139	Jan	19	9	28	A	2	5852
1140*	Jan	1	11	1	GF	3	5853

Western Era
Julian

Year	Month	Golden Number	Epact	Solar Cycle	Domenical Letter	Roman Indiction	Julian Period
1141	Jan	2	22	2	E	4	5854
1142	Jan	3	3	3	D	5	5855
1143	Jan	4	14	4	C	6	5856
1144*	Jan	5	25	5	BA	7	5857
1145	Jan	6	6	6	G	8	5858
1146	Jan	7	17	7	F	9	5859
1147	Jan	8	28	8	E	10	5860
1148*	Jan	9	9	9	DC	11	5861
1149	Jan	10	20	10	B	12	5862
1150	Jan	11	1	11	A	13	5863
1151	Jan	12	12	12	G	14	5864
1152*	Jan	13	23	13	FE	15	5865
1153	Jan	14	4	14	D	1	5866
1154	Jan	15	15	15	C	2	5867
1155	Jan	16	26	16	B	3	5868
1156*	Jan	17	7	17	AG	4	5869
1157	Jan	18	18	18	F	5	5870
1158	Jan	19	9	19	E	6	5871
1159	Jan	1	11	20	D	7	5872
1160*	Jan	2	22	21	CB	8	5873
1161	Jan	3	3	22	A	9	5874
1162	Jan	4	14	23	G	10	5875
1163	Jan	5	25	24	F	11	5876
1164*	Jan	6	6	25	ED	12	5877
1165	Jan	7	17	26	C	13	5878
1166	Jan	8	28	27	B	14	5879
1167	Jan	9	9	28	A	15	5880
1168*	Jan	10	20	1	GF	1	5881
1169	Jan	11	1	2	E	2	5882
1170	Jan	12	12	3	D	3	5883
1171	Jan	13	23	4	C	4	5884
1172*	Jan	14	4	5	BA	5	5885
1173	Jan	15	15	6	G	6	5886
1174	Jan	16	26	7	F	7	5887
1175	Jan	17	7	8	E	8	5888
1176*	Jan	18	18	9	DC	9	5889
1177	Jan	19	9	10	B	10	5890
1178	Jan	1	11	11	A	11	5891
1179	Jan	2	22	12	G	12	5892
1180*	Jan	3	3	13	FE	13	5893
1181	Jan	4	14	14	D	14	5894
1182	Jan	5	25	15	C	15	5895
1183	Jan	6	6	16	B	1	5896
1184*	Jan	7	17	17	AG	2	5897

Western Era
Julian

Year	Month	Golden Number	Epact	Solar Cycle	Domenical Letter	Roman Indiction	Julian Period
1185	Jan	8	28	18	F	3	5898
1186	Jan	9	9	19	E	4	5899
1187	Jan	10	20	20	D	5	5900
1188*	Jan	11	1	21	CB	6	5901
1189	Jan	12	12	22	A	7	5902
1190	Jan	13	23	23	G	8	5903
1191	Jan	14	4	24	F	9	5904
1192*	Jan	15	15	25	ED	10	5905
1193	Jan	16	26	26	C	11	5906
1194	Jan	17	7	27	B	12	5907
1195	Jan	18	18	28	A	13	5908
1196*	Jan	19	9	1	GF	14	5909
1197	Jan	1	11	2	E	15	5910
1198	Jan	2	22	3	D	1	5911
1199	Jan	3	3	4	C	2	5912
1200*	Jan	4	14	5	BA	3	5913
1201	Jan	5	25	6	G	4	5914
1202	Jan	6	6	7	F	5	5915
1203	Jan	7	17	8	E	6	5916
1204*	Jan	8	28	9	DC	7	5917
1205	Jan	9	9	10	B	8	5918
1206	Jan	10	20	11	A	9	5919
1207	Jan	11	1	12	G	10	5920
1208*	Jan	12	12	13	FE	11	5921
1209	Jan	13	23	14	D	12	5922
1210	Jan	14	4	15	C	13	5923
1211	Jan	15	15	16	B	14	5924
1212*	Jan	16	26	17	AG	15	5925
1213	Jan	17	7	18	F	1	5926
1214	Jan	18	18	19	E	2	5927
1215	Jan	19	9	20	D	3	5928
1216*	Jan	1	11	21	CB	4	5929
1217	Jan	2	22	22	A	5	5930
1218	Jan	3	3	23	G	6	5931
1219	Jan	4	14	24	F	7	5932
1220*	Jan	5	25	25	ED	8	5933
1221	Jan	6	6	26	C	9	5934
1222	Jan	7	17	27	B	10	5935
1223	Jan	8	28	28	A	11	5936
1224*	Jan	9	9	1	GF	12	5937
1225	Jan	10	20	2	E	13	5938
1226	Jan	11	1	3	D	14	5939
1227	Jan	12	12	4	C	15	5940
1228*	Jan	13	23	5	BA	1	5941

Western Era Julian Year	Month	Golden Number	Epact	Solar Cycle	Domenical Letter	Roman Indiction	Julian Period
1229	Jan	14	4	6	G	2	5942
1230	Jan	15	15	7	F	3	5943
1231	Jan	16	26	8	E	4	5944
1232*	Jan	17	7	9	DC	5	5945
1233	Jan	18	18	10	B	6	5946
1234	Jan	19	9	11	A	7	5947
1235	Jan	1	11	12	G	8	5948
1236*	Jan	2	22	13	FE	9	5949
1237	Jan	3	3	14	D	10	5950
1238	Jan	4	14	15	C	11	5951
1239	Jan	5	25	16	B	12	5952
1240*	Jan	6	6	17	AG	13	5953
1241	Jan	7	17	18	F	14	5954
1242	Jan	8	28	19	E	15	5955
1243	Jan	9	9	20	D	1	5956
1244*	Jan	10	20	21	CB	2	5957
1245	Jan	11	1	22	A	3	5958
1246	Jan	12	12	23	G	4	5959
1247	Jan	13	23	24	F	5	5960
1248*	Jan	14	4	25	ED	6	5961
1249	Jan	15	15	26	C	7	5962
1250	Jan	16	26	27	B	8	5963
1251	Jan	17	7	28	A	9	5964
1252*	Jan	18	18	1	GF	10	5965
1253	Jan	19	9	2	E	11	5966
1254	Jan	1	11	3	D	12	5967
1255	Jan	2	22	4	C	13	5968
1256*	Jan	3	3	5	BA	14	5969
1257	Jan	4	14	6	G	15	5970
1258	Jan	5	25	7	F	1	5971
1259	Jan	6	6	8	E	2	5972
1260*	Jan	7	17	9	DC	3	5973
1261	Jan	8	28	10	B	4	5974
1262	Jan	9	9	11	A	5	5975
1263	Jan	10	20	12	G	6	5976
1264*	Jan	11	1	13	FE	7	5977
1265	Jan	12	12	14	D	8	5978
1266	Jan	13	23	15	C	9	5979
1267	Jan	14	4	16	B	10	5980
1268*	Jan	15	15	17	AG	11	5981
1269	Jan	16	26	18	F	12	5982
1270	Jan	17	7	19	E	13	5983
1271	Jan	18	18	20	D	14	5984
1272*	Jan	19	9	21	CB	15	5985

Western Era Julian Year	Month	Golden Number	Epact	Solar Cycle	Domenical Letter	Roman Indiction	Julian Period
1273	Jan	1	11	22	A	1	5986
1274	Jan	2	22	23	G	2	5987
1275	Jan	3	3	24	F	3	5988
1276*	Jan	4	14	25	ED	4	5989
1277	Jan	5	25	26	C	5	5990
1278	Jan	6	6	27	B	6	5991
1279	Jan	7	17	28	A	7	5992
1280*	Jan	8	28	1	GF	8	5993
1281	Jan	9	9	2	E	9	5994
1282	Jan	10	20	3	D	10	5995
1283	Jan	11	1	4	C	11	5996
1284*	Jan	12	12	5	BA	12	5997
1285	Jan	13	23	6	G	13	5998
1286	Jan	14	4	7	F	14	5999
1287	Jan	15	15	8	E	15	6000
1288*	Jan	16	26	9	DC	1	6001
1289	Jan	17	7	10	B	2	6002
1290	Jan	18	18	11	A	3	6003
1291	Jan	19	9	12	G	4	6004
1292*	Jan	1	11	13	FE	5	6005
1293	Jan	2	22	14	D	6	6006
1294	Jan	3	3	15	C	7	6007
1295	Jan	4	14	16	B	8	6008
1296*	Jan	5	25	17	AG	9	6009
1297	Jan	6	6	18	F	10	6010
1298	Jan	7	17	19	E	11	6011
1299	Jan	8	28	20	D	12	6012
1300*	Jan	9	9	21	CB	13	6013
1301	Jan	10	20	22	A	14	6014
1302	Jan	11	1	23	G	15	6015
1303	Jan	12	12	24	F	1	6016
1304*	Jan	13	23	25	ED	2	6017
1305	Jan	14	4	26	C	3	6018
1306	Jan	15	15	27	B	4	6019
1307	Jan	16	26	28	A	5	6020
1308*	Jan	17	7	1	GF	6	6021
1309	Jan	18	18	2	E	7	6022
1310	Jan	19	9	3	D	8	6023
1311	Jan	1	11	4	C	9	6024
1312*	Jan	2	22	5	BA	10	6025
1313	Jan	3	3	6	G	11	6026
1314	Jan	4	14	7	F	12	6027
1315	Jan	5	25	8	E	13	6028
1316*	Jan	6	6	9	DC	14	6029

Western Era
Julian

Year	Month	Golden Number	Epact	Solar Cycle	Domenical Letter	Roman Indiction	Julian Period
1317	Jan	7	17	10	B	15	6030
1318	Jan	8	28	11	A	1	6031
1319	Jan	9	9	12	G	2	6032
1320*	Jan	10	20	13	FE	3	6033
1321	Jan	11	1	14	D	4	6034
1322	Jan	12	12	15	C	5	6035
1323	Jan	13	23	16	B	6	6036
1324*	Jan	14	4	17	AG	7	6037
1325	Jan	15	15	18	F	8	6038
1326	Jan	16	26	19	E	9	6039
1327	Jan	17	7	20	D	10	6040
1328*	Jan	18	18	21	CB	11	6041
1329	Jan	19	9	22	A	12	6042
1330	Jan	1	11	23	G	13	6043
1331	Jan	2	22	24	F	14	6044
1332*	Jan	3	3	25	ED	15	6045
1333	Jan	4	14	26	C	1	6046
1334	Jan	5	25	27	B	2	6047
1335	Jan	6	6	28	A	3	6048
1336*	Jan	7	17	1	GF	4	6049
1337	Jan	8	28	2	E	5	6050
1338	Jan	9	9	3	D	6	6051
1339	Jan	10	20	4	C	7	6052
1340*	Jan	11	1	5	BA	8	6053
1341	Jan	12	12	6	G	9	6054
1342	Jan	13	23	7	F	10	6055
1343	Jan	14	4	8	E	11	6056
1344*	Jan	15	15	9	DC	12	6057
1345	Jan	16	26	10	B	13	6058
1346	Jan	17	7	11	A	14	6059
1347	Jan	18	18	12	G	15	6060
1348*	Jan	19	9	13	FE	1	6061
1349	Jan	1	11	14	D	2	6062
1350	Jan	2	22	15	C	3	6063
1351	Jan	3	3	16	B	4	6064
1352*	Jan	4	14	17	AG	5	6065
1353	Jan	5	25	18	F	6	6066
1354	Jan	6	6	19	E	7	6067
1355	Jan	7	17	20	D	8	6068
1356*	Jan	8	28	21	CB	9	6069
1357	Jan	9	9	22	A	10	6070
1358	Jan	10	20	23	G	11	6071
1359	Jan	11	1	24	F	12	6072
1360*	Jan	12	12	25	ED	13	6073

Western Era
Julian

Year	Month	Golden Number	Epact	Solar Cycle	Domenical Letter	Roman Indiction	Julian Period
1361	Jan	13	23	26	C	14	6074
1362	Jan	14	4	27	B	15	6075
1363	Jan	15	15	28	A	1	6076
1364*	Jan	16	26	1	GF	2	6077
1365	Jan	17	7	2	E	3	6078
1366	Jan	18	18	3	D	4	6079
1367	Jan	19	9	4	C	5	6080
1368*	Jan	1	11	5	BA	6	6081
1369	Jan	2	22	6	G	7	6082
1370	Jan	3	3	7	F	8	6083
1371	Jan	4	14	8	E	9	6084
1372*	Jan	5	25	9	DC	10	6085
1373	Jan	6	6	10	B	11	6086
1374	Jan	7	17	11	A	12	6087
1375	Jan	8	28	12	G	13	6088
1376*	Jan	9	9	13	FE	14	6089
1377	Jan	10	20	14	D	15	6090
1378	Jan	11	1	15	C	1	6091
1379	Jan	12	12	16	B	2	6092
1380*	Jan	13	23	17	AG	3	6093
1381	Jan	14	4	18	F	4	6094
1382	Jan	15	15	19	E	5	6095
1383	Jan	16	26	20	D	6	6096
1384*	Jan	17	7	21	CB	7	6097
1385	Jan	18	18	22	A	8	6098
1386	Jan	19	9	23	G	9	6099
1387	Jan	1	11	24	F	10	6100
1388*	Jan	2	22	25	ED	11	6101
1389	Jan	3	3	26	C	12	6102
1390	Jan	4	14	27	B	13	6103
1391	Jan	5	25	28	A	14	6104
1392*	Jan	6	6	1	GF	15	6105
1393	Jan	7	17	2	E	1	6106
1394	Jan	8	28	3	D	2	6107
1395	Jan	9	9	4	C	3	6108
1396*	Jan	10	20	5	BA	4	6109
1397	Jan	11	1	6	G	5	6110
1398	Jan	12	12	7	F	6	6111
1399	Jan	13	23	8	E	7	6112
1400*	Jan	14	4	9	DC	8	6113
1401	Jan	15	15	10	B	9	6114
1402	Jan	16	26	11	A	10	6115
1403	Jan	17	7	12	G	11	6116
1404*	Jan	18	18	13	FE	12	6117

Western Era Julian Year	Month	Golden Number	Epact	Solar Cycle	Domenical Letter	Roman Indiction	Julian Period
1405	Jan	19	9	14	D	13	6118
1406	Jan	1	11	15	C	14	6119
1407	Jan	2	22	16	B	15	6120
1408*	Jan	3	3	17	AG	1	6121
1409	Jan	4	14	18	F	2	6122
1410	Jan	5	25	19	E	3	6123
1411	Jan	6	6	20	D	4	6124
1412*	Jan	7	17	21	CB	5	6125
1413	Jan	8	28	22	A	6	6126
1414	Jan	9	9	23	G	7	6127
1415	Jan	10	20	24	F	8	6128
1416*	Jan	11	1	25	ED	9	6129
1417	Jan	12	12	26	C	10	6130
1418	Jan	13	23	27	B	11	6131
1419	Jan	14	4	28	A	12	6132
1420*	Jan	15	15	1	GF	13	6133
1421	Jan	16	26	2	E	14	6134
1422	Jan	17	7	3	D	15	6135
1423	Jan	18	18	4	C	1	6136
1424*	Jan	19	9	5	BA	2	6137
1425	Jan	1	11	6	G	3	6138
1426	Jan	2	22	7	F	4	6139
1427	Jan	3	3	8	E	5	6140
1428*	Jan	4	14	9	DC	6	6141
1429	Jan	5	25	10	B	7	6142
1430	Jan	6	6	11	A	8	6143
1431	Jan	7	17	12	G	9	6144
1432*	Jan	8	28	13	FE	10	6145
1433	Jan	9	9	14	D	11	6146
1434	Jan	10	20	15	C	12	6147
1435	Jan	11	1	16	B	13	6148
1436*	Jan	12	12	17	AG	14	6149
1437	Jan	13	23	18	F	15	6150
1438	Jan	14	4	19	E	1	6151
1439	Jan	15	15	20	D	2	6152
1440*	Jan	16	26	21	CB	3	6153
1441	Jan	17	7	22	A	4	6154
1442	Jan	18	18	23	G	5	6155
1443	Jan	19	9	24	F	6	6156
1444*	Jan	1	11	25	ED	7	6157
1445	Jan	2	22	26	C	8	6158
1446	Jan	3	3	27	B	9	6159
1447	Jan	4	14	28	A	10	6160
1448*	Jan	5	25	1	GF	11	6161

Western Era Julian Year	Month	Golden Number	Epact	Solar Cycle	Domenical Letter	Roman Indiction	Julian Period
1449	Jan	6	6	2	E	12	6162
1450	Jan	7	17	3	D	13	6163
1451	Jan	8	28	4	C	14	6164
1452*	Jan	9	9	5	BA	15	6165
1453	Jan	10	20	6	G	1	6166
1454	Jan	11	1	7	F	2	6167
1455	Jan	12	12	8	E	3	6168
1456*	Jan	13	23	9	DC	4	6169
1457	Jan	14	4	10	B	5	6170
1458	Jan	15	15	11	A	6	6171
1459	Jan	16	26	12	G	7	6172
1460*	Jan	17	7	13	FE	8	6173
1461	Jan	18	18	14	D	9	6174
1462	Jan	19	9	15	C	10	6175
1463	Jan	1	11	16	B	11	6176
1464*	Jan	2	22	17	AG	12	6177
1465	Jan	3	3	18	F	13	6178
1466	Jan	4	14	19	E	14	6179
1467	Jan	5	25	20	D	15	6180
1468*	Jan	6	6	21	CB	1	6181
1469	Jan	7	17	22	A	2	6182
1470	Jan	8	28	23	G	3	6183
1471	Jan	9	9	24	F	4	6184
1472*	Jan	10	20	25	ED	5	6185
1473	Jan	11	1	26	C	6	6186
1474	Jan	12	12	27	B	7	6187
1475	Jan	13	23	28	A	8	6188
1476*	Jan	14	4	1	GF	9	6189
1477	Jan	15	15	2	E	10	6190
1478	Jan	16	26	3	D	11	6191
1479	Jan	17	7	4	C	12	6192
1480*	Jan	18	18	5	BA	13	6193
1481	Jan	19	3	6	G	14	6194
1482	Jan	1	11	7	F	15	6195
1483	Jan	2	22	8	E	1	6196
1484*	Jan	3	3	9	DC	2	6197
1485	Jan	4	14	10	B	3	6198
1486	Jan	5	25	11	A	4	6199
1487	Jan	6	6	12	G	5	6200
1488*	Jan	7	17	13	FE	6	6201
1489	Jan	8	28	14	D	7	6202
1490	Jan	9	9	15	C	8	6203
1491	Jan	10	20	16	B	9	6204
1492*	Jan	11	1	17	AG	10	6205

Western Era
Julian

Year	Month	Golden Number	Epact	Solar Cycle	Domenical Letter	Roman Indiction	Julian Period
1493	Jan	12	12	18	F	11	6206
1494	Jan	13	23	19	E	12	6207
1495	Jan	14	4	20	D	13	6208
1496*	Jan	15	15	21	CB	14	6209
1497	Jan	16	26	22	A	15	6210
1498	Jan	17	7	23	G	1	6211
1499	Jan	18	18	24	F	2	6212
1500*	Jan	19	9	25	ED	3	6213
1501	Jan	1	11	26	C	4	6214
1502	Jan	2	22	27	B	5	6215
1503	Jan	3	3	28	A	6	6216
1504*	Jan	4	14	1	GF	7	6217
1505	Jan	5	25	2	E	8	6218
1506	Jan	6	6	3	D	9	6219
1507	Jan	7	17	4	C	10	6220
1508*	Jan	8	28	5	BA	11	6221
1509	Jan	9	9	6	G	12	6222
1510	Jan	10	20	7	F	13	6223
1511	Jan	11	1	8	E	14	6224
1512*	Jan	12	12	9	DC	15	6225
1513	Jan	13	23	10	B	1	6226
1514	Jan	14	4	11	A	2	6227
1515	Jan	15	15	12	G	3	6228
1516*	Jan	16	26	13	FE	4	6229
1517	Jan	17	7	14	D	5	6230
1518	Jan	18	18	15	C	6	6231
1519	Jan	19	9	16	B	7	6232
1520*	Jan	1	17	17	AG	8	6233
1521	Jan	2	22	18	F	9	6234
1522	Jan	3	3	19	E	10	6235
1523	Jan	4	14	20	D	11	6236
1524*	Jan	5	25	21	CB	12	6237
1525	Jan	6	6	22	A	13	6238
1526	Jan	7	17	23	G	14	6239
1527	Jan	8	28	24	F	15	6240
1528*	Jan	9	9	25	ED	1	6241
1529	Jan	10	20	26	C	2	6242
1530	Jan	11	1	27	B	3	6243
1531	Jan	12	12	28	A	4	6244
1532*	Jan	13	23	1	GF	5	6245
1533	Jan	14	4	2	E	6	6246
1534	Jan	15	15	3	D	7	6247
1535	Jan	16	26	4	C	8	6248
1536*	Jan	17	7	5	BA	9	6249

Western Era
Julian

Year	Month	Golden Number	Epact	Solar Cycle	Domenical Letter	Roman Indiction	Julian Period
1537	Jan	18	18	6	G	10	6250
1538	Jan	19	9	7	F	11	6251
1539	Jan	1	11	8	E	12	6252
1540*	Jan	2	22	9	DC	13	6253
1541	Jan	3	3	10	B	14	6254
1542	Jan	4	14	11	A	15	6255
1543	Jan	5	25	12	G	1	6256
1544*	Jan	6	6	13	FE	2	6257
1545	Jan	7	17	14	D	3	6258
1546	Jan	8	28	15	C	4	6259
1547	Jan	9	9	16	B	5	6260
1548*	Jan	10	20	17	AG	6	6261
1549	Jan	11	1	18	F	7	6262
1550	Jan	12	12	19	E	8	6263
1551	Jan	13	23	20	D	9	6264
1552*	Jan	14	4	21	CB	10	6265
1553	Jan	15	15	22	A	11	6266
1554	Jan	16	26	23	G	12	6267
1555	Jan	17	7	24	F	13	6268
1556*	Jan	18	18	25	ED	14	6269
1557	Jan	19	9	26	C	15	6270
1558	Jan	1	11	27	B	1	6271
1559	Jan	2	22	28	A	2	6272
1560*	Jan	3	3	1	GF	3	6273
1561	Jan	4	14	2	E	4	6274
1562	Jan	5	25	3	D	5	6275
1563	Jan	6	6	4	C	6	6276
1564*	Jan	7	17	5	BA	7	6277
1565	Jan	8	28	6	G	8	6278
1566	Jan	9	9	7	F	9	6279
1567	Jan	10	20	8	E	10	6280
1568*	Jan	11	1	9	DC	11	6281
1569	Jan	12	12	10	B	12	6282
1570	Jan	13	23	11	A	13	6283
1571	Jan	14	4	12	G	14	6284
1572*	Jan	15	15	13	FE	15	6285
1573	Jan	16	26	14	D	1	6286
1574	Jan	17	7	15	C	2	6287
1575	Jan	18	18	16	B	3	6288
1576*	Jan	19	9	17	AG	4	6289
1577	Jan	1	11	18	F	5	6290
1578	Jan	2	22	19	E	6	6291
1579	Jan	3	3	20	D	7	6292
1580*	Jan	4	14	21	CB	8	6293

Western Era Julian

Year	Month	Golden Number	Epact	Solar Cycle	Domenical Letter	Roman Indiction	Julian Period
1581	Jan	5	25	22	A	9	6294
1582	Jan	6	6	23	G	10	6295
1583	Jan	7	17	24	F	11	6296
1584*	Jan	8	28	25	ED	12	6297
1585	Jan	9	9	26	C	13	6298
1586	Jan	10	20	27	B	14	6299
1587	Jan	11	1	28	A	15	6300
1588*	Jan	12	12	1	GF	01	6301
1589	Jan	13	23	2	E	2	6302
1590	Jan	14	4	3	D	3	6303
1591	Jan	15	15	4	C	4	6304
1592*	Jan	16	26	5	BA	5	6305
1593	Jan	17	7	6	G	6	6306
1594	Jan	18	18	7	F	7	6307
1595	Jan	19	9	8	E	8	6308
1596*	Jan	1	11	9	DC	9	6309
1597	Jan	2	22	10	B	10	6310
1598	Jan	3	3	11	A	11	6311
1599	Jan	4	14	12	G	12	6312
1600*	Jan	5	25	13	FE	13	6313
1601	Jan	6	6	14	D	14	6314
1602	Jan	7	17	15	C	15	6315
1603	Jan	8	28	16	B	1	6316
1604*	Jan	9	9	17	AG	2	6317
1605	Jan	10	20	18	F	3	6318
1606	Jan	11	1	19	E	4	6319
1607	Jan	12	12	20	D	5	6320
1608*	Jan	13	23	21	CB	6	6321
1609	Jan	14	4	22	A	7	6322
1610	Jan	15	15	23	G	8	6323
1611	Jan	16	26	24	F	9	6324
1612*	Jan	17	7	25	ED	10	6325
1613	Jan	18	18	26	C	11	6326
1614	Jan	19	9	27	B	12	6327
1615	Jan	1	11	28	A	13	6328
1616*	Jan	2	22	1	GF	14	6329
1617	Jan	3	3	2	E	15	6330
1618	Jan	4	14	3	D	1	6331
1619	Jan	5	25	4	C	2	6332
1620*	Jan	6	6	5	BA	3	6333
1621	Jan	7	17	6	G	4	6334
1622	Jan	8	28	7	F	5	6335
1623	Jan	9	9	8	E	6	6336

Western Era Julian

Year	Month	Golden Number	Epact	Solar Cycle	Domenical Letter	Roman Indiction	Julian Period
1624*	Jan	10	20	9	DC	7	6337
1625	Jan	11	1	10	B	8	6338
1626	Jan	12	12	11	A	9	6339
1627	Jan	13	23	12	G	10	6340
1628*	Jan	14	4	13	FE	11	6341
1629	Jan	15	15	14	D	12	6342
1630	Jan	16	26	15	C	13	6343
1631	Jan	17	7	16	B	14	6344
1632*	Jan	18	18	17	AG	15	6345
1633	Jan	19	9	18	F	1	6346
1634	Jan	1	11	19	E	2	6347
1635	Jan	2	22	20	D	3	6348
1636*	Jan	3	3	21	CB	4	6349
1637	Jan	4	14	22	A	5	6350
1638	Jan	5	25	23	G	6	6351
1639	Jan	6	6	24	F	7	6352
1640*	Jan	7	17	25	ED	8	6353
1641	Jan	8	28	26	C	9	6354
1642	Jan	9	9	27	B	10	6355
1643	Jan	10	20	28	A	11	6356
1644*	Jan	11	11	1	GF	12	6357
1645	Jan	12	12	2	E	13	6358
1646	Jan	13	23	3	D	14	6359
1647	Jan	14	4	4	C	15	6360
1648*	Jan	15	15	5	BA	1	6361
1649	Jan	16	26	6	G	2	6362
1650	Jan	17	7	7	F	3	6363
1651	Jan	18	18	8	E	4	6364
1652*	Jan	19	9	9	DC	5	6365
1653	Jan	1	11	10	B	6	6366
1654	Jan	2	22	11	A	7	6367
1655	Jan	3	3	12	G	8	6368
1656*	Jan	4	14	13	FE	9	6369
1657	Jan	5	25	14	D	10	6370
1658	Jan	6	6	15	C	11	6371
1659	Jan	7	17	16	B	12	6372
1660*	Jan	8	28	17	AG	13	6373
1661	Jan	9	9	18	kF	14	6374
1662	Jan	10	20	19	E	15	6375
1663	Jan	11	1	20	D	1	6376
1664*	Jan	12	12	21	CB	2	6377
1665	Jan	13	23	22	A	3	6378
1666	Jan	14	4	23	G	4	6379

Western Era
Julian

Year	Month	Golden Number	Epact	Solar Cycle	Domenical Letter	Roman Indiction	Julian Period
1667	Jan	15	15	24	F	5	6380
1668*	Jan	16	26	25	ED	6	6381
1669	Jan	17	7	26	C	7	6382
1670	Jan	18	18	27	B	8	6383
1671	Jan	19	9	28	A	9	6384
1672*	Jan	1	11	1	GF	10	6385
1673	Jan	2	22	2	E	11	6386
1674	Jan	3	3	3	D	12	6387
1675	Jan	4	14	4	C	13	6388
1676*	Jan	5	25	5	BA	14	6389
1677	Jan	6	6	6	G	15	6390
1678	Jan	7	17	7	F	1	6391
1679	Jan	8	28	8	E	2	6392
1680*	Jan	9	9	9	DC	3	6393
1681	Jan	10	20	10	B	4	6394
1682	Jan	11	1	11	A	5	6395
1683	Jan	12	12	12	G	6	6396
1684*	Jan	13	23	13	FE	7	6397
1685	Jan	14	4	14	D	8	6398
1686	Jan	15	15	15	C	9	6399
1687	Jan	16	26	16	B	10	6400
1688*	Jan	17	7	17	AG	11	6401
1689	Jan	18	18	18	F	12	6402
1690	Jan	19	9	19	E	13	6403
1691	Jan	1	11	20	D	14	6404
1692*	Jan	2	22	21	CB	15	6405
1693	Jan	3	3	22	A	1	6406
1694	Jan	4	14	23	G	2	6407
1695	Jan	5	25	24	F	3	6408
1696*	Jan	6	6	25	ED	4	6409
1697	Jan	7	17	26	C	5	6410
1698	Jan	8	28	27	B	6	6411
1699	Jan	9	9	28	A	7	6412
1700	Jan	10	20	1	GF	8	6413
1701	Jan	11	1	2	E	9	6414
1702	Jan	12	12	3	D	10	6415
1703	Jan	13	23	4	C	11	6416
1704*	Jan	14	4	5	BA	12	6417
1705	Jan	15	15	6	G	13	6418
1706	Jan	16	26	7	F	14	6419
1707	Jan	17	7	8	E	15	6420
1708*	Jan	18	18	9	DC	1	6421
1709	Jan	19	9	10	B	2	6422

Western Era
Julian

Year	Month	Golden Number	Epact	Solar Cycle	Domenical Letter	Roman Indiction	Julian Period
1710	Jan	1	11	11	A	3	6423
1711	Jan	2	22	12	G	4	6424
1712*	Jan	3	3	13	FE	5	6425
1713	Jan	4	14	14	D	6	6426
1714	Jan	5	25	15	C	7	6427
1715	Jan	6	6	16	B	8	6428
1716*	Jan	7	17	17	AG	9	6429
1717	Jan	8	28	18	F	10	6430
1718	Jan	9	9	19	E	11	6431
1719	Jan	10	20	20	D	12	6432
1720*	Jan	11	1	21	CB	13	6433
1721	Jan	12	12	22	A	14	6434
1722	Jan	13	23	23	G	15	6435
1723	Jan	14	4	24	F	1	6436
1724*	Jan	15	15	25	ED	2	6437
1725	Jan	16	26	26	C	3	6438
1726	Jan	17	7	27	B	4	6439
1727	Jan	18	18	28	A	5	6440
1728*	Jan	19	9	1	GF	6	6441
1729	Jan	1	11	2	E	7	6442
1730	Jan	2	22	3	D	8	6443
1731	Jan	3	3	4	C	9	6444
1732*	Jan	4	14	5	BA	10	6445
1733	Jan	5	25	6	G	11	6446
1734	Jan	6	6	7	F	12	6447
1735	Jan	7	17	8	E	13	6448
1736*	Jan	8	28	9	DC	14	6449
1737	Jan	9	9	10	B	15	6450
1738	Jan	10	20	11	A	1	6451
1739	Jan	11	1	12	G	2	6452
1740*	Jan	12	12	13	FE	3	6453
1741	Jan	13	23	14	D	4	6454
1742	Jan	14	4	15	C	5	6455
1743	Jan	15	15	16	B	6	6456
1744*	Jan	16	26	17	AG	7	6457
1745	Jan	17	7	18	F	8	6458
1746	Jan	18	18	19	E	9	6459
1747	Jan	19	9	20	D	10	6460
1748*	Jan	1	11	21	CB	11	6461
1749	Jan	2	22	22	A	12	6462
1750	Jan	3	3	23	G	13	6463
1751	Jan	4	14	24	F	14	6464
1752*	Jan	5	25	25	ED	15	6465

Western Era Gregorian

Year	Month	Golden Number	Epact	Solar Cycle	Domenical Letter	Roman Indiction	Julian Period
1583	Jan	7	7	24	B	11	6296
1584*	Jan	8	18	25	AG	12	6297
1585	Jan	9	29	26	F	13	6298
1586	Jan	10	10	27	E	14	6299
1587	Jan	11	21	28	D	15	6300
1588*	Jan	12	2	1	CB	1	6301
1589	Jan	13	13	2	A	2	6302
1590	Jan	14	24	3	G	3	6303
1591	Jan	15	5	4	F	4	6304
1592*	Jan	16	16	5	ED	5	6305
1593	Jan	17	27	6	C	6	6306
1594	Jan	18	8	7	B	7	6307
1595	Jan	19	19	8	A	8	6308
1596*	Jan	1	1	9	GF	9	6309
1597	Jan	2	12	10	E	10	6310
1598	Jan	3	23	11	D	11	6311
1599	Jan	4	4	12	C	12	6312
1600*	Jan	5	15	13	BA	13	6313
1601	Jan	6	26	14	G	14	6314
1602	Jan	7	7	15	F	15	6315
1603	Jan	8	18	16	E	1	6316
1604*	Jan	9	29	17	DC	2	6317
1605	Jan	10	10	18	B	3	6318
1606	Jan	11	21	19	A	4	6319
1607	Jan	12	2	20	G	5	6320
1608*	Jan	13	13	21	FE	6	6321
1609	Jan	14	24	22	D	7	6322
1610	Jan	15	5	23	C	8	6323
1611	Jan	16	16	24	B	9	6324
1612*	Jan	17	27	25	AG	10	6325
1613	Jan	18	8	26	F	11	6326
1614	Jan	19	19	27	E	12	6327
1615	Jan	1	1	28	D	13	6328
1616*	Jan	2	12	1	CB	14	6329
1617	Jan	3	23	2	A	15	6330
1618	Jan	4	4	3	G	1	6331
1619	Jan	5	15	4	F	2	6332
1620*	Jan	6	26	5	ED	3	6333
1621	Jan	7	7	6	C	4	6334
1622	Jan	8	18	7	B	5	6335
1623	Jan	9	29	8	A	6	6336
1624*	Jan	10	10	9	GF	7	6337
1625	Jan	11	21	10	E	8	6338
1626	Jan	12	2	11	D	9	6339

Western Era Gregorian

Year	Month	Golden Number	Epact	Solar Cycle	Domenical Letter	Roman Indiction	Julian Period
1627	Jan	13	13	12	C	10	6340
1628*	Jan	14	24	13	BA	11	6341
1629	Jan	15	5	14	G	12	6342
1630	Jan	16	6	15	F	13	6343
1631	Jan	17	27	16	E	14	6344
1632*	Jan	18	8	17	DC	15	6345
1633	Jan	19	19	18	B	1	6346
1634	Jan	1	1	19	A	2	6347
1635	Jan	2	12	20	G	3	6348
1636*	Jan	3	23	21	FE	4	6349
1637	Jan	4	4	22	D	5	6350
1638	Jan	5	15	23	C	6	6351
1639	Jan	6	26	24	B	7	6352
1640*	Jan	7	7	25	AG	8	6353
1641	Jan	8	18	26	F	9	6354
1642	Jan	9	29	27	E	10	6355
1643	Jan	10	10	28	D	11	6356
1644*	Jan	11	21	1	CB	12	6357
1645	Jan	12	2	2	A	13	6358
1646	Jan	13	13	3	G	14	6359
1647	Jan	14	24	4	F	15	6360
1648*	Jan	15	5	5	ED	1	6361
1649	Jan	16	16	6	C	2	6362
1650	Jan	17	27	7	B	3	6363
1651	Jan	18	8	8	A	4	6364
1652*	Jan	19	19	9	GF	5	6365
1653	Jan	1	1	10	E	6	6366
1654	Jan	2	12	11	D	7	6367
1655	Jan	3	23	12	C	8	6368
1656*	Jan	4	4	13	BA	9	6369
1657	Jan	5	15	14	G	10	6370
1658	Jan	6	26	15	F	11	6371
1659	Jan	7	7	16	E	12	6372
1660*	Jan	8	8	17	DC	13	6373
1661	Jan	9	29	18	B	14	6374
1662	Jan	10	10	19	A	15	6375
1663	Jan	11	21	20	G	1	6376
1664*	Jan	12	2	21	FE	2	6377
1665	Jan	13	13	22	D	3	6378
1666	Jan	14	24	23	C	4	6379
1667	Jan	15	5	24	B	5	6380
1668*	Jan	16	16	25	AG	6	6381
1669	Jan	17	27	26	F	7	6382
1670	Jan	18	8	27	E	8	6383

Western Era
Gregorian

Year	Month	Golden Number	Epact	Solar Cycle	Domenical Letter	Roman Indiction	Julian Period
1671	Jan	19	19	28	D	9	6384
1672*	Jan	1	1	1	CB	10	6385
1673	Jan	2	12	2	A	11	6386
1674	Jan	3	23	3	G	12	6387
1675	Jan	4	4	4	F	13	6388
1676*	Jan	5	15	5	ED	14	6389
1677	Jan	6	26	6	C	15	6390
1678	Jan	7	7	7	B	1	6391
1679	Jan	8	18	8	A	2	6392
1680*	Jan	9	29	9	GF	3	6393
1681	Jan	10	10	10	E	4	6394
1682	Jan	11	21	11	D	5	6395
1683	Jan	12	2	12	C	6	6396
1684*	Jan	13	13	13	BA	7	6397
1685	Jan	14	24	14	G	8	6398
1686	Jan	15	5	15	F	9	6399
1687	Jan	16	16	16	E	10	6400
1688*	Jan	17	27	17	DC	11	6401
1689	Jan	18	8	18	B	12	6402
1690	Jan	19	19	19	A	13	6403
1691	Jan	1	1	20	G	14	6404
1692*	Jan	2	12	21	FE	15	6405
1693	Jan	3	23	22	D	1	6406
1694	Jan	4	4	23	C	2	6407
1695	Jan	5	15	24	B	3	6408
1696*	Jan	6	26	25	AG	4	6409
1697	Jan	7	7	26	F	5	6410
1698	Jan	8	18	27	E	6	6411
1699	Jan	9	29	28	D	7	6412
1700	Jan	10	9	1	C	8	6413
1701	Jan	11	20	2	B	9	6414
1702	Jan	12	1	3	A	10	6415
1703	Jan	13	12	4	G	11	6416
1704*	Jan	14	23	5	FE	12	6417
1705	Jan	15	4	6	D	13	6418
1706	Jan	16	15	7	C	14	6419
1707	Jan	17	26	8	B	15	6420
1708*	Jan	18	7	9	AG	1	6421
1709	Jan	19	18	10	F	2	6422
1710	Jan	1	9	11	E	3	6423
1711	Jan	2	11	12	D	4	6424
1712*	Jan	3	22	13	CB	5	6425
1713	Jan	4	3	14	A	6	6426
1714	Jan	5	14	15	G	7	6427

Western Era
Gregorian

Year	Month	Golden Number	Epact	Solar Cycle	Domenical Letter	Roman Indiction	Julian Period
1715	Jan	6	25	16	F	8	6428
1716*	Jan	7	6	17	ED	9	6429
1717	Jan	8	17	18	C	10	6430
1718	Jan	9	28	19	B	11	6431
1719	Jan	10	9	20	A	12	6432
1720*	Jan	11	20	21	GF	13	6433
1721	Jan	12	1	22	E	14	6434
1722	Jan	13	12	23	D	15	6435
1723	Jan	14	23	24	C	1	6436
1724*	Jan	15	4	25	BA	2	6437
1725	Jan	16	15	26	G	3	6438
1726	Jan	17	26	27	F	4	6439
1727	Jan	18	7	28	E	5	6440
1728*	Jan	19	18	1	DC	6	6441
1729	Jan	1	9	2	B	7	6442
1730	Jan	2	11	3	A	8	6443
1731	Jan	3	22	4	G	9	6444
1732*	Jan	4	3	5	FE	10	6445
1733	Jan	5	14	6	D	11	6446
1734	Jan	6	25	7	C	12	6447
1735	Jan	7	6	8	B	13	6448
1736*	Jan	8	17	9	AG	14	6449
1737	Jan	9	28	10	F	15	6450
1738	Jan	10	9	11	E	1	6451
1739	Jan	11	20	12	D	2	6452
1740*	Jan	12	1	13	CB	3	6453
1741	Jan	13	12	14	A	4	6454
1742	Jan	14	23	15	G	5	6455
1743	Jan	15	4	16	F	6	6456
1744*	Jan	16	15	17	ED	7	6457
1745	Jan	17	26	18	C	8	6458
1746	Jan	18	7	19	B	9	6459
1747	Jan	19	18	20	A	10	6460
1748*	Jan	1	0	21	GF	11	6461
1749	Jan	2	11	22	E	12	6462
1750	Jan	3	22	23	D	13	6463
1751	Jan	4	3	24	C	14	6464
1752*	Jan	5	14	25	BA	15	6465
1753	Jan	6	25	26	G	1	6466
1754	Jan	7	6	27	F	2	6467
1755	Jan	8	17	28	E	3	6468
1756*	Jan	9	28	1	DC	4	6469
1757	Jan	10	9	2	B	5	6470
1758	Jan	11	20	3	A	6	6471

Western Era
Gregorian

Year	Month	Golden Number	Epact	Solar Cycle	Domenical Letter	Roman Indiction	Julian Period
1759	Jan	12	1	4	G	7	6472
1760*	Jan	13	12	5	FE	8	6473
1761	Jan	14	23	6	D	9	6474
1762	Jan	15	4	7	C	10	6475
1763	Jan	16	15	8	B	11	6476
1764*	Jan	17	26	9	AG	12	6477
1765	Jan	18	7	10	F	13	6478
1766	Jan	19	18	11	E	14	6479
1767	Jan	1	0	12	D	15	6480
1768*	Jan	2	11	13	CB	1	6481
1769	Jan	3	22	14	A	2	6482
1770	Jan	4	3	15	G	3	6483
1771	Jan	5	14	16	F	4	6484
1772*	Jan	6	25	17	ED	5	6485
1773	Jan	7	6	18	C	6	6486
1774	Jan	8	17	19	B	7	6487
1775	Jan	9	28	20	A	8	6488
1776*	Jan	10	9	21	GF	9	6489
1777	Jan	11	20	22	E	10	6490
1778	Jan	12	1	23	D	11	6491
1779	Jan	13	12	24	C	12	6492
1780*	Jan	14	23	25	BA	13	6493
1781	Jan	15	4	26	G	14	6494
1782	Jan	16	15	27	F	15	6495
1783	Jan	17	26	28	E	1	6496
1784*	Jan	18	7	1	DC	2	6497
1785	Jan	19	18	2	B	3	6498
1786	Jan	1	0	3	A	4	6499
1787	Jan	2	11	4	G	5	6500
1788*	Jan	3	22	5	FE	6	6501
1789	Jan	4	3	6	D	7	6502
1790	Jan	5	14	7	C	8	6503
1791	Jan	6	25	8	B	9	6504
1792*	Jan	7	6	9	AG	10	6505
1793	Jan	8	17	10	F	11	6506
1794	Jan	9	28	11	E	12	6507
1795	Jan	10	9	12	D	13	6508
1796*	Jan	11	20	13	CB	14	6509
1797	Jan	12	1	14	A	15	6510
1798	Jan	13	12	15	G	1	6511
1799	Jan	14	23	16	F	2	6512
1800	Jan	15	4	17	E	3	6513
1801	Jan	16	15	18	D	4	6514
1802	Jan	17	26	19	C	5	6515

Western Era
Gregorian

Year	Month	Golden Number	Epact	Solar Cycle	Domenical Letter	Roman Indiction	Julian Period
1803	Jan	18	7	20	B	6	6516
1804*	Jan	19	18	21	AG	7	6517
1805	Jan	1	0	22	F	8	6518
1806	Jan	2	11	23	E	9	6519
1807	Jan	3	22	24	D	10	6520
1808*	Jan	4	3	25	CB	11	6521
1809	Jan	5	14	26	A	12	6522
1810	Jan	6	25	27	G	13	6523
1811	Jan	7	6	28	F	14	6524
1812*	Jan	8	17	1	ED	15	6525
1813	Jan	9	28	2	C	1	6526
1814	Jan	10	9	3	B	2	6527
1815	Jan	11	20	4	A	3	6528
1816*	Jan	12	1	5	GF	4	6529
1817	Jan	13	12	6	E	5	6530
1818	Jan	14	23	7	D	6	6531
1819	Jan	15	4	8	C	7	6532
1820*	Jan	16	15	9	BA	8	6533
1821	Jan	17	26	10	G	9	6534
1822	Jan	18	7	11	F	10	6535
1823	Jan	19	18	12	E	11	6536
1824*	Jan	1	0	13	DC	12	6537
1825	Jan	2	11	14	B	13	6538
1826	Jan	3	22	15	A	14	6539
1827	Jan	4	3	16	G	15	6540
1828*	Jan	5	14	17	FE	1	6541
1829	Jan	6	25	18	D	2	6542
1830	Jan	7	6	19	C	3	6543
1831	Jan	8	17	20	B	4	6544
1832*	Jan	9	28	21	AG	5	6545
1833	Jan	10	9	22	F	6	6546
1834	Jan	11	20	23	E	7	6547
1835	Jan	12	1	24	D	8	6548
1836*	Jan	13	12	25	CB	9	6549
1837	Jan	14	23	26	A	10	6550
1838	Jan	15	4	27	G	11	6551
1839	Jan	16	15	28	F	12	6552
1840*	Jan	17	26	1	ED	13	6553
1841	Jan	18	7	2	C	14	6554
1842	Jan	19	18	3	B	15	6555
1843	Jan	1	0	4	A	1	6556
1844*	Jan	2	11	5	GF	2	6557
1845	Jan	3	22	6	E	3	6558
1846	Jan	4	3	7	D	4	6559

Western Era
Gregorian

Year	Month	Golden Number	Epact	Solar Cycle	Domenical Letter	Roman Indiction	Julian Period
1847	Jan	5	14	8	C	5	6560
1848*	Jan	6	25	9	BA	6	6561
1849	Jan	7	6	10	G	7	6562
1850	Jan	8	17	11	F	8	6563
1851	Jan	9	28	12	E	9	6564
1852*	Jan	10	9	13	DC	10	6565
1853	Jan	11	20	14	B	11	6566
1854	Jan	12	1	15	A	12	6567
1855	Jan	13	12	16	G	13	6568
1856*	Jan	14	23	17	FE	14	6569
1857	Jan	15	4	18	D	15	6570
1858	Jan	16	15	19	C	1	6571
1859	Jan	17	26	20	B	2	6572
1860*	Jan	18	7	21	AG	3	6573
1861	Jan	19	18	22	F	4	6574
1862	Jan	1	0	23	E	5	6575
1863	Jan	2	11	24	D	6	6576
1864*	Jan	3	22	25	CB	7	6577
1865	Jan	4	3	26	A	8	6578
1866	Jan	5	14	27	G	9	6579
1867	Jan	6	25	28	F	10	6580
1868*	Jan	7	6	1	ED	11	6581
1869	Jan	8	17	2	C	12	6582
1870	Jan	9	28	3	B	13	6583
1871	Jan	10	9	4	A	14	6584
1872*	Jan	11	20	5	GF	15	6585
1873	Jan	12	1	6	E	1	6586
1874	Jan	13	12	7	D	2	6587
1875	Jan	14	23	8	C	3	6588
1876*	Jan	15	4	9	BA	4	6589
1877	Jan	16	15	10	G	5	6590
1878	Jan	17	26	11	F	6	6591
1879	Jan	18	7	12	E	7	6592
1880*	Jan	19	18	13	DC	8	6593
1881	Jan	1	0	14	B	9	6594
1882	Jan	2	11	15	A	10	6595
1883	Jan	3	22	16	G	11	6596
1884*	Jan	4	3	17	FE	12	6597
1885	Jan	5	14	18	D	13	6598
1886	Jan	6	25	19	C	14	6599
1887	Jan	7	6	20	B	15	6600
1888*	Jan	8	17	21	AG	1	6601
1889	Jan	9	28	22	F	2	6602
1890	Jan	10	9	23	E	3	6603

Western Era
Gregorian

Year	Month	Golden Number	Epact	Solar Cycle	Domenical Letter	Roman Indiction	Julian Period
1891	Jan	11	20	24	D	4	6604
1892*	Jan	12	1	25	CB	5	6605
1893	Jan	13	12	26	A	6	6606
1894	Jan	14	23	27	G	7	6607
1895	Jan	15	4	28	F	8	6608
1896*	Jan	16	15	1	ED	9	6609
1897	Jan	17	26	2	C	10	6610
1898	Jan	18	7	3	B	11	6611
1899	Jan	19	18	4	A	12	6612
1900	Jan	1	0	5	G	13	6613
1901	Jan	2	11	6	F	14	6614
1902	Jan	3	22	7	E	15	6615
1903	Jan	4	3	8	D	1	6616
1904*	Jan	5	14	9	CB	2	6617
1905	Jan	6	25	10	A	3	6618
1906	Jan	7	6	11	G	4	6619
1907	Jan	8	17	12	F	5	6620
1908*	Jan	9	28	13	ED	6	6621
1909	Jan	10	9	14	C	7	6622
1910	Jan	11	20	15	B	8	6623
1911	Jan	12	1	16	A	9	6624
1912*	Jan	13	12	17	GF	10	6625
1913	Jan	14	23	18	E	11	6626
1914	Jan	15	4	19	D	12	6627
1915	Jan	16	15	20	C	13	6628
1916*	Jan	17	26	21	BA	14	6629
1917	Jan	18	7	22	G	15	6630
1918	Jan	19	18	23	F	1	6631
1919	Jan	1	0	24	E	2	6632
1920*	Jan	2	11	25	DC	3	6633
1921	Jan	3	22	26	B	4	6634
1922	Jan	4	3	27	A	5	6635
1923	Jan	5	14	28	G	6	6636
1924*	Jan	6	25	1	FE	7	6637
1925	Jan	7	6	2	D	8	6638
1926	Jan	8	17	3	C	9	6639
1927	Jan	9	28	4	B	10	6640
1928*	Jan	10	9	5	AG	11	6641
1929	Jan	11	20	6	F	12	6642
1930	Jan	12	1	7	E	13	6643
1931	Jan	13	12	8	D	14	6644
1932*	Jan	14	23	9	CB	15	6645
1933	Jan	15	4	10	A	1	6646
1934	Jan	16	15	11	G	2	6647

Western Era Gregorian

Year	Month	Golden Number	Epact	Solar Cycle	Domenical Letter	Roman Indiction	Julian Period
1935	Jan	17	26	12	F	3	6648
1936*	Jan	18	7	13	ED	4	6649
1937	Jan	19	18	14	C	5	6650
1938	Jan	1	0	15	B	6	6651
1939	Jan	2	11	16	A	7	6652
1940*	Jan	3	22	17	GF	8	6653
1941	Jan	4	3	18	E	9	6654
1942	Jan	5	14	19	D	10	6655
1943	Jan	6	25	20	C	11	6656
1944*	Jan	7	6	21	BA	12	6657
1945	Jan	8	17	22	G	13	6658
1946	Jan	9	28	23	F	14	6659
1947	Jan	10	9	24	E	15	6660
1948*	Jan	11	20	25	DC	1	6661
1949	Jan	12	1	26	B	2	6662
1950	Jan	13	12	27	A	3	6663
1951	Jan	14	23	28	G	4	6664
1952*	Jan	15	4	1	FE	5	6665
1953	Jan	16	15	2	D	6	6666
1954	Jan	17	26	3	C	7	6667
1955	Jan	18	7	4	B	8	6668
1956*	Jan	19	18	5	AG	9	6669
1957	Jan	1	0	6	F	10	6670
1958	Jan	2	11	7	E	11	6671
1959	Jan	3	22	8	D	12	6672
1960*	Jan	4	3	9	CB	13	6673
1961	Jan	5	14	10	A	14	6674
1962	Jan	6	25	11	G	15	6675
1963	Jan	7	6	12	F	1	6676
1964*	Jan	8	17	13	ED	2	6677
1965	Jan	9	28	14	C	3	6678
1966	Jan	10	9	15	B	4	6679
1967	Jan	11	20	16	A	5	6680

Western Era Gregorian

Year	Month	Golden Number	Epact	Solar Cycle	Domenical Letter	Roman Indiction	Julian Period
1968*	Jan	12	4	17	GF	6	6681
1969	Jan	13	12	18	E	7	6682
1970	Jan	14	23	19	D	8	6683
1971	Jan	15	4	20	C	9	6684
1972*	Jan	16	15	21	BA	10	6685
1973	Jan	17	26	22	G	11	6686
1974	Jan	18	7	23	F	12	6687
1975	Jan	19	18	24	E	13	6688
1976*	Jan	1	0	25	DC	14	6689
1977	Jan	2	11	26	B	15	6690
1978	Jan	3	22	27	A	1	6691
1979	Jan	4	3	28	G	2	6692
1980*	Jan	5	14	1	FE	3	6693
1981	Jan	6	25	2	D	4	6694
1982	Jan	7	6	3	C	5	6695
1983	Jan	8	17	4	B	6	6696
1984*	Jan	9	28	5	AG	7	6697
1985	Jan	10	9	6	F	8	6698
1986	Jan	11	20	7	E	9	6699
1987	Jan	12	1	8	D	10	6700
1988*	Jan	13	12	9	CB	11	6701
1989	Jan	14	23	10	A	12	6702
1990	Jan	15	4	11	G	13	6703
1991	Jan	16	15	12	F	14	6704
1992*	Jan	17	26	13	ED	15	6705
1993	Jan	18	7	14	C	1	6706
1994	Jan	19	18	15	B	2	6707
1995	Jan	1	9	16	A	3	6708
1996*	Jan	2	11	17	GF	4	6709
1997	Jan	3	22	18	E	5	6710
1998	Jan	4	3	19	D	5	6711
1999	Jan	5	14	20	C	6	6712
2000*	Jan	6	25	21	BA	8	6713

CALENDAR OF SAINTS

1 Jan

ST. ODILO
Circumcision
St. Fulgentius
St. Felix
St. Clarus
Blessed William
Blessed Hugolinus
Blessed Giuseppe Maria Tommasi
St. Vicenzo Maria Strambi
St. Telemachus

2 Jan ST. MACARIUS THE YOUNGER
The Holy Name of Jusus
Sts. Narcissus, Marcellinus, and Argeus
St. Martinian
St. Aspasius
St. Frobert
St Vincentianus
St. Adelard
Blessed Gerard Cagnoli
Blessed Stephana Quinzani

3 Jan ST. GENEVIEVE
St. Florentius
St. Bertilia

4 Jan ST. RIGOBERT or ROBERT
St. Titus
St. Benedicta
St. Pharailde
Blessed Roger of Ellant
Blessed Angela of Foligno

5 Jan ST. SIMEON STYLITES
St. Telesphorus
St. Emiliana
St. Amata
St. Gerlach

6 Jan ST. GUARINUS or GUERIN
Epiphany
Sts. Melchior and Gaspar
St. Gertrude van der Oosten
St. Peter Thomas

7 Jan ST. VITALIS
St. Lucian of Antioch
St. Valentine
St. Tyllo
Blessed Widukind
St. Canute
St. Aldric
St. Rainold
St. Cedd

8 Jan ST. SEVERINUS
Sts. Lucian, Maximinus and Julian
St. Apollinaris Claudius
St. Patiens
St. Felix
St. Gudula
St. Pega

9 Jan ST. ADRIAN
St. Marcianna
St. Peter of Sebaste
St. Marcellinus
St. Waningus
Blessed Honoratus of Buzencais
Blessed Philip Berruyer

10 Jan ST. GONZALVO
Blessed Gregory X
St. William
St. Peter Urseolus
St. Agatho
St. Domitian
St. Marcian
St. Petronius

11 Jan ST. THEODOSIUS THE CENOBITE
St. Baltshasar
St. Hyginus
St. Palemon
St. Anastasius
St. Vitalia
St. Paulinus

12 Jan ST. VICTORIAN
ST. AELRED
St. Arcadius
St. John
St. Caesaria
St. Benedict Biscop
Blessed Bernard of Corleone
St. Stephen
St. Nazarius
St. Ferreolus

13 Jan BLESSED YVETTE
ST. LEONTIUS
Blessed Godfrey of Kappenberg
Blessed Berno
Blessed Hildemar
St. Veronica of Binasco

14 Jan ST. HILARY
St. Fulgentius
St. Felix of Nola
St. Sabbas
Blessed Engelmer
Blessed Odo of Novara
Blessed Odoric of Pordenone

15 Jan ST. MAURUS
St. Paul
St. Alexander the Acemete
St. Ida or Ita
Blessed Geoffrey of Peronne
Blessed Pierre de Castelnau
St. Isidore of Alexandria

16 Jan
ST. MARCELLUS
ST. HENRY
St. Priscilla
St. Melas
St. Honoratus
St. Fursey
Sts. Berard, Otho, Accursius, and Adjutus

17 Jan
ST. ANTHONY OF THE DESERT
St. Sabinus
St. Ricmir
St. Roseline
St. Amelbert

18 Jan
BLESSED BEATRIX D'ESTE
ST. LEOBARDUS
St. Prisca
St. Venerandus
St. Volusianus
St. Wilfrid
St. Deicolus

19 Jan
STS. MARTHA and MARIS
ST. CANUTE
St. Pontian
St. Bassianus
St. Lomer
St. Wolstan
St. Henry
Blessed Beatrix of Lens
Blessed Andrea of Peschiera
St. Sulpitius the Pious

20 Jan
ST. SEBASTIAN
St. Fabian
St. Euthymius the Great
Blessed Desiderius

21 Jan
ST. AGNES
ST. MEINRAD
St. Patroclus
St. Epiphanius
St. Avitus
Blessed Inez

22 Jan
ST. VINCENT
St. Gaudentius
St. Anastasius
St. Dominic of Sora
Blessed Gauthier of Bruges

23 Jan
ST. ILDEPHONSUS
St. Raymond of Penafort
St. Emerentiana
St. John the Almsgiver
St. Bernard

24 Jan
ST. TIMOTHY
St. Felicianus
St. Babilas
St. Artemius
St. Macedonius
St. Cadoc
Blessed Paula Gambara

25 Jan
ST. ANANIAS
The Conversion of St. Paul
St. Artemas
Sts. Maximinus and Juventinus
St. Praejectus
St. Poppo

26 Jan
ST. PAULA
St. Polycarp
St. Alberic
St. Margaret of Hungary

27 Jan
ST. JULIAN
St. John Chrysostom
St. Marius or Mary
St. Lupus
St. Thierry II

28 Jan
ST. VALERIUS
ST. CHARLEMAGNE
St. Flavian
St. Julian
St. John of Reome
St. James the Palestinian

29 Jan
SAT. FRANCIS DE SALES
St. Constantius
St. Sulpicius Severus
St. Gildas the Wise
St. Arnoul or Arnult
Blessed Imaine
Blessed Gelasius II

30 Jan
ST. BATHILDE
St. Martina
St. Aldegundis
St. Adelelm
St. Hyacintha Mariscotti
Blessed Sebastian Valfre

31 Jan
ST. MARCELLA
Blessed Louise Albertoni
St. John Bosco
St. Peter Nolasco
St. Julius
St. Cyrus

1 Feb ST. IGNATIUS
St. Brigid of Kildare
St. Severus
St. Ursus
St. Sigebert
St. John of the Grating
Blessed Andrea de Segni

2 Feb ST. CORNELIUS
The Purification of the Blessed Virgin
St. Catherine de Ricci
St. Jeanne de Lestonac
Blessed John Theophane Venard

3 Feb ST. BLAISE
St. Anatole
St. Theodore
St. Hadelin
St. Anschar
Blessed Elinand
Blessed John Nelson

4 Feb ST. GILBERT OF SEMPRINGHAM
St. John de Britto
St. Veronica or Berenice
St. Isidore of Pelusium
St. Theophilus the Penitent
Blessed Rabanus Maurus
St. Andrew Corsini
St. Jeanne de Valois
St. Joseph of Leonessa

5 Feb ST. AGATHA
St. Adelaide or Alice of Guelders
St. Peter Baptist and his twenty-five companions

6 Feb ST. VAAST or GASTON
ST. AMANDUS
St. Dorothea
St. Guarinus
St. Silvanus
Blessed Angelus of Furci
Blessed Francesca of Gubbio

7 Feb ST. THEODORE
ST. ROMUALD
St. Fidelis
St. Richard
Blessed Anthony of Stroncone
Blessed Thomas Sherwood
Blessed Jacques Sales and Guillaume Saltemouche

8 Feb BLESSED JACOBA or JACQUELINE
St. Meingold
St. Stephen of Muret
St. John of Matha
Blessed Isaias Boner

9 Feb ST. APOLLONIA
St. Raynald
St. Nicephorus
St. Cyril of Alexandria
St. Sabinus
St. Romanus the Wonder-Worker
St. Ansbert

10 Feb ST. SCHOLASTICA
St. William of Maleval
St. Austrebertha
Blessed Hugh of Fosse
Blessed Arnold
Blessed Clare of Rimini

11 Feb ST. ADOLPH
St. Gregory
St. Pascal I
St. Lazarus
St. Severin
St. Jonas
St. Euphrosyne
The Blessed Peter Paschal and Catallan

12 Feb ST. EULALIA
St. Julian the Hospitaller of the Poor
St. Benedict of Aniane
The Seven Founders of the Servite Order or "Servants of the Virgin Mary"

13 Feb ST. MARTINIAN
St. Polyeuctus
St. Stephen
St. Gilbert
Blessed Jordan of Saxony
Blessed John de Triora

14 Feb ST. VALENTINE
St. Antoninus
St. Maro

15 Feb ST. GEORGIA or GEORGETTE
ST. FAUSTINUS
St. Eusebius
St. Severus
St. Walfrid
St. Sigfrid

16 Feb
ST. ELIAS
ST. JULIANA OF NOCOMEDIA
St. Onesimus
St. Honestus
Blessed Philippa Mareria

17 Feb
ST. SILVINUS
St. Mariamne
St. Theodulus
St. Fulrad
Blessed Evermodus

18 Feb
ST. CONSTANTIA or CONSTANCE
ST. ANGILBERT
St. Simeon
St. Flavian
St. Colman
St. Helladius
St. Theotonio
Blessed John Peter Neel

19 Feb
ST. CONRAD
St. Gabinius
St. Barbatus
St. Beatus
Blessed Boniface
Blessed Alvarez of Cordova
Blessed Elizabeth Picenardi

20 Feb
ST. EUCHERIUS
St. Eleutherius
Blessed Wulfric
St. Amata

21 Feb
BLESSED NOEL
St. Severian
Blessed Pepin of Landen
St. Daniel
St. Irene
St. Felix

22 Feb
BLESSED ISABEL
St. Paschasius
St. Maximian
St. Margaret of Cortona
Blessed Giovanna Maria
Blessed James Carvalho

23 Feb
ST. PETER DAMIAN
St. Florentius
St. Serenus
St. Medrald
St. Dositheus
St. Lazarus

24 Feb
ST. MATTHIAS
St. Sergius
St. Liuthard
Blessed Robert of Arbrissel

25 Feb
ST. AVERTANUS and BLESSED ROMEO
St. Caesarius
St. Walburga
St. Tarasius
Blessed Constantius of Fabriano
Blessed Sebastian d'Aparicio

26 Feb
ST. NESTOR
St. Victor
St. Porphyrius
St. Alexander
Blessed Philippa of Guelders

27 Feb
ST. LEANDER
St. Honorina
St. Galmier or Baldonor
St. Marvatus

28 Feb
ST. ROMANUS
St. Ermine
St. Proterius
St. Oswald
Blessed Antonia
Blessed Augustus Chapdelaine
Blessed Villana de'Botti

1 Mar
ST. ALBINUS
St. Eudocia
St. Simplicius
St. Antonina
St. David
Blessed Roger le Fort

2 Mar
ST. CHAD or CEADDA
St. Luke Casali
Blessed Charles the Good
Blessed Henry Suso

3 Mar
ST. MARINUS
ST. WINWALLUS
St. Kunigunde
St. Camilla
St. Titianus
St. Gervinus
Blessed Frederick

4 Mar
ST. CASIMIR
St. Lucius I
St. Leonard
St. Basinus
Blessed Humbert III

5 Mar ST. JOHN JOSEPH OF THE CROSS
St. Theophilus
St. Adrian
St. Phocas
St. Eusebius of Cremona
St. Virgilius
St. Drausinus
Blessed Romeo

6 Mar ST. COLETTE
St. Fridolin
St. Cyril of Constantinople
St. Rose of Viterbo
Blessed Agnes of Bohemia

7 Mar STS. PERPETUA and FELICITAS
St. Thomas Aquinas
St. Paul the Simple
The Blessed German Gardiner and John Larke

8 Mar ST. JOHN OF GOD
St. Pontius
St. Senan
St. Felix of Burgundy
St. Humphrey
St. Vincent Kadlubek

9 Mar ST. FRANCES OF ROME
St. Gregory of Nyssa
St. Vitalis
St. Pacianus
St. Catherine of Bologna

10 Mar STS. LEONTIUS, CANDIDUS, CLAUDIUS and OTHER MARTYRS OF SEBASTE
St. Blanchard
St. Droctoveus or Drotte
St. Anastasia the Patrician
St. Attalas

11 Mar ST. EULOGIUS
St. Benedict
St. Vigilius
St. Constantine
St. Sophronius
St. Vindicianus

12 Mar ST. MAXIMILIAN
St. Gregory the Great
St. Paul of Leon
St. Theophanes the Chronographer
St. Fina or Josephine or Seraphina
St. Muran or Mura

13 Mar ST. EUPHRASIA
St. Gerald
St. Eldrad
Blessed Agnellus of Pisa
Blessed Eric or Henry
St. Patricia
St. Rodriguez

14 Mar ST. MATILDA or MAUD
St. Lubin
Blessed Jean de Barastre
Blessed Peter of Moticello or of Treja

15 Mar ST. LOUISE DE MARILLAC
St. Longinus
St. Zachary
St. Clement Mary Hofbauer
St. Leocritia

16 Mar ST. ABRAHAM
St. Gregory of Nicopolis
St. Dentlin of Soignies
Blessed Torello of Poppi
Sts. John de Brebœuf and Gabriel Lallemand
Blessed Benedicta

17 Mar ST. PATRICK
St. Gertrude of Nivelles
St. Agricola
Blessed Thomasello

18 Mar ST. ALEXANDER
St. Cyril of Jerusalem
St. Narcissus
St. Edward
St. Anselm
St. Salvator of Horta
Blessed Fra Giovanni Angelico

19 Mar ST. JOSEPH
St. Leontius
Blessed Andrea Gallerani
Blessed Sibyllina Biscossi
Blessed Mark of Montegallo
Blessed John of Parma

20 Mar ST. JOACHIM
St. Photina
St. Cuthbert
St. Herbert or Hereberht
Blessed Maurice Csaky
Blessed Baptista Spagnuolo
St. Wulfram

21	Mar	ST. BENEDICT St. Lupicinus Blessed John of Valence Blessed Santuccia Terrebotti
22	Mar	ST. LEA St. Basil of Ancyra St. Deogratias Sts. Herlindis and Reinildis St. Benvenuto St. Nicholas of Flue St. Avitus
23	Mar	ST. VICTORIAN and OTHER AFRICAN MARTYRS St. Turibius St. Joseph Oriol
24	Mar	ST. GABRIEL, ARCHANGEL St. Catherine of Sweden
25	Mar	ST. HUMBERT The Annunciation of the Blessed Virgin The Good Thief St. Pelagius St. Lucia Filippini St. Cyrinus or Quirinus
26	Mar	ST. LUDGER St. Emmanuel St., Cassian St. Theodore Blessed Rinieri
27	Mar	BLESSED PELLEGRINO St. John Damascene St. Rupert or Robert of Salzburg St. Lydia St. John of Egypt
28	Mar	ST. JOHN CAPISTRAN Blessed Jeanne Marie de Maille Blessed Venturino of Bergamo St. Guntram
29	Mar	ST. EUSTACE Sts. Jonas and Barachisius St. Cyril St. Gery St. Berthold St. Ludolfus
30	Mar	BLESSED AMADEUS OF SAVOY St. Quirinus St. John Climacus St. Peter de Regalado Blessed Joachim of Flora
31	Mar	ST. BENJAMIN St. Balbina St. Daniel St. Guido of Pomposa Blessed Bonaventure Tornielli Blessed Camilla Pia
1	Apr	ST. HUGH St. Gilbert St. Melito St. Venantius St. Valery St. Celsus
2	Apr	ST. THEODOSIA or THEODORA ST. MARY OF EGYPT St. Urban St. Nicetius St. Francis of Paula
3	Apr	ST. RICHARD St. Pancratius St. Sixtus I Sts. Agape, Chionia, and Irene St. Burgundofara or Fara Blessed Gandulphus
4	Apr	ST. ISIDORE OF SEVILLE Sts. Agathopus and Theodulus St. Zosimus St. Plato St. Benedict the Moor
5	Apr	ST. GERARD St. Albert St. Juliana of Cornillon Blessed Eve St. Vincent Ferrer St. Catherine Tomas Blessed Crescentia Hoss
6	Apr	ST. PRUDENTIUS St. Marcellinus St. Eutychius St. Vinebaud St. William of Eskilsoe Blessed Notker Balbulus or the Stammerer
7	Apr	BLESSED HERMANN JOSEPH Sts. Epiphanius, Donatus, and Rufinus

St. Hegesippus
St. Calliopius
Blessed Evrard or Eberhard

8 Apr ST. WALTER or GALTERIUS
St. Dionysius
St. Perpetuus
St. Albert of Jerusalem
Blessed Julie Billiart
Blessed Julian of St. Augustine

9 Apr ST. WANDRU
ST. CASILDA
St. Mary of Cleophas
St. Marcellus
St. Gaucherius
St. Acacius
St. Bademus
Blessed Antonio Pavoni

10 Apr ST. FULBERT
Blessed Paternus
Sts. Terentius, Pompeius, and Zeno and other martyrs
St. Ezechiel
St. Macarius of Antioch
Blessed Maddalena of Canossa

11 Apr ST. LEO THE GREAT
St. Philip
Blessed Ulrich
Blessed Raynerius
St. Guthlac
St. Gemma Galgani

12 Apr ST. JULIUS I
St. Victor
St. Damian
St. Zeno
St. Sabbas
Blessed Mechtilde
Blessed Angelo Carletti

13 Apr ST. IDA
St. Romanus
St. Ursus
St. Martius
St. Hermengild
St. Caradoc
Blessed Ida

14 Apr ST. JUSTIN
Sts. Tiburtius, Valerian, and Maximus
St. Lambert
St. Bernard of Abbeville
St. Benezet
St. Lidwina of Schiedam

15 Apr ST. PATERNUS
St. Leonidas
Sts. Anastasia and Basilissa
St. Crescens
St. Peter Gonzalez or Elmo

16 Apr ST. BERNADETTE
St. Paternus
St. Fructuosus
St. Turibius
Sts. Martial, Urban, Eventius, Caecilian, Julia, and their companions
St. Drogo
Blessed Herve
St. Benedict Labre

17 Apr ST. ANICETUS
St. Robert of Chaise-Dieu
Blessed Mariana of Jesus
St. Landric
Sts. Elias, Paul, and Isidore
St. Stephen Harding

18 Apr ST. PERFECTO
ST. GALDINO
St. Eusebius
St. Agia
Blessed Marie de l'Incarnation

19 Apr ST. EMMA
St. George
St. Ursmar
St. Expeditus

20 Apr ST. MARCELLINUS
ST. THEOTIMUS
Sts. Sulpicius and Servilian
Blessed Harduin
St. Marcian
St. Agnes of Montepulciano
St. Hildegund
Blessed Oda

21 Apr ST. ANSELM
St. Simeon
St. Anastasius Sinaita
St. Wolbod
Blessed Bartholomew of Savigliano

22 Apr ST. OPPORTUNA
ST. LEONIDAS
Sts. Soter, Caius, and Agapetus
St. Leo
St. Theodore of Sikion

23 Apr ST. GEORGE
St. Gerard
St. Adalbert
St. Pusina
Blessed Giles of Tyre
Blessed Egidius or Giles of Assisi

24 Apr ST. FIDELIS
St. Honorius
St. Deodatus
St. Bova and St. Doda, her niece
St. Wilfrid
St. Egbert
St. William Girmat
St. Mary Euphrasia Pelletier

25 Apr ST. MARK THE EVANGELIST
St. Ermin
St. Heribaldus
St. Phoebadius
The Great Litanies

26 Apr ST. RICHARIUS or RIQUIER
ST. PASCHASIUS
Sts. Cletus
St. Lucidius
St. Trudpert
Blessed Alda

27 Apr ST. ZITA
St. Theophilus
St. Anthimus
St. Peter Canisius

28 Apr STS. THEODORA and DIDYMUS
St. Arthemius
St. Vitalis and St. Valeria
St. Patritius
Blessed Luchesius
St. Louis Marie Grignon of Montfort

29 Apr ST. ROBERT OF MOLESME
St. Wilfrid the Younger
St. Peter of Verona
St. Hugh of Cluny

30 Apr ST. MAXIMUS
Sts. Louis, Amator, and Peter
Sts. Marianus and James
St. Suitbert the Younger
St. Catherine of Siena
St. Joseph Benedict Cottolengo

1 May ST. PHILIP
ST. JAMES THE LESS
Sts. Bertha and Gumbert
St. Jeremias
St. Andeol
St. Brieuc
St. Sigismund
St. Theodulf or Thiou
St. Blessed Augustin Schoeffer

2 May ST. ATHANASIUS
St. Waldebert or Gaubert
St. Exuperius and St. Zoe, his wife; Sts. Cypriac and Theodulus, their children
Blessed Mafalda

3 May STS. EVENTIUS, THEODULUS, and ALEXANDER
Blessed Emily Bicchiere
Sts. Antonina and Alexander
St. Juvenal
St. Ausfrid
Invention of the Holy Cross

4 May ST. MONICA
Blessed Ladislaus of Gielnow
St. Florian
St. Godard
St. Titianus
St. Malou
St. Ethelred
The Blessed John Houghton, Robert Lawrence, Augustine Webster

5 May ST. ANGELUS
ST. PIUS V
St. Judith or Jutta
St. Aventinus
St. Gerontius
St. Nicetius or Nizier
St. Hilary of Arles

6 May ST. EVODIUS
St. Justus
St. Maurelius
Blessed Bonizella Piccolomini Cacciaconti
Blessed Prudence
St. John before the Latin Gate

7 May ST. STANISLAUS
St. Maillard
St. Hernin
St. Domitian
Blessed Villano
Blessed Albert of Bergamo

8 May ST. DESIDERATUS
St. Acacius
St. Dominica and St. Indract, her brother
St. Aurelian
St. Ida or Ita or Iduberga
St. Guiron or Wiron
St. Peter of Tarentaise
Blessed Amato Ronconi
The Apparition of St. Michael

9 May ST. GREGORY OF NAZIANZUS
St. Pacomius
St. Gerontius
Blessed Adalgar or Auger
Blessed Hans or John Wagner

10 May ST. SOLANGE
St. Antoninus of Florence
St. Isidore the Labourer
St. Gordianus
St. Job
Blessed William or Anthelm
Blessed Beatrix d'Este

11 May ST. MAMERTUS
St. Gengou Gangulphus
St. Majolus of Clunty
St. Gauthier of Esterp
The Blessed John Rochester and James Walworth
St. Francis of Girolamo

12 May ST. DOMITILLA
STS. ACHILLEUS and NEREUS
St. Pancras
St. Epiphanius
St. Modoald
Blessed Imelda Lambertini

13 May ST. SERVATUS
St. Robert Bellarmine
Blessed Gerald of Villamagna
St. Rolanda
St. Agnes
St. John the Silent

14 May BLESSED GILES
St. Boniface of Tarsus
St. Aglae
Sts. Justa, Justina, and Henedina
Sts. Victor and Cournatus
St. Michael Garicoits
Blessed Maria-Dominica Mazarello

15 May ST. DENISE
St. Achillius
St. Dympna
St. Reticius
St. Rupert or Robert
St. Jean-Baptiste de la Salle

16 May ST. UBALDUS
St. Honore
St. John of Ponuk or Nepomucene
St. Andrew Bobola
St. Simon Stock

17 May ST. PASCAL BAYLON
Sts. Solochon, Pamphamer, and Pamphalon
St. Adrian, martyr of Alexandria, and St. Victor, Roman martyr

18 May STS. CLAUDIA, ALEXANDRA, JULITTA, PHANIA, THECUSA, MATRONA, and EUPHRASIA
St. Eric
St. Dioscorus
St. Felix of Cantalica

19 May ST. PETER CELESTINE
St. Ives
St. Emiliana or Humiliana
St. Dunstan
St. Pudentiana
St. Theophilus of Corte

20 May ST. BERNARDINE OF SIENA
St. Theodore
St. Lucifer
St. Austregisilus
St. Ivo of Chartres

21 May ST. THIBAUT
ST. GISELA or ISBERGE
St. Hospitius
St. Maurelius

22 May ST. JULIA
ST. RITA

St. Lupus
St. Atto
St. Fulk
St. Humilita or Rosana
St. Romanus

23 May ST. DESIDERIUS
St. Guibert or Wibert
St. Florentius
St. William
St. Michael
St. John Baptist of Rossi
St. Jeanne-Antide Tourret

24 May STS. DONATIAN and ROGATIAN
St. Vincent of Lerns
St. Simeon Stylites the Younger
St. Martha
St. John of Praido

25 May ST. URBAN
ST. GERARD OF LUNEL
St. Gregory VII
St. James Philippi
St. Madeleine-Sophie Barat

26 May ST. PHILIP NERI
St. Eleutherius
St. Mariana de Paredes

27 May ST. BEDE THE VENERABLE
St. Julius
St. John I
St. Hildebert
St. Bruno
St. Eutropius

28 May ST. GERMAIN
St. Augustine of Canterbury
St. William of Gellone
St. Bernard of Menthon
Blessed Lanfranc

29 May ST. MAXIMINUS
St. Bonna
St. Mary Magdalen of Pazzi

30 May ST. FERDINAND
ST. JOAN OF ARC
St. Felix I
St. Vanantius
St. Walstan

31 May ST. PETRONILLA
ST. ANGELA MERICI
St. Silvius
Blessed Baptista Varani
St. Gabriele dell' Addolorata

1 Jun ST. PAMPHILUS
ST. CAPRASIUS
St. Claudius
St. Ronan
St. Gerard
St. Simeon
St. Theobald
Blessed Herculano de Piegaro

2 Jun STS. BLANDIAN, BIBLIS, POTHINUS, MATURUS, SANCTUS, PONTICUS, ATTALUS, and OTHER MARTYRS OF THE GAULS
St. Eugene I
St. Erasmus or Elmo
St. Stephen
St. Nicholas the Pilgrim

3 Jun ST. CLOTILDA
St. Liphardus and St. Urbicius
St. Genesius
St. Morand
The Twenty-two Martyrs of Uganda

4 Jun ST. QUIRINUS
ST. OPTATUS
St. Saturnine
St. Vincenza Gerosa
St. Francis Caracciolo

5 Jun ST. BONIFACE
St. Dorotheus
Blessed Sanctus
Sts. Florentius and Julian
St. Zenaida
Sts. Valeria, Marcia, and Cyria
Blessed Ferdinand of Portugal

6 Jun ST. NORBERT
St. Claudius
Sts. Artemius, Paulina, and Candida
Sts. Gilbert and Petronilla, and Blessed Poncia
St. Bertrand of Angouleme
St. Alexander

7 Jun BLESSED MARIE-THERESE DE SOUBIRAN

St. Robert
St. Colman
St. Wolfgang
St. Gottschalk and his companions
Blessed Ann of St. Bartholomew

8 Jun ST. MEDARD
St. Chlodulph
St. Godard
St. William of York
Blessed Pacificus of Cerano

9 Jun ST. PELAGIA
Blessed Diana of Andolo
Sts. Primus and Felician
St. Richard
St. Columba of Iona
Blessed Anna Maria Taigi

10 Jun ST. LANDRY
ST. OLIVIA
St. Margaret
St. Maximus
St. Evermund
St. Bardo

11 Jun ST. BARNABAS
St. Adelaide or Alix
St. Parisius
Blessed Paula Frassinetti

12 Jun BLESSED GUY OF CORTONA
St. Placidus
St. Odulphus
St. John of Sahagun

13 Jun ST. ANTHONY OF PADUA
St. Peregrinus
St. Rambert
St. Aventin
Blessed Gerard

14 Jun ST. BASIL
Sts. Valerius and Rufinus
St. Elisha
Sts. Anastasius, Felis, and Digna

15 Jun ST. GERMAINE COUSIN
St. Yolanda or Helen
Sts. Modestus and Guy or Vitus
St. Landelin

16 Jun ST. QUIRICUS or CIRYCUS
St. John Francis Regis
St. Vorle
St. Benno or Bernard
St. Lutgard

17 Jun ST. RAYNER
St. Avitus
St. Herve
St. Bessarion
St. Manuel

18 Jun ST. EPHRAEM
Sts. Marcus and Marcellinus
St. Leontius
St. Amandus
Blessed Marina of Spoleto
Blessed Hosanna of Mantua
St. Elizabeth of Schonau

19 Jun BLESSED MICHELINA OF PESARO
Sts. Gervasius and Protasius
St. Juliana Falconieri
St. Deodatus
Blessed Odo of Cambrai

20 Jun ST. FLORENTINA or FLORENCE
St. Silverius
St. Innocentius
St. Goban
St. Adalbert or Albert
St. John of Matera
The Blessed Thomas Whitbread, John Febwick, William Waring, John Gavan, and Anthony Turner

21 Jun ST. ALOYSIUS GONZAGA
St. Rodolphe
St. Alban
St. Eusebius
St. Meen
Blessed John Rigby

22 Jun ST. PAULINUS OF NOLA
St. Alban
St. Flavius Clemens
Sts. John I and John IV
St. Everard or Eberhard
Blessed Innocent V

23 Jun ST. AUDREY or ETHELREDA
St. Walther
Blessed Mary of Oignies
St. Lietbertus

24 Jun ST. JOHN THE BAPTIST
St. Ivan
St. Theodulf
St. Bartholomew
St. Rumold

25 Jun ST. PROSPER
ST. WILLIAM
St. Maximus
St. Adalbert
St. Gohard
St. Lucy
St. Amandus

26 Jun ST. MAXENTIUS
ST. DAVID
St. Vigilius
Sts. John and Paul
St. Salvius
St. Anthelm
St. Pelagius
St. Babolen
The Blessed Madeleine Fontaine, Francoise Lanel, Theresa Fantou, and Jeanne Gerard

27 Jun ST. LADISLAUS or LAZLO
St. Zoilus
St. Crescens
St. Emilian
Our Lady of Perpetual Help

28 Jun ST. IRENAEUS
St. Alice or Aleth of Bourgotte
Sts. Plutarch, Serenus, Heraclides, Hero, Herais, Potamiana, and Marcella
St. Irene

29 Jun ST. PETER
St. Paul
Sts. Salome and Judith
St. Emma
St. Beata or Benedicta

30 Jun ST. PAUL
St. Martial
St. Lucina
St. Bertrand
Blessed Arnoul Cornebout
St. Thibaut

1 Jul ST. THIERRY or THEODORIC
The Precious Blood of Our Lord
St. Thibaut
St. Gallus
St. Esther or Edissa
St. Regina

2 Jul ST. OTTO
The Visitation of the Blessed Virgin Mary
St. Monegunde
St. Bernardino Realini
Blessed Peter of Luxemburg

3 Jul ST. ANATOLIUS OF LAODICEA
ST. ANATOLIUS OF CONSTANTINOPLE
Blessed Raymond Lully

4 Jul ST. BERTHA
ST. ULRICH
St. Florentius
St. Aurelian
St. Andrew of Crete

5 Jul ST. ZOE
St. Philomena
Blessed Archangelus of Calatafimi
St. Antonio Maria Zaccaria
Blessed Elie de Bourdeilles

6 Jul STS. PHILEMON, APOLLONIUS, and ARRIAN
St. Dominica
St. Isaias
St. Mechtild
St. Angela
St. Justus
St. Maria Goretti

7 Jul THE BLESSED ROGER DICKENSON and RALPH MILNER
Sts. Cyril and Methodius
The Twenty-nine Martyrs of China
St. Willibald
St. Ethelburga

1 Jul ST. ISABELLA or ELIZABETH OF PORTUGAL
Blessed Peter the Hermit
Sts. Kilian, Coloman and Totnan

9 Jul ST. THOMAS MORE
ST. JOHN FISHER
The Blessed Marie Rose, Marie Claire, Marie Anne, and the other Martyrs of Orange
St. Anatolia
St. Veronica Giuliani
The Holy Martyrs of Gorkum

10 Jul ST. FELICITAS and THE SEVEN BROTHER MARTYRS
St. Paschasius
St. Ulrich
Blessed Pacificus
The Blessed Martyrs of Damascus

11 Jul ST. OLGA
BLESSED OLIVER PLUNKET
St. Pius I
St. Cyprian
St. Aleth
St. Leontius the Younger

12 Jul ST. JOHN GUALBERT
Sts. Nabor and Felix
Blessed John Jones

13 Jul ST. EUGENE
St. Anacletus I
St. Sara
Blessed Jacobus de Voragine

14 Jul ST. BONAVENTURE
St. Felix
St. Deusdedit
St. Francis Solanus

15 Jul ST. HENRY II
ST. VLADIMIR
St. Donald of Forfar
Blessed Angelina of Marsciano
St. Pompilius Maria Pirotti

16 Jul OUR LADY OF MOUNT CARMEL
St. Helier
St. Eustathius
St. Marie Madeleine Postel

17 Jul ST. ALEXIS
ST. MARCELLINA
St. Benignus
St. Fredegand
St. Generosus and the eleven other Scillitan Martyrs
The Blessed Carmelites of Compiegne

18 Jul ST. CAMILLUS DE LELLIS
St. Arnulf
Blessed Bertha de Marbais
St. Emilian
St. Frederick
St. Herve or Hervaeus

19 Jul ST. VINCENT DE PAUL
Sts. Justa and Rufina
St. Arsenius

20 Jul ST. MARGARET
St. Elias
St. Aurelius
St. Flavian
St. Jerome Emiliani
Blessed Gregory Lopez

21 Jul STS. VICTOR, LONGINUS, ALEXANDER, and FELICIAN
St. Praxedes
St. Daniel
Blessed Oddino Barotti

22 Jul ST. MARY MAGDALEN
St. Wandrille
St. Lorenzo da Brindisi

23 Jul ST. APOLLINARIS
St. Liborius
St. Anne or Susanna
St. John Cassian

24 Jul ST. CHRISTINA THE ASTONISHING
St. Christina
St. Boris or Roman and St. Gleb or David
Blessed Cunegundes
Blessed Anthony Turriani
Blessed Louise of Savoy

25 Jul ST. JAMES THE GREATER
ST. CHRISTOPHER
St. Valentina
St. Cucufatis

26 Jul ST. ANNE
St. Erastus
St. Simeon
St. Bartolomea Capitanio

27 Jul STS. NATALIA, AURELIUS, LILIOSA, FELIX, and GEORGE
St. Pantaleon
St. Desiderius
St. Celestine I
St. Ursus
The Seven Sleepers of Ephesus

28 Jul ST. SAMSON
Sts. Nazarius and Celsus
St. Victor I
St. Innocent I
St. Geran

29	Jul	ST. MARTHA St. Beatrix St. Lupus St. Olaf St. William St. Constantine St. Seraphia
30	Jul	ST. JULITTA St. Abel St. Rufinus St. Donatilla Blessed Manes Sts. Abdon and Sennen
31	Jul	ST. IGNATIUS LOYOLA St. Fabius St. Peter II St. John Colombini St. Germain of Auxerre
1	Aug	ST. BAUDARINUS or BAUDRY St. Exuperius or Spire St. Arcadius St. Jonatus Blessed John of Rieti St. Peter Advincula
2	Aug	ST. ALPHONSUS LIGUORI St. Serenus St. Alfrida or Etheldreda St. Stephen I
3	Aug	ST. LYDIA St. Nicodemus Blessed Geoffrey de Loudoun Blessed Peter Julian Eymard
4	Aug	ST. DOMINIC St. Aristarchus St. Raynerius
5	Aug	ST. ABEL Dedication of the Church of St. Mary of the Snow St. Oswald St. Nonna St. Emidius
6	Aug	ST. SIXTUS II BLESSED OCTAVIANUS Sts. Justus and Pastor Blessed Bertha The Transfiguration of our Lord
7	Aug	ST. CAJETAN St. Donatus Another St. Donatus Blessed Jordan of Padua
8	Aug	STS. CYRIACUS, LARGUS, SMARAGDUS, and SISINNIUS FOURTEEN HOLY HELPERS St. Hugolina Blessed Juana of Aza
9	Aug	ST. JEAN-BAPTISTE-MARIE VIANNEY St. Amor St. Samuel of Edessa St. Maurilius
10	Aug	ST. LAWRENCE St. Philomena St. Arey or Aregius St. Hugh of Montaigu St. Autor St. Blane
11	Aug	ST. SUSANNA St. Gerard of Gallinaro St. Gery St. Taurinus St. Gilberta or Agilberta
12	Aug	ST. CLARE St. Cecelia St. Anicetus St. Hilaria
13	Aug	ST. RADEGUNDE St. Maximus the Confessor St. Vitalina St. John Berchmans Sts. Hippolytus and Concordia
14	Aug	ST. ATHANASIA or ANASTASIA St. Marcellus St. Eusebius Blessed Eberhard
15	Aug	ST. ARNOUL The Assumption of the Blessed Virgin St. Tarsicius St. Stanislas Kostka
16	Aug	ST. ROCH St. Simplicianus St. Fraimbault Blessed Lawrence Loricatus Blessed Beatrix da Silva

17 Aug STS. LIBERATUS, BONIFACE, RUSTICUS, SERVUS, ROGATUS, SEPTIMUS, and MAXIMUS
St. Hyacinth
Blessed Jeanne Delanoue
St. Mamas
St. Elias the Younger

18 Aug ST. HELENA
St. Milo
St. Agapitus
St. Rusticus
Blessed Leonard
Blessed Aimo Taparelli

19 Aug ST. JOHN EUDES
Blessed Burchard
St. Sebaldus
St. Louis of Anjou or of Toulouse

20 Aug ST. BERNARD OF CLAIRVAUX
St. Samuel
Sts. Christopher and Leovigild
St. Philibert
St. Amator or Amadour

21 Aug ST. JANE FRANCES DE CHANTAL
St. Privatus
Blessed Hombelina
St. Baldwin
St. Alberic

22 Aug ST. HIPPOLYTUS
ST. SYMPHORIAN
St. Sigfrid

23 Aug ST. SIDONIUS APOLLINARIS
The Immaculate Heart of Mary
St. Flavian
Blessed Richilde
St. Philip Benizi

24 Aug ST. BARTHOLOMEW
St. Ouen
Blessed Emilif de Vialar
St. Maria-Michaela

25 Aug ST. LOUIS
St. Genesius of Arles
St. Genesius of Rome
St. Patricia
St. Aredius or Yrieix
Blessed Thierry I
Blessed Thomas a Kempis

26 Aug ST. ZEPHYRINUS
St. Victor
St. Pelagia
St. Jeanne-Elisabeth Bichier des Ages

27 Aug ST. CAESARIUS OF ARLES
St. Poemen or Pastor
St. Lizier
St. Joseph Calasanctius

28 Aug ST. AUGUSTINE
St. Hermes
St. Julian of Brioude or of Auvergne
St. Moses
St. Vivianus
Blessed Gobert
The Blessed William Dean, William Gunther, Robert Morton, Hugh More, Thomas Holford, James Claxton, and Thomas Felton

29 Aug STS. SABINA and SERAPHIA
The Beheading of St. John the Baptist
St. Candida or Adavisa
St. Medericus

30 Aug ST. ROSE OF LIMA
St. Fiacre
St. Pammachius
Blessed Juvenal Ancina

31 Aug ST. RAYMOND NONNATUS
St. Aristides
St. Amatus
St. Paulinus

1 Sep ST. LUPUS
St. Giles or Egidius
St. Augustus
St. Nivard

2 Sep ST. JUSTUS
St. Eleazar
St. Comus of Crete
St. Stephen of Hungary

3 Sep ST. REMACULUS
St. Antoninus
Sts. Euphemia, Dorothea, Thecla, and Erasmus
St. Mansuetus

4 Sep ST. ROSALIA
St. Candida
St. Marinus
St. Moses

5 Sep ST. BERTIN
St. Lawrence Justinian
St. Aman or Aignan
St. Urban

6 Sep ST. MAGNUS or MAGNOALDUS
St. Eve
Sts. Donatian, Mansuetus, Germanus, Praesidus, Fusculus, and Laetus
Sts. Faustus and Macarius, and ten other Christians
St. Zacharias

7 Sep ST. REGINA
ST. CLODOALD or CLOUD
St. Gratus
St. Madelberte

8 Sep BLESSED SERAPHINA SFORZA
The Nativity of the Blessed Virgin
St. Achilles
St. Belina

9 Sep ST. OMER
St. Peter Claver
St. Bettelin
St. Osmana
Blessed Aesop

10 Sep ST. PULCHERIA
St. Nicholas of Tolentino
St. Aubert
St. Theodard
Sts. Sosthenes and Victor

11 Sep STS. HYACINTH and PROTUS
BLESSED JEAN-GABRIEL PERBOYRE
St. Adelphus
St. Emilian
St. Veran

12 Sep BLESSED MARIA VICTORIA FORNARI
Sts. Leontius and Valerian and four other Christians of Alexandria
St. Bonna
St. Guy of Anderlecht

13 Sep ST. AMATUS
St. Maurilius

14 Sep ST. MATERNUS
The Exaltation of the Holy Cross
St. Odilard

15 Sep BLESSED ROLAND
St. Nicomedes
St. Albinus
Blessed Aichardus
St. Aper
St. Catherine of Genoa

16 Sep ST. CYPRIAN
St. Edith
St. Cornelius
St. Ludmilla

17 Sep ST. LAMBERT
The Stigmata of St. Francis
St. Columba
St. Narcissus
St. Hildegard

18 Sep ST. SOPHIA
ST. RICHARDIS or RICHILDA
St. Stephana
St. Joseph of Cupertino

19 Sep ST. JANUARIUS
St. Desiderius
St. Miletus
St. Lucy of Scotland
St. Marie-Emilie de Rodat

20 Sep ST. EUTACHIUS
Sts. Pirvatus and Dionysius
St. Vincent Madelgaire or Mauger
Blessed Yves Mayeuc
Blessed Francis de Posadas

21 Sep ST. MATTHEW
St. Iphigenia
Blessed Bernardina

22 Sep STS. MAURICE, EXUPERIUS, CANDIDUS, and OTHER MARTYRS OF THE THEBAN LEGION
St. Lo
St. Salaberga
St. Silvanus

23 Sep ST. LINUS
ST. THECLA
St. Hereswitha

24 Sep OUR LADY OF MERCY
St. Andochius
St. Rusticus
St. Paphnutius
St. Germer

25 Sep ST. FIRMINUS
Sts. Paul and Tatta
Sts. Aurelia and Neomesia
St. Lupus of Lyons
St. Aunarius

26 Sep STS. JUSTINA and CYPRIAN
St. Vigilius
Sts. Isaac Jogues, Jean de Lalande and Rene Goupil

27 Sep STS. COSMAS and DAMIAN
St. Hiltrude
St. Elzear

28 Sep ST. WENCESLAUS
St. Thiemo
St. Chariton
Blessed Bernardine of Feltre

29 Sep ST. MICHAEL THE ARCHANGEL
St. Cyriacus
St. Fulgentius
Blessed Charles of Blois

30 Sep ST. JEROME
St. Ambert
St. Lery
St. Conrad

1 Oct ST. REMIGIUS
St. Bavo or Allowin
Sts. Julia, Verissima, and Maxima
St. Piat

2 Oct ST. LEODEGAR
The Guardian Angels
St. Theophilus
Sts. Cyril, Primus, and Secundus
St. Eleutherius
St. Thomas of Hereford

3 Oct ST. THERESA OF THE CHILD JESUS
St. Gerard
Sts. Ewald
St. Cyprian

4 Oct ST. FRANCIS OF ASSISI
St. Aurea
St. Callistena and St. Adauctus
St. Mainfroy

5 Oct ST. PLACIDUS
Blessed Aymard
Sts. Constant and Alexander
Sts. Flavia and Firmatus
Blessed John of Penna

6 Oct ST. BRUNO
St. Mary Frances of the Five Wounds
St. Modesta
Sts. Emilius and Marcellus

7 Oct ST. SERGIUS
ST. ARTHOLD
St. Augustus
St. Justina
St. Pallais

8 Oct ST. BRIDGET
St. Nestor
Sts. Laurentius and Palatia
St. Thais

9 Oct ST. DIONYSIUS or DENIS THE AREOPAGITE
St. Louis Bertrand
St. John Leonardi
St. Ghislain

10 Oct STS. DANIEL, HUGOLINUS, SAMUEL, NICHOLAS, LEO, AGNELLUS, and DONULUS
St. Paulinus
St. Clair
St. Tancha
St. Francis Borgia

11 Oct ST. ZENAIDA
St. Nicasius
St. Emilius
St. Placida
Sts. Probus, Tarachus and Andronicus
St. Gomer

12 Oct ST. SERAPHIN
St. Eustachius
St. Maximilian
St. Wilfrid

13 Oct ST. EDWARD
St. Lubentius
St. Reimbaut
St. Theophilus

14 Oct ST. CALLISTUS
St. Fortunatus of Todi
St. Fortunata
St. Dominic Loricatus
St. Burchard or Burckhard

15 Oct ST. TERESA OF AVILA
St. Aurelia
St. Leonard of Vandœuvre or of Corbigny
St. Roger

16 Oct ST. BERTRAND OF COMMINGES
St. Gall
St. Florentinus
St. Mommelinus
St. Gerard Majella

17 Oct ST. HEDWIG
St. Margaret Mary Alacoque
St. Solina
St. Florentine
Blessed Contardo Ferrini

18 Oct ST. LUKE
St. Mono
St. Fabian of Sylvarolle

19 Oct ST. PETER OF ALCANTARA
St. Laura
St. Savinianus
St. Aquilinius

20 Oct ST. IRENE
St. Caprasius
St. John Cantius
St. Felician

21 Oct ST. HILARION
St. Ursula and the Eleven Thousand Virgins of Cologne
St. Wendelin

22 Oct ST. SALOME
St. Alodia and her sister St. Nunilona
St. Alexander
St. Mellon
St. Flora

23 Oct BLESSED MARIE CLOTILDE and OTHER URSULINES OF VALENCIENNES
St. Bonizet or Benedict
St. Oda
St. Ignatius of Constantinople
St. Severinus

24 Oct ST. RAPHAEL THE ARCHANGEL
St. Antonio Maria Claret
St. Florentinus

25 Oct STS. CRISPIN and CRISPINIAN
St. Cyrene
St. Chrysanthus and his wife, St. Daria
Blessed Francis of Calderola
Blessed Ludovic of Arnstein
St. Touchard

26 Oct BLESSED BONNE D'ARMAGNAC
St. Magloire
St. Evaristus
St. Rusticus

27 Oct BLESSED ANTONIA
ST. FRUMENTIUS
Sts. Vincent, Sabina, and Chrysteta
St. Florentius

28 Oct STS. SIMON and JUDE
St. Ludard
St. Faro
St. Dodo

29 Oct ST. NARCISSUS
St. Aelfleda
St. Theodore or Theudart
St. Zenobius
St. Eusebia of Bergamo

30 Oct ST. DOROTHEA
St. Zenobius
St. Marcellus
St. Alphonsus Rodriguez
St. Eutropia
St. Lucanus
St. Foillan

31 Oct ST. QUENTIN
St. Lucilla
St. Begga of Egremont
St. Ultan

1 Nov ST. BENIGNUS
St. Ludre
St. Amabilis
All Saints

2 Nov ST. MALACHY
St. Eudoxius
St. Maurus
Blessed Margaret of Lorraine
The Commemoration of the Faithful Departed or All Souls' Day

3 Nov ST. HUBERT
St. Papoul
St. Florus
Blessed Martin de Porres
St. Gwenael

4 Nov ST. CHARLES BORROMEO
St. Gilbert
St. Gerard
St. Vitalis
St. Amantius

5 Nov ST. BERTILLE
STS. ZACHARY and ELIZABETH
St. Guiraud
St. Lye
St. Nataline

6 Nov ST. LEONARD
Blessed Christina of Stommeln
St. Winnoc
St. Theobald

7 Nov ST. ERNEST
St. Engelbert of Cologne
St. Willibrord
St. Florentius

8 Nov ST. GEOFFREY
St. Clair
St. Drouet
The Four Crowned Martyrs
Blessed John Duns Scotus

9 Nov ST. MATHURIN
St. Vitonus
St. Ranulfus
St. Ursicinus

10 Nov STS. NYMPHA, RESPICIUS, and TRYPHON
ST. ANDREW AVELLINO
St. Alda
Sts. Florence, Tiberius, and Modestus
St. Justus

11 Nov ST. MARTIN OF TOURS
St. Bertuin
St. Veran
St. Menas
St. Theodore of Studium

12 Nov ST. RENATUS
St. Christian
St. Martin I
St. Emilian
St. Nilus
St. Or

13 Nov ST. BRICE
ST. DIDACUS or DIEGO
St. Homobonus
St. Siardus
Sts. Valentine, Felician, and Victor

14 Nov ST. JOSAPHAT
St. Sidonius
Sts. Philomenus, Theodotus, and Clementinus
St. Emmerich

15 Nov ST. GERTRUDE
St. Leopold
St. Arnoul
St. Desiderius
St. Valeria
St. Eugene
St. Albert the Great

16 Nov ST. EDMUND
St. Agnes of Assisi
St. Emilion
St. Othmar

17 Nov ST. AIGNAN
St. Gregory of Tours
St. Gregory the Wonder-Worker
St. Salome

18 Nov ST. ODO
St. Hilda
St. Mandez
Sts. Romanus and Barulas

19 Nov ST. ELIZABETH OF HUNGARY
St. Mechtilde
St. Citroine
Sts. Exuperius, Felician, and Severinus
St. Patroclus

20 Nov ST. FELIX OF VALOIS
St. Edmund of England
St. Hippolytus
St. Mamas
St. Octavius

21 Nov ST. GELASIUS
ST. COLUMBANUS
St. Albert of Louvain
Sts. Celsus and Clement

22 Nov ST. CECILIA
Sts. Philemon and Appia
St. Calmin
Blessed Tygride

23 Nov ST. CLEMENT OF ROME
St. Felicitas

St. Trond or Trudo
St. Gobert
Blessed John the Good

24 Nov STS. FLORA and MARIA OF CORDOVA
St. Justus
St. Marius
St. John of the Cross

25 Nov ST. CATHERINE OF ALEXANDRIA
St. Fintan
St. Barbary
St. Jucunda
Blessed Elizabeth the Good

26 Nov ST. DELPHINE
St. Leonard of Port Maurice
St. Basle
St. Victorina
St. Peter

27 Nov ST. MAXIMUS OF RIEZ
St. Oda or Odette
St. Achar
St. James Intercissus

28 Nov ST. SOSTHENES
St. Gregory III
St. James of the Marches
St. Stephen the Younger

29 Nov ST. SATURNINUS or SERNIN
St. Radbod
St. Brendan of Birr, or the Younger
The Blessed Denis of the Nativity, and Redemptus of the Cross, discalced Carmelites

30 Nov ST. ANDREW
St. Maura
St. Constantius

1 Dec ST. ELIGIUS or ELOI
St. Agericus
St. Florentinus
St. Nahum
St. Agnofleta or Nofleta
St. Simon of Cyrene

2 Dec ST. BIBIANA or VIVIAN
St. Constantine
Sts. Aurelia and Paulina
St. Silvanus
St. Pontian
Blessed John Ruysbroeck

3 Dec ST. FRANCIS XAVIER
St. Anthemius
Blessed Bernard of Toulouse
St. Lucy the Chaste
St. Veranus
St. Mirocles
Sts. Claudius and Hilaria, his wife, Sts. Jason and Maurus, their sons

4 Dec ST. BARBARA
St. Osmund
St. Meletius
St. Cyran
Blessed Francis Galvez, Jerome de Angelis, and Simon Yempo
St. Peter Chrysologus

5 Dec ST. SABBAS
St. Nicetius
St. Aper or Avre
St. Basilissa

6 Dec ST. NICHOLAS
St. Asella
Sts. Majoricus, Dionysia, and Aemilianus
St. Peter Paschal

7 Dec ST. AMBROSE
St. Maria Josepha Rosello
St. Gerard

8 Dec THE IMMACULATE CONCEPTION OF THE VIRGIN MARY
St. Eucharius
St. Gunthildis
St. Romaric

9 Dec ST. LEOCADIA
BLESSED CLARA ISABELLA FORNARI
St. Balda
St. Valeria
St. Cyprian
St. Peter Fourier
Sts. Philotheus and Lollian and five other Christians

10 Dec ST. EULALIA
Our Lady of Loreto
St. Valeria
St. Guitmarus
St. Miltiades

11 Dec ST. DAMASUS
St. Daniel the Stylite

12 Dec ST. CORENTINUS
St. Columba
Blessed Conrad of Offida
Blessed Callistus

13 Dec ST. LUCY
ST. ODILIA or OTTILIA
St. Jodocus
Blessed Bartholomew
St. Aubert
St. Rose Elizabeth

14 Dec ST. FORTUNATUS
St. Agnellus
St. Viator
St. Spiridion

15 Dec ST. NINA or CHRISTIANA
St. Urbicius
St. Silvia or Silviana of Constantinople
St. John Discalceat

16 Dec ST. ADELAIDE
St. Albina
St. Bean
St. Eusebius
St. Judicael

17 Dec ST. OLMPIAS
St. Florian
Blessed Yolanda
St. Begga

18 Dec ST. GATIANUS
ST. FLAVITAS
St. Desiderius
Sts. Victurus, Victor, Victorinus, Adjutor, and Quartus
St. Winebald

19 Dec BLESSED URBAN V
St. Adam
Sts. Thea and Meuris
St. Gregentius
St. Timoleon or Timotheus

20 Dec STS. THEOPHILUS, ZENO and THEIR COMPANIONS
Blessed Julia Della Rena
Sts. Bajulus and Liberatus
St. Dominic of Silos
St. Ursicinus

21 Dec ST. THOMAS
St. Paul of Latros
St. Honoratus
St. Themistocles

22 Dec BLESSED GRATIAN
St. Flavian
St. Frances Xavier Cabrini

23 Dec ST. VICTORIA
Blessed Hartmann
St. Servulus

24 Dec STS. ADELA and IRMINA
Sts. Lucian, Zenobius, and Theotimus
St. Delphinus
Blessed Francesco dei Maleficii

25 Dec ST. EUGENIA
Christmas
Blessed Nera
St. Anastasia
St. Romulus

26 Dec ST. STEPHEN
St. Theodore
St. Zosimus
St. Archelaus

27 Dec ST. JOHN THE EVANGELIST
St. Nicarete
St. Fabiola
Sts. Theodore and Theophanes

28 Dec THE HOLY INNOCENTS
Sts. Castor, Victor, and Rogation
Blessed Gaspare Bufalo

29 Dec ST. THOMAS BECKET
St. David
St. Eleanor
Blessed Regimbert

30 Dec ST. SABINUS
St. Raynerius

31 Dec ST. SYLVESTER
ST. COLUMBA OF SENS
St. Barbatian
St. Catherine Laboure
Sts. Melania the Younger and Pinianus

THE FRENCH REVOLUTIONARY CALENDAR

In October, 1793 the National Convention of the French Republic instituted a new calendar based on what it considered philosophical and scientific principles. Its epoch was Sept. 22, 1792, the autumnal equinox and the day following the establishment of the Republic. The calendar went into effect on Nov. 24, 1793. It was divided into 12 months of 30 days. Five (or six days in leap year) were added at the end to make it correspond with the solar year. The names of the months, invented by Fabre D'Églantine, were taken from nature. They were:

Vendémiaire—vintage month
Brumaire—fog
Frimaire—sleet
Novôse—snow
Pluviôse—rain
Ventôse—wind
Germinal—seed
Floréal—blossom
Prairial—pasture
Messidor—harvest
Thermidor (Fervidor)—heat
Fructidor—fruit

The five days, added in September, were considered holidays. Their names were: Virtue, Genius, Labor, Reason and Reward. The sixth day, added for leap year, was Revolution Day.

The French calendar divided the months into three Decades of 10 days each; the 10th day was considered a day of rest. The days were named: Primidi, Duodi, Tridi, Quartidi, Quintidi, Sextidi, Septidi, Oxtidi, Nonidi and Decadi. Thus the first day of the Revolutionary calendar would be written Decade I, Sexidi of Frimaire, Year One of the Revolution.

New Year's Day fell on Sept. 22 in years 1, 2, 3, 5, and 7 of the Revolutionary calendar, on Sept. 23 in years 4, 8, 9, 10, 11, 13, and 14 and on Sept. 24 in year 12. Leap year occurred in the third, seventh and 11th years.

The French used the Revolutionary calendar until Dec. 31, 1805, when they reverted to the Gregorian calendar.

Autumn	Common Year	Leap Years 1796 & 1804
Vendemiaire	= 22 Sep-21 Oct	22 Sep-21 Oct
Brumaire	= 22 Oct-20 Nov	22 Oct-20 Nov
Frimaire	= 21 Nov-20 Dec	21 Nov-20 Dec
WINTER		
Nivose	= 21 Dec-19 Jan	21 Dec-19 Jan
Pluviose	= 20 Jan-18 Feb	20 Jan-18 Feb
Ventose	= 19 Feb-20 Mar	19 Feb-19 Mar
SPRING		
Germinal	= 21 Mar-19 Apr	20 Mar-18 Apr
Floreal	= 20 Apr-19 May	19 Apr-18 May
Prairial	= 20 May-18 Jun	19 May-17 Jun
SUMMER		
Messidor	= 19 Jun-18 Jul	18 Jun-17 Jul
Thermidor	= 19 Jul-17 Aug	18 Jul-16 Aug
Fructidor	= 18 Aug-16 Sep	17 Aug-15 Sep

Name Of Day	Decade I	II	III	Holidays Dedicated To	Common Year	Leap Year
Primidi	1	11	21	Virtue	17 Sep	16 Sep
Duodi	2	12	22	Genius	18 Sep	17 Sep
Tridi	3	13	23	Labor	19 Sep	18 Sep
Quartidi	4	14	24	Opinion	20 Sep	19 Sep
Quintidi	5	15	25	Rewards	21 Sep	20 Sep
Sextidi	6	16	26	Franciade		21 Sep
Septidi	7	17	27			
Octidi	8	18	28			
Nonidi	9	19	29			
Decadi	10	20	30			

SOVIET CALENDAR

In 1918 the newly established Soviet government abandoned the Julian calendar then in use in Russia and instituted the Gregorian. That same year Finland, Latvia and Lithuania, all recently proclaimed independent of Russia, also switched to the Gregorian calendar. But in 1929, in an effort to dissociate the calendar from religious purposes, the Soviet government abandoned the western calendar and adopted a new one which contained a five-day "week." Saturday and Sunday, with their religious associations, were eliminated. The days of the week had no names but were given a number and a color. The first day was yellow, the second orange, the third red, the fourth purple and the fifth green. Each person was assigned a color indicating his or her one "day off" per week. There were five general holidays during the year: Lenin's Day, which fell on the western January 31; two Days of the Proletariat, May 1 and May 2 by Western reckoning; two Days of the Revolution, October 31 and November 1; and New Years Day, January 1. The new calendar was put into effect in October 1929.

The calendar caused a great deal of confusion. It was designed so that there would be no "weekend" and work could be carried on continually. But with no uniform day of rest, the Russians had to rearrange their lives. Families had to arrange their days off so they could be together. Friends had a difficult time meeting each other and many actually listed their acquaintances under the color which each has as a day off. By January 1930 the Soviet government realized that the system was not working and dropped the five-day week and the color system but kept the practice of labeling days by numbers. Instead they established 12 periods of five weeks, corresponding to months, each week containing six days. The first day of the month was to fall on the first day of the week. In order to make the system work, they had to make adjustments in the calendar, creating extra work days and/or extra holidays.

But by 1932 it became clear that this system, too, was unworkable. That year the government tried to adjust this calendar to the general pattern of the Gregorian calendar, but because each of the Russian "months" had 30 days, the two calendars could not be coordinated. The effort to eliminate the names of the days and designate them only by numbers caused further problems. The habit of calling days and months by name was too deep rooted to be broken. Further, for people working in situations involving foreign contacts, the Gregorian calendar still had to be used. Thus, in 1940 the Soviets abandoned their attempts at calendar change and, on June 27, returned to the Gregorian Calendar.

NEW YEAR'S DAY

The observance of New Year's day on January 1 did not become standardized until the 16th century. Ancient peoples frequently celebrated it at the autumnal equinox or the summer or winter solstice. Each group followed its own calendar based on differing astrological concepts and religious and political holidays. Thus in one area New Years would fall on the summer solstice while in another it would fall on the date of the ascension of the ruler to the throne. During the Roman period the New Year was standardized on January 1 throughout the empire. But as the empire crumbled, diversity reappeared. During the middle ages New Year's Day was celebrated in the Christian world around March 25. Following the adoption of the Gregorian calendar by the Catholic world around 1582, the day was observed on January 1.

Below is a list, by century, of when certain areas celebrated the New Year.

THE NEW YEAR DAY

I - IV CENTURY

1 Jan	Roman Empire

V - VIII CENTURY

1 Jan	Germany, generally to VIII Century
	Hungary, in part
	Denmark, in part
	Gregory of Tours, chronicler, in part
	Venice, civil and common year
1 Mar	Gregory of Tours, chronicler, in part
	Council of Verdun - 755
	France, until 800
	Germany, in part, V - X Century
	Venice, legal documents
	Thassilo of Barvaria, VIII Century
	Fredergarius, chronicler
Easter	Council of Tours - 775
1 May	Annalis Pitaviennes
12 Aug	Denmark, in part
1 Nov	Celts until 1179, 1 year early until 1014
25 Dec	Mayence until XV Century
	Alsace, VIII to beginning of XVI Century
	England VII through 1338 (one year behind)
	Cyprus
	Denmark, in part
	Hungary, in part

IX CENTURY

25 Mar	France after 800, until 996.
	Tuscany and Florence until 1750
	Pisa, Lucca, Sienna, Lodi, until 1745, but 1 year behind.
25 Dec	Genoa
	Savona
	Liguria

X CENTURY

1 Mar	Germany, in part, 919 - 1138
	Sicily
	Cahors, Rodez, Tulle, until 1290
	Aragon, until 1350, Spanish Era
	Castile and Segovia until 1383, Spanish Era
	Switzerland, until XIV Century
	Portugal, until 1420, Spanish Era
Good Friday	Delft
	Dordrecht
	Brabant
Easter	France, 996 - 1051
1 year behind	England, church records
Easter	Holland
	Flanders
	Hainault
25 Dec	Germany, general use through XII Century
	Mayence, until XV Century
	Low Countries
	Guelders
	Friesland

XI CENTURY

1 Jan	Straussburg, except 1004
25 Mar	Sicily, 1099 until XV Century
	France, before 1066, in part
Easter Eve	France, generally, when Paschal taper lighted
Easter	English holdings in France 1066 - 1453, in which case words "more Gallicano" added.
25 Dec	Straussburg, 1004 only
	English holdings in France 1066 - 1453 (without "more Gallicano")
	Note:—During the XI and XII Centuries, some chroniclers added 22 or 23 years to their reckoning.

XII CENTURY

1 Mar	Benevento
18 Mar	Liege and Treves, 1101
25 Mar	England, church documents
Easter	Gelasius, 1118 and 1119
1 Nov	Celtic calendar until 1172, after that, as English
25 Dec	Poissons
	Amiens

XIII CENTURY

1 Jan	Picardy after mid century
25 Mar	Rheims, until 1390
	Cahors, Rodez, Tulle until 1289
	Leige, until 1334
	Treves, until 1652
25 Dec	Milan, through XV Century
	Cahors, Rodez, Tulle, after 1289

XIV CENTURY

1 Jan	Switzerland
25 Mar	England, civil year after 1339
	Aragon until 1350
	Castile and Segovia until 1383
	Utrecht until 1333
	Leige until 1334

Easter	England, church from 1339
	Cologne, "style of the court"
	Rheims, after 1390
	France, except English holdings, 1363 on
25 Dec	Cologne, church
	Mayence, to XV Century
	Utrecht, 1334 on
	Leige, 1334 on
	Aragon, after 1350
	Castile and Segovia, after 1383
	England, legal year

XV CENTURY

1 Jan	Chartres, 1445 on
	France, 1455
	Switzerland, except Laussane and Pays du Vaud after 1431
25 Mar	University of Cologne, 1428
Easter Eve	Peronne, at the lighting of the Paschal taper
Easter	France, 1453 - 1566, except 1455
	Cologne until 1429
	Pays du Vaud and Laussane after 1431
1 Jul	Sicily until XVII Century
25 Dec	Portugal after 1420

XVI CENTURY

1 Jan	Germany, Venice, Alsace, 1508 on.
	Hungary, 1520 on
	Rome, 1525
	Holland, 1533 on
	France, in part, 1563 (edict of Charles IX)
	France, 1567 (year 1566, 14 Apr - 31 Dec)
	Low Countries, 1575
	Burgundy, 1576
	Beauvais, Louvaine, 1580
	Scotland, 1600
	Note:—For changes after 15 Oct, 1582, see country listings in Gregorian calendar section.

Index

D

E

F

G

H

I

J

O

P

Q

R

S